GOIN' HOME: THE UNCOMPROMISING LIFE AND MUSIC OF KEN COLYER

BY MIKE POINTON AND RAY SMITH
DESIGNED BY MARTIN COLYER

Cartoon of Ken drawn by clarinetist Wally Fawkes, better known as 'Trog'

Dedicated to the memory of Bill Colyer

First published in Great Britain by The Ken Colyer Trust

Copyright © Mike Pointon, Ray Smith and The Ken Colyer Trust 2010

The moral right of Mike Pointon, Ray Smith and The Ken Colyer Trust has been asserted

A CIP catalogue record for this book is available from the British Library

ISBN 978-0-956-29401 2

Concept and interviews by Mike Pointon and Ray Smith
Design and art direction by Martin Colyer
Editing and indexing by Rick Ball
Production by David Bann

Printed and bound in China by WKT.

"WORK, WORK ALL THE TIME. Find out about this earth, this universe, this force and matter, and the *spirit* that glimmers up through force and matter and from the maggot to the Godhead. And by all this I mean WORK for a philosophy of life. It does not hurt how WRONG your philosophy of life may be, so long as you have one and have it well. The three great things are: GOOD HEALTH, WORK and a PHILOSOPHY OF LIFE. I may add, nay, *must add*, a fourth—SINCERITY. Without this, the other three are without avail. With it you may cleave to greatness and sit among the giants."

—*Jack London*

THE INDIVIDUALISTS

Jazz? It's a matter of FAITH...

says the New Orleans High Priest

KEN COLYER ... blowing a lonely horn

WHILE the Vicars of Bray of British jazz scramble to cash in on any latest fad, one man stands obdurate—and, say some, stubbornly hidebound as a musical mule.

In the smoky Soho basement temple where the Ken Colyer band holds vespers there is no dancing. The crush is such that if Mr. Colyer breathed in deeply the front row of the congregation would be sucked up his trumpet. One's impression is that they would neither notice nor mind.

Oblivious, shirt-sleeved, waistcoat open, eyes shut, mouthpiece submerged in blond beard, this first-principler and last-ditcher, the defender of the faith that pristine New Orleans is the only true jazz, and all developments and deviations blasphemous corruptions, blows implacably at his re-creation of a 40-year-old music.

It was alleged in the past that, so assiduously did Mr. Colyer brainwash himself with ancient recordings of Mutt Carey and Fredie Keppard that he reproduced the rumble of passing streetcars and the needle-hiss.

by KENNETH ALLSOP

rapidly swallows some beer, rolls himself a cigarette and says: "My New Orleans trip was a dream come true. From listening, first-hand, in New Orleans I got definite ideas about the way jazz should be played.

"It's not just style, it's the intent. Jazz has to be honest music. The man with convictions stands out.

"This fantastic commercial boom in trad is by-passing us. But something always goes wrong with jazz if it becomes too popular. The temptations are big, dangling right there in front of you, and if a bloke grabs some of the loot I don't altogether blame him."

His group

THAT can hardly be still maintained, for ten years ago Mr. Colyer, who has been builder's labourer, milkman, and stable boy, worked his sea passage to the land of dreams.

In New Orleans—where he spent six weeks in the parish prison for overstaying his work permit—he imbibed at the fountain-head and played with the veteran clarinettist George Lewis.

Upon his return such pioneer British revivalists as Chris Barber, Acker Bilk, and Lonnie ... seemed to him to have ... and company was

... ually he assembled a ... satisfactorily purist and ... Now the plunk-plunk ... and the simple beat. ... semble sound in blues, ... stomps, and rags ... Mr. Colyer, nightly ... canon ... the gospel in London ... e provinces. ... ng 10 minutes off the ... the 34-year-old evangelist

His drive

I'M a bit older, a bit more tolerant, now. My brand of jazz used to arouse hostility and ridicule. But I'm not bitter. I draw a good audience who know I'm genuinely trying to recreate the drive, spontaneity, and authenticity of the early New Orleans.

"It doesn't make me a bomb, but I earn an adequate living. Life isn't a bed of roses. But what's ambition? I'm doing what I want to do, and I believe it's worth while."

Back in the basement, devotions resume; Mr. Colyer speaks his creed through his horn; it is again a make-believe Mississippi night in London, W.1.

A BIOGRAPHY, APPRECIATION, RECORD SURVEY & DISCOGRAPHY BY JOHN REDDIHOUGH

KEN COLYER

JAZZ NEWS

31st May 1961

THIS WEEK 24 PAGES

- KEN COLYER
- STEVE RACE
- SONNY STITT
- BRUCE TURNER
- DANIEL HALPERIN
- VIC DICKENSON
- MA RAINEY
- MIKE BUTCHER
- TUBBY HAYES

Our cover photo of Ken Colyer was taken on stage at a concert.

GEORGE LE...

accompanied by

KEN COLYER

Jazzmen

with

TERRY LIGHTFOOT'S and **MIKE DA...**
JAZZMEN **DELTA JAZ...**

SUNDAY, APRIL 28...

at 7 p.m.

STOLL THEATR...

KINGSWAY, W.C.2.

Tickets 5/-, 7/6, 10/6, 12/6 and 15/- fro...

Box Office, Stoll Theatre and usual agencies

Printed by Walter Parker (Kly.) Ltd., Wellington St., Keighley.

KEN COLYER'S CONCERT

JAZZ NEWS — Saturday, February 18, 1961
Page 3

Now your top ten British musicians list their personal favourites to make this the last of the Jazz News Polls of 1961.

winners' choice	
HUMPHREY LYTTELTON	**MONTY SUNSHINE**
Louis Armstrong	Duke Ellington
Buck Clayton	Louis Armstrong
Roy Eldridge	Count Basie
Pee Wee Russell	Barney Bigard
Thelonious Monk	Johnny Hodges
Ben Webster	Vic Dickenson
Sandy Brown	Sidney de Paris
Duke Ellington	Vince Catolica
Johnny Hodges	Ruby Braff
Dizzy Gillespie	Errol Garner

TUBBY HAYES
Charlie Parker, Duke Ellington, Miles Davis, Dizzy Gillespie, Sonny Rollins, Horace Silver, Victor Feldman, Milt Jackson, Stan Getz, Philly Joe Jones, Benny Golson, Quincy Jones

(Then are not listed in any order of preference. Also, for obvious reasons my own colleagues — Tracy Cox, Joe Temperley etc. — are omitted, not because I hold them in low esteem but quite the contrary for them being, I hope, taken for granted.)

KEN COLYER
George Lewis, Alton Purnell, Omer Simeon, Jelly Roll Morton, King Oliver, Louis Armstrong, Ed Hall, Bunk Johnson, Tommy Ladnier, Kid Ory

CHRIS BARBER
Louis Armstrong, Sidney de Paris, John Lewis, Bob Shaffner, Thomas Jefferson, Muddy Waters, Garvin Bushell, Ruby Braff, Tony Parenti, Ed Hall

ACKER BILK
George Lewis, Johnny Dodds, Omer Simeon, Jelly Roll Morton, King Oliver, Louis Armstrong, Ed Hall, Bunk Johnson, Jim Robinson, Percy Humphrey, Red Allen, Art Hodes

BRUCE TURNER
Louis Armstrong, Bix Beiderbecke, Johnny Hodges, Earl Hines, Django Reinhardt, Sidney Bechet, Coleman Hawkins, Barney Bigard, Benny Goodman (1927-33), Lester Young

KENNY BALL
Louis Armstrong, Bix Beiderbecke, Bunny Berigan, Dick Cathcart, Peter Schilperoot, Duke Ellington, Clifford Brown, Paul Desmond, Jelly Roll Morton

JOHNNY DANKWORTH
Charlie Parker, Duke Ellington, Lester Young, Gerry Mulligan, Art Tatum, Lionel Hampton, Benny Goodman, Jack Teagarden, Bix Beiderbecke, Django Reinhardt

JOE HARRIOTT
Dizzy Gillespie, Thelonious Monk, John Lewis, Shake Keane, Ken Wheeler, Miles Davis, Phil Seamen, Count Basie, Ornette Coleman

Footnote to Poll

Nearly every musician stated that their listed choice was not necessarily in the order given and for this reason we have dispensed with tabulating their choices in numerical sequence.

Vic Feldman, who came 4th in the British Poll, was unable to be contacted and Kenny Ball who finished in 11th place was included. When Vic Feldman's choice is received it will be published at a later date.

Wherever the voters have made additional comments on their ballot forms these comments have been printed.

KEN COLYER IN NEW ORLEANS

TANZ UND JAZZ international...

JAZZ COLUMN

Big Bill really sings Blues

HEARING blues-singer Big Bill ...

A 17 No. L 65 378391   *Spring* 19 64   G L 5 1025

Bank of George Lewis

or Order

Pay *Bearer Cash*

the value of one monthly payment £4 —

to a maximum of Four Pounds

GEORGE LEWIS LTD.

George Lewis

DIRECTOR

CONTENTS

FOREWORD

WHAT A CONTRAST BETWEEN KEN'S CHILDHOOD AND MINE! The three small boys living in a disused railway carriage by themselves and then ending up in Dr Barnado's. My parents were wealthy and I went to expensive schools and eventually Stowe School, housed in what was once the country home of the Dukes of Buckingham. Their town house was that now known as Buckingham Palace. The last Duke spent his vast fortune in building and laying out his garden at Stowe, with the help of Capability Brown, as a rival to Versailles so you can imagine how wonderful it was to attend such a school. George Melly was there too but before my time.

WHEN I LEFT STOWE I was invited to study at Jesus College, Cambridge but my father would not support me in this because I had insulted his second wife (not my mother). What a stroke of luck! If I had gone to Cambridge I would never have met this lad from Barnado's who changed my life. I was determined to obtain a University degree because I knew that bass players—unless they were brilliant—and I certainly was not, could not expect to earn a good living. I needed a day job. Because the Cranes often played every evening of the week and I later joined the Cy Laurie band, it took me six years instead of the usual three.

IT WAS NOT JUST THE MUSIC—playing with the Cranes was wonderful and glorious experience. Ken, partly because he thought I was younger than I was, was like a father and brother to me. He taught me to play the music and a good deal about how to conduct myself. He taught me how to roll cigarettes—they don't teach you that at a public school. In reality we seldom conversed; the communication was through the music.

I HAVE WONDERFUL MEMORIES of the Cranes and of playing with the Ken Colyer Jazzmen for several years up to his retirement. I played with many other bands including some of my own. The opportunities to do this all stem from his invitation to join the band and what I learned from him.

I HAVE READ THIS BOOK and have found it fascinating. It is the result of painstaking research and hours of interviews carried out by the authors: Mike Pointon and Ray Smith, both musicians who knew Ken well and played with his bands many times. It consists of Ken's observations and anecdotes and recollections of those who knew Ken. These stories give a multifaceted description of the man and his experiences and opinions.

THE CHAPTER DEVOTED TO THE CRANES brings back many happy memories for me and gives me a very interesting insight into how the other members of this truly co-operative band felt about those days. The fifth chapter is about the Christie Brothers Stompers, the band for which Ken left the Cranes. Many, many years later I was chatting about it with him during an interval at the 100 Club. He told me how it did not work out and how he wished that he had rejoined the Cranes which of course he did twenty years later with great success.

THE SECTION ON HIS PILGRIMAGE TO NEW ORLEANS is largely composed of his letters to his brother Bill and I am reminded of his fine literary style. When I gave a copy of *When Dreams are in the Dust* to my father he read the first chapter and remarked, "You were right not to edit it. It is beautifully written. But I will not read the rest of it because I hate Jazz !"

THE FOLLOWING CHAPTERS RECOUNT HIS ADVENTURES in developing his career as a professional musician. The formation of the first Ken Colyer's Jazzmen with Chris Barber; after leaving Chris, his experiences in Germany; the formation of the 'Classic' Ken Colyer's Jazzmen, and the tours with George Lewis and other musicians from New Orleans. These chapters give on an almost "fly on the wall" view of British Jazz and the Trad Boom.

JUST BEFORE KEN DIED HE ASKED ME TO PUBLISH HIS AUTOBIOGRAPHY *When Dreams are in the Dust*. The need to raise money for this resulted in the formation of the Ken Colyer Trust which continued for twenty-two years to promote the music that Ken loved, and to safeguard his interests.

Julian Davies
Hon. President, Ken Colyer Trust

Ken Colyer April 18, 1928- March 11, 1988

WHO'S WHO

THE INTERVIEWEES

ADAMS, PAUL Producer/sound engineer/
drummer/proprietor of Lake Records
ALLEN, RICHARD B. 'DICK' American jazz
historian and former Tulane University
archivist
AMES, KEN Bassist with the Jazzmen 1969-71
and 1981-3
ASHMAN, MICKY Bassist with Christie
Brothers Stompers
ASMAN, JAMES Record shop proprietor/
writer
BALDWIN, LEN Trombonist with the
Jazzmen (All Stars) 1972-8
BARBER, CHRIS Trombonist/bandleader
BARTON, MATTHEW Author
BASTABLE, JOHN Banjoist with the Jazzmen
1955-1971
BEECHAM, JOHN Trombonist with
All Stars 1978-1982
BIELDERMAN, GERARD Dutch discographer
BERNARD, JOHN & URSULA New Orleans
jazz enthusiast friends
BETHELL, TOM Expat British author/critic
BILK, BERNARD 'ACKER' Clarinetist with
the Jazzmen 1954-5
BILLETT, KEITH 'CUFF' Trumpeter/
vocalist/bandleader
BLACK, EDWARD Professor of
English Literature/friend of
Ken Colyer/founding member
of Ken Colyer Trust

BOATFIELD, GRAHAM Critic
BODDY, JOHN Agent/bassist
BONNER, VAL (nee Colyer) Sister of
Ken Colyer
BORNEMAN, ERNEST Critic/writer/
anthropologist
BOWDEN, COLIN Drummer with
the Jazzmen 1955-1961 and re-formed
Crane River Jazz Band 1973-80
BOWDEN, RON Drummer with
Crane River Jazz Band 1949-50 and the
Jazzmen 1953-4
BRAY, JIM Bassist with the Jazzmen 1953-4
BRYCE, OWEN Trumpeter/bandleader
CASIMIR, MIKE Trombonist/bandleader
CHAMBERS, GEORGE Trumpeter/
bandleader
CHARTERS, SAM American
author/producer/musician
CHRISTIE, IAN Clarinetist/journalist
COLE, BILL Bassist with the Jazzmen 1964-69
COLE, GEOFF Trombonist with the
Jazzmen 1961-1971

COLLIE, MAX Australian expat
trombonist/bandleader
COLLINS, LEE New Orleans trumpeter
COLYER, BETTY Wife of Bill Colyer
COLYER, BILL Brother of Ken
Colyer/washboard player/Jazzmen
manager/founding member of Ken Colyer
Trust
COLYER, BOB Brother of Ken Colyer
COLYER, CATHY Wife of Bob Colyer
COLYER, DELPHINE Wife of Ken Colyer
COLYER, RUSSELL Son of Ken Colyer
CONNOR, CHARLIE Clarinetist/ saxophonist
COOPER, ALAN Clarinetist
COX, NORRIE Clarinetist/bandleader
CRAWFORD, RALSTON American
artist/photographer
DAVIES, JOHN R.T. Multi-instrumentalist
with Crane River Jazz Band/sound
engineer/record restorer
DAVIES, JULIAN Ken's first and last bassist
DAWBARN, BOB Journalist/trombonist
DEUCHAR, PETE Banjoist/bandleader
DISLEY, WILLIAM 'DIZ' Banjoist/ guitarist
with the Jazzmen 1954-5
DONEGAN, TONY 'LONNIE'
Banjoist/guitarist with the Jazzmen 1953-4
DUNCAN, MALCOLM 'MAC'
Trombonist/vocalist with the Jazzmen 1955-60
DYER, PETE Trombonist
EYSSELINCK, WALTER Belgian Professor
of Drama/jazz enthusiast
FABRIE, COR Dutch trombonist/bandleader
FOX, CHARLES Critic /broadcaster
FOXLEY, RAY Pianist with the
Jazzmen 1957-61
FRANKLIN, DAVE Jazz enthusiast
GATWARD, ALAN Businessman/patron
of jazz/Friend of Ken Colyer

GILBERT, GEOFF Banjoist/broadcaster

GODBOLT, JIM Chronicler of British jazz

GREIG, STAN Drummer/pianist with the Jazzmen 1954-5

GRIFFITH, JOHN Record producer/banjoist

GUY, JOHN Writer

HAIM, GERALD Sousaphonist with John Haim's Jelly Roll Kings

HALCOX, PAT Trumpeter

HANDSCOMBE, LES Trombonist

HARKER, BEN Author

HARRISON, KEN Drummer

HARVEY, BRIAN Journalist/record producer

HATFIELD, FRED New Orleanian supporter of jazz

HAWES, PAT Pianist/vocalist with Crane River Jazz Band/Christie Brothers Stompers

HAWKINS, ANNIE Expat Australian bassist

HOLLAND, RAY Bassist

HOLMES, JIM Trumpeter

HONE, GERARD 'GED' Trumpeter/bandleader

HORTON, ROGER Longtime proprietor of the 100 Club in London's Oxford St.

HUBNER, ABBI German trumpeter/bandleader

HUNTER, PETER Merchant Navy Officer/friend of Ken Colyer/Education co-ordinator for Ken Colyer Trust

HUNTINGTON, BILL New Orleanian banjoist/bassist

INGHAM, KEITH Pianist

JACKSON, RAY American enthusiast/friend of Ken Colyer's

JOHNSON, FRANK Australian trumpeter/bandleader

JONES, MAX Journalist

KAEGEBEHN, CHARLES F. American lawyer

KAYE, ANDREW L. Author

KEEN, JOHN Trumpeter /psychologist

KERSHAW, REV. ALVIN American pastor/jazz enthusiast

KORNER, ALEXIS Guitarist/vocalist/writer/broadcaster (with skiffle group 1953-4)

LANDAU, DOUG Trumpeter/writer

LANE, STEVE Trumpeter/bandleader

LARKIN, PHILIP Poet/critic

LAY, PETE Drummer/bandleader/ promoter (member of Ken Colyer's final band)

LEPPARD, TONY Friend of Ken Colyer/founding member of Ken Colyer Trust

LINDGREEN, OLE 'FESSOR' Danish trombonist/bandleader

LYTTELTON, HUMPHREY Trumpeter/bandleader/author/broadcaster

LONG, JOHN Friend of Ken Colyer/promoter/founding member of Ken Colyer Trust

LONG, RENEE Wife of John Long/friend of Ken Colyer/Treasurer of Ken Colyer Trust

MARSHALL, BEN Banjoist with the Crane River Jazz Band

MARTYN, BARRY Drummer/bandleader/record producer/author

McCOMBE, MIKE Drummer with the Jazzmen 1966

McINTOSH, JIM 'GENTLEMAN' Banjoist/bandleader

McNICHOLAS, JOHN Friend of Ken Colyer/record producer

MELLY, GEORGE Blues singer/entertainer/author/broadcaster

MILES, LIZZIE (Elizabeth Mary Landreaux) New Orleanian blues singer

MORCOM, PETER Banjoist

MORRIS, LEO 'SONNY' Trumpeter/bandleader/with Crane River Jazz Band

MORRISON, STU Banjoist with All Stars 1972-6

MURPHY, MALCOLM 'MALC' Drummer with the Jazzmen 1967-71

NEWMAN, TIM Trumpeter/bandleader/promoter

O'DONNELL, ED Trombonist/bandleader/with the Jazzmen 1954-5

O'DONNELL, ANNE Wife of Ed

O'SULLIVAN, TONY Trumpeter

PALSER, BARRY Trombonist/drummer/bandleader

PARKER, JOHNNY Pianist

PAWSON, DAN Trumpeter/bandleader/writer

PENDLETON, HAROLD Entrepreneur/founder of Marquee Club, London

PETERS, MIKE Trumpeter/bandleader

PETTERS, JOHN Drummer/bandleader/promoter

PHILLIPS, TIM Multi-instrumentalist

PYKE, TONY Clarinetist/saxophonist with the Jazzmen 1965-71, 1979-83

REDDIHOUGH, JOHN Journalist

REID, BILL Bassist with Alex Welsh 1958-60

REVELL, ALEX Clarinetist/bandleader

RIMINGTON, SAMMY Clarinetist/saxophonist/guitarist/with the Jazzmen 1960-5

ROBINSON, MAC Guitarist/vocalist/longtime Colyer enthusiast

SCAMMELL, KEN Jazz club proprietor/friend of Ken Colyer

SCHNEIDER, UDO Jazz club proprietor/promoter/friend of Ken Colyer

SEALEY, PAUL Banjoist/guitarist

SIMMONS, RICHARD Pianist with the Jazzmen 1965-6

SIMS, KEN Trumpeter/bandleader

SKINNER, ERIC Drummer with the Jazzmen 1954

SLATTER, MIKE Jazz enthusiast/friend of Ken Colyer

SMITH, DAVE Jazz enthusiast/ friend of Ken Colyer

SMITH, DICK Bassist with the Jazzmen 1954-6

SMITH, KEITH Trumpeter/bandleader/friend of Ken Colyer

SOUCHON, EDMOND 'DOC' New Orleanian guitarist/banjoist

STEVENS, DAVE Pianist with John Haim's Jelly Roll Kings

STEWART-BAXTER, DERRICK Critic/journalist

STOTESBURY, BILL Banjoist, Allstars 1973-84/founding member of Ken Colyer Trust

STOTESBURY, CHRIS Wife of Bill Stotesbury/former Ken Colyer Trust Committee Member

SUNSHINE, MONTY Clarinetist/bandleader with Crane River Jazz Band and the Jazzmen 1953-4

TAIT, DOROTHY Journalist/manager of George Lewis Band

THIELE, BERND German doctor/ friend of Ken Colyer

TODD, TREVOR Enthusiast

TURNER, BRUCE Altoist/clarinetist/bandleader

WALLIS, BOB Trumpeter/vocalist/bandleader

WARD, RON Bassist with Jazzmen from 1956-64

WATFORD, CHRIS Clarinetist/ bandleader

WESTWOOD, JOHN Drummer with John Haim's Jelly Roll Kings

WHEELER, IAN Clarinetist with the Jazzmen from 1955-60

WILKINSON, BILL Drummer

WILLIAMS, TREFOR Bassist

WINNER, MICHAEL Film director

WINTERS, DEREK Trumpeter/bandleader/newspaperman

WOOD, BERTA British expat journalist

WURR, JOHN Clarinetist/saxophonist

INTRODUCTION

TRUE TO YOUR CODE
MIKE POINTON

SOME YEARS AGO RAY SMITH AND I decided to assemble a definitive biography of Ken Colyer, but it wasn't until we had completed our first book—*Bill Russell: Father Of The New Orleans Jazz Revival*, based mainly on long interviews the pioneer historian gave us—that we realised the same approach would be appropriate for Ken's tortuous life. Many years ago I had tried to persuade Ken to write his autobiography, and the first hint of this came via the abridged collection of his New Orleans letters, *New Orleans and Back*, followed by his posthumous *When Dreams Are in the Dust*.

Although both contain fascinating and, at times, quite moving insights into Ken's complex character we felt that there was much more to be said about this influential— and certainly controversial—figure. Thanks to the Ken Colyer Trust we were able to realise our project, and it has been immeasurably enhanced by Martin Colyer's creative input and David Bann's production expertise. Through contributions from many of those who knew him over the years, coupled with some of the rare interviews Ken gave, we hope a true assessment of his contribution to jazz will emerge. We might also be able to explode a few myths along the way...

I would like to express my personal appreciation to Ray Smith for being the most dedicated and meticulous collaborator one could wish for. Ray's close connection with Ken over many years is well-known but perhaps I should explain mine.

I first saw Ken on stage at the old Civic Hall, Croydon, in 1956 and decided then and there this was the music I wanted to try and play. Studio 51, the Ken Colyer Club in London's West End, became a regular haunt, and hearing the Jazzmen at that time at their peak helped direct me to the recordings that had influenced them. A highlight of those early years was seeing George Lewis guesting with Ken on his first UK tour in 1957.

Mac Duncan's superb tailgate playing inspired me to take up trombone, and when he left in 1960 I was one of several youthful deps who worked with the band and aspired to take his place. But, quite rightly, Ken decided to recruit the more mature Graham Stewart in Mac's place. Stewart's Ory-tinged style fitted the band perfectly and he stayed for about two years. I played alongside him with Ken on the occasional parade and gigged with the band again after Graham left, until Geoff Cole became Ken's permanent slide man for the next decade.

BUT KEN AND I KEPT IN TOUCH AND AFTER HE GAVE up full-time bandleading in the early seventies I occasionally worked with him right up to when he left for France and his final place in the sun. We developed an offstage rapport through our mutual love of the wry humour of the great W.C. Fields, whose biography I obtained for him. Ken was an avid reader of all sorts of books and one I particularly remember his mentioning to me was They Hanged My Saintly Billy, Robert Graves' semi-documentary account of the bizarre life of the infamous Victorian poisoner William Palmer.

We once discussed jazz in the movies, and a film Ken had particular affection for was *Reveille With Beverly* from 1943, in which the Ellington, Basie and Bob Crosby bands appeared. I recall him asking me if he might borrow my Billie Holiday LP, *Songs for Distingué Lovers*, so that he could learn the lyrics of Johnny Mercer's world-weary *One For My Baby (And One More For The Road)*, which he subsequently recorded. I think his interpretation of the wistful line "Could tell you a lot,

Mike Pointon plays with Ken, on a Floating Festival aboard the *Royal Daffodil*

The plaque on the wall in the 100 Club honouring Ken's association with New Orleans music, and with the club itself

but you've got to be true to your code," says much about Ken's approach to his personal credo of untiring integrity...

I STARTED MAKING RADIO DOCUMENTARIES ON JAZZ in the nineties and one of my BBC projects with George Melly was *Memories Of The Blues*. It was clear that we had to revisit Studio 51, as Ken's involvement with the blues through his music had helped generate what became a major force in British pop music. I remembered seeing such legends as Speckled Red, Sister Rosetta Tharpe and Little Brother Montgomery in that smoky cellar, and the likes of Long John Baldry and the Rolling Stones appeared down there when they started their careers.

It was a moving experience reminiscing with George below ground at Great Newport Street, in what had by then become a small conference suite. Over forty years earlier I'd been one of many would-be jazzers queuing to descend those stairs and absorb what we knew to be the "righteous" music.

The strains of, perhaps, *Uptown Bumps*, would drift up through the grating as we waited to pay our half-crowns (?!) and evoked the ambience of how we'd imagined such fabled New Orleans venues as San Jacinto Hall to be. Certain loyal "faces" were always sitting near the stage including Ken's close friend, journalist Pete Vince, and when the band vacated the club for the nearby Porcupine during the intervals (there was no official bar at the 51) we were envious of those in their "inner circle" who joined them.

But the real turning point was in 1959 when George Lewis brought his band over. I'll never forget the thrill of meeting them when they visited the club and being able to actually talk to such idols as Jim Robinson, Kid Howard and Slow Drag from

records we'd avidly collected...

This was indeed a time of passion for New Orleans jazz, and we believe the interviews and contemporary documentation we have assembled in this book convey much of the commitment Ken gave throughout his life to the music he loved. They also provide an evocative flashback to a more innocent time, before popular music became dominated by exploitation. Thanks to Ken's widow Delphine, his son Russell, Chris Stotesbury and Kay and Tony Leppard we are able to include the most comprehensive sequence of Ken's remarkably eloquent letters from New Orleans—which, seen for the first time in their entirety, give a vivid impression of how things were in the early fifties before integration was permitted.

The book also contains a unique collection of letters written to Ken during the mid-fifties. Often they were handwritten, and quite a number were completely or partially undated. Because of this, some of them may not be perfectly transcribed or placed. Also, idiomatic spellings have been left intact. Previously unseen letters from Edmond Souchon, who became one of Ken's New Orleans mentors, also provide an insight into this time of revelation for a young visiting, white Englishman. And the affection he was shown by members of the black community is reflected by letters from Lizzie Miles.

Ken's close relationship with his older brother Bill, whose love of jazz had originally inspired him, is apparent throughout. This momentous pilgrimage became the catalyst for the eventual appearance of George Lewis in England and, after Ken's triumphant return home, we are able to trace, through a further sequence of correspondence, how this was made possible by expatriate British jazz journalist Berta

Wood's link with Lewis's new manager Dorothy Tait. We can also see, via letters from such admirers of Ken's work as Mike Slatter and Walter Eysselinck, that his attempts to continue the principles he had learned in New Orleans were succeeding with those who understood the music.

OUR GENERAL PRINCIPLE HAS BEEN TO ALLOW THE interviewees to tell the story themselves, much as in the exemplary jazz history *Hear Me Talkin' To Ya*. Towards the end of his life, Ken planned another book, which he intended to be a masterclass. He only got as far as the note stage, which he jotted down on any sort of paper that came to hand—from the backs of airline tickets to hotel note-pads—but these give a true impression of his considered thoughts at the time, so we have included extracts of this unique and invaluable document as an appendix.

In many peoples' estimation Ken Colyer achieved much in his comparatively short career, but his innate humility still led him to reflect: "Make no mistake about it, there is nothing simple about the real New Orleans music. At its highest order it is very complex indeed, and I have no hesitation in saying that the Colyer band has never achieved the ultimate. Not by a long shot."

KEN COLYER AS I KNEW HIM RAY SMITH

N THE YEARS AFTER THE SECOND WORLD WAR, a fair number of talented musicians in Britain directed their pent-up, emotive energy into the emerging jazz-revival. It was an underground movement—an expression, perhaps, of the newly-found freedom and release from what had been a possible end to the existence of life as they knew it—but from that movement emerged a quite staggering amount of gifted musicians who produced music of lasting quality and created the traditional jazz scene as we know it today. None were more dedicated than Ken Colyer, a man whose instincts set him on a path to discovering and developing *his* perception of New Orleans-styled jazz music.

I first heard of Ken Colyer when Dick, my brother, brought home a copy of the LP *New Orleans To London* in 1954. The band, with Chris Barber, Monty Sunshine et al., had a considerable impact on the traditional jazz scene in England, and Ken's ultimate dissatisfaction has passed into legend, although the very "new" style of the band continued—and continues—to be influential. There's no doubt that their very fine music was a product of mutual compromise, and that, given the personality clashes, its demise was regrettable but inevitable.

A few years later I used to visit the local jazz club at South Harrow every week. Of all the bands that played there, my two favourites were Sandy Brown's and Ken Colyer's. Entirely

different music, but each possessing some special authority. I didn't know what it was—still don't—and perhaps the journey we're embarking on with this book will clarify a few things. Possibly not. Dissecting flowers doesn't necessarily improve one's appreciation of them.

There's no doubt that Ken—during *his* journeys—had discovered some truth that captivated all of us, some truths that have led people to say that any band that he led had the "Colyer Sound". Bill Russell said of Bunk Johnson that he never wasted a note—that everything he played led somewhere. I don't know if Ken ever wasted a note, but he definitely wasted very few. He was once heard to say to trumpeter Denny Ilett—after a display of high notes—"I know there's a felony going on up there but there's no need to compound it!"

"Deceptive simplicity" perhaps could best describe his playing—allowing the other members of the front-line to do their job in order to produce an uncluttered ensemble. I've always felt that his playing had a sort of folk-music quality to it, which may explain, in some way, his enduring appeal.

IN 1968 I WAS FORTUNATE ENOUGH TO BE ASKED TO do a concert with the Colyer band in Hamburg, which location was about the same size as the Royal Festival Hall. On the stage was a full-size Steinway Concert Grand positioned in such a way that the length of the instrument stood between me and the band, making Ken's announcements even harder to hear than normal. Before going on for the first half I asked Ken what we were going to play.

"Don't worry about it, man, you'll be alright. The first number's *Bugle Boy March*." I had never played it before. "I'll shout out the chords," said Johnny Bastable. We soon gave that up, as his voice was largely inaudible at that distance anyway. Luckily, I'd heard the band playing most of the numbers before, but had to listen very hard. And that was Ken's secret; he taught you how to *listen*. Sure, there were wrong chords from me, but that session improved my ear considerably. The method would have been seen by some as "unprofessional", but for Ken it was justified—there were moments in the concert where everything seemed to gel.

The following two years found me playing on the band's annual German tours, both of which were most enjoyable, although Ken seemed to be drinking quite heavily and was rather short-tempered at times.

Back in England, I used to sit-in with the band fairly regularly, and it was always great—Ken was always friendly, and the band was always a pleasure to play with. Ken was a different man; it was as if he really resented being on tour, which wasn't surprising if his health was bad, but as far as I know, he didn't discuss his problems with anyone in the band. Had he done, maybe he wouldn't have resented what he later described as their "indifference" to his health problems.

I started working regularly with Ken's band in 1976, some

time after the "All Stars" were formed for him to lead: Len Baldwin, John Wurr, Annie Hawkins, Colin Bowden and Bill Stotesbury. Gerry Turnham eventually joined the band in place of John Wurr on clarinet, and Ken and Gerry got on very well; so much so that at Gerry's funeral the following year Ken was more emotionally moved than I would have thought possible.

That takes me back to a jazz festival gig in Germany, in Mönchengladbach. The Chris Barber band were on in one of the concert halls adjacent to where we were playing, and when we finished our set Gerry said "Come on, Ken, let's go and see Chris's band." The reply wasn't favourable, and so some of the band went off to see Chris. I stayed behind talking to Ken, and suddenly he said "Well, I suppose we'd better go and see this Barber Band," and so we set off. As we opened the doors of the

Ken's Quartet, with Ray Smith on piano, Ian Christie and Jim Bray

hall, they were playing the last chorus of *Isle Of Capri*. Ken turned on his heels, muttering something about "...stole my arrangement..." and disappeared.

Later that evening—as we were all staying at the same hotel—Ken invited the entire Barber band, amongst others, back to his hotel room for a party. This was not a wise idea, as he had a single room which comprised a bed, a fridge, several ashtrays, and not too much room. However, there were about twenty people in the room by about three in the morning; Ken was dancing with Annie Hawkins ("let's shake a leg" would have probably been his request) and we all had a great time.

Paul Rosenberg and I were the last to leave at about five, and I cast an eye around the room before I left. The cigarette trays were full of spent cigarettes, the fridge was on its side, empty bottles were strewn about, and I believe I remember one of the curtains had come loose from its moorings.

At breakfast the following morning we weren't all there—in many ways—and Ken's absence was obvious to us all. I was sitting with Gerry Turnham and Len Baldwin when one of the cleaning ladies approached asking which one of our band was in a certain room.

"Oh, that's Ken Colyer's room," said Gerry. "Best to use your room key because he likes a drink or two." Several minutes passed before the maid came back saying, in a tone of disbelief, "That man is an alcoholic!" That she could actually have believed that one man could do that amount of damage was too much, and provided some amusement for the rest of the tour — the word "alcoholic" was enough to start the hilarity.

However, waiting at the airport for our flight back to London, Gerry could contain himself no longer, and told Ken the story. Could have been risky, but Ken was crying with laughter at the end. There were people whose company he enjoyed, and Gerry Turnham was one of them.

DURING ALL THIS TIME ONE OF KEN'S REGULAR GIGS was at Centaurs Rugby Club, which had replaced the regular Monday night at Brentford Football Club. The band he used on those sessions—different from the All-Stars—had settled into a fairly regular personnel by the late seventies and it was always an enjoyable evening, but there was trouble ahead when Ken started writing the manuscript of his book *When Dreams Are in the Dust*. He confessed to me one day that writing about his life had stirred up old problems, most of them having remained unresolved.

He started firing people from the band for no apparent reason, and one night he accused me of stealing one of his gigs—a long, boring misunderstanding at which we both felt offended, and I left the band before he decided to fire me.

The following year he guested with The European Classic Jazzband, with whom Mike Pointon and myself were playing, in Brecon, and several months later he phoned up to ask me to do a gig at the Pizza Express with himself, Jim Bray and Ian Christie. He picked me up in his car, and we chatted, had a very enjoyable evening, and he dropped me off home in the early hours. It was as if no problems had ever existed.

But that was Ken—he could view life from a philosophical standpoint sometimes, at times be quite charming, humorous, concerned and at other times irrational, bitter, and quite difficult. I remember listening to the band at the 100 Club one night when Johnny Parker was on piano. The band was on form, and on one number, as Ken played into the hat mute for the penultimate chorus, I remarked to Roger Horton "That's a sound you could die for"—not that I had any intention of expiring at that moment—and of course, the next chorus was even better.

And that's how it was to play in the band. Bound For Glory. His music hit the heights whilst his personal life plumbed the depths at times, due perhaps to frustrations beyond his control, or the aforementioned build-up of unresolved problems. Ken's was an amazing talent—his achievements made all the more remarkable considering his personal struggles. As he often said: "When the music's rollin' along good, sometimes one of those magic moments happens. That's what you live for."

Here, to begin, are some of the impressions of a few of the people closest to Ken over the years.

The display case for the start of British Jazz at the British Music Experience in London with Ken's Derby mute and trumpet at the centre

CHAPTER ONE
'SOUNDS IN HIS HEAD'

BILL COLYER The same way that George Lewis and the New Orleans kids who grew up with those sounds from the cradle—Ken's was the same sort of background; he'd got sounds in his head... I'd be indoors when I was at home playing my records and obviously those sounds were going into Ken's head.

BEN MARSHALL There used to be a regular article in the *Reader's Digest* called "The Most Unforgettable Character I've Ever Met"—Ken would be mine. His life story reads like a film script; at his peak, playing some of the most glorious jazz trumpet to be heard, and at his lowest, suffering the pain and distress of serious illness and seemingly throughout his life a victim of the frustration he felt, as crystallised in a quote from his book, which he gave me years ago, *New Orleans and Back*: **"I was born about 60 years too late, the wrong colour and in the wrong country—a misfit."**

JULIAN DAVIES There's that little bit in *McSorley's Wonderful Saloon* by Joseph Mitchell—a book that meant a lot to Ken. "The people in a number of the stories—in this book—are the kind that many writers have recently got into the habit of referring to as 'little people'." I regard this phrase as patronising and repulsive. There are no little people in this book. They are as big as you are... whoever you are."

DIZ DISLEY I used to think he reminded me of Stalin. He wasn't a very good player but he was a good bloke.

KEN COLYER Some people tend to think that I'm very narrow-minded in my musical tastes. But this isn't so. I am in what I want to play. But of course, I mean, I like other styles of jazz, as well. And I'm well aware of them, you know.

MONTY SUNSHINE Ken was very, very deeply feeling the music. That's what he felt, and that's all you needed to have, as far as I was concerned, and I enjoyed his playing, which was fine; he was a great pleasure to play with. I mean, in a way it's the same as—the Hot Fives and so on are all very well, but in a way, it would be better if Louis played like George Mitchell. I've heard that remark more or less made. Well, Ken was like that. He had *that* quality, that you don't notice.

JULIAN DAVIES I realised that for the first time in my life I was listening to a man who actually meant what he played. He wasn't just playing a tune, he was living it. "Man, you sound just like Mutt Carey." Ken turned to me and said, "Do you want to join my band?"

PAT HAWES I often got the feeling, when I was playing with him, that he'd much rather be somewhere else, or doing something else. **There is for my mind a distinct link between the playing of Ken Colyer and Miles Davis.** But I can hear it up there, rather than I can put it down on my fingers, or writing or whatever.

SONNY MORRIS Around '53 when he came back from New Orleans, he was over the moon about Percy Humphrey. That was the greatest thing ever, according to Ken, when he came back from there—Percy Humphrey.

BILL COLYER But of course, playing at sea, you got the open-air lungs, so Ken was loud. Don't forget, he'd heard Wild Bill in Condon's, who was powerful, and they were only tiny clubs in New York, so you'd sit this close to Wild Bill. That's a wall of sound. Ken was on an "Iron Chops" thing. **He learnt light and shade afterwards, power not noise.**

JIM GODBOLT All the guys that were making a lot of money out of New Orleans jazz never *went* there, including Humphrey Lyttleton, by the way—I don't think Humph ever went to New Orleans. But Ken did—he made the effort; getting on that boat, getting off the boat, jumping ship, on the bus down to New Orleans. It was like Scott of the Antarctic.

ED O'DONNELL One day I said I thought Mezzrow's book were a load of rubbish; well... Ken went up in the air. Sits down an' mumbles something and John Parker gets up and sits down between us and says "Get on with your dinner." And I never got a chance to explain.

And I thought: "You jumped your ship, took a risk, made your way down on the Greyhound, and went down to New Orleans, and Mezzrow didn't have to do that." You know, Mezzrow got some money off his father, probably, which he could've. I mean, he could've taken a train down there, or a bus down there even, and found out what it was really like to be a black man—which he would have found out—really found out.

And Ken Colyer said he couldn't go in to the boozer with 'em, because of the colour bar.

COLIN BOWDEN I know that he liked Harry James, and I know that he liked Percy Humphrey, but he probably liked all of the very New Orleans players. But he had a lot of respect for musicians outside his genre.

DOUG LANDAU His technique was well crafted rather than spectacular, but this was probably an artistic choice; he is on record as thinking Louis Armstrong's dominating flamboyance to be "not for the benefit of the band." His approach stood him in good stead when tackling the intricacies of rags, which he always carried off with authority. Stylistically he was much influenced by most of the New Orleans trumpeters that came to the fore in the revival, Mutt Carey and Bunk in particular, but he was never a slavish copyist, fashioning these influences in his own way.

KEN SIMS He wasn't a stomper. I mean, if you listen to Herman Autrey or George Mitchell—they joined the rhythm section. Ken didn't do that—he was a lyrical, melodic player. Beautiful.

PHILIP LARKIN Colyer combines a robust public personality with the tenderest of instrumental tones.

DICK SMITH He *did* sort of bully you a bit. But when you joined his band you knew what you were expected to... be like. Yeah, he told me not to do anything fancy. None of this bopping. And you could tell whether you were in with him. If you were standing behind him, you'd know.

I enjoyed it with Ken. I don't know how, but he just managed to bring the best out in you.

STAN GREIG He was alright. I mean... he was a bit grumpy, that was the only thing. I thought he was just a guy with very definite ideas. Nothin' wrong with that.

DELPHINE COLYER I think he thought everyone was against him—I don't think he thought many people were on his side. If he had a sort of magic session, I suppose he would have thought that we were all going the same way, but I think he was fighting an uphill battle all the time, really.

KEN SIMS A very kind man—he was very good to me. Without him I would have been sleeping in doorways, certainly at that time. Even with the Bilk band, it was very hard to save any money. Couldn't go home to Mum.

Ken was there—at Lillie Road—but he was having some kind of problems with his stomach. He had this lady coming in

Ken photographed at
the flat in Lillie Road,
Fulham, London in 1956

to care for him, who cooked him enormous meals, and Ken would give me most of it, so I'd eat mine and his. And he had an amazing record collection. Small groups from the Basie band, and then the next one would be what sounded to me like a second-rate Salvation Army band—and it was wonderful stuff.

JOHNNY PARKER Well, personally, I was frightened of him, because, you know, it was the old class thing of middle-class from a grammar school and there he was—rough speaking. He looked as though, you know, he'd sooner hit you than talk to you.

CHRIS BARBER His accent, to me, always sounded a bit like a cross between Australian and Birmingham, which is about the same—a funny, very strange accent.

Ken sounded about the same to me, all the time. I mean… it's a very recognisable, individual sort of accent; it's his voice more than the accent. Stu Morrison can do it perfectly. When Stu joined the band, Stu was standing behind Ian Wheeler, and Stu said "Wheeler," and Ian nearly jumped out of his skin, because he thought Ken was standing behind him.

RON BOWDEN He didn't speak a lot; but when he did, you knew what he meant.

DAVE BRENNAN I never found Ken a particularly disagreeable man. He was just forthright. Some things pleased him enormously. I once said he reminded me of Lee Collins in some of his playing. I was his friend for the whole evening. When he saw a newspaper article I'd written describing his trumpet playing as "dancing," he went into raptures, repeating it over and over again with his eyes having a distant glaze. "Dancing, that's it, man, dancing." I felt he was very sensitive to criticism but only liked praise of the right kind.

LONNIE DONEGAN I don't think we've had a jazz trumpet player with the talent of Ken Colyer. I could cry listening to him sometimes. He had so much in him— such a musical "soul" player on trumpet. But all artists have their funny psychological quirks.

PETE DYER Ken had a pretty unique sound from that point

of view, and he was quite exciting to play with. All musicians should have the "Four Ts": Timing, Tone, Taste and Technique. By technique I mean being able to do what you want to on your instrument.

ALAN COOPER He was unswerving, never mind whether it made a few bob or it didn't. I mean, he was doing something and he said this is what it's about and did it, and I have the greatest admiration and respect for that. And so the wheel moves an inch further.

JOHN KEEN He was initially a jazz fan, like a lot of us were; we wanted to play like that. But he was much more talented than most of us. And he soon found that he could play effectively, but he also had a kind of a latent potential leadership inside of him, which meant that he knew what he wanted quite early on; and from what I know of him, he actually used to go around to people's houses and say, "Look, we're gonna form a band and this is what it's gonna be like."

I don't know whether the word *crusade* is right, but he had a kind of a vision, and it also fitted in with that post-war world of: "Well, this is a democratic music and those people who weren't commercial in the United States—the black blokes who played from their heart—they never got the exposure, and perhaps it's up to us to do it."

BILL REID He *did* have a magic to him. But quite how Ken had this magic, and this awe that got over to people, I don't know, but he *did*. It was simple, and he was sincere, and he didn't deviate. He stuck to what he liked, what he could do, and it worked. And he could play very well, and it did swing. He was more musical than many thought.

SAMMY RIMINGTON Years after I'd left the band, I went up to him and said, "You're still playing with great feeling, Ken."

You know, it was the *feeling* thing that got me. The sincerity, and the heart. The feeling he played with was sincere, which is quite rare when you think about it. There's so many people like going through the motions of playing from up here [*points to head*] all the time, they don't play with any soul, you know.

He kind of *was*, though, because he had a charisma, without doing anything; sometimes quietness or silence is mystical. He had that kind of charismatic power on stage, without doing anything. A lot of the musicians were afraid to say anything to him—people get sometimes a little bit afraid, because there's no contact. So they're thinking, "What's he thinking?" So they're making the magic in their own mind—it's all happening in themselves. It's all to do with that: control.

CHRIS BARBER It's more than that. It's the timing of every

Ken with Sister Rosetta
Tharpe at the 51

phrase. Every note. That's what Ken had, you see—the correct swing and feel and timing was always there and never wrong.

MIKE CASIMIR Musically I enjoyed his playing. He had a distinctive and lyrical style reminiscent to me of perhaps Charlie Love, Mutt Carey, Percy Humphrey and a few others. I approached him on this subject once and received a blank stare as an answer.

DELPHINE COLYER Very, very sensitive person, and more complex than some people have thought. He was a great reader. I think this is where he got his knowledge from, really.

CATHY COLYER Ken was a quiet man. And he never showed any showing-off business—he wasn't someone that would say: "I'm Ken Colyer, I'm to be given a bit more respect"... and all of this. He wasn't like that. He was very modest—he wasn't a man to go into this "big star" business.

FRED HATFIELD Ken appeared to be a person that would be totally dedicated to whatever he was doing, at the time.

DICK ALLEN Another thing that I remember that Ken was very interested in, when he was here in '52 and '53, was trying to revive the English folk tradition. It shows up in things like *Bobby Shaftoe* and *Miner's Dream of Home*, which he recorded with the Cranes.

JIM HOLMES In my opinion, Ken's most telling contribution to the traditional jazz scene in Europe was leading a band that played ensemble music in good taste. At a time when commercial pressures led most other bands into gimmickry, this says a lot about Ken's integrity.

Ken's style of playing was in the early days quite strongly influenced by Bunk Johnson and Mutt Carey, and of course by many other New Orleans players. Through his career he was to develop his own very individual style.

KEN COLYER When I hear the Bunk Johnson American Musics it makes me feel warm inside—a warm feeling in the belly. No other music moves me like that. [*BW*]

CUFF BILLETT He *was* distinctive, whatever way you say it. You could hear Mutt Carey in him, and I could sometimes hear Elmer Talbert; some of the bowler-hat mute stuff reminded me of Elmer Talbert at times. And he'd probably been influenced by Percy Humphrey, being the player with George's band; and of course, at that time he would use the bowler-hat mute. He wasn't in the same league as Percy as far as power or rhapsodic playing. **But I thought I could hear Mutt Carey and Elmer Talbert in him. What I didn't hear was any kind of influence of other British players that had been before; I didn't hear any, shall we say,** **Humphrey Lyttelton coming out of him,** although they were both on the same kick, Humph being a bit before Ken.

JOHN WURR I was interested in his influences. He always quoted Mutt Carey, Bunk Johnson and King Oliver as his major sources, and all these are apparent. He also loved the Condon mob, and there was quite a bit of Wild Bill in there. I'm not sure about Louis Armstrong. He claimed not to have been influenced by Louis, and clearly Ken's style did not follow Armstrong's path.

But it is interesting to note that a large slice of Ken's repertoire came from the Armstrong 1930s recordings. More interesting to me was that Ken also loved Duke Ellington, Billie Holiday, Lester Young, Charlie Parker and Woody Herman—something the Colyer idolisers care to gloss over. He told me once, with a conspiratorial grin and obvious pride, that he had given one of his mysterious roll-ups to Dizzy Gillespie.

RON WARD Another time in Leicester we played for a Students Rag Ball. **Towards the end of the evening we realised that Dizzy Gillespie was across the hall listening to us!** He had been playing a concert the same evening, just up the road at the De Montfort Hall. He stayed listening to us for a half hour or so and at the end of the set he spoke to Ken and told him he had liked what he heard.

ED O'DONNELL I think he was exploited... even when he was living.

HUMPHREY LYTTELTON I think all musicians who worked—certainly in the traditional jazz field, and many outside it—respected Ken for the devotion to early New Orleans jazz, which he's certainly shown throughout the years.

Ken's belief was that in New Orleans the music was all part of the life, and had a particular flavour which was lost at that time. And so he came back and demonstrated this particular music, which of course had been heard on records by Bunk Johnson and Kid Ory and George Lewis.

And it really split the traditional jazz movement into two.

I suppose you could say at that time Ken and myself represented a divergence, and I went off. You see, I had the feeling that if somebody had stood at Louis Armstrong's shoulder in 1923, when he was with King Oliver, and told him what he should play, and told him to stop doing this because... that's not allowed, that's not New Orleans style... my belief is, there would have been no jazz, as we know it today.

It would have just become a 1920s music and wouldn't have developed. And I've had discussions and arguments with Ken about this. But certainly, as a representative of that style of music, which I love, you won't find anybody more devoted than Ken.

CHRIS BARBER The main thing was, he informed us about what was going on in New Orleans then... as to the jazz of twenty to thirty years before. That helped us to start off, but of course I've heard where his influences came from: from Percy Humphrey, Mutt Carey, Wild Bill Davison, and so on. With the band, we *did* find a new style, even though we didn't want to do so. We just wanted to play good jazz.

PETE LAY You know, there was never any antagonism between Ken and Chris as far as the music was concerned; he always respected Chris's band. He said to me, "There's things that Chris does, I don't do them but Chris does them well. If people come to me and say 'I want *Rent Party Blues*,' I say 'Chris's is the band to do those things; I don't do that type of arranged thing.'" He respected Chris for those sort of things. He was very respectful of other bandleaders, you know. I mean, Alex Welsh: he liked the Welsh band, and he liked the early Lyttelton band, and Bruce Turner.

BRUCE TURNER Ken's way was always to assume that the music contained its own appeal. Ken simply played the stuff he believed in, occasionally transfixing with a scowl any members of the public who did not seem to be paying attention.

ACKER BILK Ken had a lot of dynamics in his playing— I like that. He's not a trumpet player that plays in one level, you know. He drops it down, and the last choruses are up, and then the hat.

It's quite exciting to play with. I mean, I made this record last year with Ken after... thirty years or more, you know. And he's playing the same. I couldn't play the same. I mean I've

Ken on board the
SS Tamaroa, dressed ready
to take on the town

changed—it's not intentional with me; I get influenced by different people. And my style has changed a lot since. I think that's a good thing. Because, in a way, I mean, Ken Colyer is Ken Colyer, and always will be. It's good to have an institution.

JOHN WURR To be frank, we never got on particularly well. We had a shared interest in gardening, which was fine, but most of the time his legendary taciturnity obstructed any meaningful dialogue. Having hero-worshipped him as a youth, I found it quite difficult, as an adult, to accept that I didn't really like the man very much. Some bandleaders seem to go out of their way to upset those that are there to support them (sound crews, stage managers, etc.) and Ken shared this characteristic with one or two others I have worked for.

His drinking didn't help.

As a jazz trumpeter, Ken was primarily a melodist, rather than a harmonic improviser. A typical Colyer performance consisted simply of the tune played many times over. But the subtle variations in tonal colour, volume, and rhythmic placement of the notes created endless interest and variety. He was wonderfully easy to play *with*.

IAN WHEELER He didn't strike me as an abnormal person, all the time I was with him. He didn't suffer fools, I don't think. But he was reasonable to most people. He was a bit short, sometimes; they make him out—some of these people—to be either one extreme or the other. But he didn't strike me as anything other than perfectly normal. As I say, I had a good relationship with him—went on holiday with him... had a good time.

KEITH SMITH Sometimes Ken could be enjoyable company, but I often felt I was treading a fine line if I disagreed with his emphatic loves and hates for the British and our traditional class structures. **Ken loved eccentrics and often the romantic side of his character would come to the fore with enthusiasm for Judy Garland, for example,** and her various film appearances. This subject often concluded with a vocal chorus from Ken of *Somewhere Over the Rainbow*.

On the darker side, he would vent his hate for religion, authoritarianism and his contempt for graduates of private schools, which are inexplicably referred to in Britain as "public schools."

COLIN BOWDEN He didn't like to do the showbiz bit of deliberately raving the audience up. He liked to do it in his own time and in his own way. I mean, we'd go on to the stage in these big band concerts, you know, and a trad band would have been blasting away, and Ken would start with a slow blues, just to get things down to his level, which was a very clever way of doing things. I mean, those four rags we recorded showed the introspective side of his playing. And then you'd get the wild stuff, where he's going like a train. He could build up to a finale.

PETE DYER We were chatting at the end of the session and he'd say something like, "Do you know, we had two choruses in that tune where we got near there and that's all you can ask for in one evening. That's good." And he used to speak like that... quite interesting. I think *he* knew in that sense, you know.

STU MORRISON When I first met him, he seemed quite remote, and...

the legend was flying about... I mean, this was someone who had been to the mountain and come back with the tablets, you know.

And he'd come back to tell a story. The people he had played with were names on record labels, so we had a feeling that he was of another species almost, you know? In later years, when I got to know him better—a lot better—it was obvious really that it was shyness, it was the unwillingness to put up with bullshit and a load of mindless waffle.

On parade with John Keen and Sonny Morris in the Excelsior Brass Band

BILL WILKINSON When he was invited to play with the Excelsior Brass Band he bought a tenor sax. He was so quiet you could never hear him. I asked him why. He replied, "'Cause there's too many bloody good trumpet players [*Cuff, Jim Holmes, Andy Dickens*] in this band." **Every generation needs a Ken.**

BETTY COLYER He lived with us for a little while when he came back from America, and he was such a good raconteur when he was on form. He was so interesting—if you got him at a good moment, you know. He was *so* interesting. He was a very self-taught man.

I learnt such a lot from Ken and Bill with their knowledge of literature—Bill particularly.

COLIN BOWDEN I always remember him talking about Don Camillo—he used to love those stories, and he would use them as anecdotes. See, this is the way he is: classic example—somebody gave me an omnibus of all the Don Camillo stories, and of course I read them, and I thought they were marvellous. And I used to bring these anecdotes up, and of course in the end he'd never talk about Don Camillo after that.

But that was his way; he would like to find something that nobody else really knew about, I think. But I don't know—you could say that I didn't know him very well. All I knew of him was his musicality—his trumpet playing. I knew where he was going then, there's no doubt about that.

BILL COLE I can't really remember the exact first time I met him, but I remember that he struck me as being an imposing sort of person, in his own quiet sort of way.

TONY PYKE To some people Ken must have seemed abrupt if not quite rude at times. He didn't find conversation easy, particularly with strangers, and had no time for small talk. He was usually alright on matters close to his heart such as music,

the sea and, later, gardening but basically he was extremely shy and introvert.

COLIN BOWDEN In the late fifties the band used to play Eel Pie Island, and the only way across the water was by the chain ferryboat. We were all travelling together on the way over, and Mac and Ian were having a heated argument on some subject or other.

To cool the situation down a bit, Ken said for them to toss for it and produced a coin. It was an old silver half-crown piece. They grudgingly agreed, Ken tossed the coin, he missed the catch as it came down and it bounced off the side of the boat into the river. You can guess what happened: The atmosphere changed from doom to hilarity, with Ken crestfallen over his good intentions. He probably got a pint out of it though.

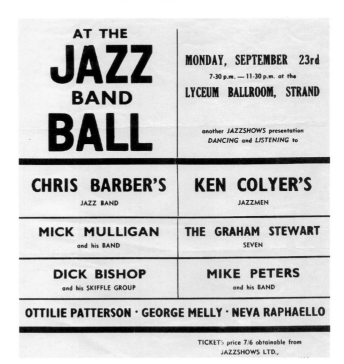

Poster for a Jazz Ball held at the Lyceum Theatre in Covent Garden

PETE DYER I can remember an instance where people used to come up and say, "Oh Ken, that last number—it was terrific. It was the best version I've ever heard." And I've heard him say, "Well, obviously you haven't listened to this version by George Lewis," or Armstrong, or something. But of course, he liked to be praised.

EDWARD BLACK Listen to the records. His fine tone, flights of melodic invention, the human qualities which empower a musician to play blues and spirituals. The great Lizzie Miles at the time of the prison incident inscribed two records "To a great jazzman."

Serious and dedicated, in touch with an ideal, Colyer was the creative artist on the razor edge of life. With his horn to his lips, he felt the contact of dead musicians motivating his playing far more than lesser artists accompanying him. Bunk had been showing the way (yet with his own distinct style Ken was properly scornful of copyists). When he played at the Düsseldorf Bier Bar the photo of Bunk on the wall appeared to smile or frown.

GEORGE MELLY At a recording session Ken went into the box to hear the playbacks and rejected the lot. "You can't hear the fuckin' inner rhythms," he told the astounded engineer.

JOHN GUY A young lady who had been reading George Melly's *Owning Up* asked Ken if he really used the 'f' word. "You can't believe everything you read in books, my dear. Anyway, we forgive George because he's good fun!" Thereafter Ken would refer, smiling, to "the *proverbial* inner rhythms!"

GEOFF COLE Ken realised that we were never gonna sound exactly like a New Orleans band. He said to me: "I'm not much on communication. I wish I could play all six instruments."

Ken was very strong on inner rhythms, as you know. You know, you maybe play the same notes, but you don't play them at the same time. They were improvising with time, rather than with notes. And he was very good at this. Bunk Johnson—he improvises with time, puts different stress on different phrases and places notes at different places over the beat.

Concerning Ken's attempt at recreating New Orleans music, I didn't think he was doing that. It seemed to me that Ken had already formed his own style.

BILL COLYER Number one: his mute work, and he's been to New Orleans enough times to know. Ken with his mutes, best mute man in the business, Ken. He's making sounds and when you are sitting behind him... I had to play washboard for some months till we found a real drummer, and I remember whenever Ken went in the bowler hat, the sound waves coming back, they turned you on.

IAN CHRISTIE I don't think Ken's actual trip to New Orleans changed the course of British jazz history. His style was already set, his ideas were completely formulated.

It did a lot for him, as he'd left the Christie Brothers Stompers, without any kind of a row or anything. I mean, he thought that we were diverging from the truth—the gospel—of New Orleans Music. I mean, he suddenly announced he was going to kind of recharge his batteries by going off to New Orleans and playing there. It reinforced his ideas rather than changed them, I think. And when he came back and started his own band, he had that unswerving dedication which he always had.

LEN BALDWIN Jim Godbolt in his book recently said about the chap who went up to Ken and, trying to be sycophantic, said, "Oh, Mister Colyer, your band's better than George Lewis," and Ken got up and punched him.

He was quite kind in some ways and was very tolerant if you had a problem, as at one time when I split my lip. The more I played the more it split. It was a problem, and he was great and very understanding: "Just do the best you can, man." That sort of thing. Whereas somebody else, I won't mention any names, would tell you to take a week off while he got someone else in.

COLIN BOWDEN I used to like him, but there were black periods. For example, if you met him and you'd go to a session in the evening, and if I didn't get the right response then I would just move on and not talk to him. Or directly he went on a tack I didn't like, I would just quietly leave the conversation. I found that better, then I didn't get screwed up. He was moody, like Mac was, really. Ken could handle his drink—I could never keep up with him.

I think really Ken used to get very nervous. Sometimes when he would start a concert he wouldn't go straight into it. I think he was very conscious of what he was doing, and I think he felt very vulnerable sometimes. And part of his whole psyche was a shield.

SAMMY RIMINGTON Ken was a bit funny. He loved loyalty: he really respected loyalty. And if anybody left him, he'd never forget it. I think he even said it to me, "You've left me now." And somebody else left the band, and he didn't take it good at all, you know. Because he felt that they'd let him down.

With Chris, he felt he got let down, I think. Because they went on a different way. The others were thinking more commercially, let's put it that way. Their main thing was to make money, where Ken's wasn't. **He wasn't aiming, as a goal, to get famous or to make money. He just wanted to spread that gospel—if you like—of that music. And to give him that feeling—himself—that he was aiming for it. He wanted to master it.**

GEORGE MELLY Awkward as an old bear, often too drunk to blow properly, he has played as he wanted to since the very beginning.

JOHN BEECHAM The things that struck me most about Ken's playing were his bell-like tone, which he was able to maintain even in the deadest acoustics, and his knack at the end of a number of squeezing out one last chorus which was even hotter than the one before.

The interplay between cornet and trombone is very important in a New Orleans band, and I always listened closely to Ken's lead and tried to complement his melodic and rhythmic approach.

He was never smug or self-satisfied, and so I'm proud to remember the times when he would smile and say, "We have a great rapport." I also admired his professionalism. He turned out smartly dressed for every engagement, whether it was a dinner suit occasion or a casual gig; his beautiful cornet was always clean and shining; the band always started on time and played the agreed length of sets.

'FESSOR' LINDGREN He was fighting for what he believed in. A man who dedicated his life to the music.

How an English newspaper viewed Ken's part in the beginnings of Pop music!

IAN WHEELER Yes, he *was* different. You could say that it was just that everyone else was following a slightly different line. So, what Ken was playing—based on what he learned in New Orleans, and what he liked—was not generally followed by most of the bands at the time. That's why he was different. Different in so far as where he left the spaces. He spaced his notes very different from everybody else.

In fact, when I left Ken, I found it very difficult to play with anyone else, because I was playing over other people's things, you know. Because I'd got so used to the way Ken phrased. You know—he phrased and you answered, type of thing, but the timing of his phrases *was* very different from other trumpet players.

GEORGE MELLY Even Humph, although he has always denied it, was affected by Ken's ideas. For a month of two he turned to look over his shoulder. The Ghost of Mutt Carey whispered in his ear. Then he turned away, and swam slowly and deliberately into the mainstream.

JOHN PETTERS Melodic—that's how I'd describe his playing, and I think he could play the blues as well; I think he could sing the blues. I remember hearing him do what he called *Lowland Blues*, which is the same as *Backwater Blues* on one of those LPs that I'd got at the time, and thinking, "Yes, this is as real as you can get... here and now." From my experience of him, he was quite open-minded musically, but I think he was locked into the way that he played. He wasn't like some musicians that can, say, turn on Louis Armstrong one minute and Bunk Johnson the next and that sort of thing. What you got when you heard Ken Colyer, was Ken Colyer.

TONY O'SULLIVAN I listened to my contemporaries who were more into the music than I was in about 1956, and kept hearing the name "Ken Colyer."

His image was that of a non-commercial bandleader with the—to me—romantic overtone of the man who had jumped ship and gone to New Orleans to learn about traditional jazz at source and play an authentic interpretation of the music. I bought an EP of the Crane River band and decided that this

27

was the sort of music I wanted to be involved with—melodic, swinging and devoid of any great pyrotechnics.

I acquired my first trumpet in 1958 and, after the usual trials and errors of the self-taught musician, began to develop a personal approach to playing New Orleans-style jazz. At this stage, Ken Colyer was the seminal influence.

I had discovered Bunk Johnson, Kid Howard and Mutt Carey (inter alia), but **the accessibility of the Colyer band through records, numerous visits to Studio 51 and concerts in the London area gave me a live model on which to base my style and technique.** I even bought a Humes & Berg "Derby" mute.

What I learned specifically from Ken Colyer, which I like to think have lasted to this day, are the virtues of good leadership (exposing the theme of a number and controlling the balance between solo and ensemble work), controlling the dynamics of a number (plenty of light and shade and gradual building to a climax), and a controlled yet lyrical "middle register" style, which seems to suit my constitution.

In addition, the various types of ensemble Ken led—the brass band and "ragtime" interpretations, inspired me to develop on both these fronts. I even did a bit of skiffling between 1957 and 1959 (which, if nothing else, taught me a bit about chords).

JOHN BEECHAM When I heard his record *The Isle Of Capri* on the radio, I saved up enough money to buy the record. The 'B'side was the majestic *Goin' Home*. This music knocked me sideways, and I decided that I'd have to have a go at playing it.

Most people who love music are happy to listen to it, but other poor devils are driven by an irrational need to play.

I would never have guessed in those days that I would be lucky enough to play professionally with each of the six guys on that recording and that I'd even get to make records and appear on TV with most of them.

As you can imagine, it was a tremendous thrill when, many years later, Ken asked me to join his band.

DAVE BAILEY I had been knocked out hearing the recordings of his late fifties band with Mac and Ian in the front line. The first time I ever met him was when I was on tour with the Yarra Yarra band in 1969. We were the backup band at, I

"Ken Colyer, who plays my kind of music."
Lizzie Miles, New Orleans 1958

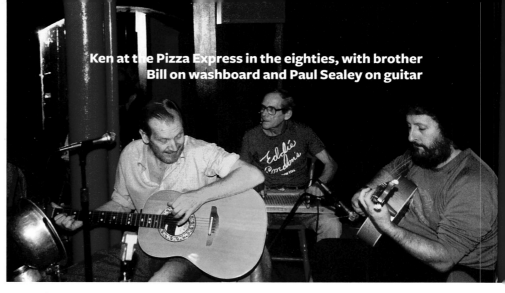

think, Osterley jazz club. He seemed somewhat remote and difficult to make contact with, but then who wouldn't, being constantly pestered by the punters during the intervals.

CHRIS BARBER I have to say that, during the year or so we were together, I learned from Ken Colyer everything I knew about timing.

For that sort of music, Ken would still be the best were he alive today. He had a perfect understanding of how to make a New Orleans band swing—while doing almost nothing. He was a marvelous musician who became a pain in the arse.

PETE DYER Well, we were both Sinatra fans. We could hear the timing, you see. Timing. And I think Ken recognised that.

COLIN BOWDEN But Ken had an ego. It was a weird combination. Ken loved that New Orleans ensemble sound... but he still liked to be in charge and be the focal point.

And the way he controlled a session to go the way *he* wanted to do it... and not the way the audience expected it. If he wanted to play four slow blues in succession, he would, you know.

BILL STOTESBURY I went in his garden, and he'd got this fishpond with straight sides; concrete fishpond. And he'd got this little ladder coming out of the fishpond. And I said, "What's that for Ken?"

"Oh... that's for the hedgehogs." And I said, "What do you mean, the hedgehogs?" and he said, "Well, they keep getting in the pond and drowning. So I put the ladder up for them to get out."

And I said, "You're joking." He said, "No." So I said, "Does it work then?" and he said, "Well, I haven't had any hedgehogs drown since."

And funnily enough there was something on the radio about a month later, and somebody—in a gardening programme or something—said, "Oh, but hedgehogs can climb, so..." And I said to him afterwards, "You were bloody right." And he said, "I know..."

MARTIN COLYER In the course of making a record in Muscle Shoals, Alabama, our band went to a club gig way out in the countryside. The bar band were tremendous, and when the musicians came down from the bandstand we were introduced to the guitarist—local legend Travis Wammack.

Travis was a slightly scary figure. He had probably been ripped off by men with much less talent, but much more business sense, throughout his life, something he had in common with many jobbing musicians in the American South (and all over the world, probably). Travis is a man whose lips smiled (in a Jack Palance-type way) as his eyes said, as Mark Pringle, our guitarist, put it later, "Just what do you want from me, boy?" The only other time he had experienced a similar look, he told me, was when he was introduced to my uncle, Ken Colyer, at the 100 Club.

ED O'DONNELL Oh, he was a funny bugger!

ALEXIS KORNER It is easier to gain liking than to gain respect. Liking, after all, makes few demands on the giver; it is so often a casual matter. Respect implies a degree of thought and, in some cases, admiration—which may not always be given too willingly. One such case is definitely that of Ken Colyer.

Here is a man of solitary nature, moody, diffident and utterly dedicated to his music, a man whose absolute integrity is admired even by those who do not like what he plays.

He does not make friends easily—Colyer is not "casually" likeable—but when he gives his friendship he expects to make and meet the demands which such a relationship must imply. His pride leaves him open to sudden wounds, his intensity betrays him into strange depressions. And all this is plainly audible in his music.

GEORGE MELLY Ken Colyer came back from New Orleans like Moses coming down from Mount Sinai with the tablets of the law. To the growing number of New Orleans purists he trailed clouds of glory, and every note he blew was sacred.

Ken with Chris Barber and Acker Bilk, probably photographed on a 'Floating Festival' on the Thames

CHAPTER TWO
MEMORIES OF THE 51

KEN COLYER A perfect band would be a delight beyond dreams, and it has always eluded me. The one chance I might have had I missed because of a misguided devotion to the British jazz scene. And now I do regret it, if you can call it that.

The 51 Club in Great Newport Street was going well, and I had what some considered my best band (I have tried to produce the best with any band I have ever had.)

I was packing up one night when a Frenchman from Paris came up and asked if he could have a word with me. It transpired that Jimmy Archey, Albert Nicholas and 'Pops' Foster were in Paris and, like Sidney Bechet, liked the climate there and wanted to stay.

The Frenchman, who must have known his music, reasoned that it would be an excellent idea to form a band, **but they lacked a leader and a lead horn. I was the obvious man for the job.** The only problem I could see was that we would have to have a French contingent in the band to satisfy the union and the authorities. I expect this could have been overcome, but I thanked him for the offer and turned him down.

JIM HOLMES I was present at the first session there, the first of many. The ensemble style of the band was the closest to N.O. bands I had heard on record. Listening to Ken's melodic style soon led me to take up the trumpet myself, and so changed my life.

JOHN KEEN He was a terse kind of player; not many notes, but what he *did* play actually meant something. The length of them, the way he pushed them in, the phrasing, the rhythm attached to it—it was all pretty good stuff. At that age—21 or so—I couldn't put my finger on what was happening... But I liked the way, the enthusiasm, the energy that someone like Colin Bowden had, and I thought, "*That drives it; that is good stuff.*"

COLIN BOWDEN I joined the band in '55 and they were already in the 51, and I think the band was still playing there when I left [September 1961].

Musically it was very, very exciting. That's the only way to describe the

Ken at the 51
with Sister
Rosetta Tharpe
and Vi Hyland

experience. You'd get mood swings, obviously, but when everything was right it was such a powerful band. When it was good it was very, very good, and when it was bad it was horrid!

It was exciting, and those years passed so blooming quickly! I've often wished I were a writer, to be able to put together the words to adequately describe the experiences.

KEN COLYER Somebody coerced Steve Race to come down to the 51; this was when the Crane River Jazz Band were holding forth. And Steve Race was very anti-trad; *well, I was anti-trad*—I always have been. This wasn't what I was up to. But fortunately, we hit a sort of series of numbers.

He was expecting to hear—a phrase that's always annoyed me—the "weary old war-horses" trotted out in the same weary old way. And we trot off about six numbers... Alright, some of the numbers he *didn't* know... but he didn't expect a jazzband—a trad band— to be playing these; you know, *Play to Me Gypsy, A Miner's Dream of Home*. And these are numbers which I was bringing in to the music *then*.

As I've said before, you've got to be moving. Even though we're learning, you've got to be moving. I mean, we're not just gonna copy what we've heard Bunk play.

BILL COLYER Look, I *was* the Cranes. I got the 51 set up...

IAN WHEELER Ken used to call numbers that we'd never played sometimes. For good or bad. If it worked, OK. I had a bit to do with arrangement, and some of the time—certainly before Ray Foxley joined—I used to work the chords out. Because, having played guitar, it gave me the sort of aptitude.

I remember Steve Race writing, and he criticised one tune for the wrong chords and another tune for the right chords. The one with the right chords was the one that I'd done. I remember in the *Melody Maker* he criticised *Over the Rainbow* because he'd worked with Judy Garland. Probably someone was saying that we sped up, and Ken said, "*No, it's controlled acceleration.*"

STUDIO '51 *presents*
THE KEN COLYER JAZZ CLUB

Every FRIDAY, SATURDAY,
SUNDAY, MONDAY & WEDNESDAY
FROM 7.30 TO 11 p.m.
WITH

KEN COLYER'S JAZZMEN
& SKIFFLE GROUP
PLUS BLUES & BOOGIE BY
BOB KELLY
AT STUDIO '51 10/11 GT. NEWPORT ST. W.C.2

GALA OPENING
Sat. Sept. 1st

KEN SIMS I joined the Cy Laurie band, and we played in Great Windmill Street. And I used to go from there to sit-in down the Colyer Club, because to play with the Cy Laurie band was very hard work—very arranged—and the stuff that Ken was doing didn't seem to have any arrangements; you just followed the lead and went with the wind—whichever way it went. And I met the guys there, and then I met Ken—in awe of, you know. It's funny, but in those days—he was only a few years older than me—he seemed like he was... a giant.

CUFF BILLETT I remember the kind of electric feel he had to the place—it was hot and sweaty. And to us then, it was wonderful. It was nothing like all the other kind of things we'd heard, like local bands playing. Wonderful.

And Stu Morrison had been perhaps the instigator of that, because he'd learned about this and joined our band. "You've got to go up and hear the Colyer band!" Looking back to what I actually remember about it, it just sounded an extremely good band.

And then we used to go to the all-nighters when he would sometimes be there—only in body! Of course by the all-night sessions, I mean if they'd already done an evening one anyway...

I remember him falling on Stu Morrison once, and Stu said: "He's fallen on me!" As if it was like "Oh, guess what! Winston Churchill's just been sick over me," or something like that. But anyway, the music had a great flow—an ebb and flow in the band, which was great.

KEN SIMS It was like being in some kind of church. I must admit I thought it got a bit out of hand—he never seemed to me like some kind of God, although I was in awe of his playing.

JOHN GRIFFITH Well to me the 51 was like a temple. You know, it was just sort of—I was new to all this. I was sort of on a late pass. I was still, virtually, almost a schoolboy. **Suddenly these sounds that I'd heard on disc I was hearing live for the first time.** I was *fascinated* by all of it, particularly, obviously, John Bastable.

BILL COLE I always found the 51 had a little bit of a sort of Mecca atmosphere. Everybody there was dedicated.

Great Newport Street in the Sixties

It was a little bit less straightlaced than Canterbury had been, where they were sort of dedicated but in a rather sort of negative way. But I found the atmosphere there great, particularly the all-nighters, of course.

GEOFF COLE As a member of the audience, it was always very exciting, because the band would start before the audience came in. So you were up there standing on the pavement, up against the railings, and waiting for the doors to open. And I would go in from the Porcupine, across the road, and then Pat Mayhew or Vi Hyland would be just down on the little step—two steps down or whatever—and they'd take your money, and then you'd go down, and the band would be playing.

And of course, while you were outside on the railings, the sound would come up through the double doors where you'd go through... and, you know, "Oh great..." You'd have to dash down to get a seat, you know, or stand around the outside at the back. **And you'd get your seat, and you'd... and that would be it. You'd sit there and just *wallow* in it. We used to just wallow in it. We used to hate it when the interval came.**

IT'S A MUST!

KEN COLYER'S JAZZ CLUB

STUDIO '51,
10-11, Gt. Newport Street, W.C.2
(next to Leicester Sq. Tube)

PROGRAMME FOR APRIL

Fri.	1st	KEN COLYER JAZZMEN
Sat.	2nd	,, ,, ,,
Sun.	3rd	,, ,, ,,
Wed.	6th	SAN JACINTO JAZZ BAND
Fri.	8th	DAVE NELSON BAND
Sat.	9th	Direct from Germany! First West-End Session HERR EGGY LEY & His Jazzmen
Sun.	10th	KEN COLYER JAZZMEN
Wed.	13th	THE RIVERSIDE JAZZMEN
Fri.	15th	MIKE DANIELS JAZZMEN
Sat.	16th	KEN COLYER JAZZMEN
Sun.	17th	,, ,, ,,
Wed.	20th	IAN BELL JAZZMEN
Fri.	22nd	SONNY MORRIS JAZZMEN
Sat.	23rd	GRAHAM STEWART BAND
Sun.	24th	IAN BELL JAZZMEN
Wed.	27th	KID MARTYN BAND
Fri.	29th	KEN COLYER JAZZMEN
Sat.	30th	,, ,, ,,

Every Thursday at 7.30
KENNY ROBINSON JAZZMEN

Every Monday at 7.30

ALL NITE SESSIONS EVERY SATURDAY AT MIDNIGHT

April 2nd
SONNY MORRIS BAND
TONY VINCENT BAND

April 9th
STORYVILLE JAZZMEN
JIMMY LOUGHERS JAZZMEN

April 16th   Easter Special!
KEN COLYER JAZZMEN
SAN JACINTO JAZZ BAND

April 23rd
TERRY LIGHTFOOT JAZZMEN
Chez Chesterman Scintilla Jazz Band

April 30th
HERR EGGY LEY JAZZMEN
and Supporting Band

EVERY FRIDAY 12-2 p.m.
LUNCHTIME

JOHN KEEN The college where I lived was stuck at the bottom of Commercial Road. And you could catch a bus there—a number 15—which took you into the West End. So I went on this bus, and people told me to go to Great Newport Street, and I did. I used to go there—after the first visit—on a sort of semi-regular basis. **And I remember seeing the band as we know it from 1956 with Colin Bowden, and it was a complete revelation to me to hear that music live like that. It was quality music.**

Other bands that I'd heard in the provinces were not anywhere near as good. So I thought, "Christ, this is good stuff!" and I used to go there on a regular basis, and then would want to play myself, which eventually I did. I bought a cornet.

TONY PYKE I always tried to get a good seat towards the front. And of course I didn't drive—there was no drink to be had, and I was reluctant to go over to the Porcupine in the interval, in case I lost my seat. Because I wasn't really too much into the skiffle, but I sat through it—I had to to keep my seat.

COLIN BOWDEN Pat [Mayhew] and Vi [Hyland]. They had the most huge Alsatian you've ever seen. They were lovely, and Vi loved Ken, there's no doubt about it. They were two lovely ladies—they'd come up the hard way, there's no doubt about that, to run that place. I used to just go in and say, "Hello Pat, hello Vi," and go and set my drums up.

I remember going down there once, and I hadn't waited to say hello, and I was half way down the stairs and the dog was coming at me the other way, barking its head off. I just froze, and Pat said, "Don't move," and she called it back down. They had a commissionaire there. I think that was a legal requirement in those days—they had one at the 100 Club too. I think it must have been a local by-law.

JOHN BODDY I did the door for a while. Delphine and Ken asked me if I would help out—I didn't get paid for it, I just used to be on the door taking the money.

It went well. Ken was popular. He got on very well with Vi Hyland. Ken being Ken and Vi being Vi. They got on very well indeed, you know. She was a bit eccentric, wasn't she?

A character. And she could be tough, but once she knew you, she had that little bottle of whisky under there and she'd say, "I suppose you'd like one of these?" And you'd say, "No… yes, please."

Because she didn't have a licence. But the other one—Pat,

the tall one—was scary, but kind. They were a couple, weren't they? I assume they were, anyway.

DELPHINE COLYER Vi was lovely—well, they both were. They were really nice ladies, and there was an old Mum—I think that was Vi's mum. She used to serve the teas and drinks sometimes. They were really helpful. They obviously didn't have any fire regulations there… I don't know. But it was after Bill had left. I was the secretary for the 51 club, after Bill had gone. We had that club magazine [see page 40]. We used to type it in a room above the 51. You went up some steps to another office and we had a funny Banda duplicator. It was just a spirit thing, so this is why you could only get a hundred-odd off. It was very effective.

RAY FOXLEY Well, about 1955 I wandered down the 51, which had ceased to be a modern stronghold and had become the Ken Colyer Club by then. Because Ken had come back and had joined up with Chris and left again and started the 51 club. And I went down one night, and Bill Colyer said, "Would you like to come and play the interval once a week?" And maybe it was fifty bob a night.

Had a beautiful grand piano down there. So I started to go along and play every week, to whichever band was there—sometimes it was Ken, sometimes it was another band. So I saw a lot of bands there. I was there for over a year, I suppose. I've played in all sorts of conditions. Used to sit-in with people in the band, and have a little blow, you know.

DOUG LANDAU Studio 51 proved to be a far more intimate place than the Humphrey Lyttelton Club in Oxford Street (now the 100 Club). At first all those people crowded into the small basement with a lowish ceiling made it seem almost suffocating, but strongly focussed on the music, the punters seemed quite unaware of any discomfort.

In contrast, "Humph's" was veritably spacious, with plenty of room for dancing. In those days the bandstand was down towards the end of the room, and the musicians could be watched without the impediment of a sturdy column obstructing the view. The acoustics also benefitted from this arrangement compared to these days.

At the Colyer Club the band could be hard to see on a Saturday night, unless you were in one of the seats in front of the bandstand; even being tall only helped a little. There were about six rows of seats, and behind them it was standing room only, everyone confined towards the sides and back of the room to provide floor space for a few dancers.

There was some seating in the adjacent anteroom, where the band could be heard perfectly well, **and soft drinks could be bought from the two friendly middle-aged ladies who ran the place, Pat and Vi.**

On this first visit it was noticeable that almost everyone seemed focussed on listening to the music in a way I had not

Pat Mayhew at the bar: Orange juice all round, unless you were especially favoured

seen before, but accompanied by a girl, I could not pay such close attention. On first impressions, the merits of the music seemed less obvious than the ebullient stuff Humph was knocking out in those days.

My second visit was alone. I managed to get a seat and was able to study the proceedings at close quarters. Some of the numbers were very long (I once attended a revived Crane River Band concert with just four numbers in a one-hour set), the band would build up to what seemed like the climax and final chorus, only for Colyer to change the dynamic and take things down before gradually building them up again. Sometimes this could happen more than once in the course of a number, and amounted to what might be dubbed "multiple musical orgasms."

IAN WHEELER It was nice to have a residency—about four nights a week we were playing there at the 51 at that time, which would be about 1955, when it started. It was a "home thing"; almost like an office job in a sense. You played the gig, went home, played there the next night and then home, and on and on. The same people would come night after night: Pete Vince and John Reddihough, John Renshaw (the bass player) and others, all sitting there in the front row. Vi Hyland, who used to run the thing, was always there in the kitchen, and Pat and the commissionaire on the door.

GEOFF COLE Occasionally, on a good night down the 51, when I first joined the band, **he would harangue the audience, tell them how wonderful the music was. He'd go on for ten minutes, and we'd all go: "Go on Ken! Tell 'em Ken!"** About the beauty of the goddamned inner rhythms and all the rest of it. I can't think of all of his favourite words, which, unfortunately, were always mispronounced.

COLIN BOWDEN Bob Kelly used to play the intervals and then Ron Vickers. Basically, Ken was trying to show the black musical influence of the Mississippi Delta. He loved Broonzy. Broonzy used to come on tours with us—what a lovely man. Ken liked that Black sound. His version of skiffle was based on that. **Skiffle was a dirty word as far as Ken was concerned, because of what it became: people trying to play the music Ken was trying to play, and they ended up with this trad phenomenon, if you like.**

It's like John Mayall, who stuck to his guns the way Ken did. The bands that liked Robert Johnson wanted to capture that. And it's very hard—you don't do it, really.

IAN WHEELER He didn't try to impose anything on you at all. Even when I picked up the saxophone he didn't say anything. Not very often. Maybe two or three times a night. I'd got this saxophone—I'd bought it in a second-hand shop, swopped for various things... an alto—and I went up with it one night; I think it was on *Gatemouth*.

I just thought, "If I get a solo I'll play sax," and I just picked it up, and he didn't say a word. You know, he didn't say Good, Bad, or Indifferent; I just played it. And after that, I just played it whenever I felt like playing it—whenever I felt it might fit. He never told me not to.

TONY PYKE **Ian Wheeler? Well, I mean, I was just in awe with his playing, because he was so very facile—weaving in and out of Ken's lyrical playing.** And a steady trombone on the other side—that was Mac. It was just a terrific band. Yeah, Ian was very high up in my estimation.

IAN WHEELER When I first joined the band we did a bit of rehearsing—not a great deal, just to get a few numbers off before we went to Germany. But other than that we didn't do a great deal of rehearsing. We did a bit if we were going to do a recording, as I remember. Even then, not a lot. We did more rehearsing when we were playing.

But with things like the rags, you need to work them out. But even then, it was only what came out. "Keep it in" sort of thing. "Oh, that's nice. Keep that in." It was all very much head arrangements. But of course, you had to rehearse how the themes came and went—that sort of thing.

JOHN KEEN And that's another thing Ken could do. He could get the right tempo. And they weren't fast, or overly fast—he never did that. And I used to envy his ability to set the right tempo for the melody, because he got away with it. I don't mean that he was taking a risk—he knew somehow that that was the right tempo for that tune. And that was an important element in getting the message across about the tune itself, and the feeling inside that tempo. That came across in his playing.

ALAN GATWARD But do you know the story about when Jim Robinson heard the Ken Colyer band at Studio 51? Oh, well, a fan took Jim Robinson down to the 51—he hadn't been out of New Orleans, I don't think. **And he heard a few tunes the Colyer band played, and Jim Robinson turned to his friend and said, "Hey, man—they're playin' our tunes."** He didn't realise they'd heard the records. But he was in a state of wonderment.

IAN WHEELER We didn't think about it, we just played, and it came out, presumably, because we played together for quite a while. And Ken—having his particular type of lead—lent itself to, perhaps, the way Mac and I played together.

> Oh, it was one of the happiest periods of my life. Really. I mean… not only being with Ken… not only that, but the fact that I was doing something I loved doing, and making a living at it, and I was doing it with a band I liked—that I enjoyed.

I mean, all of a sudden we started out. That period, when you start getting places, is a wonderful feeling. And you're so enthusiastic about everything; it was all new, and it's all coming together. Wonderful, you know.

NORRIE COX When we [The San Jacinto Jazz band] started playing the all-night sessions at Studio 51, he would always ask me to sit in for a couple of—sometimes even three!—numbers. I so well remember the first occasion, when completely out of the blue he signalled me to get my horn and join them. I only remember the terror of that first number—*Just A Little While to Stay Here*, in Ab, which at that time was not one of my strong keys. I was also in the process of changing from an Albert system clarinet to a Boehm, under the mistaken notion that this would turn me into a great player. I somehow got through it.

I believe *New Iberia* was the second tune that night. I guess, for all my screwups, Ken recognised a germ of a New Orleans flowering, because he invited me to sit-in several times after that, even though I never was in the same class as any of his regular players.

JOHN KEEN The band was so lively and there was a kind of knowledge—an understanding—amongst the audience that Ken would do this, and these are the kind of tunes they like to play, and he wouldn't do much announcing, but somehow the others knew what tune… There was a kind of… oh, we liked it because we're the in-crowd people, you know; all that stuff. You knew from the look on his face whether it was going to be a fast tune or a slow tune. He never went around saying, "Bb chaps" or "One more chorus" or any of that. They had to go along with his approach to it.

RICHARD SIMMONS All-night session at the 51 club (all a bit punchy by 4.00 a.m.). Colyer very rarely announced to the audience what he was going to play. He certainly never told me.

Delphine with homemade dress and Peter Hunter behind

repertoire-wise (who would have dared!), so the whole thing just sort of lamely petered out on the side of the road.

As far as I remember, nobody was particularly concerned or embarrassed, least of all Ken, who just rolled another fag. After a suitable pause, we all soldiered on.

DELPHINE COLYER Ken didn't really like me dancing—he didn't like that at all. In fact he banned me from the 51. I mean, you could only dance at the back of the 51 anyway. I was dancing with Pete and the interval came and he said to Pete: "Get out before I crush every bone in your body! And she's bad and you encourage her. Get out the both of you— you're banned!"

The most I ever heard was a vague murmur left and right to Geoff Cole and Sammy [Rimington], and I had to sort of catch up as we went along. However, on this particular night, he not only didn't tell me, he didn't tell Geoff or Sammy, and also neglected to tell himself: he just tapped his foot and then started playing.

Now you know that thing when you actually *have* been told what number is going to be played, but, as it is being tapped in, you suddenly forget—it doesn't usually matter because, as soon as it starts, you think, "Ah yes, of course" and away you go.

So, as Ken is tapping it in, *everyone* else in the band is thinking, "What is it? What is it? I've forgotten, but never mind, I'll noodle around for a bit until it all falls into place."

Sadly, on this occasion, that "everyone" included Ken himself. Whether he'd actually thought of a tune and forgotten it, or perhaps hadn't even thought of a tune, we'll never know. What ensued was a full (and wonderful) eight bars or so of everyone including our glorious leader completely bluffing and nurdling around (in various keys) waiting for some recognisable musical pattern to emerge.

No one else in the band had the courage to take any initiative

Yet, although we had some not-too-good moments, we had some really good times as well. Because he was ever so kind. And if you were ill, you couldn't have wanted anyone better.

DOUG LANDAU A good example of his Bunk Johnson-inspired fast descending runs, at which he was very adept, can be found on the 1953 recording of *Tiger Rag*. His skilful use of various muted effects, and the Derby hat in particular, gave much added colour. He would often punch his lead into the Derby for a whole chorus, or sometimes two, and very effective it was.

His high register work seldom went above the staff, but, only sparingly deployed and with plenty of dynamics, it lacked for nothing in its effect. It often took on a sailing, parade-like quality.

GEOFF COLE I went to an all-nighter, and people were playing, and at some stage I said, "Can I have a sit-in on trombone?" So, I seem to remember Roy Vaughan on piano, and I remember seeing Bert Murray around; he got up later. And I played with some of the guys—did a couple of tunes—and then Ken came

The 51: the view from the stage

up with Rosina Scudder, who at the time was quite often singing with Ken's band. Good blues singer, she was.

And some of the other guys got off when Ken came back. He said it was sort of a jam session, and New York jam sessions would always try to get the New Orleans "feel" going, you see. And of course, I loved it.

KEN HARRISON We [the Doug Richford band] were playing at one of the notorious Saturday/Sunday Frank Parr-Diz Disley all-nighters at Colyer's, and sometime after midnight, when his own gig had finished, the great man himself walked in. Removing his trumpet from its case and clambering onto the stage he warbled, "Richford, can your fuckin' band play *Winter Wonderland?*" and without warning, playing the first seven notes of the tune, he launched us into it.

I had never liked Colyer's music; his style of jazz did not interest me in the slightest, I could never understand what all the fuss was about. I was about to find out. He was brilliant. The moment he began playing, the X-factor clicked in and he and Doug's band swung as we'd never swung before.

Absolute perfection. His innate sense of time plus knowledge of the idiom brought everyone miraculously together. It was sensational. Ken was delighted too and remained on stage with us until the end of the gig.

Originally a post-bop drummer and still more interested in that than any other idiom, I'd never enjoyed Colyer's playing or his band and for those

reasons paid no attention him. As a matter of fact the Trad musicians' habit of referring to him as "The Guv'nor" offended me, but after playing with him I was forced to reappraise my opinion.

SAMMY RIMINGTON They used to go up the 51 Club. Everybody did—it was probably one of the only places, you know, if you liked New Orleans jazz, at that time. So, I was only young. I wasn't even allowed in there, but I used to go up there, and after I'd been playing about a year, I sat-in. Dave Reynolds—who I'd played with before Colyer—was a big fan of Ken; well, that was the kind of image then, wasn't it? You

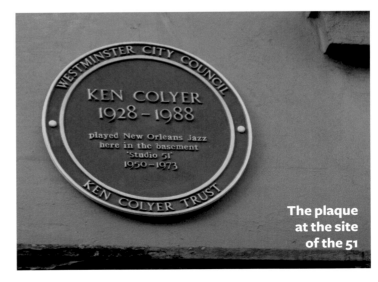

The plaque at the site of the 51

know, the kind of pre-hippie type thing, and everybody had beards. Very bohemian.

Dave loved Ken. He was his English idol, if you like, but he also liked all the other things, like Kid Howard and Bunk and all the guys we do. So Dave Reynolds liked it all, **but I think he admired Ken and respected him so much because he was honest with the music. Colyer, let's face it, you know, he wouldn't budge. And you've got to admire that, you've got to respect that.**

I remember Kenny Ball said he respected Ken a lot. He didn't say whether he liked his playing or not, but he had great respect for him. So I used to go up and sit-in at these late sessions, especially the all-nighters; I shouldn't have been allowed up, you know.

ANNIE HAWKINS When I first came to London in 1962 we used to go to the 51 club—the Colyer club—and they used to have all-nighters there, and we'd stay 'til the early hours. And Ken invited me to sit-in with his band when he found out I was just learning bass, and I gained a great deal of valuable experience, because he was quite kind and took the trouble to talk to me and… I was pretty grateful about that.

He was very keen on control in the band, and of course—being a new young player—I tended to get carried away with excitement, especially if it was Colin Bowden on drums. So he would turn around and say "Keep it down" in his funny old voice.

> And also, another thing that I learnt was that he was very keen to make us all play with a lot of dynamics. And the contrast of the light and shade was beautiful; it was very, very, very musical. Harmonics and melodies and… it was beautiful.

GEOFF COLE I sort of wandered out towards the kitchen area, not really wanting to get back. It was too early for a train, of course; six o'clock in the morning—Sunday morning—so I don't think the Underground started 'til about seven on a Sunday in those days.

And Ken was there, and I went up to Ken and said, "I was delighted to have a go and play for you,"—I'd read in the *Melody Maker* that there was a benefit for Lee Collins the following week—"and I just wanted to say I'm very glad to see that there are people helping those old guys in New Orleans who need help; that somebody is taking the trouble to do something for them."

And this obviously rang a bell with Ken. And he said, "Oh yeah, tell you what man; come into the kitchen. I think I've got a bottle of gin in the fridge." And of course, there was no licence down there. And so we sat at the table—Pat Mayhew was there with Spike Heatley the bass player, and they were talking modern jazz things across there, Ken and I were talking New Orleans across here. And never the twain should meet.

We had our conversation, we had our gin—we finished the bottle by about eleven o'clock Sunday morning. And he said, "Well, I'd better get back home to bed. My housekeeper [Vera] has taken Russell [Ken's son] down to Torquay." He was only two then. They'd gone for a fortnight's holiday. And in fact I went back to the flophouse in Paddington—Sussex Gardens, I think it was. Anyway, turned up in the evening with the trombone, and Ken says, "Yeah, come on man, come and have a sit-in."

LEE COLLINS LETTER TO KEN COLYER 8 SEPTEMBER 1959

1424 East Marquette Rd, Chicago 37, Ill. USA
Dear Ken,
What a great pleasure to write to a nice guy like you. I can never get over saying thanks to you for what you have done for me, and all the other musician's (sic) that took part in helping you with the benefit for me. I do trust that God will see fit and I will get up and can blow my horn again and be able to make a trip to England. That is where I always wanted to come and play, when the time came so I could come over there I had to take sick.

My grandmother came from Leeds, and the funny part her surname was Leeds, that is where I got the name of Leeds and when I got older I cut if off to Lee. I understand that you have a great band and I am glad to know that some of the musicians are still carrying on. Ken I thought that I would not go in the hospital but the treatments that I will take I have no other choice. I am tired of going to hospitals if I ever get well I will never go near one again even to see my wife and I love her very dearly.

I understand that Kid Ory is coming over?, he is a good friend of mine I have known him all my life. George Lewis have a piano player that made the Astoria records with me his name is Joe Robichaux.

So thanks again, the money will enable me to get the treatments that are required.

Sincerely, (signed) Lee Collins

SAMMY RIMINGTON I sat-in with Ian Wheeler. In fact, I sat-in as well when Acker Bilk came down to London from Bristol, and I think they did an all-night session or something, and then I sat-in with Acker as well there and Ken. And I used to go up

In the 51, with its dangerously wired electric sign. The line up is Ian Wheeler, Bill Reid, KC, Colin Bowden, John Bastable and Mac Duncan

there and just blow, but I couldn't play much. I mean, I couldn't play *High Society* and all them rags; forget it.

TONY LEPPARD We used to go there from '57 until well after Mac and Ian had left and Sammy had joined; until they stopped playing there, really. But you know what it was like: Marriage and work and things like that come along, and we had children, so we weren't able to go. But we used to go and see Ken as often as we could, and the great thing about that was when we went through bad times—when we were down in the dumps—you'd go and listen to Ken, and you'd come away... you'd be lifted, and it was great, and suddenly the troubles of the world had dropped off your shoulders. And the next day you were back again into it.

KEN COLYER I've been a very intense man—I've had to be; you know, intense about what I'm trying to do.

I mean, I've never been really satisfied with my music, you know. The whole thing. Because that's the important thing about a New Orleans band. It's having six, seven very good men, who all really know what they're doing. And each man reflects the other.

You know, each man sounds good in his own right, but reflects off the other man.

It's been observed that my style of leadership is sort of self-effacing, if you like. I don't believe in being out front of the band; I'm always part of it and I'm more interested in creating the ensemble, which is the important thing for me. It's creating the inner thing in the band.

I mean, my attention to the music has been *for* the music. I started out with the sole intent of playing this wonderful music and hoping we could get enough people to listen to it, and have this reciprocal thing; you know—play good New Orleans jazz to good audiences.

GEOFF COLE He said to me: "I was playing one day down the 51, and a woman came up and stood underneath me and said 'He's Jesus Christ!'"

And he told the story, about himself. And he wasn't rubbishing the woman at all. It was almost as if, at that moment, he felt that he was spreading the message in a quasi-religious way.

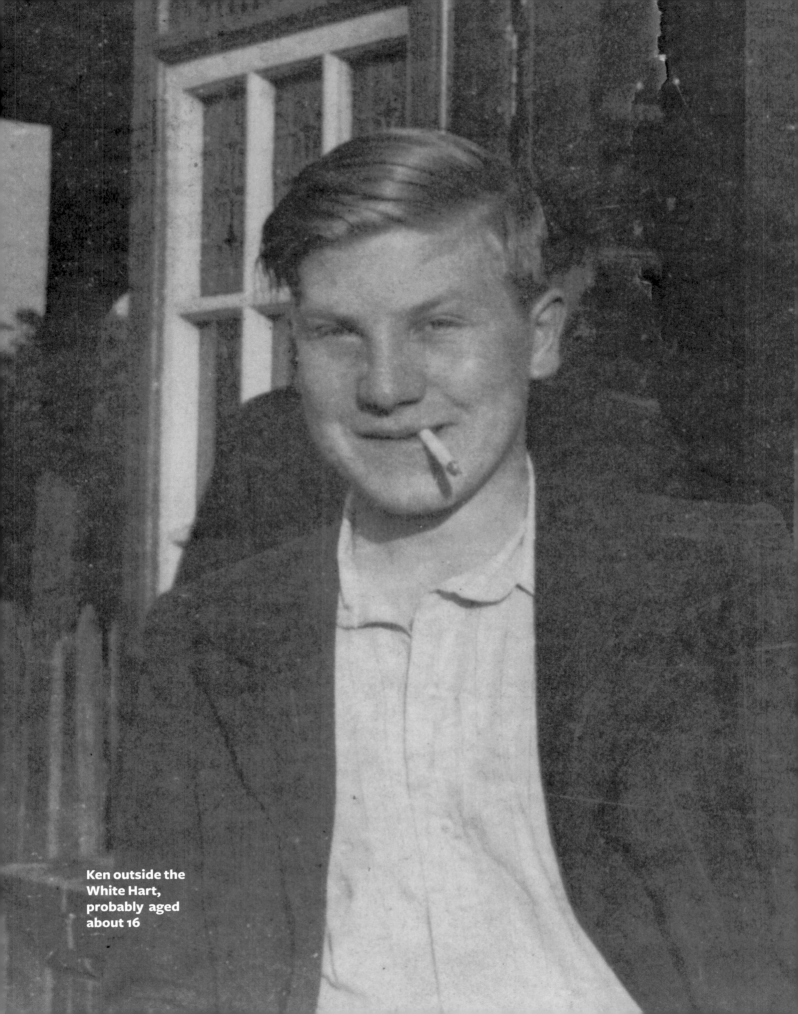

**Ken outside the
White Hart,
probably aged
about 16**

CHAPTER THREE
CHILDHOOD, FAMILY & THE MERCH

KEN COLYER WAS BORN on 18 April 1928 to Ruby Bertha (formerly Ehrhardt) and William Edward Colyer, at 53 North Market Road, Great Yarmouth. It was the home of William Ehrhardt, Ruby's brother. The details of Ken's early childhood are fairly sketchy—none of the three brothers were forthcoming about their early years, possibly because it was a traumatic time for all of them.

Ken's parents were both in service at the time of his birth, at The Old Manor, Twyning, near Tewkesbury, Gloucestershire: Ruby as a cook and William Edward as chauffeur. Presumably Ruby had moved temporarily to her brother's home to give birth to Ken, and it would seem that Ken's brothers Bill (6 years old) and Bob (4 years) were put temporarily into care at this time.

A sister, Daphne, was born in April 1930, by which time the family had moved yet again, to 18 Kings Road, Laindon, Essex. Ruby was hospitalised with liver failure, probably around this time, and baby Daphne died at the Isolation Hospital at Buttsbury on the afternoon of 16 December 1931, the cause of death noted as "Diphtheria—no P.M. (post-mortem)," the father being given as informant.

The family then moved to London—a third-floor flat in Fitzroy Square—where Ken attended Marylebone Road Infants' School. Yet another family move, this time to Dagenham, happened around 1935. In 1936 their young sister, Valerie, was born. The three boys were found to be living alone in a railway carriage sometime shortly after, and were put into a Dr. Barnardo's Home for a short period. The family were then reunited and moved back to London, to Marshall Street, Soho. In 1938 came the move to Cranford, Middlesex, where Ken attended the William Byrd School, Bath Road, moving on to the New Road School in 1939.

CERTIFIED COPY OF AN ENTRY OF BIRTH   GIVEN AT THE GENERAL REGISTER OFFICE

Application Number 983997-1

REGISTRATION DISTRICT		YARMOUTH AND FLEGG	
1928	BIRTH in the Sub-district of Yarmouth Northern	in the	County of Great Yarmouth C.B.

CERTIFIED to be a true copy of an entry in the certified copy of a Register of Births in the District above mentioned.

Given at the GENERAL REGISTER OFFICE, under the Seal of the said Office, the   25th   day of   February   2009

BXCD 719365

CAUTION: THERE ARE OFFENCES RELATING TO FALSIFYING OR ALTERING A CERTIFICATE
AND USING OR POSSESSING A FALSE CERTIFICATE 'CROWN COPYRIGHT'
WARNING: A CERTIFICATE IS NOT EVIDENCE OF IDENTITY.

CATHY COLYER Ken *did* have a rough time, really. The mother was always out working, the father was always chauffeuring—the boys were left to their own devices. Sometimes there was no food in the place for them.

KEN COLYER I know that I used to remember incidents from when I was about three years old (shipmate Eddie used to say "Tell me your life story since you were three years old"). Being scalded by hot fat from a frying pan when my two brothers and I were trying to fend for ourselves. Being in hospital with impetigo for the same reason. My sister Daphne falling down the stairs and dying within twenty-four hours of diphtheria. I was broken hearted and inconsolable for days. It's hard to have to come to terms with death when so young.

CATHY COLYER Daphne was buried in Rainham, on the hill. It was diphtheria… partially neglect as well. Because Ruby went into hospital due to liver failure—she was on a waterbed for a year, apparently.

And of course they told her that she couldn't have any more children, and of course then she went on and had Valerie. And the boys—what happened was, when she went into hospital, they lived in a railway carriage; in Laindon, near Basildon.

They were quite young, because Bob and Ken were put in to one Barnardo's place and Bill went into a much nicer one somewhere. And of course they were making out they were pining for Bill, and he cursed them when they got him into this other one because he was being treated really lavishly wherever they put him, but Bob and Ken were in Barnardo's. The father couldn't look after them, you see. He was a private chauffeur. Bob was actually born over the Manor at Esher. And we always said he was never like the other two.

KEN COLYER Memories become clearer of Fitzroy Square and the bug-infested flat. Bernard Shaw had lived in the house at one time. My mother had obtained it by subterfuge and a friendly rent collector. Children were not allowed; she had three. We used to have to creep in and out, trying not to be seen by the other tenants. We learnt to be quiet as mice.

My father was a chauffeur to some gown makers. My mother cooked for Clarice Mayne, Teddy Brown, Nervo and Knox—top entertainers of their time.

We moved to Dagenham and a change of environment and pest. There it was damp and we were plagued with mosquitoes and all sorts of flying insects. I believe the estate had been built on old marshland.

I had gone to Marylebone Road Infants' School and, on leaving, the teacher gave me several packets of flowers and seeds and wished me luck. I hadn't seen a garden before, so promptly planted the seeds. That summer I grew the largest sunflowers for miles and was very impressed by them.

It was all wide-open country by then, and the whole place would be ablaze with hollyhocks, lupins and many other flowers, all growing wild. You didn't really need to plant flowers, they were everywhere in the summer. Nostalgia has been so strong sometimes that I have felt I was back there with the lovely scents and the countryside atmosphere. I have no bad memories of school days there.

CATHY COLYER I know they were down in Essex. They lived in a railway carriage there for quite some time, then they came to Marshall Street in London, because Bob won a swimming certificate twice and they all got free swimming there for a month or so.

KEN COLYER We moved back to the slums of London: a mouse-infested flat above Finkle's sweet shop and Reece's the Furriers. Our house sloped with the street and we had to take the castors off the table as it would roll down and crash against the wall. I liked it there though, but I didn't like climbing the stairs at night. There was no light and we had gaslight only in the rooms, although Marshall Street power station was only yards away. I used to have an imaginary guard of resplendent soldiers to escort me in case of attack.

BILL COLYER All round here there are similar dwellings: they were called St. James's Dwellings then. There's one in Brewer Street, there's one in Marshall Street near the baths.

KEN COLYER I think the houses were condemned then but, as far as I know, they are still standing. Marshall Street ran along the top and Broadwick Street ran down to Brunswick Street market.

The area had a polyglot society: Jews, Chinese, Italians and many others crammed into a small area. Oh, there were Londoners too. We considered ourselves Londoners although we had lived in many parts of the country before settling for a while in Soho. Refugees used to be absorbed. Once there were some Russian families who had fled some purge or other. They couldn't speak any English when they arrived, but within two weeks the kids knew every swear word and curse in the vocabulary.

The three of us went to St Anne's School on Dean Street. It was allied to St. Anne's church but wasn't a religious school, as such varied denominations went there, but mainly Jews and Christians. We are Church of England, whatever that is. The Jews just did not attend our morning service and brief weekly religious lessons. The headmaster was a wonderful man and disliked by nobody. During the dinner break his study door was open and we could wander in at will. Children would sit on his lap or play around him and he loved them all.

Old pupils would come to see him, and Blackie and Son sent him all his schoolbooks at no charge. Whether it was by luck or what, I don't know, but Bill, Bob and I came top of our classes in our first term there. The headmaster was delighted and congratulated my mother.

Ruby in service, aged 18

St. Anne's church took their choirboys from the school and I managed to pass muster, much to my delight. I only made up the numbers, but I liked the pomp and splendour of some of the services. At the end of the first quarter I received six shillings. I was dumbfounded, wealth was mine: three brand-new florins. I was getting paid for what I liked. I rushed home and gave my mother four shillings, then gorged my mates and myself with the other two.

My father made some jeering remark about my choir singing one Christmas. The worst thing you can do is to shatter a child's fantasies. The period of innocent youth is all too brief and is often an important moulding time.

The idyllic life ended when we moved to Cranford. I went with the removal van, sitting in the back with two of Vignall's ham rolls and a bottle of Tizer for sustenance.

BILL COLYER I was buying the records. I must have had that early HMV windup gramophone when we lived in Soho, Broad Street, but I know that when we moved down to Cranford in about '38, I took my records down there. I must have had twenty or thirty 78s by then, and the gramophone.

You know that in the old days there were orange boxes with two compartments... well, I cleaned one of those up and put my 78s in it and the windup on the top. So, Ken would have been about 10 years old. Well, of course I wouldn't let a younger brother go near that. I mean, I was a teenager, wasn't I? You know, I ruled the roost with the kids.

Anyway, he and his school chums looked on me as the crazy big brother with the windup gramophone, but the music was obviously going into Ken's brain.

I had my set times when I got home and I would play some records; the old Songster needles: change the needle for every record and wipe the record, all this bit, you see. Well, Ken was doing his own thing with his school chums; they would come home occasionally and I'd tell them to shut up or clear out because I was playing my records.

KEN COLYER The kids (in Cranford) were suburbanites, neither true country people or townies. I hated it and would save my money and go back to my mates at weekends on the Green Line bus. I eventually had to get used to suburban life and make friends with some of the boys.

At eleven years of age we had a final exam before we went to senior school. This sorted out the intelligent ones from the dullards; A, B and C. I went into the A class.

From what I see today, there was nothing wrong with the "Elementary Education" of the day. It taught you how to read and write, how to spell, composition and how to write and address a letter correctly. We had as thorough a grounding as they could give us in all the basic subjects. If they couldn't get it into our thick heads, it wasn't their fault.

I was an avid reader by this time and had read Mark Twain, Alexandre Dumas and much classic material out of my own interest. I read Bram Stoker in the hope of being terrified, but didn't realise that it is the idea that is terrifying. I found *Dracula* pretty boring, though I persevered in the hopes that it would scare the wits out of me.

BILL COLYER Well, then the war broke out in '39 and we got issued with Anderson shelters. We dug a big hole in the garden and put the corrugated iron in. That became Ken's hidey-hole with his mates and he was keeping rabbits. He'd be playing his harmonica and they'd do their own thing by candlelight in the shelter. I'd be indoors when I was at home playing my records, and obviously those sounds were going into Ken's head.

Now this is very interesting. When I was called up—I'd volunteered twice for the Navy and the Army but I was deferred for months because I was doing ARP work, putting

Ruby in her later years

out the incendiary bombs and all that stuff in 1940—I went in the Army; finally I got my call-up papers. I ended up at the end of 1941, I think, doing my twelve weeks basic training in North Wales. After twelve weeks you are a pretty well trained soldier for openers, before you get into the real stuff.

So, I excitedly wrote home to my mother and said, "I'm coming home on leave on such-and-such a date, but I'll be coming home with everything—my kitbag, my rifle—because I'm being posted to Southampton, to the Hampshire Regiment."

I got this letter back from my mother saying, "Now don't be angry whatever you do, but Ken's been playing your records." I'm sitting in the barrack room: "The little sod! Wait till I get home!"

But he has done exactly the right thing. He's wound the thing the exact number of times, then he's wiped the record and he's changed the needle. That mollified me a bit. Then she said, "But also your brother Bob took your racing bike out from the shed." Of course I'd hung it up fully greased ready for the halcyon day when I could ride it again; he'd taken it down, had

an accident and buckled the front wheel. So my mother said, "But we got the money together and we've had the wheel repaired." So now I've got two brothers I'm coming home to clip round the ear holes.

VAL BONNER NEE **COLYER** I have so many childhood memories of Ken and me during the war years. He used to take care of me many hours while our mother worked in the munitions factory. He was quite a disciplinarian, even then, and I had to toe the line even though I was mischievous at the first opportunity—hence, me becoming a typist. Ken had acquired an old manual typewriter from somewhere and threatened me not to use it when he was out—needless to say my fingers *burned* to touch that keyboard.

CATHY COLYER I think his mother and father separated before the war—the father, I think, drifted off with somebody else, and it was a totally dysfunctional family. And Robert—very kind man. They were all younger than Bill. It was Bill, Robert, Ken and then Val.

KEN COLYER Mr. Hopkinson took the music class, which was a pleasure. We learnt one or two songs from the school music book. The toughest was *The Good Ship Arethusa*, a sea shanty with a melody line that I still can't remember correctly. But then Mr. Hopkinson would teach us the pop tunes of the day: *The Woodpecker Song*, *Over the Rainbow*, *I Know Why And So Do You.*

With no piano accompaniment, we would sing with gusto. Even people living in the vicinity of the school would say how much they enjoyed the singing lesson.

Mr. Hopkinson had a fine voice, but not as good as the baritone who would lead us on the BBC once a week. We would assemble in the main hall and the headmaster would have a radio there for a BBC schools broadcast. The singer would lead us through The Twenty-third Psalm to the *Brother James* air, which I think is the greatest thing the Bible produced. Perfect poetry. Blake's *Jerusalem* is another piece of perfect poetry.

Mr. Hopkinson took us for gardening, arithmetic, music and philosophy. The latter did not feature in the school programme but, nevertheless, he and Mr. Barnes did teach us this subject. Mr. Hopkinson was eventually called to the war to fight against tyranny, but it is still with us.

He came to the school in uniform. He was a handsome man with a very reserved air of authority and soon rose in the ranks. I vaguely heard at some time that he was killed in the desert campaigns. The last "Gentlemen's War." I hope I am wrong, for I hate to think of his bones bleaching in the desert air in that miserable country.

Mr. Barnes was another fine teacher. These men had the best qualifications; why they tried to teach us deadbeats I will never know. I have tried to teach deadbeats and it's a frustrating waste of time.

Mr. Barnes, I realise now, was a dying man. His heart was giving out, but he soldiered on because of the hostilities. He must have been well past retirement age. I learnt much from him but was headstrong and rebellious by this time. He was another that I shook by my self-taught knowledge when I was the only one in the class who knew the names of the Three Musketeers and D'Artagnan. To cap it all, I told him that I had read the sequel, *Twenty Years After*, and Victor Hugo's *The Toilers of the Sea*.

> I constantly annoyed teachers by my knowledge, and by this time I considered that I could learn no more from school. I was 13 years of age. I didn't like Geography and am still hazy on geographical direction, except for places to which I have sailed.

I didn't like history and don't give a damn when the Battle of Hastings or Waterloo took place. It's a boring lot of shit as far as I'm concerned and I just switched my mind off. However, I was always top of the class for composition.

You could go on from Elementary School to Secondary School if you could pass an exam to go to a Technical College. The system was very good, and it has only been changed for the worse over the years.

Most of us were interested only in getting to work. The crack was on and you had to be a bread-winner. I was earning a pound a week whilst still at school, doing two paper rounds a day and collecting money on Saturdays. I used to give my mother ten shillings a week.

At least one time Mr. Hopkinson was sympathetic. I told him I had had a bilious attack (if you have never had one, then I wouldn't wish one on you). My mother had a growth developing inside her liver when she was carrying me, but nobody knew. Maybe this was something to do with it.

These attacks would come on for no apparent reason. I would feel the beginnings, a general feeling of unease that slowly built until I collapsed in bed and went through twenty-four hours of purgatory just vomiting green bile. Afterwards I felt very shaky for some time.

We left school at fifteen unless we went on to higher education. Most of us weren't interested in higher education.

Bill and Val, Bill on leave

The Spitfires and Hurricanes were flying out to fight the Battle of Britain; we knew how many were lost by the return formation. The war was on and we couldn't wait to get out to work. I applied immediately to join the Merchant Navy. I never would have been any good in the Army. **Left-handed, yet you can handle a Lee-Enfield rifle with improvisation. In a right-handed world us left-handers have to learn how to improvise.**

Faulty eyesight—born with a congenital disorder in an otherwise sound body. With resentment of authority on top, I would have been a loser (but then I am a born loser anyway).

I started work at the Dick Honer foundry on the Slough Trading Estate.

DELPHINE COLYER The first thing that I remember about Ken was when we played ha'penny-a-bake with milk. And I went to school with no milk-money. So I escaped from school to get milk-money—crying my eyes out, because I was a really spoilt little brat. And Ken and his mates were out on the road—and I was about eight. "What's the matter...?"

"I haven't got my milk-money." And I can remember Ken in short trousers: "It's alright—I'll give you the money" and... "No, no, I want my Mum." And that's my first memory of him, trying to give me my milk-money. He was only about 15 I suppose.

He lived at 38 Eton Road, Cranford and we were at 54. I knew him but he didn't know me. And Bill was living in Hornby Road—about three doors away from where I was born.

BILL COLYER So I didn't have a family life. Ken had. Oh, and Valerie—that's my sister Val—they both had a bit of a family life because my mother was a remarkable lady.

She was an incredible lady. In Ken's book, *When Dreams Are in the Dust* you can see that wonderful picture of her in her skivvy things; she'd have been only about 17 or 18 then. Beautiful lady, an amazing woman; I don't know how she put up with my father.

CATHY COLYER I don't think the father was a violent man. He used to shout, but I don't think he was a violent man; that's why I couldn't understand why they put him in the asylum.

I saw him, because I worked then, and he came in the shop. And I was always very quiet in those days, you know... and... come and chat to me... I don't think he was a violent man.

Well, they went back together for a while. But she was what I would call a tease.

DELPHINE COLYER I always felt quite sorry for Ken's father, because he had a... breakdown. He went into the local asylum, and when he came home, he came home to an empty house, because Ruby and Val had left. But, he met a very nice lady, and they were really, really happy and they had a daughter, but what happened to her I don't know.

But it does make you wonder if things run in families, because his father had a nervous breakdown.

Yeah. See, these are only... vague ideas... but he was sitting upstairs at the bedroom window with his feet dangling out the window, so I don't know. But when he came out, Ruby and Val had gone; I suppose they couldn't stick it any longer.

CATHY COLYER The father was a very attractive man—he was like Ken, basically. The mother was... I'm not speaking ill of her, but she was... loud, and the father was always a quiet man. But of course, when *he* came home from work, he didn't want all this blaring music—jazz music.

Bill was playing drums in the front-room—they lived in Eton Road, opposite the White Hart there. And it was a very small house. I think they had two bedrooms upstairs, and the boys had the room downstairs. And of course, he'd come home from work, and all this noise would be going on; there'd be Bob playing the piano, Ken blowing his trumpet... and of course the mother stuck with the boys because she was being show-bizzy, you know. And the father wasn't a bit like that. He was very much like Ken.

And I thought it was dreadful when he had the breakdown. I mean, he *did* have a bad breakdown—the father. As I say, they *were* so much alike, those two... very much alike. Both quiet. And if they're too much alike it doesn't sometimes work. I think Bill always got on alright with the old man, right up until he was older. He would say things about the old man, and the boys would stick up for the mother.

They all loved Val—they were very, very fond of her, all the boys were. She was the only girl with three grown-up boys, you know. They really protected her, in a way.

BETTY COLYER It was a totally dysfunctional family.

JULIAN DAVIES Ruby, yes. Well, we didn't call her that, we called her Mrs. Colyer. She was a lovely lady.

BEN MARSHALL We met Ken's mother and spoke to her, but didn't get to know her well really.

The impression I got was that they didn't think a great deal of their dad—neither Ken nor Bill; nor Bob, for that matter, but I'm not sure about Bob. I think the family had split up some years earlier, but I don't know any details about that at all.

CATHY COLYER Well, the boys were playing in there [1949-50], and the mother had suddenly decided she wasn't having any more of his

Bob, Ken and Bill, possibly outside the Cranford house

nonsense, as she called it, and she went up to Staffordshire—friends up there. She left him overnight—he didn't even know she was gone; the boys put her on the train, and that was it.

And of course, then they started playing over the club and he wanted to know where she was, so he came into the club one night, caused a bit of a scene, really, and... I found it slightly embarrassing, but it happens with families.

> And one of them threw a punch—I'm not sure which one—and of course, father was on the floor, and he was shouting and cursing and everything else, at the boys; they'd encouraged the mother to leave him and everything.

They'd taken all the stuff out of the house and all of these bits and pieces—it *was* bad. And of course, I've always been the one with more common sense than... and I said to him "Now calm down."

To... Hanwell... Yeah, he was in there for a good few months. He played the piano, and they sold the piano, because they needed the money to give the mother to keep her going while she went up in Staffordshire. And of course, she went into service up there.

And then Valerie went up there with her to Staffordshire, and met some lovely people up there—she had a good education. But the mother was always in service, and she was what I would call a tease with the men. I moved her... three times.

But as I say, I always found him very, very pleasant. He was never nasty or aggressive—not to me he wasn't—and I think he just wanted a quiet life.

Ken was very much like his father—he did anything for a quiet life.

KEN COLYER Music does run in families. My father was taught as a child. He was a very popular pub pianist. He could play a ukelele and anything similar, and he could play a bit of clarinet and violin. My Uncle Bill was a well-known classical clarinettist. This had no influence on me.

My father didn't turn a finger for his kids or my mother. He was an idle bastard as a family man but always did alright for hisself. When my mother was absent we led a very miserable existence, until I started work. When I finally became a milkman I was earning relatively good money at fifteen and a half years of age. I was the second youngest on the LCS (London Co-operative Society). I gave my mother as much as I could without being asked.

THE MERCH*

BILL COLYER Anyway, I get home with all this gear—your kitbag (there's your whole life in your kitbag) and your rifle and your five rounds of ammo—and I chastised Bob and then I was going to belt Ken, and all of a sudden I thought, "Hold on." I said, "What records did you play?"

I was knocked out. He'd done the Sleepy John Estes; he got into the blues records, which tells a story. I had several by then. The names, they're all legendary: Sister Rosetta Tharpe, Red Nelson, Champion Jack Dupree (which were American because none of his were issued over here at that point in time) and many more. But the things you'll see on Brunswick mainly, I had them all.

Well, it turned out that Ken had mainly played all my blues 78s, the Brunswicks and the Vocalions. What would he have been then? Twelve years old and he's already steeped in this music. He played them himself. He had heard them played by me—that's probably why he picked them out—but for all the twelve weeks I was away, the ones he'd been playing were the blues records. What a grounding he was getting.

KEN COLYER I had always carried a mouth organ around with me since a friendly neighbour had given me one, and I quickly learned to play simple tunes on it. As soon as the war started, like all things, they quickly became hard to get, and of course they were all German made.

By accident, and to my amazement, I saw a brand-new ten-hole Hohner chromatic for sale in a tobacconist's shop window. It was two pounds ten shillings, an enormous sum of money. But I went in to enquire and explain how badly I wanted it. The lady agreed to put it to one side for me and I paid a shilling a week or as much as I could until it was paid for. By this time I had got interested in brother Bill's jazz records and tried to play some of the tunes as I got familiar with them.

BILL COLYER Oh, yes. I remember on another leave I came home and he was already trying out a cheap, secondhand trumpet and I brought him home as a present the Nat Gonella trumpet book. I've forgotten whether it was 7/6 (37.5p) or 12/6 (57.5p), but it had photographs in it and how to play the trumpet. Ken never learnt music, never learnt to read it or anything, you know.

---

* *The Merchant Navy consists of registered commercial civilian ships, which can be used by the Navy during wartime*

If you look at Ken, his posture, it's exactly like Nat Gonella's. The way he holds the horn and the way he sits. He learned from the photographs.

> Of course, when he got down to New Orleans in '52 he was a damn good player by then. And don't forget, I've often wondered what would have happened if I'd not talked him into leaving the Merchant Navy.

He got a cheap guitar. Don't forget, he had a tough war because the blitz extended way past Cranford. The East End of London and the docks got the hammering, but those Jerries were dropping their load and pissing off. Even Reading was getting bombs dropped on it in 1940, the blitz period. So, although you are twelve miles from London, you have still got the searchlights, the ack-ack guns roaring up and down Cranford Lane. They had a hazardous time.

By now Ken is the man of the family, because father is in the Middle East, brother Bob has gone into the Navy (no, that was later), so Ken is looking after Valerie and my mother. And my mother is getting only her allotment from me and my father; I think about seven bob a week.

My mother rarely used the Anderson shelter. She slept under the stairs; that was the recommended thing in houses without shelters. She had a little bed under the stairs, but Ken and his mate Len would be down in the shelter for hours on end with their candles, and I suppose somewhere along the line he got a cheap guitar to play down there. He was working as a milk roundsman, so he was earning a few bob, and in those days a penny was saved, wasn't it?

Ken would get a bus to Shepherds Bush market; that was a great big, busy market, which had a record stall with a jazz section with 78s in it, and it also had a couple of secondhand music shops. You'd see something in the window, like a pawn shop, thirty bob or two quid sort of thing.

So Ken bought one of those to while away the hours in the Anderson shelter in addition to looking after the rabbits, so he simply taught himself to play. But he was left-handed and had to restring, which, of course, can lead to a lot of string breakage.

Ken, the minute the war ended—and father was being demobbed from the Middle East (I also was demobbed from the Middle East; I ended up out there after the shit, shot and shell)—joined the Merch straight away. Then, of course, he used to keep in touch with me endlessly, because he looked up to me as the guru. Obviously because I was the one about rhythm, nuances and dynamics, all that stuff. It was all down to me.

KEN COLYER That was the first boat—the *British Hussar*. Well, we got into Ancona on the Adriatic coast in Italy. We were the first British boat to sail into Ancona immediately after the war when peace had been declared... and of course, the money was useless, because the Italian Lira was so useless we couldn't even *get* money on the ship, so everything was barter.

So the first things to go were our fags—our cigarettes; we had a pretty good stock of cigarettes, so it was all barter. And we got this exceptionally good Cognac. They'd had it buried all through the war, to stop the Germans getting it.

So, for a carton of fifty Woodbines, you could get a bottle of this delicious Cognac. And of course, eventually, the cigarettes start running out. So one thing leads to another. We're still thirsty. Blankets are excellent barter material at times like this... so one by one, all our blankets go. And by the time we left Ancona, we didn't have any blankets at all, we just had our sheets, and just had to make do with coats or what-have-you at night. And it was fairly cold then, as far as I can remember. It was near winter.

So we eventually sailed to Haifa; it's baking hot during the day, but it's freezing cold at night, and we had no blankets. And we're freezing to death... until we could steal them one by one, when the officers changed blankets. You know, the stewards and so forth. One by one... each week we could finagle a blanket on the living chain, so we eventually got our quota of blankets back. But it was pretty cold until we did.

KEN COLYER LETTER TO RUBY COLYER UNDATED

Dear Mum,

I'm just dashing off a few lines as I have managed to get the money to stamp this and send it from Aden.

I received yours and Val's letters O.K.

I hope you are keeping alright and getting rid of your colds, it may seem strange but most of the boys have or have had bad colds here. We sweat like hell and then stand around in draughts and breezes and end up with all sorts of chills. I'm keeping pretty well myself and haven't had any new complaints yet except a little boil on my head, I don't remember having any there before.

We've got about another three weeks now to home and I certainly won't be sorry to get off this old tub.

I won't be staying long when we get back as I have been told that one can get jobs on American tankers from a port near Liverpool called Hesham and I don't want to waste any time if this is true. I should tell Bill this when you see him as I didn't have the information when I wrote to him. Well I'm sorry this is so short but there isn't much space left.

Tell Bob I will try and write to him as soon as I can.

All my love to you and Val,

Ken

P.S. Tell Val I'll buy her a gramophone when I get back.

Young Ken in the Merch; his identity card

FICHA DE IDENTIDAD
FICHA DE IDENTIDADE
IDENTITY CARD

Nombre / Nome / Name — KENNETH

Apellido / Apelido / Surname — COLYER

Nacionalidad / Nacionalidade / Nationality — BRITISH

Edad / Idade / Age — 19

Estatura / Estatura / Height — 5' 4"

Color del cabello / Cor do cabelo / Colour of hair — FAIR

Color de los ojos / Cor dos olhos / Colour of eyes — BLUE

Color de la piel / Cor da pe / Complexion — FRESH.

Nariz / Nariz / Nose — STRAIGHT

Señas particulares / Sinais particulares / Special marks — NIL

KEN COLYER [In Montreal] I decided to buy a new mouthpiece, so I found a musical instrument shop. When I entered, a good-looking, well-dressed Negro was talking to the shop owner. The shop owner was talking about bands and musicians. I heard him say that they were going to get Gene Krupa up shortly. The Negro said cheerio and left.

I asked to see some mouthpieces. I didn't know anything about them at the time, only ever having had the one that had come with the first horn I had bought: a Rudy Muck cushion-rimmed job. I looked through a selection, took a chance and picked one out and bought it.

After I had paid the fellow I asked, "Is there any jazz in town?" "That was Louis Metcalf that just went out," he said. "He is playing at the Café St. Michel." He gave me the address. I thanked him and went back to the ship. I couldn't wait to get finished that evening. I had a good grey pin-striped suit but

suddenly thought, "I haven't got a tie." I had never bothered with ties and didn't even know how to tie one.

I happened to mention this to Ken [ship's carpenter]. "Come in my cabin. I have got one you can have. It was given to me as a present and I have never liked it." It was a nice blue paisley pattern tie of good quality. He tied it for me and later taught me how to tie a Windsor knot.

I spruced myself up and set off to find the Café St. Michel. I did not have any trouble finding it and went in. It was dimly lit and quiet. There was a barman behind a small bar cleaning glasses. I ordered a beer, which he got me, and I asked when did the music start?

"Oh, you're far too early. They don't start 'til around nine-thirty." I had a long time to wait. "The main hall is upstairs but you can wait down here." I thought, "I will have to pace my beers," as I didn't have too much funds. I asked him about the band. "Louis has an international band."

He named the musicians; there were only two I vaguely recognised: Al "Cheekum" King on bass and a tenor saxist whose name I have since forgotten. He had a Japanese trombonist. I thought it strange, a Jap playing jazz. "But if you stick around 'til about one-thirty, Oscar Peterson usually looks in after he has finished his hotel job." He was playing solo piano at some hotel. "He's the greatest, he's good."

I had never heard of Oscar Peterson, and I doubt if anyone else had in England at that time, as he was a Montreal boy and about the same age as myself. I was around nineteen.

I was sitting sipping my beer when a man came in wearing an expensive-looking gabardine topcoat and a sharp-looking Cadé. The barman knew him and they started talking. The man did most of the talking. From the gist of the conversation it appeared that a gang were after his blood.

"I've been to the police for protection but they won't. So I've brought my own protection." With this he reached inside his coat and produced a .45 automatic. The bartender quietly said, "Now put that away and calm down. They are not going to come for you here." The man said something else and left.

Time went by and they opened up upstairs. I went up and sat at a table and ordered another beer. The band eventually got on the stand and started to play. They coasted through a couple of numbers. There weren't many people present, it was still early. The rhythm section was good. King was a fine bass player.

The drummer was like Les. He had a sharp jacket on with very wide padded shoulders, only when he twisted about, the padded shoulders seemed to stay in the same place. Another coat hanger. The Jap was awful, probably playing Jap music. His trombone had an enormous bell but nothing much came out of it. The sax-man was nice, with a lovely tone. I wish I could remember his name, as he was on many early records.

The cabaret artists had a long table beside the bandstand. Girls began turning up and sitting there. They were dancers in the floor show. A slim, dapper, well-dressed Negro arrived. "Snookums!" they all cried. He was the star singer of the show and obviously very popular and I should imagine homosexual, as was Frankie "Half-Pint" Jaxon, another very good cabaret artist.

Louis Metcalf played a very nice, easy-paced *White Christmas* with a beautiful tone, then the band took a break before the cabaret started. The dancers did some numbers to build things up for Snookums. He made a dramatic entrance with the lights dimmed down and a white spotlight on himself. It was very effective. He had a pleasant voice, did some patter then went into *Shine*.

He sang a couple more numbers then a little more patter. He said he was now going to do a number that had made him famous sometime in earlier years: *Brown Boy, Chocolate Boy*. He was very good and got a big hand.

As I was having a drink I noticed that there was a hush in the place. A whisper rustled round the room: "Oscar's here." I looked around and then saw this giant of a Negro walking toward the bandstand. They all greeted him warmly. The pianist immediately left the piano and the front line got off the stand. Oscar sat down at the piano, looked over at the drummer and *Cheekum*. Then the place started to rock.

He was powerful and used both hands, all ten fingers. The rhythm section was swinging superbly. As he warmed up, his massive frame leant further over the keyboard. The atmosphere was electric. "You see them fellows standing behind him?" someone said. "They are all pianists trying to watch his hands." I had never heard piano playing like it and the place was in an uproar after each number.

BILL COLYER Ken even brought a 78 back of Oscar doing two Albert Ammons numbers. Of course, he started as a boogie man, a real left hand and power, and Ken brought back a Victor 78 of boogie-woogie stomps.

Ken was on leave and, do you know, he and I walked round Charing Cross Road, where there was a load of music shops, to take this record round and rave about it, but none of them were interested. That really hurt me and Ken because by then we were deep jazzers and we'd heard this piano. We had some good piano players here, but nothing of that stature.

So there's Ken, only into his teen-age, hearing all this, and he knew all the names because I would tell him personnels.

I was a bible. I knew every personnel; I even knew the string players on the Artie Shaw records because of the Edgar Jackson booklets. I was a walking mine of information; that's why I ended up in that first jazz store.

It's a hell of a story—Communist Party and all that bit.

Anyway, back to the guitar. Now, obviously because he'd listened to all those blues records while I was away, what does he teach himself on the guitar? The blues licks. Nothing to do with guitar playing as such, it was the sound and the rhythm. Of course, that stood him in good stead in his early days in the Merch because he took the guitar to sea with him. And so, in his little boot of a cabin, he always spent a couple of hours playing his guitar.

He was on the *Port Sydney* quite a while in the finish. He loved that old tub. She was 34 years old and she only got her Lloyd's certificate for each trip. A ship at a certain age has to, well, *all* ships have to have a Lloyd's certificate, but those old coal burners, leaking in every pipe, they were checked out each time they docked in England; they were given a thorough going over by the Board of Trade officials before they could get a certificate to go to sea for one more trip. That's when I joined. Bloody leaking tub!

But Ken loved her; he was second cook by now. He had been on other ships, always taking his horn and his guitar with him, and some of those ships he was on were on the Aussie and New Zealand runs. You were at sea for weeks then. But Ken religiously went to his cabin, seven days a week, to play his trumpet and guitar. He got fans among the crew, and I know when I joined the *Sydney* there were a couple of Liverpudlians; they were early Rock and Rollers, and Ken would join in with those two. They'd do some marvellous stuff.

If the weather was good you'd be out on the top deck, and all the other guys would sit around: Tex, Ken and Len strumming away and singing tunes of the day, but Ken would always go into the twelve bars and the eight bars when the others would be strumming other stuff—popular tunes of the day, Bing Crosby numbers or whatever.

KEN COLYER Ken, the chippy, had bought a nice guitar in Montreal, and I had a cheap one that cost considerably less. Though Ken had also bought a very good chord tutor, it was too advanced for us and we weren't getting anywhere. We were both left-handed and had struggled to learn right-handed as it saved changing the strings round. But finally we both agreed that our left-hand instinct was too strong and laboriously changed the strings round.

Sea air plays havoc with strings. When we were at sea and had no spares we would tie knots in them when they broke, as long as there was enough string to tie the knot above the nut. This works with the wound strings but not the first and second. Ken worked on this and devised a knot of his own that would grip and not slip. Just before we were ready to leave, the word went round that we were bound for New York.

The trip before, one of the stewards told me he had been to New York and had heard Bunk Johnson at the Stuyvesant Casino. He wasn't a jazz fan but had thoroughly enjoyed the band and thought they were terrific, especially Bunk. But Bunk was to be gone by the time we got there. The trip was uneventful, except for some fog. The Captain hated fog and would not leave the bridge until it cleared.

To my surprise Ernie [a shipmate] called us out on deck as the New York skyline hove into view. It is a magnificent sight, especially when seen for the first time. We tied up at Fourteenth Street pier. Almost as soon as we tied up, the horse flies honed in. They were ferocious and either stung or bit. Once again I attracted them.

I got washed and changed, once again forgetting that nightlife doesn't start 'til later this side of the ocean. I put on Ken's tie and shined my shoes and I was ready to go with my sub in my pocket. There were still four dollars to the pound. **I had read about Eddie Condon's club and heard their once-a-month town hall concerts on the BBC at home. I had no idea where the club was. New York is a big place.** I got to thinking as I walked. I saw a news-stand and asked if they had a *Downbeat*. "No, don't you know it's not due out 'til next week?"

Then I saw a telephone kiosk. I didn't know about the *New Yorker* then, which has an excellent section devoted to nightlife with Whitney Balliett's pithy descriptions of each place and its style of entertainment. I found the Condons in the directory: the list was endless. There must be more Condons in New York than Smiths. I didn't know whether it was Edward or Edwin. There were long lists of both. I gave up, figuring that I would never make a detective.

I walked on until I saw a cabby tinkering under the bonnet of his cab. "Do you know Eddie Condon's club?"

"Hop in; I'll be with you in a minute." He didn't want to lose a fare.

I got in the cab. It had seen better days, in fact it was a wreck. But I didn't mind as long as it got me there. I was sure I would find the place like a homing pigeon finds his home. The cabbie finally got the engine going and we started cruising.

"What was the name of that place?" I told him. "If you don't mind me cruising around I'll try to think of it." I didn't mind.

"What sort of musicians play there?"

"Jazz musicians."

"Who's playing beside Condon?"

He'd got me there. I didn't know Eddie's present lineup. I mentioned a few names, then Pee Wee Russell.

"Pee Wee, he's a friend of mine, know him well. I took him for his medical when he got drafted. He told me to wait; he was only gone ten minutes. They threw him out because he was seventy proof. Now I've got an idea it might be the old Howdy Club. Used to be a burlesque joint, they've got these marvellous old dolls in the chorus line, not one under sixty. Want me to try there?" he asked, eyeing the clock.

"Go ahead," I said. We drove into Greenwich Village, turned a corner and there was the 'mutton chop' sign David Stone Martin designed for Eddie hanging over the entrance. I was elated. I gave the cabbie a generous tip. He told me not to

55

forget the address: West Third Street. Before he pulled away he called: "Don't forget to tell Pee Wee his old friend Al brought you here. So long, pal."

I waved him away. On the street, there was a billboard advertising the band and a list of rave reviews, like you see outside theatres. There was a commissionaire in livery standing by the door looking dignified. He saw me reading the board.

"Are all these people playing tonight?"

"Yes, but it's a little early yet. They don't start playing 'til nine. Why don't you go to that little bar down the road and have a drink. Come back about eight-thirty and you'll get a seat right by the band."

I said, "Thanks, I will."

He was no hustler. I found out later that Eddie wouldn't allow it. He had played enough clip joints himself and also considered it was important to encourage youngsters to listen to the music. Also they turned a blind eye if you were obviously under age.

On each table was a small green card. On one side it gave the personnel: Pee Wee Russell, clarinet; Wild Bill Davison, cornet; George Brunis, trombone; Gene Schroeder, piano; Sid Weiss, bass; Maurey Feld, drums; Eddie Condon, guitar, and Joe Sullivan, intermission piano. On the other it proclaimed: "Jazz in its finest flower," a quote from my favourite critic, Whitney Balliett.

As I sipped a beer the band turned up. George oiled his slide with an elaborate flourish, then the band kicked off. Within a couple of numbers they were playing with a power, swing and tonal quality I would not have believed possible. It struck me for the first time that the gramophone record is badly misleading when it comes to jazz. No recording could ever completely capture the greatness of this music. As each number got rocking I seemed to be suspended, just sitting on air. And when the music finished I flopped back on my chair as though physically exhausted. If this is Chicago jazz, I told myself, then it is better than expected—and not far from the New Orleans pattern and sound.

The sensation I got from hearing Wild Bill for the first time was a sort of numb joy that such a man lived and played. If Louis Armstrong was better in person, then it was beyond my imagination. His teaming with Brunis heightened this reaction.

When Edmond Hall took over from Pee Wee, playing his cutting electric phrases, it was almost more than I could bear.

Brunis was entertaining to watch. While playing excellent trombone, he constantly screwed his body into the most awkward-looking positions, sometimes jamming one leg against the piano. If there was a drunk in the room he would play snatches of *I'm Forever Blowing Bubbles*, or something equally appropriate, in the most syrupy manner, during the breaks.

Then crack back in with glorious golden-toned tail-gate. I was to see a joker try this and make a fool of himself. I have never heard a trombonist in England come anywhere near the way Brunis was playing then.

Pee Wee, with his broken comb moustache and a slightly distant look in his eyes, was also entertaining. I was told he had a select band of fans, who follow him mainly to watch his weird expressions that contort his face while he plays. Also he is a little eccentric and difficult to get to know, but if you knew anything about poodles, he would open up and be friendly.

As nightclub prices go in New York,

Ken's Merchant Seaman identity card

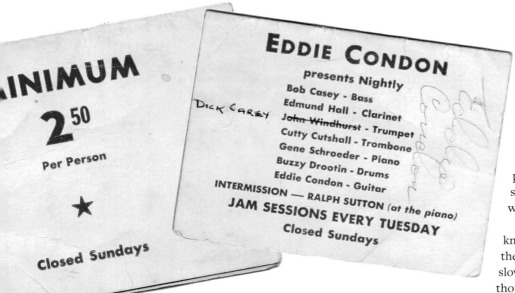

A signed Condon Club card from a later date

Eddie's were very reasonable. But I still had to make every beer last as long as I could. The waiters didn't like this too much.

The first night I left comparatively early. I felt a little sick but hadn't drunk very much. It was the emotional impact that was making me feel groggy. The old Negro toilet attendant was sympathetic and understanding. "That's OK, son, I know how it is."

I said I would be back tomorrow night. "See you then," he said with a smile, and I got a cab back to the ship.

Unfortunately I hadn't really converted Ken and Les at this stage and they never came ashore with me. They regretted it on later trips.

Work was a little harder the next day and my head was still full of the music, but I got through the day and had a nap. I knew I didn't have to get ashore so early.

I was amazed at Wild Bill's seemingly relentless power, his glorious tone, when he wasn't roughing it up. I didn't know about King cornets then but have played them for many years now. Muggsy Spanier always played a King and also Harry James and Red Allen. But at the time I was reasonably happy with my French Sioma trumpet. I only wish I had known about mutes then for practising. I even used to go in fear of someone throwing my horn over the side sometimes.

I fretted 'til it was time to go to Condon's. I got a cab, not realising that the subway went to West Third from Fourteenth Street. I said good evening to the commissionaire and went in to the same small corner table and sat down. There was a bar at the far end of the club where drinks were a little cheaper, but I preferred to sit at a table while I could.

A couple of young fellows came into the club and sat down alongside me. We chatted a little and they said they were from Baltimore. They happened to say that Cuba Austin played in one of their local bands. They were surprised I had heard of him.

The reason I knew his name well was because one of my favourite records was (and still is) McKinney's Cotton Pickers' *Rocky Road* with its magnificent intro of just Cuba Austin snare drumming and Rex Stewart playing a tightly muted solo that still stands among the finest on record, along with Red Allen's *Feeling Drowsy*.

They were surprised at my record knowledge and seemed to know very little themselves about the music that was slowly becoming an obsession with me. My thoughts were mostly on music, not cooking.

I was feeling better from now on and had got over the initial shock. The music was giving me a happy mellow glow and I was all set to stay until the end of the evening.

Joe Bushkin sat in for a few numbers and also Roy Shelton on trumpet, but it was lightweight stuff after what had gone before. Miff Mole sat in but Brunis ruthlessly carved him, though it didn't seem to bother Miff.

Musicians looked in, this was living. These men had only been names on records and personnels in HMV and Parlophone catalogues, and here they were in the flesh: Bobby Hackett, Lionel Hampton, Cliff Jackson and probably many I didn't recognise. I stayed until the band finished for the night. It was about 5.00; I was still on cloud nine.

The band were sitting near the bandstand, chatting. Cliff Jackson rose and sat at the piano. Then he commenced to play the most remarkable *Ain't Misbehavin'* I had ever heard.

"That was terrific, Cliff," someone said.

"All you got to do is relax," he replied.

I left the club and looked for a cab. One pulled into the kerb. I thought he had stopped for me. I jumped in and said "Fourteenth Street Pier."

"Jeesus fella. I've just finished for the night. Why don't you take the subway? It runs all night and I'm bushed."

So I discovered the subway, which costs cents instead of dollars.

I went down on the platform. There weren't many people waiting. A large, well-dressed Texan approached me. He asked something and I recognised the Texan drawl. I said I was English and I had only been in New York a couple of days. I like the American openness. They will engage a complete stranger in conversation, and it is accepted. But this time it could have been a little dodgy.

"I like the English," he said in a loud voice to everybody in general. "They're not like these Yankee northern nigger-lovers."

He was very drunk and I slipped away as he was haranguing some people walking past. I made sure I got into a different car to him and got out at Fourteenth Street.

The city was quiet as I walked back to the ship. A large dustcart was crawling down the street at a walking pace. Dustmen either side of the pavement were throwing trash cans up to men on the cart, who emptied them and threw them back, all in one smooth operation. I admired their strength and skill.

Something made me think of Tallulah Bankhead and her favourite poem: 'I burn the candle at both ends; It will not last the night; But ah, my foes, and oh, my friends—It gives a lovely light.'*

I was physically and mentally exhausted. I was dropping off to sleep peeling potatoes. Washing the pans, I woke up with my head nearly in the sink. Ernie gave me some odd looks and Les thought I was raving the nights away somewhere. He was right. I was.

I suddenly realised it was the first of the month. Eddie Condon had a Town Hall concert on the first of every month. I finished work as quickly as I could, got changed and hurried ashore. I got on a bus and asked for the Town Hall.

Immediately a conversation started as to which stop was for the Town Hall. A drunk staggered and slipped as he got on the bus. "Sorry, I'm drunk."

"No," a chirpy fellow said, "you're not drunk until you are flat on the pavement and just cannot get up."

I was fascinated and enjoying this glimpse of the New York people. There is an exhilarating atmosphere there.

"What are you going to the Town Hall for? They only have highbrow stuff there."

"Jazz concert?"

He laughed. "They don't have that sort of music there. Now if I was free tonight I would take you around the hot jazz joints. Nick's, Eddie Condon's, Jimmy Ryan's."

They all bade me a friendly goodbye as I got off the bus. Wonderful people. Joseph Mitchell said, "They are the little people and they are as big as you are, whoever you are."

I asked a policeman for the Town Hall. He looked at me quizzically. "Town Hall, son, it's just across the square."

I found the Town Hall; a group of people were quietly talking. **There was a notice board informing of the day's events. I read from the top. Eddie Condon concert, special guest Huddie Ledbetter, then something about some Viennese Music.** My heart sunk. I realised the concert was just finished. Of course, the men had to work in the evening so the concert had to be early. If I had only known. I could easily have got a couple of hours off work. But so we go.

I ambled around, then thought I would go to Nick's, where Muggsy was playing, which I knew was on West Tenth Street, in Greenwich Village.

I thought it would be easy to find, the city being planned on the block system, so I proceeded to cross the avenues. The blocks were much longer than I realised. It seemed simple at first but, once off the grid, New York is a maze, like London.

I asked one or two people the way, but it is the same the world over: they either didn't know or weren't sure. Eventually I was in the Village. I stopped to ask an old gentleman. He drew himself up with a dignified air.

"Sir, I have lived in the Village all my life and Nick was a personal friend of mine. Just go to the next corner and turn right."

"Thank you very much."

"It's a pleasure, sir."

At Nick's it was Philadelphia all over again.

"How old are you, son?"

"Twenty-one."

"Where's your draft card?"

Thinking quickly, I said, "I'm a merchant seaman; I've left it aboard ship." I had my seaman's identity card in my pocket but daren't show it, as it showed my age.

"What ship are you off?"

"The *Port Sydney*. She's lying at the Fourteenth Street pier."

"If the police came in and you were lying we could get into a lot of trouble. The law is very strict in the State of New York."

I almost pleaded with him, explaining my situation. "Well, keep at the bar where I can see you."

I gratefully bought him a drink and continued buying him one every time I had one. Muggsy's band was much quieter than Eddie's but he punched out that fine lead and the band increased the intensity and got very hot.

When I went to the toilet I noticed the old Negro attendant, listening to the band intently, head slightly bent, tapping out a terrific rhythm with his foot as though willing the band on. I felt that he had more rhythm than the rest of us put together. Hank Duncan played fine intermission piano. As had Joe Sullivan at Eddie's. This was an added pleasure and I was to do the same at the Studio 51.

Ernie Caceres was the only man I knew in the band apart from Muggsy, but if they were unknowns they were still very good.

This is what makes good jazz. Having a very high standard improves the musicianship and the deadbeats fall by the wayside. In England the deadbeats carry on as if they are of some good.

Money was running short, so I bade the bartender goodnight—we had got quite friendly by this time—and went back to the ship. I decided to stay aboard the next night, partly because I was nearly broke and because I needed some sleep.

Later at home I was telling Alex Revell of my experiences in New York. "Oh," he said, "I wouldn't have gone to Condon's or Nick's, I would have gone to hear somebody good like Sidney Bechet." He was quite shocked when I said that taking it easy had cost me about three pounds a night, and worth every penny. Little Lord Fauntleroy wouldn't have even got his foot in the door.

The cruiser HMS *Sheffield* came in and tied up across from us at the next pier. They were on a goodwill tour. Some Jews picketed their dock gate. They were quite orderly, they were probably protesting about British oppression somewhere in the world.

Sunday came and the docks were quiet and peaceful. The officers were having a tea dance on the after deck of the *Sheffield*. They had a small orchestra playing Victor Sylvester-style dance music. I was in my cabin building up a head of steam to the detriment of my lip.

I looked over; they were all out of step and the orchestra's tempo and timing were getting erratic. I was smiling to myself, but I saw Captain Pedrick come round the corner frowning. He wasn't amused and I thought I had better pack up for the day and wrestle with the guitar.

A couple of ratings on the *Sheffield* came back roaring drunk and decided to borrow the captain's barge and go for a cruise up the Hudson. I dread to think what their punishment was.

We had a shock on the Monday. Without notice the pound was devalued to $2.40 to the pound and everybody was hopping mad. This diminished funds considerably.

I managed one more night in Condon's. The band was on fine form, my ear was more attuned. Sid Weiss's tone floated through the room. I've rarely heard bass playing like it since. One of the best brass teams ever. I heard different drummers on different nights—Maurey Feld, Johnny Blowers—but I noticed they all used the same beautiful Zildjian top cymbal. It had a tone like a guitar chord, not the usual noise produced by most I've heard.

It's a pity that Eddie was becoming more the host and leaving the band to it, because he was a fine rhythm man and really added to the rhythm section.

I had read about Gene Schroeder earlier in one of the jazz magazines. A dedicated man who had come up the hard way.

Edmond Hall, one of the most brilliant clarinetists, plays the perfect New Orleans foil.

Pee Wee, probably the most unique individualist that jazz has ever seen, his seeming eccentricity covering the thoughts of a very intelligent man.

Brunis, brash, a bit of a comedian, but playing tail-gate with a dexterity that probably only Ory has matched.

Wild Bill, whom I had never heard of until I saw his name on the billboard outside the club, soloing on *I'm Confessin'* with a vibrant power that was incredible. He filled the whole club with pure tone and literally pinned you to the wall.

Joe Sullivan standing with his little tune book in his hand, looking like a benign preacher, but getting on the piano and playing what would be unplayable for many pianists. "He can reach for a tenth and a drink at the same time," Condon said. **I never got to Jimmy Ryan's, where Bertha 'Chippie' Hill was knocking them out every night. It was frustrating being in New York penniless, and not being able to hear the glorious music that was being played. The joint was jumping and I wasn't able to get in on the action.**

I still hadn't done any shopping. It was obligatory because of conditions that still appertained at home after our glorious victory.

I hunted through my gear and hustled up various currencies left from previous trips. There was a bar on the waterfront where the bartender would change any negotiable currency. I went down to the bar; he was doing a brisk trade. Of course he charged a few cents commission.

"You guys are crazy. Why don't you hang on to your money?"

To my surprise, my South African pounds (I had kept a couple because they were such pretty notes and I hadn't needed to spend them and then forgotten about them) commanded a very good rate, far better than the British rate.

New York was a wonderful city for shopping. Free enterprise and competition really work there to the benefit of the customer.

I was slightly amazed at what I was able to buy for the money I had. Shirts for my brothers, real sharp ones. Leadbelly's Asch album. A first edition of

Mezz Mezzrow's *Really The Blues*. Dorothy Baker's *Young Man With A Horn*.

Dorothy Baker has been much derided by some musicians, but it is very difficult to write a good fictional story with a jazz basis (Garson Kanin's *Blow Up A Storm* is a good effort) and she makes some very good valid points about the problems of a creative artist that often end in death and the terrible waste of talents that will never come again.

BILL COLYER I'd been playing with Ken all that time in the Merch. Seven days a week when he came off duty, he went down to his cabin and practised, played his horn. The chippie would be on a guitar they bought in Canada, the baker would hold his guitar and pluck the bass string and I would be on wire brushes on a stainless steel kettle and a suitcase.

The greasers—that's the guys down in the stoke hole who'd oil the stuff—the two of them used to complain bitterly to the skipper because they were in the cabin opposite Ken's. But that skipper, old Pedric (I was told this by one of the seamen), he was up on the bridge leaning over with the first officer and they saw Ken walk up the deck, hobnailed boots and his white trousers, his second cook's gear.

He said, "Look, there he goes, young Collie, right on the dot every day, even Sundays, and he sits and plays that bugle for two hours and the greasers complain, but as far as I'm concerned that man is dedicated and it's his time off and he always works by the clock. He can carry on playing his horn."

We were stuck in Buenos Aires for weeks without a cargo; Peron was having an argument with the British government over something, and he held the whip hand because that was where all the beef was coming from for starving Europe; it was still starving in the Forties after the war.

Oh, the things we got up to! I remember the nearest bar—the "First and Last" we always called the nearest bar in the docks—was the Norgie; it was run by a Norwegian, and I remember going in to him and they'd swear that the ladies of the night did their off-hours thing there, and I talked him into letting us in there.

We used to go in there and play, our quartet. Each trip was three or four months long, so you are away a long while, and most of it's at sea. You only do about nine knots and you are going thousands of miles, just work out how long it takes to get to South America: weeks. And you break down, being that old. She'd break down and all our energy had gone up the safety valve.

In the stoke hold we'd go mad. Saw the needle go back, the engineer daren't come in because we'd have smashed him. That's our energy gone up there. Same with fog: When you're in fog and you see that needle go back, that's your sweat gone up

Ken Colyer

Ken cooking in the galley

there, all that coal. Anyway, I remember sitting with Ken, talking. I said, "Listen, Ken. You're getting so good now, you've only got to hear a tune a few times and you can play it." Like we'd hear stuff coming over the radio when we coasted down to South America; the radio man would tune in to shore stations and I remember that's where we heard *Rum and Coca-Cola* by the Andrews Sisters. And, do you know, on those two or three days coasting down there, Ken had learnt it. Oh yeah, there were several tunes.

Ken had a hell of a mind on him, and if he didn't remember all of the tune, he improvised. If he didn't remember a middle eight, he made one up. He had some innate sense of harmony and... it was just unique.

But a lot of it is definitely that Merchant Navy experience and seven-day-a-week playing; your chops are in and your mind's working on it all the time. Anyway, I said, "Ken, do you want to take another trip?"

Ken by now was a merchant seaman; he'd been halfway round the world—the Australia run. We had some very in-depth chats and I said, "Listen Ken, I've got lots of contacts back in London; we're bound to get some gigs there." Not talking about forming a band, and that was my view. I know we came back from this trip and went to King George's Hall where the George Webb Band was playing.

There used to be people like Albert McCarthy who would do a record recital in the interval, some of them very old-fashioned, but there were things going on like Regent Polytechnic on Regent Street, lunchtime sitter-in jazz things. So after hearing Webby and then one or two sit-ins, Ken decided to leave the Merch.

The early
Cranes play an
American air
base, 1951

CHAPTER FOUR
THE CRANES

GEORGE MELLY The emergence of Ken Colyer led to a great deal of soul-searching throughout the whole revivalist jazz world. I first heard him on a riverboat shuffle. Like most people at the time I thought he was joking.

There was no question of the Mulligan band playing that year; Mick had only just formed the band. Even so, he had brought his horn, because on the way back we were to tie up for an hour at Eel Pie Island, and there was to be an open-air jam session. Ken Colyer was on board, and seeing Mick had his trumpet with him, asked if he could borrow it when we went ashore. Mick said yes, imagining that he would blow a couple of numbers and then give it back. Not a bit of it. After about half an hour Mick asked him for it back and Ken refused! Mick told me about this later and added, "And have you heard him?"

KEN COLYER I was looking for an in on the jazz scene. We used to go to record recitals at a pub on the corner of Windmill Street and Lexington Street. We heard Jimmy Asman, Sinclair Traill and Albert McCarthy among others give recitals there. Ken Lindsay and Pete Martin ran the sessions. Ken was always very helpful. I told him I was learning trumpet and thought I was good enough to start getting some band experience.

I met up with Mick Mulligan somewhere and he let me sit-in a couple of times. Then Johnny Haim, who had his Jelly Roll Kings with his brother Gerald, dramatically died in his sleep at 19 years of age. He had burnt the candle at both ends and in the middle too. I think Johnny would have been a major force on the jazz scene. He was rough and had that certain something that you can tell as soon as you hear it. Shortly after, Ken suggested I try and replace John. He knew Gerald and arranged for me to play at one of their rehearsals.

He went along with me.

CHARLIE CONNOR Ken Colyer and Ken Lindsay attended the audition at Belsize Park and Ken Lindsay introduced K.C. I was not impressed. It was terrible—not, as K.C. said years later, "because I didn't know enough tunes" but because he didn't have any idea of stage etiquette and would not stop blowing; he seemed to think that it was to be one long ensemble.

KEN COLYER We tried a few tunes but I didn't know them properly. Having played at sea from memory I used to make bits up to fit. I would change key without realising it. It must have sounded bizarre but years later on, reading Wingy Manone's book *Trumpet On The Wing*, he says he did much the same thing when first learning. Some of the band were so damned superior I took an instant dislike to them.

I failed my audition dismally. But some time later when I had got the nucleus of the Cranes going, Ken told me the reason they didn't want me was that I was too good for them, and they didn't like it.

DAVE STEVENS In his book Ken comes across as quite modest about the occasion, and his feeling that we acted 'superior' comes from poor communication—Ken said very little to us, and we responded the same way. Ken Lindsay's comment was of course absurd. I know we all *wanted* Colyer to fit in with us, as it was our only chance to continue with the band.

JOHN WESTWOOD Sadly, none of it reflects well on Ken. Dave Stevens hit the nail on the head with his conclusion that it was a "communication problem." None of the Jelly Roll Kings present really talked to Ken, nor he to them. I had the same experience with him when I joined the Cranes. I don't think we exchanged more than a couple of dozen sentences in the whole time; the 'sorting' was done by Bill.

BILL COLYER Ken was turned down by Gerald Haim and… I've forgotten, it was somebody else he auditioned for, didn't work, so I know that, although he was doing a bit of sitting-in, it wasn't fitting in with the other guys; they were all Condon or Lu Watters things.

> Of course, Ken had a different thing going. A born jazzman if you like. Not learning Hot Fives and Jelly Roll Mortons— he played any damn tune, like the New Orleans men did.

HAROLD PENDLETON All I can remember from an early audition is that the trumpet player was very modest and… a sort of shambling bear, and the mouthpiece—the articulate one doing all the talking—was his brother Bill. And Bill talked so much that he probably lost him the job, I would have thought—who knows. All I know is, he didn't get the job.

BEN MARSHALL Well, there was a bunch of us young lads in our mid-teens, all hanging about together. One day we were in my house in Cranford, and talking about music, and what we'd like to play. But it cost so much to get the instruments. And my father suggested—he said, "Well, why don't you all chip in so much a week, and when you've got enough, buy your first instrument, so that one can start learning that, and keep going, and eventually you'll all have an instrument—and you can form a band."

So, in fact, we started to do that. We bought a clarinet and a trumpet. I was going to be the piano-player because we had an old piano—and the guy that tried the clarinet, he tried it, and got nowhere, after weeks and weeks of trying. Didn't have lessons— should have gone for lessons really. He would have found out then, because I tried it and could hardly get a note out of it.

Finally found out that it was a two-piece thing—that it was a high-pitched mouthpiece and a low-pitched barrel, or vice-versa. And it didn't seem to work. But we got a trumpet— another fella, Reg Burgoyne—and he'd drifted away from the crowd and didn't want to play anymore, so it was floating about. And that was the trumpet that was floating about when Sonny came back from Palestine in the Army.

KEN COLYER Brother Bob met up with Teddy Peacock. He had lived three doors from us at Cranford. He had just left the Merchant Navy after spending some years as a steward on the P&O Line. He told Bob there was some fellows he knew over the bridge who were trying to get going and why didn't I sound them out.

I contacted them and went to see them. They had heard George Webb's band and quite liked it. I said that was the sort of sound I was after. My reaction on first hearing the Dixielanders was one of elation that here were guys in England trying to play the music. Then the snag came. They had formed a quartet with Ralph Dollimore who lived nearby, but he was after a different style of music.

We had a few blows together and bit by bit I weaned them away from Ralph. I would have been pleased to have had Ralph with us but I think he had modern leanings and it just wouldn't have been any good. He was a thoroughly trained pianist and would have been invaluable.

I knew nothing about chord structures and was never too sure what key I was in. At sea I would take a tune and play it with as many difficult valve combinations as I could find, not knowing what they were.

BILL COLYER It was Ken back in Cranford who was thinking he'd got to find some local guys; there must be somebody. Then somebody mentioned to him that there were some guys in Waye Avenue or wherever, all on the local patch; it's only a small place, and it was Ken who caught up with Sonny and Ben and Ron Bowden, who were into a sort of mainstream trio. Ben was taking lessons from Bert Weedon, Ron was taking lessons from Billy Eyden, I think—he was great mates with Billy, a fine drummer, but they were kind of… I can't think of the word… *hot dance,* if you like; and Sonny was learning a bit of trumpet. Ken met them and, of course, when I went down there, Ken introduced me to them.

There were only three pubs, and then it was halves— we couldn't afford pints, too many pints.

> But, yeah, I became the focal point, because I could talk about the stuff and I had the records.

We used to go round to Sonny's house in Waye Avenue; I

Bill as MC tells the crowd what the Cranes are about to play

went there years later to take him to the Reading Festival, and when you think there would be five or six guys in a room smaller than this and I've got my box of 78s... So I was playing them the Ellingtons, the Dorseys, the Woody Hermans, the Bunk Johnsons, the Mutt Careys. So it was widening their knowledge of the music and no prejudices.

BEN MARSHALL Then Ken appears on the scene. An afternoon, which I believe was a Saturday, there was a knock at my door. I opened the door, and there's this guy—Ken. He has a case, and he said, "Oh, hello. My brother knows your brother, and he tells me that you play guitar." So I say, "A bit." By that time I had bought a guitar, but for flash rather than quality. It was a big white thing. That was the bee's knees! Sounded really good, and a beautiful thing.

Anyway, he says, "I hear you play guitar, is that right, because I'm looking to get a band together." So I said, "Well, come in, come in." And he came in and we had a chat, and he was telling me that he wanted to get a band together playing New Orleans music, which meant nothing to me at that point, really. And he says, "I play trumpet," and he got his trumpet out. So I said, "Ooh, that's nice," and the piano was there, and he said, "Do you play the piano?" and I said, "I can do a few chords, that's all..." And he said, "Let's try a twelve-bar."

So I'm just sort of thumping this out, and he's blowin', and I'm thinking, "Ooh, that's nice... Yeah, I like that." Anyway, we chatted, and got along quite well. Very enthusiastic he was—keen. A little bit introverted, as he always was—he couldn't **really open out to you.**

He was very quiet and reserved. And lived in this world that he'd created for himself. And he said, "Would you be interested?" So I said, "Well, it's not on really, because the group that we're rehearsing with at the moment already has a trumpet player. So it wouldn't work. You know, we can't leave him out."

So then he pondered it for a moment, and he said, "Well, we could use two trumpets in the band." And so I said, "Well, that might be on." And that's how the two-horn Cranes appeared. Not because of Oliver or anybody else. Purely for that reason.

After a chat and a cup of tea or whatever, we said we'd arrange to meet in a couple of days. I'd bring my brother Bill along and I'll have a chat with the lads. I think we met in the Berkeley Arms a couple of days later.

It was early '49, yeah. I talked to the blokes; I'd got nothing to lose by talking to them. So they came along, open-minded, and again were caught up in their enthusiasm, and said, "Well, let's talk to Ralph and see if he's interested." But when we did he said, "No, not really. My inclinations are the other way. But you go ahead—no bad feelings." And so we did. Said, "Well, lets give it a shot." So that was it—that was when the listening to records started. And talking. And it was almost every day we were together, because we all lived in Cranford, you know... It was only five minutes walk, and we were all talking.

And so we said, "Well, where do we play?"—We were playing in each other's houses initially. We used to go to Ron's, I think, and Sonny's and mine. That's where the *Miner's Dream Of Home* came from, actually. We were playing one day and said, "What sort of tunes should we do?" and my dad came in and said *Miner's Dream Of Home*." That's 'cause after he'd had a few jugs he always used to sing that, my dad. "*Miner's Dream Of Home*, that's a good tune. How does it go?" and he sang it for us. "Yeah, yeah, yeah, we'll try that." And we did, and that became one of the numbers of the Cranes.

There was no talk about "You do this and I'll do that." None of that at all. It was just: "We're gonna just blow and enjoy it." And one would take the lead and the other would try and harmonise behind that, or fill in—sometimes getting in the way of the clarinet or the others, but it didn't matter. And the more they did it, the more Sonny was figuring out. He didn't know how he was doing it, but it used to work. And they'd swap the lead.

SONNY MORRIS Ben, Ron Bowden, Ralph Dollimore and a fellow called Reg Burgoyne—he was going to be the trumpet player—they were going to form a dance band. Ben was playing guitar and Ron was drums. By the time I came home from the Army, Ben had heard George Webb's Dixielanders, and Reg Burgoyne had decided he wasn't cut out for that sort of thing, so would I buy the trumpet? Two pounds ten shillings! So I did and I started to fiddle about with it. Bob Colyer knew Don Marshall, Ben's brother, being in the Merchant Navy, and Ken decided to come round and talk to Ben about forming a band.

So Ben said, "Well, we've got a trumpet player"—meaning me—trumpet player! I don't think Ken was really interested in the two trumpets, but because I was there, I suppose he thought he didn't like to break up...

So Ken suggested we use two trumpets. So that's how that came about; the two of us went in. **Ken and Bill, of course, they had a Dansette record player and a pile of records. They would come round here very often and we used to play these records, mostly Bunk's, and that's what started me off.**

And then, I suppose, Wooden Joe [Nicholas] came along, didn't he? And Kid Shots Madison, without a doubt. They were mainly my influences at the time. We started off with the Cranes at the White Hart, Cranford. There were Ken and myself, Ben on banjo, Ron on drums and that was it for a start. Ken and Bill, they'd heard about John R. T. [Davies] and contacted him and John turned up with an armful of instruments—as you can imagine!—and we wanted a trombone player at the time. Brother Julian turned up with a sousaphone. We still never had a clarinet player. Cy Laurie was going to come down and do an audition. For some reason or other he couldn't make it so he asked Sunshine to come down and do it instead, and that was alright. Monty had this little metal clarinet. He seemed to suit and that was it. He was in.

We started playing without piano, of course, and then Pat Hawes was demobbed from the RAF. Suddenly he was in the band. Ron left very early on—we couldn't find a regular drummer so Bill came in on washboard. We were playing stuff like *Moose March*, *A Closer Walk With Thee*—all those spirituals. Ken was a great lover of spirituals, you know.

RON BOWDEN Ben lived about half a mile away in another street. Ralph Dollimore lived opposite Ben in another street. You know: all that Cranford crowd. We used to hang around on a Sunday morning at a cafe called the Continental Cafe, run by an Italian lady. And we used to meet there, and talk about it and sit on the seat... go to the pub, and things like that.

We were only seventeen or eighteen or something. That was during the war we used to go in the pub—we shouldn't have been in there really. Ben's dad and his uncle used to do a Flanagan and Allen act—all that stuff. And at the end of the night at the pub everybody was well-pissed. It was great, you know—all that sort of thing was going on then. And, I thought, it was a sudden switch to New Orleans.

SONNY MORRIS The very first session we had at the White Hart, Cranford, was 12 March, 1949. It was a week after I came out of the Army, so I remember it well. And then, some local people came along and heard us and they formed this club. Ken was very keen on Bunk Johnson at that time.

KEN COLYER When I first cottoned on to Bunk, I admit I slavishly tried to copy him. Bunk was a wonderful teacher, which I realised. It wasn't just to try and copy him, it's a waste of time becoming a carbon copy of anybody.

BILL COLYER Ken came up to me—by now we'd got the quartet, we'd got the Cranford three and Ken, so we'd got four of us, we'd play out in the open or in road menders' huts; anything—and Ken said, "Hey, I've just found out there's two brothers. There's a brother out at Longford"—that's up the Bath Road. So we got a bus up from Cranford to Longford, knocked on the door and a very well spoken lady said, "Yes, what do you want?"—flat hats and duffle coats obviously out of the norm for them. I said, "Is John Davies in? We'd like to see him." "Oh, the boy's in the garage doing something."

So we went to the garage, quite a big garage, and he was sitting there, headphones on and a cylinder machine and some wires and a turntable. He was trying to fake a Buddy Bolden cylinder. **He was playing a King Oliver 78 and trying to transfer it to an Edison Bell cylinder that he'd bought in Shepherds Bush market, and that's how we met John.** We got talking to him and said that we had

Monty's designs for the Cranes' label; the Cranes play Camberwell School of Art

got the makings of a band down at Cranford and would he like to come and join us.

Of course, I knew about him because John started playing trombone with Mick Mulligan and could play banjo and that. So he said, "Oh, my brother Julian plays tuba." So I arranged for them to come down to the White Hart. On Monday evening this Austin 7 pulls up outside the White Hart and on the roof it had got cases: the tuba and a trombone and something else and a banjo case. In they came and they get all this stuff out and we started playing.

It turns out that his big influence was Eddie Edwards of the ODJB, but he knew chords; that was the thing, because Ben was only learning things. So he and John would always be heads down for Ben's chord book; yes, John R.T. was invaluable in his way. He would even play a swannee whistle solo, you know, without saying anything to Ken, this cornucopia of instruments.

JULIAN DAVIES I remember when Ken came to the door. I'd just got home from work, and I have to confess, I couldn't understand a word that he said. I'd just come from a public school, and this guy has got this London accent... I thought he had a cleft palate or something.

But I eventually understood that he wanted to come and see my brother, so I invited him in, and a little while later John came back from work, and we went up to his room, which was right at the top of the house, in the attic. And they both got out their horns and just started blowing, just to see if they could fit together. Funnily enough, my father—who hated jazz—gave John a trombone for his Christmas present some time in the past. And it had lain idle for years. John was in the Army and he didn't take the trombone with him, and this trombone lay around. But anyway, he had the trombone, so he played.

And I heard—in listening to Ken, I suddenly realised that I'd heard quite a number of musicians "live", but he was talking to me with music that wasn't a sound that sounded like jazz or anything. This man was talking to me. And I said, "You sound like Mutt Carey," who happened to be his hero. And he said, "Do you want to join my band?"

Just like that. And I had actually only just left school at eighteen, and I had bought a sousaphone from Mike Daniels for three pounds. And I said, "Well, I've got this sousaphone." I also played clarinet. I also played cornet, actually. But he said, "Well, bring it all along." Of course, they didn't want the cornet because they'd got Sonny. Ken was playing trumpet in those days, and Sonny was playing cornet.

But anyway, I brought the clarinet, and I was absolutely hopeless on that, so Ken said, "Try the sousaphone." And he stood it for about three weeks. And then he said, "Why don't you get a string bass?"

67

KEN COLYER Almost as soon as we started, John had to keep putting me right where I had mis-learned the tune.

"There's no key change in that tune."

"What key change?" I didn't even know I had changed key.

The few sessions we had had before, Ben on guitar had just followed me, assuming it was right as he didn't know the tunes either. It might have been interesting if we had carried on like that. We were playing 'free-form' and didn't know it. But John got us sorted out.

BILL COLYER We were quite a team. We were a family really. John didn't drink and yet we were bitter drinkers, and by the end of the evening you're ticking a bit. But John would be ticking with us on orangeade.

Julian did like the bitter, and I remember when we got our first Nottingham or Sheffield gig, I had to go down to Longford and get Mrs Twiston Davies's permission for Julian to travel, and she said, "You will look after him, won't you? He's only a young lad, you know." Little did she know that he could shift that beer as well as any of us. John was marvellous in his way, always part of the scene.

Pat Hawes had come home on leave and, being a jazzer, he had gone down Piccadilly Arcade where Sinclair Traill and Steve Appleby had a little record shop; Jimmy Bryning was their gofer. He was doing transfers—some of those early Tempo releases are Jimmy's work—but it was Jimmy who brought Pat to us. He'd got us a gig at a drinking club in Ealing which had a piano, and Pat was on leave. Of course, the minute we heard Pat, Ken and I looked at one another and said, "That's our man."

PAT HAWES They had very different ways of playing. I mean, in those days, Sonny was a bit of a blaster, you know. He'd grab the number by the scruff of the neck and give it one. **Ken was, I don't know if *subtle* is the right word. He was different.** I remember something he said to me—where this came in the sequence of things, I don't know. I was playing a record, and he said, "Who's that?" And I said, "Well, listening to it, it's either Mutt Carey, or you trying to play like Mutt Carey. Or some Japanese bugger impersonating both of you." "Right," he said. But we never did make clear which it was.

MONTY SUNSHINE That was my first thing—the Crane River. We were great purists, we had the blinkers on. We used to listen to all the contemporary music of New Orleans, and it was great fun. A great part of my life actually. And I look back with great fondness.

Ironically, with Ken we had an understanding it was always, you know, from afar. But the strangest thing is that

whenever I used to do guest spots with Ken, or play with his band or whatever, I always used to say to him, "Well, come on son, it's time we went and played," and he used to always turn around to me and say, "What do you keep calling me son for?" And I said, "Well, I'm older than you are, aren't I?" and he said, "Oh that's right, yeah." He had a good sense of humour as well, you know.

BILL COLYER I was the gofer, and I went along to the White Hart, because there was this big, corrugated-roofed hut in the small gardens by the pub and I knew it was used for British Legion weekly meetings, odd weddings and whatever. I had a word with Clarry Brinsden, and out of that came the Cranford Jazz Club. And then with local youngsters, one volunteered to do the door for us. I think we charged about 1/6 [7^{1}/$_{2}$p] or 2/- [12p]then, and it became the focal point.

But prior to me doing that, we used to rehearse in the open air because we had nowhere else to rehearse, and, of course,

John R.T. records an informal session

locals were taking the mickey and saying we were crazy bastards and we were a local nuisance. But we got on *Picture Page* on television and we became national heroes by then because everybody had a little black and white telly and *Picture Page* was an *in* programme. They were what nowadays is everybody's *Coronation Street* or *Eastenders*, in those days.

I know that by now we are part of the local scene and, me always having the latest records, we'd go round to Sonny's, maybe twice a week sometimes. See, they had day jobs. I think they worked as panel beaters for Duplex, the coach builders, Sonny, Ron and Ben. But I know they had day jobs. Ken by now was a carriage cleaner at Acton Underground Depot, I was obviously working in the bookshop, and Julian and John, they had their own thing going—don't forget, they were upper crust. How they swung with us! They were an amazing couple, those two.

BILL REID I was at Harrow County School—and there was an art teacher there called Paul Oliver (later to become a distinguished writer on the blues). I joined his class about negro music. And he played some music from the American Music sessions. You know, schoolkids didn't know much about music except for the Hammersmith Palais and listening to Joe Loss, and so we were onto the in thing—Grammar School and Art School types, you know, we all got into it—New Orleans jazz. It was a fresh, invigorating sort of folk music. Bunk Johnson, George Lewis and that sort of thing.

And we would hear all these records, and we had a marvellous idea of the music from the States, Jim Robinson and all those.

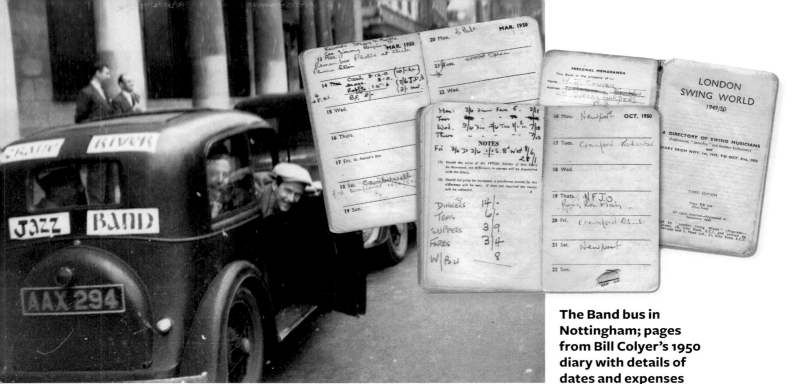

The Band bus in Nottingham; pages from Bill Colyer's 1950 diary with details of dates and expenses

And then somebody said, "There's a band that plays like this down at Cranford at the White Hart."

And I know I wasn't eighteen yet so it would be 1949 or '50. And we went down there, and it was like a shed behind this pub, and the pub was on the edge of London Airport. And they came on... and they didn't stand up, and it was incredibly uncommercial.

There was Sonny Morris—they were all there: John R.T. Davies, Pat Hawes on piano, Monty Sunshine—they were all playing. It was wonderful stuff, and I remember a fight took place—there were a couple of kids fighting at the back of the hall. The band were very impressive. He had a magic about him—Ken—he was so into that sort of music. It was so uncommercial, but attractive. You'd go home with the tunes running through your head.

MONTY SUNSHINE We used to pay to rehearse. We went into this little hut beside this pub in Cranford, and somebody would look through and say, "Oh, sorry about that..." and he'd sit in the corner, sit there drinking beer. And suddenly a few more would come in. And then on a Friday a chap came over to us and said, "You know, while you're rehearsing, I'll go around and collect some dibs for you."

So he'd go around and collect. People would put in a shilling, two shillings. And it paid for our beer. Well eventually this chap—Ted Schrift his name was—said, "Look, we might as well get people come in and they'll dance." And they came in, and as long as they were quiet, we would stop in the middle of a tune and say, "No, we want to try it again." The people didn't mind—they liked to hear the music. And gradually it started to build up, it was tremendous.

KEN COLYER The band kept wood-shedding, and that glorious summer we spent almost every evening by the banks of the Crane in a friendly farmer's field, rehearsing.

After the long summer we started using the annexe (at the White Hart) more often, chipping in a shilling each and keeping a kitty to pay for the hall. Youngsters started gathering outside. So the Crane River Jazz Club started. I didn't want the band to play in public—we didn't consider the White Hart public. They were rehearsals people were allowed to listen to, until we were proficient and knew our material.

George Melly arrived in a long astrakhan overcoat, smoking a huge cigar. He had style even then. I liked the Mulligan band at that time. I could mentally imagine a dustcart hurtling down the street out of control, when they were going under full throttle. Steve Lane was playing guitar then and would come regularly to our sessions. Sometimes he would put us right on a tune. If anybody showed any resentment, I would point out that if he was right then it was up to us to correct the fault and we had learnt something.

SONNY MORRIS Bill had a collection of records—he used to bring round his record player. He used to leave it here most of the time, because I think Bill was living in a flat somewhere in town. I know that he played us the Bunk stuff that came out on HMV, you know? *Dark Town Strutters'*, *The Saints*, *High Society*, *Snag It*, *Franklin Street*, *Sister Kate*. And I was quite taken with that, so I thought that was nice, you know. And so we went on from there. The thing about it was that Ron Bowden didn't stay long—it wasn't really what Ron wanted to play.

And so for a long time we had no drummer at all. We tried various drummers, but **we used to get regular bookings at the old Camberwell School of Art, because Monty was a student there, and any time they had any sort of a do, we were there, you know. We used to get a lot to drink, but not a lot of money.**

MONTY SUNSHINE I had been trying to play for about eight or nine months. I had met up with Cy Laurie purely because I used to go along to Wood Green Jazz Club primarily to dance. Although I was interested very much in the jazz, to me it was super to be able to hear the music I liked and to be able to dance to it. I got chatting to Cy Laurie and Charlie Galbraith and they told me about a band out at Hounslow who were looking for a clarinet player. "Oh, that's interesting," I said, and anyway I took the address, put it in my wallet and forgot about it.

There was this chap who was at art school with me who played trumpet and he lived over at Hampstead and had quite a good collection of jazz records. **We used to go over and listen and try and emulate the sounds coming from the records. In other words it was like "I'm going this afternoon to play with Louis Armstrong"—or something like that.**

On this particular day, I can remember it was a great turning point in my life because I'd gone along to Hampstead, dead keen—really dead keen—about this playing-the-clarinet, although I hadn't got a clue as to what was happening, what the notes were or anything like that. And I hadn't even got a clarinet case—I just used to have it in a rotten old piece of paper, rolled up.

I got to this chap's flat, and there was no reply. It was about 4.30 in the afternoon and he said that he'd be there then. I waited until 5, quarter past 5, and I thought, "Oh dear," and I was really brought down because I really wanted to have a blow, as they say. I suddenly remembered about this band out at Hounslow. I got my wallet out and had a look, and thought, "What the hell... I'm going to go there," and I got the tube; following the directions Cy Laurie had given me, I came to a pub: The White Hart at Cranford.

Now in those days I didn't touch a drop of beer or anything, but I thought I'd get a half-pint, at least look part of the pub scenery, and I could hear this band playing, but they were playing in a green-painted hut with a tin roof—I remember a corrugated roof—and I sat outside on a bench, sipping my half pint of beer, and I thought, "I don't know, I suppose I ought to go in." And then I heard a clarinet playing as well, so I thought, "Ah well, they've got themselves a clarinet player. I might as

well sit out here and listen to them playing," and it was terrific.

A chap came out of the hut with a tray with a load of empty beer glasses, and he walked past me and I was listening away to the band. Then he came back with a load of pints of beer, and he said, "Do you like this kind of music?" And I said, "Oh, I think it's terrific. I'm a clarinet player..."—just blurted it out. And he says, "You are? Well, come on in!" And I went inside and there was this band of guys. They all looked like thugs—it was the only way I could describe them.

They were all enormous great fellows, and they didn't look at all like musicians—or my conception of what musicians looked like—and there was this clarinet player, you see, wearing RAF uniform.

This chap who'd brought me in—who incidentally was Bill Colyer—said, "Hey look guys; here's a clarinet player!" And I thought, "Oh dear, I've really got to do something." So anyway, they said "Come on—sit-in." I didn't know any of the tunes, so I just blew and tried to hear what I was supposed to do. After they finished playing the first tune, they said would I like to join the band.

I said, "But what about this fellow here?" "Oh no," they said, "he's stationed at Uxbridge." Or Stanmore—I can't remember. "And he's only just come along to sit-in." So I said yes, and that was a great turning point because that was the Crane River Jazz Band.

STEVE LANE Yes, it was known as the Crane River, but Ken was the leader, wasn't he? I don't think anybody argued with him. Well, he took it seriously. When he played, it

JULIAN DAVIES: 19-year-old "baby" of the band, who is also known as their "tame-mad-man". Plays three-string bass and tuba, is ex-public school. Hobbies: bass and radio. Bearded.

BEN MARSHALL: One of the finest rhythm section men in British jazz. Playing banjo and guitar he, too, is a founder member. Has been playing several years and (dare we say it?) we have heard him called "Marrero"!

PAT HAWES: a fine pianist, and, also knows how to handle that old washboard. Fond of quoting Chaucer coupled with well-known Anglo-Saxon words, Pat has been prominent in British jazz a long time. Began playing with John Haim's Jellyroll Kings—contemporary with the George Webb Dixielanders. From Haim Pat went to Lyttelton, leaving to join the R.A.F. Demobilisation saw him joining the Cranes.

Now we have told you about their music and about them, take our tip and make a point of getting an earful of that Crane River Band. It is rapidly becoming the most worthwhile sound in British jazz—even Steve Race says nice things about this band (Musical Express 18/8/50). We wish you, then, many happy hours "Down by the Riverside".

Ken Colyer

Cranes caricatured, left, and in action at the White Hart, Cranford

was important to him to get it right and nice. And his skill at leading the band, building the numbers up as he went along, was tremendous. I think what he did so good was playing the lead... he did that so good.

JOHN BODDY I don't remember it being really a holier-than-thou attitude down at Cranford, though. Because there were a lot of locals as well. I mean, they weren't all the sort of back-to-New-Orleans-or-die audience, you know... they just came because they enjoyed it, and I took friends from school—we went down, and it was good fun, you know. And after a while, jazz *did* become the music of young people, didn't it?

JULIAN DAVIES My parents were recently divorced and I was living with my mother. I was working for EMI at Hayes as a trainee electronics engineer for a little over two pounds a week, most of which my mother took for my keep. I was desperate for some decent clothes and persuaded my father to send me fifty pounds so I could get kitted out.

We used to visit George Beaumont's shop—alas no more—which was in Great Newport Street, and it was on that morning and in that shop that temptation came my way: George had a double-bass for sale for forty-five pounds including the cover. My father was amazingly furious when he heard how I had blown the money.

I put paint marks all the way up the neck of the bass where the finger positions should be and started to teach myself how to play it. After I had been struggling for about three weeks, I turned up for a rehearsal with my sousaphone as usual. Ken said, "Can't you play that string

bass yet? Bring it along next time." I thought that was a bit rich coming from somebody who had spent three years in the Merchant Navy learning his instrument; nevertheless I did as I was asked and, thanks to his patient coaching and encouragement, began to make progress.

Every time I played a right note he grinned at me, and every time I played a wrong note he frowned. And I can remember the first time that he actually congratulated me. It was one of those magical moments where you're playing, and you just go off into a sort of a trance, and you wake up, and say "fantastic." It's a matter of relaxing and letting the music come out.

MONTY SUNSHINE I found him very, very—I won't say sullen but he didn't have a lot to say outwardly. A lot of machinations inwardly. And when he *did* say something, I was pleased to hear what he had to say. In fact, he got me onto George Lewis. I was interested in Bechet, and I'd never heard of George Lewis. The only time I'd heard of George Lewis was the HMV things with Bunk Johnson, as we all did. And then, I suddenly received these recordings of *Ice Cream* and so on, and I was completely gone.

But really, my *being* with Ken Colyer was very, very favourable. Bill had access to the American Musics, and we'd been hearing lots of this playing that other people hadn't heard. You know, people like Big Eye Louis Nelson. The clarinet playing, as far as I was concerned, they were all very much the same. And Dodds and George Lewis and Sidney Bechet were all walking the same road.

I mean, I used to get up—I was supposed to be painting... going to Art School—and I used to stay awake... nine in the morning playing 'til ten o'clock at night. You know, trying different things all the while. And my mother used to say, "For God's sake, be quiet!" in the other room.

And subsequently, of course, when I eventually started getting better and better, I went along to rehearsal rooms—different thing. But there was... a sense of pathos. You know, it was the blues which was the music that I loved... very much so. *Burgundy Street*—oh, that floored me, that did. And there were things like Johnny Dodds and Omer Simeon playing the beautiful blues.

PETER HUNTER I heard records of Bunk Johnson and at that time I was absolutely sold, and that was my future music. I was waiting to go into naval college and I met a couple of old cadets who had been at sea and they said to me, "Look, there was a guy on our ship on the last voyage that plays your sort of music—a guy called Ken Colyer." I thought, "Never heard of him," and they said he was supposed to be quite good and that he had a jazz club out near Cranford somewhere. I thought: *Where the hell was Cranford?*

Eventually I must have found out where Cranford was—and off I went on safari at the age of 13 to find Cranford. I eventually did, and there was Ken and the rest of the Cranes playing away, and of course, being only 13 years old, I wasn't even supposed to be there—but that didn't really matter. I just listened and once again I was sold on the music.

As time went on I went to naval college and I took up playing the cornet, and my interest grew and grew in the music, buying records by this time—Bunk Johnson, the Crane River Band and Humphrey Lyttelton, of course, who by now had formed his own band as opposed to George Webb's Dixielanders, who I had also listened to, and then I went away to sea.

DELPHINE COLYER I used to get off the bus on my way home from school and go into the White Hart and listen to the music and think "Oh yeah, this is alright." Then I got friendly with Mike Peters. And we got records, and we got the HMV Bunks and some George Lewis ones and a few American Musics. I think this is what really impressed Ken, because the first time we went out he said "There's something called American Music Records," and I said "Yeah, I've got some of them, and he thought, "Oh, I haven't found one of these before..."

BEN MARSHALL Well, there were bits of writing, and bits in the *Melody Maker* and so on that were anti—no doubt about it. That it was out of tune, and everything wrong with it. It might have been true. But it was exciting enough for a lot of people to like it. And I think that was—what most people liked was the rawness, really. And not knowing what might happen. And that was a bit of excitement, you know.

But some nights it would take a long time, and some nights it would really take off, and things happen.

Like the first time we did *Do What Ory Say*—where they did the two-trumpet break—Sonny's doing a bugle-call and Ken's riding over the top of that with another break. And they did it at the same time. I think that came about because each thought the other one was going to take the break, so they both did it. And it happened, and everyone cheered and I think we did it on a record somewhere, and you hear Bill yell out when it happened. The first time it happened by accident. Of course, they kept it in.

So, we've now got the full band. And looking back at all the paperwork I have, I didn't realise that that was almost a year when we were discovering everything, really—1949 when we started—well, we opened that little club at the White Hart on the 12th of March '49. And from then on it was not a lot happening out in the big wide world, but it was all going on— we were getting the band together.

RAY FOXLEY I'd met Ken once in Birmingham, actually. In that we were playing—we used to have plays in the parks, to keep people entertained towards the end of the war years—and we were playing in a tent one day... and the Crane River band wandered into town. They were going back to Nottingham so they called in to see us.

We were all rather frightened by all these rough, aggressive-looking individuals who'd come to see what was going on. But Bill Colyer still reminds me of it every time: "Do you remember that first time we saw you? And you were playing in a tent?" I said only the other week, "We were scared stiff of you," and he said, "We were scared stiff of you and the way you played." But we didn't really have any connection at all.

KEN COLYER The band were raring to go and were given the opportunity to play at the Wood Green Jazz Club, which was one of the strongholds. I grudgingly agreed as I still felt we needed more wood-shedding, but all playing is experience and we had to get it sooner or later. I was terribly nervous playing anywhere other than Cranford for a long time, and though a little nerves are a good thing, you can't play well if you are ashake and not relaxed.

IAN CHRISTIE I knew of the Cranes, but I can't think of when I first heard them—I was kind of impressed by their single-mindedness of purpose and the relentless rhythm section that they had, and of course Ken on trumpet.

JOHNNY PARKER I came out of the Army in 1950, and while I was in the Army I'd met Mick Mulligan... all that lot, and I'd joined his band when I came out of the Army, and that was all kind of arranged. And the Crane River Band were around at that time, so I knew Ken as the trumpet-player with the Crane River Band, without actually knowing him personally; I just knew of him, as it were.

But that would be, probably, about 1951. I think I was already with Lyttelton when I went down there. I went down one Christmas, and they had Christmas dinner there—at the Crane River Club—and it was quite funny. When we finished, Ken said, "Well, come back; we'll all go back to Bill's place," which was nearby—Bill Colyer's.

So, there was Ken and one or two others, and I know Jim Bray and I were there and Chris Barber. So we all go back to Bill's place, and—thinking that Ken had got permission and everything was fine—we tucked into booze and stuff we'd found there, when the door opened and in came Bill and Betty. **They went absolutely spare because, apart from being uninvited, we were drinking all his Christmas booze,** and then he goes into the kitchen and he explodes because Ken's sitting there eating a slab of butter with a knife and fork. And in those days, of course, butter was rationed, and

he probably had about a month's ration for two there.

And, anyway, we got slung out of there. So Jim and I went back to Chris Barber's place, and proceeded to tuck in to Mrs. Barber's Christmas pudding in the early hours of the morning.

JIM BRAY People used to assert—the Crane River sort of people used to assert—that Louis and Oliver and Jimmie Noone and all those had gone commercial, you see, because they'd gone to Chicago.

CHRIS BARBER I saw Ken and met him, I think it would have been with the Crane River band when they first started. I don't know whether it would have been the time they played on the amateur jazzband contest at the Hammersmith Palais. One track of theirs and one track of ours came out on Esquire records.

They did a better job than we did, but then they were setting out to play a much more simple sort of music, so they had a right to get closer than we did—possibly. But, shortly after that—around that time—I went down to the White Hart and saw them down there, and I joined in, if I remember rightly.

And then, not long after that, was when Alex Revell and I—it was OK what we were doing but the Oliver thing was getting more difficult; if you had to replace anybody, you had to find people that could understand what you were talking about, otherwise you were wasting your time.

But we thought—really speaking—that it would be the right idea to try and get together with Ken and some of the

73

other people there who were clearly a strong force in that. **And we couldn't really say, as it tends to divide people into two halves—it was bad enough dividing Traditional against Modern, which was absurd in the first place, let alone having traditional against traditional.**

You know... nonsense. And we had a couple of nice sessions at a pub in Goodge Street which had Dave Stevens on piano, otherwise it was Ken and Sonny and Ben and Ron and Alex Revell and myself, and we just played some Oliver tunes and some other tunes and different things, and after a couple of weeks of that, Alex and I got talking about it.

KEN COLYER There was a tentative merger with Chris Barber and Alex Revell, but they changed their minds and wrote Bill a slightly ridiculous, pompous letter stating that they didn't think we would suit them or some crap. We laughed about it at the time.

ALEX REVELL I remember Ken and Sonny failing the Barber band audition. Being a nicely brought-up middle-class lad, Chris wrote a very polite letter to Ken, saying something on the lines of we didn't think they were quite suitable for the kind of music we had in mind. Ken was very sniffy about it—the contents—in his book. I remember saying to Chris that I thought anybody who didn't seem to know if he was in the middle of a chorus of *Sister Kate* or at the end, would never amount to much.

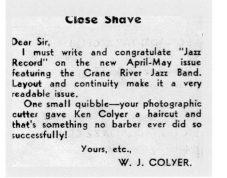

Close Shave

Dear Sir,

I must write and congratulate "Jazz Record" on the new April-May issue featuring the Crane River Jazz Band. Layout and continuity make it a very readable issue.

One small quibble—your photographic cutter gave Ken Colyer a haircut and that's something no barber ever did so successfully!

Yours, etc.,

W. J. COLYER.

BILL COLYER Well, in addition to the band—and this is the term I've always used—The Breakdown Group was born. What happened was that we had an evening to fill, and don't forget we're playing then to local kids, not to any vast audience from anywhere, just the locality. Because it was something to do and it was entertainment. We're talking about kids 15, 16, 17, you know, no adults as such in the beginning. To fill an evening the band would do a few numbers, play for 45 minutes even.

Then they've got to take a break. They're all young, learning and only playing once a week, so lips get tired or banjo strings break, whatever. So it's the band's time for a break.

They would go to the public bar of the pub and I would then go on stage, and by now I'd got an electric turntable: the Colaro. I would take that along and

I would play the 78s in the interval, entertaining if you like, but teaching. I had access to an awful lot of good records working in the record store, and I was teaching them; not just New Orleans but the whole spectrum of jazz.

If there was a good Mills Brothers record or a good Bing, I played that, but always something that swung; the old Ralph Sutton dictum: "Warm tummy and a patting foot." That's always wonderful. I played the music I liked; it made me happy and it made other people happy and it always used to go down well. I'd do my thirty minutes, or whatever, and then the band would come on again.

When Ron Bowden left us and we had no access to a drummer, I started on the washboard. Because in the Merchant Navy I'd always kept rhythm for Ken with wire brushes on a suitcase, the washboard was the next obvious choice. So I actually ended up professionally, would you believe it, on the washboard; I played for about three months. Julian Davies bass, Ben on banjo and me on washboard: that was the rhythm section.

Anyway, at Cranford I said to Ken that maybe we should make a change from playing the records. "Why don't we go back to the old Merchant Navy days? I'll keep rhythm going on a washboard, you on guitar, and if Julian wants to have a go on bass, we'll have a breakdown group." And so that's what we became: The Breakdown Group.

I used to announce it as such when we would do a concert or whatever. I'd say, "And now, ladies and gentlemen, I'd like to introduce you to our special, The Breakdown Group. By the way, you'll have to put up with me on washboard"—that kind of thing.

When I sang with the Cranes I could make up twelve bars on the spur of the moment. This is an oddball one. Humph by now is at 100 Oxford Street—it's the Humphrey Lyttelton Club. The Cranes are an obvious threat (we're talking about 1950/51), and I remember that one night at the 51 Jimmy Asman, who always sat right by the stage—you know, he was the pundit there, and he says, "Bill, look down the end of the club."

It was only a small place, wasn't it, the 51? And there was Humphrey Lyttelton, George Webb and a couple of other guys, maybe the Christies and Wally.

Freddie Randall and Ken meet Princess Elizabeth. Inset; Bill's Festival Hall invite, complete with printing errors

MONTY SUNSHINE The thing was that we'd decided that we wanted to play in the New Orleans manner. And as regards the style, we were just interested in how they played. There was no such thing as we were going to be evangelistic and shriek to the pillars that we're going to come and invade your territory. Nothing like that at all.

In fact we had no idea of trying to vanquish other bands. In other words, the other bands played their things. In fact, so much so, that Wally and Humph used to come down and hear us. They'd heard a lot about us. And we never interposed our method.

KEN COLYER Much was made at the time of a big concert at the Festival Hall at which all the major bands played, and some minor ones. The Cranes were grudgingly allowed to play, although there was strong opposition from some quarters. We were a bunch of roughnecks playing a purposely primitive music. We might dirty-up the place and offend the ears of Princess Margaret and Princess Elizabeth, who would be there due to the efforts of Lord and Lady Donegall.

JULIAN DAVIES I was hoping to do the Festival Hall concert—they'd had Denny Coffey playing bass in the band at various places. I was on the photograph of the band. I was very disappointed, particularly as I was probably the only

monarchist who could have been presented to the princess.

John had taken a job with Minimax—working in East Anglia—so he couldn't make the gig. And I was studying for my Bachelor's degree, and I had taken time off from the band ready for the exams.

SONNY MORRIS Denny Coffey came in on bass and Ray Orpwood on trombone when we recorded *I'm Travelling* at the Royal Festival Hall. **I think we actually played four numbers on the session and the recording company just picked *I'm Travelling* and put it on the back of the Saints playing *I Want A Girl*.** July the 14th— I'll always remember the date because whenever we play it we mention it. I've always thought it was a nice tune to play. It was on a Bunk Johnson record. Lottie Peavey was the singer and I'm told now that it was called *When I Move To The Sky*. I think the first line is *I'm Travelling* so that's what we called it.

DELPHINE COLYER At the Festival Hall, when Princess Elizabeth was there, she wanted all the members of the band— all the bandleaders—to sign the visitors book at Clarence House. Well Ken was off on a bender somewhere, and Bill was looking for him, and eventually he found him—looking pretty awful, I imagine—and Bill said; "You've got to go and sign the visitors book at Clarence House" Well, there are sort of big metal gates with a little door—a door within a door. "Come to sign the visitors book"—these two bums! And: "What's your occupation?" And he put "Underground Train Cleaner!"

KEN COLYER Records were issued by Parlophone and—thank goodness—the engineers did a good job for a change, though we made this easier for them by having no drummer. Bill was on washboard. One track was put out of each band. Our track was *I'm Travelling*. Though this was not my choice it remains one of the best British jazz records ever made and shows what the Cranes were capable of.

BILL COLYER George Martin recorded that, and we broke the rules because *I'm Travelling* is only half of the number. It's backed by the Saints Jazzband playing *I Want A Girl Just Like The Girl That Married Dear Old Dad*. But that's what made the money and sold the record which, as I say, is only half the number. It starts with Pat Hawes—he's on that grand piano and we've only been on stupid uprights, out of tune. Pat's on a high, but we are supposed to keep each number to under three minutes.

> George Martin was the recorder. And what did I do like an idiot at the rehearsal when he said, "Can you give me the composers of your tunes?" Then I, with a chip on my shoulder, said, "All 'traditional', mate." What an idiot!

I'm Travelling came out of a lift-off of an acetate I got from America, a 10-inch acetate, one of the floppy ones, and I realised that it was Bunk Johnson but I couldn't figure out who the rest were. It was actually the West Coast stuff he did with Lu Watters' boys; Turk Murphy. But what I didn't realise was that they were playing the spiritual *When I Move to the Sky*. All we could hear on our terrible dubbing—it was like it came down a rainwater pipe! I didn't know that it was a spiritual.

COLIN BOWDEN That record of *I'm Travelling* was the first major recording I ever did, because I was in the audience!

KEN COLYER They ran a national jazz band competition at the Empress Hall by Earls Court. The hall was an ice-skating

rink then, and it was damned cold. The whole thing was a farce and the winning results of the judges a joke. Lord Donegall was on the panel and Ernest Borneman. Len Beadle's band won Best Band in the Land. They made some records afterwards and even Sinclair Traill in his critique said the joke had gone far enough.

Ernest Borneman said in his column in the *Melody Maker* that the Cranes should have been among the top three winning bands. For its fire and feeling. He liked the Cranes and said that, though there were a lot of things wrong, by some alchemy it came out sounding very right. He knew what we were after.

I had to drill it into them men—they weren't avid about the music like I was, but I coerced them and influenced them. I don't know today whether it was ever to their regret! It was my

Detail of George Melly's painting of The Cranes

personality and driving force that made the band what it was.

PAT HAWES Well, the 1951 concert, that was certainly one of the best things I ever did, without a doubt. I think we were more impressed with the thought of playing at the Festival Hall than the music which was actually being created at the time.

KEN COLYER Things have to take their course; it's useless to have regrets and think what might've been or could've been. All those guys in The Cranes—we're all a bit more staid now, more experienced, and maybe the better for it.

In the beginning we were all so hepped up, so intense—

naturally—we were discovering the music together! For me it was just a wonderful revelation; but in hindsight I was probably in too much of a hurry to get it right and get on with it.

Getting back to what I was saying earlier, **I knew these "sounds" which I wanted us to produce. And we did a pretty good job, actually; but we just didn't have the ability, the exposure or the experience to progress as fast as I wanted us to. That was essentially the crux of my personal disenchantment and feelings of unrest at the time.**

The Christie Brothers Stompers experience might have been short-lived—and maybe it was inevitable that it would be—but at its best it was a wonderful experience for all of us in that band, and some really good music was produced.

**London Jazz Club
Riverboat Shuffle
from Richmond
to Chertsey,
Summer 1951.**

CHAPTER FIVE
THE CHRISTIES

KEN COLYER Keith and Ian Christie used to do odd sessions with pick-up groups, calling them the Christie Brothers Stompers. This was a band they had had in their hometown before coming to London. They asked Pat, Ben and myself if we would do a job with them. Keith was the first man I heard call it a job. I never looked on it as work in those days. The rest of the band was Mickey Ashman and George Hopkinson. They were all still with Humph. We played at Wood Green. I kicked the first number off and it was as if a charge of electricity went through us. There had never been a band sound like this in England. Humph knew something was afoot. I had been surprised to see him turn up but hadn't thought about the implications. I would sooner he hadn't been there.

The session was super-charged (those first kicks are the killers). I saw Humph's behind drop back on his seat after one number, as mine had when listening to the Condon band. But I wish he hadn't sat right in front of me in the first row. Maybe the old devil did it on purpose.

Sometime after, Ian got together with me and I got the story. Both Ian and Keith were due to leave Humph. They wanted the Stompers to be a full-time group. They would try and get Mick and Hoppy to leave with them if Ben, Pat and I would come in.

The Christie Brothers Stompers: Ken on cornet, Keith Christie on trombone, Ian Christie on clarinet, Pat Hawes on piano, Denny Coffey on bass Ben Marshall on banjo and Bill Colyer on washboard

We were at a fork in the road. I had achieved much with the Cranes but, now I knew where I was going, I was in a hurry to get there. The decision wasn't an easy one.

There was nothing underhand done (as is often the case). The Cranes got together and discussed it openly, weighing the pros and cons. The decision was made. We would leave Sonny and Monty to run the Cranes and we would join the Stompers. Naturally Humph did what he could to thwart us. We were pulling the rug from under him and I don't blame him. Mick wouldn't leave Humph and Humph had some hold over Hoppy and he couldn't quit. We were off to a bad start.

PAT HAWES Early in 1951 seven jazz musicians from the Crane River and Humphrey Lyttelton bands got together to make some records for Carlo Krahmer's Esquire label—Ken Colyer, Pat Hawes, Ben Marshall from the Cranes, Keith and Ian Christie, Mickey Ashman and George Hopkinson from Humph's band. All shared a mutual admiration for one another's playing, and Keith and Ian, who had starred with Humph's band since RAF National Service brought them to London from Blackpool, shared a desire to start their own group.

Quickly on the market, these records were well received by the critics both here and in the USA, and such was the enthusiasm of the players that we decided to make the Stompers a permanent working unit. In the event, Mickey Ashman and George Hopkinson decided that their future lay with the Lyttelton band and withdrew; Denny Coffey came in from the Cranes on bass, and the drum chair remained temporarily vacant with Bill Colyer, Ken's brother, sitting-in on washboard.

The two Esquire sessions featured some fine, roaring, uninhibited jazz, but the sound left much to be desired. So we were delighted to record a first session for Melodisc in April 1951 under studio conditions. Unfortunately the sound jinx was still there—*Creole Song* and *Heebie Jeebies* were mastered, pressed and issued as Melodisc 1173, but this record was quickly withdrawn because of previously undetected distortion. Investigation of the remaining titles, *Don't Mind Dying* and *Old Grey Bonnet*, revealed similar deficiencies. Both titles were rejected, but thanks to Bill Colyer you can hear *Old Grey Bonnet* for the first time ever, taken from a really beat-up acetate.

The Stompers came together with no preconceived ideas or prejudices as to our repertoire. Prevented from live contact with American stars by the Musicians' Union ban on their touring of Britain, our influences and inspiration came perforce from records.

We were familiar with much of the classic Oliver, Morton, and Louis' Hot Fives and Sevens, and to this we eagerly added the traditional sounds then appearing on small American labels: Art Hodes' Blue Note sessions, Rudi Blesh's *This Is Jazz* shows, Tony Parenti's Ragtimers, the Kid Ory Exner, Crescent and Columbia sides, plus the Condon and Wild Bill Commodores and, of course, all the American Music discs of Bunk Johnson, George Lewis, Wooden Joe [Nicholas], Louis de Lisle et al that Bill Colyer could find for us at the International Bookshop in Charing Cross Road where he worked.

I myself regularly trawled the racks of Doug Dobell's rapidly growing stock at 77 Charing Cross Road and Dave Carey's Swing Shop in Streatham for yet more delights.

From all these varied influences I would imagine that the Kid Ory band came out on top: Keith played powerful tailgate trombone without aping the Kid's phrases, Ian concentrated on fluid, Creole-style clarinet à la Albert Nicholas, and Colyer fans may well be surprised at the sheer power and drive of Ken's lead horn.

At the beginning of the fifties jazz was becoming increasingly popular, although noone in 1951—noone—could have yet foreseen the "trad" boom of a few years later. The Christie Brothers Stompers soon became established as a strong attraction amongst the ranks of the bands operating on the London scene. This was consolidated by a sudden stroke of good fortune.

Stan and Bert Wilcox offered us a twice-weekly residency at their London Jazz Club, 100 Oxford Street—an offer which we delightedly accepted. Bert and Stan had the justified reputation of being decent guys, jazz lovers, and above all honest in their financial dealings. This was not always common in the business, as we had already discovered—young as we were!

They then made a historic masterstroke by booking Big Bill Broonzy for a season at the club and a series of concerts. We all have happy memories of Big Bill at 100 Oxford Street: one foot on a chair, singing, talking, and playing his unamplified guitar. The club was regularly packed out. More than three hundred

fans listened in silent, rapt attention—magic moments indeed, and personal contact with the real blues—an experience never to be forgotten!

BEN MARSHALL The end of the Cranes in its original manifestation was the result of some records made as an experiment, using a mix of musicians from the Cranes and the Humphrey Lyttelton band. They were such a success that many offers came in for the band to perform, including a twice-weekly residency at the London Jazz Club, which later became the 100 Club.

After a lot of heart-searching, it was decided to break up the Cranes, and I became a member of the Christie Brothers Stompers. The personnel on the first six of the recordings was Ken Colyer, Ian Christie, Keith Christie, Pat Hawes, Mickey Ashman, George Hopkinson and myself, but when the break came Mickey and George decided against, and Denny Coffey came in on bass. Once again, I was in a rhythm section without a drummer. The date was June 1951.

NORRIE COX My first exposure to Ken Colyer's playing in the flesh was unforgettable. It was in December of 1951. Gwen, my future wife, and I had travelled up by train from Brighton early morning. We shopped all day, and then to 100 Oxford Street where the Christie Brothers Stompers were appearing in the evening. Anyway, we walked from Lyons and hurried down the steps into the club and into a wall of the most glorious music I had ever heard.

I didn't at first recognise the tune, as it was the verse to *Bill Bailey* and I just stood there transfixed as they swung into the chorus. Now I probably wouldn't cross the street to hear anyone's version of *Bill Bailey* but to this day I can still re-experience that wonderful moment by playing their version on the Esquire EP.

I don't recall much else specific about the evening, except that I was absolutely overawed by Ken's masterful lead and his wonderful use of mutes, particularly his old tin mug. I don't recall whether at this time he was using a metal Derby, but at later sessions I always enjoyed the way he "coaxed" the notes out of the bell by waving the Derby to and fro. I don't recall anyone else on the revival scene being as expressive as Ken in his use of mutes.

I remember that the two hours or so passed in what seemed like a flash and that we only made the train by a matter of minutes. I know that, had I been on my own, I would gladly have stayed till the end and travelled back on the first milk train out in the morning.

BEN MARSHALL It was exciting. Ken really took to it. I loved Keith's playing. He slipped into the Ory mode just like that. And Ken used to love Mutt Carey, so with Pat on piano, Mickey Ashman and George Hopkinson—how could you go wrong, really? I just sat in the middle.

From left, Keith Christie, Ben Marshall, Ken sans beard, unknown and Ian Christie

The Wilcox Brothers were running what's now the 100 Club. Getting together and doing the recording was just a try-out to see what it would sound like. People were—well, we—were interested just to see what that mix would create. And the records came out and were so successful, they decided to do some more—and there were the ones that were done on Melodisc as opposed to Esquire. They then came out and were also very successful, and people started talking. It was the weekend of Sunday the 1st of July. That weekend was decided, well, it was the band that made the decision. We'd all finally decided that "Yeah, we'll go for it." So that was when it became a unit that was gonna become permanent; well, as permanent as any of these things do. And that was the 1st of July '51.

MICKY ASHMAN That's the best New Orleans band there has ever been in this country. It was absolutely super. It couldn't possibly work. I mean, there was no way Ken could work very long with Keith and Ian Christie; it was absolutely impossible.

So, when the band decided to go on the road I said, "No, not for me; it won't last for five minutes." There was such a clash of —what's the word I want? Not egos. I have never thought Ken Colyer had an ego; he just wanted to play trumpet, and did all he wanted to do playing trumpet. Really and truthfully, listening to the records, even now, it was the nearest thing to New Orleans music this country has ever known.

IAN CHRISTIE Keith played like Ory, but it wasn't quite him. Well, what was quite him? I don't know—anything he played was always very good jazz, and always recognisable as Keith Christie, whether he was doing Ory, or to be more mainstream, or something a bit more modern.

I was impressed with all these New Orleans players. Albert Nicholas and then later Ed Hall. Bechet was formidable, of course. Too unique, I think, to imitate. Although I absorbed that. Yeah... Nicholas and those New Orleans players.

JULIAN DAVIES The only time I saw them "live" was when I turned up at the Crane River Jazz Club at Great Newport Street to find another band there, and Bill told us that Ken was joining this band, and that was it. And then Humph came in and I thought… and of course, there was half his band, and I said, "What are you gonna do about this?" and he said, "I'm gonna get my band back." I don't think he did.

He was a bit angry. And I was flabbergasted to turn up for a gig and find that there wasn't one. They never told me.

I think between them they decided that Ken needed to play with better musicians, and so they formed the Christie Brothers. But I stayed awhile, heard the band, and then went home. But that's the only time I heard the Christie Brothers. I mean, in recordings, the band sounded an awful lot like the Cranes. But I haven't got any of those recordings.

BEN MARSHALL When it was decided we were going to form the unit, the Wilcoxes were looking for another band to put in the 100 Club—or the London Jazz Club. And that's when the job was offered to the Christies, for the Monday, I think it was, and the Saturday—apart from when we got out-of-town jobs and they put deps in. And the money we were offered for that—for those two jobs—meant that I could stop work. Heaven! So I packed my job in. I was making leather handbags in Soho.

Well, when we thought that this band that had done the recordings was now gonna become a band, we thought, *well that's three, four people out of Humph's band—he's got to start again.* But in fact, it didn't turn out that way, because George [Hopkinson] didn't come with us.

Two reasons for that: one, that he was offered more money to stay with Humph, and two, that he was under some sort of contract, so couldn't leave. And Mickey Ashman didn't want to leave. We thought he was offered more, but whether that's true, I don't know. But he felt that—because of its composition—it wouldn't last. And that's why he didn't join it. So, Denny Coffey came in. Mick was more of a driver. Denny was a bit of a slaphappy character—lovely man.

He was one of the rare black musicians in the country. But it meant no drummer again.

JOHNNY PARKER Ken didn't last all that long—I don't know how long he lasted with them. But the band was sort of politically motivated really. There was trouble. Lyn Dutton, who managed the Lyttelton Band, was trying to negotiate with the Wilcox Brothers to get more money for Lyttelton, I think, for playing at the 100—what is now the 100 Club. And Bert wouldn't pay any more, and so they said, "Well you can't have Lyttelton."

They bribed Keith Christie to leave Humph by saying they'd pay his Guildhall School of Music fees. And they got a band together, with his brother Ian, and Ken was around then.

It was a good band, I thought—of that sort. They played all the Kid Ory-type tunes.

Well, Humph was above it, you see. "Oh no, doesn't bother me. No!" He was above all that. It didn't really affect Lyttelton.

IAN CHRISTIE Originally we made this record, and it got—amazingly—very good reviews; I don't know quite why. I tell you who was over here doing reviews—Ernest Borneman. And he raved about it. Which was much to our surprise, because it was a one-off kind of thing. And so we decided to form the band on a regular basis. I think Humph had left to go on tour. Humph was the resident down at the 100, and after that we took over. In 1952, I think it was. That was a great place to be. It was indeed. It was a home to the band, playing twice a week.

And then we decided to tour. It was great fun.

We did have rehearsals. Ken established the thing.

BEN MARSHALL Bill was on a couple of the recordings with washboard. You know, it was the bane of my life, really, because without a drummer, you're trying to lay down that heavy beat. You know, to sort of make it compensate for no drums. Pat's the same.

So, I don't know whether that was a good thing—whether that created the sound that was a bit different, because there were no drums, but you need 'em really. And lots of things we did without drums.

And then Bernie Saward came in. Again, lovely man—very quiet. I always remember when he did a roll, he used to rise up. I always remember that.

IAN CHRISTIE As far as I remember, I think it was Carlo Krahmer, whose record label was Esquire. That's when he gave us the proposition. Very interesting idea, and we thought, well, it's a new thing; interesting.

We liked the idea of that—a combination of the two groups would be interesting, and it turned out to be. There was Ken doing his straight lead and the rhythm section—straight down the line without any deviations. And that was what Ken wanted, of course. More or less without solos. That's what the New Orleans pattern seemed to be in those days. We would come to the forefront occasionally, but there was always something going on in the front-line and we liked that. It worked very well. It was an exciting band.

JOHN BODDY I got to chat to Ken when he was with the Christie Brothers Stompers in '52. **Personally, I think the rhythm section was—as all rhythm sections were then—wasn't that brilliant, but the combination of the brass—of Ken and Keith—was the hottest New Orleans brass I've heard. It was fantastic, you know. And they only sold Coke down there at that time, so it wasn't the beer talking. But it was so hot, you know.**

And that *Rum and Coca-Cola* which I've got on 78

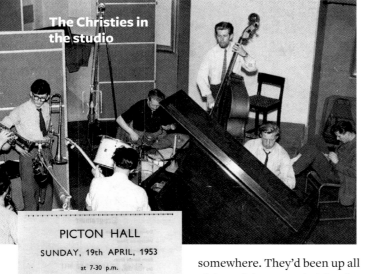

The Christies in the studio

jazz better than anyone we could speak of—*that* kind of style. He played like, let's say, Mutt Carey. He could play all that lovely shakey stuff. Exciting, kind of vibrant.

He could play any tune and of course, he had these big kind of metal bowler hats. He was very conscious of getting different sounds out of the thing. He was very good at all that.

JOHN BODDY It was still a great band—Keith was the best person that's played alongside Ken. He was so good at what he was doing then. I mean, he went on to become more of a modern player, and a very good big-band player. Keith, when he died, he was drinking too much and whatever, and he collapsed and died; that was terribly sad. I mean, they got on like a house on fire, those two. You could tell that... the rapport was really terrific.

The interplay and the heat, you know. It wasn't mouldy-figs, though, if you know what I mean. It was fresh. I mean, what Ken was doing, using those Mutt influences. A bit of Bunk more than Mutt, and sort-of Red Allen—I mean all of those things were in there, but the two of them together, they really gave it a lot of wellie. But they were creative as well and that was very good, you know.

GEOFF COLE I'd heard what he had been doing with the Christie Brothers Stompers, which was very, basically, like the Kid Ory band. With Keith, who was terrific. I remember Bill Colyer saying that when he and Graeme Bell's brother Roger were backstage at one concert where Lyttelton's and all the combined bands were playing, Keith Christie played a solo on such-and-such a blues and it brought tears to their eyes.

And I could well imagine it; he had a wonderful tone, a wonderful concept of what to do, and I suppose, really, it was inevitable that he would progress further. Because he had the technique, and obviously wanted to use it—wanted to develop his ability. A wonderful big tone.

JOHN LONG The Christie Brothers Stompers with Ken was the first live Colyer I saw. And that was about 1951.

Well, it intrigued me greatly, because the style that the Christie Brothers were playing I didn't recognise, because I'd been listening to completely different American stuff.

BEN MARSHALL Although the band was received extremely well wherever it performed, it was not long before doubts began to creep in as to whether the move had been the right one. **Ken was getting uneasy; I think he felt he had**

somewhere. They'd been up all night and they recorded that for Krahmer—didn't they?—one Sunday morning. *Rum and Coca-Cola*, and there were about four tracks including *Creole Song*. But I mean, that sort of captured it a bit, but when you were there live, at that age, with the excitement that Ken used to generate with Keith, you can imagine.

Keith was as hot as hell, and the interplay between them, and Ken's use of the mute, and the hat and that aluminium cup he used. And Keith and him—the interplay—the way they sparked each other off!

I mean, the rest of the band it was a bit like listening to Louis with that big orchestra he recorded with in Chicago. Erskine Tate. Like Louis was well away—he was in front of the orchestra and he's sort of dragging the whole band with him. Well that was rather like Ken and Keith Christie together. I mean, they were just so hot, and the rest of the band were like in tow, trying to keep up with that.

IAN CHRISTIE I liked Ken very much. He had a wry sense of humour as well. Sometimes, you'd never know whether he was joking.

No, he was an interesting guy to be with, was Ken. We used to play all the good places, you know. Sunday nights in various towns where they had cinemas—films during the week, then they'd have a concert on Sunday. We used to play all these places. We were very big in Liverpool. We played the Cavern before those guys with guitars came in.

But Ken played the music that we thought was New Orleans

Bill rolls a cigarette on a riverboat shuffle, with the Christies, including Denny Coffey on bass, Ken in cap and Keith on trombone, circa 1951

taken a wrong turning down the road to the ideal band that he had in his head.

It happened sooner than expected; some three months from the band's inception, Ken said he was leaving to rejoin the Merchant Navy in the hope of getting to New Orleans. The Christies brought in Dickie Hawdon as a replacement, an excellent player from the Yorkshire Jazz Band who had been playing with Chris Barber's Jazz Band.

My diary from that time says: "…Portland Place. Dickie Hawdon replaces Ken Colyer. *I'm So Glad*, plus Bernie Saward on drums." So it looks as though about the time that Ken went, Bernie came in, then. With Dickie it just stepped out of New Orleans for me. Excellent player. Great technique—it was a cleaner sound.

PETE LAY Something had been put together by some guy, who'd put the old Christie Brothers Stompers band together, with Ashman and Ian and Keith Christie, Pat Hawes, and I don't know if George Hopkinson was on it—but it was basically the old Christie Brothers Stompers. And Ken had done it.

And Ken told me about this session, and I said, "Well, how did it go?" And he said, "I had a bloody great time, I really enjoyed playing with the guys." And I said to him, "Well, why did you leave the band in the first place, in '52." And he said, "Because they were far ahead of me, musically. I wasn't in their league." And he intimated then—at that session—he said: "The buggers are still better than me."

IAN CHRISTIE I just think he felt we were getting a bit too

Ken Colyer

modern. We had one or two good ideas—or Keith did—to get out of just that strict Ory type thing which we all loved—and he loved—but Keith wanted to get with more solo kind of bits in it, more moving towards the more Chicago Condonesque.

I think Ken liked all this kind of music, but eventually, I think, he got a bit restless—I don't remember him actually saying so. There wasn't any kind of mutiny, there was a settled change, and we wanted to do things that Ken didn't want to do. A bit off the beaten track. But it was a kind of pleasant straitjacket to be in—the New Orleans format that Ken had in mind.

And he left and went to New Orleans, and when he got arrested for overstaying his visa, that's an ideal thing—to be arrested in a New Orleans jail—what a background! A pedigree for a jazz player...

KEN COLYER The brief brilliance of the Stompers was short-lived. I was down in the dumps, *Everything's Wrong, Ain't Nothing Right* (Lil Armstrong). We had been getting the American Musics recorded by that marvellous man William Russell. Bunk Johnson is the greatest teacher I have ever had. Squire Gersh some years later, when he was over with Kid Ory, was to tell me of the times Bunk played with the Lu Watters Band.

He said they didn't really understand Bunk until one day he was playing so good that like a shaft of light it hit Squire. "The old man was showing us the way. Straight down the middle of the road."

Then I thought: These men were still playing in New Orleans —they weren't that old—they must still be playing, so the logical thing was to get there while they *were* still playing.

I checked into the visa business. The problems were insurmountable. Unless you were Brian Rust or a man of means, you had no chance. The only way I could think of this at the time was to rejoin the Merchant Navy and somehow or other find a boat that took me to New Orleans.

The big snag was very few British boats went to the Gulf ports. They were looking for crew for the *Empire Patrai* which was sailing out of Mobile, Alabama—that's near enough—I daren't take any more chance. This is as near as I'm going to get.

I made my decision. I explained to Keith how I felt and what I had decided to do. He agreed amicably and I worked out my notice until Dicky Hawdon came in.

I went to the Victoria Docks to see about getting signed back on the pool. The Seamen's Union reared its ugly head. I went to the union office. **I tried to argue that I had been a member of the NUR and the MU for some time, but with the "brotherly love" that these people have for the workers they said I would have to pay the back dues from the time I had left the Merch up to the present. Bill helped me out and I paid up and got reinstated.**

First I went to the Port Line office on Leadenhall Street to see if I could get back on a Port boat. After a while I thankfully got a standby job on the *Port Lyttelton*. Thankfully, because funds were running low and also I would be glad to get out of the dreadful place I was living at just off Lancaster Gate. I had had insomnia ever since I had been there. The place gave me the heebie-jeebies.

The guys gave me a farewell session at Cranford and I took the train to Newcastle, getting aboard the ship in the early hours of the following morning. The *Lyttelton* was to me a brand-new ship. She was a motor ship built in 1947 and very civilised compared with some of the tubs I had sailed on. [This was the start of a succession of ships that would take Ken to the *Empire Patrai* in Mobile-Ed.]

Ship's Name	Official Number	Capacity in which he served	From	To	Trade*	Ability†	Conduct‡
PORT SYDNEY	136660	Assistant Cook	21 Aug 1947	3 Oct 1947	F	VG	VG
PORT SYDNEY	136660	Assistant Cook	1 Nov 1947	17 Dec 1947	F	VG	VG
PORT SYDNEY	136660	Assistant Cook	8 Jan 1948	24 Feb 1948	F	VG	VG
PORT SYDNEY	136660	Assistant Cook	6 Mar 1948	13 Jun 1948	F	VG	VG
PORT SYDNEY	136660	Assistant Cook	25 Jun 1948	26 Oct 1948	F	VG	VG
PORT LYTTELTON	181590	Assistant Cook	20 Nov 1951	3 Dec 1951	H	VG	VG
LLANDOVERY CASTLE	148678	Assistant Cook	19 Dec 1951	13 Mar 1952	F	VG	VG
TAMAROA	144805	Assistant Cook	9 Apr 1952	25 Jul 1952	F	VG	VG
EMPIRE PATRAI	181702	Assistant Cook	21 Aug 1952	25 Nov 1952*	F	VG	D

*When the seaman is reported to have failed to rejoin at Mobile

Ken in front of the Halfway House in New Orleans: "The colour bar was very strict at the time and there were problems, but I've often felt that the old saying "Fools go where angels fear to tread..." I took chances sometimes and even the bands did, because they were aware the colour thing was a problem.

CHAPTER SIX
NEW ORLEANS: THE PILGRIMAGE

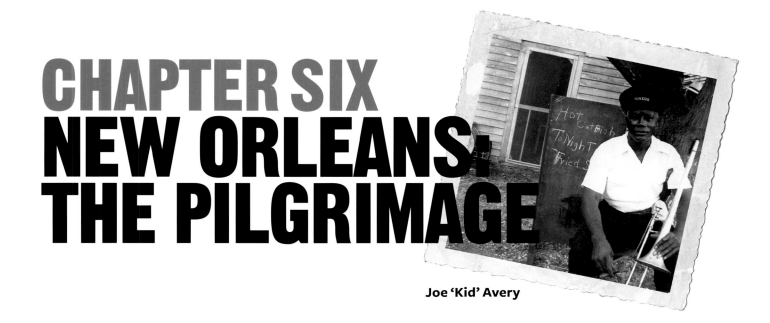

Joe 'Kid' Avery

**KEN COLYER LETTER TO BILL COLYER
8 OCTOBER 1952**

K. Colyer Asst. Cook, S.S. Empire Patrai, c/o Page and Jones, First National Bank Bldg, St. Joseph Street, Mobile, Ala. USA
Dear Bill,

We just docked this morning and I got all the mail together as we must have just left before the first arrived. I got the lolly O.K. and thanks, any odd buck will be welcome as I want to save a little kitty so that when I pay off here or somewhere on the coast I can ease off down to Noo Awlins and find my own way home. You see I won't collect my pay-off 'till I reach home so I'm going to sub to the limit all the time and save up what I can.

We'll be a week or ten days loading so I will try my damnedest to get a quick trip to N.O. if only to contact Souchon and whoever I can so as to pave the way to a longer stay in January. From what I gather they are not too harsh on British seamen on the beach in N.O. The *M.E.* clipping should be a handy intro to anybody too. The N.F.J.O. had quite a blow-up eh! I bet that shook things up considerable.

The trip has been stinking hot though Mobile is quite cool now. We hit a bit of a blow a couple of days from here but had no other bad weather.

There was quite an interesting chain of events after we left Port of Spain which I will recount.

We were laying at anchor picking up our oil and water, which the Officers have somehow managed to pollute to a mixture looking like something between a brick red liquid and stale urine. Still nobody's died so it can't be plain poison.

The usual boys were aboard peddling souvenir trash, Coca Cola (Jim my bunkmate wangled a crate off a fellow without paying for it) and rum. I laid off the hooch altogether but most of the crowd were buying all they could lay their hands on and were drunk in no time at all.

It must have hit the bosun the wrong way, unless he's always mean when he's drunk. He went on the bridge after the old man first, and the shipping master was there. It seems they had a hell of a time holding the bosun down. He eventually came off the bridge and then went for the chief engineer. After that he just ran amok, went for Nixon, a coloured seaman who had a file in his hand. If it would have been a knife the bosun would have been dead meat the way he was stabbing him with it. Things quietened down a little then and they had a recess for a drink.

The next thing I hear is that Nixon is a little berserk and he's hiding somewhere laying for the bosun and he has got a knife this time. The old man knows what's going on but hasn't set foot off the bridge or his cabin. He then gets the anchor pulled up and heads for sea and you could practically smell the blood in the air!

During one of the forays the mate had armed himself with a very light pistol as there were no other arms on board, got excited and fired the thing, luckily hurting nobody.

This had all started about dinner time and we left shortly after. Peter, an English A.B., went to do his trick on the wheel. After he'd been steering for a while he told the Captain that the crew requested him to turn back and put Nixon off as he was still hidden somewhere with a knife and things weren't safe. The old man didn't even hear him out but started raving and ordered him off the bridge. In the meantime the bosun had been beaten up by a Norwegian seaman and was now out of the scene spark out on his bunk.

By the time the 4 to 8 should have been turning-to, Peter had got them into a mutinous frame of mind and nobody went on watch. The second Engineer was in a panic as the '12 to 4 had gone up and the 4 to 8 hadn't gone down so he stopped the engines but the Chief talked a couple of greasers into turning-to and we carried on. Even the sparks did a trick on the wheel that night as they held off until about ten next morning but finally sobered up and turned to.

There were all sorts of loggings and we all fully expected them to be jailed when we got here but nothing has happened.

I think the Old Man's scared of his job and has hushed it up as this is his first command and he's making a bit of a mess of it. He's no saint hisself and hits the bottle too much now and then. He got boozed in Porto Orday one night and tried to smash the bond door down and set about the customs guard who remain aboard all the time there, he nearly got jailed for that, then coming down the Orinoco he tried to throw the pilot off the bridge so you see he's a bit of a rum guy.

We have a new mate joining and a new chief, second and fourth engineer also all the firemen were signed off today and I hear that all the new ones are Greek, also Jim signed off today. He's not letting any of the deck crowd sign off and yet four of his mutineers are there, I don't figure it at all. The cook is dead set in getting off her but they won't let him go and he's browned off with the lot but he may let me get away this week-end for a few short hours in the City.

I'll close this now Bill but will write again in the next couple of days.

All the Best, Ken

KEN COLYER The weather was fine and we sailed back to Mobile for another cargo. I had some New Orleans phone numbers… Somebody had discovered a phone book in the Westminster Public Library and had made a note of all the men he knew. Among them was Doctor Edmond Souchon's. I thought it worth a try and phoned him from the Seamen's Club. He was completely bewildered as I tried to explain to him who I was and how I came to be in Mobile. Eventually he told me there was to be a session at the International House, Gravier Street, if I could make it.

Mobile is about 160 miles from New Orleans and I didn't know how long it would take to get there. When we finished work I got ready as quickly as I could… then went to the Greyhound Bus Station.

It took longer than I expected to get there, and part of the session was over when I got to the International House. Doc was a nice fellow with a bluff, hearty manner. He had played guitar with the Johnny Wiggs band. Paul Barbarin's band was there with Kid Howard and Albert Burbank. Richard Maclean on bass was the most powerful man I had ever heard, playing with a big tone and plenty of drive. I was in a daze. I had finally made it. It had been a long haul but I was finally there talking and listening to the men.

KEN COLYER LETTER TO BILL COLYER
FRIDAY, 10 OCTOBER 1952. 1.50 P.M

Am taking a flying visit to New Orleans, will get hell for it, as the boat's due to leave at any time, and the cook's skinning out tonight (but they don't know)— but I guess it's worth it.

Just talked to Dr. Souchon on the phone again (phoned last night). I am going to meet at Journalists' reception at International House, Gravier Street. George Lewis Band will be there, and another group. Will give you results of trip as soon as I can…

Doc Souchon was irascible but lovable. He blew hot, he blew cold. He was an eminent figure in New Orleans and a practising surgeon. He showed me great kindness at times. He took me round the old historic places. The ruins of Spanish Fort, where Armand Piron used to play. Bucktown, which he assured me was really wild in the early days, and several other places of interest. Where Mahogany Hall had stood. Doc remembered his young days well. He said he was a heller until he knuckled down and studied medicine.

He remembered King Oliver in New Orleans and also heard him in Chicago. He maintained that the band was never as good in Chicago as it was in New Orleans. He saw Tom Brown's band off on a northern trip before the O.D.J.B. went north. He remembered booking Jelly Roll Morton's band for his college dances. He said they had to treat Mr. Morton with respect, even then. Jelly would take no truck from anyone.

KEN COLYER LETTER TO BILL COLYER
SATURDAY, 11 OCTOBER

Seamen's Club of Mobile, 350 St. Joseph Street, Mobile, Alabama
I arrived back at 8.30 a.m. this morning from my flying trip, and man, was it worth it! When I got back this morning they were all frying their own breakfasts as the cook had gone, and I have been on my own all day. I'm one tired man right now, still, I'll relate more of the ship news later, as I'd like to get my teeth into important stuff right now.

I got into New Orleans at 7.55 and headed straight for this journalists' meeting at the International House on Gravier Street. Doc Souchon was sorry that I had just missed the Johnny Wiggs session. (He plays guitar with them.) The Barbarin band, who had to replace the Lewis band, as they had just left for California, were lined up and being presented to people, so I promptly joined in and made with the handshakes like an octopus. **I nearly dropped when I met Kid Howard, but I managed to control myself, though you can imagine the emotions on meeting so many greats at once.**

The set-up was very informal and very fine and friendly, people would recognise you like an old friend the second time you saw them, and the Doc is one of the finest guys I've met for a long time. The band eventually kicked off on Weary Blues. The Kid damped down and muted all the time—probably just as well

Ken walks in
New Orleans with
Dick Allen

else I might have died of happiness. Burbank—a quiet retiring man. He didn't respond at all when I tried to converse with him, even though I mentioned Ralston Crawford; but he really plays wound-up clarinet—great stuff. The bass player was the man that really knocked me out. God! What a tone and power and slapping technique (Richard McLean). He really rocked the band and some.

Lizzie Miles sang three numbers, *A Good Man Is Hard To Find*, *Bill Bailey*, and *Darktown*. She sings first in English, then Creole, and generally mixes the two, has a really fine voice and a great personality.

Buglin' Sam was about the last person I expected to meet. He's a really nice guy, and he got a great kick when I told him how we used to rave over his Basin Street on that airshot. Another surprise for me is that he is white. When the Barbarin band finished their short set they took a couple of photos which I managed to get in on. I'll have to see if Doc can get hold of them for me. Then Johnny Wiggs, Raymond Burke, Lester Santiago, St. Cyr and Barbarin backed Buglin' Sam on *Bugle Call Rag*. The guy's great and one hell of a bugler. I was chatting with Kid Howard then, and he urged me to get up and blow with them.

I had my mouthpiece with me, so he lent me his horn. Souchon formally introduced me to Sam on the stage, and I joined them in backing him on *How'm I Doing, Hey, Hey*, then without Sam we wound up on *Jelly Roll*. The damned thing was in C, and I've hardly ever played the tune, but I didn't make out too bad, and Lizzie Miles and Howard seemed to like it. A journalist from England (I think his name was something Lewis) wound up the thing with a really good speech, and that was it.

Doc Souchon then drove me to the new Pan American Life Insurance building, where he has his surgery and office. It's an ultra modern building and really lush, the sort of place that makes you feel that your suit's cheap, and you could be looking a little smarter.

Over a couple of bourbons we had quite a conflab. During that time he gave me sad news that Dr. Leonard Bechet died a couple of days ago, and showed me a wonderful photo that Ralston Crawford took of him. He also mentioned a time he had dinner with Wild Bill Davison and his wife, and that he's about the dirtiest mouthed cuss he's ever met, and don't give a damn who's in the company. He surely is a wild one.

Doc Souchon presented me with an LP of the Wiggs band with Papa Jack Laine and Tom (?) Brown on, about the oldest white tram man. It should be interesting. The notes on the back are written by Doc Souchon too. He also gave me a whole pile of *Second Line* mags, and asked me if I would draft him some gen on the London clubs for printing, so if you could send me the latest gen it would be handy. We talked about the faction and camp situation in the jazz world, and it seems it's just the same in New Orleans.

We left eventually and he drove me down to Basin Street, and to where Lulu White's used to stand. It's all gone now, and

there's just new brick walls and buildings. We drove down Bourbon Street, which holds most of the hot spots, and we stopped outside the Paddock Bar as the band were knocking out *High Society*.

"Listen to poor old Picou," Souchon said. "They've had to slow that number right down so's he can finger it." I said nothing 'cos the band was rocking along and it sounded pretty fine to me, and I had a sneaking feeling that I wasn't going any further that night. I said cheerio to a wonderful guy, and went in. I walked around the bar, which is U-shaped, to get a seat and wham! That trombone swung round and I knew that it could only be one man—Bill Matthews.

I didn't know whether to laugh or cry, so I just ordered a beer, and soaked up some of the Octave Crosby band, and the kicks came just about every other second. **I sent a photo up to Bill for the autographs of the band with a dollar for the kitty, and he was tickled pink when he recognised me on the photo.** I went into the back room with them when they had finished their first set, and Snookum Russell took over.

Picou is a great old man and still plays some great clarinet. Those wonderful patterns, like a piece of pretty embroidery, and those figures coming down the harmony, like a sweet young thing delicately walking down a flight of steps. Yes, he still plays a lot of clarinet for my money. Those boys have got some wonderful personality, as has Ralston Crawford. They seemed as glad to see me as I was to see them.

Alvin Alcorn is a great little guy, and I had quite a chat with him. He plays quite quietly, using a burbling melodic technique a lot of the time, but can punch out a fine clear tone when he requires it. The rhythm section was just great! Fine drumming, again great bass, and the man himself on piano, rocking right along with them. He does a lot of vocaling, and Alvin does one or two too. They don't waste any time on the stand. One number finished and they are straight into the next. They also have some nice little twists on some of the old ones.

The people seemed really appreciative too, applauding solos, not too loud so that you could hear what was going on all the time. Earlier in the evening at the mention of Bill Matthews' name, someone remarked, "He's another Ory." Man! But he's great. Plays all the time just like on the discs—stark, simple patterns, with a rock and a punch that makes the ensemble go to hell.

I was really sorry to leave when the time came, and when I got to the station I had just missed a bus and had to wait a couple of hours, but I didn't go back as I was feeling a bit rough by then, and I think I had done pretty well in a few hours.

Well, I've just about covered the evening now, though I'll probably remember a few odd things later that I will jot down, but that's about all for now. The job and the ship are a bit ropey right now, but whatever happens I should get down there at least once again, and I'm sure that I haven't heard the greatest yet by a long way.

Cheerio for now, Ken.

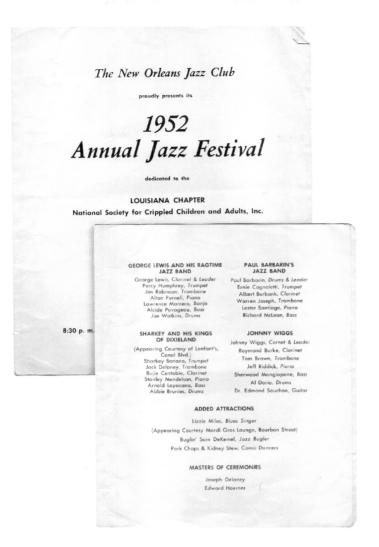

KEN COLYER Lizzie Miles had a wonderful dynamism and she liked to talk. For me it was a delight. She had worked with all the great men. King Oliver was once her backing horn. She said once that she told Joe that if he realised how much he had been cheated by promoters, he would take his 38 and shoot them all. He always carried a 38 pistol in his case.

She had known Ethel Waters well. I mentioned that I had read her book *His Eye Is On The Sparrow*. Lizzie flared, "Don't you read them stories, that woman led a notorious love-life." The Mardi Gras was quiet. There was just Sid Davilla, Joe Robicheaux, Lizzie and a couple of other people. It was late and we had been yarning. Bessie Smith's name came up.

"The record companies come to me," said Lizzie. "Can you find us another Bessie Smith?" Lizzie told them, "You will have to go to Mississippi. That's the only place. That's where all the great ones come from."

Joe was still sitting at the piano. Lizzie got up on stage and started singing Bessie's numbers. After a while there was a magic moment and if you closed your eyes, there was no distractions, no idiots around that think they are at a football match. It was Bessie Singing.

…I arrived back in Mobile with my eyeballs hanging out, and just had to have a cup of coffee before I went back to the ship.

3136 Octavia Street, New Orleans
Dear Bill

Thank you for the second letter about Ken. It was I who should have written to you to tell you how much we enjoyed him, and how we are looking forward to his return trip. Under separate cover, I am forwarding a photo which was snapped with Ken in the bunch. I don't think you'll have much trouble picking out his beaming countenance.

I would have written sooner, but have been abed with a good case of the flu. It has laid me low for the past 8 days. Just today I was able to leave the house and get down to the office to run over my mail, and to get another 'shot' of penicillin in my fanny. It's beginning to feel like a well used pin-cushion.

Here's Ken's story—he phoned me from Mobile (about 175 miles from New Orleans, eastward) to tell me he was heading my way, and so I gave him the address of the 'International House' on Common Street where the N.O. Jazz Club had been asked to meet at a "Special Meeting" in honor of representatives of the N.A.T.O. (England, France, Italy, Denmark, Sweden, Norway—and I believe a representative of Germany was there—of this I am not certain).

The club had given the 'all out' sign to the members, and those of import really showed up with bells on. Paul Barbarin's group was there in full force (Paul, Johnny St.Cyr, Ernie Cagnolatti (trumpet), Burbank (cl), Richard McLean (bass), Lester Santiago (pno), a trombone and second trumpet that I could not identify. All of Johnny Wiggs group (Wiggs, Mangiapane (bass), Raymond Burke (cl), Tom Brown (tromb) of "Tom Brown's Band from Dixieland"; Stanley Mendelson (pno); Souchon (guitar and banjo); Santo Pecora (drums—yes, you read correct—nephew of t-h-e Santo Pecora of trombone fame). Papa Celestin was there; so was old Papa Jack Laine (the Father of White Jazz), and too many other local celebrities in the music world that it would bore you to continue.

Ken left Mobile by bus at 4p.m. and made it into the International House at about 8.15. The Wiggs group had just finished their set The Paul Barbarin band held sway for a half hour.

This was followed by a 'mixed' session with both bands playing together—and here is where Ken couldn't stand it a moment, and borrowed the 'second' trumpet player (with Barbarin's) trumpet—fortunately he had brought his mouthpiece along! I cannot recall all the numbers we played, but sort of recall a spiritual, then, *Ain't Gonna' Give Nobody None Of My Jelly Roll*— and that's all that jumps to my mind.

Ken was quite equal to anyone there, or better, and I am only sorry that with all that din I could not single him out well. But what I did hear was enough to want more—and this we shall have at a later date, I am sure, that is, if Ken keeps his promise to return.

The show at the International House broke up early, and so I took Ken over to see my new and wonderful offices at 2400 Canal St. We swapped yarns, hoisted a few, and then I took him down to the Vieux Carre, where we rode around the block several times identifying the places he *must* see (or rather, hear. **I warned him too keep away from those 'dives' with the life-size portraits of nudes advertising the wares inside, as he was here to listen to music and not to see 3rd rate whores shake it up to inferior music. And I believe he listened to me!**

He wrote and told me he parked himself at the first place I showed him (The Paddock) with Alphonse Picou and all of Papa Celestin's old band (sans Papa)—Apparently he was fascinated—and got all the listening he wanted for the first night! George Lewis is on his way out to the Dixieland Jubilee in California, and then to remain at Beverly Caverns to play for a month. I know he will play for a dance given by the S.C.H.J.S. (Floyd Levin). Sharkey leaves N.O. the end of this month for Colombus, Ohio for a 4-week engagement—then he forsakes Lenfant's to re-open with a new drummer (Abbie Brunies, nephew of the real Abbie) at the swank Blue Room of the Roosevelt Hotel. And that's all I can squeeze in on this page— except to say that I enjoyed meeting Ken so much and look forward to hearing him play in the sanctity of my own living room—and to RECORD him with some of us backing him up.

My very best to you and Betty—your American friend, Edmond

P.S. Must tell you that *The Anthropologist* arrived in good shape—in fact 10 copies of him! Thanks no end!

P.S.2—I forgot to say that Lizzie Miles was there in all her glory, and really put on the heat for your boy Ken! Also—Buglin' Sam De Kemel, who plays such hot music on a simple army bugle (no valves please!)

The spokesman for the N.A.T.O. was a youngster from Wales —he did a nice job thanking us for their group. ES

KEN COLYER LETTER TO BILL COLYER OCTOBER 1952

Seamens' Club of Mobile, 350 St. Joseph Street, Mobile, Alabama
Dear Bill,

I hope you were home to receive the letter with autographed photos etc. and not in Devon, and will you write to say you got the same? I guess you will anyway, but I will feel easier when I know.

Well man, I'm still full of the wonder of having been to the dear old city, and it's going to be tough waiting for the next visit. Doc Souchon told me that Bill Russell has been down recently and recorded a whole stack of stuff, so I have written to him asking for the gen and will try to get hold of what I can when we get back. I may have to hold on to the LP I have for now, as it's not convenient at the moment to send it. I think that Ralston C. gave us the wrong impression of Doc Souchon. He is a bluff, good natured, and pretty down-to-earth fellow, though admittedly he

may be more interested in white New Orleans jazz, but I guess that's understandable, as he is actively participating in it and living among the men and the music all his life. He is bound to have a different outlook to us.

I must recount a little incident of the journalist session. Just before I joined in the last couple of numbers, old Doc came down the room saying, "To Hell with this, I'm getting in there. I'm going to have a ball on this one." And he certainly did, joining St. Cyr on guitar. In the middle of *Jelly Roll*, Johnny Wiggs asked him if he wanted a solo, and he promptly got up, dived through the front line, sat on the edge of the stage in the front of the band, and gave out a fine raucous vocal. He's a real live wire alright, though he said to me later, "You could be doing this every night you know, but I'm getting a little too old for it now."

He has a strong personal interest in Raymond Burke, the clarry man. He says that it's good to see him coming up and getting more recognition, and more money, as he could certainly do with it. There's some fine stuff in these Second Line magazines, including a fine article by Albert Glenny, with a terrific photo of him. He remembers Buddy Bolden well, and says, "He played louder than Louis Armstrong with the microphone turned on." He mentions him quite casually. Amazing isn't it?

I think now is our chance to get much closer to New Orleans and I don't think we should miss it. I'm pulling the finger out and am going to do all the corresponding that I can manage. I feel that a barrier is being broken down, and I think it is.

Just another little thing I've remembered. The Barbarin band were playing Basin Street and I was talking to Margie and Buglin' Sam and we were looking at and handling his little slender bugle, when poor old Sam exclaimed, "Hey! Do hear that? The bastards are playing my tune." And he was pretty sore over it.

Another thing I've just remembered is that I've worked out a nice little blues called Going Home. I think that it is inspired by my great liking for Cisco Houston's Chilly Winds though it's nothing like it. I've only got three verses to it, as I haven't studiously written them, but just let them come as I've been working it over nightly. I will write it down and if anything comes to you spontaneously, just get it down and we might build something, though I don't think you'll get much inspiration without the melody, but, still, here it is.

I've tried to illustrate the intervals on the repeat lines (first two). I hope that you get it. The melody's really pretty and I think that you will like it.

Going home...
Going home...
Leaving town, going away from here,
'Cos if I don't leave now,
Won't be going nowhere

Where you from....
Where you from...

Tell me, tell me 'fore I'm gone
Cos if I don't leave now,
Won't be going nowhere

What you say...
An' what you do...
It's tight like this, An' I'm telling you,
Cos if I don't leave now,
Won't be going nowhere

Have just read a bit out of *Second Line Magazine* for August 1951, about Myra Manville receiving a present of some discs from the Wood Green Jazz Club. They include Eh La Bas and the Stompers Weary Blues. She thinks that they are great.

I guess I'll close now Bill, so all the best and here's to a brighter jazz future.

Yours, Ken

KEN COLYER It's a funny thing about probably the most popular tune I have ever written, *Goin' Home*. I started the idea on the *Empire Patrai* and thought up three verses but felt I needed a fourth, but couldn't think of anything so I shelved it.

Pacing up and down in the day pen at the Parish Prison I suddenly thought *If home is where the heart is, then my home is New Orleans, take me to that land of dreams*. Then I thought "Why the hell am I thinking that, the situation I'm in?" But I had observed myself long before this. The real prison bars are in the mind.

KEN COLYER LETTER TO BILL COLYER MONDAY, 20 OCTOBER 1952

We left Saturday round about midnight and hit a little rough weather straight away. The old weather man must have said "Just look at that dirty stinking little tub, let's clean it up a little." And that he did. He washed all that shit and grease off of them decks and cleaned her up considerably.

They must have just about renewed them boilers to see all the rusted scrap iron that came out of that engine room.

When they finally put the steam on, a joint started leaking in our cabin and nearly cooked us. The captain and I had to fix it ourselves with a Stillson as the engineers were busy putting boiling water and steam through the cold water taps.

The Greeks are taking this ship over in January, they say, but it seems they've taken it over right now.

Engineers and Firemen (except Henry, a Trinidadian fireman) were indiscriminately sacked to be replaced by Greeks and they run this tub from the old man down. They've even had Henry put on deck as an A.B. to get him out of the fireman's quarters. He's coloured by the way and used to be a champion boxer in the Navy.

The Yank bunking with me has just got over his sea-sickness and is more his sprightly self tonight.

He's strumming away on the Git. Right now, I'm afraid he's no Jazzman though he likes *Careless Love*.

I'm going to get paid off when we get back if I possibly can. I'm writing a report on the 'Old Man' to use if he won't let me go.

Man! They are breaking more Board of Trade and Union rules aboard here. It's murder, it's a farce and it's a dirty racket and the sooner I'm quit of it the better.

The Finnish Cook is twenty-three years old, has only one finger on his left hand. That was either bad luck or bad judgement, I'm inclined to think it was bad judgement.

He's got plenty of ego if nothing else. Not a bad cook but I've pulled him out of a few holes already.

I'm the only Britisher in the crew now (not including officers) on this British ship. There are 7 more among the officers and I wouldn't give you two fucks for two of them.

One's the captain and the other's the chief steward. The C.S. seems to delight in treating everyone under him like shit, especially the Trinidad (coloured) 2nd steward and next the Yank (Peter).

He doesn't ride me too much and I hope he don't 'cause he's as strong as an ox and used to be a A.B.A. or something and sure as Christ he'll mash me if anything starts but even if it comes to it I don't care; I'm not standing any shit from that sonofabitch.

I've tried to be fortuitous and stick to my job. I've touched hardly any liquor and I think I've done well but this set-up is running me ragged. Somebody's just shut the engine-room door. There'll be an argument over that. The G.'s insist on it being open all the time and we have to try and sleep with that Goddammed racket in our ears all night.

Well to change the subject them Second Line mags have some great stuff in them. I'll send them on as soon as I can. I have written letters to Ralston C., Bill Matthews, Bill Russell, Souchon. I hope there's some replies when I get back.

Still practising on the horn though I can't do much as I get pretty tired not getting any decent sleep.

Well I've got a little off my chest Bill and maybe will be calmer for it. If things get worse I'll just have to let off steam through the pen and wait quietly till we get back.

I just can't seem to write straight on this goddamned paper so excuse me if I straighten up a little now and then.

You know that banal 'Blushing Bride' bit in *Breeze*. If you change it to 'Easy Ride' it sounds O.K. Did we ever think of that before? I can't remember myself.

21 October

Was awoke this morning with the news that the cook had reported sick at 12 last night. I saw him at 11.30 and he was all right then. That bastard can bake all his own bread now, he ain't laying about on me.

Told the C.S. that I am quitting when we get back and I think I've got him worried. He gave me one of the five new camp beds today for sleeping on deck.

Found out today that the Chief Engineer is part owner of the vessel but even the G.'s are fed up with her. I hope they have a belly-full before they're finished.

25 October

Things are quieter now now and going a bit smoother. Weather is pretty warm, quite a good breeze but it is dead ahead.

The Finn's bread is terrible but I'm saying nothing. He thinks he's so goddamned good that he needs pulling down several pegs so I'm working accordingly to do just that.

26 October 8.30pm

We picked the pilot up early yesterday morn and proceeded up the river.

The savage splendour of the jungle which comes right to the river's edge is still something to see even a second time.

I knocked off yesterday after dinner and had just laid down for an hour's sweaty snooze after trying to patch two damned great holes in my checks which I burned when a cigarette dropped into the bucket they were in (of course the damned things had no boogie in the bucket at that time). When the most Godawful racket emits from the engine room. The dear boys had broke a piston rod. We had to anchor where we were while they disconnected the piston so as to run on the remaining three.

That night the other ship passed us that is on this run.

We have just arrived at Porto Orday. I'm hoping we'll limp back to Mobile and not stop at Trinidad as I've no faith in this tub making it at the rate we're going. It has taken us a little longer to get here this time than the last.

Man I'm pining for Noo Awlins and won't rest easy 'till I'm back there.

27 October

The old tub still plods its weary way across the Caribbean. Nobody seems to know when we'll get there but I guess it must be some time this week. This is the hurricane season. It's still pretty warm with frequent squalls and blows but we've hit nothing really bad as yet.

The damned wind is staying on the other side this trip and the cabin gets pretty hot. The camp-bed is really handy and I've slept on deck the last three nights.

Even with the stack blowing soot down on you and the odd showers during the night it's good to get a couple of hours' decent sleep. **Pete cut my hair two nights ago and Brother! It's the shortest it's been for many a long day but don't worry I'll have it back to normal before I get home.**

The apprentices were telling me last night about a queer cook who was on here once. He had a glass eye and false teeth, his name was Jim nee Rose. I haven't laughed so much in a long time. It appears he used to be real slick when going ashore yet he used to cut the pockets out of his galley trousers so that he could wear them inside-out when they got dirty. The crowd got him paid-off in the finish.

It seems the old tub is all to cock down below despite the thousands of dollars of repairs they must have had done. She's burning oil like nobody's business now and they are wondering if we'll have enough to make Trinidad on the way back.

1 November 8pm

We went alongside this afternoon but nobody knows for certain yet when we are unloading.

I've just been practising on the horn. Did a mean 2.19 and a *Canal St* à la Wooden Joe and sweated about a gallon a minute. I guess it's never cool in this place though there's not so many wee beasties this time.

I sliced a piece clean off of my right hand thumb today. Sure glad it wasn't my left because I pick with that one on the guitar.

The customs caught some of the crew on the other tub with marryano or some such thing yesterday. She looks about on a par with this crate. I don't know what nationality she is yet, probably a death-ship.

I've just started reading *Return To Paradise* by James Michener (wrote *Tales of the South Pacific*) can recommend it. Have also read Oscar Levant's *A Smattering of Ignorance* which is very good in parts. Another I've read on here is *The Path of an American*, which is really great in the best Hemingway class.

I cleaned the stove out last night (evil bastard) and it started burning worse than ever this morning though it improved somewhat later on.

16 November

I'm afraid I'm way out of date now. I guess I would never keep a good diary.

Had one good toot in Orday with a bottle of Bols gin which the sparks got off the other ship, a tub just about on a par with this one.

She has a Dutch crew. Saw Glenn Miller's *Sun Valley Serenade* at the camp pictures. Some very good band stuff in it.

We paid off all our Trinidad fellows at T.D. and signed on 5 more (greenhorns) who will probably sign off there next trip a little sadder and a little wiser.

We shipped out of TD. With no clearance from Lloyds for the… engines and are four days out now wallowing along on three pistons. We hope to get in on the 22nd.

Have had some good laughs with the two apprentices and the sparks this last couple of weeks. We play a lot of crazy poker and pontoon and manage to forget this tub for a while.

My bunk-mate has gone on deck now and I have one of the TD cabin boys with me now.

I developed a cold-sore on my lip today. I hope I'm not going to have a run of them.

The wind is on my side now thank God and it's comparatively cool in the cabin now.

Those Caribbean sunsets are glorious. I've never seen so many glorious pastel shades in a sunset at one time.

Monday, 17 November

"It is with considerable honour at a time like this when
men are subservient to the gun and the orator, that these
should have spoke.
The time was not their choice but what they made of it was.
The time was a vehicle for their variations."

That sure is a profound piece of prose, it keeps running through my mind.

It's taken us since last night to crawl past the islands of Jamaica, the day has been the hottest since we left Orday and I'm sure getting me a tan. I get plenty of sun now to ease that old prickly heat.

The days are full of bickering and ill feeling as stores are running short. We have no clean linen, we are down to our last bag of flour and what eggs we have left are 90% rotten. On top of it all the Steward is still penny-pinching and won't give a little extra of what he's got such as milk, coffee and sugar to make things easier.

He thinks he's putting me ship's cook next trip but he won't if I can't get paid off. If I can't I shall take it and go A.W.O.L. down to N.O. and to hell with them.

I don't trust this tub so I'm grasping every opportunity to get to N.O.'s. After all, it may be the only chance in a lifetime.

If you could get the back copies of *M.E.* with our little shindig in I should like them Bill, thanks.

Have tried to practice tonight but my lip is puffed up still with this damn cold sore.

The generator broke down last night and the old engine sounds as if it's on its last legs, still five or six days more and we'll be there.

It would be bully if she cracked up just outside Noo Awlins eh!

Tuesday, 18 November

Cooler today with a good stiff breeze on the starboard side (my side). Still have them good old following seas pushing us along. I got your letter from Orday by the way and a very old one from Mum addressed Hellenic Lines.

Two TDs scrapping yesterday—one bopped the other with a lump of wood and bust his head open.

If you should get a telegram anytime with just two words 'I'M OFF' you'll know I'm paid off of this crate and I shouldn't write until I send a fresh address.

Lip still swollen tonight, practice hopeless, still keeping the old guitar work going though and improving with my limited technique. Was hitting some mean boogie in Mobile one night with the door open and was really sending a couple of them coloured boys and when I see coloured people enjoying my music that really bucks me.

Wednesday, 19 November

Time drags slowly on. We should make it by Sat. or Sun.

Am in a bit of a quandary about getting paid off. I guess I'll just have to wait and see what develops when we hit Mobile.

We'll just about make it on stores and no more. I'll be glad to see the back of this yarpy of a cook; I've just about a bellyfull of him. It's been raining for the last couple of hours and the wind has changed to the port quarter.

Friday, 21 November

Weather has cooled right down
and the seas are livelier. The old tub is rolling all over the ocean and her speed is down to two knots. God knows when we get there now.

Had a row with the second engineer this morning and most everybody is at somebody's throat. There's going to be some fine old barny's if this ship don't darn soon get there.

I'm messing around with Dusty Bottom on the guitar today, it sure is restful. Practicing again on horn though my lip isn't in good shape yet.

Sunday, 23 November

The weather has been glorious this last two days and we must have been doing every bit of five knots.

We pick the pilot up at 1 a.m. in the morn.

Told the 'old man' that I want to pay off today and he's asking me do I want to sign on again!!! (in January) He says he won't pay me off but we'll see about that.

Roll on Mobile and let's get to dear ol Noo Awlins.

KEN COLYER We made our way through the docks, caught a cab to the Greyhound Bus Station and I bought a single ticket to New Orleans. This was it, there was no turning back.

We finally arrived at the depot. I left all my luggage at the station in a locker. I would have to travel light until I found somewhere to stay. I was dog-tired from nervous exhaustion and lack of sleep. I felt a little like a man on the run. I was wondering if police messages had been sent out from Mobile and they were looking for me. Eventually it was evening and the night life was starting up. I went into the Paddock Bar remembering the brief visit I had had before. There weren't many customers but the band kicked off and sounded fine. They had different interpretations of numbers I had never heard before and have never heard since. They had a break and went into a small band room.

By way of introduction, I asked the waiter to get the boys a drink. They asked me into the cramped band room.

I said I was from England. They were delighted and asked me all sorts of questions.

I told them a little about England and that I had run a jazz band there. When they got back on the stand the difference was dramatic. They had an audience of one among the punters who just wander in for a drink.

Bill Matthews had a glorious tone and range, like Ory and George Brunies. His style was starkly simple yet effective.

Alvin Alcorn had a nice tone and lilting style. Alphonse Picou, though getting on in years, played that nice Creole style and still knew about counterpoint.

Octave Crosby sounded much like Alton Purnell at times. I wondered about the style. McNeil Breaux played fine bass. Wellman Braud was his brother and had changed his name when he went North. [in fact, they were cousins—Ed]

Happy Goldston was a good drummer, highly respected in New Orleans. I heard him play patterns on snares and cymbals that I have never heard any other drummer play...

This would be Papa Celestin's band but now went under Octave Crosby's name.

KEN COLYER LETTER TO BILL COLYER
THURSDAY, 27 NOVEMBER 1952

Dear Bill,

Have finally gotten down to writing to you. I tried to get paid off the ship when we docked on Monday, but the Old Man said "No", but I got a twenty-nine day clearance from the Immigration Officer, and he said, "You look after No. 1." So I did.

I packed my bags Tuesday night and slid out and was in New Orleans by midnight. I left all my gear at the bus station and grabbed a cab to the Paddock Bar. There was only two or three people in there, as I guess they have their slack nights during the week. Bill Matthews gave me a big "Hello" as soon as he saw me. He had received my letter and had shown it to the band. I went into the back room with him when they had finished their set. There was some amusing talk about this and that, and odd chatter about the trip. Picou just sat there looking at his hands and drinking his gin most of the time, laughing now and again when the conversation was amusing. He keeps his bottle in the clarinet case I notice.

"Remember Simon?" asks Bill. "He was so mean, even when he was making good money he never had none. I think that cos wife, Goldie, used to take it all off him. Don't matter what was wrong with him, when he was ill he would never see a doctor, but always used to drink that Cola." (Some sort of cheap medicine I believe.) "'Warms a man's bones," he used to say. I think that's what killed him, all his bones dried up."

"You could never get Simon angry," said Happy. "He was a most mild tempered man."

"Hey, Ken," said Alvin, who had been dozing in the corner. "The George Lewis Band are playing at the Mardi Gras tonight and it's pretty late, so I should get down there if you want to hear them."

I said "Goodnight" to the boys and floated down to the Mardi Gras.

The Lewis band were playing when I walked in. I sat down.

Then I ordered a drink and almost went into a trance. Marrero was about five feet away from me, with Drag just behind him. Alton Purnell on piano just to the right (facing the band). Drummer in front and to Marrero's left, Joe Watkins. Marrero plays beautiful solos on most numbers, and lifts like a dream when he comes back on that soft, yet biting, driving four. They all play unpretentiously and so wonderfully. At the end of their set I met them in the back room. They all shook hands, but were very quiet, and didn't want to talk much. Drag lit up a cigar, and a fellow came in with a lady and started talking ten to the dozen. He was an ex-Whiteman drummer and was yarning about Bix and Gillette and so on.

"Do you use any of so-and-so's arrangements?" he asks.

"We don't use no arrangements," said Joe Watkins, quietly but tersely. "We just play."

"That's the way it ought to be, man," I said quietly in reply. The fellow heard me, laughed and went on talking, but I don't think he liked it.

Lizzie Miles came in as the band went to go on. She does the intermission spots with Joe Robichaux on piano. She remembered me from last month and started yarning straight away. She is a wonderful person and is helping me considerably, and has put me onto a room, which I have taken for a week for twelve bucks, and it's fine. A big bedroom with a small double bed and nice furniture, with a swell bath etc. I would like to keep it if I can manage it. I have fifty-five bucks left in my pocket, so I am OK for the next two weeks at least.

Wednesday morning, about 4 a.m.

I had to get a 3-90 room in an hotel. I saw Souchon about noon at his surgery in the Pan American Insurance Building on Canal Street. He was pleased to see me and we had a chat and then drove to his home and had a great record session and general conflab. He drove me to the Mardi Gras and here I saw Sid Davilla and the porter who sees to the rooming for him, and I got my gear and moved in. I got a letter from Ralston Crawford telling me to contact Dick Allen—a young fellow here who works for Mercury Records and knows just about everything about New Orleans musicians.

I met him last night and he's a good man to know; he also introduced me to Bob and Dick Greenwood. Bob is another man who is right in the centre of things. His brother is a Merchant Seaman, a nice guy and a Lewis band fan. I am going to meet a couple of people this evening through Dick Allen who have some of our records. I think it will be interesting. If you could, would you mail me a box of Stompers and Crane River records, and copies of some of the good acetates like *Bobby Shafto*. Also any

more of our paper clippings, especially the *Mirror* article and the *MM* blow up when we quit.

I don't know whether to get my mail forwarded from Mobile yet, as I don't particularly want them to know my address yet, so let me know if there is anything of importance there. Souchon is trying to fix me up with a job, and I'm also trying to get hold of a bloke who jumped the *Patrai* here in New Orleans and is working here on the tugs, so there is hope that I might get employment here. I would like to stay for a few months if things turn out OK. The "Bunk Talking" is about to be issued, also some more Wooden Joes and Eureka Brass Bands.

Will close for now. Give my best regards to everybody, and here's to the future.

Ken Colyer

KEN COLYER I had met Ralston Crawford, an American artist, between ships, through Alexis Korner, and spent a pleasant evening with him at Alexis' flat. He was also a good photographer and had a mass of superb photos of New Orleans and the musicians. He was a mine of useful information to me. He told me where to contact Dick Allen at an eating house on Bourbon Street, which Dick frequented. I went there and had a couple of cups of coffee and enquired after Dick. Nobody knew where he was so I left a message.

That evening I went back to the Paddock bar. I was talking to the band in their back room when I mentioned George Lewis. Alvin, who had been dozing in his chair, opened a sleepy eye. He worked all day as a gas station attendant. "George is playing tonight at the Mardi Gras, just a couple of doors down." I couldn't believe my luck. They only played the relief night for Freddie Kohlman. And Lizzie Miles was there too, doing their intervals with Joe Robicheaux on piano.

You could hear the band as you approached. It sounded fine, superb swinging music with a lead horn like I had never heard before. I went in and sat at the bar—there weren't many people in. The band weren't very well positioned on the awkward shaped stage. I knew all too well they never seem to think about the band when they build stages. But it didn't seem to make any difference. The band would start with one of Alton's beautiful intros and within three choruses everything was working perfectly.

Percy Humphrey was on trumpet, George clarinet, Jim Robinson trombone, Alton Purnell piano, Slow Drag Pavageau bass, Lawrence Marrero tenor banjo and Joe Watkins on drums. I hadn't heard of Joe or Percy before.

Percy hadn't recorded much with George, as he was an insurance collector during the day and was tied to his job, so Kid Howard toured with the band, when they usually did their recordings.

The music gave me the same warm feeling that the American Musics do.

Walt Whitman put it well: "I hear the keyed cornet it glides... It shakes mad-sweet pangs through my belly and breast."

Lizzie had been tucked away in a sort of room by the stage next to the lavatories. She recognised me and when her set was finished, beckoned me into the room. She was delighted to see me again. She was always bubbling over and was a delightful personality. When I said I had to find somewhere to stay, she immediately said Mr. Davilla has rooms upstairs. She went to talk to Sid. She came back. "There's a room vacant at twelve dollars a week."

Sid came through and Lizzie introduced me. He was a small dapper man, very smartly dressed. I took the room after he had shown it to me. It was quite large with its own bathroom and a double bed and enough furniture.

I went to the bus station and retrieved my case, my horn and my guitar, then got a cab back to the club. Thanks to Lizzie I was fixed up within the hour and back listening to the band for the rest of the evening. **I wrote to Bill as soon as I got to my room and then turned in. Everything that was happening filled me with adrenalin and for a while I didn't need much rest.**

Dick had got my message and when I went to the Bourbon House the following day he had left his address on Royal Street. I told him about Ralston, who he knew well from his periodic visits. We had a long talk and he was to be an invaluable friend while I was there. He has a good sense of humour, even about his home town, Possum Trot, Georgia.

I met John and Ursula Bernard through Dick. They were devoted Lewis fans. They were particularly interested in me because I knew Bob Wallis. Bob's brother Peter had been in the MN and had been fortunate enough to get there on a British Tanker. A bit different from my experiences. They had shown Peter as much as they could in the short time he was there, and they were to be wonderful friends to me.

One night at their apartment, Ursula casually said, "Why don't you ask George if you can sit-in?"

I looked at her. "That's what I came here for, but what about the colour bar, and how do I go about it?"

"It won't be any trouble at Manny's Tavern. It's away from the centre and there's only local people go there. I'll ask George, we'll take you there Friday."

I was elated. Friday came and I couldn't wait for the evening. We went to Manny's. It seemed to be a quiet, dark area but the pub was pleasant and had a nice atmosphere. We heard a few numbers and had a drink. I was familiar with the band but not Percy—the more I heard him the more I liked him. I noticed Alton had a smile tonight; he was usually frowning at the Mardi Gras. He told me it was because the piano was so bad, but this one was pretty good.

Ursula went over and spoke to George. He nodded and pulled up another chair. I could sit-in. I was nervous and my lip wasn't in very good shape. But once again, "Those first kicks are the killers." But the pleasure was mutual. I've never known Percy to show much outward emotion but Jim and George were chuckling and Drag had that lovely smile. We all had a good time.

As they were packing up at the finish, Lawrence asked me, "Where did you learn our music?"

"From your records."

He had to think for a minute before he could remember the American Musics and Bill Russell. That's what makes them so good. Bill captured them at their best; when they are completely unselfconscious and playing for the sheer pleasure of it.

As we got in the car the band were loading their gear. "Keep up the good works, Ken," Joe called out.

KEN COLYER LETTER TO BILL COLYER FRIDAY, 28 NOVEMBER 1952

Room 3, 335 Bourbon Street, New Orleans, Louisiana, USA

Last night I spent the evening with Dick Allen, Mr. and Mrs. Bernard and a Swiss fellow who is working here. He's a bit of a jerk, but tolerable. The Bernards are really nice people, and great lovers of the music. I am going with them to Manny's Tavern tomorrow to hear the Lewis band. They dropped me back there and I got an earful of the Fred Kohlman Dixieland Band, who are not so hot I'm afraid. They are the resident band and George just does the Tuesday.

After hearing them, I dropped down to the Paddock to catch an hour of the Octave Crosby Band over a long beer. They are not the greatest band, but are still pretty good. Alvin (Alcorn) plays some beautiful lyrical horn and has a fine tone. Matthews style you know, he punches it out like that all the time, and is great to watch. Old man Picou sits with his head down most of the time when not playing, with a faraway look about him; now and again he becomes animated for a second. I think that he was pretty boozed last night. He sang the vocal on *Eh La Bas* with great spirit, with verses that were aimed at the crowd. He sang one making a big belly sign to some dame with a fellow at the bar, and she must have taken offence.

I came back to my room and got some practice in. My horn fell off the rack on the bus coming down, and took quite a belt; it's a bit bent but working OK. The Dukes of Dixieland are pounding and screeching away while I write this. I'm afraid they are pretty God-awful, and only play anything decent once in a while.

I went with Dick Allen to see Emile (Mile) Barnes today, and

had a couple of interesting hours with him. Dick has a half-an-hour radio programme on Sunday evenings at 6.30 and wanted to get some information off him, as he is going to give him some publicity and try to help him. We met Slow Drag outside the Tumble Inn, a hang-out of Drag's and Marrero's. He told us about an out-of-town job that they did the other night. He said that the place was packed, and the people loved it, but it was so cold that he had a tough time fingering his bass. There was a fellow with him— a tailor by trade— who is a nephew of "The World's most great clarinet and saxophone player—Sidney Bechet." He was telling us about the wedding in Paris, and is really proud of his uncle. Drag didn't know about Leonard Bechet's death until it was mentioned then.

I'll have to get Dick's notes of the Emile Barnes meeting to write a full account, but I'll give you what I remember now. He mentioned many names unknown to me, of men he had played with in the old days. He started playing on a tin flute, and one night made a mess of money gambling, and stayed up the rest of the night drinking with Bunk Johnson who, he says, was really great in those days, but was a gone man when he came back. They used to call him "Willie the Pleaser," and it seems he was just that, and they used to come flocking whereever he played. Well, they waited for Fink's to open, and then Bunk brought him his first clarinet.

He says that he started playing and working straightaway. The first tune that he ever played, which seems to be as soon as he got the clarinet, was a thing that goes something like the main theme of *Black Cat*. He is a mattress-maker by trade by the way. His all-time favourite is Chris Kelly who, he says, was a great leader. He stresses the importance of every man knowing his part in the band and that, no matter how good a man thinks he is, he's always got to be "chastised from the outside." He reminisces of the time he and Johnny Dodds went to an after-hours session, and they both sat-in with the band.

When he finished playing, everybody started yelling and clapping and he found out that they had unwittingly taken part in a contest, and he had won and was crowned "King of the Blues." There were one or two other good clarry men besides Dodds there too. He says that he doesn't like playing the blues now, also that he's not been playing much these past years and is a little corroded now.

Charles Love, he says, is a great ragtime man and knows most of the old rags, and has the music to a lot of them as well. He is rehearsing a band with Love, and Brazeley on trombone, and Glenny I think. I am hoping to meet Love next week, and some of the others too.

Dick Allen lives in a hole-in-the-wall just round the corner from here on St. Ann Street. Bed, records and rubbish leave just about enough room to swing a not too big mouse— if you have a short arm, that is. He plays trombone and has sat-in with Burbank, Barnes, Lewis, and various others. I can't hear him play as he had his trombone stolen. The police have it, but are keeping it as evidence at the trial of the thief. He reminds me of Bob

Milne a little.

Some of his friends have opened a jazz record shop here on Bourbon Street. I was in there today and heard some not so good Basin Street Six, Johnny Wiggs, and the Yancey LP, which is pretty fine of course. *The I* and *How Long* are quite different from the others.

Memo: It was a regular flute that Mile started on, given to him by Bab Frank. The tune that he first played was *Got Good Booty, So They Say*. Well, I guess that's all for now. Will write again as soon as I can.

All the best, Ken.

PS written by Ken later [*back in London.*]

In my letter from New Orleans, I'm afraid I mixed up the Dukes of Dixieland with Freddie Kohlman's band. The powerhouse band that I could hear as I was writing was actually Kohlman's and not the Dukes. I never got to meet the Dukes, but did hear them occasionally. They had a rather commercial Dixieland style, though the trombone sounded promising and they usually had a good clarinettist, such as Raymond Burke or Harry Shields, brother of the famous Larry, member of the Original Dixieland Jazz Band.

FRED HATFIELD My memories of this are kind of hazy, but my wife at the time and I had an apartment. And we met Ken, and we knew the background: that he had jumped ship, and he was here in town on his own because he loved New Orleans music.

> And of course, we loved him, because of New Orleans music, so... we were very proud to show him around, and he stayed with us for a couple of weeks. He had a place to sleep, and we knew he was broke and didn't have a job.

So at night we would take him to different locations to hear music and hear the bands and so on. And I recall one occasion: Papa Celestin and his band used to play on the docks for ships that were coming in—like to tourist ships; when they would arrive in New Orleans the band would be down on the docks, and he would be playing, you know, some New Orleans tune to greet the people.

Well, at the same time there was a group from New York coming down— they were filming a series called *The March Of Time*. It used to be a very popular documentary-styled programme. And they wanted to film Papa Celestin greeting the ship as it docked, and so on. So we told Ken about this and decided to bring him along, and we went to the dock, and sure

enough there was the band—Papa Celestin with all the band. And Ken got a chance to meet them. In fact, he brought a pint of Jack Daniels with him, and he passed that on to the members.

When the ship finally docked, we went on board the ship. And Ken stayed on the dock, because they would only let myself and my wife on the ship. And they were filming from the balcony of the ship. You know, if you stand looking down to the band playing, Ken was right there next to them—so he may have been in the shot. I just got the idea recently that I should try to locate that film. Because now on the internet you can find those things. It was a *March Of Time* about New Orleans.

Later on they wanted to film a sequence on Bourbon Street—one of the nightclubs. And at the time the owner, Sid Davilla, was a clarinet player, and he had this club—the Mardi Gras Lounge— and at the time he had George Lewis' band playing there. And so we filmed a sequence in the club itself, and—if I recall correctly—there were some shots of the customers, which... we were the customers, mainly. There may be a shot of Ken in there too.

But he did meet George Lewis, and the rest of the band.

There was definitely a labour-shortage here in World War 2, and finding somebody to play music at dances and social events was very difficult, because most of the musicians were in the Army. At least the young ones were. So some of the older ones— especially some of the older black musicians—began to appear on the scene again. And that's when Don and I began to hear some of the old-timers. We started hearing that really great traditional music, you know, instead of the tunes of the day.

And we made an effort to find parades and funerals and so on, so that we could hear some of these people. And that's when we discovered the Eureka Brass Band and some of the great brass bands that were playing. Most of the time we were the only white people in the group, you know, following the bands around, and we were always looking for these obscure dance-clubs where bands would be playing. So, we had a whole string of them, you know—Manny's Tavern and Kohlman's and... well, there were quite a few.

We had a regular string of neighbourhood places we would go to, just to hear the music, and sort of watch the people. One of our favourites was Luthjens, where the average age there, I would think, would be about ninety. And we were always amused, because there was a big sign on the wall that said "No Jitterbugging."

We would do that Saturday nights when we had the money, and we rode streetcars to these different places—didn't have an automobile.

So we had places like The Barn on Franklin Avenue; that was usually a white band—white musicians. Luthjens was black, of course, and it varied, depending on where you went, but we never saw blacks and whites playing together. That was sort of verboten... Well, there were special occasions where it would—sort of private—where people would do that. **But I always looked forward to the day when we** could have... have a mixture, you know, of good musicians playing together.

DICK ALLEN There was no mike at Luthjens where we heard musicians like Billie and Dee Dee Pierce and Harrison Brazely. A mike was usually only for singing when there was one. There was no ear-splitting music. Substituting volume for feeling is a major change. The musicians of the fifties relied on strength not wattage.

KEN COLYER LETTER TO BILL COLYER 30 NOVEMBER 1952

Room 3, 335 Bourbon Street, New Orleans, Louisiana, US.A
BILLIE AND DE DE PIERCE AT Luthjens

Got to bed at four this morning, and here I am, up, bathed, and feeling fine. I didn't know the time, mind you, when I woke, as I have no clock at present. I dropped my watch in the galley, and it done broke. I phoned Doc Souchon yesterday and he told me about getting the cable from Donnegal inviting the Wiggs band over for the Coronation do. They can't make it, but he is very pleased with the gesture. He is sending someone, but he hasn't told me who yet.

Last night I went with the Bernards (John and Ursula) to hear George at Manny's Tavern. It was a foul night and George wasn't feeling well, so the band wasn't playing. Nobody else was there and I thought that the evening was ruined, especially as I had my horn with me to sit-in with them, but they decided to go to Luthjens to hear Billie and De De Pierce and, Man Oh Man!, I heard some of the greatest music and singing, and plenty of it.

Luthjens is a wonderful, dingy old dance hall, the type of place the White Hart could be. It's quite a big place, but gets very crowded, and often one can't even get in the place. There's dancing in front of the band and tables either side. They just about squeeze the band into a tiny pen, with an almost chest-high fence around it, and Harrison Brazeley's trombone is sticking over or resting on it most of the time. The place is mostly patronised by "Boogleys" (country people—but don't let them hear you calling them that), who get drunk, do some of the funniest fox-trotting and waltzing I've ever seen, and have the time of their lives. They are mostly very friendly and good natured, but now and again one will annoy Billie by slapping her on the back while she is singing. She always manages to twist the vocal line when they do this to show them that she is mad with them. Like on *Baby Won't You Please Come Home* she snapped out "I need some money." And on another one, "There's someone pimping on me."

The only beer sold is 55 cents, and soft drinks which are very nice. We managed to get a table down near the band (the Swiss bloke was with us and turned out to be a bit of a jerk). Billie plays with her back to the floor at the battered old upright, which has a lovely pub-tone. George Henderson is to her left, playing the best drums that I think I've heard yet, and he looks like he is enjoying himself all the time. He's got a squeak in his bass drum pedal, but it doesn't bother anybody.

De De on horn is in front and between George and Billie. He is always active while playing, and a good showman. His control and dynamics are superb, his tone and vibrato are to be heard and wondered at all night long. His singing ranks with his horn playing and the two are very much alike. His *Tout de moi* vocal you know, and his *Eh La Bas* is equally good. De De to me looks quite unlike a horn-man, and yet he is a fine one. It is truly an education to hear him. Some of his muted work is colossal, and can he growl; but he uses his effects sparingly and effectively.

Last but not least, Brazely sits on Billie's right looking a bit like Archey, his head well back and his glasses giving him that slightly moon-eyed look. He plays quietly and sparingly, hitting his notes with a lilting bounce, keeping close to the harmony and melody. He opened up more on *High Society* and took two fine choruses. On certain notes he has that poignant vibrato that Jim Robinson gets sometimes. He sits very quietly and unobtrusively, and yet is ready to talk to you as soon as you approach him. He asked me if there was much jazz in England, and I told him the music was doing fine and so forth.

Then he leant over and asked me, "You read from music?" I said, "No, I'm a head man, I learnt everything from Kid Ory and Bunk Johnson records." He looked surprised, and then laughed and remarked, "Oh, you understand this stuff then." Before we left he hoped that we would get together and play and I certainly hope so too.

The band play in the highly individual style of the Emile Barnes AM (American Music record) and they play anything, mostly pop requests, laced with blues and the old jazz standards. They play a beautiful version of *Love Song Of The Nile*, which Billie says they recorded, but can't remember who for. We stayed till three o'clock when they finished, and I am certainly returning for another truly wonderful evening.

Dick Allen has his radio programme at 6.30 this evening on WNOE. I helped him to prepare the script the other night. That fellow is pretty terrific, and I'm beginning to realise he knows more about the music than Blesh will ever know. When you send some stuff over he is going to do a programme with me. Tell the folks that I'm sorry that I'm not writing to them, but I've got to watch every cent at the moment, so these letters will have to do for all. I'm looking round for a job and I'm hoping to get work of some sort this week.

Of all the coloured musicians here, there are only one or two who own phonographs or records. Lewis's favourite record is Jelly Roll's *Winin' Boy* piano solo, and he really cherishes it. There are some that say that Picou didn't really create his famous solo, but Mile says that he was the first man that he ever heard play it, and Picou taught him how to play it.

I'll sign off for now, but there'll be plenty more coming.
Cheerio for now,
Ken Colyer

**KEN COLYER LETTER TO BILL COLYER
2 DECEMBER 1952**

Room 3, 335 Bourbon Street, New Orleans, Louisiana, USA

Well, Bill. I'm hoping to hear from you any day now. The weather changed yesterday, we had some rain and it's a lot milder.

Had a great night last night with Phil Ennis, a researcher who is on a nationwide tour interviewing disc jockeys. He loves the music and has latched on very fast. He bought 4/5ths pint of Bourbon and we spent most of the evening listening to Octave Crosby's band and drinking the loon-juice in the can, as they don't allow you to take a bottle in these places and they would be very annoyed if they knew.

The band was playing fine. The more I hear Alvin, the more I like him. He has a rich mellow tone and pretty lilting style, besides a very good technique. He can hit the high ones clear as a bell when he wants to.

Matthews never ceases to send me and I think he is the joy of everyone who hears him, whether they know a thing about jazz or not. He plays like natural man and punches a real living horn.

I think the Band Wagon records give a pretty good picture of the band.

Pork Chops came in the other night and tap-danced around the place to the band. He's a real colourful character. He comes around with the hat and mumbles something about the wife and family being ill.

We came back to the room after the last set and I played Phil a mess of blues on the guitar. He was tickled pink about my Southern accent when singing. We must have wound up about five this morning.

George Lewis is playing here tonight so I'll be able to hear more of the man's great band and also see and hear Lizzie Miles. I haven't seen her since last Tuesday.

Sid Davilla is a nice guy and I think I'll be all right here.

I had lunch with Doctor Souchon today, he's one swell guy and treats me real fine. He's still waiting for that telephone call from Donegall. He's a little peeved over it, I think they've been messing him about and he's wondering what the hell goes on.

I saw Francis Murray today and got some gen about jobs. I've hit on nothing yet but probably will do soon.

**KEN COLYER LETTER TO BILL COLYER
3 DECEMBER 1952**

Glory be! Mine ears have heard the glory of the George Lewis Band once again and I'm going to sit-in with them Saturday night at Manny's.

Can you wonder that, though dead beat last night, I have only slept three hours and am now up writing this at 8.

The kicks were greater than ever on the second hearing. Practically every other stomp reached the intensity of *Climax Rag*. The P 38 (aircraft) is like a model T against them boys.

Slow Drag stands behind Marrero looking rather imperious with eye-lids half lowered and a sort of knowing smile hovering around his lips. There is a touch of the majestic about him, although he's dwarfed by his bass a little. He watches Marrero's every move and works with him beautifully.

Marrero sits solid as a rock creating a rhythm and banjo tone that no other can. He solos frequently and always gets a spontaneous applause no matter how square the audience (the bars are patronised mostly by tourists). The theme he and Purnell play on *Chimes Blues* is the sweetest thing I have heard in a long time.

His fingering hand moves as if there is all the time in the world, but them chords always come out right, rich and clear. Ben (Marshall) had the same style. When they get rocking I expect to see that stucco clown fixed on the wall start jitter-bugging.

Purnell, from where I was sitting, seems to have a half worried look all the time, but I guess they are all so damned natural, there is very little showmanship with any of them, except the handclapping they do when they are not playing (front-line). The Octave Crosby Band do the same. George claps a tricky double beat instead of the usual off-beat.

Purnell's playing is not quite what you would expect from records (strangely, Octave Crosby has more of that). He fits the section fine. He also shares the vocals with Joe Watkins.

Joe sits and plays clipped, efficient drumming and I noticed he was sweating, though the evening was comparatively cool. Again, there's no showmanship, though he's in front of the band, yet they are all too great to watch. He does some great accenting with his bass drum, always on definite patterns.

Percy Humphreys is funny. He's a big fellow and squirms on his chair, giving the impression that he's half shy and a little embarrassed. His head lowers a little and his boyish eyes open wide as he looks around. The Bernards thought he seemed ill at ease one night and asked him if anything was wrong. "My feet hurt," he said. He is an insurance collector, and they say he's a much happier man altogether when his old "dogs" have had a day or two's rest.

His playing is fine, hard to liken to anybody; it's light and never too loud or dominant. He just blows up more on the last chorus to drive them down. He and Robinson play some nice muted riffs (hand muted) like Mutt and Ory somewhat on one or two numbers.

Big Jim just sits there calm and unpretentious, blowing great trombone. It's great when he stands for a solo and the bell of that horn swings right at you.

The bands are very smart, by the way, and all wear identical suits, shirts and ties. The Octave Crosby Band wore evening suits the other night and sometimes light grey and green ties. The

Lewis band were in brown last night and George cuts a really sharp figure, being the slimmest in the band. Their ties were glaring red with one of those splurge designs.

George plays beautifully all the time, but not with the power I think he must be capable of. He is always controlled and blends right in with the horns, with just the odd flash standing out.

They play plenty of pops and plenty of jazz standards that they have never recorded, such as *Savoy Blues* (Big Jim plays a great version of Ory's solo, also of Brunies, on *Tin Roof*), *Dippermouth* etc.

I was talking to Sid Davilla last night, and he's beginning to realise how phenomenal the band is, though he admits many things baffle him and says they are unique, even in New Orleans.

He heard me practising yesterday afternoon and has invited me to sit-in with the Freddy Kolhman band any time (will do tonight). I am going to sit-in with Sharkey's mob at noon at Joe Mares, 522 St. Louis Street, at just a get-together. It appears Johnny Wiggs has spoken highly of me. I also have a wonderful note of intro to Joe from Lizzie, who is great, just great as a singer and a personality. I'll send you the note later.

Got to move now, am anxiously waiting for your first N.O. mail, none yet.

Keep on the ball man. Love to everybody.

One happy man, Ken

KEN COLYER It seemed to me that at times there was a telepathy running through the band. When I sat in with them I noticed that even at the most exciting moments there was an inner calm that was quite uncanny. I liked Kid Howard with the band, but in a way it might be unfortunate that William Russell caught him on such a glorious peak when he recorded him on the Climax session, that after, he pales on comparison. But unlike some knowledgeable fans who dismiss a man when they happen to hear him on a bad night, I still dug what he had to say. Whitney Balliett and Ernest Borneman are the only two critics who understand this. Most of the others are bums and should devote their time to Victorian crockery.

George played beautifully all the time, but not with the power he has on the American Musics. After his accident—his chest was crushed by a bale that slipped off the hook—he worked as a stevedore during the day and there wasn't two-pennorth of him. I think he often had to conserve hisself. I know too well myself what a terrible strain it can be playing when you are under the weather, and still have to earn a living.

Alton Purnell always brought the band in with perfectly timed swinging intros. There was never any discussion about tempos. Those lovely rolling chords, and again a seemingly simple style, set the pace, and within two choruses it was all knitting together perfectly, like the fingers in a glove.

Lovers of the Lewis band, and I use the word in the true sense, who had been listening to the band for years, said that they had never heard the band better and that they had seemed to have reached a peak. They were playing better than they had ever heard them.

Raymond Burke was an unusual musician for a white New Orleanian. Apart from being a delightful man, he knew no colour bar. He talked of playing with Mutt Carey, Wooden Joe Nicholas, Bunk Johnson in years past. I asked him one day how on earth he managed it with the colour bar. He was vague about it. It seemed he just ignored it.

Although he was a white man, born in New Orleans, Raymond just talked about musicians. It never occurred to him that this isn't a thing to take for granted. All white musicians in New Orleans aren't like this. Well, they never used to be. But old Raymond, this music was in him. When I used to play with him, and he'd say, "Man, when I used to play with Papa Mutt, he sounded like that."

And this time he was saying, whatever he was doing, if he hears music, he has to follow it, to find out where it is. Don't matter if he might be going that way, if the music's this way. He said "I heard this sound, and I knew something was going on, and I walked a couple of blocks, and I turned around, and there was this float with Bunk on there and George Lewis." In fact, there's a photo of it somewhere. They were trying to revive the oldstyle of taking a float around New Orleans to advertise the San Jacinto Hall, or somewhere. And I said to him, "Well, how did Bunk sound?" you know, and he said, "Oh man, he was marvellous. Bunk was playing so good, you know, and the band was terrific. And I just stood there and listened until he'd finished playing."

I was to be given a quiet word of warning one day, that it was going around that I was a nigger-lover and should play with white musicians more. I quietly explained that that was what I had come to New Orleans for and nothing was going to deter me. So be it.

I sat-in with the Freddie Kohlman band at the Mardi Gras. It was ideal sometimes, rooming above the club. Thomas Jefferson was on trumpet and Willie Humphrey, Percy's brother, on clarinet. I can't remember the bass and pianist's names.

At the time Freddie was playing good, powerhouse drums, but I thought he would be ideal for driving a big band rather than a small group. He was very nice and helpful, and they toned it down when I stood in. But I got a terrific attack of nerves and didn't think I was playing very well. But when we came off, Willie said it reminded him of the old days. He warmed to his memories, and talked of the early days. He sang me a simple dirge they used to play at funerals, called *In That City*.

Every time I played with George was an adventure, and I fitted better each time, because Percy never stepped down. So with nothing being said, we worked as I had done with Sonny. He would just flip his fingers when he wanted me to take the lead, otherwise I would play underneath him, in loose harmony, or on a variation of the melody. They took *Sister Kate* in at a lovely drag tempo.

> I took the first break. I heard Lawrence say to George, "Ain't that Bunk, George. That's Bunk man." I had a big warm cavern of sunshine in my belly and not a worry in the world.

I took three breaks and they all fell perfectly. What I had been searching for was there.

Dick Allen was to say that he had heard many white men sit-in with George, mostly to prove that they could play the music. But I was the only white man he had heard that contributed something to the band. The wonderful thing was it was a mutual delight.

These men weren't always very literate but they immediately knew what was going on without a word being said. I just loved the pleasure of their company and nothing needed to be said. "A haircut and no conversation," as the man used to say to the barber. Or in bad times, as Robert Service said, "What's the use of talking when you ain't got a cent and you're walking."

I had walked the desert and sailed the seas, and here I was.

KEN COLYER LETTER TO BILL COLYER 4 DECEMBER 1952

Room 3, 335 Bourbon Street, New Orleans, Louisiana, US.
Well, it's 3.10a.m. and time to narrate. If I didn't put it down as I go along I would never keep the record straight.

Was going to look for a job today but went to hear Sharkey, Buglin' Sam and Lizzie rehearse for some recording dates under the supervision of Dave Dexter instead. He was asking where Peter Tanner is right now and whether he'll be going out to the coast. Could you find out and let me know?

The boys were too busy rehearsing to do any jamming, and I just blew a couple with the pianist when they had finished.

Monday there's a session at Mares' and probably Lawrence and Drag will be there too!

Saw Dick Allen (he comes from Possum Trot, Georgia). We tried to contact Milé, but couldn't get him.

Had to grab a couple of hours sleep this afternoon, I was real beat. Have spent the evening here listening to Fred Kohlman's band. Sid Davilla sat-in with them for a couple and blew some

nice Shaw-style clarry.

I sat-in and did *Margie* or something. They were already started when I joined in and I'm damned if I could think what tune it was; talk about fake!

We then did a fine *How Long Blues*. I did the vocal and gave it the business and finished up with *Streets*. Their accompaniment was great and I felt fine, except my legs were a bit rubbery. They are fine musicians but I think Willie Humphrey is the only old-time musician there. They play a good brand of Dixieland on all the old standards but go best when on a modern kick, then they can be really terrific but tiring. Willie Humphrey plays his same style all the time though, and is quite good at times, quite a clown too. They're a fine bunch of fellows, Sharkey and his boys too; Fred even bought me a beer, which is much appreciated at 65 cents a time. Sid bought me rum and coke last night.

There's a big do at the Old Artesian Hall on the 14th. Will find out more about it.

Joe Mares sends his regards to Humph. He still thinks his brother's (Paul Mares) outfit, the NORK, was the greatest.

4 December P.M.

Just got your letter with the clippings; great stuff man, and it only took two days!!! I still can't figure out how it got here so fast; that's certainly express. But my first letter must have taken five days. I can't figure it at all, but not to worry.

I sent to Mobile today for my mail, so I should get it in a couple of days unless they are sore at me. I hope not.

Got my emergency Social Security Card today. The proper one will come through in about ten days. Tomorrow I must look in earnest. Dick said he will help me out if I get stuck, but I want to try to keep on my own two feet if I can.

The bands have all started up. It's a pity I can't hear the best from my room, but it could be worse I guess. Have you seen the article on Bunk in this month's *Record Changer*? Very interesting.

5 December. [Odd notes]

When Souchon made the Paradox session he said the engineer asked Elmer Talbert to blow quieter. He drew his self up and said, "No sir, I'll stand another ten feet away, but I won't blow one tone softer." His horn is bent in that photo. He bought a new one just before he died.

Fred Hatfield was telling me that he used to be a clothes presser. They used to go round and chat to him and he would take their coats off and press them while they talked.

Good Time Jazz have reissued some of the Ory Crescents, they've been gone over with an echo chamber and sound pretty good. Bunk's *Down By The Riverside* with vocal is also out.

Fats Domino's *How Long* is very good. I don't know what it is on yet. Played it on a juke box.

The Lottie Peavey on GTJ is wonderful.

5 December 2.30 A.M.

Just got back from a fine evening with Dick Allen, checking

his Sunday programme with him, yarning and playing records, so many of which I haven't heard before.

I tried for a job this morning with no luck; that's about the sixth so I'll go to the Labour Exchange tomorrow.

Went to see Tony Almerico this afternoon. He was pleased to see me and before I knew where I was I was the guest on his 45-minute afternoon jazz record show, which is well laced with ads, but he does manage to play some good stuff. He's invited me to play on his Sunday Jamboree which is also broadcast. It's strictly Dixieland, but what the hell! I'll be there even if I'm the nigger in the woodpile; it will be one more opportunity to get known and be heard.

Seems I've done the "Dicks of Duxieland" (Dick's pun) a slight injustice: it's the Fred Kohlman band I hear blasting away most of the time in my room. They certainly sound better in the bar than they do up here.

Is there any chance of getting a few bucks through Ken Lindsay for buying records and such to send over? I'm just aching to buy some of the stuff I see, that is unless you are getting it over there. Let me know.

Have just read Ron Staley's article in September's *Jazz Journal*. Would you write and tell him that he would be surprised and pleased at how much Bessie there is in Lizzie Miles voice, and it's pretty good to be able to hear an old trouper singing with all the vitality and charm that Lizzie has, besides, as I say, an almost uncanny likeness to that great lady Smith.

Guess I better get this one off, so long Bill, Ken

KEN COLYER LETTER TO BILL COLYER 6 DECEMBER 1952

Room 3, 335 Bourbon Street, New Orleans, Louisiana, USA
Dear Bill,

Am keeping OK and still waiting rather anxiously for your next letters. Right now I have an important plan for coining me a few bucks. Will you send volume 4 of *Jazz Directory*, and the rest of the volumes as they come out, to Dick Allen, 928 St. Ann Street, New Orleans. He is giving me the dollars for the nine volumes. I will probably be getting about another six orders for single issues which you can send to me direct. Also, can you send me a complete list of all the jazz and folk books the shop carries. I can probably get orders for some of the stuff.

I'm hoping there will be some lolly off reports I'm sending to cover anything like this. Let me know if the scheme's OK. Also find out if anybody will publish photos of the clubs and bands etc, then I could get them off the clubs themselves and send them.

[Odd notes]

Heard a wonderful tape last night of Herb Morand being interviewed by Bernard Steiner and Bob Matthews. It's really good to hear them men talking.

Also heard the album of Wilmoth Houdini and Gerald Clark's Night Owls; Jesus! That stuff's great. Also a little like

Lyttelton's band at times, and that stuff was recorded in the twenties. Did they say they were doing something new??

Al Morgan, the bass player, is the only N.O. man on them and the rest are West Indies men.

7 December 8.20 a.m.

Got to bed at 5 this morning and here I am hopped-up and up again. I guess you just can't sleep with the news I've got whirling round in my brain, and I don't wonder either.

To kick the evening off well I received your wonderful letter from Mobile, also one from Jim Asman. I didn't know what was in that letter, but somehow that's what I have been itching to get. Thanks man, it done me the world of good. I drove over to Manny's Tavern with John and Ursula Bernard and Elizabeth, a lady from the Symphony (cello player) who is just digging the music (but good too). Dick Allen went home as he has had flu and is still getting to bed early to fix up some.

Manny's is the place where you go through a big bar-room into the dimly lit hall, tables and chairs are all around a floor for the dancers (no jitterbugging!) and the band are on a stand against the wall facing the entrance. It takes a minute to get accustomed to the dimness and then it's real restful and conducive to good listening. As I got a fresh pack of cigarettes in the bar-room, I could hear the swingingest band in the City rocking away on *The Sheik Of Araby*.

I immediately realised that Percy Humphrey was playing so much better here than at the Mardi Gras, so quiet at times that you could feel him as much as hear him, then he would come out with electric, clear, stabbing phrases, rocking the band along like nobody's. When he plays into his tin derby fixed on a little stand it's more like that big toned muted Papa Mutt than anybody else.

They play quietly with all the drive and heat in the world and I could have willingly sat and listened all night, as much as I wanted to sit-in.

I said "Good evening" to George and Lawrence; big, beaming Lawrence, his face is wonderful when it lights up with a smile or a chuckle. George said he would give me a wave when I could sit-in.

I sipped my beer and got sent with every number, the beautiful changing tone colours are a wonder to hear and their effortless, seemingly casual, teamwork works uncanny wonders at times.

George gave me the wave and I got my horn out and tootled a little bit by the piano till they finished the number. George then gave me his chair next to Percy and put another on the stand next to me. I felt absolutely calm and played like a dream from the first kick off. First though, old Percy tooted an A without saying anything and I tuned up to him. "What kind of little old cornet is that?" he asked after the first number and I explained that it was a mezzo trumpet etc.

George decides the numbers and the next one was *Yes Suh* with Joe Watkins doing one of his knocked out vocals (no mike there, but you can hear him fine).

Percy would just flip his finger at me when to take the lead and, man, it's a dream to play with them men, no fighting, no carrying, just sit back, relaxed blowing easy and play the greatest horn of your life.

The next one was *Dallas Blues*; Percy put the music on his derby mute as they were just working it over. I offered to sit that one out, but George said to stay and I just eased along behind Percy.

On *Sister Kate*, played at a real drag tempo, I took the first break and heard Lawrence quickly turn his head and say to George, "Ain't that Bunk." I had a big warm cavern of sunshine in my belly and not a care in the world. I took three breaks and each one was a pip; now I know what I've been practising for all these years.

"You're all right man, you're all right," said George, beaming and patting my knee. Lawrence was chuckling away and I nearly floated off the stand. The Bernards said they've never seen me so happy. I don't wonder, I could feel myself almost lighting up. I finally knew that I was right, so right, and those other bums... well!

George next asked me what I would like to play and we did *Gloryland* and, man, I was nearly there. Them two horns just fitted, although there was no third harmony.

My lip isn't in great shape and I would have been worn out normally, but ended fresh as when I started and fit to play all night.

We did a great *Bugle Boy* at my request. Ha ha, them two horns in unison on the intro bugle call man! I would willingly go through all that frustration and yearning again to experience playing with them men. That's my music and they knew it too well. John Bernard said of all the men he's heard sit-in with the band, and that's just about everybody, I'm the only one that has contributed anything , and that's all I could tell him why, "Cos that's my music."

Whew! Just had the fright of my life. I thought there was a copper knocking at my door and it was the postman with an express letter from you. Just read the letter, man, but why haven't you sent me *NME* article of mine and what reply coupons are you talking about? By all means use any cash we earn as you see fit. I realise the expense must be a strain but it's worth it, man, even if you land in debt. We've got to make hay while the sun shines with a vengeance. I can't possibly buy a camera as I'm nearly down to my last buck and will have to go to Dick after all.

I'm still living in Room 3 and will do so as long as I can.

Please send me Bechet clipping.

See if you can get an option on White Hart hall for me so that whoever is in there has to go when I get back. The Cranes did a bad thing there, what the hell's Lindsay up to? And ask Ben why the hell he's quit playing and shake Sonny's hand for me.

Have heard the Lawson Jelly LP, pretty good in spots. Souchon has it.

To continue. I had quite a yarn with Lawrence and Drag when we had to quit at 1.30 a.m. Lawrence sends his best regards to Len

Page and thinks a lot of him and likes the record fine. Also met the manager of Premier drum agents here and he sends his regards to Mr. De La Porte (I think) of shop in Regent Street. Would you phone him and tell him (all good connections).

Well, Luthjens was the obvious place after such a great time. As we were going out to the car, the band were packing in theirs and shouting good nights, Joe Watkins yelled, "And keep the good works going" and I'm feeling fine.

Wonderful Luthjens, same happy, drunk boogleys having their weekend spree; same fine little combo; Elizabeth was sent, never seen nothing like it. Notice on wall "No smoking while dancing!" She expressed admiration for Billie Pierce's piano playing. Wonderful Billie, square jawed, looks like she could floor an ox, fag butt rolling from side to side in her mouth; and Harrison's quiet fine tone trombone, never a wrong note, correct harmonies and beautiful Archey-like lilting punch.

De De still sends me, dynamic control of a master, wonderful animated stances no matter what position he's playing in, vitality of a ten-year-old, chews gum in his craggy jaws; and he's still my favourite vocalist on *Eh La Bas*.

George Henderson with that big, happy gold-filled smile, very handsome fine forehead and features.

The old Spanish dame who has the vitality and actions of Mum (and looks a little like her) was there and did one of her numbers, pacing up and down in front of the band with great zest and shadows of greater stages.

My God, if only there were a Luthjens in London. We left when they closed and went to Elizabeth's for coffee and a yarn about the evening and this and that. Got home at 5 and slept like a log for about 2 ½ hours. What a night, what a night!!

Tell that dog Asman I had to pay 10 cents on his letter and I'll send it back if he does it again. By the way, I hope you are all working amicably in the shop together. Thank Jim for his letter and I will reply soon; but what's to do? I'm giving you a pretty full account of everything, so tell me what to write to Jim as I don't want to ball any works up.

I'm seeing about getting some photos of parades etc, and will ask the Bernards to take some of me. Vic's (Roberts) my boy and give him my regards, I think he's the best Delta horn man till I get back. Lawrence plays the short-necked banjo. I think probably you could only get that tone on that type.

All the best, Ken

KEN COLYER I could work on the same wave-length as George. I mean, this is what knocked him out when I first went to New Orleans. You know, they'd had white people sit-in with the band before. That was nothing new. To try and prove that there was nothing to this sort of New Orleans business.

So I was with John Bernard, and he said afterwards—actually, it was his wife, Ursula—she said, "Wouldn't you like to sit-in with the Lewis Band?" I said, "That's what I'm here for. But how do I go about it?" She said, "Oh, I'll ask George." So I'm in the same boat there. She said, "We know George. It'll be alright." And I said, "Are you sure? How do I get to have a blow with them?" Sort of revering them.

She said, "Oh, come to Manny's Tavern on Wednesday night, that'll be OK." So, sure enough, we got to Manny's Tavern on this Wednesday night—lovely little pub-type place, just a bit out of the centre of New Orleans. Nice relaxed atmosphere. And they—the band—get stomping along, and they're playing and they have a little break. Ursula goes up and chats with George, and says, "There's this English boy, and he'd like to play a couple of numbers."

And she came back and said, "Oh, when George gives you the signal, it's OK. You sit-in." But, you know, I sort of wasn't a bundle of nerves, but naturally I was apprehensive. So he finally gives me the signal, and pulls another chair up.

Percy's sitting there. You know Percy. Lovely bloke—he was always a good man. Sort of looks down, with that funny little frown sometimes. So he says "What you gonna play, man?" I could only think of all the obvious numbers, you know—*Gloryland*. And he says, "Alright."

Stomps off, and Alton does a beautiful swingin'intro, and away we go. By the time we finished *Gloryland* old George says, "What you gonna play now, man?" and I said *Isle Of Capri*. So we played *Isle Of Capri*, because I'd heard them play it a couple of nights before. And I'd never heard *Isle Of Capri* played like this before—it really opened my eyes.

When I came back to England and played it, that's the way I'd learned it from them. So George said, "Where did you learn the *Isle Of Capri* ?" And I said, "I heard you play it the other night." And he said, "Oh, did you?"

I'd never played it before in my life. But I was so knocked out by the way they played it. And then it just went on and on, you know. So then we're having a ball. If that band could have come to England, I know it's an exaggeration, but it would have altered a lot of courses you know, or musical arguments. See, when the Lewis band eventually came to England, unfortunately, it was a little too late.

That unique band that was going so good had been disrupted, and, unfortunately, you can't replace these things. Let it go. It might still be good, but the quality they had then with Marrero and Drag and Purnell, it was real New Orleans music personified.

Well, the way I put it, I said there must have been better bands in New Orleans in the past, but it's beyond my comprehension. If they were better than that, then I just cannot imagine it. I'm willing to accept the fact that all of them, sort of twenty years before, were terrific, superb. But I just can't comprehend them swinging more. The subtleties and nuances of swing that that band had at that time.

The Lewis band was playing so good! I'd played, and Davilla had played with them too, and he said, "That band is unique. It's unique even for New Orleans." That's the way he put it. You know, this isn't a typical New Orleans sound.

I've heard that band, and the tone colour has been so powerful you could see it, you know. Your imagination is so lit-up, you can see colours to the tonal quality of the playing. Because it all hinges on this important thing: the three-part counterpoint harmony all playing just as it should be, and it suddenly produces colours. Not just sounds. The same with the rhythm.

And Davilla put the best description. He said: "That band. It swings!" And you could hear it. They'd hit a certain sort of propulsion, and it would sound almost effortless. This propulsive, effortless, striding swing. And then suddenly you'd hear all these inner-rhythms going on. It's not all just a four-four. It's rhythms *within* the pulse. And he said: "It's like a watch. All them little cogs going around going tick, tick, and it's all coming out right— the time's coming out right." But it's a very rare thing now. It's the sound. It's orchestral. Because they play orchestral— they're not playing as individuals.

EDMUND SOUCHON LETTER TO BILL COLYER 7 DECEMBER 1952

3136 Octavia Street, New Orleans
Dear Bill and Betty,

I was so pleased to get your note of the 3rd, that I hasten to answer. Yes, I have had plenty of contacts with Ken, and must say I find him one swell fellow. From the very start, we seemed to hit it off well together. At least, that's how I felt about it. We have had two very pleasant dates, one of them to listen to records, and the other simply to lunch together, & we didn't stop talking a moment!

Ken has taken a room over the Mardi Gras Lounge, a place in the French Quarter (Vieux Carré they call it here—similar to The Village in New York). He has made friends with Sid Davilla, who owns the Lounge, and who incidentally is one of the very greatest clarinettists in America today—**In the Mardi Gras Lounge, Sid has playing nothing but the very best bands—Paul Barbarin, George Lewis—and Lizzie Miles singing with Joe Robichaux on piano. It couldn't be more ideal for Ken to absorb the stuff he came to America for!** He says the room is reasonable, it's warm—too warm, in fact—and clean. And he has many restaurants around that are also in the reasonable class.

Up to now he hasn't landed a job, but we are all looking for him. Personally, I am quite friendly with the officers who own this fine building where I have my offices, and have asked that they keep him in mind for anything that might turn up. But Ken has also been doing himself some good. He has made friends with another musician, (sax) man by the name of Francis Murray, who is also "boss" of a gang on the docks, loading and unloading ships. That seems to be Ken's love, anyway. He loves those ships, and still wants to be close to them! I hope he lands something, as everything in America is so expensive, and his pounds or $$$ would run out right fast if he didn't do something to replenish his coffers! Meantime, I hope too he gets a chance to play some music. As soo n as our old gang gets together, we are going to invite him to sit-in, and possibly cut a few tapes together. If we do, I promise to shoot some acetates over to you immediately.

Thanks for the information regarding the release of our Papa Laines album over in England. I am enclosing $10 (as a starter) for you to buy me 3 complete sets of the 78's. If they have issued all of the L.P. on singles, there should be 6 records. If it is possible, since you are in a position to purchase these records at something of a "dealer's price," it would help me a great deal. They have only issued our records on the 33 1/3 with one (Ella Speed-Bucket) on 78's.

In other words, I am ordering 18 records, 3 sets of each, and would appreciate if you would send them to my office. Whatever charges over and above the $10 which I am enclosing, please either send the stuff collect—or forward the bill which I will take care of at once. (Yes, I plead guilty on all "vocals" for the session! God help me, they even pay me for groaning like I do!)

We are waiting anxiously for our first pressings of an LP with Raymond Burke, clarinettist extraordinary, and Johnny Wiggs, with our bassist Sherwood Mangiapane and myself on guitar. Bill Russell of American Music recorded us a month or so ago, and Bill (John) Steiner is releasing us on Paramount (a worthy label, and we are proud to be on it! In company with Joe Oliver, Ma Rainey, Johnny Dodds and others!) As soon as they "hit" I will forward one to you.

Well, I have overrun my time, but I did want you to know that we had a great deal of fun with Ken, and that he is heading in the right direction. I am certain that he will get what he came to N.O. looking for. I hope that he brings home to you great memories of his visit here. There is a remote possibility that me and my old band might be in London a short while before the Coronation, but this is not for publication, and up to now is simply a dream...

I am looking forward to seeing the article you wrote with the picture I shot of the NATO group and us. In fact, I am always looking forward to the journal, as I consider it one of the finest (if not THE finest) of its kind in the world.

My very best wishes to you both for Christmas, and here's hoping that our paths will actually cross. You seem so friendly and good fellows!

Most cordially, Edmond

Send records here: Dr Edmond Souchon, 11 Pan-American Life Ins. Co. Bldg., 2400 Canal Street, New Orleans, Louisiana

KEN COLYER LETTER TO BILL COLYER 9 DECEMBER 1952

Room 3, 335 Bourbon Street, New Orleans, Louisiana, USA
Dear Bill,

About all I can find out about Petrillo is to write to Chicago. The guy's well known so it's bound to get to him. Souchon says they're doing everything they can and progress is more favourable than expected. Johnny Wiggs and Souchon are going, so you see that I can have no influence over any decisions. I would suggest, though, Raymond Burke, Tom Brown and Mangiapane, a very fine bass player. These men will probably be picked anyway.

I went over to a session at Joe Mares yesterday evening. Slow Drag, Lawrence, Abbie Brunies, Stanley Mendelson, Jack Delaney, Alvin A., Bill Matthews and Raymond were there. Alvin Alcorn played really fine and Bill was punching it like always. Drag and Lawrence really carried Abbie and Mendelson along. Them boys sound OK in Sharkey's rhythm section but I'm afraid D and L really show up their lack of swing. Delaney, Sharkey's tram man, played much better than he usually does too. That boy will be fine if he's influenced enough by them men.

I sat-in when Bill and Alvin left to go to work. Bill received your letter and was in a little wonderment when he told me, I think. Albert Ortega, a white horn man, was playing. We didn't get along at all and the few numbers we did were pretty much of a shambles. Various drummers sat-in, none of them much good.

Got the news last night that there was a funeral parade today at Gretna over the river. I went with the Bernards and Dick Allen in their car.

We got to the Wolves Aid Social and Pleasure Club about an hour before they were due to start. Things are pretty rugged in that area, which is the coloured quarter. There are very few paved roads; most are just dirt and gravel and there are short stretches of pavement here and there; otherwise just grass and mud, as there has been showers all day. This made it heavy going following with the Second Line at times.

The lodge hall is a low, flat-topped, breeze brick building standing on its own between a cafe and a house. I suppose these are the suburban districts of New Orleans and most of the coloureds live there.

Willie Pajeaud (trumpet), Kid Avery and Wilbert Tillman (sousaphones), were already there. John Casimir (Eb clarinet and leader), Kid Howard, Bob Thomas (tram), Ernest Rogers (snare drum), the bass player and the sax player turned up in about half an hour in a grey car.

The band was then John Casimir's Young Tuxedo Band. They went into the lodge and warmed up on *Just A Little While To Stay Here* and it sounded real fine. The swing and style is just the same as George L's band.

The bass drum player has a cymbal fixed to his drum and hits it on an off-beat with a loop of wire fixed to a handle. Dick tells me they all use this. (Pouring with rain now). They came out to

me to Willie Pajeaud.

They assembled again and started marching with that swinging little strut they have. They kicked off with a fine *Panama* then *St. Louis Blues* with two wonderful minor choruses. *Jambalaya* fits the music perfectly, also *Bourbon Street Parade*. There was a bigger second line going back, though Dick and Ursula dropped out and went back to the car.

We arrived back at the lodge, muddy, tired and me, anyway, very happy to have seen my first parade and not, I hope, my last. I'd walk till my legs dropped off to hear them men.

Well, I held off finishing this to go down and dig the Lewis band and to play a set with them. Man, that was something, sitting there with George standing right alongside me and blowing all them beautiful things right in my ear. Percy is sitting on my other side and I'm matching his tone and we're weaving all around one another; first he takes the lead and then me and it's really something. Jim is next to Percy blowing like a demon, and Joe is right in front of me telling me to "Blow it out, kid" when I take a solo. We play an *Isle Of Capri* that's the prettiest thing I've heard in a long while, and a very pleasant *Careless Love*, and of course that good old *Bugle Boy*.

I sat-in the back room the rest of the time, except for a couple of drinks with Joe Delaney, talking to Lizzie Miles. She loves to talk and I love to listen. She even invited me to Xmas dinner with her, God bless her, while we're eating some fried chicken, toast and a small beer, but as much as I hated it, I had to turn it down as the Bernards have already asked me.

Do you know, when Lizzie's husband died she sold his Buescher trumpet to Buddy Petit for $85 and never did get all the money for it, as wages were pretty low then, but, boy, she's telling me what they did with a dollar in them days.

Huey P. Long said on the radio: "If I took a chicken and gave all the pure white people in the state of Louisiana a piece, I would still have half of it left."

Clarence Williams' book-keeper once told King Oliver: "If you knew how much them record companies have done you out of, you'd take your pistol, go right out now and shoot 'em dead."

She's just full of little anecdotes and experiences. She slugged one of her managers once for crossing her up on a record deal. Says she was so mad she hit him before she realised it.

A fellow comes in who knows her and just about every blues singer. Doesn't stop talking Bessie Smith, but the guy even heard Ma Rainey!

Well, I must to bed, so more anon Bill.

Best to everybody, Ken

KEN COLYER LETTER TO BILL COLYER 11 DECEMBER 1952

Room 3, 335 Bourbon Street, New Orleans, Louisiana, USA
Dear Bill,
Getting registered at Labour Exchange this morning, go back

assemble and Dick introduced me to Wilbert Tillman, a fine, tall man with a very pleasant nature. Dick remarked that it would be rough going with the mud and wet; it didn't rain during the parade though. Smiling he said, "Well, I've been parading for thirty years so I guess it won't hurt me none."

The parade got in line, man with a black umbrella in front. Two trombones, sousaphone, clarinet, two trumpets, snare drum, bass drum, sax, man carrying lodge banner, two more holding banner with strings either side, man carrying Stars and Stripes. This order isn't exact but near enough.

They started off with a fine *Saints* and were off to the church. Avery blows some tremendous trombone; records don't do him justice.

The snare drummer doesn't stop once the parade has started.

Gloryland, Sing On, The Lord's Been Good To Me and a couple of others saw them to the church. The overall sound is great but not quite like the Zenith or the Bunks.

They played *The Saints* again very quietly and did a little back and forth march in front of the church, then broke up to go and have a beer while the service was on. The church was a pretty sad place with no outward resemblance to such places, more like something off *Tobacco Road* [Erskine Caldwell's novel, Ed.]

I wanted to go and have a beer with them but Dick said it wasn't wise, so we tramped about half a mile to a white cafe. When we got back we had missed them. By the time we caught them up, they were at the cemetery and we only heard one beautiful dirge, *Saviour Lead Me*, which they played by the graveside.

When they came out of the cemetery, Kid Howard, who still remembered me and still says I'm a fine horn man, introduced tomorrow. Had to use my ace in the hole today, the three Canadian bucks. Was down to 10 cents; borrowed the rent from Dick and Harry (Jazz Centre). Got a dollar and one cent apiece for C dollars.

Had my chest x-rayed at a public mobile unit this morning, they mail the results.

Odd Memories

Wonderful, tall, stately man carrying the banner in the parade. Little kid's wonderful animated hand-clapping as he watched the parade go by. Big, gangling fellow trucking in front of parade going back.

Cousin Joe playing wonderful guitar in back room as Kohlman's band play *Honeysuckle Rose*.

Lizzie knocking herself out for her own sake 4 o'clock one morning singing *Go Back Where You Stayed Last Night*—Kid Ory's *My Regular Man Now*.

Lizzie telling of a time Bessie Smith was on a night out, went into a club to drink but wouldn't sing, until the compere announced Mary Faith as the world's greatest blues singer. She soon got up to show that hussie just what she thought she was (that's what the manager figured and it worked fine).

> The jazz scene isn't rosy here, mind you. It's much the same as it is at home—warring factions, misunderstandings and what have you, but there's still enough good to make it still the only city.

There must be dozens of old-timers lying idle and neglected, not playing through lack of work or recognition or because, as Milé Barnes says, they won't pitch in there and assert themselves. I hope that someday someone with the right ideas and the money will do something about it. Let's hope there will come a time.

Interesting point for John R.T.; Willie Cornish did say that Bolden made a cylinder, but the quest for it has been given up.

Wilbert Tillman and Thomas Jefferson heard me talking on Almerico's radio programme; looks like it did a bit of good.

Just received your big envelope, great stuff manny. I shouldn't send any more miscellaneous clippings unless I ask again though. What is very important is the topical stuff and anything printed of mine about these men. I am still wanting the first *ME* article, or was there just Souchon's letter? I am in good with the Crosby and Lewis bands and any good publicity I can show them and give them (always send two) puts me in better. I also want the Bechet clipping.

Am working on the club angle but am flat broke (may get a job today, have my Social S card and am registered at Labour). Have got a great pic of Sid D playing in the Mardi Gras with Fred K but need a better copy. Will also work on Paddock when I can (and Luthjens).

Have some sad info on Elmer T. The night he died, they say his brother walked out and left him dying in agony and hasn't been back since. They say Elmer was on his knees praying when they found his body.

Kid Howard is a bouncy, genial little fellow. It seems he did lay-off at one time and his playing and lip were bad for some time. He sounds pretty good to me, but he is not held in very high esteem here now.

The purists here are inclined to be worse than us in some

ways and are a little blasé about some things. I guess it's understandable when they live right here and can hear all the men fairly frequently.

Congratulate Monty for me for his success in the art world; it's good to see the boy get a break.

Went to the Latter Library on St. Charles Avenue; they have a fine collection founded by Doctor Souchon and wonderful playing facilities. Heard some wonderful L of Congress stuff including some Sonny Terry, who only plays a cheap mouthorgan (not chromatic) and can just see enough to distinguish night from day. His *Fox Hunt* is one of the greatest things I've ever heard.

Have to report to Exchange again tomorrow, hope to Christ I get something.

Don't worry about Page and Jones, I got your letter from them so they will either send me the other stuff or return it to you. I hope Mum is better. Tell her I will be writing soon and I hope she can make out OK for the time being.

Sid Davilla is a really nice guy, a small dapper man with a quiet charm. Has been a professional musician with many big bands (sax and clarinet) and did the first published orchestration of *The Saints*.

Steve Valenti I haven't met yet but I know that he is a racehorse owner and luminary of New Orleans, probably likes jazz.

I don't try and pump any of the men for views and such like. I figure they've had enough jerks bending their ears and the best way to secure their friendship is to be casual with them and not force oneself; and I think it's working and I'll probably get that sort of stuff anyway sooner or later [queries from Bill. Ed.]. Right now most of them know me and I think they like me and that's fine and if I never get any more I will still be perfectly happy to have known them, seen them and heard them.

John Bernard has some photos of the parade and of me. I will be getting copies.

I looked at Sweet Figlio's diatonic, double-ended washboard from every angle until I looked on the back and found out what it was. God! It's wonderful; first, how can we steal it? second, where can we find a man to play it?

KEN COLYER LETTER TO BILL COLYER 12 DECEMBER 1952

After much bullshitting and red-taping I got a job and start tomorrow as a roofer's mate, you know, repairing roofs and whatnot. The pay's a buck an hour, which is fair, and I'm working the weekend.

I went up to see good old Doc with two cents in my pocket and he lent me a ten spot with no messing. I've had to get a pair of rubber sports boots as the guy won't let you work in leather soles. It's only a one or two man business I think, and the job should be OK.

I passed San Jacinto Hall on Dumaine St and didn't know it

until I saw a bill-poster. I must go back and look at it sometime and think about all the wonderful music that was recorded there. A bus named "Desire" runs down our street.

Doc was telling me they are getting along fine fixing things to go over. Definitely going are Souchon, Wiggs, Harry Shields (Larry's brother), Mangiapane (very good bass), Tom Brown, one of the original white creators (where's Rust and the boys?) who hates Ory and most coloured tram men, he originated it all you know. Possibly Ray Bauduc if they can get him. Oh, and Stanley Mendelson (pianist) who says he is willing to quit Sharkey to go.

I gave Doc the *NME* clipping; he was chuffed with it.

Well, that's all for now, Brother Bill, so I'll get this one in the post.

So long for now.

All the best to everybody. Ken

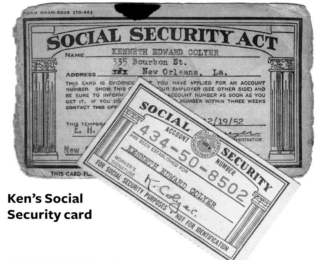

Ken's Social Security card

KEN COLYER Funds were running short so I started looking for work. I went to Woolworth's but you can't compete with coloured labour at a dollar an hour. Then I went to the Employment Bureau. I had an interview with a delightful Southern Belle, Miss Molydeaux. She started asking me about education "Well I only had an elementary education." She was puzzled. I explained that in England you went to an elementary school unless daddy sent you elsewhere. I mentally thought to myself that I have known a few 'educated' people that go to college twits, and come out educated twits, but they acquire that essential accent in the process.

"What does an elementary education entail?" The basic grounding, you are taught to read and write and spell, English, Geography and a little chemistry, music, physical training (which is the only thing I enjoyed at school). She was impressed. "That's a lot higher than elementary in America." I was impressed.

But it didn't do me any good. She had a job for a short order cook, which I turned down. I said I had had enough of cooking for a while, but with hindsight I would have been better off taking it. The only other job going, and I needed a job quick, was roofing. So I took it.

It was a two man business. I saw the boss and he explained that I must have rubber soled shoes like baseball shoes. They only cost five dollars. I barely had five cents. I went to see Doc Souchon and he kindly lent me ten bucks. I jumped on a tram after seeing Doc. His surgery was at 2400 Canal Street. **I proferred the ten dollars to pay my car fare. The ticket collector had a fit. He couldn't change ten dollars. So I had to hop off, change the note and get another car.**

They have an excellent system in the States that should have been copied here. If you have to break your journey, you can get a transfer ticket and continue on the one ticket until you reach your destination. I should know better than to suggest they copy it here. We never do anything sensible. The idiots always put idiots in charge.

I should never have gone roofing with the lifestyle I was leading, but I was committed. These professionals are like cats on a roof. I was more like an elephant and usually still half asleep when I turned to at 7.

KEN COLYER LETTER TO BILL COLYER
14 DECEMBER 1952

Room 3, 335 Bourbon Street, New Orleans, Louisiana, USA
Dear Bill,

Thanks a lot for the lolly, as you must have guessed, it came in the nick of time and saved me having to borrow again. I also received the journal and like the article; you made a good job of it. There was only one mistake and that was the bass player's name: it's McNeal Breaux (his autograph is on one of the photos). He is a relation of Wellman Braud, who changed his name for some reason or other. Jim Robinson's sister was married to Jimmy Noone, by the way. Could you send a couple more journals, I showed it to the Crosby band and Octave and Alvin would like them.

Fred Hatfield of The Jazz Center, 706 Bourbon St. is interested in buying some of the English discs, so would you write to him?

Friday night I was going out and bumped into McNeal who was just going to work. We were chatting and I happened to say that I hadn't been in because of no lolly and that I had just got a job and the guy slips me a buck to get some smokes. Wasn't that something?

That night Fred took me to play at the Superior, a coloured joint that I frequent, but they wouldn't let us in. It appears they were mixed up in the Zachary Scott business somehow or other and they are scared of getting closed down if they tangle with the law at all. They did tell us where Kid Sheik (George Colar) was playing though, so we went there.

It was an ordinary tavern with a fair-sized, echoey back room.

Ken sits in with the George Lewis Band, colour bar notwithstanding

Nobody can remember the name of it, not even the Kid. He had drums, sax, electric guitar and his self on trumpet. I have their autographs but can't decipher them. I will get them off Dick sometime, he lives next door to the guitar player.

The drummer is a gnome-like fellow and one of the most startling showmen I've seen. He reminded me of one of the characters in Eudora Welty's story. He was playing a real beat-up kit with the fervour of a Krupa. His bass drum would have rocked over if it weren't for his carrying case propping it up, and his snare drum had a coating of dirt and grease on it that must have been as thick as the skin itself. He sang *Eh La Bas* during the evening and if any Afro Joes had been there they would have been entranced, it was really savage and with different words, it took on a totally different meaning as he spat it out.

The guitar player was similar to St Cyr, who plays electric guitar on them AMs and Paradoxes, and was really fine. The sax man was a bopper yet pleasant and they seemed to fit together OK. Kid Sheik is a real easy going guy and very likeable. He has a mouth full of gold and a lip on his lip; that boy must have done some hard blowing in his time. He still plays in the Superior Brass Band.

I sat-in with them the whole evening and thoroughly enjoyed it. We played the old assortment; pops, standards, waltzes and God knows what. We even paraded around the room and the bar-room playing *The Saints*. The manager loves me like a brother and buys me two beers.

The nearest I can liken this stuff is to the Kid Thomas AM, and Sheik plays very much like him. I shall be going again. I just love those tonks where nobody gives a damn.

The Kid took us to the coloured Union Local from there, to see if anybody was jamming. There was no one playing when we got there so we had a couple of beers and waited to see who would turn up. Albert Burbank's son was there but he doesn't play anything. Alton Purnell came in but couldn't stay. Finally, a trumpet player gets on the piano and a man pulls his sax out and they hit a 32-bar bop thing. **I joined and really blew some great stuff, as the tune was straight enough for me to understand. We did a twelve-bar blues with me blowing good old melodic horn against a flattened sax. It knocked Fred out to hear me playing such stuff with a couple of cool-cats.**

After they had gone, the Kid was fooling about on piano. I asked him if he knew an eight or twelve-bar sequences. "This is the only one I can play," he says and goes into *How Long Blues* in A♭. If I wasn't sitting there playing with the man I would have sworn it was Jimmy Yancey. When we finished I asked him to play the same thing slower and I enjoyed it just as much the second time. That's the kind of 88s I like playing horn with.

A couple of men from the Teddy Bears—that's the band with the Dukes at the Famous Door—had come in and were having a drink. One was the pianist (Hernandez). He sat down for a quick couple of tunes; *Careless Love* and one other; he's a pretty good pianist but Fred is nuts on Kid Sheik now.

Hernandez drove me back to Bourbon Street in his car. It was 6 am when I got in and I set my clock for 6.30, but just couldn't make it. I got to work at 8.45 and the boss just said, "Good Morning" and set me to work. We were putting Ruberoid shingles on a slate roof of a decaying tenement house on Dumaine, not far from San Jacinto (pronounced "Assinto").

I got home at 5 yesterday afternoon, just about beat, had a bath and turned in for a couple of hours before going out to Manny's to play with George.

I was in fine form and played for about two hours with them. The session was greater than ever and was really glorious. Highlights I think were *Snag It*, *Ice Cream*, which we played twice, *Just A Little While*, which Percy led into, *Sing On* and just about every dilly number I guess.

Bob Huntington, who was taught by Lawrence, sat-in for a while and is pretty good. A little like Wilber was when Bechet had finished with him. Dick Allen also sat-in for a *Tiger Rag* on tram, but is pretty rusty I'm afraid, as the police still have his horn.

I got in at four and managed to get to work at nine. The boss said, "Good Morning" and put me to work. This was on a different job on General Taylor Street, roofing a new wood-frame wing to a house. The boss went about 12 and we carried on till two (the fellow who was sick is back) and practically finished the roof. It's asbestos shingle and you can slap that stuff on pretty fast.

I hurried home, changed and went to Artesian Hall (memories of Wooden Joe) where Joe Delaney was giving a free concert with Kohlman and George L. I was late and missed George's set. Joe D. was taking it all on tape for something or other. Kohlman was playing his usual powerhouse drumming and Jefferson blowing his torrid Windhurst-like horn. Cousin Joe was there and did a very amusing *Saints* with a long preaching piece full of humour that had the mostly coloured audience in stitches. They did an all-in jam at the end, but I'm afraid the Lewis band couldn't assert themselves very well; still, it was interesting. The Hall is a stone, box-like affair little bigger than the White Hart hall. There is a big banner over the stand with "Go forward with God" or something on it.

The first man I bumped into when I went in was good old Kid Sheik. Alton Purnell saw me and introduced me to the president of their Union Club. I got a big hello off George's boys and Willie H, who is Percy's brother. The Bernards took flash photos of the Lewis session, so I will get copies as soon as I can; I'm hoping they got some good ones of the front-line.

I also saw Mrs. Valenti last night and am getting two recent shots, one of the band, one of the Paddock, on Thursday, so I'll get them sent off as soon as possible.

I guess I'll stop in tonight now and catch up on my sleep.

I had a letter from Val and have written to Mum, also Jim Asman just giving him a general account of things. I should try and vet anything he might use now though, as it's no good balling any *MM* stuff up is it? I hope it will bring in enough lolly to stave off expenses you are incurring. I know it must be tough trying to do all that I keep asking you, but we've really achieved something this time, eh?

> # I still can't figure how so much has happened and I haven't been here three weeks yet, yet there are still many men to see and hear. If only I can stay till Mardi Gras. Man that would be something!

I like this job and will keep it now, so that might help me get a time extension. I've heard nothing more about that new bill that comes into force this month.

Guess I'll sign off now Gate, so all the best to one and all. Ken

FRED HATFIELD Ken played with the black group that we brought him to, where George Colar was playing. I brought him to that particular place. And the music was very primitive there, because it wasn't really Dixieland or traditional—it was just music, you know—but it was very primitive, as he expresses in that little article he wrote about it. And then afterwards, well, he actually sat-in with them and played some tunes which really delighted them—everyone was delighted with Ken sitting-in and playing—and then he played with a group at the Musicians Union Hall—afterwards.

But that was the only time I can remember that he sat-in and played with anybody—at least when he was with us. I think later on he may have done more...

KEN COLYER LETTER TO BILL COLYER
16 DECEMBER 1952

1407 Prytania Street, New Orleans
Dear Bill,

As you see, I've made a move and have moved my gear to the new place. The fellow I work with, Nick, rents it and asked if I wanted to come in with him. Well, it will be fifty per cent cheaper, so I figured it would be silly to refuse and it's still only about ten minutes from Bourbon Street. It's a self-contained flat with nice, big kitchen with fridge and washing machine and I can feed myself most of the time once I get organised. The job went easier today and will be OK once I get back into training.

Last night I went with Dick A. and the Bernards to the New Orleans Jazz Club's club night as Doc's guest. It was held at Perez's on the Airline Highway, a slightly snooty joint.

Doc showed me your letter and was very pleased to hear from you. Thanks for telling him about the lolly, he's a great guy and won't mind that arrangement at all, I'm sure.

I met Myra Menville there, Joe Delaney once again, Mangiapane, who is quite a fellow. Big raw-boned guy, talks like a Texan a little. He was in England during the war, loves that booze and is looking forward to returning. My band was there (who else? G.L.). Also Lizzie Miles, Red Mott, Johnny Wiggs and many others. I had a few drinks (on the club) and talked to Joe D., Tony A., Doc and Myra.

The Lewis boys did a parade around the club with everybody marching around. George told me to get my horn as he passed me, so I asked Doc if it was OK, as I have been wised up to some of the club members who frown on mixing it up. Doc said certainly and I joined them in the middle of a *Saints*. We accompanied Lizzie on about six numbers then did a terrific 6/8 time *Gettysburg* while they gave Xmas presents out to members (they had brought them themselves, but I expect everybody got a different one).

Jim Robinson was in great form and a little canned I guess. He was joshing me and clowning like I've never seen before.

Doc S. sat-in with us on his Vega banjo for one or two, and Raymond Burke joined George for some fine two-clarinet stuff.

Fred Hatfield was telling me one time he got drunk with Jim in a bar and Jim got out his tram, marched up and down playing tailgate to everything on the jukebox.

Percy was a little tight and pretty lively, which is something I haven't seen before. Old Doc must have been fixing them up.

I'm afraid the majority of the club members are pretty square. I like to hear Dick expounding on them; he's got them all taped and hasn't got much time for them. That boy has got a mountain of notes from men like Milé Barnes etc, also dozens of anecdotes. He could probably write a really authoritative book on New Orleans jazz and men, but the guy won't. He has no time for Blesh and shows a knowledge of the stuff that makes you realise he's right.

Heard the Bunk Columbia last night and think there's been too much bull slung about it. Bunk is fine but the band isn't the best by a long way; not bad but definitely not great.

Dick backs up a lot of what Ralston says about Bunk. Says he was a snob and that was the reason he disliked the Lewis band. He wanted big names around him, to catch a little reflected limelight I suppose. Another fact that is true is that Bunk never had a band of his own until he fronted the Lewis group.

Well, I'm going to hear the men again tonight and play with them I hope. There's a little Jim Crow at times that makes things delicate, but it's not too bad.

Will write again tomorrow.

All the best Gate,

KEN COLYER LETTER TO BILL COLYER
17 DECEMBER 1952

1407 Prytania Street, New Orleans
Dear Bill,

Have just been to the Mardi Gras and got the other *Jazz*

Journal and your letter with *Melody Maker* clipping. I am extremely irritated over the article, as I think you are. Anything I put in letters like the Picou incident or anything derogatory is, like as I told you, highly confidential and personal just between you and me.

Don't give (Max) Jones any more of my mail, but vet it and re-write it yourself. What does that bloody oaf think these people are going to think if they see that stuff written about them? Here I am, trying to be diplomatic and friendly with everybody, and he's going to land me in the shit.

Explanations are no good afterwards when the damage is done. And I think his re-writing is bloody lousy, the man is clueless. If it wasn't for the fact that we couldn't sell the stuff I'm writing to anybody else, I would say to hell with Max Jones. I trust you will see that nothing like that happens again.

I'm hoping to get your next letter tomorrow. I think you got me wrong on Dick A's jazz directory; he has the first 3 and wants volume 4 and all future editions, but never mind. He only fixed this arrangement to help me out by giving me dollars, which he has done.

Well, now to some more pleasant news. I sat-in with George last night at the Mardi Gras for the last time. You see, technically it shouldn't be done, and the trouble is Alton Purnell is a Union delegate. I know he has told George about it before, but the guy's so damn good natured, I suppose he hasn't liked to refuse me; also Sid Davilla has never said no when I have asked him, probably for the same reason. Still, Manny's is still OK, as things don't matter so much out there.

The band know me well now and greet me like a brother, also the Kohlman boys and Crosby's band. McNeal Breaux is sick at the moment; I hope it's only a cold or something. Kohlman has a new pianist now, Batiste (might not be correct), I haven't heard him yet.

The set with George last night was a corker and *Panama Rag* tremendous; Jesus, the beat them boys produce when they are really rocking. You can feel the terrific surge and impetus like I've never experienced before. The more I hear Joe Watkins the greater I realise the guy is.

I was sitting in the back talking to Lizzie when Sid told me that there were a couple of people would like to talk to me. I went into the bar and met them and they bought me a drink (very welcome) and expressed admiration and delight at the way I fitted in with the band and played so well (you can't go wrong with Percy alongside you).

They were Charles and Anne Kaegelbehn from New York. He is an Attorney at Law and they were leaving for New York this morning, much to their regret. They frequent Nick's a lot in New York and know the late Nick's wife very well; also Hank Duncan, who is still there.

After hearing all but the last set of George's, I took them to the Paddock to hear a little of the boys there. They had a pretty good relief bass who I didn't know.

They insisted on taking me back to their hotel to have a gin fizz because I had not heard of or had one. It was the Roosevelt Hotel, "Home of the Original Ramas Gin Fizz," the neon sign outside said. The bar was closed so we had to go into the blue room, a very swank night club in the hotel. They made me put on a tie before they would let me in and regarded me very dubiously, the management that is. The tie was bright blue with white spots and clashed beautifully with my maroon shirt and brown suit.

We managed to wade through the waiters, who looked more expensive and smarter than the people, to a table. This gin fizz is made of egg whites, gin, lemon and juice of rosebuds or something, and really is a wonderful drink. We had three all together and who do you think was playing there? Tommy Dorsey; yes, old T. D. his self. It was typical club stuff though, bags of cabaret acts and singers, T. D. only featured his self on one number while I was there, *Marie* done in real *Getting Sentimental Over You* style.

I got in at three this morning and the day has been a tough one, so I'll have to close.

Just one thing. While I was quickly perusing your mail outside the Mardi Gras, I heard old Bill's trombone shouting out, looked up and he emerged from the door of the Paddock with Alcorn and Picou behind him pumping out *The Saints*, did a quick parade round the pavement and marched back in. Great, eh?

Well, I hope to Christ no one gets hold of that *MM* down here.

All the best for now, Bill, Ken

KEN COLYER LETTER TO BILL COLYER 20 DECEMBER 1952

1407 Prytania Street, New Orleans

Dear Bill,

Have just received your letter of the 14th. Damn thing's taken 6 days, I don't know why.

I'm glad you've fixed things up with Max J. I'm still a bit burned up over it, how stupid can that guy get? I'm also sick of Lyttelton after reading that *Journal* article. I've no time for any of them dumb bastards any more. I guess they never will know what it's all about.

I hope I get some of the discs before Xmas, as Dick is waiting for them to work a programme out and there's no guarantee that I'll be here after Xmas. I am going to write to the immigration officer to see if I can get an extension of my time.

I heard a record of Bob Huntingdon, Merriweather (drums) and the George L. emulator last night. It's not bad at all though it drags a little. The clarry man has good tone but hasn't the rhythm or vibrato of Monty.

I can't tell you much more about the boys coming over, though I would definitely rather see them go than Sharkey. Souchon, Burke, Mangiapane and Wiggs make a very good quartet, so a band with Mendelson (Sharkey's piano), Shields

Ken Colyer

and Tom Brown and Bauduc should be OK.

They hear Bix in Bunk's playing on the LP, It's every inch Bunk, somewhat like his playing on the "Days Beyond Recall" session.

I had an Xmas card from Dick Werlich today and he says the article is on its way.

I can't get hold of any photos till next week; I will send them off as soon as I get them.

I was surprised at Alex wanting to play legit guitar and it reminds me of Lizzie Miles asking me if I had learnt to read. When I replied "No" she gave a satisfied nod and said, "You play better when you can't read as long as you've got a good ear."

I haven't got Monty's letter yet, Souchon hadn't received it when I asked him.

21 December

Did my sixth session with George and the boys last night. I was pretty tired but enjoyed it immensely. That band gives you a really deep kick and memories I will always cherish.

George has received your letter and showed it to me last night; he says that was real nice of you and thanks you.

The band hit some great stuff and Alton was playing the best I've heard yet. Joe Watkins does most of the vocals and makes a pretty good job of them, he also likes to yell encouragement to the band now and again with a "Blow it out, kid," or "Let me hear you, boy."

George is the boss and picks the numbers, tells them if they are not quite playing to his liking and picks tempos. Nobody argues but does as he says and they all get along fine. They are great kidders and always joshing one another and have a great sense of humour. I hope they always stay together because I think they have something the old Ory band had, and that's what makes the difference.

Drag gets their drinks from the bar, he always has that quite humorous smile and his eyes are wonderfully youthful and laughing.

I've played many numbers with them that I have never played before and which I never thought they played; there seems to be no limit to their repertoire. Percy is a thorough musician and reads well; also I think Alton and Lawrence.

We found out from the boys last night that there was to be a

funeral today. I was going to work but that news soon changed my mind. The Bernards were going so I met them at midday. It has been a fine day for parading, bright sunshine, though a little chilly as the evening wore on. Algiers is also better for parading as the roads and paths are good. I guess Jefferson must be a poor district.

We got to the Youngmen's Protective and Charitable Association of Algiers Hall in good time. Some of the Eureka Brass Band were already there. The full band was Percy Humphrey, leader, Kid Sheik, Willie Pajeaud (trumpets), Albert Warner, Sonny Henry (trombones), Emanuel Paul (tenor sax), Ruben Roddy (alto sax), Joseph "Red" Clark (tuba and manager), he's the tuba player in the dead front photo in *Jazzways*, Robert "Fewclothes" Lewis (bass drum) and Alf Williams (snare drum).

We had a talk with Sheik; he's a great guy, really loves his music and is so damn good natured, loves to laugh his head off at the least provocation.

They were eventually ready and did a warm-up on *Just A Little While*, then got into line; a smart looking leader with a big sash over his shoulder leads, then the trombones, saxes, tuba, bass drum and snare drum and, last, the three trumpets. Then comes the double file of Association members with white gloves on and smart Sunday suits, some of them carrying the club banner and a furled Stars and Stripes.

They started marching to *Gloryland* then they played another hymnal that I don't know. *The Saints* saw them to the church, where they do a little back and forth parade, then stand and play, getting quieter as the people file under the banner, up the concrete steps and into the church.

I then went to a coloured tavern with Sheik and Ernest McKinney, who is Sheik's drummer usually and also Sheik's boss during the day. McKinney is a plasterer and cement finisher. There I met Red Clark, Roddy, Henry, Warner and the rest. It was only an ale house and Sheik don't like beer. I guess most of them are whiskey men mainly, so we went down the road, McKinney and Roddy gave me some money and I went into a white bar and bought a pint of Old Forester. We took this back to the church, which is on the second floor; underneath is a big, long kitchen and tables and chairs and all sorts of bric-a-brac and what-not.

Sonny Henry came back with a half of Old Stagg (terrible stuff) so we all had a couple of shots and a good old natter about this and that. Sheik introduces me to everybody and I can never remember half of them.

Sheik showed me the Eagle Eye Club House; Red Allen senior belonged to that and they had four bands at his funeral when he died. Sitting under the church as we were, you could hear the singing and the preaching fine.

When the service had finished the band got set. "Listen to this carefully," said Sheik, and I certainly did; as the coffin was brought down the steps and put into the hearse they played *Westlawn*, a dirge. It was the saddest, most beautiful thing I think I have ever heard. The tenor sax solo passage, the tone and vibrato of the trumpets and trombones sent shivers down my spine and almost tears to my eyes. Sonny Henry said he cries sometimes when they are playing them tunes. I think it's true that they only play with that depth and beauty of tone on them occasions. They played another slow one which hasn't a name, it's just called number three tan (tune P) or something.

They quickened up the pace again after this and played another number to the cemetery gates, and filed into the graveyard. As the coffin was being put in the grave they played a sweet, sad *Closer Walk*, and then the preacher was giving the graveside sermon as we walked back to the roadway.

They quickly shake off the gloom of the occasion and swing back to happy-music. The trombones lay down some glorious tailgate and rip and punch like hell. The saxes fill the sound out between the brass and blend well. The horns are whacky and fine. Percy sounded as great as ever and played some wonderful stuff.

We got back tired but satisfied; you certainly hear a mess of music on a parade and I pray that the custom will never die.

Will sign-off for now, Bill, so all the best and a merry Xmas to one and all. Ken

EDMOND SOUCHON LETTER TO BILL COLYER

New Orleans
Dear Bill—and Betty too!
[*Excerpt*] The fact that we have received good write-ups (especially from you), is very pleasing to us—but I assure you that the music you are hearing was not meant to be commercial—we were simply playing the way we ourselves know to be the exact and correct way we did—35 or 40 years ago. The fact that anybody liked it, amazed us and made us happy, but we were not trying to sound like anyone else—we were simply having "old mans fun"—and—it was not one of those "let's get tight and play just like we used to!" We have recorded several times for the *Voice of America*, for the N.O. Jazz Festival, and lastly, a group of 4 of us for Bill Russell and John Steiner and Rudi Blesh.

KEN COLYER LETTER TO BILL COLYER 25 DECEMBER 1952

1407 Prytania Street, New Orleans
Dear Bill,
I got your letter telling about the flat and Preston. Great news about the flat, I hope everything works out OK. I will write out a note for Preston with proviso that no changes are made. I want nothing derogatory printed or aired, if this is done again I will make a printed declaration denying all quotes from me. I may be wrong but that's the way I want it. I would like a mention of Dick Allen put in if possible, also the Jazz Center, 706 Bourbon Street where he now works and lives (in the back room). They specialise in the stuff and can build up into something like the I.B.S.

Dick Allen also asked my advice on Orin Blackstone merging with Dave Carey and Albert McCarthy on Jazz D. I said go ahead

so I think they will do it. They just want to make sure they were merging with no bums and bludgeons. I didn't think so and said I thought it was a good idea.

I've been feeling pretty low this last few days, I have a bad cold and neuralgia in the right side of my jaw and can't seem to get rid of neither.

I will have to write or contact immigration tomorrow to see about extending my time.

McNeal Breaux has left Octave and James Davis is on bass. The band were fine Tuesday night; Happy Goldstein was drumming great and using cymbals like I've never heard before. Alvin was still playing that pretty, rich-toned horn and Bill M. popping that tram in fine form.

Monday night George Lewis was at the Mardi Gras instead of Tuesday because of Xmas, and Kid Howard was here instead of Percy, playing fine bubbling, boisterous horn. The man's a fine singer too.

———————

I, Kenneth Colyer, authorise Dennis Preston to use parts of my letters/material for B.B.C. programme purposes and further authorise any monies due to be paid to and signed for on my behalf by W.J.Colyer

Ken Colyer, New Orleans, December 25th.

KEN COLYER Before I had left the ship, first I had seen Captain Black at the seamen's club to see if I could get any advice off him. He knew the ship well and didn't like it. He said it had been nothing but trouble since sailing from Mobile. He was sympathetic but personally could do nothing as it was outside his jurisdiction. He advised me to go along and see the immigration officer. He gave me his home address and I went there. "As far as I'm concerned, I have given you twenty-nine days clearance, so just look out for number one." This clinched it for me and I had left.

The time limit expired on Christmas Day, which meant the office wouldn't be open until the following Monday. We were working on the Monday but finished at five p.m. because it was coming on to rain.

We had been repairing an old roof just off Rampton Street.

Nick said he would go along with me, so still black and grimy from our labours, we walked down Gravier Street on to St. Charles Avenue and into the offices.

We were shown into an office and told "Mr. Peterson will see you in a minute." We sat down to wait and I rolled a smoke. A man at a desk was attending to someone and seemed to be keeping an eye on me all the time.

Through an open door I could see a fellow in a wire mesh pen. He kept giving me signs gesticulating with his hands and patting his behind. I thought he was some kind of nut and ignored him. I was to find out later that he was frantically trying to warn me to get the hell out of there. He was a Canadian and had just been picked up.

Finally this Mr. Peterson saw me. I explained my situation

Xmas in New Orleans

and asked for further time in order to find a ship sailing out of New Orleans. He went away for a while.

When he came back he said "I'm afraid I'm going to have to arrest you under the new act." I was thunderstruck. He allowed me a moment with Nick, who was looking scared.

I asked him to look after my gear until I knew what was going on and said that I would get in touch with him. Also to explain to the boss what had happened and to pick up a few bucks that was due to me.

Then I went into an office with Peterson. He gave me a cigarette and we chatted for a while. He said the McCarran-Walters act was now in force, but was so complex they couldn't unravel it and were following it as best they knew how. It was causing them a lot of headaches.

They had kept Federal detainees in situations such as mine in an old hotel until recently. You lived there under a sort of house arrest, and it was pretty free and easy. But the authorities had decided to discontinue this practice and pay the sheriff to keep us in the Parish Prison.

Eventually a plain clothes Federal man came for me and we went to his car. These people were friendly and civilised, but it was to be a different matter with the local law.

A & H TEM 7577

Friday 16

WILLIAM CRANE HALL
KEPA RD
ORAKEI
AUTO PURNELL
V13239
N. ROCHER BLVD

Saturday 17

Nottingham

KID SHEIK
G. COLLAR
939 DESLON DE ST
BY2098

LONNIE D. LAR 2687

Wednesday 3

K.C. ...
Ja ja ja
Kind County Bucket
...
Winn Boy
...
JIMMY B.
PER 2518 SPRINGBRIDGE
ROAD
PHOENIX CLUB FAME ROAD

Thursday 4

JOHN WISE
RIV 5407 (BOB)
GLA 7204

Tuesday 9

Glasgow Broadcast
Up jumped the Devil
Creole Song
Harlem Feelings
Cush Bob?
Ja ja ja
NAM JONES TEM 2463

Wednesday 10

INK River ...
BBY SHORTO
R'N GNOSY LAMP
RAY ...
YT SCARE ME RIGHT YOU
RATTLING SNAKE
or on the Fence
NIGHT FUNCTION

4th in Advent Sunday 23

LIVERPOOL
VAGABOND
2609 ONZAGA
FR9846
SAN JACINTO
1422 DUMAINE

Monday 24

Friday 21

ALL OF ME
F | F | A | A | D | D |
E♭ | Gmi. | A | A | Dmi. | Dm. |
G | G | Gmi. B♭ | C | F | F |
A | A | D | D | E♭ | Gmi. | Gmi. |
Dmi. | F | D **Saturday 22** D2C | F | F |
MANCHESTER

2400 CANAL ST INSURANCE ADA Souchon

INTERNATIONAL HOUSE GRAVIER ST.

Quinquagesima Sunday 4

Dr. ED. SOUCHON
3136 OCTAVIA
UNIVERSITY 3700 (HOME)
RAYMOND 4460
FRANKLIN 4144 (ALIBE)
G. LEWIS { 2873-4
{ ...
AVERY HOWE 1112 ST. PHILIPE
RAYMOND 6577

Shrove Tuesday Tuesday 6

SID DAVILLA
MARDI GRAS LOUNGE
HYP GUINLE
FAMOUS DOOR
PADDOCK (RICOU)
PEREZ (AIRLINE HIGHWAY)
CELESTIN (BOURBON ST P)

Monday 5

MARRERO 907 BURGUNDY
MAGNOLIA 0661
ROBINSON 1720½ M.DROSAT
BYWATER 8815
PURNELL 1524 DUMAINE
TULANE 9053

Ash Wednesday Wednesday 7

TONY ALMERIO
PARISIAN ROOM
(SUNDAY AFTERNOON)
BONANO L'ENFANTS
BRUNIES WA5602
2808 GREEN ST
UN 1913

KEN COLYER LETTER TO BILL COLYER
30 DECEMBER 1952

531 Broad Street, Parish Prison, New Orleans

Will commence to keep the record straight and recount what will probably be my last musical experience in the Crescent City. I sat-in once again on Saturday night with George Lewis and the music was as great as ever.

Sunday there was a parade with two bands. The societies were "The Daughters of the Universal Grand Charter" and the "United Most Worshipful St. Johns' Grand Lodge." The Tuxedo band and the Eureka Brass Band were the bands. Andy Anderson and Vernon Gilbert were on trumpets with Kid Howard in the Tuxedo. Percy Humphrey had Kid Sheik and Willie Pajeaud in the Eureka. I think Percy is the best parade horn I've heard. He has a high swinging tone and plays a fine, clear lead.

The parade was in great style and the lodge members were out in force wearing their colourful lodge regalia; the Daughters wearing a light grey uniform complete with grey stockings and grey fezes. I noticed the youthful participation of the oldest women; they all really enjoy these occasions, and there's nothing half-hearted about it. The St John's men wore black suits with red aprons and colourful trappings. Their head man was done up like an admiral, similar to the man in *Jazzways*.

Though it had been miserable and damp Friday and Saturday, the Sunday morning was bright with sunshine, and the air was clear and crisp. The parade was due to start at twelve-thirty not far from our apartment in Prytania, so I walked over. The musicians and lodge members were turning up when I arrived. I was in good time so went to have a drink in a coloured bar with Kid Howard and Andy Anderson. They were finally ready to start and the bands tuned and warmed up on a couple of numbers and then got into line with the Eureka leading and the Tuxedo in the rear.

The parade must have been 100 yards or more long, as you could just hear one band when following the other, so they were each playing different tunes all the time. Only when the band stopped could you faintly hear the other one playing around the corner, in the rear or up the front. I would listen to one for a while and then the other to get a good earful of both. All the good old numbers were played and the Eureka do a fine job of *Lord, Lord, Lordy You Sure Been Good To Me*.

We finally arrived at the church, the First African Baptist Church. The bands played outside while the lodge members filed up the stone stairs and into the church. The musicians then had a rest before going into the church to play, so I went with Andy Anderson to have another drink. One always receives a firm handshake from these men and it's fine to be in their company. I met Kid Clayton (tpt) in the tavern but

Pages from Ken's diary from his time in New Orleans. He was frugal enough to use a diary from the previous year. He mostly used it for note taking: of phone numbers and set lists

didn't get a chance to talk to him.

I went into the church with Aaron Kahn, another follower of the parades, and we sat not far from where the bands assembled on the balcony at the rear. The church was a fine, big building and the acoustics were good. The Eureka first played *The Saints*. The three horn work left me in pleasant wonderment as they warmed up to the number. Their improvising produced some astonishing and beautiful effects.

The Tuxedo played *A Closer Walk With Thee*; John Casimir's clarinet work was really inspired and he seemed to be having a great time. Kid Avery really let rip and tore off some really earthy tram work on some choruses. Kid Howard and Vernon Gilbert and Andy Anderson kept the volume down during the church number, though they were really socking it out during the parade.

They were going to play again but there was to be a long service first, so I left, not realising that this was to be my last earful of living New Orleans music.

Monday, Nick and I quit work at 2 p.m. as it started raining, so I went to the immigration. At 5 p.m. I was residing at the present address. I was taken into custody as soon as I had made a sworn statement. It appears that I have broken the law by obtaining work here for a start. I will be kept here now until they find me a ship or deport me. Looks like my luck's run out.

It's OK in here though, naturally, boring; we don't work on anything.

I have left a lot undone but have achieved much, much more than them bums who might come down here and might just as well have gone to Southend or somewhere. If someone was down here who had a little time and capital, the scope is tremendous still. There is so much that hasn't been recorded and might never be. There are a few youngsters here, all white to my knowledge, who are learning the music, but there are no coloured musicians carrying on the tradition. New Orleans jazz is going to be in a funny old position in ten or more years time.

Ken

KEN COLYER We went to the Parish Prison and I was signed in. I had to empty my pockets but I didn't have much on me. Anything metal and such was put into an envelope. My comb, handkerchief and what few cents I had on me were returned. I was taken to the cells.

I was a nuisance and had disrupted their routine. The men were in their cells and the evening meal long gone. The Captain—all the officers are called Captain—opened the electrically operated gate and I went into the day-pen. They brought me a meal from the kitchen. The food was atrocious. I pecked at it and was then put into a cell with three other fellows. There were two bunks either side and a bare lavatory bowl by the gate with a light shining on it, and a wash basin. There was very little room for anything else.

I chatted with the other inmates for a while then turned in. The bunk just had a mattress, a pillow and a rough blanket. The place was clean enough. And that's about all.

I slept well enough with thoughts in a turmoil until rudely awakened at five thirty. We had a hurried wash and were herded into the day pen. We were to spend from six to six in the day pen, then from six pm to six am in our cells every day. There is always a certain camaraderie amongst prisoners. I was found a plastic spoon to eat with. There were no metal objects allowed at all, and no eating irons issued, so the spoons were kept as prisoners left and given to the next inmate. I was to find out later that there had been a vicious crackdown, as a murder had been committed in the wing I was in.

Life suddenly didn't look so rosy. I wonder what Little Lord Fauntleroy would have done?

There was no reading material and only a couple of decks of cards. There was always two card schools going. I have never found playing cards very interesting. I managed to get cleaned up a little. There was a shower in the day pen but no soap and no towels. A commissary came round twice a day. He sold cigarettes, some odd candies, soap etc., if you had any money. A penniless inmate was in a dire situation.

The food was uneatable. The only decent thing I ever ate in there was the individual packet of Kellogg's Cornflakes we got for breakfast once or twice a week. The milk wasn't milk but some powdered rubbish, and the coffee wasn't coffee, but some horrible concoction that must have been floor sweepings. Men finally ate because there was nothing else. You could feel the energy draining from your body as the weeks went by. Some men tried to keep up any sort of physical exercises. Some just walked back and forth like caged lions all day long, others played cards. The day pen, being all steel, was like an echo chamber, and the noise would get intolerable. But the heat of the day would be exhausting and things would quieten down.

I was to meet some of the most interesting men I have met. Villains, but some with sterling qualities, and seamen in the same plight as myself.

Federal detainees were supposed to be kept separate from the prisoners, either serving short terms or awaiting trial, but once inside, the sheriff did as he pleased. Anything you might read about corruption in the penal system is perfectly true. Exposure only creates a momentary stir, then it goes on as usual.

I was sitting pondering after a couple of days. I had written a couple of brief letters, one to John and Ursula to explain what had happened, as they were bound to wonder about my sudden disappearance from the scene.

A tough raw-boned man sat beside me and we chatted. "You got any friends on the outside?" "Yes, quite a few."

"Now let me put you wise, so's you can start getting used to the idea. Once you are in prison you've got no friends."

I started to remonstrate. "Forget it kid, and remember what I said."

John soon came to see me. It's impossible to hold a conversation with a visitor, as you have to shout through a little grille and look through a thick pane of glass. Everybody can hear what you have to say. It is only with special privilege that you are allowed into a room with a lawyer or similar person. Surreptitious notes are shown through the window, although this isn't allowed. John left me a couple of bucks. The Captain loudly explained this to everybody as he handed it to me. It is important to some, to know who has money on them.

These Captains are mostly loudmouthed ignorant oafs. They have a little power and glory in it. Whoever the sheriff is hands out the jobs to his friends and those who grease his palm.

There was an exercise yard between the wings. We were supposed to have a period of exercise, also newspapers, but these had all been stopped since the murder.

The wing opposite was for coloured inmates. It was at least good to hear their voices and their singing, sometimes at dead of night. The best singer would start up a song and maybe a hundred voices would chant the chorus, all in perfect harmony. Sometimes during the day something stompy would start, they would get it going until the whole place would be rocking and it would he joyous. Even hardened men would stop and listen. "Them goddam niggers sure can sing." But at night it was always the wailing blues and "You'll be a long time dead."

Once a Mormon choir came to entertain us. They stood in the yard so that both wings could hear. They were quite good and we gave them a big hand of appreciation. But the men laughed their heads off when they had gone. "Jeez, fucking useless. They should a stuck around and heard our boys."

Ralston Crawford came into town. He was mortified at my predicament and ashamed at the system.

Fred Hatfield said, "We should be treating you with honour, and we throw you in jail." But people really do go in fear of the law and you can understand why.

Lizzie, bless her soul, came to see me, dressed in her black finery with a heavy black lace veil over the face. She left me a

Ken with Johnny Wiggs, composer of 'Postman's Lament'

dollar and some music, which I wasn't allowed to have. She was nervous and told me afterwards that it wasn't done for a black Negress to visit a white inmate. The Head Captain happened to see her leaving. "What are you doing in this wing?"

Lizzie gave him a dressing-down and finished with, "And you mind your manners mister. I'm Spanish." She laughed, but said she was shaking with fright at the time and was glad to get out of there. Dick Allen came to see me and did try hard to get something done, but it's tough trying to buck the system.

The raw-boned fellow came up to me shaking his head with wonderment. "You really do have friends, but how?" I tried to explain about the music. It was slightly beyond his comprehension. He didn't know anything about New Orleans music. "I've never seen anything like it in my life, and I've spent a lot of time in jail."

EDMOND SOUCHON LETTER TO KEN COLYER
30 DECEMBER 1953

New Orleans
Dear Ken,

Received your note and was sorry to hear of your whereabouts! However, I do hope that it won't be for too long, and that something could be done to keep you here for a long enough while so that you could learn the thing you came after. You are so close to it now that in a short while you'd be the most authentic thing on that stand besides "Slow Drag!"

I had a call from John Bernard, Ursula and Dick Allen after they had visited you, and they were concerned with the contacts, the food and the fact that you were suffering with a neuralgia (untreated). I wish there was something I could do to help you—I have never had experience with immigration authorities and am at a total loss to know in which direction to turn nor who to go to.

I do not intend to write your brother until things are set one way or the other—I mean, that either you are "sprung" and can can stay here, or they chase you back to England. In any event, getting home won't be so bad—especially when you have drunk so deeply from the fount! But let me tell you one thing! You have drunk enough Mississippi water to *make* you come back. You'll not be able to help yourself from doing it.

I would be happy indeed to get a story from you about your musical life and your experiences in N.O. I have one picture of you and would appreciate your sending more—likewise your records. You have already become very definitely identified with New Orleans music and are a great musician.

Do let me know the score as the game progresses—and I will write your brother accordingly.

Cordially, Edmond S.

KEN COLYER LETTER TO BILL COLYER
31 DECEMBER 1952

531 Broad Street, Parish Prison, New Orleans

Dear Bill,

Will have to condense this. Am being deported in two or three weeks time, kept in custody until then. Write me but don't send any clippings etc. Don't tell Mum if you think she will worry. Am keeping fine, nothing to worry about. Read *MM* clipping on Luthjens, very good. Use T.D. stuff as you will. Write to Bernards asking for any photos. John B. 543 Gov. Nichols St, N.O. Am hoping to see Dick Aleen, am trying to contact Doc Souchon. Will arrange for mail, records etc. to be cared for.

I thought I wouldn't have enough space on one page but looks like I will so I'll relax a little. It was good to get the mail, two from you, one from Max J (card), one from Mum. I have written a report on a parade (see letter of 30 December) I went to Sunday but can't post it yet as I need my lolly for tobacco etc. I was interested in what you say about the jazz scene. I agree with White Hart hall but I must try and reach professional status again. **Music is all I have in life and all I want to do is play that stuff. You could start looking for a job for me though, as I will probably land broke.**

I am working on the book project now. Am writing a condensed life story, was going to send it to Souchon for *Second Line* Magazine, but may keep it or work more on it.

The Bernards have some good photos of me and the parades but it's been hopeless trying to get them and stay diplomatic so if you could write a nice letter it might move them. I am writing them tomorrow, also I am willing to tackle any article writing or literary stuff when I get home. To hell with them all, I'm getting in on the act when I get home. If you write me immediately you get this, I should get the letter OK.

I will be sent to Ellis Island eventually I think and be sent home from there. Don't worry Brud, everything's OK and I should be home within the next two months. If you see Lyttelton you can tell him there's some good boppers down here; they never go off the chords or mumbo-jumbo. Don't ever try to enlighten them bums, it's not worth it and I didn't come here for the likes of them M.P's benefit.

All the best Bill,
Be seeing you, love to everyone, Ken

KEN COLYER LETTER TO BILL COLYER
2 JANUARY 1953

531 Broad Street, Parish Prison, New Orleans
Dear Bill,

I want you to note this carefully. If Lord and Lady Donegall could arrange my passage back through Ropners on the *Deerspool* or the *Daleby* as a passenger or a working member of the crew, this could be done.

The immigration would allow me to do this. Otherwise my stay in here is indefinite. If they can do this, tell them to contact the Immigration Officer at Masonic Temple Building, 333 St Charles St., N.O., LA.

I guess you'll have to work on them, but it's worth a try. I am on a $500 bond but would not impose upon Souchon to bail me out and I am not allowed to work, so that would mean more borrowing and I don't want to impose on anybody's friendship.

I have written to Dick A., the Bernards and Doc but it's too soon to see or hear from anybody. Maybe I'll see Dick on Sunday, which is visiting day. I'll have to get Dick to pick that manuscript up and send it to you. I have told him about the records.

The parade last Sunday was fine. The Eureka and Tuxedo playing that usual, wonderful marching music. The section of town and the weather were good for parading. The bands played in the church (First African Baptist) and sounded out of this world. I have a fuller report written on this.

We've just got to build a marching band when I get home, that's the music man.

Tell Mum I got her letter OK and hope everybody is still doing fine. I have not heard from Bob; don't he want to know me?

I hope the flat project is working out OK. Don't forget the Donegall biz, this may be a break.

So long for now and all the best to everybody, Ken

KEN COLYER LETTER TO BILL COLYER
11 JANUARY 1953

531 Broad Street, Parish Prison, New Orleans
Dear Bill,
John and Ursula and Elizabeth came to see me this morning. John told me that he put my bond up through a lawyer but it was refused as they said I would be shipped out by next week. Now this has been done to other fellows here and they've still been here weeks later, so I'll just have to wait and see if I do go.

I received your first letter and am awaiting a second. In case you have done anything about my passage, I will try and wire you if I go to Ellis Island anytime in the near future. What I want to tell now is that I've learnt a lot since I've been here about "The Greatest Country in the World" and in particular Louisiana, and I could cook up a good story if you can get anybody interested (Odhams Press?).

The way I feel now I would just love to blow the lid off this rat-trap when I get home, and a good article in a daily paper would probably do it. Don't ever mention anything in letters, as all mail in and outgoing is censored and I've already been tipped-off by a trusty that if there is ever a shakedown and I'm caught with any written reports on me about this place, I'll be taken up to No. 5 and worked over. Pleasant, isn't it? And it just shows you that they're scared of anybody knowing what's going on in here.

There is a little humour though with a couple of characters. This letter is being taken out for me by a friend. If you can sell a news item of my being down here, do so, but tell Mum I'm doing fine. The B.s are sending you some wonderful photos of parades; will be very good for publishing. I'll just say again, don't mention anything in letters, as what I tell you is the truth.

All the best Bill.

Hope to see you soon, Ken

BRITISH EMBASSY, WASHINGTON, LETTER TO
BILL COLYER, 12 JANUARY 1953

Dear Sir,
I have to acknowledge receipt of your letter dated 7th January about your brother, Kenneth Bolyer [!], and to inform you that I have forwarded it to Her Majesty's Consul-General at New Orleans for his attention. He will communicate with you direct on this matter.

On the face of it it would seem that your brother has contravened the immigration regulations and is now subject to deportation proceedings. These regulations allow a seaman 29 days ashore in order to find a berth on another ship but he is not allowed to seek employment ashore. If he does, or exceeds the period of 29 days allowed ashore, he becomes liable for deportation.

Yours faithfully, (signed) D.W.T. Smithies
H.B.M. Consul
Mr. W.J.Colyer, 52 Charing Cross Road, London, W.C.2.

RALSTON CRAWFORD LETTER TO KEN COLYER
14 JANUARY 1953

60 Gramercy Park North, New York 10, NY
Dear Ken,
Thanks ever so much for your good letter. I am sorry that you have had what seems to be a very bad piece of luck. I don't know whether you will be out of there by the time this arrives, or not.

Of course I hope you will be away from your immediate residence, and whether they forward mail or not, I don't know.

There is a chance that I may be in New Orleans within the next ten days. Of course I shall try to find you. Do you need legal representation? Is your point of view being taken care of in a satisfactory way? If you tell me about these things, and if there is anything I can do, I will certainly try to do it.

If you get up this way before I get down there, or afterwards, communicate in whatever way is allowed you, and if you can't get over here to Manhattan, we'll come over to Ellis Island.

Yes, I am sorry you are in such a spot, but as you say, the experience has had its solid and constructive qualities. I know exactly what you mean by that. Here's luck to you, and write again to tell us how things are going.

Sincerely yours, (signed) Ralston

KEN COLYER LETTER TO BILL COLYER
16 JANUARY 1953

Parish Prison, 531 Broad Street, New Orleans
Dear Bill,
I received some forwarded mail Wednesday, three letters from you with the *MM* and *NME* clippings, one from Mum, one from Val, one from Bob Wallis, a horn man from Yorkshire, and

one from Bill Reid of the Eagle, Pinner. I should try and get Max Jones to check tune titles and names more accurately, or is it the printers?

I thought I was on my way Weds, but they changed their minds and I'm still here. The Immigration claim that the shipping company must pay my fare. Why they've only just found this out I don't know, and I think they are wrong anyway. When John B. put my bond up a week ago, they refused to let me out as I would be going this Weds. It seems the tape is just about as red here as it is at home.

John B. has sent the photos, so let's hope you get them soon. I asked him to put in an explanatory note with them. They're a pretty good selection and you should be able to use them all. The March OT [*March of Time*] film was for TV but I should imagine they use the same stuff for the overseas serial.

We'll have to talk over what to do when I get home, but tell Monty he's my man whatever the set-up. I was thinking of building a unit without 88 [piano] on the A.M. [American Music] Climax styling, also the parade band. I was also thinking of opening up again down the Studio Club. You could chat to Costas on this possibility.

I also have a business angle to work on that may save me having to slog my guts out for a living and give me a little independence.

Let me know when you get your new place. I shouldn't send any more stamp coupons as I can't use them in here. I have enough money to get a smoke and stamps with. Did you get the other letter OK?

Will close for now.

All the best, Ken

N.O. CONSUL-GENERAL LETTER TO BILL COLYER 17 JANUARY 1953

A.D. Francis, H.M. Consul-General, British Consulate-General, 1022 NATIONAL BANK OF COMMERCE BUILDING, New Orleans 12, LA.

Dear Sir,

I have your letter regarding your brother, Kenneth E. Colyer, and I am aware of the circumstances of his case. It is true that your brother left the *Empire Patrai* and in due course was picked up by the Immigration Authorities. He testified to them that he left the ship with the intention of proceeding to New Orleans to study jazz music and to seek employment while in the United States in order to maintain himself. Unfortunately this was contrary to the United States Immigration laws so he was sentenced to be deported.

Your brother was visited by a member of the staff of this consulate a few days ago and I have been in touch with the Immigration Authorities who will arrange for him to be sent home as soon as possible. I understand that this may be in the next week or ten days. Your brother stated that he was suffering from neuralgia possibly caused by dental trouble and at his

request arrangements were made with the Chief Warden of the prison for him to see a doctor and subsequently a dentist.

Yours very truly, (signed)

KEN COLYER LETTER TO BILL COLYER 25 JANUARY 1953

Dear Bill,

Received a letter from you today. John and Ursula were here and I read your letter to them also. You say you haven't heard from me since Jan 2nd. I have written at least two letters since then so I don't know what goes on.

The Immigration refused my bail two weeks ago on the grounds that I would be gone in a couple of days, but that midnight special ain't been round yet.

So long for now, Ken

N.O. CONSUL-GENERAL LETTER TO BILL COLYER 26 JANUARY 1953

British Consulate-General, 1022 NATIONAL BANK OF COMMERCE BUILDING, New Orleans 12, LA.

Dear Sir,

Upon receipt of your letter of the 21st January I rang up the Immigration Authorities to find out how the deportation of your brother, Ken Colyer, was proceeding. The people here had everything fixed for him to leave on the 14th January but received instructions at the last moment from their superiors that this was a case in which the transportation with the shipping company that brought him into this country. This has held up matters, as the Immigration Authorities have had to correspond with Mobile and it will probably be necessary to send him on a ship from New Orleans or Mobile. I am sorry this delay has occurred but there is not very much more one can do except to keep the case well before the local authorities by reminding them every few days. I will take care to do this.

Yours very truly,

(signed) A.D. Francis, H.M. Consul-General.

KEN COLYER LETTER TO BILL COLYER 29 JANUARY 1953

Parish Prison, New Orleans.

Dear Bill,

I saw John Bernard yesterday and things don't look good for a quick passage from here. All he knows is that the immigration wrote a letter to Mobile and have received no reply. I told John to tell them or the consul to get in touch with Fenton Steamship Company of London; their office is about a minute from Leadenhall Street, Aldgate end, but I can't remember the address, maybe Mum would have it. I was wondering if you could phone them under some pretext and see if they have been contacted. The phone number is AVE 2763.

Now, this joint is really bum, the food and treatment is bad, us IM men are treated just the same as criminal prisoners; though we are only supposed to be detainees, we might as well be doing time. The old graft and corruption is rife; you are OK as long as you've got plenty of money, otherwise it's just too bad. Now, would you write a letter of complaint to the U. S. Attorney General, Washington D.C. to the effect that though everybody (consul, immigration) says they are doing their best to secure me a quick deportation, they are doing literally nothing! I have been here 31 days today. My bond was refused over three weeks ago on the grounds that I would be gone in two or three days and here I am with no knowledge of when I'll get out of here.

After a month of requests I am finally getting some effective treatment for my neuralgia, but I've been going through bloody hell with it up to now. If you start worrying them from your end maybe we'll get some action, otherwise I can see me having a long stay in here under this "Military Dictatorship."

You may get a small package from Cuba for me some time at the shop, also will you mail the letter back for a friend of mine.

Dick Allen let me down through not intercepting the MSS and maybe the records at Bourbon; you see, my roommate moved and has never been to see me; but John B. is trying to track him, so I'm hoping it will turn out OK.

All the best for now, will write if anything develops, will try and wire if I leave without notice.

January 30

Just a few more lines as I've bought a new pad and I can't get this smuggled out till tomorrow anyway.

The vice-consul came to see me today and said they had had a letter from you. It was probably the one you sent to Washington so it does shake them up a little to get letters from outside. I didn't get much satisfaction out of him though, the same old smooth talk that seems to go for nothing, but if you keep worrying them it will stop them from forgetting me and should finally move them; to hell with being here three or four months. I gave the consul the works again—the bad food and conditions, and it was a different guy this time, so I hope he tries to do something.

I had another letter from Lizzie Miles today. Wait till you read the first one, it's really great.

I keep the normal letters short, as the paper and envelopes are so damn heavy I'm scared they'll be overweight and get sent back.

Also I can't write what I want to say as things are so rigid here and these lawmen down South here are mean bastards.

I think you might as well tell Mum where I am, then I can write her, so let me know if you do. I may also get charged when I get home, but I'm not worried about that as I have a good case against them, the way the ship was being run.

Will sign off once again.

All the best, Ken

UNDATED LETTER FROM KEN COLYER TO BILL COLYER FROM THE PARISH PRISON

Dear Bill,

Guess there's nothing much new to relate, I have been waiting for a third letter from you for the last half of this week but haven't received one. I had a letter from Bob saying you had moved into your new place, that Val had moved in with you and the joint was pretty fine. He didn't send the address though.

John Bernard told me Wednesday that the immigration were waiting on three letters from England before they can ship me out, so I have no idea when I will be leaving.

I had a letter from Lizzie Miles yesterday, one fine person. I expect John B. will be here to see me tomorrow. Ralston Crawford is due down here soon, by the way. I had a letter from him early this week saying he'd be here in about ten days time; looks like I'll be here too. Remember Jackson T's "I'd rather drink muddy water?"

There's another Englishman in town named Lane, from Kent. Do you know him?

Could you contact Art Saunders and Costas in view of future plans as I'm thinking of concentrating on a few local places and try and build up a week's steady work in the district. **Tell Monty to keep plugging and I'm just itching to get back with him and we'll "Get it Right" this time and no mistakes.** An odd point of interest, Wooden Joe plays with a perfect no-pressure system.

I haven't seen or heard from Dick A. for over a week. You probably won't hear from Fred K. as he has left the J. C.

Guess there's no more to write about at the moment so I'll sign off hoping to hear from you soon.

All the best, Ken

BILL COLYER LETTER TO KEN COLYER 2 FEBRUARY 1953

78B South Ealing Road, London W5

Dear Ken,

Thanks for your last letter. I'm sorry about the delay since my last letter, but I've been up to my neck in things. I was hoping you were on your way by now. Hard man, it's really hard. Now here's the real gen but don't get too worked up if the days drag out. I got to tell you this.

The Cranes have broken up completely through not being able to get competent replacements, and now Monty (this is only known to me and the blokes concerned) and Chris Barber are going to Denmark, approx. March 31st or a day or two later. Also with them will be Ron Bowden, Jim Bray on bass and Lonnie Donegan, (no piano) all of them double other instruments. They will be doing three weeks or so there, then maybe work back through Holland and France. They need a horn player and are sweating blood hoping it's going to be you. Final aim is to arrive back in England a hot unit and move into their own club; this to be worked out by me in their absence.

I might as well tell you—since the first week you've been in, I've been bombarding the Ambassador in Washington and the Consul in New Orleans with letters asking for results. The New Orleans Consul has been very cooperative, but regrets he can only keep prodding the powers that be. He told me about your neuralgia and teeth.

Your newsletter goes out on the BBC on Saturday; I'm arranging to have it taken down on acetate. I'm at Dennis Preston's tomorrow night to work out the final programme. Max Jones has arranged a small pictorial feature as a tie-up. I'll post copies to John and Dick. I've not had any answers from Fred or Dick. I managed a very good write-up of Kohlman and Sid Davilla in *Jazz Journal*; I'll post them copies at the weekend. Have now received all mail from you so don't worry. I've just got the first money from the *Melody Maker* (4 guineas); I was down to my uppers.

England has been smashed by the greatest gales for centuries; wind reached 125 mph. Known dead 300, missing nearly 600 or 750. Gale worked its way right round from West to East Coast. Canvey Island washed out, Yarmouth, Kings Lynn, Southend, Clacton, Jaywick, all smashed and flooded and many others. Scarborough has no power, light, water, food; is virtually under siege. No communications; God, the old British Isles really got hit. While that was all happening we moved in here.

It's a new, modern block next to South Ealing station on the Piccadilly line. Self-contained, never been lived in before. Two bedrooms, living room, kitchen, bathroom, loads of cupboards, new furnishing, big windows. Manny, it's great and we can't wait for you to see it.

I wrote to Edmond; as yet no reply. It was nice of John to send so many great photos. I got an odd buck in the shop and sent it on to him. Wondered if you would have got it if I had sent it to you; guessed not. Having undergone censorship for five years in the army I strongly object to it now.

I've had a lot of work to keep up with these last weeks and it's

kind of late, so I'll close up for now Ken. I hope it's not going to be long now. I still haven't told anyone, but it's getting difficult.

Love from all, your old Brud, Bill

BRITISH JAZZMAN HELD IN NEW ORLEANS GAOL FOR 38 DAYS
Melody Maker

Ken Colyer, the British Jazzman who made a story-book journey to the Crescent City, has just been released from a New Orleans Gaol. He was held for 38 days for over-staying his visitor's permit.

Colyer, who played cornet with the Crane River Band, became a seaman to get to the birthplace of jazz. Within a number of days he was sitting-in with his jazz idol—George Lewis—at Manny's Tavern. His newsletters created great interest with *MM* readers, and eventually reached half a million listeners through *World of Jazz*. Then, suddenly, they ceased. Ken was in gaol. A bribe in the right quarter succeeded in his being able to smuggle out a letter that gave his story to the outside world.

"My permit expired at Christmas he wrote," and therefore I didn't get to the immigration officer until the Monday (29th) to ask for an extension. By five p.m., thanks to an over-zealous official, I was in the Parish Prison on Broad Street.

'Worked Over'

"Don't ever mention anything about this (letter) in your letters to me, as all letters are censored. I've already been tipped off by a 'trusty' that if ever there is a 'shakedown' and I'm caught with any written reports on me about this place, I'll be taken up to No.5 and worked over. They are really scared about anybody knowing what goes on in here." Bill Colyer, Ken's brother takes up the story: "A $500 bond was set on Ken he tells the *MM*, "but when this sum was raised by John and Ursula Barnard and Dick Allen of the New Orleans Jazz Club, the authorities refused to accept it.

John Bernard offered the money three times, but was told that Ken could not be released as he was being sent to New York for deportation.

While John chased up all the appropriate departments in New Orleans, I bombarded the Embassy in Washington and the Consul-General in New Orleans from this end.

Although Ken was technically an Immigration Detainee, he was treated at all times as a criminal. Finally, I heard from John Bernard—who had been to see Ken each visiting day (twice a week)—that the Immigration Department was thawing out a little and might allow the bail.

"Then, early last week, came the news from Ken: 'Well, at last I'm sprung from the place, thanks to John and Ursula. I'm on bail and staying with the Bernard's, waiting for a ship to bring me back.'"

Many of the New Orleans jazz lovers are indignant about the treatment given Colyer, Doctor Souchon, president of the jazz club there, wrote to Bill Colyer.

"Needless to say how distressed we have all been about Ken's coming afoul of some stupid clerk. For what has been done to him, I am greatly depressed, and apologise for those who are concerned."

Wanted To Stay

A local newspaper, *THE NEW ORLEANS ITEM*, ran a photo of Ken with the headline: "British seaman held 38 days—Why?" And the answer they gave was "New Orleans Jazz."

"Was there any other reason for not releasing Colyer on bail?" asked the *ITEM*. In reply they quoted Edward Ahrens, Immigration Officer in charge, who said:

"Yes. He (Colyer) told us that he would like to stay in New Orleans to study jazz; he wanted an extension. He practically admitted that the only reason he came here was to study New Orleans jazz. We were afraid he'd try to stay illegally."

Ken is expected back in Britain in two or three weeks.

Another of his "New Orleans Newsletters" will appear in next week's *MELODY MAKER*.

DICK ALLEN Ursula Bernard was important in many ways. Ursula encouraged Ken to sit-in with George. Ken was immediately and enthusiastically accepted by the musicians. When he got out of Parish Prison, he lived with the Bernards.

KEN COLYER LETTER TO BILL COLYER 5 FEBRUARY 1953

534 Gov. Nichols Street, New Orleans
Well Gate,

I'm finally sprung from the "place" thanks to John and Ursula and, boy, does it feel good to be in civilisation once again.

It appears they are still balling about trying to get the company to pay my passage and, as they are sending another batch of eight men to Ellis Island tonight, they finally agreed to release me on bail. John came and got me at twelve o'clock today and I am staying with them until I leave.

I am seeing the Doc tomorrow and hope he can fix my neuralgia, the damn thing gets worse all the time, but let's hope I can finally get it beat. I phoned Doc and he says he has received the records. I've lost track of them you sent me but will try and find out where they have gone; also the manuscripts, that boy I was living and working with has really let me down. You see, he has moved from Prytania and the dog seems to have left a phoney address.

You can imagine that I'm delighted to get the 'reprieve' and

the chance to get one more glorious earful of the men.

Ralston came to see me on Sunday with Dick (besides the Bernards), he's not leaving till Sunday so I should see him again. Lizzie Miles also came to see me for a minute; there's one wonderful woman, people like that give you a renewed faith in humanity. She left me two of her records, autographed, some music, some of it good, and a buck. **Her first letter to me is something I will always cherish, she thought I was in real trouble then and really wrote a wonderful epistle. As she says, "The sun will always shine when the clouds do seem the darkest" and I reckon she's darned right.**

Well, let's hope there'll be some more reports before I leave, I still have the last one, I'll copy it out and send it on, but right now I want to throw this in the post and get it to ya.

One relieved Gate, Ken

PS. All the best to Monteh and them that's interested and love to Mum.

KEN COLYER LETTER TO BILL COLYER 7 FEBRUARY 1953

543 Governor Nicholls Street, New Orleans.
Dear Bill

The Bernards have just gone to the races so I figured that it was a chance to sit down and write at greater length, as I want to get that parade report copied down. It feels really great to be out and I am recuperating fast. I saw Doc Souchon yesterday and he gave me a shot of penicillin and some pills; he says that it is sinus trouble that's causing it, but since I've had a couple of decent nights' sleep it hasn't bothered me.

Poor old Doc was pretty burned up over the Donegalls. I don't know whether you know, but they calmly telegraphed him to say that they had booked Sharkey to do the job and "Thanks for all you've done." Now this is a lowdown dirty trick after Doc had practically arranged everything. Wiggs had received permission from the school board to go, Mangiapane had fixed things with the bank he works for, Mendelson was going to quit Sharkey and Harry Shields was going to quit the Dukes, so you see the mess it's left them in. I'm sure there's going to be no love for the Ds from now on in New Orleans, and there's enough wrong with the jazz world now without people making things worse.

The way Doc feels now, he's going to quit all his activities in the jazz game and get out of the picture. If you have any further news on this business I would like to have it. Doc gave me another fine copy of the Lewis band picture with me sitting-in. He told me that he sent you one and that you should have it by now.

I saw Ralston yesterday, also Dick and Fred Hatfield. I may be seeing a reporter on the *New Orleans Item*, as Fred knows one. Ralston was pretty disgusted with the set-up and agrees that something should be printed about it. I will be seeing him again tonight at a Lewis session that has been organised by John, Hughie Marone, who is part owner of Jazz Center, and some fans. George isn't at Manny's anymore, so this is the only way they can get to hear him now, except for the Tuesday Mardi Gras session. They have found a place where the management will pay half the cost of the band and they chip in the rest. If they can get 30 people to go and chip in a dollar each, this covers costs. John was surprised at the "peanuts" the band have to work for, but you will probably remember Ralston informing us of this.

I think Ralston will be taking some photos tonight. I'm getting a little practice in today, so I think my lip will be all right if I nurse it.

I have just contacted my old boss's wife and have got track of Nick, so there is hope of getting the manuscript yet. I phoned the Mardi Gras and it seems the records have not turned up, so there is hope for them too. Doc has received his though, with the acetates. Have you any other copies of *Bobby Shafto* and *High Society*? Doc is going to try and get that session organised and taped before I leave. Once it's made we can get a copy somehow or other later. It won't be with the "men" but, at least, it will be something.

I met another Englishman in the Prison, a Scouser and quite a character. I'll give you a brief outline of him, Peter Chatfield. Joined the army at 14 years of age. Had served in Korea and was sent to Japan for demob on completion of ten years army service. Deserted in Japan, joined a German ship as a stowaway and worked his way to Canada. Was working there as a lumberjack, saved a thousand dollars and decided to have a holiday in the States. Made his way to New Orleans through Los Angeles and was picked up here by the immigration.

Point of interest is that he met and heard Dink Johnson in Maxwell's Cocktail Lounge in Los Angeles. He thought Dink was shooting him a line about his musical career until I told him of Dink's career. It appears Dink is in and out of Lincoln Heights jail occasionally and bums and plays for drink around town when he is out.

One thing about the Parish Prison was the wonderful singing from the two tiers of coloured prisoners across the yard from us. I am wondering if Professor Lomax was ever there to record them. One number they were always singing was *You'll Be A Long Time Dead*.

Well, I think I will write down that last report now, just as I wrote it in the Parish Prison.

Well, it looks like you never know how things are going to turn out and this reprieve should give me a chance to achieve a little more. The Bernards have been wonderful and I am hopelessly indebted to them for all they have done.

The fellow, Lane (I must get his first name), will be there tonight. He is taking tram lessons from Sonny Henry while he is here, wise fellow.

Well, I think that's all for now Bill and I should have more news tomorrow.

So long for now, Ken
PS. I hear the weather has been terrible at home lately.

KEN COLYER LETTER TO BILL COLYER 9 FEBRUARY 1953

543 Governor Nicholls Street, New Orleans.
Dear Bill,

I figure you should have received my letter with the good news this morning and I'm hoping to hear from you this weekend. Any mail that goes to the Parish Prison, by the way, will now be returned, as the lousy bums don't forward it.

The session Saturday was really great and was a success all round. They are hoping to make a regular thing of it if the management are willing, as Percy has a band of his own when George leaves on his tours and John says they are pretty good, except for an electric guitar, so they could do the session until George and Co. return.

The place is called Trio's. It is smaller than Manny's Tavern and is more modern in fitting etc. The acoustical quality is sharp and clear, and the band is inclined to be just a little loud at times, though not enough to worry about. George can be heard better here than anywhere I've heard him, and that's a real treat.

They were playing *Tin Roof* as we got out of the car and, brother, did that music sound sweet to these old ears.

The place was pretty dark inside and you could hardly make out who was there, though I think just about all the George Lewis fans had turned up. The band looked terrific as you can imagine in this semi-darkness and were playing as great as I have ever heard them. You know that *Climax Rag* tempo when you begin to wonder just how much hotter the band can get before they take right off that stand, well that's the way just about every ding-dong stomp was going. Man! That band's a fresh revelation to me every time I hear them.

After a few numbers George spotted me and I went over to them. I had a big, warm feeling in my belly as I shook hands with them all; they were real pleased to see me out of the jug and Big Jim nearly shook my hand off.

My lip was pretty weak when I sat-in but I managed to hold out and more people were congratulating me at the end of the session than there's ever been, so it must have sounded OK.

Bill Huntingdon took the last part of the session under Lawrence's watchful eye. The boy's good and is well on the way to being Lawrence's equal, which proves what can be done.

Dick played his speciality *Tiger Rag* on Jim's trombone and got a big ovation.

The piano there is a good one, and Alton was tremendous and I have never heard him better; in fact the whole darn band were right on top form, Percy blowing fine and Jim having the time of his life and really getting the crowd going.

Ralston stayed for about an hour, but took no pictures, as his gear was packed ready for his return to New York early Sunday morning.

The fellow Lane was there, and he feels the right way about the band. He seems an intelligent bloke and I hope he makes something of them tram lessons from Sonny Henry. Sonny taught Jim, so if he's got anything in him that ought to produce it, don't you think?

Coming home, John calmly told me that George had said he wished he could take me to California with him. Jesus! You can imagine my emotional reaction to that; alas, I guess that sort of thing will always be a pleasant pipe-dream, but at least it's nice to know that it could be a reality. As it is, Kid Howard is going with him.

Yesterday afternoon I went with the Bernards to a Wax Wing meeting; these are the monthly record sessions that the New Orleans Jazz Club holds. It was at Doctor Strange's house. Nobody seems to know him but he's a very nice unassuming man, and it was an enjoyable afternoon. One of the founder members of the club gave a recital on Rod Cless and he had the advantage of actually having known the man, so he was interesting to a great degree.

Good old Doc was there also; his brother Harry and Peter Miller had brought a Decca LP copy of the Royal Festival Hall concert which has just been released here, and Johnny Wiggs and the Souchons congratulated me on the Cranes' number and thought it was very good.

Yesterday evening we visited the Purnells and man! what an evening. I could never put it all down so will have to save it till I get home. The main thing at the moment is that any time the money could be raised, a recording session of the Lewis band is a comparatively simple procedure.

Now, I was thinking of the set-up that Ken Lindsay had with Woody Guthrie and if he would be interested in a similar one down here in New Orleans. John Bernard would only be too pleased to record the session and fix everything at this end. The set-up is pretty good, as John has a tape recorder and also Alton and the band are only too pleased to record all they can, but it must be a regular Union date as they are pretty strict on recording.

It would take roughly $300. I don't know whether that could be raised by Ken, but I have also thought that maybe Melodisc or Vogue might be interested. The idea is certainly worth a try as I should think the records would sell well, especially with the fact that they would be specially made for release in England.

No matter when I leave, this could always be done through John, so let me or John know if there is any hope of pulling this off.

The Delaney session at Artesian Hall is being released sometime on Decca, and I think the Lewis numbers should be good from what John says. If you remember, I missed their set as I was working that Sunday; I expect the Kohlman band will get the most numbers as I think Delaney is plugging them, but there's a chance to hear Percy Humphrey, so it will be worth getting.

Well, I'll close for now Bill.

So adios, your old brud, Ken

KEN COLYER During an evening with Alton Purnell at his Dumaine Street home, we had discussed the possibility of recording the Lewis band. It seemed that there were no difficulties providing the Union were notified, and Union rates were paid. I tentatively suggested that I would like to record with the band but Alton said he didn't think this could be done as I didn't hold a Local card. Also, because he is a Union delegate, he couldn't very well participate in non-union activities.

> I felt a little frustrated, as I realised that there might not be another chance of playing with those supreme creators and having it recorded as an all-time memento of an ultimate achievement.

I mentioned the talk to Dick Allen who is an impressive authority when it comes to New Orleans music and is also a personal friend of most of the City's musicians. He sympathised with me but said we could still get a fine band together as he knew many good men who would be willing to record for us.

KEN COLYER LETTER TO BILL COLYER 11 FEBRUARY 1953

543 Governor Nicholls Street, New Orleans
Dear Bill,

[The start of this letter is missing, but Ken is talking about the evening at the Purnells mentioned in his previous letter.]

We arrived a little late. We should have been there at seven but it was nearer seven-thirty. We had left the Wax Wing meeting at six and it hadn't left us enough time to get back home, get something to eat and arrive on schedule.

Alton was waiting, Jim and Lawrence hadn't arrived, and he

was afraid that nobody was going to show up, so he was probably a little relieved to see us.

Alton is a little on the short side but well built, though not too heavy. He has a roundish pleasant face which quickly breaks into a wide smile when he animatedly laughs at something amusing. When he is playing though, he has a slight frown of concentration which wrinkles his forehead and which might be mistaken for annoyance, but which is the sign of a serious musician really working at his job.

Alton introduced us to his wife, a Creole woman with a quiet charm and beauty. She speaks softly in a voice that is fascinating in its quality, and her hands make poetic gestures as she talks. There is a suggestion of some quite peaceful dream world about her that held me fascinated when she was speaking.

Their home is well furnished and neat, with a feeling our own used to have.

Alton brought a bottle of Champagne in, that he had discovered that day and John opened it, being the only one knowing how. It had a pleasant, dry taste that I recognised as similar to various types of vino I had drunk in Italy and Buenos Aires.

Alton produced a tape recorder which he intends to use to record little-known artists and talent for his own benefit. He had one very fine number he had recorded of the band with his brother sitting-in on sax. This is the same Purnell that is on the Collins-Jones Hot Eight side. They were playing *Heebie Jeebies* and it was good, except that Alton's vocal hadn't been picked and he sings this one really well. His brother takes a fine solo and plays in the true New Orleans sax style.

Alton showed us his scrapbook and photo album which has some amusing and interesting photos of the band at Ward Kimball's place when last in California. There were photos of the celebrated Kimball locomotive and fire engine, also a great shot of George Lewis, wearing a top hat, astride one of them little rail buggies that are manually propelled along the tracks, with the rest of the band standing around wearing porters' caps. They certainly looked like they had some fine times in California.

Alton likes to talk and is a good conversationalist. He takes a serious interest in our present-day environment and has some sound views on the state of affairs.

The talk drifted to the Bunk band and its various adventures. I was beginning to realise that one cannot assess these men on a nodding acquaintance on a bandstand, as first impressions are sometimes accurate but often misleading.

It appears that when Bunk came back he was a hard man to get along with. He was conscious of his age and had a fixation about being young and staying young; as Alton says, he wanted to be eighteen years old all the time and was very aggressive about achieving this. It seems he didn't get along with the band because he didn't want to, and they couldn't please him whatever they did. He didn't like Baby Dodds because he couldn't dominate him

and order him around, whereas the others were a little afraid of him and would do their best to keep the peace.

An example Alton gave of Bunk's temperament sums him up fairly well. If he approached you and demanded you buy him a drink and you bought it and said nothing, he would like that, but if you offered to buy him one he would aggressively say, "I'm a man, I'm old enough to buy my own drinks" and walk away.

Alton told various anecdotes of Bunk's bad manners and eccentricities, but did add more than once that he was a great musician. It surprises me that the band produced such great music with this situation being prevalent through most of its career with Bunk.

He was not the great reader it is sometimes thought he was; he knew all them rags fluently from his days in the Eagle band, which specialised in rags.

Before the band played *I Can't Escape From You*, Bunk practised it for about two weeks before rehearsing it with the band. Alton heard him and learnt the band the tune, so that when Bunk finally came to a rehearsal, put the music in front of Alton and kicked the tune off, expecting the rest of the boys to make a complete mess of it, it instead went so well that he ended up liking it and included it in the repertoire. What he normally did was to throw the tune out on the grounds that he was the only one that knew it. He also liked all the limelight and didn't like the fact that Baby, George and Jim had many fans.

John had asked me to take my guitar along; I did but was rather dubious of playing to a jazzman of Alton's calibre. As it happened it turned out fine and Alton, his wife and John and Ursula liked it fine. Alton also revealed a secret ambition to be a guitarist; he said he knew all the chords from playing the piano and had taught several guitar players, but when Smilin' Joe tried to teach him guitar he just couldn't manipulate his fingers on them strings.

As the evening wore on, both he and his wife reminisced about the old days. Now, Alton is only forty-one but, as he says, he has a good memory, and with that and what older men have told he has a clear picture of early New Orleans; here is yet another man that says the true history of New Orleans has never been told. In what time and experiences I have had here I am beginning to realise that there is a lot of truth in this statement.

Well Bill, that is a rough outline of that evening. Don't use this till we can work on it some more as I have left some information out. I think this stuff would make a good article in a sort of reply to the *Changer* article and show another side of the Bunk angle. I don't want to run Bunk down or anything, and I still think his music is as great as I ever did, but I'm sure that what these men say is the truth and their side of the story should be heard.

After talking with John I think you should get the news printed of my imprisonment as soon as possible, as this is better than trying to suppress it, which I think serves no purpose and will only lead to unnecessary complications; so go to work Gate, and let some of them bums know that I have had to pay my price for my taste of millennium.

I will have to curtail my writing once again to just you, as the Bernards are not particularly well off and finances are slender. I have written to Mum, but would you explain this to her, also to Bob and Val as they are inclined to get the wrong impression that I am ignoring them.

Also, would you drop a line to Bob Wallis in Bridlington, East Yorkshire; he's a good kid and writes me great letters and signs off with "Always for our kind of jazz".

Last night I saw Lizzie and Lewis band with Howard at the Mardi Gras. Howard was playing better than I've ever heard him, though still not quite on form. Sid was telling me that at the time he was making the Climaxes, he was in the process of blowing himself to a standstill and he now has a lot of lip trouble and is having a tough time getting back into shape. Well, he certainly sounded well on the way last night and was executing some great stuff. Sid says he has had a couple of letters from you but hasn't yet had time to write, but I think he will soon.

I saw the *Item* reporter this morning and had my picture taken, so will hold this until tomorrow when it will be printed. I don't think the article will be anything big, but it might shake things up a bit.

Thursday 12
The article wasn't printed, no space I guess, and so I better get this mailed. So cheerio for now.

All the best, Ken

DICK ALLEN The jam sessions were held in various places. The Jazz Record Centre was one of the most popular. One of the owners—the late Harry Mayronne—had wonderful and funny stories to tell about the musicians. His widow Phyllis sadly doesn't remember many. The *Unknown Sessions* (504CD) includes one at Albert Artigues' home. I believe Artigues' sessions were weekly affairs. Albert owned the French Market Hardware and Fishermen's Supply on Decatur Street., but he had been a professional musician. He reformed! Now, he sounds wonderful to me on the CD. We should be thankful for this and not just for Ken. He was responsible for several New Orleans Musicians being issued for the first time. Maybe the only time.

KEN COLYER LETTER TO BILL COLYER 11 FEBRUARY 1953

543 Governor Nicholls Street, New Orleans.
Dear Bill,

Received your letter this morning. Lady D pulled a lousy blunder there, but I guess it's done now and all I hope is that they learn better someday; as you say, it's not much good you stirring up anything over. Doc has taped the acetates and also taped them for me, so I will give Dick the dubs, as the Bernards have also taped them for their collection. Doc also gave me a very fine bottle of Cuban rum; it's fifteen years old and man, is it mellow! Some nectar.

Myra Manville phoned me this afternoon. She has just received a letter from an English collector with all the latest news. Main point of interest was the breakup of the Cranes; is this right? If so, I would take the name over again when I get home.

We had a jam session at the Jazz Centre yesterday with me, Raymond Burke, Billy Huntingdon and a very young friend of Billy's on drums. It wasn't too bad, except for the drummer, who is too immature. Ursula came down and taped four of the numbers and they sound pretty good. It's a very good machine they have.

Monday 16
Must now condense this to get it off. Watch your addressing man, I nearly lost letter with clippings and dollar, you put wrong number but I have just this minute got another with address OK, so I guess it was just a slip.

Them readers' letters (*MM*'s) make you think, eh? I think best thing to do is ignore them and forge ahead, they might learn one day. Coverage looks pretty good from clippings and publicity is tremendous, so they are achieving the main aim I guess. Could you send copies of *MM*'s Lewis, the one just about sitting in with them, and the one about Kid Sheik; I would like to give them each a copy of these.

Now don't bank on this, but I am getting a recording session sponsored (non-union, sh!) with Milé Barnes, Manuel Manetta, Glenny etc. so keep fingers crossed.

Will also try Koenig for Lewis session. I have been through all possibilities of being recorded with them and there seems to be no hope. That's why I thought of the other angle, which should come off.

World of Jazz programme sounds fine to me and records played very good, congratulate Dennis (Preston) for me.

I like the Denmark idea, hope I'm home in time.

What do you think of Wilcox' offer? I appreciate it and it would eliminate looking for a job. I'm afraid I'm a little excited and nervy at the moment, Bill, and also have things to do, so will write coherently as soon as I can.

Keep up the good works man and I'll do the same this end.

All the best, Ken

PS. Saw best parade yet yesterday (Eureka), weather and music were glorious. (it's Percy Humphrey).

DICK ALLEN Ken and I were at many parties and jam-sessions. He describes the party at Aaron Kahan's apartment on Mardi Gras. This was the only Mardi Gras party given by a rabbi I ever attended. Aaron loved jazz and the black preachers. Somehow it all moved him so much that he contributed to the *Ken Colyer in New Orleans* recording. Later, he hired bands when he ran Bonds for Israel rallies.

Ken and I busked on our way to Aaron's party. I met fellow-students who didn't recognise me. I had only a cheap bowler and a false nose to disguise myself. Good fun and little money.

KEN COLYER LETTER TO BILL COLYER
18 FEBRUARY 1953

543 Governor Nicholls Street, New Orleans
Dear Bill

Thanks for your last letter. I should have replied a couple of days ago but I'm afraid I've been feeling a bit rough and couldn't get myself to write coherently, as you can judge by my last poor epistle. I had a nice letter from Mum, she doesn't seem to be in too good health; also had a good letter from Bob and one from Mont which I answered immediately, explaining the situation as best I could. I just can't push things and must trust that I get deported and get home in time.

I'm glad you are getting the jail saga published; that *New Orleans Item* article is pretty good, don't you think?

I did Dick Allen's radio programme with him tonight on W.N.O.E. John has taped my little bits of talking. We played some Bunk's etc. first and then *Do What Ory Say, I'm Travellin', Slow Drag* and finished up with *Miner's D.O. Home*. Harry Souchon and Billy Huntington rang up the station to say they were liking it, and I think it went over well.

I'm afraid I can't write much about the Mardi Gras as it's a bit beyond my writing skill, but I am enclosing a paper report that you can rehash and I will put down some odds and ends.

The atmosphere on Mardi Gras day is wonderful, there's a real good-time feeling in the air and the majority of people are in wonderful fancy dress. All the bars are open and serve the liquor and beer in paper cups and cans so that you don't have to worry about the glasses and can wander about with your drinks at will. **The floats are magnificent and depict just about everything one can think of; most floats carried a band and among them we saw Toca (Milé Barnes LP), Kid Ernest, a very good clarinet player, and many other fine coloured musicians; they are all out playing somewhere carnival day.**

Raymond Burke was at the "Famous Door" on Bourbon with Monk Hazel, Chink Martin and Geoff Riddick. Raymond's about the best white N.O. clarinet player in town and plays consistently good inspired clarinet.

Dick and I played at various parties and places: Dick plays tubaphone, that's a galanised washtub with a broomstick and length of clothes line, as you probably know. I'm a bit vague about most of the day, as I was ticking like a bomb fairly early and I guess you know the old old story. I kept on my feet 'till four the next morning but it's all rather misty now.

I would like to just note that parade I mentioned. Wilbert Tillman, usually on tuba, was playing alto sax that day, otherwise the band was the same as the other Eureka line-up I told you of.

When them saxes soloed it was strongly reminiscent of the Sam Morgan band—can you imagine that? Man! What a kick, they played *Salutation March* and the greatest *Maryland* I've ever heard. It's hard to explain the sound of these parades but it's definitely different fro m the Bunk B.B. or the Zenith B. Band's.

The Eureka have been recorded by Russell so let's hope he releases them someday.

KEN COLYER LETTER TO BILL COLYER
19 FEBRUARY 1953

Dear Bill,

Am in a bit of a flat spin owing to Mardi Gras. I had a wonderful time but was bilious yesterday and am still a little shaky.

Doc surprised me yesterday, he phoned to say that he has received a tape of the W.O.T. program from Scoop Kennedy, who recorded it in Paris. I am going to hear it tonight.

I am going ahead with Milé Barnes date, as this is something that can possibly be pulled off in the next few days.

George goes on tour Monday and will be gone about two to three weeks (Indiana and places North) so it's pretty hopeless to arrange anything while I am here and there's so many damned union technicalities to be ironed out.

Would you send Raymond Burke a *Jazz Journal* with N.O. log article in? Thanks.

His address is 905 N. RAMPART ST.

George Lewis told me Monday he had received another letter from you when I saw him for a few minutes. I meant to say before, don't use any too technical lingo when you write as they might not dig it.

Lizzie Miles address is 1214 N. TONTI ST.

I'm enclosing a couple of paper reports on MG day to give you an idea of what goes on, also the one on me that was in Sunday *Item*.

Dick Werlich is sending MSS direct to you sometime.

I will write again before the weekend and I also want to write a short letter to *MM* after reading criticisms again.

What do you think of Doughty? I have come to the conclusion that he is a frustrated jazz musician and his reactions are mean and vicious and Burman is still pretty much of an oaf.

Well I'll close now, Bill, and I hope to have some definite news on recording date when I write again.

All the best, Ken

While I think of it, as far as I can figure, the records you sent have gone back to England unless they've been snaffled somewhere along the line. Did you send Jazz Directories to Dick to Bourbon Street or Dick's old address ST ANN? You know that Dick now lives and works at THE JAZZ CENTRE, 706 BOURBON besides attending Tulane College to study anthropology.

That's something we could do for John Bernard is send him the J.D.'s. He hasn't got any of them and would really appreciate that.

We went to Luthjens last night, and about all I can say is that that quartet play more and more and greater New Orleans music every time I hear them.

Noone and Sam looked in the shop this afternoon. Noone, besides playing fine guitar (Kid Sheik session) also plays "bazooka," which is an instrument he built his-self many years ago out of two brass bed-posts and a paraffin funnel. He slides it like a trombone and it has a soft mellow bass tone, a little like Cy St Clair's tuba. Sam plays guitar and sings, Noone sings with him and plays his bazooka.

I tuned my guitar to Sam's (I had left it at the shop from Mardi Gras ramblings) and we played awhile with Dick on tubaphone. That was real skiffle music and quite a kick.

I heard some more musicians a couple of nights back when Emma Barrett, who is a friend of the Bernards, snuck us into a private social do. Emma, who is just a name in the personnel listings of the early Celestin recordings in England, is however still a very active pianist. She is renowned for her tremendous knowledge of tunes and memory. She is never stuck for the words of songs, no matter how old or obscure. She is a slim pleasant woman who organises her own bands besides playing in other groups.

She was playing in Fats Houston's band at this do, and there was Fats on drums, Emma piano, Kid Howard trumpet, Andrew Morgan sax and clarinet and John Handy sax.

The crowd were strictly square and the band had to play mostly waltzes and Foxtrots but I think they could have played some good stuff if given the opportunity.

Kid Howard did a fine vocal on *Stardust* and played flashes of very fine horn. I couldn't get to meet the band as I intended, as we had to keep out of the way down the opposite end of the hall.

Well I'll push this off for now Bill and dig up some more stuff later.

All the Best to everybody,
Your old Brud, Ken

DICK ALLEN There were several Brass Bands then, playing mostly for neighbourhood functions. The Eureka was considered standard, even though it had alto and tenor saxophones and no clarinet. They read well by New Orleans standards and played by ear too.

John Casimir

This reminds me of a bass player who bragged about reading music. It turned out that he couldn't sign his name. This was in another band, but it tips us off to braggarts. A lot were "spellers." Listen to the Eureka CD on American Music and the Eureka's Folkways LP if it has been reissued. I don't know. The recordings let us know who could read.

Some of you may have heard the Young Tuxedo Brass Band on Atlantic. It was a wilder band, usually with screaming trumpets and more riffing by the saxes. One member enjoyed clowning in the late fifties. Personally, I enjoyed their excitement, and particularly John Casimir's Eb clarinet. His wailing suited the stomps and the dirges.

Most of the jazz lovers, including Ken, preferred the Eureka, But Bill Russell liked the George Williams Brass Band best. It had a clarinet, and Russell hated the saxophone.

It had an alto sax too. I liked the different bands for different reasons. George Williams sometimes had Buster Moore or Robert Thomas on trombone. Both were red-hot, much more exciting than their recordings.

Now brass bands are not so organised. A friend told me about an older trumpet player talking to a young, up and coming star. The older one asked the younger if he wanted to play first or second. The youngster didn't know what he was talking about. This speaks a book about a different approach.

Back in the fifties, a novelist used to follow brass bands. One day, she commented, "What I like is the pageantry." Now every day is Mardi Gras when a band hits the streets. There is no distinction between a parade and a procession. The form of a funeral is almost gone. Changes of mood are gone. I appreciated the ability of the bands, the organisations, and even the second line to capture the sorrow and the joy. There was great dignity, especially from the Grand Marshalls. By the way, I don't remember Marshals carrying umbrellas. I think this was started by someone giving his fancy second-line umbrella to Slow Drag Pavageau. You can see this in photographs from about 1961.

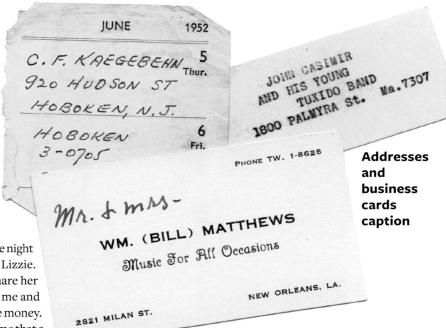

Addresses and business cards caption

KEN COLYER After sitting in with George one night at the Mardi Gras, I was in the back talking to Lizzie. She was wonderful. Sometimes she would share her delicious southern fried chicken lunch with me and get me a beer. I think she knew that I had little money. Sid's wife, who waited on the tables, had told me that a couple had come in and invited me for a drink. Lizzie looked pleased; I went and sat with them. They were very pleasant and I had a beer with them. They were Charles and Anne Kaegebehn from New York on a periodic visit, as Charles was a lawyer and travelled a lot. Charles said, as they walked down Bourbon Street, they had heard the band, thought it sounded good and gone into the club.

> They were amazed to see me sitting-in. My hair was almost white from the sea air, and the contrast must have been most marked as I sat among those dark negroes. They were even more surprised to find that I was English.

The McCarthy witch hunt was under way and I knew the McCarran-Walter was coming into force. Peter, a seaman on the *Empire Patria*, has assured me there would be no problems. There were always seamen on the beach. He said, if I wanted to bother, just go to the immigration authorities, tell them you were still looking for a ship out, and they would just keep extending your time, indefinitely. I thought Charles was the ideal man to ask, being a lawyer. He admitted nobody knew how the act would work and typically of governments it was complex and complicated. He advised me to do what I was going to do anyway, but if he could be of any help to let him know, and he gave me his Hoboken address.

CHARLES KAEGEBEHN LETTER TO KEN COLYER FEBRUARY 17 1953

Charles F. Kaegebehn, Patent Attorney, 111 Broadway
New York 6, N.Y. Rector 2-9400
Dear Ken

Your letter mailed from New Orleans February thirteenth reached us yesterday, February sixteenth. We were dismayed to learn of your unfortunate experience with the immigration authorities. We are in complete agreement with you concerning the McCarran Act. It is really a vicious law. Its sponsor, Senator McCarran of New Mexico, is a horrible example of demagoguery. It was our hope that Senator Stevenson would have been elected President last November with a working majority of Liberal Democrats in the Congress, in which event, the McCarran Act might have had a chance of early repeal. Now that the country is going to the right under the Republican (we hardly think Eisenhower knows where he is going), I am afraid it may be some time before there is any real important change in the McCarran Act.

Be assured that Anne and I will want to see you here very much in New York. Please let us know when you will be leaving New Orleans, how you will be travelling and when you expect to arrive in New York. If you are assigned to Ellis Island prior to embarkation for England, will you be permitted to go about in New York City? Will the bond, under which you are now at liberty, hold good for your stay at Ellis Island?

If you will promptly, upon receipt of this letter, write me again giving me as much information as you can as to what your prospects are for arrival at Ellis Island, how long you will be there and what you may know about the liberty you may be accorded, I will try to make some plans for your stay. It may be possible, either through the British Consul here in New York or through the immigration authorities, using connections that I might be able to develop, that we can insure you some time free in the city. If not, Anne and I will certainly come over to Ellis Island to see you.

In any event, we will probably see you in England this spring. Anne and I are planning to get over, I on business and Anne with me. We will try to avoid London during the Coronation, but we expect to spend about a week there sometime in May.

Anne and I send our very best regards and hope that your sojourn in the Parish Prison did not embitter you and give you the wrong impression of all things American and all Americans.

Cordially, (signed) Charles G. F Kaegebehn

KEN COLYER Dick Greenwood, merchant seaman and brother of Bob Greenwood, who helped organise the Lewis Good Time Jazz session, had just left on a short trip. His parting words were if he had enough money on his return he would sponsor a recording session for Billie Pierce, whose great admirer he is. A few days later I was taken into custody by the immigration officials for violating the law under that strangely Un-American activity, the McCarran-Walter Act. After thirty-eight long days the Bernards—John and Ursula,—were finally successful in having me released on their bail of $500.

I knew that I was due to leave for New York at any time. Fortunately Dick Greenwood returned from his trip so I immediately asked him if he was still interested in backing a recording session with myself and some local men. He was, but was doubtful that he had enough money, so Dick Allen rounded up some other enthusiasts to help bear the expense.

Emile Barnes and most of the men were now contacted, but Mardi Gras was due and it was several days later before anything could be done.

After the hectic Mardi Gras carousel, we were finally all set to go with Emile Barnes, clarinet; Harrison Brazely, trombone; Albert Glenny, bass; Albert Jiles, drums; and Billy Huntingdon, fifteen year-old white protégé of Lawrence Marrero, on banjo.

Dick Allen had suggested we use on piano, Professor Manuel Manetta (teacher of music and multi-instrumentalist), a remarkable man capable of prodigious musical feats, one of which is the ability to improvise on two trumpets simultaneously. He was, unfortunately, unable to make the dates we had fixed, so we decided to go ahead with a three-piece rhythm section.

We had tried to secure a suitable place to record but had been unsuccessful. We finally settled for Emile Barnes' (known as Milé) living room, which seemed to be in the best "William Russell" tradition, and the rehearsal date was fixed for the 23rd February. The tape recorder we were going to use was found at the last minute to have developed mechanical trouble, so the Bernards offered their machine and services. We decided to tape both rehearsal and the actual session and later on were thankful that we did so.

Everyone arrived at Milé's home on La Harpe Street more or less on time, and as some of us were not sure of some of the tunes that had been chosen, rehearsal started without delay. As the evening wore on, it became pretty warm in that living room. I didn't realise how hot it had become until Albert Glenny staggered and we had to move him quickly into the cool air of the passage to sit down and rest awhile.

Albert had stood there all evening, straight-backed, playing magnificent, swinging bass, and I wondered at the strength and youthfulness of this man, eighty-three years old, who has played bass right from the very birth of jazz.

I feel that he will go on defiantly independent until the end of his days. I respectfully salute him.

Though I was willing to use Albert the next evening, a majority vote decided that we use another man, and Milé suggested a very capable young bassist named George Fortier.

We met again and taped the tunes we had rehearsed, then took time out for a beer and a rest before taping the most surprising tunes of the session. These were decided on the spot with no previous run through. *Winter Wonderland*, a pleasant pop from some years back, I remembered for no apparent reason. Milé suggested *Ciri-biri-bin*, quite possibly because he remembered an old New Orleans tune that was similar, the same way that he remembered *Frankie and Johnny* under a different name and only knew *Hiawatha* as a tune he used to play with Chris Kelly (his all-time great on trumpet) as *There's a Lizard on the Rail*!

How Long and *Buddy Bolden* were done after Billy had insisted I do a couple of vocal numbers.

The evening ended with everyone in good spirits and Milé, I felt, was recapturing something that has probably been slipping from him through the years. Dick Allen had remarked to me previously that he had heard Mile when he was playing as well as George Lewis. I was a little dubious at the time, but after two evenings of playing with him, realised, as the records will prove, that here is another New Orleans clarinettist who is being virtually lost to the jazz world.

The same also applies to Harrison Brazely, the trombonist, whose name should be there with Jim Robinson in the Hall of Fame.

I should like to acknowledge here the names of the sponsors who made this session possible and to whom I am deeply grateful for enabling me to leave New Orleans with such wonderful evidence of my stay there.

They are: Dick Greenwood; Harry Souchon, brother of Doctor Edmond Souchon (Harry, though not widely known, is an old-time lover of the music who has done much behind the scenes to help it and its exponents); Lee Cavin, an ardent fan of the George Lewis Band and follower of the Parade Bands; Aaron Kahn, a very fine person and sincere jazz lover; and last, but not least, John and Ursula Bernard, who gave unstintingly of their time and helped me immeasurably.

KEN COLYER LETTER TO BILL COLYER 25 FEBRUARY 1953

543 Governor Nicholls Street, New Orleans.
Dear Bill,

John got the news this afternoon that I am leaving Monday night for Ellis Island. I report back at the Parish Prison midday and leave that night according to information given to John. If they don't keep me on Ellis Island too long, it looks like I'll make it home for the Denmark deal. Are there any passports and visas required for this, and how long will it take to get them? I would like to know because if it means cutting it fine on time, I could fill them in and mail them back so that things would be ready by the time I came home.

Last night we got another session in the can. We tried hard to get a first-class tape machine but were unable to, owing to slim finances. Nevertheless, I think John's machine has been good enough to do a pretty good job. I haven't heard the second tape but, going by judgement, I think some of the stuff is not as good as Monday's and some is better. We had to use George Fortier on bass last night instead of Glenny. I was a bit doubtful about him at first but he turned out fine; once he got the idea of things and taped his fingers, he made out fine. On playing some stuff back he remarked that he sounded like "a sousaphone in them old bands."

There are two takes of some numbers, three and four of others, as we taped practically everything, and at a rough guess I would say 11 numbers could be used with a little editing.

Here is a list of the numbers taped:
New Orleans Hop Scop Blues
Frankie And Johnny
Panama Rag
Gravier Street Blues (1 & 2)
How Long Blues (vocal by me)
Buddy Bolden (vocal by me)
Climax Rag
That's A Plenty
Winter Wonderland
Black Cat On The Fence
Ciribiribin

Ciribiribin is pretty terrific. It was the last number done and I wouldn't have dreamt of playing it if Milé hadn't suggested it. As it is I think it turned out the best number of the evening. The

stuff on the whole is a little rough in places but, taking things all round, I think the two sessions were highly successful and, as fast as I have tried to work on this, it looks like we only just got it done in time.

There are two *Gravier Streets*, different enough to be used as two different numbers, that's how I make eleven numbers. One is at a slow tempo, one much faster and quite different.

Frankie And Johnny, *Buddy Bolden* and *Ciribiribin* were all thought up on the spot. My original plan was to really whip the main five numbers into shape, but the lip wasn't in too good shape through lack of practice and playing, so I decided not to press these numbers, and when Milé started suggesting numbers to take it easy on, I figured he knew best.

He was enthusiastic about the band, and it's a shame in a way to do something like this and realise what another few sessions would produce. Milé would feel it more, as he is a purist and won't play with bands he doesn't rate. His clarinet on these tapes will prove to you what a great instrumentalist he must have been, and hearing Brazeley play like this I almost wonder who is best, him or Jim Robinson at times.

Have just heard the tapes again and some of the stuff is terrific. We could safely use two takes for issue on some like *How Long*, as there is so much fine collective improvisation that has "The Master Touch." The drummer is a little loud at times, but the rhythm section really swings when it's going.

With a little editing and good quality dubbing, there is nothing to worry about, but I feel the job must be done right and think you'll agree when you hear the stuff. I will leave it to you to advise on best people, but it must be done with plenty of co-operation. We may only have this chance in a lifetime, so I guess you understand, Bill.

I guess it's no use going into any eulogies, but now I know I'm on my way I just can't wait till I get home for you to hear it, man. Glenny is tremendous on first session and Fortier is very good on second. Fortier is a comparatively young negro and I don't think he's been recorded before.

> On hearing *Ciribiribin* again, I would say that, if I didn't know it was me playing, I would swear it was Bunk, and the number as a whole is a dilly, absolutely a dilly.

My vocals are good and the band back me fine. Billy will prove to you what I said before: at fifteen years of age the kid's a phenomenon. As a person he tends to get a little unbearable— Dick sometimes calls him "That brat"—but he's very young and let's hope time will learn him humility and humbleness.

I will write Ralston so I may see him once again when I get to

Second day of the Milé Barnes recording session

Ellis Island. The Kaegebehns offered to go my bail when I get there, but I don't think it can be done. I think I've been fortunate in meeting so many fine people; it even upsets me a little at times when I think of how cynical I tend to get at times, but I guess that to appreciate friendship when you do find it is the main thing.

I've heard nothing from anybody about the article, as they probably haven't seen it down here. There's very few people get the *MM* in these parts.

Will have to close now Gate, but will probably write again before I leave here and will do as soon as I get to New York, so let Mont know the news when you see him.

All the best for now and love to everybody, except those goddam ofays.

Your old brud, Ken

ALEXIS KORNER Should anyone require it, this EP, together with LDE. 161, are the permanent proof of an ambition fulfilled. In years to come people may well wish to dispute that Ken Colyer ever went to New Orleans. Such things are wont to happen, and, when all other proof is invalid, this will show the truth, for here is a set of recordings which Ken made in New Orleans during his stay there. Not only had Ken fulfilled

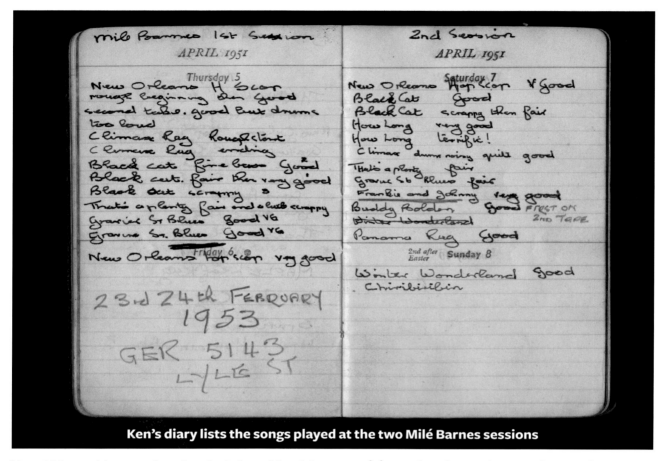

Ken's diary lists the songs played at the two Milé Barnes sessions

his ambition to visit New Orleans but also he has achieved the distinction of being the only British musician, playing jazz today, to have recorded with New Orleans musicians in the Crescent City itself.

It would be impossible even to attempt even a description of Ken's fanatical feelings on the subject of New Orleans jazz, but the sincerity of his emotions is, in some way, proven by the fact that he achieved his aim; as indeed he deserved to.

The recordings were made on a portable tape recorder in a back room and, under the circumstances, the balance is extraordinarily good, revealing a freedom of atmosphere which is rarely, if ever, heard at recording sessions made in Britain. There is, no more, that tension which is inevitably brought on when musicians consciously try to recreate a music. This music is not forced in its execution, for it is being played by people whose learning has not been restricted to the medium of the gramophone record.

There is here an inherent knowledge which so few jazz musicians in this country possess; it is the true knowledge of the blues. If you cannot play the blues then you cannot play New Orleans jazz, for the blues are there all the time, and Ken Colyer's life has given him many opportunities to understand the blues, an understanding which shows even more when, as in this case, he is playing with musicians who, themselves, understand.

Although none of the musicians playing on this E.P. are great, they produce, with less technical ability, a sound which none of their more fluent European counterparts have yet succeeded in doing. No pretence is made that this music reaches the standard of the best George Lewis recordings but, despite occasional mistakes and poor balance, this set of recordings must surely serve as an ideal indication of the sound which Ken intends to produce in Britain.

If, after all this striving, a truly successful New Orleans style band does come together in this country, a band made up of British or European musicians, then, almost certainly, Ken Colyer will be leading it. Even if, for some reason, Ken should not be in this band of the future, then it will, nonetheless, owe its existence largely to his efforts, for it is Ken's ardour, more than any other single element, which has created a demand for this music.

A fanatical devotion to New Orleans jazz has urged Ken on to bring this music to a public which was, for some time, most unreceptive; such a devotion has brought with it an uncompromisingly high set of of criteria by which to judge his own efforts. It is the dissatisfaction with his work which has enabled Ken to progress to the stage where he may seriously be considered as an extremely fine trumpet player, even if one were to judge him by his own high standards.

> Ken has never played 'self satisfied' jazz, for none is worth the playing; Ken has never played 'compromise' jazz for neither is that.

DICK ALLEN I must add a few words about recordings. *The Unknown New Orleans Sessions* with Raymond Burke are a miracle of good taste and engineering. The bass can hardly be heard on the first ten numbers. I was a lousy wash-tub player.

After he got out of jail, we discussed making a record. I have almost always found the union officers cooperative, but scale was high. I was concerned about raising money to pay the musicians, but people like Bob Greenwood, a librarian (or possibly Bob's brother, Dick Greenwood, who was a seaman), lawyer Harry Souchon, a television repair man, and the bond salesman Aaron Kahan came through. I have to explain that Ken mixed up the Greenwoods... all admired Ken.

John Bernard had his home recorder. Of course, professional engineering could have helped, but this was what we could afford. I thought that John helped choose the musicians and numbers. He said that Ken and I did that. I had helped out at a George Lewis and Herb Morand session; however, Ken had more experience with recording than anyone else. Of course, he didn't know all of the musicians, but we worked out the band members with Emile Barnes. The most surprising to me was Harrison Brazley. He said he was sick when he recorded with Barnes in 1951, so we are lucky to have the Ken Colyer recordings..

I was especially impressed with Brazley's playing on *Ciri-Biri-Bin*. This was a new number for Ken, and he thought it was the best. Some of the numbers were new to the other musicians, who did well by them. The old New Orleans tradition was to play any request, from a dancer or a musician. Ken knew lots of unusual numbers which were somehow no challenge to the band.

MONTY SUNSHINE LETTER TO KEN COLYER 17 FEBRUARY 1953

45, West Heath Drive, London, N.W.11, England
Dear Ken,

I believe I am pretty well up to date as to what you have been doing the last few months, as Bill has kept me posted.

As you know the 'Cranes' have disbanded and Ron and I have struck out on our own, whilst the rest have re-formed under Ray, calling themselves the Phoenix Jazz Band.

The basic reason for the breakup is, of course, the obvious one. Ron and I intend to make jazz our full-time occupation, while the rest of the 'Cranes' and the men who have replaced us, are only interested in jazz as a side line.

Ron and I, anticipating your return to England knowing (from Bill) your wish to make jazz your full-time occupation here, have formed a group which at present is a secret known to only a few people, which we have been rehearsing twice a week for a month, and all the members of which have the same outlook on our music as Ron and I—which I believe is very much the same as yours e.g. NO PIANO. The people in the group are :- Ron and I you know – plus the following.

Chris Barber, who is a much improved player and can hold his own with anyone playing our music playing in England, and his style is now very much turned towards what we always wanted to hear from a trombone. On banjo and guitar we have Tony Donegan, who is a much soberer and better banjoist than he used to be and who also sings well now. Our bassist is Jim Bray, who even Bill considers to be the finest in the tradition in the country and plays tuba very well also.

As you can see by the above, we really mean business, and we planned to go to Denmark for the entire month of April for our pleasure, for a chance for the band to really get to know each other, and of course to get some real public playing experience together. We have a series of dates arranged for us there and free accommodation, and the trip will not cost a cent. Those who still have daytime jobs have planned to leave them on our return to England.

Before we heard from Bill that you planned to return to England in the very near future to take an active part in jazz again here, we had found a very capable trumpeter (Pat Halcox, now playing with the Albemarle) who was willing to come to Denmark with us and to turn professional on our return—he is willing to come to Denmark even without a permanent job with the band afterwards, but he probably would not be able to stay away from his job for a full month without leaving it, and we would not ask him to do that without being able to offer him a permanent job on his return.

Ever since we heard of your plans from Bill, we have been more or less banking on your returning here very soon and taking the group over under your leadership (we had planned to call it Ken Colyer's All Stars).

However, the time for our departure for Denmark (March 30th) is drawing very near, and recent news from Bill leads us to wonder whether we can count on your returning in the near future, and we should like to hear from you by return Airmail (Reply Coupon enclosed) as to what you think of our various ideas.

We would of course rather have you in the band as leader than anyone else, so we would very much like you to send us your answers to these questions.

(1) Have you any idea when you will return?

(2) Assuming you can return fairly soon, does the idea leading the group appeal to you?

(3) If the above are OK, what do you feel about coming to Denmark?

All the fellows send their best wishes and hope that your troubles will soon be over – and please write me by return post— COME HOME SON WE NEED YER LIKE MAD—

The very best to you Ken. (signed) Mont.

KEN COLYER LETTER TO BILL COLYER 27 FEBRUARY 1953

531 Broad Street, Parish Prison, New Orleans
Dear Bill,

I was surprised to see that my letters are taking five days now. Four is usual for yours and this one has only taken three. You should have my main mail by now, I should think, with Mardi Gras clippings and recording news. I hope Monty has also got my letter; if I'm no longer than a week on Ellis Island I should make it home. Be sure to send any applications for passports etc. if they are needed.

What did you record of the W.O.J. programme? If it's just talking I should send it, as it's not so easy for the Bernards to get stuff off Souchon. They will already have the records played, as they have quite an impressive collection of discs, practically all on tape. If it's going to entail more expense though, you can say you can sell the stuff; I should do so, as the Bernards already have twelve numbers by me singing with guitar on tape and they really cherish that, and I think that will suffice. They also have me talking, taped off Dick Allen's programme.

I have been thinking about the Milé Barnes session and talking it over with Dick, and I think it would be better if we could get it done on LP. If you talk to Whitton, see what he thinks. I know you can't figure much till I get the stuff home, but I should imagine Vogue is the best bet for issuing it; still, maybe we better leave it under wraps till I get there.

I guess I must talk about it, as my head is so full of it. There is a possible fourteen numbers with the three repeats. *Gravier* could safely be put out twice, also *How Long*. I would like to call the fast *Gravier*, *Milé's Blues*, as he suggested doing it again at a faster tempo. The repeats show the fine collective improvisational qualities of the band. Some of that stuff is really going to have you hopping, Man: Milé's wonderful, silvery tone, Glenny's driving bass, Harrison's glorious tram and more.

In my playing I would say there are shades of Howard, Bunk and Papa Mutt, and Billy's banjo is almost Marrero. I just think of the age span on some of them numbers, 15 years to 83.

I'm getting photos today; I hope they come out OK. Will close now, Bill; don't forget I'll be on Ellis Island March 3rd.

All the best Gate, see you soon, Ken

KEN COLYER LETTER TO BILL COLYER 3 MARCH 1953

Ellis Island, New York
Dear Bill,

Just a few quick lines to let you know that I arrived here this morning OK. The Immigration said that I am all clear to leave and should go on the first available passage out, so I'm hoping it shouldn't be more than a few days before I'm on my way home.

This place is certainly a different story to the Parish Prison; food is good, treatment is good and we are not locked down. There are plenty of men here, a wonderful, motley group, but also plenty of room.

I received your letter yesterday with Festival concert news and P.S. that you had received Mardi Gras clippings. I hope they haven't come too late. You should have news by now of the wonderful fifty-odd minutes of millenium (I think this is a play on Milé) I have on tape. Don't mention to anybody what type of kit it was recorded on because if they don't know I don't think they'll ever know the difference.

I have some negatives of photos taken at the session, but they aren't very good, but might come up a little if a good man works on them. Fortunately the group shot taken at the end of the session is the best one.

Wilcox's idea sounds OK. What is their new place like?

Will sign off now, Gate, and let's hope I make that deadline.

Ken

KEN COLYER As soon as we were on Ellis Island we were told to line up and were then given a short talking-to by an official. He was polite but firm. We weren't in the South now and he knew what conditions we had been held under. We would get three good meals a day and a clean comfortable bed. As long as we behaved ourselves, we would be treated with respect. They didn't want any trouble, was that clear? It certainly was.

The dining hall was run on the cafeteria system and every meal was a banquet. You could help yourself to whatever you wanted. The coffee was excellent and banished memories of the muck we were given in the Parish Prison. The beds were wide and comfortable with spotlessly clean sheets. The vista from Ellis Island again is magnificent. It gives you a grandstand view of the approaches to the piers, the ships coming in and the New York skyline, also the Statue of Liberty gazing out with her sightless eyes.

We were given cards to send to anyone that might want to see us. I sent one to Ralston Crawford and Charles Kaegebehn. I was slightly surprised when they both turned up to see me. They had bought me some cigarettes, which was most welcome. I was still looking after one or two of the men. Ralston didn't stay long, but said he was glad to see me finally on my way home.

Charles chatted for a while, then I casually said that rumour was strong that we would be going home on the *United States*, America's crack liner, in a few days' time. His jaw dropped. He pulled a folded paper out of his pocket. It was a twelve hundred dollar bail bond. He was all set to surprise me and take me home with him, but for a day or two it was hardly worth it and they probably wouldn't allow it.

I felt terrible at disappointing him. I certainly wouldn't

Feb 17th.

45 West Heath Drive,
London. N.W.11.
England.

Dear Ken.

I believe I am pretty well up to date as to what you have been doing the last few months, as Bill has kept me posted.

As you know the 'Cranes' have disbanded and Ron and I have struck out on our own, whilst the rest have re-formed under Ray calling themselves the Phoenix Jazz Band.

The basic reason for the breakup is of course the obvious one. Ron and I intend to make Jazz our full time occupation, while the rest of the 'Cranes' and the two men who have replaced us are only interested in Jazz as a side line.

Ron and I, anticipating your return to England knowing (from Bill) your wish to make Jazz your full time occupation here have formed a group which at present is a secret known to very few people, which we have been rehearsing twice a week for a month, and all the members of which have the same outlook on our music as Ron and I — which I believe is very much the same as yours e.g. NO PIANO

2

the people in the group are :- Ron and I you know — plus the following.

Chris Barber - who is a much improved player and can hold his own with any one playing our music playing in England and his style now is very much turned towards what we always wanted to hear from a trombone. - On banjo and guitar we have Tony Donegan who is a much soberer and better banjoist than he used to be and who also sings well now. - Our bassist is Jim Bray who even Bill considers to be the finest in the tradition in this country and plays Tuba very well also.

As you can see by the above we really mean business and we planned to go to Denmark for the entire month of April for our pleasure, for a change for the Band to really get to know each other and of course to get some real public playing experience together — We have a series of dates arranged for us there and free accommodation and the trip will not cost a cent. Those who still have day time jobs have planned to leave them on our return to England

---

3

Before we heard from Bill that you meant to return to England in the very near future to take an active part in Jazz again here, we had found a very capable trumpeter (Pat Halcox now playing with the Albermarle) who was willing to come to Denmark with us and to turn professional on our return — he is willing to come to Denmark even without a permanent job with the Band afterwards, but he probably would not be able to stay away from his job for a full month without leaving it, and we would not ask him to do that without being able to offer him a permanent job on his return.

Ever since we heard of your plans from Bill we have been more or less banking on your returning here very soon and taking the group over under your leadership (we had planned to call it Ken Colyers AllStars)

However, the time for our departure for Denmark (March 30th) is drawing very near and

---

4

recent news from Bill leads us to wonder wether we can count on your returning in the near future, and we should like to hear from you by return Airmail (Reply coupon enclosed) as to what you think of our various ideas.

We would of course rather have you in the Band as leader than anyone else so we would very much like you to send us your answers to these questions.

(1) Have you any idea when you will return?
(2) Assuming you can return fairly soon - does the idea leading the group appeal to you.
(3) If the above are o·k what do you feel about coming to Denmark

---

All the fellows send their best wishes and hope your troubles will soon be over — and please write me by return post —— COME HOME SON WE NEED YER LIKE MAD ——

The very best to you Ken.

Mont.

have minded a week or two in New York before going home. I thanked him for all he had done and we bade farewell. I was to see him and his wife Anne in the not too distant future in London.

I had met Fred Hatfield through Dick Allen and he came along with me. Fred was interesting. He was a native Orleanean yet he hated the colour bar and bucked the system. This had its dangers. He would go into a coloured bar and drink. If they tried to evict him he would insist that his great grandmother was jet black therefore he was coloured and he had a right to drink in a coloured bar.

> **I got onto a streetcar one day and, not thinking, sat down next to a negro… He shuffled nervously for a while, then he asked politely if I would sit in front in the white seats. I apologised and moved.**

It was a white pub of course; only the band was coloured. They played a few numbers. It was a rough-and-ready group, but sometimes this can have a great charm. Fred said that he thought that was true New Orleans music. I didn't try to get into any arguments. They had electric guitar, a sax player who was playing bebop and a drummer who was one of the most startling showmen I have ever seen. He was a gnome-like fellow playing a beat-up kit, with the fervour of Gene Krupa. His bass drum was propped up by a case. His snare drum head had a coating of dirt and grease on it as thick as the skin itself.

They played *Eh Las Bas* and it was pure African. It was savage, his Creole was guttural and obviously the words were different. De De, Albert Burbank, Alphonse Picou, all have different versions.

The session was very casual. People just drifted in, had a drink and drifted out. I played a few numbers with them and was thoroughly enjoying it. Anybody who cannot understand this, then it's a waste of time trying to explain.

I needed a drink and noted that the boys didn't move from where they played. One or two had a half bottle in their cases and sneaked a drink now and then. I thought what the hell, I only had a couple of bucks, but went to the bar. "Six beers, please." The barman put six beers on a tray with some glasses. As I was about to pay, the governor came up and said, "Are you buying them for the band?"

"Yes," I said, expecting some sort of trouble. "That's OK, they are on the house. Do you usually play with these people?" he asked. "Yes, as much as I can," I replied. "That's wonderful. I love them, but I can't alter the situation. Order what you want anytime." And he told the barman to serve me anything I ordered. I didn't take liberties, but got the band several rounds. They were slightly bemused by this turn of events and it made their evening.

When we finished for the evening, Fred and I were having a final drink. The little drummer came up. He had written his name on a card. I had trouble deciphering it. Paul Letau. I also had trouble understanding him. It was harder than Drag. Finally I realised he wanted me to say how good he was. I patted his shoulder and assured him it was the best drumming I had ever heard and in a way it was. He was just one step from Africa. A true primitive. He bade me goodnight and went home with a beaming smile on his face. Everything was just fine.

JOHN BERNARD I was born and raised in the North of the United States, lived in England six years, and settled in New Orleans in 1950 when I was in my thirties. Like anyone of my background I was appalled that coloured (this was in the years before "black" was used to describe Afro-Americans) were mandated by law to have different toilet facilities, drinking fountains and space on a bus—to name but a few of the regulations in force. New Orleans, however, has always been an oasis in the South, with a combination of cosmopolitan veneer and laissez faire attitude. As a result, segregation was not as 'violently enforced' as in other areas of the South.

The color problem was definitely bad, although the black and white races were not as polarized as they seem to be at present. In the fifties most Southern whites approved of segregation, and most of the colored bore it as something inevitable, akin to death and taxes, since they felt virtually powerless to change their condition.

Ken did not need a lot of nerve and courage to go in and play with Lewis etc., and to get accepted by the bands and the black audiences. Ken spoke to the members of the various bands as musician to musician, friend to friend, and was readily accepted. Once he began to play, his talent was immediately evident. Incidentally, Ken played to white audiences, mostly at kitty halls such as Manny's Tavern; it is possible that he played before 'black audiences' but I am not aware of any such occasion.

Ken's legal problems were with the Federal Authorities and not the police, since he did not have the proper visa to stay in this country. When he went to the Federal Authorities to resolve his visa problem, their response was to put him in jail immediately. Since the Federal Authorities had no jail of their own in New Orleans, their normal procedure was to put their prisoners in the city's Parish Prison, where Ken was incarcerated with the "lowest of the low"—and undoubtedly the highest of the low as well.

I was finally permitted by the Federal Authorities to put up the $500 bail bond for his release from the Parish Prison. For the remaining weeks of Ken's time in New Orleans on that trip,

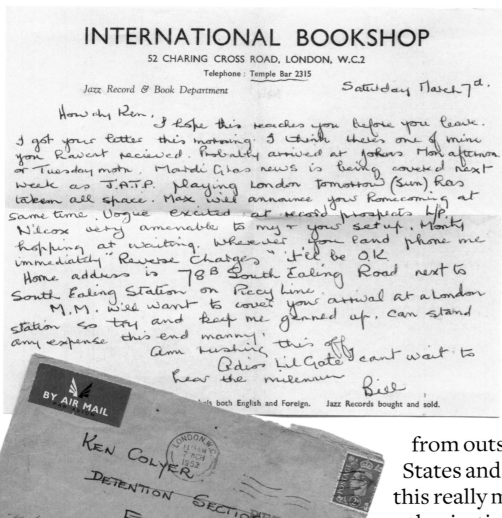

playing, so we went to their home, and we brought them over to the jam session, and they walked in. And the management was very upset. But they played with the white group, and everybody loved it. So we tried to encourage that, you know, when we could.

I loved Ken because, as of today even, anyone that comes from other parts of the country to enjoy New Orleans or to whatever, I'm very enthusiastic about showing them around, or answering their questions or taking them out, you know.

And Ken was one of the first people to come here from outside the United States and then, of course, this really made us enthusiastic about him.

PETER HUNTER So, anyway, I went off to sea—and where did I go? New Orleans. Once again, I was in my element. I walked down Bourbon Street and heard Sharkey Bonano playing in the Paddock Bar and George Girard playing in the Famous Door. As I walked further I found this club called the Club Slipper. Echoing out through the doors was the George Lewis Band with Percy Humphrey and once again I went into orbit over this band.

Although I had a beer reserved in three of the main venues, I would nip over there during the intermissions from the Club Slipper and there one day the manager... came over to me and said "Are you English?" and I said "I like to think so." He said, "Well, would you like to come and meet the band, there is another English guy here, he plays trumpet, perhaps you would like to meet him?"

I hadn't got a clue who he was and I walked into the inner sanctum to be confronted with God and, as you can gather, that was Ken who was sitting in with the George Lewis Band. Then I actually got to speak to him and talked about these two cadets who had been on the ship with him and he said "Bloody

he lived with us (my former wife Ursula and me) and played music as before until he was deported.

FRED HATFIELD A lot of times the black bias was very prevalent among the populace, you know. And it was very common for that to happen, so anyone who had a liberal attitude towards blacks, as myself, was an exception. I recall one meeting of the New Orleans Jazz Club. We got together—Donald Perry and myself—and we decided that we would go and ask some blacks to join the jam session. And so we went to Luthjens, where Billie and De De Pierce would play, and we got Billie and De De to come play at the jam session.

Well, the jam session was on a night that they weren't

officers—can't stand them."

But that was not really true, and over the years he became a very great friend and I think we had a lot in common, apart from music, as we never talked about it very often. We talked about the Merchant Navy and odd comments about what they said about him aboard ship, which was usually, "Stop playing that bloody trumpet!" He used to play his trumpet and his guitar whilst he was at sea. We used to reminisce about all the ports we had been to, as sailors do.

It was in late 1952, I was 16 years of age at that time and, well, it was a wonderful experience

It was not a tourist a trap in those days, I mean there were a lot of rhythm and blues clubs and a lot of the usual strip joints and whatever you would expect to find, but it was still very much a jazz city; there was the Paddock , the Famous Door and the Slipper and all that sort of thing...

And I did actually manage to get to a funeral to which George Lewis invited me. Then, in 1954 , I was back in New Orleans, long after Ken was back home.

BILL HUNTINGTON There were two attitudes towards Ken. I guess some people just thought he was an eccentric, sort of crazy, bohemian. And then other people, like myself, and the Bernards and people who were more into the music, felt like he had done an incredible thing—a courageous thing. There were jam sessions, and there were parties that people would have at their houses, and he was part of that, and so was I.

And there was an institution called the New Orleans Jazz Club, which was formed by some very courageous, heroic people. The place where most of us went was a place called Manny's, which was basically a white establishment, but we began to invade it. And Ken and I would both sit-in.

I think it *was* unusual for Ken to do this—playing with African-American musicians; wanting to play with them, wanting to listen to them, because he did it with so much intensity. In fact, he was criticised by a lot of white musicians —some who were prejudiced—about doing this.

> I think Ken felt that that was the real music. I think he felt like the African-American musicians—as I did—felt that the music had more potency, it had more strength, it had more feeling, and that's what I was attracted to.

I think that jazz research and hearing all these great blues singers and blues players was a very exotic thing, and a very important thing.

DICK ALLEN Everyone's perception of racial segregation in the fifties is likely to differ, and depends in part on the background of each individual. For my part, I was born and raised in the North of the United States, lived in England six years, and settled in New Orleans in 1950 when I was in my thirties. Like anyone of my background I was appalled that coloured (this was in the years before 'black' was used to describe Afro-Americans) were mandated by law to have different toilet facilities, drinking fountains and space on a bus—to name but a few of the regulations in force.

New Orleans, however, has always been an oasis in the South, with a combination of cosmopolitan veneer and laissez faire attitude. As a result, segregation was not as 'violently enforced' as in other areas of the South. The color problem was definitely bad, although the black and white races were not as polarized as they seem to be at present. In the 50s most Southern whites approved of segregation, and most of the colored bore it as something inevitable, akin to death and taxes, since they felt virtually powerless to change their condition.

LIZZIE MILES LETTER TO KEN COLYER UNDATED 1953

Hello Ken

It was nice hearin' from you as I was wonderin if you was still here or had gone. So when I read your letter I was happy to know you will be on your way home. 'Cause I guess you're tired of the whole thing. They should of let you stay right here with us. Same here—nice knowin you hope to be reading about you and your great Jazz band, Ken Colyer and His Jazz Coelies in America for an indefinite stay and when I come to hear you you'll be smiling just like a real dixielander ha! Ha! I wish you could always keep in touch with me.

If you run across Spencer Williams, writer of *Basin Street Blues*, tell him you and I used to sit & talk. He use to be my ole sweetie but when he got rich he forgot me cause I helped him to get rich. He's a $10,000,00 a year man in ASCAP. Tell all who knows me hello.

I'll always write you what's goin on in N.O. and send you music when I can. I'll pray for you to have a fine trip and a safe landing so until next time be sure and write.

As ever your friend, (signed) Lizzie Miles

KEN COLYER That's why I went there—to confirm the courage of my convictions. I thought: if I'm wrong, I'm wrong, but am I? It's the only way to find out—go there and play with these men and they fully restored my faith in humanity, music and everything.

WARRANT

FOR ARREST OF ALIEN

United States of America

DEPARTMENT OF JUSTICE

~~WASHINGTON~~

New Orleans, Louisiana

No. R-15555

To Any immigration officer

~~Or to any Immigrant Inspector~~ in the service of the United States.

WHEREAS, from evidence submitted to me, it appears that the alien
KENNETH EDWARD COLYER

who entered this country at Mobile, Alabama
on - - the 22 day of November, 1952, has been found in the United States
in violation of the immigration laws thereof, and is subject to be taken into
custody and deported pursuant to the following provisions of law, and for the
following reasons, to wit:

Section 241(a)(1) of the Immigration and Nationality Act, in that,
at the time of entry, he was within one or more of the classes of
aliens excludable by the law existing at the time of such entry,
to wit: An immigrant not in possession of a valid immigration
visa, in violation of sec. 13 (a) of the Act of May 26, 1924, and
not exempt from the presentation thereof by the said Act or regulations made thereunder.

I, by virtue of the power and authority vested in me by the laws of the
United States, hereby command you to take into custody the said alien and
grant him a hearing to enable him to show cause why he should not be deported
in conformity with law. The expenses of detention, hereunder, if necessary,
are authorized payable from the appropriation "Salaries and Expenses, Immigration and Naturalization Service, 1953 ." Authority has been granted to
release under $500 bond the alien named.

For so doing, this shall be your sufficient warrant.
Witness my hand and seal this 29 day of December, 1952.

Horace A. Nabers

HORACE A. NABERS
ACTING OFFICER IN CHARGE

16—54531-1

CHAPTER SEVEN
NEW ORLEANS TO LONDON

KEN COLYER We are going to try to popularise New Orleans music without distorting it, aborting it, or slapping any gimmicks on it. I am very glad to have Ron Bowden, who is the best British drummer I have played with.

SAM CHARTERS I can give you an interesting perspective as to what happened in New Orleans when Ken came. It was marvellous; I was not there while he was there, but I came down to New Orleans a couple of months afterwards, and the air was still vibrating with the effect of Ken's visit. In New Orleans, the breakthrough hadn't occurred; George Lewis was still working as a stevedore, still playing in the little club.

So there had been people who had come to New Orleans, like I'd come to New Orleans in 1950, American white musicians who kind of came up through the world of Dixieland, which was enormously popular.

But when Ken came, this was something totally different. He was not American; he wasn't one of these Dixieland players; he was English, for God's sake, you know. He really was from that other world, which for them was still totally unknown. No one had any idea, even, where it was. And here this kid showed up, and he was really a genuinely sweet guy. And he played very, very well. And his sincerity, and his honesty and his determination really stunned the people of New Orleans.

I remember he stayed with John and Ursula Bernard, and Ursula had really become very, very, very fond of Ken; but there was absolutely no concern from John's side, because he saw the same things in Ken that Ursula did.

> But when I came, the musicians were still talking about him: "Yeah, this man he came over from England— somewhere like that—and he played that trumpet, and my... he played like we did. I don't know how he learned... I don't know where he got that music from, but he could get that music."

And then of course, the incredible drama of being arrested and being thrown in prison —"And then they throw him in prison..." And that's *really* somebody who loves his music. And this fact that Ken had come... that he had really done this. All the rest of us had arrived by something like the train from California. But he had jumped ship! He came over, and got out that horn and played so well.

I think the thing that Ken learned in New Orleans and this was so crucial—which he brought to English jazz and which nobody quite understood—was its quality of informality. In New Orleans the musicians were just used to being called up for a job; they were expected to play in each others' bands, and they were all expected to know the same basic 500 tunes.

But I'm sure Ken had the same experience I did when he sat-in. I sat-in at Manny's and it was the same band that had been at the Stuyvesant Casino with Bunk; we had Lawrence Toca, but it was everbody else. Toca wasn't a great trumpet player, but he knew a thousand tunes, and he could play them all, and we were playing requests. Nobody ever stood up to take a solo, we didn't play a single jazz number, we just made our arrangements on whatever anyone asked us to play. And, I mean, Lawrence and Drag had a wonderful rhythm—it was really like just lying in a hammock; I could have played a scale, and it would have sounded beautiful.

I sat behind George, and just played, and I really felt like I

was just being rocked along. We were a dance-band, in a neighbourhood restaurant where you went, meet with a party of friends, and you came to dance. You wanted to dance to songs you knew, and the band bloody-well better be able to play them, and Ken brought that to Britain! Some of the sense of the music that should be part of the community... which should be allowed...

His sense of melody... his sense of the lyricism that really was at the heart of New Orleans Jazz; it should sing, and it should be danceable, and Ken had never, ever, lost that. And he had—as in New Orleans—heard and learned great tunes. You were never bounded by a certain repertoire—you could play anything.

MONTY SUNSHINE I wanted to turn pro, Ken wanted to turn pro, I think Sonny might have done. But then, I don't think we had sufficient gumption. We wanted to learn to play music. But then when Ken went to New Orleans, I and Chris and Lonnie used to play quartet things with no drums. Like an Eclipse Alley Five. Possibly Chris played trombone and Jim Bray played bass. But we still had no drums at that time.

CHRIS BARBER Monty and I in the first place, having realised that the amateur bands all around us had very little chance of learning the ability to produce the free improvised three-part front line which was for us the key to New Orleans jazz in its basic form—because they were not able to play together often enough to get hold of it—decided that we must get a band together which played this music as if their life depended on it. (Strangely, that is the definition of a professional musician!)

It was the summer of 1952. We quickly found several candidates. Ron Bowden was in Monty's "last of the Crane River Band" and was in fact not working but living at home on the odd gig money. Lonnie was playing banjo in my hitherto basically "classic" New Orleans orientated band but had his own band too (so he could play twice a week!) with Jim Bray on bass. Jim actually had a real day job (being a brilliant scientist) researching flame-thrower fuels for Shell, I think, which he did not wish to perpetuate!

So we had an Eclipse Alley Five line-up.

We found Pat Halcox, hopefully to be our trumpeter, about September 1952 and began practising every chance we had. At that time we met a group of Danish fans headed by Karl Emil Knudsen, a very influential and dedicated promoter of jazz and blues all his life who, hearing of our plans and liking the sound we were making, invited us to visit them for a few weeks shortly before "turning pro" the next year.

They could find us lots of clubs to play at and could put us up with different friends as guests for, say, three weeks. We accepted and carried on practising. We played just two public sessions, at Harold Pendleton's Club Creole in Gerrard Street, Soho, the 24th and 31st of December, 1952.

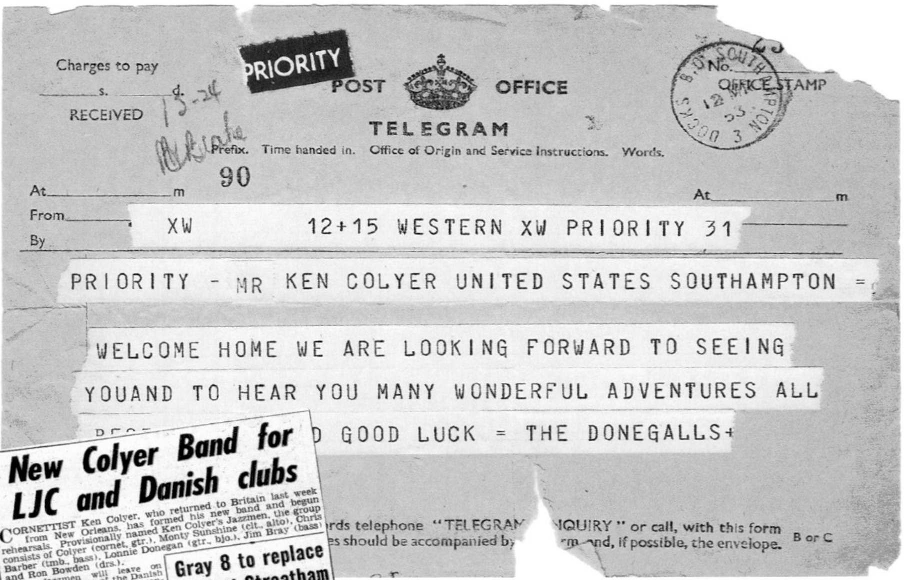

Charges to pay
______s. ______d.
RECEIVED
PRIORITY
POST OFFICE
TELEGRAM
Prefix. Time handed in. Office of Origin and Service Instructions. Words.
90
At______m
From______
By
At______m

XW 12+15 WESTERN XW PRIORITY 31

PRIORITY - MR KEN COLYER UNITED STATES SOUTHAMPTON =

WELCOME HOME WE ARE LOOKING FORWARD TO SEEING
YOUAND TO HEAR YOU MANY WONDERFUL ADVENTURES ALL
BES... D GOOD LUCK = THE DONEGALLS+

...rds telephone "TELEGRAM ENQUIRY" or call, with this form
...s should be accompanied by ...rm and, if possible, the envelope. B or C

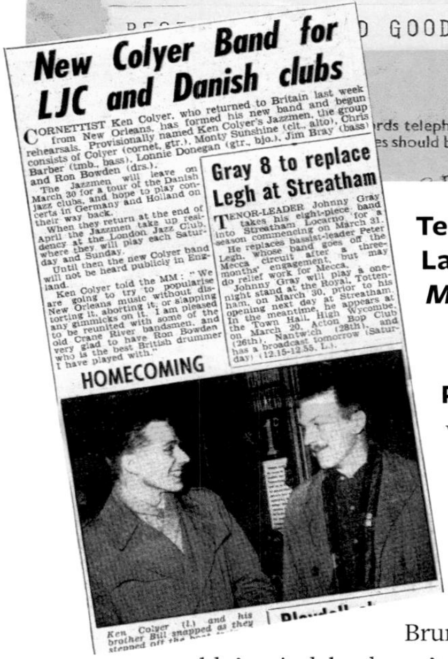

New Colyer Band for LJC and Danish clubs

CORNETTIST Ken Colyer, who returned to Britain last week from New Orleans, has formed his new band and begun rehearsals. Provisionally named Ken Colyer's Jazzmen, the group consists of Colyer (cornet, gtr.), Monty Sunshine (clt., alto), Chris Barber (tmb., bass), Lonnie Donegan (gtr., bjo.), Jim Bray (bass) and Ron Bowden (drs.).

The Jazzmen will leave on March 30 for a tour of the Danish jazz clubs, and hope to play concerts in Germany and Holland on their way back.

When they return at the end of April the Jazzmen take up residency at the London Jazz Club, where they will play each Saturday and Sunday.

Until then the new Colyer band will not be heard publicly in England.

Ken Colyer told the MM: "We are going to try to popularise New Orleans music without distorting it, aborting it, or slapping any gimmicks on it. I am pleased to be reunited with some of the old Crane River bandsmen, and very glad to have Ron Bowden who is the best British drummer I have played with."

Gray 8 to replace Legh at Streatham

TENOR-LEADER Johnny Gray takes his eight-piece band into Streatham Locarno for a season commencing on March 31.

He replaces bassist-leader Peter Legh, whose band goes off the Mecca circuit after a three-months' engagement, but may do relief work for Mecca.

Johnny Gray will play a one-night stand at the Royal, Tottenham, on March 30, prior to his opening next day at Streatham. In the meantime, he appears at the Town Hall, High Wycombe, on March 20, Acton Bop Club (26th), Nantwich (28th), and has a broadcast tomorrow (Saturday) (12.15-12.55, L.).

HOMECOMING

Ken Colyer (l.) and his brother Bill snapped as they stepped off the ...

Telegram from Lord and Lady Donegall, and *Melody Maker*'s report

PAT HALCOX I met Jim Bray when he came around and sat-in with the Albemarle band, and he was very good. He told us that he was playing with Lonnie Donegan's band, and he said why don't you come over, Bill Brunskill's playing with them and he wouldn't mind, he doesn't mind sitters-in, he's a nice guy. That was at a club in Abbey Wood. I went round the same night, and Ian Wheeler was there. I'd met Ian a couple of times.

We had Sonny Morris in the Albemarle band, the perfect trumpet player to play alongside. I loved playing with him, and we carried on being good friends. I miss Sonny.

JIM BRAY Monty and Chris had got together quite a bit. And Chris had always been interested in classic jazz but he did have a great interest in the New Orleans revival as well. Much more than I did. That's despite the fact that he's got a classical training, Guildhall School of Music.

It was a very small world. Everybody knew everybody. I'd never played with Chris at the time, I don't think. He had his own band then with two trumpets. They used to do classic jazz, but Chris was getting more and more interested in revival—the New Orleans Revival.

But we got together, and I was very friendly with Monty and already played with Lonnie and then Pat Halcox, who played in Southall—where we frequently used to play; he was a splendid trumpet player then as now. He became interested as well, though in fact he never joined the band as a regular thing. He was working as a chemist at the time—in a laboratory—and he wouldn't give up his day-job. We all had daytime jobs, but we packed them up, and we did some jobs with no trumpet at all, which were very successful.

Well, the band was very good, and it did very well.

PAT HALCOX Monty Sunshine came along, and what I didn't realise was that he and Lonnie were looking for a trumpet player and they liked what I did. They asked me if I would be interested in joining the band. I said, "Well I don't know, I'm quite happy doing what I'm doing, but I'll have a go at anything." I didn't realise then that Chris, Lonnie and Monty had decided to stop what they were doing and try and make a go of it for a living.

I was working at Glaxo Laboratories in the research department, and studying in the evenings, getting a day off every week. But to tell you the truth, I wasn't getting through any exams, because I was spending too much time playing music. Anyway, they said, "Would you be interested." So I said, "Well, let's see." We played one or two places as a band.

We weren't a rich family, and my dad had saved up to get me through sixth form, so I thought I'd better finish my studies.

We were sort of secret about the band. But of course Ken came back from New Orleans at the time, and that was the ideal opportunity.

There were quite a few trumpet players about, but once I had heard the band with Ken I thought: "What a lovely band."

RON BOWDEN We knew that Ken was in New Orleans. I mean, there was so much publicity on that—at *that* time, you know. It was sort of the front page of the *Melody Maker* and things—how he'd come back, and he'd been put inside.

Pat wouldn't turn pro—didn't want to turn pro—so that was how Ken got the gig, really. Because, you know, he was a good player, and Chris said, "Oh yeah, we should..." And he had a name, anyway, of being out there, and had been playing with the guys out there and everything. So some of that rubbed off on all of us—we hoped. And it was a good band, wasn't it?

JIM BRAY And that's when we heard that Ken was coming back from New Orleans, having been released from prison for immigration offences, and Chris thought it would be a very good idea to get him in the band, and... everybody else agreed that it *would* be a good idea.

CHRIS BARBER Our group had no name as yet, and we could imagine that Ken's name would bring people to hear what his sojourn in New Orleans had brought. We were a cooperative group—i.e. nobody owned it and we would share any income equally—but we wanted Ken to be the Leader in musical terms. Through Bill Colyer's good office we wrote a letter to Ken explaining the situation and we heard back that he would be happy to meet and have a go, as it were.

And we had this rehearsal, which went very well indeed—it was superb, and he was in good spirits; he was laughing, and—there's a picture of that session, where he's clowning about like an old picture of the O.D.J.B. where he's playing the trumpet like this with the bell round the wrong way. And you wouldn`t think Ken would do that, but he did, quite happily; he was enjoying himself —it was good fun.

ED O'DONNELL Bill wrote to me saying Ken was coming back to England and he'd been in New Orleans. And it *used* to be "…'kin' Barber." You know—that's what it were like when we were talking: "Barber and Sunshine," you know. And then in this letter—it was "Monty and Chris." They weren't supposed to be called that, you know. **The letter said Monty and Chris had had a talk, and they were going to form this band that Ken's going to join when he comes back.**

BILL COLYER During that period, almost daily, somebody like Chris or Lonnie Donegan would show up, pick my brains. They already had a band formed. Chris Barber had formed a band with Pat Halcox that was going to do a couple of weeks in Denmark but Pat was not able to go. So of course Chris could see the possibilities here.

Ken's name was big because of his letters that I was getting published every week in the *Melody Maker*. And I even did a broadcast; Denis Preston did a broadcast called *Letters to His Brother Bill* and I supplied all the records. Anyway, now the news had reached the *Melody Maker* via me that Ken was being deported to Ellis Island and his deportation was under this terrible Act by these two names, McCarran and Walters, where anybody who had not taken out American citizenship or wasn't born there was going to be deported, no questions.

By now, Chris, Lonnie and Monty were regularly coming into the International Book Shop to ask when Ken was due to arrive in this country. I would say, "Any day now, the USS *United States* is docking at Southampton."

I remember I took a train down to Southampton with Chris and we were in this big shed, tables laid out, and we were behind some barriers and I saw Ken come through the end of the shed with his suitcase. I burst through shouting out, "Hey, Ken!" And these customs officials bundled me back the other side and they threw the book at me because of all this bureaucratic crap. "They are deportees; they have still got to be searched for anything."

KEN COLYER We returned to London, talking about the group Barber had and hopes for its future. I heard a session with Pat on trumpet. It sounded just like another mediocre band. There was a lot of work to he done. We found a pub on York Way, up from Kings Cross station.

> The first rehearsal, Donegan made his self comfortable and said, "Now tell us all about New Orleans." I thought we were there to start work on a repertoire. The danger signals were already there.

As I was to say later, "I had sailed half-way round the world and done my share of evil." These jokers were still wet behind the ears.

MONTY SUNSHINE When Colyer came back from New Orleans, he went to the Porcupine and had a drink before he got on the train to go to Cranford. And off we went to Cranford, and he was pissed as anything. When he got there and sat down and picked his horn up, he couldn't play.

BILL COLYER We kept the original '53 band under wraps at first. Ken was back and nobody was going to know, and dear old Max Jones of the *Melody Maker* helped to keep it a mystery. People were already phoning him and asking, "When are we going to hear Ken Colyer?" All the weeks of publicity which I had been supplying was building up.

CHRIS BARBER On his return we speedily organised a series of rehearsals at a pub in York Way, behind King's Cross station. The only onlooker once or twice was Johnny Chown, a photographer friend of Lonnie's, who also had had a go at playing trumpet at a practice before we met Pat. The music was great. Ken's lead was, as always, the best lead I ever played with in a band of that instrumentation—and I have played with quite a few highly-regarded trumpeters!—and the band was rarin' to go.

And go we did.

JIM BRAY The band rehearsed for some time without playing in public. A month, or a few weeks or something, and then we went... did a month's tour of Denmark, and recorded in Denmark; 78s they were. And then came back to London and started playing in London, and we recorded practically straight away for Decca in London. Which was the *New Orleans to London* LP, which was very successful. I think there had been some publicity but it wasn't because of Colyer's name, it was because of the band... the quality of the band.

Colyer didn't really have much of a name at all. Not a popular figure with the crowds. Never was, as you know. Never changed. But there were some good bands about at that time. The Lyttelton band was of course excellent—he had had a very good band for some years. Keith Christie had left, but Johnny Picard was with the band, and they had Wally Fawkes and Bruce Turner on reeds. Johnny Parker on piano. Mike Daniels had a very good band. Freddie Randall had a very good band.

We decided to call our band under Ken's name. But it was a cooperative band.

He wasn't really the leader in much more than name. Though of course he had considerable influence on the band, because he was a man of very strong views.

But his views were very influential, but so then were Chris'. And everybody in the band were people of strong views. And the band *was* cooperative, and... nobody dominated at that time.

NEW COLYER BAND FOR LJC AND DANISH CLUBS *Melody Maker*, 21 March 1953

Cornettist Ken Colyer, who returned to Britain last week from New Orleans, has formed his new band and begun rehearsals. Provisionally named Ken Colyer's Jazzmen, the group consists of Colyer (cornet, guitar), Monty Sunshine (clt, alto), Chris Barber (tmb, bass) Lonnie Donegan (gtr, bjo) Jim Bray (bass) and Ron Bowden (drs).

The Jazzmen will leave on March 30th for a tour of the Danish jazz clubs, and hope to play concerts in Germany and Holland on their way back.

When they return at the end of April the Jazzmen take up residency at the London Jazz Club, where they will play each Saturday and Sunday.

Until then the new Colyer band will not be heard publicly in England.

Ken Colyer told the *MM*. "We are going to try and popularise New Orleans music without distorting it, aborting it, or slapping any gimmicks on it. I am pleased to be reunited with some of the old Crane River bandsmen, and very glad to have Ron Bowden who is the best British drummer I have played with.'

COLYER IN 'WOJ' AIRING BUT DOESN'T PLAY
Melody Maker, 4 April 1953

Following the sudden collapse of Lonnie Donegan with rheumatic fever, two unsuspected changes took place in last Saturday's 'World Of Jazz' broadcast.

A frantic last-minute search for a suitable deputy for banjoist Donegan resulted in several well-known traditional musicians being contacted only a few hours before the actual broadcast.

Ex-Crane River banjo-man Len Page finally took over the vacant place in the new Colyer group, which made its BBC airing with Pat Halcox, of the Albemarle Jazz Band, on trumpet in place of Ken Colyer.

Colyer, who was introduced over the air by 'World of Jazz' editor Denis Preston, obeyed decisions made by manager/brother Bill Colyer and did not play.

His first public appearance in England will be when the new outfit take over the resident job at the London Jazz Club on May 2, following their trip to the continent.

Until then, with the glamour of his famous New Orleans adventure behind him, Ken Colyer will remain the mystery man of the British traditionalist jazz world. Secret rehearsals are taking place daily with many of the latest Tin Pan Alley hit tunes replacing the old evergreens in the band's repertoire.

CHRIS BARBER So... I'd already planned since the previous summer to start by going to Denmark for a few weeks. We were going to leave our day jobs... and I was going to get out of the college and Monty was going to get out of *his* college—Camberwell Art School—and, as I say, we had it all planned out. And this summer it had gone pretty well; some of the people had said it was very good, and we'd arranged to go, at the end of March, to Denmark. **And we did, and arrived to see a banner saying "Chris Barber's Crane River Jazzband" and luckily, Ken didn't take offence. He might well have, but it was just so funny, that obviously... so he didn't bother. Which just shows that he could be quite amenable.** But... if there was someone there to prod him into being unreasonable—namely his brother—that could be another matter. Or worse: tell him what he'd said when he hadn't said it, and leave it to Ken not to actually shoot him down by denying it—which he never did. Brotherly love is a great thing, isn't it? I haven't got a brother, so it's all right.

JIM BRAY Well, we started in Denmark on a month-long tour of the whole of Denmark; we did by train. We had one of these one-month rail passes, and we used to go everywhere by train and stay at the station hotel. And very enjoyable it was, as well.

Ken's relationship with the band was good at first. We knew the sort of music he liked, and what he wanted, and he was very good at getting his points across both verbally and by demonstrating. But he was always... difficult, you know.

He was critical. Unable to accept people that didn't do what he wanted.

There wasn't any friction until much later, when Chris more or less wanted to assert himself more.

There was more friction between Donegan and Ken than there was between Chris and Ken. Well Ken found it hard to hit it off with anybody, really.

RON BOWDEN Storyville Records recorded us there twice.

Chris had the connection out there. Because he took his old band out there first of all. He made his connections out there, with Karl Emil Knudsen. That was used as a way to break the band in, that tour of Denmark.

It was all trains and things like that. On and off trains, trying to get a connection. But the people were so marvellous, anyway—they really were. We stayed at their places .

I loved that band—it was great. It was what I wanted to play. And when we'd done that tour out there, we got paid for it. I thought, "Wow!" Not that the money was the big thing.

When we got together and played, you got those great nights when you knew everything was clicking—which is what you get in jazz, isn't it? Which I think is proved on *New Orleans To London*—on that LP.

And there were several nights like that. And it just developed that sound, didn't it? With the six different guys in it. I mean, Chris being the musician of the band—really technical type, Monty being a nice, free-flowing clarinet-player, Ken doing the thing, and Lonnie wanting to do that. And me having all these other things going round in my head, and Jim doing his nice bass notes... and it just jelled. It wasn't something we strived for, it just happened.

KEN COLYER We *did* whip the band into shape, and Barber had already got a Danish tour lined up through Karl Knudsen.

Donegan was unreliable. He would be sitting at home when he should have been at the station waiting for a train. He missed a ferryboat in Denmark through his own ineptitude. It was only through a reporter paying the Captain that he turned back for him. He had a good story. He would be sick and miss jobs through a broken toenail or whatever.

SWEDISH CUSTOMS 'SEARCH' BRITISH
Melody Maker, Undated, 1953

A Swedish Customs official searched Jim Bray's Sousaphone as the Ken Colyer band arrived from Denmark on a special riverboat tour arranged by the Danish Storyville Club...

When time came for the boat to leave Landskrona and return to Copenhagen, guitarist Lonnie Donegan was found to be missing, and the boat left without him. However, the *MM*'s Danish correspondent (Hans Jorgen Pedersen) had the boat turn back when Lonnie arrived on the quayside.

LONNIE DONEGAN We went straight to Denmark and worked night and day for six weeks to rehearse and get the band in shape before anyone would hear us in England. We slept on floors and played for hamburgers, bacon butties, or whatever was going, and in that six weeks we created what was then known as Ken Colyer's Jazzmen.

Unknown to us, we made two albums, because there was some little Viking with a tape recorder following us and everywhere we went he recorded it. And that later became the Storyville Jazz label, and I am still waiting to be paid for it! I haven't even been given a cassette of the record, which has been selling ever since.

KEN COLYER Barber was about as pleasant and jumpy as a flea. Inquests after every number. "Are you going to keep that augmented G7 in?" I would say yes. Involved chord changes would be made, then I would play it different the next time.

We casually made some tapes in Copenhagen. Tape machines were still a novelty then. Knudsen started his Storyville label with these tapes. I never received a thank you or a penny. One number was on the Danish hit parade, but it wasn't selling or making any money. I hear that Knudsen is now a rich man. Bad cess to all parasites.

CHRIS BARBER During our time in Denmark Karl Emil Knudsen was always there and he arranged a couple of sessions at the Gentofte Hotel near Copenhagen, where there was a ballroom to play in... a rather echo-y sound, oddly like that on the Bill Russell recordings at Artisan's Hall (Artesian in New Orleans-speak) of George Lewis. We knew full well—and hoped!— that Karl Emil would try and make records to sell, and he did start Storyville Records with our recordings.

We had some money for the gigs in Denmark but Karl put all his money into building the label and died many years later a far-from-rich man, but the records he made with Ken and later by the same band (except one) under my leadership were the foundation for the (some say "would-be") New Orleans revival in Europe, to all our benefit. After all that I realise I did not categorically state that the Storyville recordings paid nobody, including me.

BILL COLYER They took off for Denmark and I didn't know at the time that Knudsen recorded everything. I don't know whether Chris got anything out of it but to my knowledge Ken never got a cent from those Storyville records. I certainly didn't.

I didn't go on the trip over there but I was Ken's guru still. Anyway, they came back and then the buildup really started. They had done all that Danish thing, working up as a band; they had about three weeks playing daily as well as the commercial concerts and they wanted to gain everything they could from

Ken's experience of playing with the gods.

But what actually happened was there was a guy called Hugh Mendl of Decca who came up to me—I was now the band manager and we had that regular gig for the Wilcoxes at Bryanston Hall under a church at Marble Arch—and I learnt that Decca wanted us because we were cleaner and more musicianly than the other bands on the market. And that's how we did the Decca session. But all we got was £70 for that recording, and that's between seven guys so that's a nothing.

But Decca were doing their "ffr" [full frequency range recording] thing so they had got top bands like George Evans with all his saxophones, Ted Heath and so on. They said that they wanted a Dixieland band: us. **What a fool! Why didn't I go for royalties or the usual things that they do today to keep control of the session? £70!**

CHRIS BARBER One of my closer friends among the record-collecting fraternity since 1946 was Hugh Mendl, who later worked for Decca Records. He heard our band with Ken and was very impressed, so I pointed out we would love to record and he checked with "Head Office" who accepted the idea and I sent him to Bill, who had (uninvited!) become the manager on behalf of Ken. We recorded for them at the beginning of September 1953 and the record was every bit as good as James Asman's rave review says. Oddly enough, when we parted company with Ken, Mr Asman started to criticise that record continually!

At that time nobody got royalties from the major labels unless they were artists who were essential to have and had to be persuaded financially to record.

JIM BRAY Well, we used to play at pubs, but also the London Jazz Club, which had moved from 100 Oxford Street at the time to the basement of the Bryanston Hotel. And that was a successful club… used to draw good crowds.

The band was of considerable impact.

MILLSTONES: TONY MILLS LOOKS ROUND THE TRADITIONAL SCENE
The New Musical Express, Friday, 1 May 1953

A little hope for the future was derived by London jazz purists at Ken Colyer's residential L.J.C. debut which coincided with the Club's fifth anniversary on Saturday.

From the first stomp the six piece Colyer outfit went with a swing which the packed enthusiasts greeted with the fervour it deserved; it was some little while before the first bearded gentleman ventured to dance and not listen.

Carried along by the unobtrusive but solid beat of the pianoless rhythm, Monty Sunshine, Chris Barber and Colyer showed well-nigh perfect co-ordination, and any little faults they may have in ensemble work can obviously be ironed out in time. Individually the front-line provided first-rate musicianship. The usual effortless Sunshine clarinet took more solos than anyone else; too many, I thought, because although Monty's playing was fresh and clear throughout, it did tend towards the mechanical occasionally.

In all the blues numbers, Ken's cornet was the epitome of self-restraint and feeling; particularly did I like his bowler-hat muting of *Just A Little While To Stay*, and others. Holding everything together was the earthy trombone of Chris Barber, who sounds better at every session.

Bert Wilcox tells me he hopes to introduce a little more of the "jazz for listening" element on Sunday nights. If Saturday's package is anything to go by, he won't be lacking ear-lenders.

THE MAGIC TOUCH OF NEW ORLEANS
James Asman, *Unknown magazine*, 2 May 1953

The neon lights glowed hotly on the sweating faces of the dancers as the band stomped *Gravier Street Blues* followed by an earthy version of *Isle of Capri*.

The atmosphere was hot and exciting. Movement swept band and dancers alike into a rocking, swinging motion.

Hundreds of gleaming faces crowded around the bandstand, nodding and staring, grinning with appreciation and roaring with unrestrained approval. The scene could have been Manny's Tavern in the heart of New Orleans where George Lewis holds court each week. It could have been King Oliver on a Chicago date or Ory sending the fans on the West Coast.

But it was, in fact, the fifth anniversary of the London Jazz Club in their Bryanston Street, Marble Arch premises.

On the stand was cornettist Ken Colyer with his Jazzmen. And most of the fans at this LJC session wanted to listen, not to jive. Colyer, fresh from the veterans of New Orleans and flushed with the phenomenal popularity of his band during their continental tour, was leading his musicians into a revival of jazz. The lessons Ken had learnt at the expense of a jail sentence and a mutiny at sea had been taught to a whole band of English 'revivalists'. The magic touch of New Orleans was in the shining trumpet of Ken Colyer and there was something like a beat in the rhythm section.

This was the nearest thing we had heard to genuine New Orleans music. The spontaneous applause, and the entranced faces of the crowds at the LJC on that 5th anniversary told us that Ken's adventures across the Atlantic had not been in vain.

The lessons learnt in the famous city of jazz were being applied to the decaying music of British 'revivalism'. It was a much-needed shot in the arm.

In fact it was the best thing we have yet heard by British musicians. It sounded very much like jazz.

MIKE CASIMIR The first time I recall ever seeing Ken Colyer was in London at the crypt under the church in Bryanston Street in 1953. The event was the inaugural session of the band that had been assembled by his brother Bill (we were told) for Ken to lead on his return from New Orleans. That was the band with Chris Barber, Monty Sunshine etc.

The London Jazz Club,
Bryanston Street

Ken Colyer's Jazzmen

Many of us there that night had been waiting in great expectation since the event had been announced. I imagine we were anticipating a performance verging on the sensational. As it happened, it was something of a letdown. The sound of the band was much more British than New Orleans, different to the originals we had grown accustomed to on records. We were all young then and limited in our knowledge of the music, but nevertheless very aware of the New Orleans style.

KEN COLYER We came back and worked the clubs. We took the dead night at what is now the 100 Club. We built the Mondays into the best night of the week. Bert Wilcox opened the Bryanston Street Club. It was very popular. **But all the money was going into Bert's pocket. I found out afterwards that the cloakroom attendant used to go home with more money than the band were getting.**

I had realised that Barber still considered himself the leader. All they wanted from me was a little reflected glory until the novelty wore off. I tried to meet Barber halfway musically. He was more interested in arranged numbers, all nice and tidy. A few tightly arranged numbers are OK and authentic rags must be arranged, but I have always been more interested in developing the important things that make New Orleans music unique.

The free interplay on the three-part counterpoint harmony—a rhythm section that lays down the right beat, that swings right whatever the tempo, correct control of diminuendo and crescendo until the climax of the tune is come to, a true feel for the blues. Humour too, but in the correct manner.

Finally, through a friend with influence at Decca, we secured a contract to make a ten-inch LP (*New Orleans To London*). We had Decca's top engineer. (I was never able to work with him again.) The session went well and the LP was soon on Decca's bestselling list. We made the record for a flat fee, which is normal for firsttime artists. I remember I received twelve pounds.

Monty got fifty for designing the cover, and good luck to him, but I find the values a little ironic. Inept management didn't help matters.

CHRIS BARBER It's funny: I just can't believe that Ken thought I wanted to be the Band Leader. I particularly wanted Ken to be the leader—not the "official drinker!" I just wanted to do whatever my abilities might do for the band's sake and be led by a great musician who valued others as much as himself (which he obviously didn't).

LETTER FROM URSULA BERNARD TO KEN COLYER 13 JULY 1953

Dear Ken,

When your letter arrived today, I determined not to keep you waiting so long again for a reply from us. So here I am, right on the job. One factor that helps considerably is that we are having nice cool weather this evening. After several weeks of temperatures in the upper 90's, it becomes difficult to even think, much less write. But tonight the weather is cool and we are fairly active.

John is sitting across the table writing to Peter and Bob Wallis, who must have given us up for dead long ago!

In his letter of last night (mailed this morning) John brought you up to date on the news, so I'll stick more or less to your letter.

I'm glad you met the Wallis boys. We are anxious to hear Bob someday on records, and hope the time won't be too far off. We haven't met Bob, but his letters make us feel like old friends, and we certainly did enjoy meeting Peter who was extremely likeable. We trust he will pay us another visit, because we are in a better position to take him around to hear bands and to meet the musicians than we were a year ago, when he was here.

Please give Dick Lane our regards. We have pictures to send him and will write him soon. If all your "New Orleans Alumni" get together I imagine you could have quite a session in London! And please [underlined] if Jim Asman's article is printed, send us a copy. I'd love to have it (especially to read what is said about Doc.) I could write a good article on the same subject, but between you and me—I can't as long as we live here in New Orleans. Maybe I could adopt a pseudonym.

Let us know how the parade band session went. At the baseball games. Did you stick to your cornet, or did you double at third base between numbers?

Your statement that your LP isn't out yet, but will appear shortly, more or less contradicts the "inside information" I received from Doc. His informant—whoever he is—must have stayed out too long in the fog! Anyway, when it does come out I hope it will be very popular and lead to lots of good things for you. The same goes for the Decca recording... If these latter are not to be distributed in the U.S.A. could we get a copy—or copies —from you or Bill at the Bookshop?

Your "confidential" news is terrific, and I surely hope it will come true—although why England should want Sharkey is beyond me. Couldn't someone put in a good word for George? Or Barbarin? Oh well, if your band comes over here, I'll not worry too much about who goes over. If things do work out right I'm extending, as of now, an invitation to bring your group up for a Gumbo supper. We are both feeling fine and hope you are too. Friday night we are leaving for 2 weeks in the Smoky Mountains. John's parents are driving down from New York and we will spend our vacation with them.

Keep us informed of all the news.

Best regards from Both of us,

Ursula

P.S. John asked me to add something which he forgot in his letter to you of yesterday, which he thought might be of interest in your parade band activity.

Several weeks ago at a street parade in Algiers he 'timed' the Eureka both as to beats per minute and steps per minute. During the entire afternoon they kept to a beat of 102 per minute, varying by only one or two beats over the hours—even after their several stops and pauses during the marching.

COLYER'S JAZZMEN ON DECCA LP
Melody Maker, 1 August 1953

Ken Colyer's Jazzmen are soon to make an LP for Decca Records.

The Colyer band, formed when Ken returned from New Orleans early this year, has so far recorded only for the Danish Storyville label. An LP of New Orleans jazz by a British band would be something of a departure for the local companies. And the record might well get American release on the London label.

Bill Colyer (the Jazzmen's manager) commented: "No contract has yet been signed, but a provisional date has been set for a Decca session, and we are hoping to make an LP for that company next month."

RON BOWDEN Ken never sort of rammed it down our throats, saying "Oh, you should play this" or "Baby Dodds would have done that." He would tell Monty—I mean Monty was already on a George Lewis kick. It was a natural thing for Mont, wasn't it? He didn't have to listen to a lot of other clarinet players to get that sound.

The most musical man was Chris, you know. Because he'd studied; he wanted to play jazz anyway. But he had studied bass as well, which he played.

CHRIS BARBER As far as I could see, Ken's problem was that he squashed things up inside of him and got angry, maybe because he realised he wasn't very articulate. He knew an awful lot about the music but was totally unable to communicate his knowledge to other people. So the band would be hanging on his every word, hoping he was going to teach them what they were doing wrong—and all he would do was grumble or swear at them for doing it wrong.

I spent the whole time with Ken trying to get help from him —for all of us—to play the music better; without much success, because he largely seemed to not want to explain anything. He may well have been afraid of using technical language which he was not really confident of.

But Ken did not realise that a leader has to sometimes help guide the musicians toward the best way of playing. So I tried to get him to explain what he expected of us in particular musical situations. He became abusive every time. And somebody has to take responsibility and stay sober and calm down unhappy promoters who don't like obvious drunks playing to the public in their premises and insulting people into the bargain.

MONTY SUNSHINE Chris is a very good teacher, but Ken was more an avid doer. He couldn't teach, but he could play it. That was the difference. But Chris could pick a trumpet up and play the notes, and Ken would follow it—pick the trumpet up and play it.

And Chris would try and show how to do certain things. And he'd say "Now play this..."and Ken would go "Oh, yeah..." He knew the sound of it, but he couldn't quite get the—not the polish—the method. He also played guitar and he could do all sorts of things, play flattened fifths and all sorts of things like that. But he never knew it.

> *New Orleans To London...* I'm very proud of that album. We sat down and we were learning—Ken was learning as well with Chris teaching us things. Terrific.

There were so many diverse things. When we started playing it was terrific. And they started the skiffle, and they got into it. But when we went to Denmark—strange thing: we'd start the evening off as a concert, then there'd be a pause. People would go out and drink and so forth; then there would be the skiffle, which would last about twenty minutes, then Jim and Ron and myself would go back, and we'd play for dancing, or for drinking. And it would be good, because people would hear us as a band listening, then the skiffle later on, and then of course, the dance at the end of this great thing.

CONGRATULATIONS TO COLYER
Melody Maker, 5 September 1953

Current popularity of Ken Colyer's Jazzmen has won them a recording contract. Bill Colyer recently completed negotiations with a major recording company for eight of the group's best

Lonnie, Bill, Ken and Chris

numbers to be released on an LP. Distribution of the disc is scheduled for early November, and judging by the high standing of the Colyer boys with the fans, it is likely to be followed by more.

L.J.C. EVICTED; PREJUDICE TO BLAME?
Melody Maker, 5 September 1953

Complaints from local residents are forcing the London Jazz Club to quit its premises under the Church of the Annunciation, in Bryanston Street, London, W.

The club holds its last session there on Sunday September 13th. From then on it will have to seek new surroundings.

Proprietor Bert Wilcox told the *MM*: "The trouble started a couple of weeks ago. Powerful outside sources complained to the Church, our landlords, about the noise and cheering emanating from the Club. Now the Church has taken up a clause in our contract forbidding us to commit a 'public nuisance.'

"The solicitors acting on behalf of the Church have told us we must quit by September 13th. We are therefore compelled to look around for new premises—and these are very difficult to find in the West End. Personally, I am inclined to think that some jazz-prejudiced parties have got to work."

The London Jazz Club, a favourite haunt of jazz aficionados for the past five years, first operated at Mac's Club, Gt. Windmill Street, W., until those premises were taken over by a night club. The LJC then moved to 100 Oxford Street, and finally settled in Bryanston Street last February.

Resident band at the LJC is Ken Colyer's Jazzmen. "Ken will, of course, still be with us when we do re-open," added Bert

Wilcox. This week, Ken Colyer's Jazzmen made two sessions for Decca, on which they cut eight sides of New Orleans jazz for early release on LP.

The titles were: *Isle of Capri, Harlem Rag, Cataract Rag, Too Busy, Stockyard Strut*, and three band originals—*Goin' Home, La Harpe Street Blues*, and *Early Hours*.

LJC SWITCHES TO THE MAPLETON
Melody Maker, 12 September 1953

The London Jazz Club, which closes its present premises at Bryanston Street, Marble Arch, on Sunday (13th) has not yet found a permanent home.

However, proprietor Bert Wilcox told the *MM*: "So that we can continue without a break I am temporarily holding Monday meetings at the Mapleton Restaurant, Coventry Street, commencing on September 21."

Ken Colyer's Jazzmen will continue as the club's resident band. For the last session at Bryanston Street, 15 year-old trumpet prodigy Nigel Carter guests with the Colyer outfit.

JAMES ASMAN REVIEW: *NEW ORLEANS TO LONDON*

Goin' Home, Isle Of Capri, Harlem Rag, La Harpe Street, Stockyard Strut, Cataract Rag, Early Hours, Too Busy. Ken Colyer's Jazzmen *Decca LF 1152*

It is not often that a critic has cause to correct a publisher's or producer's own 'blurb' for understatement. This is just one occasion when he can. The back of the sleeve on the new Ken

Colyer Decca LP states, "This is one of the most exciting records ever issued by a British jazz band."

Let us not carp, gentlemen. This is the most exciting record ever issued by a British jazz band without exception.

At a time when British jazz has steadily but surely descended into the doldrums; at a time when the early promise of such groups as the George Webb Dixielanders, the Yorkshire Jazz Band, the Saints Jazz Band, the Cranes and the Lyttelton outfit with Keith Christie had not been fulfilled, along comes this swinging and startlingly authentic music.

Goin' Home is a delightful Colyer original featuring Ken himself on the vocal. *Isle of Capri* swings infectiously from the first note and the muted work is very effective behind the easy riding clarinet of Monty Sunshine who, incidentally, was responsible for the cover design.

The two rags, *Harlem Rag*, and *Cataract Rag*, are taken at an easy, lilting tempo with intelligent attention being paid to the intricate chord sequences. *La Harpe Street* is yet another composition by Ken Colyer, taken at a relaxed tempo and possessing a wealth of melodic invention.

Keppard's *Stockyard Strut* has immense spirit and swing. Clarinet descant figures add an attractive treble voice to the fierce trumpet work of the leader and the exceptionally fine trombone of Chris Barber. *Early Hours* is a stately blues flavoured piece and *Too Busy* provides the LP with a bouncing finish.

The band is well on form, playing in the New Orleans idiom with certain apologies to George Lewis and his colleagues but claiming a life and style of its own. As a result this is no mere revivalist band imitating the notes and phrases of the record it has heard. Instead it is an integral unit producing healthy uninhibited jazz with discipline and taste.

One last word—this disc is quite likely to attract a much wider market than the purist jazz lovers can provide.

JIM GODBOLT Jack Payne was one of the major names, right from the late twenties when he became the director of the BBC Dance Orchestra. It was very much a commercial band—there's hardly a record that you could play which has got any, what used to be known as "hot" content.

Whereas with Lew Stone, with Roy Fox, Ambrose and Billy Cotton there was the occasional example. But somehow or other he seemed to get latched on to Ken's record of the *Isle Of Capri*.

And there was this pre-war dance band leader, who ended up broke like a lot of them did in fact, he ran an off-licence, which was a bit of a come-down for him, I would have thought. And it must have been *something* that tickled him—that *Isle of Capri*. It may have been because it was a Tin Pan Alley tune which he played in the past. He found this version entrancing and plugged it. And because he was on the radio week after week—I forget the name of the programme—it became a bestseller. Well, I say a bestseller. It got to number eight or nine in the charts I believe.

KEN COLYER I was wandering around the Gloucester Road area one day when something led me down Queen's Gate Terrace. There was a notice outside one of the old houses: "Handyman wanted for rent-free room." "Just the job," I thought and rang the doorbell. I noticed that a Doctor Prince lived on the ground floor and the Baroness Huzzar was in residence. "Pretty good," I thought, "things are looking up."

A tall woman answered the door and I explained that I had seen the notice and was a very handy man. I waited a while and then she said the Baroness would see me. **The Baroness was a handsome Hungarian woman. She drove a snazzy light blue MG, which was parked outside. She oozed charm and I got the job.**

I was to have a room in the basement, where her maid lived, and redecorate some of the rooms. Although I had worked a bit in the building trade, my knowledge of decorating was sketchy, although I knew about having my back broken by falling bricks. Bill was working in the International Bookshop and found me a cheap book for handymen.

Later, I came back off a trip and there was a letter in the kitchen telling me to pack my bags and go. Unfortunately I have never bothered too much about keeping letters once I have read the message and, having to travel as light as possible, carrying a guitar, a horn case and a suitcase doesn't encourage one to keep anything considered unnecessary.

Although we have never worked together regularly, Johnny Parker was a good friend to me when I was scuffling and didn't have a decent place to live. I saw Johnny Parker somewhere and explained my predicament. "My spare room's free, come and stay with me. The rent's a pound a week." Not long after this I read that the Baroness Huzzar had been arrested in Canada selling counterfeit dollars. She got out of this one by feigning illness and being brought home on a stretcher, leaving all her lawyers with unpaid bills. You've got to hand it to her, she had style.

JOHNNY PARKER Well, by that time, Maureen—my first wife—and I had a spare room in our little flat in Grosvenor Avenue, Highbury. And Ken had taken over the spare room, because he wanted somewhere to stay, and that was exactly at this time. That's when I got to know Ken. And he was a delightful lodger, as it happens. Never entered the room without knocking first; would always say "Is it OK to make a cup of tea?" You know—rent was always paid meticulously on time. And Ken would say "Is it all right if I come and do this?" and then he'd brush his hair. And I'd say "What are you rushing for?"

"Well, I've got to be there, because, you know, I've told them to be there at two-thirty, and..."—they used to pick up at Madame Tussaud's in Baker Street. "Yeah, but you've got plenty of time." "Oh no, I have to be on time." "Yeah, but you're the bandleader." "That's all the more reason to be on time." That was Ken's attitude. As opposed to all the other bandleaders. There was this rather old-fashioned hairstyle he had. Apparently because he wanted to look like Wild Bill

Davison.

When we used to come back, usually after I'd finished my lot with Humph, and he'd finished with his, and we'd get back home, and play some records and drink. We used to drink rum-laced toddys—a spoonful of sugar and top it up with hot water—which he used to drink in the Merch. Yeah, we used to play things.

> He liked all sorts of things, like Artie Shaw was one of the things we played, and there was a Woody Herman record that he liked, and he professed to like Chopin. So, you know, people may think that all he wanted to hear was Bunk Johnson, but far from it. He had quite catholic tastes.

And we got on... fine, it was just one of those things—we hit it off. I seem to remember he kept on about Mile Barnes, which was Emile Barnes, of course. But he certainly said he was worried about the Barber Band. He wasn't happy with the band. And he couldn't put his finger on it, but he didn't know quite what to do.

DELPHINE COLYER I thought there was something not quite right with it all. Little things that Ken said: "I'm not very happy here." I think he may have felt that they were jumping on the band wagon of his name; because he *had* done those things. And I think that Chris was really a little bit too technical; very clever, but not earthy enough really for Ken.

MONTY SUNSHINE During the time we were playing, there were lots of arguments—reasonable arguments: "No, we shouldn't do this" and so forth. And after a while, I think Ken got... unnerved with Lonnie. Because Lonnie—he'd put you up and put you down. So, in the end, he couldn't stand Lonnie. And I'm afraid that the rhythm section started to get on Ken's nerves. I mean, it was terrific; Jim played lovely bass and... I dunno, it wasn't what he wanted.

CHRIS BARBER There'll always be tension with Ken and Lonnie in the same band. I mean, any band that Lonnie was in there was. First of all, he was a small person, with a small person's inferiority complex; trying to make himself big, sometimes. He was a dedicated cheeky chappie; his idol was Max Miller.

Now, this put him exactly at odds with Ken Colyer, who disliked cheeky chappies more than anything else in the world, because he was the kind of person who could never think of the riposte that wins the day against a cheeky chappie's smart-Alec remark.

So he was always swallowing it, and hating it. So, he didn't like Lonnie, and there was always going to be a difficulty with Lonnie—he was an awkward person, you know. I mean, it wasn't difficult to find Lonnie annoying. And that was all. He didn't seem to criticise anybody much else. The difficulty was that you didn't know, because Ken never said anything to anybody, really.

RON BOWDEN Tony Donegan—he took his name from Lonnie Johnson. And Ken probably thought, "Oh, what is this little white guy like that trying to call himself after a black guy?" He somehow took against Lonnie.

Lonnie was basically a blues man, you know. He really was. He loved the Big Bill Broonzys and all those, and Lonnie Johnson. Which is what he was doing, you know. And taking up and playing guitar, but the banjo as well. But when it was a band thing happened, you needed a banjo in the band.

Lonnie was more commercially minded, the same as Chris was, when the split came.

> Because Ken wanted to play that straight ahead New Orleans—and just sit there and play. Whereas with Chris—and probably the rest of us—we all thought: "Oh, God, we're making music, and people need to be entertained."

And it's gotta be that way, you know? If you're gonna go out and get paid for a gig, people wanna see something happening onstage.

MONTY SUNSHINE I found that Ken had very good showmanship, in the sense that he knew when to put his horn through, to put it out, put it down and perform in front of people.

LONNIE DONEGAN Wherever there was a gap I would sing my little songs and people, generally speaking, either liked it or went for a beer—and I got better at it. And Chris would join in on the bass when he felt like it, Ken would join in on the guitar when he felt like it, and his brother Bill would join in on the washboard, or sometimes my bass player would play—it was very much an ad-lib situation. But it is all on record—on the "Danish" record.

Ken left primarily due to a personal private division. It wasn't a musical one. We all wanted to play the same music—we even played at one time some Modern Jazz Quartet which horrified everyone; we played ragtime, which was Chris' idea—he actually got sheet music before people knew what ragtime was in this country, and he wrote the parts out; Monty, Ken and Chris all played the parts and it all worked out extremely well, as you can hear on record. So there was no problem musically.

But as you may know, he was not an easy person to get on with when you have to live with him night and day, and was very

moody and psychologically a very complex person. Whereas I am not, I have no depth. Chris knows everything and is also a good psychologist, so he was quite able to not be condescending to anybody, which must have been quite hard for him because he was in such a position, but he wasn't.

One of the reasons he wasn't is because he gave everybody the full value of what they were doing on their own instrument—he realised Ken's values musically as a New Orleans trumpet player; he knew their failings, their drawbacks, where they were playing wrong, but he balanced that against the good effects.

I am talking in hindsight now, after the ball was over. There would be rows with Ken which was often nothing to do with the music. One night there was an unholy row and he fired me, and the band said, "You can't fire him because it's not your band."

He said "Yes it is." But we said it wasn't, it was a cooperative band and you couldn't fire anybody. The next morning he sent Bill around to tell everybody that they were fired, so we said "OK, we accept it." We phoned Pat Halcox and he wasn't in that night. And that was the end of that.

HAROLD PENDLETON Ken was afflicted with a poor lip, and the way I saw it was that in order for Ken to rest his lip, they started to do rent-party music in the middle of the set. I cannot remember when it changed from rent-party to skiffle, and I can't remember who thought of it; whether it was Chris, whether it was somebody else—Donegan maybe.

All I know is that you had this interval in the middle of an evening when Ken played his left-handed guitar, like Paul McCartney, and Chris seized the opportunity to jump on bass, which he'd studied at the Guildhall School of Music, and Bill or Beryl Bryden banged away on washboard. Just to give Ken a rest—in my opinion; it wasn't intended to be a feature.

COLIN BOWDEN Ken and Lonnie were like chalk and cheese. They were two completely different personalities, and it was inevitable that they would fall apart. They were at completely opposite ends of the spectrum. Ken would swear about Lonnie occasionally, as Lon would swear about Ken. I put this in my diary: "Spring 1954. Sonny and I went down the 100 Club; a row between Tony and Ken." And then later: "Another row. What a waste of beautiful music…" Because it *was* a good band. There's no doubt about it.

And that was the second time. And then about a fortnight later it says: "I went to the White Hart, Southall to sit-in with the Albemarle. Pat's ever so worried about joining Chris in a fortnight's time." And that's in the middle of May. And of course, on the first of June 1954: "Pat joined Chris Barber band." And then Chris based his style, I think, on those early Decca recordings. He never had a piano player, and that's why his rhythm section had that clipped sound. That's the sound that he was after.

CHRIS BARBER Ken often got drunk and played badly. He'd offended everybody in the band. People were going to leave because Ken was so disgusting; **when he was drunk, he was so terrible, you know. So it was just stupid. We thought we were going to be a professional band— to be professional; make sure you're in good condition, and do your work properly. And he wasn't some of the time.**

On the other hand, he *did* value people that behaved properly. He expected people to be dignified, but when he got drunk, he wasn't, that's the point. When he was drunk, he didn't know how to comport himself; when he *wasn't* drunk he was OK.

The difficulty was, he was a very incoherent person, as regards speaking. He didn't have the gift of the gab— the opposite. And he felt, I feel, very embarrassed.

I remember Monty and me— particularly me—asking him how to play. He'd just come back from New Orleans— he knew. His phrasing was impeccable all the time, and ours wasn't; and I'd say,

"What's that phrase; how do you get that?" and he would mumble something— not exactly helpful.

He was probably afraid that he'd be using a word and I would laugh because it was the wrong sort of word, you know; I wouldn't—I wouldn't in the least. But nevertheless, he was a bit like that. And he'd just get frustrated because you weren't playing it right, and when you'd draw attention to it and ask him for help, he would blast at you on the trumpet in the middle of a number, you know. Which is stupid, but I mean, that was how he was.

But it was a psychological thing really, that he felt embarrassed that he wasn't articulate. He *was* inarticulate. I mean, people who are in that sort of situation frequently *do* have that sort of feeling. When they get drunk.

Bill Colyer finally got himself rowed back in. It was a condition from the beginning that he wasn't going to have anything to do with the management. Well, all of us felt the same way, and in the end he rowed himself back in again.

HAROLD PENDLETON Around that time everybody was starting to talk about Bunk Johnson and New Orleans, and Bill was on the air all the time. Transmitting! I happened to have a club in Old Compton Street which bands like Mick Mulligan and so on played at.

And Ken was there one night, and he got spectacularly drunk, and I helped him up the stairs into the open air, which was probably the worst thing to do. And we sat on the wall of a bombsite, and Ken—unusually, because he and I had never really got on—suddenly talked to me. It was not what he normally did.

And apart from declaring his undying love, he told me that his hero, and the man he always wanted to play like, was Wild Bill Davison, which took me totally by surprise. Because it was totally unlike the way Ken played. And I think it was pursuing this dream of playing like Wild Bill that led him to join the Christie Brothers Stompers.

JOHN BEECHAM I think one of the problems between Ken and Chris was this: Chris knows all the nuts and bolts of music and can arrange numbers, whereas Ken could only play instinctively and wasn't able to explain in technical terms what he wanted. So Chris could impose his musical ideas more quickly and more effectively on the band than Ken could. Chris would analyse the music. Ken would call these analyses "inquests".

In later years Ken would describe these "inquests" to us, using a nerdy, whiney voice when quoting Chris Barber. Ken would say, "Barber... 'Ke-en. Are you going to finish the number on that note, Ke-en?' And I'd say yes, and Barber would rush round the band changing everything. Then next time we played it, I'd play it different."

Why was he so anti-Chris? He wrote: "Barber has never stopped maligning me through the years like some petty schoolboy." But it's not true that Chris went around bad-mouthing Ken. I think Ken was jealous of Chris' abilities. Ken resented Chris' musical arrangements because he, Ken, couldn't work things out technically the way Chris could.

Ken could play the notes that Chris worked out, because Ken had a very good ear, but that meant that he would have to do what Chris said—and that was something that Colyer would never like.

KEN COLYER Things came to a head after about twelve or thirteen months. I tried to split the band, taking Jim Bray and Monty with me. But they knew which side their bread was buttered, so I left on my own when Barber tried to dictate ridiculous terms to me in Harold Pendleton's presence. I told them what they could do with their terms, and Pat Halcox rejoined the band. I had wasted a year's work.

A fan of mine took two Americans to hear them the week after I left. They listened for a while, then one said, "They are good, but somebody has taught them."

The fan explained who had taught them, but my influence didn't last. It never does, as events have always proved. The clubs and promoters didn't do me any favours. Barber's star was in ascendancy.

BRIAN HARVEY It was a Friday early in May, 1954—warm but not hot, with a hazy sky over central London. The commuters—all but the late-drinking stragglers—had fled down the rat holes of tube stations, and the streets of Soho were now only populated by the over made-up, heavily lipsticked regulars awaiting business and the first evening visitors in search of thrills in London's "naughty" district.

Even though it was a fine night there was an almost thundery electricity in the air, however, and out on the pavement for a break I wondered if it might thunder. And then, back at my desk, listening to the band, I began to wonder whether the almost tangible electric feeling of oppression, of tension, I was experiencing was not the weather at all but something subtly psychological that I'd sensed but not understood—a near subliminal signal I'd received from someone, or a group even, but not been conscious of at the time.

The band was playing on. They sounded great, with their climaxes echoing round the room sounding for all the

world like the Bunk Johnson band in San Jacinto Hall.

There was a joy about them as they went through *Lord, Lord, Lord, You've Sure Been Good To Me*, with Ken's unique vocal twang being unmistakeable, and yet the intervals between numbers were longer than usual. I went into the hall for a moment, leaving the cash desk open to a helper, and there (it became obvious) was the source of the tension.

The bandstand itself and the musicians—they were arguing in whispers but with heat and waved arms. This was clearly not a disagreement about what to play next or who did what on the last number, but something more serious. I was worried, frightened even, that they would come to blows and I'd be lumbered with a club full of people and a band that didn't play—or even couldn't.

I'd better explain. Having dropped out of college, Harold Pendleton, a pioneer London jazz entrepreneur, had given me a junior managerial job in his attempt to create London's first seven-days-a-week jazz club, The London Jazz Centre, at 14 Greek Street. We had different bands every night, but Ken Colyer's Friday session was the star attraction and vital to the club because few other nights would break even financially. That night—if my memory is not now too blurred by my age—I was mainly on the cash desk in the foyer.

The evening continued, but the band became somewhat ragged and uninspired. The breaks between numbers became longer, and by the end of the evening the atmosphere on the stand was really bad.

Chris Barber, Monty Sunshine, Lonnie Donegan, Jim Bray and Ron Bowden left, I think, together. Ken and his brother Bill followed later—all looked downcast—but being junior I didn't ask what had happened, what was going on. And then I was told the shock news—Ken had fired the band, sacked them to a man.

At that time I was more concerned with my job and keeping body and soul together than with the actual music. And my main concern was how the hell do we find a band to replace Ken on Fridays and a band that would fill the place?

In truth I needn't have worried. Within days, Harold Pendleton—always a man to come up trumps in a crisis—had installed the new Chris Barber band, with Pat Halcox on trumpet (Ken's old band minus Ken) on Fridays, and Ken's new band came in on Sundays.

Chris' band was brilliant, but Ken's was abysmal. Acker was at that time the worst clarinettist I had ever heard, Ed O'Donnell was very poor, and Ken sounded dispirited. Their sound was, frankly, appalling—but life moves on and so did I.

The factor in all this that has bothered me over the years is this: just what did happen that night? What was it all about and were there any rights and wrongs that haven't been explained? Ken Colyer's band at that time (1954) was perhaps the best-known jazz band in Europe —maybe in the world. He had a recording contract with Decca, they were unprecedentedly giving him wide publicity, and through the national radio "plays" every Sunday lunchtime of *Isle Of Capri* by former bandleader Jack Payne, that track became an enormous "pop" hit with a consequent national explosion of exposure (and work) for the band.

The band sounded great to most of us. It was exciting, rhythmic, inventive and very fresh sounding. What on earth could have happened to break it up? Could it have been money—many band bust-ups have been. Or was it something far more fundamental?

A chance conversation not long ago with a musician friend who was close to the events of the time threw light on the subject. I hadn't thought that he would be willing to discuss it or reveal what he knew, but the forty-five years since those dramatic scenes have mellowed some people's feelings towards the participants. "Yes," he told me, "I remember it well. Ken fired the band—or the band fired Ken; it depended on who you listened to. But I knew it was going to happen two weeks before." That threw a whole new dramatic light on the happenings of May 14, 1954. My informant told me that Pat Halcox was earmarked to take Ken's place weeks before the actual row onstage. "It was a conspiracy," he said, and would say no more.

CHRIS BARBER So Bill Colyer said, "Well listen, Chris. Ken's going to fire the rhythm section." So I told him, "What the hell... He can't! What's wrong, anyway?" He said, "Jim Bray doesn't swing and Ron Bowden's too modern. And he hates Lonnie's guts."

Jim didn't swing on his own, but he made it possible to swing—he was a very good bassist; Ron wasn't a mouldy-figge drummer—he never had been. From the very beginning with the Crane River he wasn't. He was a sort-of Gene Krupa-y—not quite modern jazz. And Lonnie was a great banjo player. Terrific banjo player... and he provided the bounce, you see, and Jim Bray was the basis, and Ron swung—great swing to it. But it worked. The point was that it worked. So, OK, Lonnie could be difficult...

But I mean, we had been putting up with Ken's drunken, absurd, objectionable nature for the sake of the band for ages. And didn't try to do anything about it—you couldn't.

We just hoped he would stop, or manage it better, and improve as he went along. So, it didn't make sense, so I just said "Well, it's a cooperative band, here's five of us, and one of Ken. We're firing him. Two weeks' notice."

By the time that all happened we were playing six nights a week—we had six residencies. So I said, "You're fired—two weeks' notice." So Bill Colyer kept the band fund. There wasn't much in it—about ninety quid or something—and Ken kept his band-jacket. Only he kept the wrong one—he kept the one that he thought looked like a bandleader's jacket

As for the idolatry, Bill built it. I mean, Ken just wanted to play. He liked playing. He never put himself forward in anything, ever. I mean, the fact that we were in the band with him, we wished he *would* put himself forward and say something. We said from the beginning, "We're going to have a band that get on the stage, and you're going to be on time and just say what we're going to play, and start." And he always did that. Very keen to be a professional musician. And you couldn't take exception to it. At first.

BILL COLYER It seemed that what Ken was trying to teach the 1953 band by example and by demonstration, it just didn't work with Barber. But Ken never verbalised his disenchantment; I was the one who'd have a go at the guys about dynamics and nuances and rhythm and volume, light and shade. I often wished Ken would have spoken his mind and got into in-depth conversation with the others.

Ken had gone through that war the tough way, so by the time he joined the Merchant Navy, even though still a very young man, he was already an adult and knew what he wanted. You didn't mess with him if you didn't want a right hander. But then he still looked up to me because I had a very good knowledge of the music and people. If he did express dissatisfaction to me, I'd try to pour oil on troubled waters. But, bottom line, he was right!!

COLIN BOWDEN I used to see the band at 14 Greek Street and the 100 Club. I was in Sonny's band at the time—that was in the spring of '54. I used to sit-in; I knew there was something going on. There used to be a sort of tense atmosphere.

Well, Ron Bowden used to say "Do you want a sit-in?" And then he didn't come back, and... I seem to remember one night finishing the session. But this was when they were playing their last knockings. And whether Ron was lining me up to get the

NOTTINGHAM JAZZ CLUB
Thursday August 13th

KEN COLYER'S
JAZZ MEN

FROM LONDON JAZZ CLUB

This is the first appearance of the new Ken Colyer Band outside of London. Besides featuring Ken Colyer, the band also has two other famous instrumentalists Monty Sunshine - Clarinet and Chris Barber - Trombone. Another interesting feature of the Band is that like many of the authentic New Orleans bands they do not use a pianist. This presentation of a famous London band will be followed by many more throughout the winter season, all on normal Thursday meetings and for the relatively small subscription of 2/6d.

Thursday August 13th

KEN COLYER'S JAZZMEN

Admission that evening only......2/6   Still the cheapest prices in the land!!

job, I don't know. Later on he may have been told how to play, the way Ory dictated how Ram Hall played on recordings. And when you heard Ram Hall on live concerts it was a different ball-game… Ron was playing… he would have liked the Dixieland players like George Wettling.

Because I knew Donegan as well. Because I'd been rehearsing with Donegan in '53 while they were waiting for Ken to come back. I wasn't in on the scene—I was on the outside of it. They were forming a band; I remember playing with Monty a few—clarinet, banjo and drums in an East-End pub near Mile End.

I used to play down at 14 Greek Street and I used to play at 44 Gerrard Street, and in the intermission I used to run up the road and go and sit-in with Ken's band at Greek Street and come back. And when I wasn't working anywhere I would often play a full set. But it was at the time when all the trouble was going on within the band, but I didn't really know what it was all about. I was working myself with the Trevor Williams band, and the Phoenix band used to play down at Gerrard Street and so did Mick Mulligan.

RON BOWDEN When it happened was down at the 100 Club when Bill Colyer came in to the Blue Posts—there was no bar down at the 100 Club then, in those days. You used to go up there in the interval, and Bill says, "I think that Ken's gonna sack the rhythm section." He said that to Chris.

But there was something that Ken didn't like—or was it Bill? But Bill said that it was Ken gonna do the sacking—he didn't like the rhythm section. He was happy with the front-line—Monty and Chris—and of course, Chris realised that Ken was *not* as commercially minded as he was. He had this thing of being a bandleader, anyway—Chris. And Chris was happy with Lonnie and myself and Jim, and Monty. So both of them said "No, we don't want to go that way—the way Ken wants to go—of just playing straight-ahead New Orleans music."

So with Chris having the ideas and wanting the range—doing all those things that he came out with: *Echoes Of Harlem*, those songs that nobody ever played… So Chris had all these ideas, so he thought he wouldn't have been able to achieve that with the way Ken was gonna go.

And he said, "Who is Ken to sack the rhythm section? He's in no position to, so we'll sack *him*. And we'll get Pat Halcox in."

I mean, I didn't want to play like Baby Dodds—nobody could play like Baby Dodds, anyway. So it's no good sort of thinking that way. It wouldn't have satisfied him anyway. I know he used to go on about my cymbal—I used to play too much cymbal. But the thing that knocked me out after that was when George Lewis came over with the Barber Band, and I played and George used to turn round—believe or not—and say, "Oh, I like that. Can you play that?"

So, that was one of the things. Maybe I wasn't—I was doing the snare-drum thing and all that. That was OK, but you couldn't do that all the time. You just had to think of playing different things behind different solos. And not stick to the Baby Dodds things that I couldn't do anyway.

> ## Some of me had to come out… well it does in everybody's playing, surely. Everybody listens to everybody else. But, deep down, it's you that's coming out.

Then it all started happening with the Chris Barber Band. And everybody was happy.

Then we went to Denmark with Pat.

COLIN BOWDEN This is my diary for 21st May, 1954: "I went down to the London Jazz Centre (14 Greek Street) to hear Colyer. The band were playing really well, it's a pity it's one of their last sessions."

I used to see the band at Bryanston Street with Pat Halcox while they were waiting for Ken to come back from New Orleans.

May 19th, 1954: "In the evening met Harry at Gloucester Road. Went to the White Hart, Southall. Albemarle were playing very well. We had a sit-in for a couple of tunes. Got home at 11.30."

Pat Halcox was very worried about taking Ken's place in Chris' band. I just thought Pat was as good as Ken. You didn't analyse people, they were just two trumpet players. Pat played in a similar style.

JIM BRAY Pat Halcox, who was of course in the band really before Ken joined, left his daytime job and joined the band in his stead. But I mean, as the records show at that time, it didn't really very greatly change the style of the band. That had become an established thing. And had very much a style.

To a certain extent Pat's playing *was* like Ken's.

Ken asked me to join his new band, but I thought that life would be a lot more peaceful with Chris—without all the tearing passions. So he got a good collection of musicians with him. Ed O'Donnell down from Leeds, Disley, Acker Bilk, Stan Greig. But the band was a very rapidly changing composition. People would leave quite quickly. Ian Wheeler was with the band, wasn't he?

But of course, everybody admired Ken very much, but he was a very difficult person to get on with, and remained so until he died. He always had to have an awful lot of people he hated. It was very necessary for him to hate people. And none of those people that he hated did nothing but admire and like him.

I found him difficult to be with, of course, as everybody did. But he liked me. I was never an enemy of his. But I worked with him off and on for the rest of his life. Odd gigs here and there when he was short of a bass player.

PAT HALCOX I liked Bunk Johnson because there was this divide with, on the one side, the roots thing, and on the other, Humphrey Lyttelton playing classic jazz. I hate these labels, but you have to use them sometimes, and I could see beauty in both of them really. When I joined the band I realised it had its basis as a New Orleans-style band, so I'd better get stuck in and buy the records and see what happens.

I was quite influenced by Ken in those days, and also by Humph. I didn't know which side of the fence to go down on, and I didn't particularly want to go down on either side.

CUFF BILLETT I didn't really listen to the Barber band. I remember hearing some with Ken with his next band, and I thought it had a great feel to it. The one with Chris *did* sound a bit more mechanical. It seemed always that Ken jutted out. A bit like—I'm not putting this as a parallel really—but the way that Bix would suddenly jet out of the Whiteman band; there was that. He sounded different to the rest of the band, that's what I thought; thinking back on it... the dim and distant past.

JOHN WURR I was mightily impressed by the Colyer/ Sunshine/Barber outfit, appreciating its tidy musicianship and variety. But it's now easy to see why Ken soon became frustrated by its rhythmic sterility and its rather "British" sound. As Humph so perceptively said on his radio show at the time of Ken's death, Ken was "light years ahead" of the rest in terms of phrasing, rhythmic drive and real jazz feel.

DELPHINE COLYER I thought there was something not quite right with it all. Little things that Ken said: "I'm not very happy here." I think he may have felt that they were jumping on the band wagon of his name; because he *had* done those things. And I think that Chris was really a little bit too technical; very clever, but not earthy enough really for Ken.

HAROLD PENDLETON Lonnie Donegan was a difficult person, and he was rather prone to upsetting people. And I always remember this particular night, before the band played; Lonnie managed to upset Ken by some sort of an uncalled-for remark about the virtue of his wife Delphine, or words to that effect. I wasn't present at the actual argument but I *did* watch Ken chase Lonnie all over the club with a view to strangling him, which I thought was a good idea, because I'd had enough of Lonnie myself.

Lonnie was a *very* difficult person to deal with—very, very difficult. Anyway, Ken got him—cornered him upstairs, and proceeded to throttle him. The rest of the band pulled him off, and Ken was—quite rightly—enraged, and said, "Right, you're fired" to Lonnie. But then, encouraged by it, Ken then turned

around and said "And that bloody modern drummer!" —Ron Bowden.

And Chris then went, "But, but, but, but Ken, it's a cooperative band." And Ken said, "No it isn't. It's *my* band— *I'm* the famous person; I am the leader and it's my band." So Chris said "But, but, but... Ken, I don't know about this." So anyway, he calmed down, they did the set, and Chris and I were talking about it afterwards, because it was *my* club.

"I don't know what to do. We can't continue like this. Ken wants to take over the band. That's not on." So I said, "Well, why not ring Pat and see if he's still up for it." I don't remember the details too much. They talked to Pat and Pat *was* up for it, and Monty—to my surprise—sided with Chris not with Ken, with whom he'd been in the Crane River. And, before you could say knife, Ken was out and the band got Pat in and was going to carry on just the same, unfortunately with Lonnie still there.

And Chris said to me, "Well, Harold, what do you think will happen next?" I said, "Well, I've got a concert at the Royal Festival Hall. You'll be top of the bill. And I'll tell all the other clubs that you're now resident here at the London Jazz Club, and we'll see if they go like dominoes." And they did. So before you could say knife, Chris had got all the work, and Ken's out on his ear.

JOHNNY PARKER So he sacked the entire rhythm section. Namely, T.C. Donegan, James Bray, and Ron Bowden. But I don't think it *was* the fault of the rhythm section. That wasn't what the problem was. It was the front-line, if anything.

And they—Monty and Chris—decided that they would go off and stay with the rhythm section, so, effectively, they fired Ken from his own band. And there was a split there, so... A lot of us—most musicians—took Ken's side. The Sandy Brown lot, and Humph and Wally, as much as they talked about it, they weren't involved. But the rest of us, like me, gathered around and tried to help Ken out.

What had happened, all the contracts of the band were in Ken's name, but then Chris had got the band. Ken had got the contracts, so provided that he could turn up with *A band*, he'd got the work, you see. Chris had got the band, but no work. And I don't know why, but we took Ken's side, and tried to gather around and form a band just to help him through, and I helped him sort out a band. We got Acker Bilk up from Bristol; there was a guy, a funny drummer, came up from Portsmouth; Eric Skinner.

He approached Ken saying he could do this, that and the other and whatnot, and he turned up with his funny-looking wife. And he wasn't much cop at all. But he'd come up from Portsmouth, I think it was. And of course, Ed O'Donnell.

KEN COLYER It was great living with Johnny. He had a piano. We used to have a handsome dinner in a nearby working man's cafe—they would even ask you if you wanted any more veg—have a pint in the

local and a game of darts, then go back and yarn, play records and work tunes over.

Johnny was still with Humph and I was about to bust up with Barber. I played the last job at The Shakespeare, Woolwich. In front of the audience he gave me a bottle of rum. If it had been in private I would have broken it over his head. As it was, Johnny and I drank it that night.

JOHNNY PARKER We were sharing the flat, and it was exactly at that time that he was in my spare room. And he was worried about it, and unhappy about the band, and… muttering. And he came back one night and told me that he'd fired the rhythm section. And I didn't query.

> And *then* he came back and said that, you know, they'd sort of fired *him*. Or, you know, they were all going. He just thought, *better get another band straight away.* He was glad to get rid of them. I don't think he was particularly happy with them.

But the last job that he did was on the Sunday night, down at the Shakespeare at Woolwich—George Webb's club. And George Webb was giving half a bottle of rum as a goodbye present, and the band had clubbed together and bought him a bottle of rum. So he'd come back that night and he'd got a bottle and a half of rum. And he said, "Those bastards have given me this." He wouldn't taste it until I had tasted it, because he thought they'd probably poisoned it.

He said he wouldn't put it past them to have poisoned it.

Oh, I don't know if he really meant it. But I had to pour some and drink it first! But I didn't show any signs of fainting or whatnot, so we sat up drinking it. Made it into hot toddys.

DELPHINE COLYER I think perhaps he didn't realise that he'd be *really* all on his own. I think maybe he thought Monty and Jim would stay with him.

COLYER BREAKS UP

Melody Maker, 23 May 1954
BARBER TO LEAD

Ken Colyer and his Jazzmen have parted company. In the thirteenth month of its existence this band—which rapidly became one of the country's leading traditional groups —and its trumpet playing leader have decided to go separate ways.

The split, the result of musical and personal differences within the band, leaves trombonist Chris Barber fronting the former Colyer Jazzmen while Ken Colyer looks for new players with which to reorganise his unit.
UNANIMOUS

The cooperative band known hitherto as Ken Colyer's Jazzmen has severed connections with Ken and Bill Colyer by unanimous decision of its members.

"With the addition of Pat Halcox (formerly of the Albemarle Jazzband) on trumpet, the group will in future be known as Chris Barber's Jazz Band. The policy and style established by the band will remain the same.

"The group will continue to do all its regular club jobs, at least until Ken Colyer has another band to offer, and we shall be playing at the NJF's concert at the Festival Hall on Whit Monday."

Questioned by the M.M., Ken Colyer explained: "This may come as a shock to a lot of people, but I feel a certain amount of relief.

"While the band has made great progress in the year that it's been going, I have been well aware of its shortcomings from the New Orleans jazz point of view. We have tried a variety of styles, playing ragtime, Ellington numbers and so on, and I think that has been a mistake.
CONFIDENT

"Last week-end I gave the rhythm section notice, and this break has been the outcome. There have been differences of opinion that have nothing to do with music, but I don't wish to comment on them.

"I intend to re-form my band as soon as I find the musicians. If necessary, I'll search the countryside. I feel confident that there are enough men who share my purist aims to band around me and produce a much better New Orleans sound as far as I personally am concerned."

Ken Colyer says he will be arranging auditions immediately.

The M.M. understands that the present Colyer band makes its final appearance at the Hot Club Of London, Woolwich. The following day Chris Barber's band plays at the Humphrey Lyttelton Club.

The Lyttelton Office comments: "The successful policy inaugurated by Ken Colyer on Mondays will be continued with Chris Barber's band for the moment. As soon as Ken has re-formed, we shall be glad to give his band a hearing."

WHAT NEW ORLEANS THINKS OF COLYER
By Derrick Stewart-Baxter, *Melody Maker*, 5 June 1954
Decca's first LP of the Ken Colyer Jazzmen (LF 1152) showed a marked improvement in Ken's playing (to be expected after his four-month sojourn in the Crescent City).

But, inspired no doubt by the enthusiasm of its leader, the whole band produced a relaxed JAZZ sound and an easy beat which hitherto had been the prerogative of the best New Orleans musicians.

Furthermore, the music of this British group, although firmly

No more: the line up that couldn't be—Donegan, Bowden, Sunshine, Colyer and Barber and Bray

based on the archaic style of the Bunk Johnson and George Lewis bands, was no pale carbon copy. Here was originality allied to good musicianship and an understanding of the chosen medium.

At last Britain had produced something worthwhile in the New Orleans style. The Colyer group, with a repertoire ranging from original blues themes to rags and marches and long-forgotten 'pops' had brought a welcome freshness to the revivalist movement.

Our waning enthusiasm was rekindled. But was loyalty to a home-produced noise dulling our critical faculties? It seemed unlikely that one of our bands had 'caught the spirit'.

Their background and environment were so vastly different. Is it any wonder, then, that some of us began to doubt the evidence of our ears? The question was: What would those on the New Orleans jazz scene think of Colyer and his band?

JOE MARES

The next step was obvious. With the cooperation of the Decca Company, I was able to air-mail the LP direct to Joe Mares Jr., in the heart of the New Orleans jazzland.

As in the past, Joe was eager to help. In spite of commitments with his Southland label (soon to be made available in this country) he spared no effort to help in my search for an unbiased opinion of the boys' performance. He played the disc to many of the great names, and what follows is a report of what they said.

First, from Mares himself, come these encouraging words: "Naturally, we are always happy to hear European jazz bands that draw so much of their inspiration from the Crescent City. The Colyer band heard on the new LP is very close to the real New Orleans, particularly that phase of the music representing the George Lewis group.

"The trombone work of Chris Barber is particularly impressive. These boys should go on to produce more and greater New Orleans style jazz. Perhaps a little too much ensemble work. A few solos might help the album."

Sharkey Bonano, veteran trumpet man of the white New Orleans school, was also pleased with what he heard. His message to Ken was: "It's good music in the right way. Keep up the good work, boys." Stanley Mendelson, the young pianist who can be heard on the Papa Laines and other well-known records, was less demonstrative. But after listening carefully, he gave his verdict: "The band sounds pleasing, most promising. Very good harmony."

That grand old-timer, Chink Martin, is still going strong. And Joe was able to obtain his judgement: "A nice, clean album, with a nice beat." Sharkey's trombonist, Jack Delaney, was highly delighted with all the tracks, and had this to say: "After meeting Ken last year, I can truly say I'm happy that he came up with this fine job." Pianist Armand Hug was next. While not "carried away" he thought the disc, "A very enjoyable record to listen to."

GEORGE LEWIS

Alton Purnell, pianist with the Johnson and Lewis bands, was also buttonholed by Mares. After hearing all the title, a broad grin spread across his face. "Mighty nice, I like it"; but with an even broader grin he added: "A piano would help a lot." Perhaps it would, if Colyer could find the right man.

It was only fitting that the great New Orleans clarinet player George Lewis should have the job of summing up: "They sound pretty fine. Look out there! These boys will be putting me out of work soon." There is the opinion of some Crescent City musicians—the Colyer Jazz Band is good. Now it is up to Decca to encourage the boys with more recording dates.*

A final thought: Let the MU ponder this. Ken Colyer learned much in four months, mixing with his kind of musicians. How much could the rest of the British players (of all styles) learn if they were able to mix freely with musicians of all nationalities?

*Last weekend Ken Colyer played his final date with these men, now playing as Chris Barber's Jazz Band. Colyer is rehearsing a new line-up in preparation for his next Decca session on June 25.

CHAPTER EIGHT
BACK TO THE DELTA

JOHNNY PARKER I was with Humph in those days. I don't think Ken could read music. I honestly don't know. He'd got a very good ear; he could pick stuff up, and he could play in keys like G and Db, which was quite amazing. But whether that was because he'd got a good ear and could hear the intervals... And we used to play together sometimes—I had a piano. We worked together—just the two of us—at a concert at the Royal Festival Hall, which we'd practised for. Just Ken and I—some duets; I think we did *Tomcat Blues*—and *Breeze* was one of them.

So... we go on to the stage to do our duets, and I think it was Harold Pendleton, who was something to do with running it, saw just the two of us there, and thought: "Good God, there's no bass and no drums!" So he was in charge of a band with somebody like Tony Kinsey on drums and... I don't know who it was on bass, Sammy Stokes or some bass player. And he said, "Go on. Go on to accompany them." So we're just about to start up, and these other two come on, and the voice of Ken Colyer was heard right across the Royal Festival Hall: "Get those bastards off the stage."

And that was typical Ken.

KEN COLYER I had a tough time regrouping. There has always been very good musicians who do not care for the vagaries of the professional life, and I don't blame them. This limits the field. I eventually discovered Acker through another Bristol clarinet player. He had the good grace to tell me that he didn't think he was good enough but he knew who was. I liked Acker right from the start.

Eddie O'Donnell came down from Leeds. Diz Disley came in on banjo, a fine swinging musician. We had drum trouble until I got Stan Greig to come down from Edinburgh. Dick Smith was on bass. The band improved until it was pretty good, and we had one or two electric sessions. We made another LP for Decca, *Back to the Delta*. I chose the title for obvious reasons. We had a regular night at the Studio 51.

ED O'DONNELL The first thing I heard about it was one night in the Scarborough Taps, which was a boozer up at Leeds City Estate, with Bob Barclay. They'd got this Jazz Club—it was awful you know... a jazz night... and I met Malcolm Duncan in there, 'cos he was me mate like. And he said, "I'm gonna jam with Ken Colyer's band," and I said, "Oh yeah?"

He said: "In the *Melody Maker*, it said that Ken Colyer has sacked the Barber band and is gonna search the country, and find some proper musicians." And Malcolm said, "I'm the best choice for trombone." So shortly afterwards, I got a telegram from Bill Colyer saying "meet us down in Oxford... job there," you know, to join the Ken Colyer band. Anyway, I went down there. It was a college job—a University job—and Ian Christie was on clarinet. And Bastable was on banjo, but he hadn't joined the band. It might have been Bill on washboard, because it was first on the list—skiffle music.

Ken did *Take this Hammer,* I remember.

KEN COLYER My mother, through a friend, knew of a basement flat in Lillie Road, Fulham, which I eventually acquired. It was the first settled place I had had since leaving home.

Fred and Tilla Bull were really nice people. I soon got to know them and we had some great times, as they liked company and any excuse for a party. Sometimes in my place, sometimes upstairs in theirs; it was always open house and made for a very pleasant atmosphere. For a while, Acker Bilk and Eddie O'Donnell lived with me there.

Telfer's pie factory was just a few doors down. There was a stall outside for the staff to buy reject pies etc. There was nothing wrong with them, just that they were imperfect in some way; just as they have seconds in the garment trade. Tilla finally told me that it was quite alright to buy the produce. Although there was a sign saying "Staff Sales," they sold to the general public. There were many times when I subsisted on a few pence worth of Telfer's rejects. Their bread wasn't much good though.

BILL COLYER So on to the band with Acker. If Acker hadn't have opted out of it, who knows what would have happened to his life? But we put that band together in a hurry, and it was hard work! I did all that, because we had one more contract to do: another 10-inch LP for Decca. **That was the driving force to get this band together—we had to make this second record.** Finally I got Acker, Eddie O'Donnell— who was down in town—Greiggie, Disley.

ED O'DONNELL So I was in the band then, and Bill Colyer was managing it. Six pounds a week, that's what we got. I think Bill Colyer got more. I don't know whether he knew—whether Ken knew—that that's all we got. I don't know. But it was… terrible.

Ken's mother told us, I think, about this gaff in Lillie Road —66 Lillie Road—next to that pie Factory.

Ken in coversation with Ed O'Donnell at Studio 20 in Leeds

ANNE O'DONNELL [*Ed's wife*] You [Ed] and Acker and Ken were on the bottom floor… and Delphine . That girl Lilliane was on the top floor; I was next to the top.

ED O'DONNELL At first me and Ken and Acker were in that big bed, like… "You're a lot like children, you two," and so we went and lived in this cell—sort of—next to t' kitchen.

DELPHINE COLYER He wasn't really, really very robust. And after the break-up of the Barber band—I presume it was some sort of nervous reaction—he came out in this awful… a bit like acne, all over his face. And this is how the beard came in, because he couldn't shave. No, he was never really very robust.

ACKER BILK We were getting six quid or something a week. We were living in this terrible old gaff in Lillie Road, Fulham, me and Jean in one room, sharing a kitchen with a load of old geezers who had the other rooms. If I'd thought it was going to be fame and glory, man, I was soon disillusioned with London.

I just hated the place, and the money was hardly enough for us to eat on. It wasn't Colyer's fault, he was building up a band again and it takes time in this business to get a band swinging together and to get the fans to hear about it.

DELPHINE COLYER I mean, we only had six pounds a week with the band. We had two pounds ten for rent, so we had three pounds ten left. Well, he thought Humph was spoilt: "I had to get the money from my milk-round to get my trumpet"— you know?—"and go cleaning underground trains."

ED O'DONNELL I remember Acker joining. His first influence was Wally Fawkes. And Bill Colyer lent him a load of George [Lewis] records and… but he certainly got it off, like, you know.

ALAN GATWARD Well, nothing could compete with that band, with Eddie O'Donnell and Acker Bilk.

ACKER BILK Oh, it was a good band, I thought—I quite enjoyed playing. I was very new to the jazz scene, apart from

Party at 66 Lillie Road. Delphine behind Ken, and their landlords, Fred and Tilla Bull. Ann O'Donnell is on Ken's left

Somerset, which was a different scene altogether from London. The first gig I played was the Royal Festival Hall. I said to Ken—because I didn't know any of the tunes much— you know— I knew them vaguely, but I didn't know the keys. Ken doesn't know much about keys either, **so I said, "What key are we in, Ken?" He said, "Don't worry about it man, just play jazz... Feel your way around." It was like that in them days, you know.** It was good... good fun; I enjoyed it.

MIKE CASIMIR When that band broke up, Ken's new line-up, which included Eddie O'Donnell and Acker Bilk, sounded completely dissimilar to that of the former. It was much closer to the New Orleans sounds we were growing increasingly familiar with. I think it would be fair comment to say that their first concert at The Royal Festival Hall had us all hooked! It was definitely a rousing success.

DICK SMITH I think Johnny Bastable and I had heard on the grapevine that there was going to be this all-night party, in East Sheen —and we played with Ken all night long.

And a couple of days later, I was working at the Office of the Admiralty, which was near Staples Corner, and the 'phone rang, and it was Ken: "Hello man... would you like to join my band?" Then I had the longest five minutes of my life—I can still remember seeing a guy walking up and down the road on the other side of the street—while I thought about my future, and this chance to play with Ken. Then I knew that I wanted to do it, so I said "Yeah." So that was that.

Then I went back to see all the guys from around the Trevor Williams band—Jeff Williams, Trevor Williams, Tony Eglin, Johnny Hunt, Johnny Bastable, Kevin Sheldon; we used to go to a coffee bar in Rayners Lane, and I told them that I was joining Ken, and they were all aghast, and saying "Don't do it; it won't last," but I knew that I'd got to do it, you know?

JOHNNY BASTABLE I answered an ad in the *Melody Maker* for a banjo player. I went along to the audition and was accepted. This band was led by Trevor Williams and was called the Eagle Jazz Band. I played with them for four years, and we really had a great time. That group used to swing like an old boot, and when Colin Bowden joined us on drums, the band rapidly got to the top of its form.

I was still with Trev when Ken started forming a new band; he asked me to join but I refused because I didn't fancy the life of a professional musician, and I also had what is known as a "good safe job." I did help him out on a few sessions however, during which time I was privileged to meet those two great jazzmen, Acker Bilk and Ed O'Donnell.

DICK SMITH At that time the band consisted of Ken, Acker, Eddie O'Donnell, Diz Disley, Eric Skinner and myself. I'm not sure whether we actually had a rehearsal before the first gig—we may have—but if so it was a close-run thing. Anyway, rehearsals were pretty basic affairs—mostly establishing key signatures, chord sequences and tempos—nothing much in the way of arrangements. **Bill Colyer was invariably present, listening intently and making critical suggestions.**

ED O'DONNELL Eric Skinner—I don't know why they brought him in but he was the only one that Ken said could do press rolls on drums, you know. I remember Disley used to shout at him, "Cymbal! cymbal!" and if he did a break, he couldn't get out of it. And Diz would shout, "You can't get out of that!"

ERIC SKINNER LETTER TO KEN COLYER 23 MAY, 1954

14 Cumberland House, Portsea, Portsmouth.
Dear Sir,

With regard to the item in this week's issue of the *Melody Maker* regarding the break-up of your band, I notice that you stated that you are going to reform when you find the right men for the job. In view of that statement, I would like to be considered for the vacancy of drummer with you. I have been playing drums since I was 12 years old & possess a good understanding of New Orleans & other styles of jazz. I am able to read or busk & can improvise a rhythmic backing instinctively. If you feel that I might be suitable for you, I can audition for you at your convenience. Hoping that I shall be receiving a favourable reply from you,

I remain, Yours in anticipation,
J.H.Skinner.

JOHNNY PARKER Well anyway. Ken got the band together. And it sounded O.K. They made a similar noise to the band with Chris. Probably a bit more authentic if anything, except... it wasn't all worked-out like the Barber version.

Chris gave it more form. It was all a bit like a jig-saw puzzle... yeah, knocked off the rough edges, and... they *did* do arrangements and things which wasn't really Ken's thing at all.

DICK SMITH I don't know how, but Ken just managed to bring the best out in you. Perhaps he just picked people who he knew would be alright with him. But I mean, the first band, we had Acker, Eddie O'Donnell, Disley, and Eric Skinner.

So that was a good band, I thought—there wasn't much work around, but then we got this TV series which was a good boost.

ED O'DONNELL Kevin Sheldon—I met him one night in this boozer in Soho, and I think he was a bit scooped, like. He'd had one or two glasses. So, he was on about he'd got this idea for a television thing on a Paradise Island. And he wanted the band, like, and as the Monte Grande Nationale Band.

He said, "Yeah, it'll be great... do all the marches and that. But what we need is one of them big things—tuba!" And I said, "Oh, Disley'll play that." I knew that Disley had affected the trumpet, and I thought, "It's the same, isn't it?" Anyway, Bill Colyer comes back afterwards—he'd fixed this television programme, and I thought... but it was good fun, and good money.

We loved the medals, and Disley borrowed that thing [Sousaphone] of Jim Bray's, you see. Yeah. Of course, being Disley, he turns up late. He said, "I dashed out, caught the bus, then put the tuba down... and it rolled... I've been chasing up and down the streets, and the mouthpiece went down the drain, and I had to get the corporation out."

The "Monte Grande Nationale Band" (publicity photo from the *Paradise Island* television show)

Colyer's Jazzmen to act in TV

Ken Colyer's Jazzmen create a precedent in London traditional circles on Tuesday when they appear in the serial "Paradise Island" on Children's TV as actors as well as musicians.

Ken and the boys will play the official police band in a fictitious South American State called Monte Grande—complete with South American accents!

The band is being fitted with comic uniforms and goes into intensive rehearsal today (Friday) for their Tuesday appearance. The boys will appear in the serial for the rest of its five-week run.

MM artist Disney, regular banjo player with Ken, plays sousaphone in the serial.

Last Thursday (July 29) the Colyer Jazzmen started their new residency at the Amersham Arms, New Cross.

Anyway, the next day Ken said, "You have to get there on time." So he comes in, said, "I got no sleep, and on the train...right to the far end, and I woke up—coming back I fell asleep again?" "Did you really? Well tomorrow you will either be here on time or you won't be coming back."

But the thing was, we got paid the earth for that. Unheard-of sums— fourteen pounds! We got fourteen quid, and I think another fourteen quid on transmission. Of course, they hadn't invented videotape, so there's no record of it.

I think Eric Skinner was still the drummer then. Yeah, I think he got the bummie after that... and started crying.

DICK SMITH We soon started touring around the UK. This was only made possible by a very close liaison with Johnny Swinson and his coach. Johnny was a great guy—absolutely invaluable. He always got us to the venue in time for a meal beforehand. Afterwards he managed to round us all up, shepherd us back to the coach and drive us all to our homes, then wake us up and deposit us and our belongings there.

This was no mean feat, as the coach had certainly seen better days (unfortunately quite a long time previously), and

in fact as far as I know none of us could ever find any evidence of a heating system. Accordingly, individual arrangements to keep warm had to be made, since we often spent half of the night sprawled across the seats.

It needs to be mentioned that none of us owned a car, and these journeys took place some time prior to the invention of motorways. A typical trip to play, for example, in Manchester would involve meeting in a Soho pub at about 11.30 am, arriving at Paddy McKiernan's Bodega Club at 5 or 6 pm. After the gig, the drive home would commence at about 11.30 pm and with any luck we would approach London at 3 or 4 am.

The band was gradually improving, and we were given the date of our first recording session which was to be on Friday 25th of June at Decca's West Hampstead studio.

When it came to making that record, I had been feeling ill for a few days, and we had a rehearsal a couple of days before. I remember carrying my bass back up the stairs, and Eddie O'Donnell asking what was wrong. I said I'd got some pain, and he said something about "I think you should go to the doctor." I remember saying that I would after the recording session, and Eddie said, "Don't worry about the recording session, think of yourself."

Then that night, the doctor was called in, and I ended up in hospital with a burst appendix. So they got Micky Ashman to do the recording session. Then, Ken decided he wanted to do it over, and that's why Micky plays bass on the skiffle numbers—Ken thought *they* were OK.

It was a few weeks before I was fit enough to resume touring with the band, and by September Eric Skinner had been replaced by Stan Greig and we visited the Decca Studios again to re-record the six numbers that I had missed out on.

ED O'DONNELL I didn't like the first record we made—it was awful. As I say, I knew about two numbers in A♭.

And I really over-blew on trombone at first—*"Too much trombone"*—so I played it really underneath. I don't know why—nerves. I remember Disley was on the second one—he was on drugs, like; I think he was on Dexedrine. I remember at one time he said, "I got this good thing for a cheap high," and it was Doctor Brown's Cough Medicine.

DELPHINE COLYER Of course, the first time Ottilie Patterson came over [from Ireland], she was singing at Greek Street. She was lovely. We got married at Fulham Town Hall at quarter to one on a Wednesday, and we had to go to Ireland—he was playing the next night. And we just got the train as it was going out of the station, because there'd been quite a lot of Merrydown flowing.

And we got to Ireland, and unfortunately Ken—in the wedding celebrations—had forgotten his trumpet. Left it under the bed. So he had to borrow one from the local music shop. It was a little bit hectic that day.

We had a rather drunken evening with Ottilie at the Festival in Belfast. Ken thought Ottilie was great.

He tried to teach me how to play the guitar once. Showed me the shapes, and I was getting the chords alright.

STAN GREIG I was playing drums at that time—I was playing a bit of piano, but with Ken Colyer I was on drums.

Well, I had a drum kit, but I didn't have anything other than a bass drum which was very old and a twenty-eight inch, which was big for a bass drum. So I got another bass drum when I got to London.

Disley was impressed by my playing, and that was a good start! **Since I was a professional piano tuner, when they tuned-up I was the only one around who could tell them "that's flat."**

ED O'DONNELL Every day we rehearsed, I think—twice a day—near Kings Cross. And we were in this rehearsal room. And I remember at one time we were playin' *Ballin' the Jack*... well, the verse, I knew not. It was a funny sort of a thing, and I've never figured it out since.

Anyway, you know Greiggy—he's a piano tuner—he was with us after Skinner got the bullet. And he was there drumming, and we were three hours messing about. And he taught me the tune of that, you know. And it was dead right. So I thought *what a fantastic musician you must be!*

But, what he used to do was he'd go down t' jazz clubs and say, "I'll be down tomorrow morning to tune the piano." And he used to go down and tune it.

When he came down, he was like a teddy boy.

DICK SMITH Of course, Stan Greig was a tremendous drummer, and any time we were playing a new tune that I didn't know, he would shout the chords out to me as we were playing. I've never met another drummer who can do that. Tremendous. Then of course he left and we got Colin—just before I left.

STAN GREIG I remember when we went into the recording studio with him for that first album, *Back To The Delta*, it was

66 Lillie Road photographed in 2010, little changed from when Ken lived there in the mid-fifties

a bit tense, and half way through someone suggested but I've no idea who it was, probably the engineers—that the front-line all sit down to play. Bill was always there.

And Sandy Brown came up with the fact that he liked the band, how it played. Sandy and Ken were similar. Very dedicated people.

SLEEVE NOTES, *BACK TO THE DELTA*

The first long-playing record by Ken Colyer and his Jazzmen caused considerable talk and, no doubt, this one will come under even closer scrutiny. Comparisons will be made, conclusions will be drawn, but one fact will remain. The first recording had much obvious pleasure to offer, whereas this one will require a more genuine appreciation of the truly unselfconscious New Orleans jazz.

When Ken Colyer produced this new band many persons may have wondered what he would be able to do with it, a group with no star sidemen and with but little experience. What these six men did produce was astonishingly true to its origins. One may feel in this music an atmosphere of relaxation which has never before been created on record by Europeans playing in this idiom.

The loose, shifting beat and clarity of emotions approach, far more closely, the music of George Lewis and Elmer Talbert, which one has in the past few years come to accept as the basic New Orleans jazz, rather than the music of Joe Oliver and Louis Armstrong.

At the start of this session the music would not flow; the tension was too stringent. For the other five members of the band it was a case of "first night nerves"; for Ken it was more difficult. The record had to disprove the criticism which had been generally levelled at him for disbanding his first group.

Many people had accused him of wilfully breaking up the finest jazz band that England had produced and, furthermore, they said that he would never find five other men in this country who could play this music with any degree of success. Part of this criticism was justified for Ken did, after much thought, leave the first band; he did so, however, for a very good reason. He wanted to get back to the original jazz with a more buoyant beat, less arranged passages, and a freer atmosphere: a retrogression in time but not in quality.

Understandably, this did not help towards the necessary relaxation. The mounting tension of this important session was suddenly relieved by the simple suggestion that the band

'Mac' Duncan, Delphine and Ken Colyer, George Melly, Delphine's father, Micky Ashman, Ken's mother and Bill Colyer at Ken's wedding, Fulham Town Hall, 24 November 1954

sit down instead of standing in front of the microphone as they were accustomed to doing. This they did, with the inevitable exception of Dick Smith, the bass player. The worrying ceased and the music started; the beat became richer and the front line more assured until the six final takes came through one after the other.

All are familiar melodies which Ken has played often but never has he had with him musicians who understood better the atmosphere of this music. The feeling of recreation is stronger here and Ken is doing that which he has always wanted to: he is playing his own music within the limits of true New Orleans jazz. This is his answer to the critics.

JIM GODBOLT Bill Colyer was a great propagandist. He was a lot more ruthless than Ken was. "I'll wear these knuckles to the fuckin' bone, mate! I'll get these knuckles bleedin' to the bone, mate! I'll tell you... Anything to help the guv'nor fight those bastards." And I can remember what part of the Blue Posts he came in, all guns blazing.

DIZ DISLEY Well, I remember one wonderful session. It was on a Friday night, and we played at a place called the Florida Restaurant, which was down at the bottom of the Haymarket somewhere. And it was the first night that Stan Greig joined. Because before that he had a bloke called Eric Skinner who came from Southampton. He wasn't a very good drummer, but... I shouldn't say that in case he's still alive, but it's true. **Anyway, that was the most exciting night that the Colyer band played, and people were screaming, or something.** Anyway, Gatward was there. He'd remember it.

ALAN GATWARD Eddie O'Donnell came down, and there was a session in which everybody played at that session, and everybody who heard it reckoned it was the best session they'd ever heard.

PETER HUNTER The start of the Acker Bilk, Eddie O'Donnell band, there was... that little something that makes the difference.

It had a very loose beat with the "bounce" which Ken always talked about. He was so emphatic about this bounce business. Nobody really knew what the hell he was talking about, but over the years I think most of you have probably learnt what he meant. **As you know, he was very, very abrupt to a lot of people, but he was a very great friend to me. He actually played—and, I might tell you, for nothing—at my wedding, which was a**

great privilege. To get Ken to play for nothing took some doing!

So anyway, time once again went on and I was home on leave quite frequently in those days. Then in 1956 I came ashore to study for my qualifications as Third Officer and my Cadetship was over. I played a lot around London with odd bands, and a dreadful noise was probably made, but I thought I was doing okay.

I used to sit in with Cy Laurie on occasions. And quite often I used to go down to the 51 Club and sit down in the middle of the crowd with a dirty great big tape recorder —reel-to-reel— and plug it in to one of the lights, which usually blacked out the whole place.

Delphine Colyer, as quite a few of you will know, used to sit there with a microphone held up and we would record the

Acker, Dick, Ken and Ed

band. I used to get words from Ken: "That's for your mates on the ship, not for bloody publication!" and that's about all I got out of him. He would always give permission.

ANNE O'DONNELL Ken's humour was on the quiet—that little twinkle, you know. Like he was having a quiet joke to himself.

ED O'DONNELL Well, we had a chance to go to New Orleans. Lord Donegall—I don't know if it *was* him—he was a jazzer, and he was gonna sponsor our fares, I think. And we were gonna go, and the

VALENTINE—8-3-58

Valentine Magazine's version of Ken meeting Delphine. Delphine dances aboard the Royal Daffodil

American Musicians' Union put the block on. I think they didn't want us playing with black bands. Because they had two Unions over there— a black Union and a white Union. So the trip was off.

JOHNNY PARKER I knew Ken over a long time, but not particularly deeply. He was my lodger for about three months, I guess, and on several occasions we'd stay up late-night drinking. But I mean, we weren't in each other's company all the time. We weren't sharing a flat. He had his room and I was with Maureen in ours, you know. But he used to pop in. As I say, he was always punctilious in his behaviour. Couldn't fault him at all. When it came to anything important, he was... He did everything, you know... Turned up on time, always looked smart.

And of course, there were Alan Gatward's parties.

Oh, there was that lovely letter you've probably heard about, from Alan Gatward's mother.

ALAN GATWARD *The 29th of June 1954. Mr. Ken Colyer c/o Lynn Dutton Office (address).*

"Sir, I regret having to write this letter, but this is to inform you that for reasons which must be well-known to you, you or any of your friends are not to visit this house in future under any circumstances or excuse whatsoever. I am responsible for the conduct of this house, and the invitation of my son or daughter will be of no avail. Yours faithfully, Edith Gatward."

That gives you an idea of the kind of parties we had. And that's when I moved to Plaistow in the East End.

JOHNNY PARKER I don't know what the behaviour was. There was one where... he got up in the morning, and was pissing in the fire, I think.

As one does. Except not when it's an electric fire.

And when I mentioned this to Gatward the other day, he said, "No he wasn't. He was spitting in it." I said, "No, you couldn't have been in the room." It was one of those with the day-glo. You know, the coals which glow, and yeah, he had a pee in there. Whether that was the behaviour for which he was... But that was the mother's house at Devonfield, as it was called, up at Palmers Green somewhere.

ED O'DONNELL Chris had taken all the corners off, but I

thought that was *the* ideal band for his sort of music. We were just playing that music that we knew. I was trying to play like Jim Robinson style, and Acker was playing like George. The music was becoming more relaxed.

DICK SMITH Well, you were wary of Ken, definitely. But his lead wasn't leading in the way that a lot of people would; he would do things that made you feel that this is the right way to go. Then he would break loose, and you would feel you've got to go along with him. I don't know, but it was a different technique... I think it was just his natural way of playing.

DIZ DISLEY I went to see that picture with him: *New Orleans* with Louis Armstrong, you know? Yes, and all he said afterwards was, "Oh, he's alright." That's all he said.

He was definitely a non-showman.

ALAN GATWARD Ken always drank a fair bit, but it never seemed to effect his playing as it does some musicians. And he was only a sort of heavy-ish drinker—not an alcoholic.

DELPHINE COLYER At Alan Gatward's place at Plaistow, one of the usual parties... I don`t quite know how it came up. He was playing his guitar at the time. I said, "What's the matter with you? You haven't said two words to me all night." And he said, "Well here's two: Fuck off!" Whack!—the guitar was over my head. And I was sort of sitting on the floor with all these sort-of wood splinters and strings all around me. I think they kept that as an exhibit.

There wasn't anything left of the guitar. I would think it was probably the Merrydown, really. Just fortunate that it wasn`t his metal one.

ALAN GATWARD Ken Colyer had had the band for only a few weeks, actually, which consisted of Acker Bilk on clarinet, Mac Duncan on trombone, Disley on banjo, Stan Greig on drums and Dick Smith, bass, and they played a gig underneath the Astoria in Leicester Square. And everybody who was on that session said this was the greatest. So the audience knew it, and the musicians knew it. And then they finished a number— "Ooh, what are we gonna play next?"

Eddie had gone back to Leeds. Because normally Eddie O'Donnell never plays outside Yorkshire.

ED O'DONNELL I didn't like London. Oh, it was a drag I thought... Acker... he didn't really like it neither. He stopped on a bit longer than me.

Hated the tubes—he wouldn't go on them. "Aarh, thee tubes make moi hair fall out." You know how far it is from Lillie Road to Kings Cross Station? He used to go on 't blinkin' bus. And it was miles, and hours.

ACKER BILK The funny thing was that, more or less as soon

as we decided to go back to Pensford, Colyer began to get the band going together and it was just beginning to get more dates.

DICK SMITH Autumn was with us when Ken and Bill mentioned that the band was going to Düsseldorf for two months commencing on 1st December. Eddie and Acker reluctantly decided that it wasn't for them, so Ian Wheeler and Mac Duncan joined. I thought I would go, because I'd left my job to join Ken.

ED O'DONNELL Well, I told them, that's the guy you want— Malcolm Duncan. And I remember that night. We were up at some do. Malcolm was there. I mean, people said I taught him to play trombone. He taught *me* to play trombone. He was far better.

MAC DUNCAN LETTER TO KEN COLYER UNDATED

M.L., 50 Hillcrest Ave, Leeds 7, Yorks
Dear Ken Colyer,
I see from last week's *MM* that you are looking for musicians to form a new band. I would like to have the opportunity of playing trombone for you and am willing to travel up to London anytime in the near future.
I have played trombone for several years now, and until recently have been leading the Pine City Stompers of Bournemouth (we were on a George Lewis kick) but this has now broken up and I have left Bournemouth (for good, I hope). I would like to live in London and at present am a free agent.
I have always admired your ideals, and style of playing, greatly. Incidentally, Monty Sunshine may remember staying with me in Bournemouth one night (but perhaps you two aren't speaking).
I'll put a stamped addressed envelope in this just in case you get around to answering.
Best Regards, Mac Duncan
42 High St, Plaistow, E 13

IAN WHEELER Mac joined the same day as I did. Eddie O'Donnell went back to Leeds and Acker went back to Bristol. It was the first time I'd met Mac, when we both joined Ken.

MAC DUNCAN In mid-'54 I left Bournemouth and returned to Leeds. Just about then, Ken broke with Chris Barber, and I surprised myself for daring to write to him asking for an audition. Ed. O'D beat me to that one however, but he did leave me a ready-made band—The White Eagle Band. It was quite a good band too, though it was a struggle trying to learn a couple of rags (especially as rags have an alarming habit of not being in Eb or F).

Then I heard on the grapevine that Eddie was not going

with Ken on the German tour, and a couple of days later Ken wrote that he was playing in Leeds the following Saturday (as if I didn't know) and that he would like to have a chat. The Saturday dance turned out to be formal, and so, pooling of resources with the chap I was sharing a flat with, I turned out in a tuxedo—I owned the shirt, socks and shoes. I'm sure that Ken thought I was one of the idle rich, but despite that, the next week found me on the way to London.

Those first sessions with Ken were great. I was playing in keys I didn't even know existed, but somehow it wasn't hard work at all. Acker Bilk was a great help to both me and Ian (who joined about the same time) and displayed—and still does display—great understanding for New Orleans music.

One thing I do believe is that if any band from this part of the world makes the grade, it will be led by "the master." I hope that I'm still with it.

CATHY COLYER When Ken was in a good mood, or relaxed... he lived with us for a little while when he came back from America, and he was such a good raconteur when he was on form. He was so interesting if you got him on a good moment, you know. He was so interesting. He was a very self-taught man.

You know, reading... I learnt such a lot from Ken and Bill, you know, with their knowledge of literature. And Bill particularly. But Ken was morose sometimes—very morose. And quite difficult. He was such a complicated character. Absolutely. And then of course, Ken married Delphine, which again was a volatile marriage. Because when they were all in Germany they had a bit of a volatile relationship.

KEN COLYER Unbeknown to me, a German had come over from Düsseldorf looking for a British band to do two months at the New Orleans Bier Bar in Düsseldorf. Lyn Dutton , my agent, took him around to hear the bands. He chose Alex Welsh, whose band was very good at that time.

On his last night he said to Lyn, "Oh, is there anybody else I haven't heard?"

"Oh, there's only Ken Colyer, he's at the 51 tonight."

He listened for awhile and then said, "I've changed my mind. Would you ask Ken if he would come to Düsseldorf?"

I accepted with alacrity, assuming that the rest of the band would be enthusiastic. Acker felt he couldn't go for domestic reasons. I was sorry, because we were just getting it together. But we parted amicably and I got Ian Wheeler in and Mac Duncan, another Leeds man, came in on trombone.

For the first two weeks nothing much happened. They didn't know what we were doing. Then something clicked and the crowds rapidly built up until there was an almost permanent queue outside the club.

DICK SMITH I don't remember us having any rehearsals. I remember a few before we went to Germany, but usually, when he wanted to do a new number, he'd ask if anyone knew the chords, and start playing. It was... well, it was a bit like that when I joined Chris Barber's band at first. I mean it was never a real arrangement. But, as I say, I think the main thing about Ken was that he was inspired. There were inspired noises coming out of that trumpet, which was really exciting. He had that edge.

KEN COLYER When we first went to the Düsseldorf Bier Bar I admit we were shaking down, but the crowd didn't know this. They just didn't understand what we were doing. The waiters disliked us; our routine was different to Fatty George's. But after about two weeks, something clicked and they were with us. The waiters work on commission and work hard. Some nights, if it was quiet enough we were allowed to finish early, say 1 a.m. The waiters weren't interested in hanging about if there were no customers and would be annoyed if we hit form, ignored the time and just carried on playing. But we finally converted them and on odd nights there would be just one or two customers and the waiters having a ball with us.

We were all crazy and we liked it.

Charley, the head barman, was a nice fellow and we got along well. But he put us wise. He worked behind the bar and knew who the free-spending customers were. He told us not to play *Maryland, My Maryland*, which is derived from an old German folk tune, *The Saints* and *Just A Closer Walk With Thee*, until he gave us a certain signal. He assured us that we would be rewarded for this.

Sure enough, he gave the special signal and we played the set. Up would come trays of cognac, sometimes champagne, beer, sometimes all three.

One night nobody could get served 'til we finished the set. Every waiter was carrying a tray of drinks for the band, and there was no room to put them down. That is the only time I have played the same set two or three times in an evening.

Some of the younger fans were very thoughtful. We didn't expect anything from them, but if they could afford it they would buy us packets of ten Juno or tobacco for me when they saw me rolling my own. It's a pity that you don't see much of that in England.

Our reputation spread and people were coming from far and wide to hear us, making a special journey, as they had at

Cranford for the Crane River Jazz Band.

Every Saturday was an all-night session. Yet we never received a penny more from the management. We got twelve pounds a week, and no extra for the leader. I had spent my first Decca royalty to take the band out there.

Drink prices were too high in the club so we would keep bottles in the band room downstairs. I made a habit of going into a grocery store for my liquor.

There was no tax on spirits then, and the cheap was very cheap and the expensive reasonable, but I couldn't afford the expensive. I used to vary my diet from time to time with Anisette and such but usually drank cheap brandy. Oh, for some Limousin! [an expensive French brandy]

One day I was waiting to pay for my liquor. The middle-aged cashier started haranguing me in German. I couldn't understand what she was angry about. It transpired that she realised I was drinking all this booze and was giving me a dressing-down. I changed my liquor store.

A strange thing happened one night. I was walking home alone, it was dark and the early hours of the morning. There was a strange oppressive atmosphere. Then a thunder and lightning storm erupted at ground level. Lightning was flashing down the streets, followed by deafening claps of thunder. I have never experienced anything like it. I wasn't frightened, but wondered what the hell was going on. It subsided and started pouring with rain.

We recorded a broadcast for BFN; we did this for the forces,

Ken and Bill leave for Germany, seen off by Max Jones

no pay. But Bill Crozier promised us plenty of publicity in repayment. He was as good as his word, and when my blues, *Goin' Home*, caught on with the forces, he fully repaid me.

Decca did nothing, and we missed a golden opportunity to cash in on our popularity. They flatly refused to let me record for a local company because I was under contract to them. Big deal.

Horst Geldmacher and Disley did some decorating and art work for the club and got well paid for it (here we go again).

There was some very good blown-up photos on the walls of the club. The acoustics weren't very good but Horst had done a wonderful job of decorating. He is a talented artist.

There was the fine picture of Bunk Johnson on a wall opposite the stand, the one where he is very smartly dressed, Homburg on his head, cigarette and holder in his hand and a lovely smile. It felt when we played good the smile got broader. But when things weren't going so well, the smile faded and he frowned a little.

Most of the young British officer types were a pain in the arse. I was walking to the bar to get a drink. One tapped me on the shoulder; "I wish I could shimmy like my sister Kate."

"And so do I," I replied, and brushed passed him.

Late one night a party of older people came in. They kept requesting waltzes. It was advertised as a jazz club and we were a jazz band.

However, Diz said, "Let's play *Over The Waves*."

Well, there's only two choruses in waltz time. One old fellow just returned from the toilet as we were finishing the second chorus. He approached his lady with a flourish and as they took the floor we swung into four-four. Diz was having mild hysterics and the front line were having difficulty playing. I apologised to him afterwards and said it wasn't intentional. He took it in good part. And I believe we did play a waltz for him.

A fellow in Hamburg heard what was going on and came to Düsseldorf to ask if we would open a New Orleans Bier Bar in Hamburg.

Thanks to inept management I believe we accepted for the same money. Long after we got home I would periodically get requests to return to the Bier Bars. I told my agent Lyn Dutton that I wanted treble the money if I returned, and some decent accommodation.

"Oh, they won't accept that."

My agent, my friend! I now realise I have no friends. I would sooner have enemies. I have more idea where I stand with them. My friends

always end up doing me more harm. Mutual hatred is healthier.

We went, except for Dick Smith, who returned home because he was homesick. Mukki Herman came in on bass. Mukki (a German nickname, his Christian name was Wolfgang, but I never heard it used) was a fine fellow.

IAN WHEELER We went straight out to Germany for the residency in the New Orleans Bier Bar in Düsseldorf. Long hours: 9:00p.m. 'til 4:00a.m. at weekends. Actually it sounds worse than it really was. We'd play three numbers, then take a break—although we didn't leave the stage at that point: just enough time for a roll up, then another three numbers. Then, after three such sets, we'd leave the stage for half an hour. So really we weren't playing that much more than, say, a two hour session in Britain. But it was hard enough. After the first week we were all pretty shattered, then we got used to it.

DICK SMITH We travelled to Düsseldorf overnight via the Harwich-Hook of Holland ferry. On disembarking next morning I saw that a porter had picked up my bass—unfortunately he carried it balanced over his shoulder, holding the neck of the instrument; by the time I caught up with him

Disley's Drawing of the band: Ian Wheeler, Dick Smith, Ken, Diz Disley, Bill Colyer, Mac Duncan and Stan Greig. Used here as a Christmas card to send from Germany

and retrieved it, the damage had been done and resulted in the need of some expensive professional TLC when we arrived at our destination (not a very auspicious beginning as far as I was concerned).

The playing schedule at the New Orleans Bier Bar was pretty exacting—I think that we commenced at around 8 pm and continued more or less nonstop until 2 or 3 am for 61 of the next 62 days (we had Christmas Day off). They didn't like gaps, they liked people buying drinks, and so the breakdown groups came in. The Stan Greig piano trio and the skiffle group, the Disley duo. But there always seemed to be a bass in everything. **It was certainly tough, but in retrospect one realises that it was an important factor in the transformation of the band.**

Stan, Ian, Mac and I were most fortunate in being allocated to 28 Quirinstrasse (the house of Frau Schmitz in Düsseldorf-Oberkassel). Admittedly it was quite a walk over the Rhine Brücke at about 3 am, when we'd missed the bus, but it was worth it, and we couldn't have been in better hands.

Frau Schmitz was a star—everything was impeccable, so when we surfaced at around midday she would announce

"Frühstück ist fertig" (breakfast is over!) and we enjoyed a meal that kept us going until we met the rest of the band in the evening—normally at Fischl's, a large, bustling restaurant near the Bier Bar which served up huge portions of good, honest German food (and large steins of Pils at prices even we could afford).

Kay came over, and we had Christmas together, and we decided to get married... and then there was an offer of two months in Hamburg. So I said, "I'm going back to make arrangements to get married," but that I would return for the whole of the last month (March).

I don't think Ken was too happy about it, but Mukki Herman depped for February and so I got the train and ferry back to England, made all the arrangements, and then had to get a job digging ditches to get the money to get back to Hamburg.

And then about two days before I was going, I happened to be in London and I bumped into Sandy Brown, and he needed a bass player. He'd needed a bass player for about three weeks. So I got one gig, and I earned as much as I would in a week digging ditches—more fun, as well. So anyway, **I got on the train and went back to Hamburg, and they all met me—they'd all grown beards by this time, so I felt out of place;** it was mostly because there was no hot water where they'd been staying. And the next morning... woke up, and we found an empty bed which had had Disley in it.

But he'd decided that he wasn't going to stay with the band any longer—he left a short explanatory note. However, we were extremely fortunate that local banjoist Peter Hunck agreed to replace him whilst we were in Hamburg. Peter fitted in both personally and musically. And then of course Johnny Bastable joined for the last week. He *flew* over. And we all got taxis out and greeted him at the airport. And the band had become more established... that was a good band then.

DIZ DISLEY I remember once when we were playing in Germany... a club up in Hamburg somewhere. And Ken called me a cunt because he thought I was reading the newspaper. I left a note the following day saying, "Next time don't be so fucking rude." Trying to think who replaced me when I left Ken...

DELPHINE COLYER Poor old Diz. He was busy reading the *Melody Maker*. Still playing perfectly well, but reading the *Melody Maker*. Didn't go down very well. Then there was Peter Deuchar, and by this time they'd talked Johnny into joining.

DIZ DISLEY Well, we were a very untidy band. When we went to Düsseldorf, we just followed the Fatty George band, who came from Austria somewhere. Anyway, we had all dirty jeans and dirty shirts and that sort of thing, so the Germans must have thought we were pretty disgusting, I should think.

But it all went down very well. I remember one night we were playing *Over the Waves*. You know it starts in three-four

time, and this German couple got up to dance just at the moment we went into the four-four, and they had to stop dancing... with disgust. I left, rather than be kicked out, and I went back to Düsseldorf. And on the way I saw a huge yard full of wrecked trains from the war.

JOHNNY BASTABLE One day when I was at work I had a phone call from Hamburg. It was Bill Colyer and he wanted me to join the band. Well, after he had spent all that money to get in touch with me, I was afraid to refuse, so I said yes. **In a week's time I was out there and, after the first number I played with the band, I knew that I hadn't made a mistake, and we have been raving on ever since.**

KEN COLYER Then Johnny Bastable came out and things looked up. Near the end of our two months, an oldish fellow turned up with a very young chick. She liked the band. Would we go to their club before we returned home? They offered us very good money to do three days in Luneberg. We accepted and went to Luneberg. He plied us with champagne every night and about six people turned up. The crunch came when we went to get paid. He was broke, and owed the brewery for all the booze.

We had to wire home for train fare and I owed about two months rent on my flat in Fulham. When we got home there was no big welcome, and it was difficult to adjust to the neighbours after playing four months in two clubs.

KEN COLYER Decca ignored my pleas to record in Germany. Was under contract, they refused permission. Didn't know what was going on. Dumkopfs.

THE COLYER MEN IN GERMANY
By Klaus Berenbrok. *Collector's Corner*, **Edited by Max Jones And Sinclair Traill**

When jazz fans over here heard that Ken Colyer would be playing in December at Düsseldorf's well-known New Orleans Jazz Bar, only a few people knew what to expect. We had heard something about the fanatical purist who was imprisoned in the New Orleans jailhouse, but he was not widely known.

On his first evening, let us face it, curiosity had filled the place with people. But, after Ken Colyer's Jazzmen had played the first few numbers, applause broke out of a kind seldom given to a band here. Real New Orleans jazz! The original jazz style heard in this city for the first time.

Never has a band impressed Düsseldorf more than Colyer's Jazzmen. Since Ken started playing in the Jazz Bar on December 1, jazz fans have had a difficult choice to make. Either to begin work the next morning after a good night's rest, or to spend all night hearing music that is almost unbelievable.

Since December 1, Düsseldorf's jazz spot is so over-crowded that one is lucky to get a place. The porter is unhappy because

Dick Smith bids farewell to Hamburg and Ken and welcomes his replacement, Mukki Herman

he now has to welcome guests not only until three a.m. as usual but till five a.m. And Ken Colyer plays so well that even the manager has become a jazz fan.

The financial situation of jazz in Germany is very bad. Therefore the greater the surprise when the Jazz Bar opened on May 18, 1954. Rudolf Vortmann, the owner, had engaged for the décor Germany's "New Orleans Style painter" Horst Geldmacher.

He equipped the Jazz Bar in the architectural style of New Orleans' old French Quarter, with ancient lamps, wooden balconies and swinging latticed doors, an antique bandstand, and pictures of Bunk Johnson, Bessie Smith, Armstrong and Oliver on the walls.

Since opening night, many bands have played there, including the Dixie Jazz Pals from Paris, the German-Austrian Fatty George band, the Dixieland Pipers from the Hague, and the Feetwarmers of the Hot Club, Düsseldorf.

They played in the manner of the Armstrong Hot Five, modern Lawson-Haggart-Dixieland, and Chicago jazz—but none of these played an authentic New Orleans style like Ken Colyer does.

The Colyer Jazzmen have soon established friendships with

many members of the Düsseldorf Hot Club. Disley accepted Horst's invitation to live in his studio, and now both artists work together.

The traditionalists listen not only to Ken's music, but also to his and his brother's theories about New Orleans music.

And German jazz fans wish nothing more than to be able to hear Ken and the band very often, and, if possible, in concerts too. The German Christmas folk-song *Oh Tannenbaum* generally known as *Maryland* has proved the band's biggest hit over here.

KEN COLYER Bill Coleman had been playing at another club when we were in Düsseldorf, so we never saw him. He had come to Hamburg as we had. His job finished earlier so he often used to drop in with Curby Alexander, his sax player.

Curby didn't like the South, he told me, when I said I had enjoyed it. I had to explain that the music was the only attraction for me. If music that good had been at the North Pole, I would have gone there.

But he was a troubled man and committed suicide about a year later.

Wallace Bishop was on drums with Bill. "But he's a little modern now," Bill said. Wallace had played with some of the greats in the past.

Kurt Edelhagen's lead trumpeter used to come in, in the early hours of the morning. They were a very popular big band at the time and did a lot of radio work. He was always earning good money and always bought us a drink.

He borrowed my horn and sat in. He didn't fit but was a brilliant trumpeter. Also my mouthpiece was wrong for his style of playing but we had some laughs and used to like to see him.

The Hans Radijski Quartet were at the "Box." This was in Hamburg itself. They used to finish earlier than us some nights, and look in. "Crazy" Otto was his bass player. He wasn't crazy and was a very good bassist. They played a sort of modern style but used to join in with us. Hans Radijski could also play very nice gypsy guitar in quiet moments.

We had two breakdown groups to give each other a rest. Skiffle was still popular. I would switch to guitar and Bill would come in on washboard. Mukki would stay on bass. Then Stan Greig would switch to piano and Diz to guitar and they would do half an hour or so. They used to play a fine version of *Get*

Happy, which I liked very much.

When things were very quiet and the management still insisted on us playing I would sometimes end the evening with a skiffle session.

It was winter in Hamburg and one of the most bitter they had in years. The packed ice and snow stayed permanently frozen, it was that cold. Diz discovered that they sold glühwein opposite the club. When we could afford it, a couple of these were excellent warmers on a bitter night.

DELPHINE COLYER When we went to Germany, I suppose I'd only just left home really; certainly couldn't speak German. The music was fantastic. There was a different atmosphere. I suppose it was more like the American thing. Well, I suppose Ken thought, "Six months ago I was by myself, and now I`ve got something I can work on here."

KEN COLYER Bill Crozier came from Cologne, and we recorded another session for BFN. Bill capitalized on *Goin' Home* and it was more popular than ever. A lot of the Forces were just waiting for their demob. I also did a far better version of *Take This Hammer* than the one I did for Decca. I wanted Decca to release it but their engineers decided the technical quality wasn't good enough. What would we have done without these people?

A week prior to finishing at Hamburg a little oldish man came into the club with a very young girl friend, or wife. She thought the band was terrific. The head waiter said we were onto a good thing as he brought us up a tray of drinks.

The old fellow said we would go to Lüneburg for three days after finishing in Hamburg for good money. We owed Lyn Dutton commission on the four months we had spent in Germany, I also owed several months' rent on my flat in Fulham. It seemed an ideal way to pay our fares home. The money we had earned left nothing over for such trivialities as commissions, rent etc.

We accepted and phoned Lyn Dutton, telling him of the change of plans.

The fans were nice on the last night, presenting us with small mementoes and packets of cigarettes.

We managed to finish the job without being owed any money. Lüneburg isn't far from Hamburg and we took the train there. The fellow had arranged a hotel there for us. The three nights were disastrous business-wise.

He had expected to attract the officer class, as there was still a strong military presence in the area. The officer class consisting mainly of twits, we of course, didn't attract them. Three or four Germans came and they comprised our audience. The fellow plied us with wine but it transpired that all the drink had been supplied by a brewery on credit. He tried to deduct the cost of this from the money he didn't have, to pay us.

DICK SMITH Then we finally returned to the UK at the

Bill Coleman drops by the bar, Sarah Vaughan on the wall

beginning of April, a very different and more mature group than the one that had departed four months earlier—extremely well seasoned and well on the way to being transformed—in fact the nucleus of Ken's new band at long last.

KEN COLYER After four glorious months of transforming the German jazz world and waking them up to another form of music we were stranded and practically broke. We had to phone Lyn Dutton for our fare home.

So I returned home owing several hundred pounds in commissions, rent and train fares. Long after, I finally repaid all this money; I believe I was one of the few bandleaders that honoured his debts to Dutton. I barely got a thank you for my honesty.

The jazz world had practically forgotten about us and it was a hard slog making a comeback.

We established a reputation in Germany that stood British bands of lesser calibre in good stead for a long time afterwards. Yet they wouldn't re-book me for realistic wages.

DELPHINE COLYER They really were magic. Because when they came back and hit the town it was really something. Everyone was, you know, waiting for this band: "Why are they in Germany?" "Why aren't they over here?" "Ooh, we wanna hear 'em!" And it was great. A lot of the enthusiasm was through the build-up to it all.

ABBI HUBNER Colyer's appearances in 1955 really knocked us out. He introduce a totally new type of New Orleans to us, a New Orleans jazz going back to the folk-lore of New Orleans, showing a strong feeling for cooperation within the band and collective.

Ken *did* show us that a jazz band can swing, and he especially showed us that a jazz band can play dynamically.

Until that time, the bands in Hamburg used to start very loudly, and they ended even louder. **Ken taught us that in jazz there are, of course, quiet notes—neccessary to underline the stronger notes—and that an escalation should occur at the end of the music.**

IAN WHEELER Then came the crunch: We thought that when we returned to England we were going to blow everybody off the stage with these marvellous lips we must have. It didn't work that way! Those circumstances at the Bier Bar were actually so relaxed that, when we did get back and played our first concert —in Bristol, I think—we were all shattered at the end of two hours' continuous playing, as compared with the four or five hours in Germany, playing intermittently.

BILL COLYER The moment we had the LP made, Lyn Dutton (who had an agency that Humph was part of in Newman Street, I think) said to me, "I can get you a couple of months in Germany; they are opening a new club in Düsseldorf called The New Orleans Bier Bar." So I got on to the guys and asked, "Will you turn pro and take the gig?" They all agreed. However, just a matter of days before we were due to go, Acker had to back off, due to a family illness.

The grapevine told me there was a guy due out of hospital after a car crash, whose name was Ian Wheeler. So I went down to Catford to meet Ian, and I sounded him out pretty thoroughly, like "Who do you dig on clarinet?" And he named all the right names, so I said he was in. It turned out that he was driving a sports car and it meant that he had to attend a court case or a coroner enquiry, but that wasn't for five weeks, so he was free to come to Germany with us.

That Düsseldorf stint was our saviour. There was a German guy called Klaus Berenbrock who set it up with Lyn Dutton—a good cat! He took us under his wing.

The gov'nor of the Düsseldorf club was a very nice man. The photographs exist of us all lined up there at his bar. All around the club were photos of Sarah Vaughan, Bunk Johnson... It was Ian Wheeler who stood up on a stool and photographed the whole club. Somewhere I've got the negs, or Ian's got 'em. We were a real success there; British servicemen would queue for hours. And when the Brits would come in in civvies, I'd always be sitting with them. The band became very, very good during this gig—and of course the Breakdown Group!—and out of this successful gig we got two months in Hamburg.

It was in Hamburg that Bill Coleman showed up with Curby Alexander, his saxophone player, who used to play with Lucky Millinder. Bill had a lovely Swiss wife called Lily. I already knew Bill from the Dobell days when he'd come over and play— another wonderful man. It was a good band but they were doing these tea-dance things for the German Hausfraus eating their cream cakes. We caught his daytime set once and he played a Dixieland number for us, but because of the audience they had no chance to stretch.

That's where I bumped into Timmie Rosencrantz (the Danish Baron) and he brought Bill Coleman and a couple of the other guys over to our gig in the evening. Bill leaned over to me at the table: "Hey, d'ya think Ken'd let me sit-in?"

I said, "But you haven't got your horn." "I'll play his," says Bill. We were dressed like Mississippi gamblers then: string ties, black waistcoats, black denims. Up gets Bill in his tuxedo. Ken agreed to let him use his (Ken's) horn. Ken had the King cornet then, Bill was a trumpet man—and I never used the camera! What an idiot!

The requests could get tedious. The barman would hold up two or sometimes three fingers, which meant you had to do the same tune over again—*Tannenbaum*, *The Saints*—but you had to make it good, and from the requests came free drinks, so you did it!

They were long sessions, which is why The Breakdown Group was so important, so that lips could be rested for 15 or 20 minutes.

Ken kept it flexible: if a number was ticking Ken would stretch it for maybe 10 minutes, and the audience loved it.

Sometimes I'd think, "Hey, Ken, kick it into touch!" But uncannily he was always right, even though my arms would be aching like hell sometimes.

Pete Deuchar had lasted only a couple of days—didn't have the swing we needed. On the first night the beat was dragging, slowing; even though Greigie was doing his best to keep it going, the banjo is dominant. **Ken leaned back and said, "Pick it up! Pick it up!!" And Pete said, "My fingers are aching, Ken." Ken says, "Play till the f****** blood comes!!"**

He was a lovely guy, but just not very good. Ken and I went out to the airport on the coach to pick him up and on the way back Ken's asking him, "Do ya know this, do ya know that?" He'd had a Newcastle band called the Vieux Carre but they were amateurs, playing once or twice a week.

But it was a most interesting band. Mukki Herman was on bass, and of course Greigie: a tower of strength on drums and a very good piano man as well.

CHAPTER NINE
WALKIN' WITH THE KING: THE 'CLASSIC' BAND

KEN SIMS In Liverpool, Ken used to do concerts at the Picton Hall. And the concert prior to Ken was the Alex Welsh Band; they climaxed their show with a Lenny Hastings drum solo called *The Battle of Hastings*. And it was fast and furious, and went down a bomb. And then Ken turned up without a drummer—they had Bill on washboard, and it swung like mad and he was the exact opposite. He didn't play anything fast, turned his back on the audience, didn't smile; I don't think he announced the tunes either.

I was immediately converted to the non-flashy type of music, because it was swinging nonstop; it swung, swung, swung and swung. Didn't force anything. I must admit that at the time I thought I could play technically better than Ken, because he didn't play anything.

> He played a very lyrical lead, and without seeming to try very hard just dominated the band, which is not easy to do, especially with the two side-men he had—strong-willed persons, particularly Mac.

COLIN BOWDEN Ken didn't like "two-beat tank drumming". I never talked to him about it, but I suspect that it was the type of drumming that Ory had Ram Hall play on his recordings—very heavy off-beat and two-beat bass drum. I tried to put a hi-hat on the stage when I first joined the band, but he didn't want it. When I didn't do sessions with Ken, I used the hi-hat. But when it was his band, he didn't like two-beat, he liked a light four-four drumming like Baby Dodds or Joe Watkins.

There were other drummers around doing that other style, and it's good when it's done properly, but Ken didn't want it in *his* band. And being very brusque and to the point, he told me so.

MICKY ASHMAN I always think that, not because I was there for a short time, it was the best band that he ever had. I was always very happy with it.

It was a very good band Colyer had there.

Well, actually and truthfully, I was never *in* the band. You must understand that I'm not the best bass player in the world, but I've always been in the right spot at the right time.

DICK SMITH We now resumed our tours of UK pubs and clubs—plus the occasional concert, broadcast and recording session. We also went to Gibraltar for six or seven days. Two things stand out in my mind. Firstly, how short the runway seemed from the air, with the sea at both ends (time for a prayer!) Secondly, being woken in the hotel by the rain pouring through the ceiling onto my bed. When I went to inform the owner (expecting a different room) he, with great presence of mind, told me to move the bed—and also handed me a bucket to catch the water!

IAN WHEELER Colin Bowden joined a bit later; originally it was Stan Greig, then Stan went to join Humph after we came back from Germany. For quite some time we had Bill Colyer on washboard until Colin joined. Dick Smith was on bass before Ron Ward and Diz Disley on banjo before Bastable joined. Diz left us in Germany because he met a beautiful redhead! Typical Disley.

COLIN BOWDEN When I did that session with the Omega Brass Band—the very first one—in July 1955, made up of Sonny Morris's band and Ken's band, that was for the Soho Fair. And at the end of that, down in the cellar of the Star Restaurant in New Compton Street, Bill Colyer offered me the job. He just said, "Ken would like you to join the band." I don't think I really spoke to Ken before I joined. It was always Bill.

I was playing with Sonny, and when they joined together to form the Omega, to me it was just a one-off session.

John Bastable was playing bass drum on that session. We used to listen to Bunk's brass band. The beat wasn't so broken up as it is now; there were a few cross-patterns and that was it. And even with Bunk's brass band, where Lawrence Marrero plays bass drum—that was even a simpler style, and that would have been the bass drum line that Johnny Bastable would have taken.

The Baby Dodds sound was what I was after. I wasn't particularly bothered about whether it was a New Orleans style or not, it was the sound that I was after. So there

was a pointer for us all, and we took it our way and put our stamp on it.

But you have to be careful not just to copy because then you can seize up; but really we were dependent on the records for our inspiration—there were no cheap flights to America to hear contemporary playing. Our parameters were narrow.

KEN SIMS Omega Brass Band. I couldn't afford a white shirt and a parade hat. It was Ken Colyer, Keith Smith, and me. And again, I was amazed by the strength of Ken's lead when he didn't seem to be doing anything. And we were all likely to give it one, but he didn't. There was the lead there.

He was very kind to me. He said, "I used to play like you, on top of the band with the Cranes. But when I got to New Orleans, they weren't playing like that. And I listened to what they were doing." He always had that funny accent—in Liverpool we call that Western Ocean Cowboy accent.

COLIN BOWDEN When I got the job with Ken, every time Stan Greig came in the room I was worried stiff. Or any other drummer, I was worried stiff. I still am, actually!! You can never get complacent; you know you've got to do your best each and every time and get it as tight as possible.

People would ask me: how did I know how a particular tune was gonna go, the endings and so-forth? I just knew instinctively.

Johnny Bastable, Dick Smith and myself had been the rhythm section with Trevor Wiliams' band. We thought we were the best rhythm section in the world. It broke my heart when we found out Dick was joining Chris. I said, "You can't... you just can't!!!" Ken himself was upset, I think, and Bill Colyer too. But people move on and you adjust.

DICK SMITH In April 1955 I decided to leave the band and gave the obligatory three weeks' notice—I now had much broader musical horizons and had been invited to join Chris Barber's band. Ken was a wee bit grumpy—though not too bad—well, until the last night, that is. When I had said farewell to the band he suddenly refused to pay me for the last week, pretending that we were paid in advance!

IAN WHEELER We were certainly very friendly towards one another especially Mac and myself—he was my biggest sidekick; we'd do all kind of things together... well, some things! But musically, it just happened, it just developed. In fact sometimes you read things in the press about a particular band, and you say to yourself, "We didn't think that way, we just did it!" And it's very difficult to analyse as to how or why.

We certainly didn't do a great many rehearsals—not for most of the tunes. Of course if you're playing a rag where you

The Omega Brass
Band on parade

have an arrangement, you have to rehearse but, generally speaking, you find your way as it happens. And you work things out over a period of time.

IAN WHEELER I don't ever remember Ken telling me what to do. He was more likely to tell me what *not* to do, although I can't remember a specific even then. He let you play your thing and never tried to alter what you were doing. Ken led the band by demonstration, by example; he assumed you knew what to do.

COLIN BOWDEN If things were going well Ken could be fine; if things weren't and he'd had a couple, he could be quite abrasive to the punters. **People put it down as a crusade, but you just hear a sound and think, "That's what I want to do." You just want to play the music you like playing.**

KEN SIMS Ken's band was Ken's band. It didn't, to my ears, sound like the George Lewis band.

He sounded very different—to me—from Bunk and George Lewis, and any of the Chicago bands. It was Ken Colyer, and that was it. I mean, he didn't sound a bit like Kid Howard or Bunk, to me. He sounded a lot like—when I heard the records of the Kid Ory band—Mutt Carey.

PAUL SEALEY Mac Duncan was a very good player. Within that front-line he and Ian worked really well together, and I would say in terms of that style he was certainly one of the best around, and certainly very influential to a lot of younger players. But he was also very broad-minded; he liked Lester Young too.

When I used to come to rehearsals, after he'd formed his own band with Keith Smith, he used to be practising Lester Young things to play on his trombone—for solos within the band, and those kind of things. And he was frustrated—I know that—because he couldn't read or write music, he couldn't put it together, and there was a sense of frustration because he would get quite angry with himself, and I would sort of suggest something to help and he would cut me short and… "no, he wanted to do it himself." He felt like he needed to do it. And he had his down moments, but I put that down to him being older, although he would have only been in his early thirties. But no, he was lovely—I liked him very much.

CUFF BILLETT Ken liked Jimmy Archey… I remember him liking Jimmy Archey. And I once mentioned the fact that I thought he was a bit like Mac Duncan… And I said, "Did you want him to play like that, or did you pick him because he played like that?"

And I once said, "He's got a lot of drive"—in Jimmy Archey's playing, and he said, "No… swing". We had a slight argument, where drive was not quite the same as swing. But I know that two or three times he mentioned Jimmy Archey. I don't think I got any sensible comment as to whether or not Mac Duncan was attempting to play like Jimmy Archey.

But whether he was asked to play like that, or Ken picked him because he *did* play like that…

COLIN BOWDEN Mac Duncan, of course, wanted to be a Vic Dickenson-style trombone player. In fact he was a wonderful New Orleans-style trombone player. He and Wheeler bounced off Ken like wildfire. Mac was always very up and down.

ALAN GATWARD Well, I had this factory in the East-End of London that made paper bags and carrier bags by day, and became a jazz-club by night. So… nobody else wanted to live there, so I took in jazz-musicians as lodgers. The first one was Mac Duncan, who was the trombone player with Ken Colyer.

That's how I met him. I had become friendly with Chris Barber, and used to give him a lift home because he didn't have a car, and then when Ken Colyer came back from New Orleans, the Chris Barber Band became the Ken Colyer Band. And I used to hear that band whenever I could, and I became friendly with the musicians. And after Mac Duncan, there were a succession of musicians who were involved in what Ken Colyer would call New Orleans music.

Alan Gatward (right) with Mac and Ian

Mac was a very good-looking guy who had a likeable personality. He was a bit—shall we say—conservative about spending money. But he had lots of girlfriends who he would bring back, and he had at least two wives—married and divorced. And then he had a beautiful German girl, and then there was the television producer—Gwen.

He was very pleased once when an American musician came and heard the Ken Colyer band—this was in the early days with Mac Duncan and Colin Bowden. And… they never had band-uniforms—fairly scruffily dressed. And the American musician said, "Well, the band's playing OK, but you look like you've just come off the rods." And Colyer was pleased about that—he recounted it as an amusing anecdote, and chuckled.

JOHN GRIFFITH I saw the best and the worst of Mac: his wonderful, wicked humour, which affected his playing, and, rather like Ken, he could be reticent about certain things in the past. But at times, he would remember something, and open up with a story. With very different personalities, Mac and Ken had a *great* deal in common, and they both reacted to events and experiences in the same way. Two very different personalities.

There's an interest there. I remember Ken once saying—talking about those early times—"One or two of them were even more fanatical about the New Orleans effect than me." I think he was referring to Mac probably, when he was really bashing into that plunger mute and pouring his heart out. With absolutely the right technique and expression to serve it.

Well, it's often the case, isn't it? You know, I mean, you see it in all sorts of partnerships, arrangements, marriages—you know, people are horrifyingly similar; it's almost as if they don't like what the mirror gives them.

MAC DUNCAN LETTER TO KEN COLYER UNDATED

Dear Ken

Many thanks for the most satisfying year of my life. It's been great—and I hope we have plenty more together.

All the very best for Christmas (including Delphine) and a New Year better than this last one (if possible).

Sincerely (signed) Mac

PETER MORCOM It was in mid-1956 that through a friend of a friend I was invited to a meal at the Universal Chinese restaurant in Charing Cross Road with Mac Duncan and John Bastable. I had owned a tenor banjo for some time and talked with John about St Cyr and Marrero and about his own playing. The ice had been broken, and from then on John and I became firm friends.

The train service back to Ipswich meant that I had to hurry away from the 51 after the last number and so, one evening, John suggested that next time I should come back with him to

Ken, Bob Wallis , and Trevor Williams lead the Omega Brass Band

Croxley Green, and insisted that I bring my banjo with me.

I went back to John's place (6 Links Way) on a number of occasions. We ate the supper John's mum had left out for us and the next day listened to records of, amongst others, the 6 and 7/8ths String Band and the Trevor Williams band, whose rhythm section had gradually become the Colyer section.

John's mum seemed to like having me there and I did my best to incorporate everything from those master classes into my own playing.

One day John suggested that I sit-in with the band. His persuasion overcame my reluctance, and after the first three numbers of the second set it was my turn. Ken seemed pleased and from then on it became customary for me to sit in for three numbers and eventually a whole set. "Stay up, man," Ken would say. I dared not refuse.

John, whose instrument I played on these occasions, was pleased to be able to remain at the bar, his only caution being, "Try not to break a string."

JOHN WURR Worthing High School, Autumn 1956. I'd still not heard any live jazz, but the Colyer band is coming to Worthing Assembly Hall. We all go along. I am blown away. It's the classic 50s band of course—Ian, Mac, Colin etc., and they seemed to me to be on sensational form, although I realise now that it is probably just another routine night for them.

I can honestly say that my desire to become a jazz performer dates from that night.

JOHN REDDIHOUGH ON KEN COLYER'S JAZZMEN *Jazz Journal*, 1956

There have been several occasions recently when people who have been fortunate enough to have visited New Orleans, or other parts of the States, have come along to hear the present Ken Colyer band. It is a mark of the greatness of this band that in each case praise has been lavished upon them, for praise from those who are able to make first-hand comparisons between them and Louis, Kid Ory or George Lewis is especially noteworthy. After a particularly memorable session recently, one of these fortunates told me: "I have had two greater kicks in my life than tonight, and both of these were when listening to the Ory band in San Francisco."

In May, 1954, Ken Colyer became dissatisfied with the band he was then leading and decided to disband it. A period of uncertainty followed whilst Ken tried to build up a new group to take with him to Germany. Mac Duncan and Ian Wheeler were hired shortly before the band left the country and John Bastable made the trip to join the band early in 1955. The only original man from Colyer's first group was bassist Dick Smith.

THE DRUMMER

The present band has been together now for nearly eighteen months. A lot has happened in this time, but the biggest strides have been made in the last nine months or so. This may be due to the extra impetus given to the band since Colin Bowden, on drums, joined them at the end of last summer. Colin's drumming was just what was needed; he really swings, having the good sense not merely to lay down the beat, which bass and banjo can do perfectly well, but to concentrate on accentuation and polyrhythm. His drumming is in the Baby Dodds vein, full of light and shade. It is also extremely logical, without those outbursts of sound for no reason at all that are so typical of British drummers. His grasp of the New Orleans style of drumming, enables him to generate the wonderful driving beat which is characteristic of the best New Orleans jazz.

The rhythm section which Ken Colyer has built up is truly remarkable and for sheer swing, it is without precedent in this country. Rhythm sections have always been the bane of European jazz, but here, at last, is one that breaks with that grim tradition. Apart from Colin Bowden, there is John Bastable on banjo and Micky Ashman on bass. It is John Bastable who lays down the basic beat: I have never heard a more rock-steady banjo player. In most cases banjo players, in endeavouring to stabilize the rhythm, end only by dragging lamentably. But this is not the case with John Bastable. Nor should it be imagined that his firm beat is in any way mechanical. If the tempo of a number increases, as it is bound to do if a band is really swinging, John Bastable is right with it, ensuring that the advancing tempo is controlled but not erratic.

Micky Ashman's bass playing has a wonderful buoyancy combined with great drive which imparts a tremendous lift to the band. But the main thing about the rhythm section is its inner cohesion. The Ken Colyer rhythm section fits together and, combined with its natural drive, generates a real, swinging beat.

The front line, which started so shakily when the band was first formed, is now playing with complete assurance and mastery. From the point of view of pure technique, they are the equal of any group playing traditional jazz in this country:

Mac and Ken in musical conversation

from the point of view of JAZZ technique, they are far in advance. The tonal quality of the front line is quite exceptional: there is none of the raucousness which we once expected from European traditional bands , nor the dullness which the professionals bring with them when they turn to jazz; nor that strident blasting which so often covers a lack of tonal subtlety. In addition, the front line do not leave it entirely to the rhythm section to provide the beat, the swing in the Colyer band comes from all sections.

The biggest surprise in the band is trombonist Mac Duncan who, over the past few months, has improved to such an extent that I would not hesitate to describe him as the most outstanding traditional trombonist in this country today. He has become a tremendously rhythmical player, with the appropriate swinging phrase and tone to complement the rest of the band. His use of that neglected and much spurned thing, glissando, is highly rhythmical, sometimes covering, as an extension of vibrato, whole phrases.

IAN WHEELER

Clarinettist Ian Wheeler has now settled down and plays with a full and mellow tone. With his considerable technical ability, he is able to provide a flow of ideas which are the perfect foil for the brass horns. His playing is not a copy of any New Orleans clarinet player, for he has managed to develop a distinctive style of his own, without losing his highly rhythmic quality.

Lastly, the man who sparks the whole band and who has moulded it around himself, Ken Colyer. He has never played as well as he is doing right now, and this is undoubtedly because he has at last found a group of men capable of playing New Orleans jazz in the best tradition. Ken visited New Orleans largely to find out how the music he loves so much really is played, and to study jazz from those who created it—hence his knowledge of how a band really should sound. I have been with Ken when he has been explaining the techniques peculiar to New Orleans jazzmen, and have seen the improvements which his knowledge has produced. It is not of the slightest use endeavouring to incorporate into New Orleans jazz the tricks used in subsequent jazz styles: they just do not fit into the pattern of New Orleans jazz music. Ken realises this, and believes that to understand the music at all it is necessary to approach it with a certain humility. It is a pity for jazz that no one else has acted on this simple truth.

FREEDOM AND RELAXATION

He himself has succeeded in becoming a first-class New Orleans lead horn player. The elements of his playing are the traditional and really worth-while ones, best suited to an improvising New Orleans group. There is a sense of freedom and relaxation in the way he maintains the basic melodic structure of a number—the melodic line always being patterned in such a way that a real swing is developed. He has the ability to accentuate the rhythm so that the music is loosened and really starts to flow, and his excellent tone—fully rounded yet highly personal—constitutes a style which is at all times highly rhythmical and inspired.

It would be wrong, however, to think only of the individual playing of the jazzmen: the important thing is the band as a whole. The Ken Colyer group is a New Orleans band, but it is not just a bunch of imitators. They long since left the stage of imitation, of learning the rudiments: their music now is sure and authoritative—they are playing in the true New Orleans idiom.

Mention should also be made of the skiffle group. Ken has been doing skiffle numbers for several years now and has developed a distinctive style of his own. I remember Big Bill Broonzy, when he was over here a short while ago, saying how much he liked Ken's style. Ken sings and plays guitar in the same relaxed way that he leads on trumpet. His delivery is soft and 'lazy', the way good blues singing should be.

BOB KELLY

Talk of the skiffle group brings us to the latest addition to the Ken Colyer group, blues and boogie pianist Bob Kelly, who at present does all the intermission work. Bob Kelly's rendition of such traditional numbers as *Fisherman's Blues*, *East St. Louis Blues* and *Honky Tonk Train Blues* shows great promise. He achieves considerable swing, produces a fine tone, and his voice and diction are excellent.

Lastly, a word about recordings. The present group visited the studios on March the 8th when *Maryland My Maryland*, *Dippermouth Blues*, *All The Girls Like The Way I Walk* and *The World Is Waiting For The Sunrise* were recorded. The band was playing well that evening, and some good record resulted, although the sound of the band was not completely satisfactorily captured. Decca have promised to consider recording a live club session, and, as this is probably the only way in which to achieve really satisfactory results, I hope that they will do this.

The critic can only make comparisons and draw his conclusions from them. Comparatively, the present Ken Colyer group is far better than any other group that I have heard in this country. Ken, I realise, knows of improvements that could be made, but to know what they are one would either have to be psychic or to have visited New Orleans and learned from its creators all about the idiom.

JOHN GRIFFITH John Alvey Turner had designed a brass mute copied from an impression of drawings that he took from Lonnie's mute that Ken had

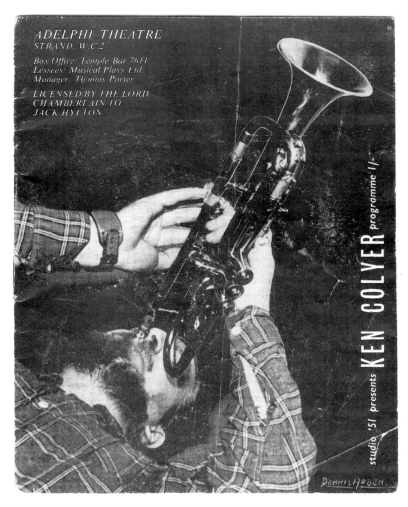

ADELPHI THEATRE
STRAND. W.C.2
Box Office: Temple Bar 7611
Lessees: Musical Plays Ltd.
Manager: Thomas Porter
LICENSED BY THE LORD
CHAMBERLAIN TO
JACK HYLTON

KEN COLYER

studio '51 presents

Programme 1/-

DENNIS ARDEN.

brought back from New Orleans, which of course is the famous Lawrence Marrero Mute. So John Bastable copied that in weight and dimension, virtually *in* brass, and that had helped to produce that forties Marrero sound.

Later, particularly when Ray Foxley joined, things got a little bit more frenetic at times. He changed his tone, and played more *on* the bridge, and then later produced this wider, brass/copper mute. And it all changed the sound and changed the effect of how he played. But that early John Bastable—which is my favourite time—was very near the Marrero sound, only slightly sharpened up.

And it is that period when Ken had Ian and Mac, Colin, Johnny and dear old Ron Ward, who is much maligned, and I don't understand why. You know, because he was very solid, effective—he worked very well with that whole outfit.

CHRIS BARBER I tried to teach Ron Ward the bass, you see. I had three students from the jazz world: Dick Smith, Ernie Price and Ron Ward. I mean, nice people. Ron was a lovely guy, but I mean... his hands were misshapen, which made fingering the bass very difficult. He was very enthusiastic.

RON WARD Every year we took part in a Riverboat Shuffle

from Tower Bridge Pier to Margate. These were arranged by George Webb of "Jazzshows."

Two boats were hired, the *Royal Sovereign* and the *Daffodil*, each carrying approximately 2,000 jazz fans; some of whom had travelled from as far away as Scotland just to attend.

I think I took part in seven of these, and every time we had perfect weather—quite a miracle!

With six or seven bands on each boat, it was a wonderful experience. On one occasion two characters, somewhat the worse for drink, dived fully clothed into the water at Margate, before the boat had docked! Much to the amusement of the spectators.

PAUL SEALEY The first time I sat in with the band I was thirteen years old—Colin Watson and I sat in. Colin Bowden and Bastable were very supportive. John knew I could play and Ken knew that Colin Watson could play. The only person who objected was Ron Ward, who didn't like him coming up to use his bass, and I remember Colin Bowden saying, "Oh, go on, they're only young—give them a break." And I think Ron—in retrospect—didn't want him to know the bass wasn't tuned up properly! Anyway, he allowed it to happen and we got up.

COLIN BOWDEN When I first joined the band I think we did Nottingham, and there was a clarinet player up there used to run a band, and we went back to his place for a party. And this clarinet player was basically a white fanatic. And so he said, "I'll play you something," and he played one of the Bunk A.M.s—a blues—and Bunk's playing was slightly off key, or something like that.

And then he said, "Now I'll play you some real jazz," and he put on the best recording he could find of the Original Dixieland Jazzband. So I said, "For Christ's sake, you play Bunk and then you play…" and I'm in the middle of this, and from the back of the room I heard this voice saying, "All these clever, clever musicians that just join a band and think they know everything," and I was furious.

I stood up, and I pointed at him and I said: "For Christ's sake man, I'm defending the music you love, not destroying it." And I sat down, and I was thinking, "The miserable old bastard." The next thing I know is, there's a tap on my shoulder and it was Ken. And I turned around and saw him slumped to the floor and I said, "Oh for Christ's sake, go away," and I wouldn't talk to him, you see.

Anyway, we're going back, and it was in the days of

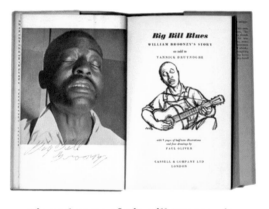

Signed copy of Big Bill Broonzy's book, given to Bill Colyer

Swinson's Coach, so there was loads of room. And it's early hours of the morning, and it was just daylight, and he comes down the coach, and he says, "Oh Colin, sorry about last night." And I said, "Sorry I lost my temper," and that was the end of it. But after that he knew what I was like. The ice was broken, as far as knowing each other pretty well was concerned. But, if he was in a grouchy mood, I'd just leave him to it.

We did things with Big Bill Broonzy. He played either solo or he did things like *I'm Looking Over A Four-Leaf Clover* with the band. Broonzy was lovely. Speckled Red and Brother John Sellers did tours with us. We did a BBC broadcast which I'd love to get hold, of when I played with Little Brother Montgomery.

IAN WHEELER Personally, I like playing with a piano. It sort of fills-in the background. Because Ray was very much in a sort of Jelly Roll Morton style, you know, which was a bit strange to start with, I think, until we got used to it. We adapted and probably Ray adapted a bit as well.

COLIN BOWDEN Musical conversations were on the stand. When Ray Foxley came into the band it broadened the sound. You can't get so many drum fills in because there's not enough room, there are not so many gaps because Ray filled out the rhythm section beautifully, especially on the rags. I think he and Ken must have done a lot of wood-shedding for that Ragtime EP—which was the front-line bit—but I didn't dig out records to find out what ragtime drummers did, I followed my instincts, and probably Mutt Carey's New Yorkers had a lot to do with the way I played on those things, and the other band members too.

When you listen to Mac you can hear Jimmy Archey, no doubt about that. And Ken's stuff was influenced by that, especially on the rags.

I think that what happened on those four tracks was bloody marvellous. Because it was a… jazz band playing rags in a style. Not that all jazz bands should play rags that way; it was the way Ken Colyer's Jazz Band played rags, and it was a little bit of poetry, to me. The musicians bouncing off one another like wildfire.

RAY FOXLEY Ken was running a piano-less band at the time; he always had, apart from the Cranes with Pat Hawes. But he used Bob Kelly, who played in the skiffle group only, and also solos sometimes. But not with the band. And one morning I read in the *Melody Maker* that Bob Kelly had had an accident, and broken his hand.

Well, it happened because the bandwagon was driving

Ken opens Dobell's Record Shop in Brighton, 1957, by smashing a 78 on the counter as Doug Dobell and Bill Colyer look on

through town, and Bob was waving out the window, and a taxi managed to catch his arm. Any rate, I thought, "I wonder if Ken would like a piano in the band?" And I said this to my wife and she said, "Well, ring him up, and ask him."

So, I took the bull by the horns, and rang up Ken. So I said, "Have you thought about having a piano in the band?" "Hadn't really thought about it, man. Come around and see me." So I hobbled down the next night to 99 The Drive, Hounslow. I mean, I'd never played with the band, except that Ken used to come back with the band and sometimes sit-in with what I was playing.

So I went in and sat down, and he put a George Lewis record on, and a bit of Bunk Johnson after that, and then he put another George Lewis on. And I thought, *How long is this going to go on before we start talking shop*, you know. Anyway, after about half an hour he said, "Do you reckon you can do that?" And I said I'd have a good try, you know.

And he said, "You start on Friday then." I went home and hastily learnt the Purnell introductions, which were somewhat alien to my style, and never used one of them.

[The following is from Ray's sleeve notes to a 504 CD]

Ken was a cunning old fox. He let me play it my way, work out my own salvation. He was canny enough to know that if I was given my head I would find out for myself, by trial and error, how I could best fit in with the band. I'll always love him for that.

Ken was a man of great integrity. He was scrupulously fair in all his dealings, both financial and personal, and was fiercely loyal to his musicians in the face of criticism.

His one great failure was lack of ability to communicate lucidly with his sidemen. He knew exactly what he wanted from us and expected us to know too. If we didn't come up to scratch on a particular occasion, there was rarely a shout-up at the end, or indeed, any sort of inquest.

Usually it was the grim silence, so we went off and got drunk, wondering what was wrong now. And the next night when we felt the whole thing was a shambles, he'd end up by beaming approval all round. So, within this unsound and unpredictable framework, the band existed and worked—by and large quite successfully, as the records show.

This was September '57. Then I stuck with the Colyer band until August 1960.

JOHN GRIFFITH Ray Foxley. Of course. Dear old Ray, who probably, I think, at times, is my favourite piano player perhaps for this style, but he always gives the sort of signal sometimes, that he didn't really understand what the hell was going on. Despite that, he produced this amazing barrel-housey, raggy effect within, you know, that thing. So I mean. Ray's always been an enigma with all this.

And as Ray tells us, you know, when he joined Ken, he thought he was going to be expected to do this Alton Purnell stuff. He started doing the thing that he knows, which was from the Morton tradition, taking in ragtime, with flavourings by early Erroll Garner even, at times. And various other influences. Rolled it all together into this wonderful barrelhouse effect, which Ken adored, and it worked so well. But it was almost accidental. Not calculated.

COLIN BOWDEN Bob McCracken and Squire Gersh came and sat-in with Ken at Hampton Court. And I can always remember Squire Gersh was saying to me, "Wait, boy, wait," because I was pushing the beat.

We did Leeds Town Hall. I went in early, set up and all that. And I sat, playing a rim-shot and chucking my stick up in the air. Well, I got it up to about fifteen feet above me, and that night—it was when Graham Stewart was in the band, and the audience were around the side of the stage, and it was a tune with breaks in. And I was throwing my sticks in the air, and of course there was all this applause coming from the side. And Ken thought Graham Stewart was doing something, and kept looking at him... and he never *did* know what it was.

Coming back from a Bath all-nighter in the bandwagon, we had to go to Germany in a couple of days. And we're going along the A4 in the early hours of the morning, the sun just coming up. And Ken leans over and says, "Yeah. And on this next trip there'll be a modicum of sobriety."

RAY FOXLEY It was reasonably well paid, actually. Well, I think so, for the time. When I joined, we were getting twenty pounds a week regular—however much we played or didn't play—and usually something extra for something like television things or concerts, you know. So it wasn't bad money at all for the time. Well, this was the beginning really of the Trad Boom, wasn't it? Or maybe just preceding it. But all the concerts were always filled. We played a lot in Germany. I mean, the Germans always went mad over the Colyer band. He was already a legend in Germany. So we were never short of an audience.

We used to play—initially when I joined—three or four times a week, actually. A good residency. It was only towards the end of the time that we had to go out on the road more,

because the basic enthusiasm at home had waned a little and we found that we had to spread around the country to get more work.

A certain amount of social life, but it wasn't one long glorious spree by any means.

We made lots of records. I think they stand up quite well. To a certain degree. I mean, I had problems with the rhythm section from the time I joined, actually.

If it went well, and everyone was happy, Ken didn't try to sort anything out. And I mean, you just had to suffer in silence. I really regret that I couldn't enjoy those years, because although it wasn't ostensibly my music, I enjoyed playing—like I do with anything—for its own sake. And when it was going well, which was occasionally, it was fine.

JOHN WURR The band I saw in 1956 was, most would agree, the best he ever had. It had a great balance between the individual brilliance of its star performers and the overriding sound and sense of direction that were unmistakeably Colyer's.

The drive and dynamism of Colin's drumming was a key factor too. To my mind the energy level of many of Ken's later bands was far too low; this criticism could never be levelled at a band containing Colin Bowden.

BERTA WOOD LETTER TO KEN COLYER 23 AUGUST 1956

2904 ¾ So. Hillcrest Dr., Los Angeles 16, Calif., USA
Dear Ken,

I wanted to answer you much sooner but my job gets tough this time of year and takes about everything I've got. I've been working my off days for weeks. If I hadn't had columns written a couple of months ahead I would have missed the column. Also when I wrote you I wanted time to do it right.

I know that you would like news of the Lewis band. They are here now and will be here for some time, perhaps until New Year's Eve when they are booked into the Hangover in San Francisco. Then again, perhaps not, as they are loosely committed with options, and if George gets homesick for New Orleans, he may go back for a while.

We were at the club last night and I have never seen him look

JAZZSHOWS present THE
FLOATING FESTIVAL OF JAZZ
SUNDAY, 16th JUNE, 1957
"ROYAL DAFFODIL"

Band Playing Rota to Margate

IN LOUNGE ON "B" DECK

10.00 a.m. — 11.00 a.m.	KEN COLYER'S JAZZMEN	
11.00 a.m. — 12.00 noon	SANDY BROWN'S JAZZ BAND	
12.10 p.m. — 1.20 p.m.	HUMPHREY LYTTELTON & HIS BAND	
1.30 p.m. — 2.00 p.m.	LES JOWETT SEVEN	

ON REAR OF "B" DECK (if wet in Foyer on "C" Deck)

10.00 a.m. — 10.40 a.m.	MERSEYSIPPI JAZZ BAND	
10.50 a.m. — 11.30 a.m.	RIVER CITY JAZZ BAND	
11.40 a.m. — 12.20 p.m.	LES JOWETT SEVEN	
12.30 p.m. — 1.10 p.m.	KEN COLYER'S JAZZMEN	

FOYER SESSIONS ON "C" DECK

11.00 a.m. — 11.30 a.m.	JOHNNY DUNCAN & his Blue Grass Boys	
12.00 noon — 12.30 p.m.	KEN COLYER'S SKIFFLE GROUP	
1.00 p.m. — 1.30 p.m.	JOHNNY DUNCAN & his Blue Grass Boys	

Band Playing Rota from Margate

IN LOUNGE ON "B" DECK

5.00 p.m. — 6.00 p.m.	AVON CITIES JAZZ BAND	
6.15 p.m. — 7.00 p.m.	TERRY LIGHTFOOT'S JAZZMEN	
7.15 p.m. — 8.30 p.m.	CHRIS BARBER'S JAZZ BAND	
8.30 p.m. — 9.30 p.m.	CY LAURIE JAZZ BAND	

ON REAR OF "B" DECK (if wet in Foyer on "C" Deck)

5.00 p.m. — 5.00 p.m.	MIKE PETERS STOMPERS	
7.00 p.m. — 6.50 p.m.	CY LAURIE JAZZ BAND	
8.00 p.m. — 7.50 p.m.	ALEX WELSH AND HIS BAND	
9.00 p.m. — 8.50 p.m.	TERRY LIGHTFOOT'S JAZZMEN	
	9.30 p.m.	AVON CITIES JAZZ BAND

FOYER SESSIONS ON "C" DECK

5.30 p.m. — 6.00 p.m.	DICK BISHOP & HIS SKIFFLE GROUP	
6.45 p.m. — 7.15 p.m.	AVON CITIES SKIFFLE GROUP	
7.45 p.m. — 8.15 p.m.	DICK BISHOP & HIS SKIFFLE GROUP	

This rota has been prepared in the expectation of fine weather. In the event of rain, we have an alternative schedule (see above) and we hope that you will bear with us during any delay which may occur while this is being put into operation.

better in all the years he has been coming here. Ever since we have known him he has had that disturbing deep bronchial cough and he did not feel well—slept too lightly and did not eat well. Now he has gained weight, eats well, sleeps well and feels good. He is up to 110 pounds and is going for 114 which is his heaviest weight. Isn't that wonderful news? George Lewis may be with us for a lot more years.

As you may know by this time, the band started on this trip without George, Marrero, Big Jim and Kid Howard. We had a letter from Laurence and he is much improved in health and the doctor says that he can play again. Some more good news. However the doctor said that Laurence could not make this trip when they left some months ago. At first the doctors thought that Laurence had high blood pressure and oooh how he loves to overeat. But now the doctors think it's something else and we hope that he will be well as ever again.

It is unfortunate that the clubs have found out that they can save the expense of the banjo or guitar man in the band. Six men instead of seven appeals to club owners these lean days so Laurence has not been replaced. The same thing happened when Bud Scott died. He has never been replaced in the Ory band when they play clubs. I miss that rhythm man always. Also it makes it tough on Johnny St. Cyr who is living here now but not getting any work playing. Isn't that hard to understand?

Kid Howard had a job playing in New Orleans and he perhaps outsmarted himself on this trip, most likely figuring that it would be a short run with substitute musicians. The doctors told George that he had to take a six week rest and that is why he was not with them until the last part of the San Francisco booking. Tony Parenti filled in for George in Ohio and a fellow by the name of Clem Raymond filled in for George in San Francisco. Poor Clem. Although one could tell that he had once played in the great tradition he was as rusty as I have ever heard.

Jim and Howard are drinking buddies and most likely Howard was the influence that kept him from making the trip. How I miss Jim for Bob Thomas can never hope to fill Jim's place. Howard's drinking makes his lip go flubbery, sometimes before the first set. Jim's drinking never affects his lip nor does it affect him adversely in any other way. Rarely does Jim get so full that he cannot play well. On the other hand Howard seldom plays well in the clubs but he does manage to play better on recordings. When Jim fell off the bandstand it was the last set of the last night of their engagement here. Jim misjudged his liquor by about 6(?) minutes. Chuckle. It is odd and I have seen before how one man can drink and another cannot. Each trip George says that he will never bring Howard again. Oops!!

Thomas Jefferson is playing trumpet this trip. Perhaps you know him. He has an iron lip and sings exceptionally well—very much like Louis only smoother and more flowing. Oddly enough. His mute work is good and often his open horn is good but he is not consistent. He has been called erratic and that is about it. When the band played *Mac The Knife* he put a *West End Blues* intro on it that was startlingly good and played the entire tune in a fine style and also sang a fine solo.

He can play in a very wide variety of styles and does but I wish he would pick out a style of his own and stay with it. Perhaps that is his main trouble. He plays all of them without the necessary conviction. He perhaps considers himself an all round-professional musician who will play any way the job demands. Perhaps he doesn't understand the difference between that attitude and playing traditional New Orleans jazz. I can't imagine how he played with Freddie Kohlman.

Joe Watkins, Alton and Drag complete the six man band. Bob Thomas doesn't make it any kind of way that I can see. Last night Drag was complaining about how much he misses Laurence and how much heavier his load is without Laurence. I hope that it works out that Laurence can rejoin the band. For Drag's sake too.

I hope that you will get to hear Ory and Minor Hall and Wellman Braud. Braud is not nearly as old as one would expect and it is a joy to watch him play. He is a wonder! Phil Gomez has fallen down very much since I wrote him up. He was playing well when he started with Blakeney but he has eyes for more modern jazz now and isn't playing at all well. I wish he hadn't done that. It makes me look as though I don't know what I'm talking about. Oh well.

There are a lot of things I would enjoy discussing with you but I thought you would enjoy most hearing about the Lewis band. I heard that there was printed in the *Melody Maker* a rumor of the death of George

Lewis and that the U.S. press could neither confirm or deny it. Perhaps they asked among themselves, "Who is George Lewis?" I am most happy to report that George has never looked better or felt better in the years he has been coming to the coast.

Did you know that George got his version of *Nobody Knows The Way I Feel This Morning* together in New York? I heard a tape of George being interviewed on the radio and he told about it. "I got it together when I was sick. I thought I was goin' to die." His voice got husky and broke in the middle of it. The first time I heard the tape I sat down on the bed and cried like a baby. George played it at the Jubilee last year and I didn't know the story behind it when I wrote it up. You could have heard a pin drop in that massive auditorium. Without exception, everyone seemed to get that intense, powerful blues message. It was one of the most intensely beautiful things I have ever heard. In my book *Nobody Knows* will always be George Lewis' special number. I thought you would like to know.

I hope not to be so long in answering you next time, Wishing you Good Going, (signed) Berta Wood

MIKE SLATTER LETTER TO KEN COLYER 20 SEPTEMBER 1956

New Orleans, LA.
Dear Ken,

I am very pleased to finds myself, once again, after more than a year, writing to you from New Orleans. Many of your old friends, as you shall hear, send you their warmest greetings. In particular it was a pleasant surprise to run into an old friend of yours who spoke so warmly of your band and of the pleasure he had received listening to the boys at the Fishmongers Arms, Ralston Crawford of New York. We shall get together in New York later on and I shall play him all the latest records that Ken Lindsay has sent me. We met listening to Paul Barbarin's band who have been appearing at the Dream Room on Bourbon Street. They have now finished there and open tonight at Pier 600. The boys all send their best wishes, Paul Barbarin, MacNiel Breaux, Lester Santiago, Willie Humphrey, Clement Tervalon, and Andy Anderson.

The day before yesterday I was listening to Kid Howard's band at the Paddock. During the interval I talked with the boys in the band room and they join with me in sending their good wishes—Kid Howard, Jim Robinson, Manuel Crusto, Joseph Robichaux, Josiah Frazier and James Davis. Next Sunday there is to be a parade starting at Josephine and Liberty at noon in which George Williams, who plays drums with Bill Matthew's band will be marching. Don't know yet who will be out except Jim Robinson said he'll be there.

Last Monday I did a short broadcast on Tony Almerico's radio program and put in a good plug for you. I sent to New York for some records to suit the occasion though I must admit that he did play examples of Barber and Lyttelton's as well. I have left the records with Tony and he proposes to play one or two of the records every day while I am here. So the people of New Orleans have once again been able to hear you... Before I leave for New York next Tuesday I hope to be able to find Hermann Deutsch, though it may not achieve anything.

Well Ken get some new records out soon. Certainly miss those sessions in London and hope that I will be able to get over again before too long.

The next weekend I am going out to Dee Dee's place, Luthjens, though in advance I cannot tell you who will be there. I shall also be going over to Gretna to hear Kid Thomas' band with Louis Nelson on trombone. Most likely I shall go over with Bill Russell. Before leaving I hope that Joe Mares will be able to hear the records that I brought from New York.

No doubt you will be hearing Ory before long, I believe that he has taken Alvin on trumpet, as I understand that he has left California for Europe. Too bad I missed Lizzie Miles who is also in California along with the George Lewis band.

New Orleans remains the same, retaining that magic quality that it always possesses. It is sad though to think that its life is now definitely limited to a few more years at best and already is losing some of its vitality. **Then the old musicians in those remaining marching bands, the Eureka, the Tuxedo and George Williams die off. There is no one left to carry on the tradition. It will be up to the bands in Europe, particularly to people like yourself to keep things alive.** Best regards to Bill, hope you saw my earlier letter to him and that the band is still blowing at Studio 51 and around the country.

If you can find the time, drop me a line in New York,

Best Wishes Ken,

Yours ever, (signed) Mike

P.S. I am already to make some recordings, but now the damned union are after me and it looks like being impossible. Still keep trying.

BERTA WOOD LETTER TO KEN COLYER 3 OCTOBER 1956

2904 ¾ Hillcrest Dr., Los Angeles 16, Calif.
Dear Ken,
A thousand and two things have come between me and get-

Mac Duncan, Ian Wheeler, John Bastable and Ken take a break. Bob Barclay looks on

ting your letter answered. This morning I huffed and I puffed and I blew them all down. Jazz people are the busiest people, surely.

Dorothy Tait, who is the West Coast Manager of the George Lewis band, asked for your address, and I gave it to her. She didn't say what she wanted with it but I thought you wouldn't mind being in touch with someone very close to George Lewis. She is very close to him and since George NEVER writes letters you could be in touch with him through her. George telephones or sends telegrams.

I showed Alton Purnell the very nice write-up about the Lewis band that you sent to me and perhaps she wants one for George. I pasted the article on cardboard so we wouldn't wear it out. The writer, Howard Lucroft, is associated with Jazz City and *Jazz International* that is most boppish and most cool and modern, so I was very surprised that he had written the article and also gotten last-minute pictures to go with it. I want to thank you very much for it. Alton asked me to send you his best regards. I saw him for a few minutes at the Jubilee and afterwards at the club but it was so crowded I couldn't get through the mob to talk to the band. Floyd Levin has one of the few letters George has written, I told him to "frame" it because it surely was a rare item.

I had a letter from Laurence and he says he is feeling fine and ready to re-join the band any time. George and Drag, somehow, got two weeks off to go to New Orleans and Buddy Burns, a New Orleans bass man, is subbing for Drag and Bob Shea is filling in for George. I am very glad they took the time off. Since Laurence is not with them, Drag must carry a much heavier load. Joe Watkins is not the steady rock he should be and Drag must hold him up and keep him straight and without Laurence that makes his work twice as hard. The band opened the Jubilee this year and *Maryland*, the opener, started off cold for the Lewis band. Drag was magnificent in sparking the band.. I have watched him do that before and sometimes it seems as if he is carrying the whole band on his back. The band caught fire in the second number, *Old Spinning Wheel In The Parlour*, and the wheel was spinning in the finest Lewis style.

One of the things I wanted to write you about is this controversial matter of pitch in the New Orleans Music. Perhaps you can help me with it. It is a very touchy subject and I haven't felt like laying it on the table for discussion with the Lewis band. There are always too many people about and too much activity for serious discussion anyway. The time hasn't fallen right to bring it up, although I hope I can get something definite and quotable on it before the Lewis band gets away. Alton is no help and I think he would resist any such ideas as he resists other good, creative things about New Orleans Music. He doesn't understand George Lewis at all.

I'll set it up the way I got into it. A few years ago, some of us took a course on jazz at the local University under the professorship of Nesuhi Ertegun. One of the interesting things I learned was that the regional African Scale has FIVE tones instead of seven and what happened when the transition from the five-scale to the seven-tone scale was evolved. This was an attempt to explain BLUE notes. Records of African ring-shouts and accurate documentary African recordings were played. The pitch is far different from a "classical" pitch, of course. It is this pitch that interested me and gives me a basis for a defence of the most maligned New Orleans Jazz Men who have ever been accused too often of playing out of tune.

Some time later I heard a recording of George Lewis and other New Orleans musicians playing a funeral in New Orleans. It seemed to me that the pitch was extremely African and FAR MORE SO than in the way Lewis plays most often. I wondered if it could be possible that some traces of the five-tone African scale had remained in the tradition of funeral music. Not having the record and not being a musician I could not tell. I only knew that the music had a stranger, unfamiliar sound but I knew certainly that they were not "playing out of tune" although by classical standards they are playing out of "classical" tune. I want to make the definite statement AND PROVE IT that for jazz music it is equally correct to play with African OR classical pitch.

Jazz need not adhere to classical pitch any more than jazz should adhere to other classical rules in order to be good jazz. Mainly I want to establish the fact that George Lewis and other New Orleans Jazzmen do not play "out of tune" and why.

I think that you played a funeral with them, didn't you. I can't trace where I read it or got the idea and perhaps you can help me with my "pitch" problems... Also let me know whether or not you want to be quoted. Let me know definitely what I may quote and what I may not quote for I would not want to do anything of which you might not approve.

Tell your Belgian friend that he may have anything he likes from the three years of *Jazz Journal* columns. However, it must be printed in his book somewhere that it has previously been published in *Jazz Journal*. If he wants any kind of special material, tell him to let me know what he wants and I will be glad to write something for him.

I always have an idea about the foreword by GEORGE Lewis. I can take excerpts from his recorded interviews, and do very nicely. Also I will see him as soon as he gets back from New Orleans.

I am very happy that you are doing so well in London. Very happy indeed. I hope that it remains that way for a very long time to come, and I believe that it will. You and your band are most heartening to a lot of people and I am one of them. We won't let the world forget about New Orleans Music, eh? (Smile).

You mean the Right things to a lot of young jazz musicians. The young Jazz Men think very highly of you and are very proud of you. Bill Brennan wrote me that there are 13 New Orleans style bands in the North of England AND HE MEANS NEW ORLEANS STYLE with 3 Dixie, 4 Lu Watters and 1 Mainstream. I wish we had a band that compared to yours locally. We have a lot of youngsters trying for it and perhaps in the future we will make it. We have an exciting young trombonist and a good drummer.

I must get towards the end of this letter if I expect to get all of it into an envelope.

Wishing you wonderfully good going in all kind of ways
Happy Breaks, (Signed) Berta Wood

MIKE SLATTER LETTER TO KEN COLYER 7 OCTOBER 1956

West 70th Street, New York
Dear Ken,

I was delighted to receive your letter and to hear all your good news of the band. I certainly hope that the recording session was a success, as I am always anxiously waiting for new records, missing those evenings at the 51 more than I can say. I left New Orleans on Thursday Sept. 27th, and, shortly before making a dash to the airport, was able to hear the opening set of the Kid Howard Band. The last sound I heard as I ran back down Bourbon Street was the closing bars of *Walking With The King*. Well here I am back in New York feeling that I have let you down badly as I was unable to get hold of Hermann Deutsch.

However, I sincerely hope that, if I can afford it, I will be able to make a short trip down to New Orleans again at Christmas time. Meantime I am going to talk to Ralston Crawford to see if he can't work out something. He and his wife are coming over this evening to hear the Eureka tape and some of your records. I shall ask him to add a few lines to this letter. I hope to get the tape off to you this week if I can. Unfortunately it is only a short one, but I think with luck I may be able to get my hands on the other four that are in existence. These tapes were originally made by Doc Souchon and Sam Charters, a good friend of mine. Unfortunately, Sam had left the other tapes at his mother's home in California. When he gets hold of them I shall ask him to dub them for me and send them to New York.

I told Sam that I was going to send you the one he gave me and I think that if you have to write him a short note after receiving the first one from me he would greatly appreciate hearing from you. His address is: Sam Charters, no. 203, 638 Royal Street, New Orleans. The whole thing is complicated by the fact that Sam is just getting a divorce, but I will send him sufficient money for the tape and keep my fingers crossed that he gets it dubbed!

Perhaps I should tell you that this tape that I am sending was made at one of the Eureka band rehearsals. They rehearse every Thursday evening on Dryades Street. They have not got a full band, though the personnel includes the following:

Percy Humphrey, Kid Sheik, Willie Pajeaud (tpts); Sonny Henry (tbn); Ruben Roddy (sax); Red Clarke (sousaphone). As the tape is such a short one, I have added a record from Dick Allen's collection that I think you could use. The reproduction is not too good I'm afraid as the record was a quite old one. The words are rather hard to hear, but it rather tickles me: "Take your fingers off it, don't touch that, it don't belong to you."

Wonderful to hear that the Omega band are going to appear at your concert. Unhappily, I was only lucky enough to hear one street parade, at Coronation time in 1953. Is there any chance Ken that you could get someone to sit backstage and take a tape for me of the whole concert? I should be more than willing to meet the expense. Of course, the tape would be kept purely for my personal use. I know it's asking a lot Ken, but still I think it

could be done. It would give the Crawfords a great thrill too. We all feel like exiles as there is no music in New York worth hearing at all. Most of my records are all but worn right through. Perhaps you could ask your brother Bill to sit backstage and record the music for us. I feel sure that he'd do it, if he can't perhaps John Reddihough might help. If it means hiring a machine and a good microphone, that can't be helped. I'd be more than happy to pay the expense. Please do what you can.

If that is impossible, you might be able to do the same thing at one of your 51 sessions. It would mean a great deal to me personally and to the small group of my friends in New York who await your record releases as anxiously as I do. If all goes well, I should be able to make it back to England next year for three weeks or so, but I'm keeping my fingers crossed. Well I'll sign off now and turn it over to Ralston.

Yours, With Best Wishes, (signed) Mike.

Dear Ken,

Peggy and I have had a fine evening with Michael Slatter hearing your records. We are sorry we can't hear your concert at the Adelphi. We hope you'll send Mr. Slatter some tapes. Good luck to you, sincerely,

(signed) Ralston Crawford.

DOROTHY TAIT LETTER TO KEN COLYER 10 NOVEMBER 1956

THE GEORGE LEWIS JAZZ BAND, 1630 First Street,
De Armas Street, Rt 1 Box 10D, N.O. 14, Louisiana
Dear Ken Colyer,

Believe me, I feel as though I were writing to an old friend.

I have listened to your music on records, met many people from your country who know you, and heard George talk about you for years.

As you probably know, George has to be hypnotised, then anaesthetized before he will sit down and even write a postcard. A short time back, when your name had cropped up in the conversation, George said to me, "I sure wish you'd send Ken that picture I had taken in Bakersfield, and write to him for me. Ken's my friend."

When George Lewis says, in that gentle, quiet way of his "Ken's my friend," I know Ken must be quite a person. George doesn't bestow that accolade lightly.

First, let me introduce myself... for the past several years end-all and be-all of my existence (aside from a full-time job as a continuity director of a TV station!) has been George Lewis and the George Lewis Band. What my title might or could be I do not know... they're my uncles and my grandfathers and my great and good friends; and I seem to have become their sister, mother, aunt, and have tried, in my place, to be their good friend to the best of my ability.

As the band came to the West Coast of California more and

more frequently, and as a number of things occurred which would take too long to relate, I found myself first acting as their go-between on engagements... and now their manager, representative... and official "snarler." Inasmuch as George doesn't know how to snarl, this latter role is very important amongst the ravening wolves and phonies of Hollywood and other spots. INCLUDING, most definitely, New Orleans. I travelled seven thousand miles with them on tour a little more than a year ago, when we went through the mid-west, on to New York and Boston, and return. More recently they have been playing San Francisco and Los Angeles, and just returned to New Orleans after a seven-months stint out here. They return, I hope, in a few weeks.

It disturbed me greatly when I learned a while ago that the rumor had hit the jazz circles in England that George was very ill, that the band had broken up, etc.etc... He WAS ill. The little man was stricken with virus pneumonia in New York, never gave himself time to recover but instead went to work, when he returned to New Orleans, for two months in one of those damnable Bourbon Street sweat shops. He slid backwards in health, and finally wound up in what the doctor described as a state of "complete exhaustion." Heart, blood pressure, blood-count... everything at so low a point that he was forbidden to work for many, many weeks. I sent him a plane ticket, and he flew out here to California. My town of Bakersfield is in the desert, with dry (usually, except when it hits 112) invigorating air, and he remained here more or less incognito for a month doing nothing but eat and sleep. He returned to work very gradually, coming back here weekends... and now, thank God, is in fine shape... back to 110 from 98 pounds. But he has been told that he must never again work past a certain point. If he remains on the regime that the doctor has placed him on, the doctor says he should continue for many years.

When the band came to the coast, Kid Howard and Jim Robinson elected to remain in New Orleans. Therefore we have Thomas Jefferson on trumpet (and he is great) and Bob Thomas on trombone. When you hear Thomas on the new Cavalier records, I KNOW you will agree that it is one of the greatest trombones ever recorded on a New Orleans jazz record. So much for the "breaking up" rumors! The picture I enclose was taken during his stay in Bakersfield.

When the band was playing in Los Angeles, I went down each weekend to be with them. Their last weekend there Berta Wood told me you had written her and mentioned a book on jazz being written by a Belgian author, who was interested in having George do the foreword. Ken, I'm sure you know that (when I have to 'phone him long-distance because I can't get even a postcard out of him on an important business matter) George would (and did) almost faint dead away at the prospect of performing what to him would be an impossible feat! Nor would he take kindly to a 100% "ghosting" job. **For above all else, George hates to sail under false pretences, and to him this would be a "phoney" thing.** He wasn't too happy that the article appeared in the English magazine with the impression that he had written it, though terribly pleased at the interest. "Shucks," says George, "everyone knows AH didn't write that."

Would this work out? I have earned a fair, and sometimes good, living for 20 years by writing. Presently I hope to be at least to the middle of a biography of George. I perhaps am closer to him and know him better than anyone in the world. A foreword of general background... with liberal quotations... (from George, that is), might be an acceptable substitute. When I said "general background" I meant general background of jazz as it was in the beginning... is now... and we hope, always will be!

Can you tell me more about this project?

Before I close, I do want to tell you how much YOUR music is appreciated in your country. This I hear so many, many times from visitors.

It is appreciated in our country too, through records... but your compatriots have told me so much of you.

I would deeply appreciate hearing from you... I repeat, when George says, "Ken's my friend" it is a little like being knighted. He says it of very few people.

Perhaps someday, somehow, all our paths will cross. I hope so.

Won't you let me hear from you?

Most sincerely, Dorothy F. Tait.

P.S. This will interest you.

George has just bought a new clarinet—which was made especially for Jimmie Noone shortly before Jimmie died.

(signed) Dorothy F. Tait

BERTA WOOD LETTER TO KEN COLYER 25 NOVEMBER 1956

2904 ¾ Hillcrest Dr., Los Angeles 16, Calif.

Dear Ken,

The Lewis band has gone back to New Orleans and left a big hole in our town. With Ory away too we haven't got much good jazz. We keep hearing rumors about racial tension in New Orleans. Then too, the Coloured union has raised it's union scale and the club owners are fighting that. I wish that the Lewis band would move to Los Angeles and work out of here, or at least somewhere out of the South until this thing simmers down.

The Lewis band will be back through here during the holidays and will stop over for a few days. Then they go on to San Francisco and open at the Tin Angel the first week in January.

I was very much interested in your brass band description and I do hope that you can manage to have it recorded. I would be delighted. I hear from my young friends the Eric Batty Jazz Aces

more the merrier, eh?

Your new L.P. sounds wonderful. I hope that it goes over in a big way. I wish that they would have it distributed over here for I know many people here would like it.

How did your concert opposite Lionel come out? I heard that Lionel went over big in London but flopped in the provinces. I hope that you drew a good crowd.

I've got a dozen things crowding me, so I had better cut out now.

Wishing you Wonderful Going, (signed) Berta

MIKE SLATTER LETTER TO KEN COLYER 7 DECEMBER 1956

198 East 70th Street, New York
Dear Ken,

Many thanks for your last letter. This is just a brief note to tell you that I am flying down to New Orleans on Saturday Dec 22nd for about ten days. I will say hello to all your old friends of course and will gather at the places of interest that I can. If it is humanly possible try to get a copy of your latest record to me so that I can broadcast it while I am there. I know that it is not due for release until January but do your best to. Hope that my brother will be at the concert at the Adelphi on December 16th and you may see him. Best of luck and do try and get TAPES or recording of some sort made. As I've said before, that music is too great to dissolve like the air! So far I have found none of the good music that you mentioned can be heard in New York. Perhaps you can give me a few leads. I'll talk it over with Ralston, though he has been very busy driving the past few weeks organizing an exhibition of his paintings—I am going to look at them this evening.

Hope my tape did not sound too bad—afraid that it was very poorly dubbed in the beginning. When I am in New Orleans I will try and get Sammy Charters to let me have his tapes—but it's by no means certain that I shall obtain them.

Well Ken that's about it for now—just hoping that you manage to preserve that next week of yours so that those like Ralston and myself that are unable to attend don't be denied the pleasure of hearing the Omega and your present band.

Best Wishes to you, Bill and the boys,
Yours, (signed) Mike

that New Orleans style jazz is very popular and being well supported in the north of England. I'm glad to hear it. They sent me a dub of their first record and it sounded very good for youthful jazzmen.

I asked George when he was here how the New Orleans drummers got that wonderful live sound in their drumming and he told me that they never used a muffler on the drums and that they tuned the bass drum to the open E on the bass or the low E on the piano. Perhaps if I put it in the column it may do some good. I am very tired of flat sounding bass drums and cymbal riding. I would love to have really good drumming become established again.

Did I tell you that I was asked to do a chapter for a book to be published in England? My subject was George Lewis and Kid Ory. How about that! The title of the book will be something on the order of New Orleans Music Today. Sinclair Traill is getting it together for Davies.

I have also been asked to write for a new Jazz magazine in Belgium. It has been started by Yannick Bruynoghe—the collaborator on Big Bill's Blues—and a few of his friends. The

Tuesday night

Dear Ken,

Thanks so much for your letter! The news in this one will come as a surprise and a joyful one, providing it is borne out by future events... And I am praying that it will be... Let me start at the beginning...

On Saturday morning bright and early I received an air mail special letter from LA with a cablegram in it which I quote below:

"Ask George Lewis if prepared solo British tour March 10th to 24th... playing jazz clubs concerts with British rhythm section or British New Orleans styled band suggest terms we will suggest British soloist for later US visit to satisfy Union early reply appreciated."

Paddy McKiernan Agency
30 Heaton Moor Road,
Stockport, Cheshire, England.

Now, Ken, I am relying on you and your friendship for George to keep this letter in strict confidence. You can see that it might offend this agency/whatever it is/to know I had immediately written for advice and to sort of check on them.

My reply was this (after checking by long distance phone with George)... that Lewis would probably be available and an air mail letter would follow.

In my letter, sent Sunday air mail, I said... and I quote, "Were you considering the Ken Colyer band, if a full band is used? Ken Colyer and George are old friends, have played together in New Orleans and the Ken Colyer band is the closest to the Lewis band of any traditional group playing on either side of the Atlantic..."

I pointed out that concert dates for a clarinettist with NO front line were extremely difficult. It was just too much blowing for one man. In clubs it's different, for there are 20 minute sets and then intermissions. Two or two and a half hours concert playing is something else again!

It was a hellish job trying to arrive at a figure. If George makes the trip it means sacrificing four weeks of the most lucrative job that we have here... and it may look awfully high to them.

Do you know this agency? Is it OK? **If so, having been tipped off about this, could you not see if the Ken Colyer group would be the one?** By now there must be rumors afoot in jazz circles about this, and you could always have picked up a rumor somewhere. Only please, please... not from me... inasmuch as it would look as though we were trying to run things from six thousand miles away. Certainly, I did my best to indicate that your group was the one George would prefer... And perhaps you could carry the ball from there.

And I will be eternally grateful if you'll answer this as quickly as possible with anything you know about the McKiernan Agency, etc. etc. And do hop onto it and see if George can't have

the same pleasure you had, in reverse... that of sitting in with the Ken Colyer band!

Thanks again for your letter... if this arrives in time... A Merry Christmas... if not, then a Happy New Year with the heartfelt wish that it may bring us all together!

Sincerely, Dorothy

Dear Ken,

Your letter, George Lewis, and a cable from Paddy McKiernan all arrived on the same day—an eventful one as well as a happy one.

Thanks ever so much for the information, timely tips and pointers which your letter contained. McKiernan's cable read "Cannot see any obstacles to tour... detailed letter follows."

It would be worse than ironic for George to come to England and not play with your band. Now that the thing is at least semi-official there is no need to "play possum," as we say over here.

Perhaps you have already heard from Paddy. If not, could you not have your agent contact him? Here is the set-up... he asked for two weeks, March 10 through 24. In my reply I pointed out that for two weeks only the expense was great... all of the transportation cost must be borne in that short period. I set what seemed to me a fairly high fee for that two weeks, and then cut it very sharply for an additional two weeks. Perhaps your agent and his agent could get together on that second two weeks, if he has not already contacted you for the first two weeks.

George doesn't want to fly. Neither do I. Sixteen hours with nothing but water below, and no emergency landing fields is not my idea of relaxation... though George flies all over the country here.

You will be hearing from me again soon... Meanwhile, write me if there are any developments.

A Happy New Year to you from George... and from me.

Sincerely, (signed) Dorothy

DOROTHY TAIT I received a telegram from Berta Wood, jazz writer in Los Angeles, relaying a cable she had received from Manchester, England, asking her to find out if George would consider a tour of England in the spring, playing as guest artist with a British band.

That this had never happened before had always puzzled me. True, I was aware—painfully aware—that not only did the big agencies control most every major outlet for jazz in this country, but the British-American exchange programme and European tours as well. Yet I knew from the fan mail and press cuttings George received from England that his appearance in that country would be the next best thing to a happy judgement day for the jazz-conscious Britons. The offer came from a young Manchester promoter, Paddy McKiernan.

The problem, of course, was George's health, and the

certain knowledge that not to take the trip would come close to breaking his heart. I laid down certain rigid restrictions on playing time, begged McKiernan's cooperation in curtailing social activities, in fact, any activities besides the actual playing, and received his complete agreement. Stuttering with excitement, I called George.

George had a characteristic manner of receiving good news. There was at first a barely perceptible phase while the quick mind turned the news over, examining it for flaws, not quite trusting its validity. Then, satisfied that it was what it appeared to be, the wide, warm smile, and the assent: "I'd LIKE that!"

Over the telephone I felt the pause, heard the delighted assent, then a sudden misgiving. "If," said George, "I can play with Ken Colyer."

There was more red-tape-type trouble involved in getting the trip underway than it would be possible to recount in just one book. It was necessary to guarantee, by contract, a similar number of concerts for Ken in this country; and , to make sure that the contract would be lived up to, necessary for Ken to receive a visa. The State Department, for several weeks, took a dim and discouraging view of Ken's previous unofficial sojourn in the United States. Finally the tour had to be postponed for thirty days, but at last all needed approval was secured. [*from Call Him George*]

BERTA WOOD LETTER TO KEN COLYER 7 JANUARY 1957

2904 ¾ Hillcrest Dr., Los Angeles 16, Calif.
Dear Ken,
Should have answered you sooner but I got lost in the holidays for a bit—as did other people. I must make this a short one as I am going back to work and time is running out. I have also been struggling toward a finish to my book. If I don't get it out looking for a publisher it will NEVER see print. Wheww! What a lot of work it is. Months and months.

The chapter in the book to be published by Peter Davies in England in July took quite a good deal of time but I am quite satisfied with it. At last hearing it will be called *Just Jazz* but the title may be changed again. Sinclair Traill and Gerald Lascelles are co-editors and my assignment was to write about Kid Ory and George Lewis in the present time. It is all fresh material and quite tough on racism and also the Negroes' attitude of being ashamed of and disowning jazz music. I don't believe that many people understand about that. If I hadn't moved in with them and lived with them for a few years I wouldn't have known about it myself. One learns so much more by being on the inside looking out than being on the outside looking in.

The Lewis band is opening in San Francisco at the Tin Angel Jan. 7th. That's today. One never knows how it will turn out but I have it on good authority that they will only be there a few weeks. You don't know how I am hoping that they will be booked into a club here in Los Angeles afterward. Thomas Jefferson and Bob Thomas are playing with the band again this trip. I had hoped for Jim's return. Although we were not sure of him, Drag also is playing with the band. Buddy Burns, another New Orleans bass player, relieved Drag for a while last trip. With Laurence out the load is much heavier for Drag and he isn't young.

Enclosed is a bit from the St. Louis Jazz Club bulletin. It is an old one but I thought that if you keep a scrapbook you might like to have it.

(Hand-written) Bob Koester still the Editor. Has a Jazz Club Record Label and a Jazz Record Shop.

WISHING YOU "HAPPY BREAKS" IN THE NEW YEAR,
(signed) Berta Wood

P.S. Will this matter of Lyttelton and Sandy Brown going mainstream throw a lot of their jazz following into YOUR lap?

DOROTHY TAIT CABLE TO KEN COLYER 16 JANUARY 1957

M316 WU SC406 BAKERSFIELD CALIF 21 16 0928A
COLYER 66 LILLIE ROAD SW6 LONDON
CAN GET CABLE TO US EMBASSY NOT LATER THAN MONDAY NIGHT FOR FEBRUARY ENGAGEMENT REGARDS TAIT

DOROTHY TAIT LETTER TO KEN COLYER 23 JANUARY 1957

Dear Ken,
This is going to be a lengthy letter, so best sit down in a comfortable spot and relax! First, before I get into anything else... will you write George immediately (it needn't be long) at the Grant Hotel, 753 Bush Street, San Francisco, 2... and after expressing yourself regarding the tour... tell him of the necessity to bring WARM CLOTHING ! I have tried my level best to convince him that it will be C/O/L/D in Scotland and the North of England until at this point he thinks, I know, that I am a clucking old hen.

Second: Would you make reservations for us in some WARM Hotel in London. Two have been suggested to me as being not too expensive, and centrally heated as well as centrally located... the Athenaeum, and the Green Park. Two singles with baths. You may have an even better suggestion, and I leave it to your judgement.

We arrive March 4 in Liverpool, and I have suggested to Paddy McKiernan we take the boat train to London immediately... George is anxious to get to London to see you, and, of course, to get together with the band for some blowing before the tour starts. If we do that George will have a sort of central headquarters, and will not have the problem of carrying his baggage around the country, etc. Perhaps the hotels make weekly rates... some of them do here. Our return reservation is for the same ship—*Empress of Britain*, and I believe it sails on April 4, but I left my schedule in San Francisco. Perhaps you could check with Canadian Pacific... and make the Hotel reservations for us. If at all possible, George wants to get to Paris for a day or two and see some of his old friends who are there. You wouldn't by any chance have Sidney Bechet's address, would you?

I'll be leaning heavily on you Ken, for help in protecting George from the death by kindness of which you spoke. Am writing Paddy along these same lines...no social engagements during the period of the tour—but NONE. No personal appearances at jazz clubs, etc.etc... no jam sessions...(other than with your group!) **I almost lost my mind on our college tour... EVERYWHERE we went, starry-eyed and ardent fans had arranged for the band to "come over to the fraternity house for a few minutes after the concert. Bring your horns, of course!"** The band was dead beat from tiredness, and I acquired a horrible reputation as a snarling and disagreeable spoil-sport. Occasionally, I was adroit enough to sneak George out back ways and down alleys so he could get to bed....

Then, if we remain an additional week or ten days, after George has had a couple of days rest, we could fit in a social engagement or a non-professional appearance or two. George, of course, is utterly without the ability to protect himself... would agree and say "shoo, he'd be happy to..." then turn to me plaintively later to get him out of it.

I read with great interest, and a certain amount of apprehension... your comments on McKiernan, and also on the possibility of a full-band exchange. Your letter, of course, was written before the whole thing had "jelled," I imagine. For a cable from Paddy (in fact several) indicates that the thing is set and substantially so, and bookings have already been made. I am PRAYING that one of these is in London.

You suggest I contact one of the agencies on this band exchange. But Ken, don't you think it would be a sort of stinking thing for me to do, inasmuch that as to date I have no complaint with McKiernan, and he has apparently worked very hard on this thing, and for me to make a surreptitious query behind his back on future band bookings would, I think, start us off on the wrong foot for sure. **Now. Is there any way that you can ascertain HOW MUCH, either including transportation, or**

net, these American bands are getting over there... Condon, for instance?** In that way, if he approaches us on a band exchange, or if we work through one of the other agencies, I'll have some idea of what to ask. This caught me flat-footed, because I had nothing to gauge it by.

What I would want to see would be concerts in England, followed by location jobs for a week or two at a time on the Continent. No doubt this is idle dreaming... the big agencies won't even discuss it because they can't make enough money on it. I warned you this would be a long letter!

If you'd shoot that letter off to George air mail as soon as you get this, it would be appreciated! Air Mail seems to take longer to get to us out here from England, than from here to there... If you have time to write me—that will be fine, but I will understand if you don't! Mainly I want George to be impressed with the need for warm clothes! And I'll trust in you for the Hotel reservations... Am anxious for two things on those—warmth and a central location, the latter because of the ease in sight-seeing! Above all else, I want to have lunch or dinner at the Cheshire Cheese... will you be our guest on this happy occasion!?This whole thing has a feeling of unreality for me... I simply can't believe it!

My very Best Wishes... and believe me, words just can't describe how much George and I are looking forward to this experience...!

Sincerely (signed) Dorothy

1630 First Street., Bakersfield, Calif.
You asked about Lawrence. It's a tragic and unhappy situation. No, there is absolutely no possibility of Lawrence ever rejoining the band. Twice he has been flown home in dangerous condition after what appeared to be strokes suffered on the road. The last time he collapsed on the stand, and I was, fortunately, there... I got him to a hospital and when he arrived he was paralysed completely on one side. They did extensive diagnostic work, and when the paralysis wore off diagnosed what is called "cerebral anaxia"—periodic interruption of oxygen to the brain, plus a very, very high blood pressure.

What makes it difficult is that between these attacks he feels well, although each attack leaves its mark on him mentally, for a certain amount of brain tissue is destroyed. The doctor has told him he can work at home, but poor Lawrence (for whom I have a deep affection) cannot understand why, if he can work at home, he cannot go on the road. The doctor has told George and me that these attacks will recur again and again and he must not take him away from home. Just two weeks ago, in New Orleans, Lawrence suffered another attack of some sort, and his blood pressure was found to be way in the 200's.

We tried George Guesnon in his place for a while, but it didn't work out. We have great difficulty (I am bruised and battered from the attempts) in getting sufficient money from the club operators to pay for a seven man band... and unless it is Lawrence... it has seemed better to go with six.

(signed) Dorothy

Dear Ken,

I have done so much corresponding these last weeks that I am "plumb out" of stationery, and don't even have any thin flimsy left for writing air-mail!

I'm sorry your letter was delayed. The postman delivered it to the wrong house and they apparently held it for a few days before giving it back to him... **Last night when I finally got to bed I was so discouraged by the whole situation and the general awkwardness of BOTH the American and British unions I was on the verge of giving up!** If you think your union can be difficult you should try the American Federation!

First... I wrote to the Federation the first week in January outlining the entire thing, and asking for an immediate reply. THREE WEEKS later I get the reply... not even sent air mail but just ordinary postage (five days across the continent).

The local in San Francisco had told me that of course we could have an exchange musician in the band whilst at the Tin Angel... they'd be happy etc. to extend a welcoming hand across the seas. This I told the Federation. Three weeks later I get a letter bawling me out for even thinking about such a thing. It MUST be concerts or not at all. Meanwhile I have, of course, to go ahead with plans. I was literally sick/a/bed about the whole thing.

Very obviously the concert-night club situation is vastly different over here. Here concerts are used, as a rule, as "fill-ins," a chance to keep the men eating between steady club engagements; they are hard to come by, not very profitable (in fact, frequently turn up losses) and with traditional jazz they are doubly difficult for it is at present "enjoying" a very severe slump in the face of the heavy commercial plugging for the modern and progressive groups, and for the big band stuff... Welk, Goodman, Kenton et al. Even Louis Armstrong flopped in Boston at a concert not too long ago.

The big bands have a big financial backlog to rely on to absorb concert losses and are usually handled by very wealthy (and greedy) agencies who promote the concerts usually to boost record sales in certain localities.

Four or five concerts during a given period is very good going here. Those generally in the same locality, because travel distances can vary from 150 to 10,000 miles... and when groups do barnstorm it is sometimes done by dint of NO sleep between dates, sleeping in the automobile, or just a couple of hours sleep. George can't do this, nor can the others.

Hence, when I got this ultimatum from the Federation you can understand my consternation and, to use a word of George's "worriment." Sixteen concerts in the United States for a traditional New Orleans jazz group would be a physical impossibility... a Cal Tjader or a Dave Brubeck MIGHT be able to work it, but not a traditional group.

Now, the dates I gave McKiernan on your trip were May 10 to June 1 before I finally got word from the Federation. Obviously these dates can't be worked for it takes far longer than that to work up even two concerts. However, I have suggested to McKiernan that he let those dates remain, and that I will personally, if necessary, contact the British Union and ask that they approve a series of dates a little later in the year (but still, of course, in 1957). Surely they will not be so unreasonable as to refuse. (I don't know why I say that so optimistically; neither your union nor ours has shown themselves to be a shining beacon of reasonableness!)

McKiernan stated they would pay your transportation. He asked me for a figure and said he must have a reply immediately (which was no doubt true). I picked one out of thin air... a 1000 dollars exclusive of transportation and including expenses. This was for union sight, he said in his cable.

Here is the problem, and I KNOW you understand it. A thousand dollars is all George makes in Los Angeles (less-$925) for a full week for himself and his men, with union tax of $70 a week and transportation to pay. In San Francisco it is a little better, although not a great deal, for we try to make the additional San Francisco money make up for the low Los Angeles money.

On concerts it's a toss-up. Ken, if we're able to scrape together a thousand dollars it will be a miracle. We had a chance of doing it if we could have put you with us in San Francisco because we could put a little aside each week until we had it. Now, with the necessity of somehow managing some concerts (there couldn't be sixteen) I can't see it.

Ken, I can't understand this hassle between these two unions. When you come over here it will be of assistance to us in booking concerts... they are hellishly hard to book, but with an added feature, it may make it easier.

> George's presence over there means probably more work for your men. Yet those unions are making a tremendous, big fat project out of one little man going to England—to me it is ridiculous and unworthy of a union.

Don't you agree, or have I pulled a Dulles and put my foot in my mouth again?

Please let me hear from you as soon as you can. At this point I'm wondering whether we really will get there or not, but it is no doubt discouragement at these frustrating evidences of red tape and unnecessary obstacles, and it will probably wear off!

With very best wishes... (signed) Dorothy

P.S. George is concerned that he will not be able to get together with your band to run through some numbers before the first concert. This can be arranged?

DOROTHY TAIT TELEGRAM TO KEN COLYER UNDATED 1957

BAKERSFIELD CALIF 25 23 85 1P VIA WESTERN UNION LT—KEN COLYER 66 LILLIE ROAD LONDON SW6=

PLEASE SEND AIR IMMEDIATELY EXACT DATE AND PLACE OF BIRTH FOR PERMIT FORMS FOR MAY ENGAGEMENT REGARDS = DOROTHY +

SC 606 BAKERSFIELD CALIF 25 30 240P VIA

= LT KEN COLYER 66 LILLIE ROAD LONDON SW6 =

YOUR LETTER REGARDING FEE DELAYED REPLY IS IN MAIL CHECK EMBASSY FRIDAY AND MONDAY FOR CLEARANCE REGARDS = DOROTHY

BERTA WOOD LETTER TO KEN COLYER 1 FEBRUARY 1957

2904 ¾ Hillcrest Dr., Los Angeles 16, Calif.
Dear Ken,

I am writing this note on my desk at work. Everything seems to have fallen on me suddenly and I'm up to my ears but I am determined to write and ask that you consider me for pictures of yourself and your bands. I want to have some on hand for when the time comes and I need them.

My book has been sent out in search of a publisher. It has been at Doubleday's and I do not know if or when it will be accepted. I want to be ready anyway. If you ever get an extra photo of the marching band, I would surely like one.

Yannick Burgoyne has asked me to write for him—his Belgian Jazz Magazine—and one always needs photographs.

I certainly hope to see you with the Lewis Band over here. That would be fine. Also I would like to hear about George's trip to England to play with you. George doesn't like to write letters and Dorothy Tait is kept busy at other things so I don't get much news of the band when they are out of town (I'm trying to do two things at once and it's not working out very well. Chuckle.)

So excuse the shortness of this answer but don't forget about the photographs. Frederick Ramsey just produced a marvellous hour-long documentary on a major television show called "Odyssey." It began with New Orleans and went BACKWARDS FROM THERE. It was truly magnificent .

Dig You Later, (signed) Berta

MIKE SLATTER LETTER TO KEN COLYER 1 FEBRUARY 1957

New York
Dear Ken,

I must apologise for not having written to you for so long but I have had a good deal on my mind since my return to New York. While I was in New Orleans I met the British Consul General who happened to know my family. In conversation I happened to mention that I had always wanted to live in New Orleans and that had it not been for the good job I was offered in New York, I should in fact be living in New Orleans. He then told me that there was a job in the Consulate that might interest me. The news of George Lewis' trip to England is very encouraging and I do hope that it will come off. Had I been definitely offered the New Orleans job, I had myself intended to get over to England in March, but that now looks very unlikely. However it is almost certain that Ralston and Peggy will be going over in March and Ralston seems more confident every day. If they do go I shall probably send my new tapes with them. After two years silence, I have finally had a letter from your brother Bill. I had learned months ago that he had left the band, but still ???????????. Ken Lindsay casually mentioned it in one of his letters. I have been thinking ever since then why on earth Bill should have done a thing like that.

Thinking that he might be interested, I mentioned it to Ralston and he was very shocked indeed to hear the news. All Bill said in the letter was that he had not seen you for six months. From that I realised that you must have had some kind of a disagreement. I hope that whatever it is is not serious, though I confess that I find the news very disturbing indeed simply because I, and Ralston too for that matter, have the highest regard for both of you and find it hard to believe that anything sufficiently serious could have happened. To produce such a division.

Please forgive these comments, Ken, but they are heartfelt, believe me, even though it is none of my damned business.

Well, it's snowing like hell this miserable Friday night. I wish I had that new record of yours to put on the turntable. I hope that you will be able to make that return trip in May. You can certainly count on my support in every way. If you run into any difficulties with the authorities or immigration I'll see what can be done. Meanwhile I shall keep my fingers crossed in the hopes that George Lewis will be able to get over to England—that would be sensational! That's about it for now Ken, all the best—hope to have some good news soon,

Yours as ever, (signed) Mike

BERTA WOOD LETTER TO KEN COLYER 16 MARCH 1957

2904 3/4 So. Hillcrest Dr., Los Angeles 16, Calif.
Dear Ken,
It is too bad the Lewis deal fell through. At first, the word got around here that you were ill and unable to play. I was very relieved to hear from Traill that the American Embassy was at fault. AGAIN!

George Lewis and Dorothy
Tait in Great Britain

I hope that they're not giving you a bad time over there but I suspect that they are. Ignore them as much as possible. I don't suppose that it will occur to them to put the blame where it belongs—on the Embassy. If you have an extra clipping of the press interview I would like to see it as I only got a rough outline of it.

The same pattern of behaviour is repeating itself over here among the negroid people... The target of slanderous attacks is Louis Armstrong! Would you believe it! I am embroiled in a defence of Louis—and jazz music. A small part of it will appear in a future *JJ* column.

I have a spread coming up in *Ebony* magazine pointing out some of the vital facts to the negroid people about jazz music. People I don't know will be very angry at me I'm sure, but if it does some good then I don't mind. It will be in the April issue and I'll send you some clippings. The staff photographer must have taken 40 pictures of the Teddy Buckner Band, Johnny St. Cyr, Paul Barnes, myself and my son and I couldn't get a single print for myself. It's a shame that the Lewis band or Ory couldn't have been in town at that time.

Lizzie Miles is very fond of you and asked that I send you her good regards and to tell you that the Library of Congress has accepted her Cook, Sounds of Our Time recordings. I put that in a column too. Traill liked it so much that he plans to use a photo of Lizzie on the cover and to feature the column about her.

Lizzie is wonderful, and one of the most honest people I have met. She doesn't give a damn what people think. She will be honest come hell or high water and how I love her for that.

I got my book back from Doubleday with a rejection slip and am getting it ready for a try at another publisher. I would still like to have some photos of you to include in it if and when it connects.

Wishing you good going and "Happy Breaks,"
(signed) Berta

BERTA WOOD LETTER TO KEN COLYER 28 MARCH 1957

Dear Ken

The photographs arrived O.K. but you didn't need to send them airmail. It's too expensive. The marching photos were fine and I was delighted with the Omega Brass Band as was every one else who has seen them. **Thank you very much for the autographed photo. I am very happy to have it and I'm going to put it next to Hugues Panassie and Madeleine Gautier on my wall.**

I want to do a piece about you for *Record Changer* and the *Second Line* too, written around the brass band photos. It may take some time before I can get your photos back to you as everything moves slowly and the pieces aren't written yet. I may have some copies made so I can keep the big street scene with crowds and a couple of others for my book. I haven't heard from it and can't tell when I will get word from it one way or another. That crowd scene was splendid. Somehow England seems the last place people expect to see a marching brass band. More power to you and the other musicians.

The attacks on Louis Armstrong are very sad. The coloured people are attacking him too. They even went so far as to boycott a performance because he was playing to a segregated audience. People have forgotten utterly that he has spent 30 fruitful years in breaking down racial prejudice here at home and who can estimate how much good work he has done. It's not fair and I'm doing whatever I can to defend him. The *Ebony* article may help somewhat and I hope that it does. *Ebony*'s Editor's, who understand my point of view and are sympathetic, although they have not been sympathetic to jazz music in the past.

The bitter and heated attacks on Louis are really attacks on Negroid jazz music and Negroid ways of speaking, acting and thinking. He is attacked because he refuses to give up his Negroid manners and playing. That's what the critics are doing when they call his actions and playing "Uncle Tom" and "Clowning." IT ISN'T REALLY. NOT AT ALL. He is expressing his happy, Negroid self and he has every right to. The inhibited critics, boppers, cool etc. are beginning to really hate him because he is warm and uninhibited and insists on staying that way.

Louis is really hurt, because so many of his own people have turned their backs on him and don't understand how much he has done for them. Hugues Panassie calls it "being corrupted by the whites"— i.e. Puritanism. What's new about Puritanism? Or progressive? Ha! Panassie is printing a strong version of the *Ebony* chapter in the *Bulletin du Hot Club de France*. People ought to know how bad it really is here for it may change some progressive opinions. (I hope so.) I figure if I can tell the truth— then the truth will fight a lot of good battles.

Louis is wonderful and it is a shame that they are trying to tear him down— AND THE JAZZ HE REPRESENTS TOO.

Lizzie Miles left Scobey to go back to New Orleans. Scobey was going into the Tin Angel following the Lewis Band. The woman who runs the Tin Angel still owes Lizzie over $40 from the last time she worked there and she had trouble getting as much money as she did. The Lewis band—or rather Dorothy Tait—had the owner before the Labor Board and the union too to get their money. So Lizzie went home.

I don't keep up on releases here so I haven't seen your LP (*Club Session With Colyer*) announced here yet. I'll check back with the *Down Beat*'s I have and let you know. I wish Decca would give you that "sympathetic recording" you want. I know what you mean. It's too bad.

The picture looks lots brighter today than formerly, doesn't it? With all our difficulties? I have a feeling that it's going to get better now that the cools are falling by the wayside. Don't you?

Wishing you Good Going

And "Happy Breaks" (signed) Berta

P.S. I'm glad you thought to send me a programme from the Adelphi Theatre. I'm enjoying showing it around. Nice. Thanks

MIKE SLATTER LETTER TO KEN COLYER 8 APRIL 1957

1928 East 70th Street, New York
Dear Ken,

Your last letter came as a great surprise, the news it contained was sensational. How I wish I could be in England during George Lewis' visit. From the sound of things Ralston will have missed this historic visit too. I hope that you have taken adequate steps to ensure that the music that is made will be preserved on tape or record. It would be a terrible tragedy if no monument were preserved, especially as so great an opportunity may never occur again. For God's sake Ken, stop at nothing! F— the union, F— Decca just save that music!

I was delighted to know you will be flying to the West Coast on May 9th. You are certain to pass through New York and even if you only stay here just long enough to change planes, please let me know your flight no. and an idea of how long you will be on the ground, as I can certainly get into the airport. Don't forget, Ken, just give me the flight no. and I'll be there somehow.

The reason that I had not written sooner was that my own plans were not settled. However I can now say definitely that I shall be flying to London on May 20th. Therefore I will only be able to see you on your way TO the West Coast. If you stick to your plans I shall be in London on your return on June 9th. So if all goes well, I shall be able to see something of you during my last week over there.

From all your good news I can only conclude that you have been able to square the immigration authorities. I must say I did not understand your reference to Miami in one of your earlier letters. You mentioned it in connection with your attempts to straighten out your papers.

Well Ken we must keep in close touch as I particularly want to see you and hear the band too. If you have any unexpected change of plans let me know at once. If you arrive in New York unexpectedly my phone number between 9 and 6pm is DIGBY 4-6580. So give me a call.

I'll be very amused to hear how your virtual monopoly of George Lewis has been received by Lyttelton and Barber! Anyway, I wish you and the boys the very best of luck—how I envy those who will hear you playing with George. It's no use if you don't make any records for the poor bastards like me who can't make it in person. Same goes for the West Coast too. I imagine that you will be making a broadcast or television appearance during the next few days. When the excitement's over let me know all about it. On Monday June 3rd I shall be down at Studio 51 complete with recorder—nothing will keep me out, at least, I hope not.

No sign of the record yet. We tried Sam Goody, so far without success.

Look forward to hearing how things are going, Yours, (signed) Mike

COLIN BOWDEN When George Lewis came over in '57 it was wonderful. Ken had arranged this rehearsal in Manchester, and George said, "We don't need no rehearsal, we're musicianers."

Ken welcomes George Lewis

We just played anyway. Ian went out and found this Grundig tape recorder—he was lazy, he just didn't want to play—only kidding!

It was a marvellous experience: that *St Philip Street*, I was floating; it just flew along, I was after him like a jack rabbit. You didn't have to drive George, he just *flew*, he was incredible. And he was such a gentle, gentle man in the truest sense. Such a quiet man. The first time we ever heard him play live we had met him in Manchester Airport and visited him in his hotel room. He was sitting on the edge of his bed playing low-register runs and it just sounded like water bubbling over round pebbles, just a tone you couldn't believe.

You listen to *Corinne Corinna* on that rehearsal we were just talking about; Ian has picked up George's tone to the extent that in places you can't tell the difference in their playing; an amazing rapport and it happened instantly.

George just had a tremendous effect on all of us, he was a very powerful player. On that *St Philip Street* he shouts from the side of his mouth, "Yeah!" But you don't hear a note change on his clarinet; I've listened and listened and I cannot hear him say it.

BILL COLYER I think Paddy McKiernan booked George first, up in Manchester. I did have a hand in that, certainly in

publicising George's name like mad! Of course one read the Dorothy Tait book later (she used the pen name Jay Allison Stuart), and she did become his manager. But he was really something else to hear in the flesh. No wonder Ken had flipped back in 1952 when first hearing him in New Orleans!

DOROTHY TAIT And so on April 10 1957, George boarded a BOAC plane in New York as a first-class passenger, settled down in the deep comfort of its seats, ate of the many-splendoured meal it provided, and drank its excellent liquor. Then, yawning contentedly, he settled back for the remainder of the trip, an over-all thirteen hours in those pre-jet transport days.

"Excited?" he said. "Of course not." And never closed his eyes till the plane set down in Manchester. As it taxied to a stop, a familiar sound could be heard faintly. The stewardess rushed to a window.

"It's a band!" she cried. "A brass band. They must be

meeting someone on the plane." Then she caught sight of George, who was managing somehow to look vaguely guilty.

"Why!" she gasped. "It's you! You're—you're George Lewis. I mean THE George Lewis!" Flustered that she had not connected the name on his ticket with the name she had seen for weeks on the hoardings in her country, she fluttered about like an excited wren.

The plane had stopped. The doors were opening. Far in the distance against the hangars, a crowd of people had gathered. In front of the crowd was a smaller group, close together. Even at that distance, the blond beard of Ken Colyer was recognisable.

"It's Ken," breathed George, and as he stepped through the door and stood for a moment on the top step, tears welled to his eyes. The sound of the brasses and the drums of Ken's band rolled across the intervening space, warming the air, chasing the fog, hurting with its gladness, as the boys wailed and shouted with their instruments the grand old hymn—Gloryland.

IAN WHEELER George Lewis's first visit. Oh, it was absolutely marvellous. It seemed we had waited so long. Paddy McKiernan, from the Bodega club in Manchester, was instrumental in bringing him over. The day he arrived, April 11th, we went up to meet him off the plane at Manchester. We'd played a session at the 51, then drove overnight because his plane was due in around 7 o'clock and, of course, there were no motorways in those days; it took us about seven hours to get there! We didn't play him in, just stood there waiting for him, shook hands, then a couple of hours sleep, then we had a rehearsal in the pub.

I was out of the band for a while because George was playing, so I rushed around to find a tape recorder, from Johnny Roadhouse, I think. Then I joined in later in the rehearsal and it was just a marvellous feeling playing with him there for the first time. The results are on a CD.

He was lovely. At first, for a couple of days, he was rather reserved. He was polite, but somewhat withdrawn and called you "Sir" which, of course, you didn't want. He was a quiet man anyway but, as we got to know him, he became a friend rather than someone who just happened to be working with you. He really was a lovely, gentle man in the true sense. He loved what he was doing and, even more to the point, loved what we were doing.

I wasn't going to say he was overwhelmed by the reception he got in this country but, actually, he probably was. So many people came to see him; they'd longed to see him. We had longed to play with him. And there he was!

One little anecdote about the time with George: we did most of the tour with him, but Chris Barber did a couple of the gigs as well. At the end of one of their gigs they presented George with a double clarinet case—there's a good part and a bad part to this story: at the end of the tour George gave me his old clarinet case—a small case with a crocodile skin-type casing. George told me that it had belonged to Jimmy Noone, and he said to me, "Use it well!"

So I did... and I used it too well, because over the years it became more and more battered until, in the end, it fell apart. Had I known what I know now, I never would have used it at all! That was the bad part.

COLIN BOWDEN George Lewis? That was something else, that was. That was like flying. All I know is George Lewis was a fantastic person, because of being with him when he was playing.

That's the link. If you could write it down you'd be a marvellous author, wouldn't you? I mean, the *St. Philip Street Breakdown*. I mean, I play the recording and... I was just chasing him all the time, you know. And at one stage he shouted at me out of the side of his mouth as he was playing: "Yeah," he went. Like that, you see. And then I found out that he'd told Joe Watkins not to play woodblocks, and that's the most incredible thing. And if I'd have known that I wouldn't have played them!

DELPHINE COLYER When George Lewis came over it was lovely. You know, they were just sort of together. And when I first heard him playing I remember Ian Wheeler saying, "Cheer up'" because I was crying. But he was a lovely man—he really was.

BERTA WOOD LETTER TO KEN COLYER 22 APRIL 1957

2904 3/4 So. Hillcrest Dr., Los Angeles 16, Calif.
Dear Ken,

You can imagine how glad I am to hear that George is playing beautifully and being well received. I can hardly wait to hear some of the caustic and cynical critics take back some of the mean things they have said about him. Mmmm hmmm.

I had a letter from Lizzie Miles and she asked that I tell you that she thanks you for the book you sent. You didn't put an address on it so she couldn't write and thank you herself. She wasn't happy with Scobey and she feels much better back in New Orleans. The Almerico band had a big Birthday Party for her—fine big cake and everything—and Lizzie said, "Everybody got the feeling." Chuckle. It looks like Scobey has gone commercial and is gone for good. The band is ragged and dull and spiritless and awful. They had a very bad fill-in drummer I can't help

The Manchester Free Trade
Hall concert, 1957; photo
taken from the side of the
stage by Bill Colyer

feeling bad about it, remembering how he used to play.

I want to ask if I may quote you: "When that plane door opened and I saw him emerge I had a job playing for the lump in my throat." I think it is fine, but if you'd rather I did not use it just say so. In *Hear Me Talkin' To Ya*, Duke Ellington said of his musicians, "I like to see great big ol' tears."

I hope that the enclosed *Ebony* article may do a bit of good among the Negro musicians and jazz public. I was rather surprised that *Ebony* would print it at all but Lerone Bennett Jr., the editor who handled it, is an Ellington man and a real one and it hit him in the middle too. It's a condensation and he tailored it somewhat to fit the *Ebony* public but most of it is mine and the general idea is the same.

Wishing you Good Going and Lucky Breaks,

(signed) Berta

P.S. I put in the column that I didn't believe that George Lewis would have made the trip to England alone unless he had known you so well and that a lot of credit for his coming goes to you. I hope Traill doesn't cut it. Traill is such a strict, middle of the road, mainstream cat that I disturb him often and he has gotten very angry at me a few times. Chuckle. I wrote some stuff about Trummy Young that really upset him. He took it to Louis Armstrong to prove me wrong and I suppose that Louis set him straight. Ha. Personally I think that Traill would like to chuck me off the magazine but he's business man enough to know that the trad following in England is not to be slighted. I hope that George Lewis in person bowls him over. Oh but I do.

Bestus, (signed) Berta

DOROTHY TAIT LETTER TO KEN COLYER UNDATED 1957

Saturday

Dear Ken...

Glory be! I have my hands on a typewriter again...

We got back from France last night to be met with the news that the Denmark date had fallen through. It put us on a hell of a spot, as our return sailing was for the eleventh... and it might have meant nine days of staying here with no income and all outgo! However, this morning I rushed up to the Cunard Line and after much eloquent pleading secured two sailings on the *Mauretania* from Southampton on the eighth.

That knocks out what I hoped would be a chance to be in London again. We'll take a sleeper from here the night of the seventh... arrive London early A.M., go to Waterloo Station from Euston and take the boat train to Southampton... sailing from there Wednesday the eighth.

I have given Paddy the dates for your coming to the United States as either May 30 to June 15, or the last week in June till July 15... as I gave them to Colin on the telephone when we were in London. The June-July dates are preferable if the Union will

agree. George is pretty "beat" as we say... and after Arras, while at dinner in Paris the next night, had a severe attack of Angina in the restaurant and was quite ill... it is well, from the health standpoint, that he can stay completely quiet till we leave. He might not have been up to another playing chore in Denmark.

The French band in Arras (a local group) wasn't so hot, tho' they tried hard. As George said "Ken and his boys could blow them guys off the stage..."

> We just haven't the words to tell you all how much we want to be with you... nor could George describe, or I, either, his happiness over being with you...

I am going to ask Paddy to give me a check for Fifteen Pounds (I'll give it to him) and send it to you... as soon as I see him. We never did complete arrangements for getting the hundred dollars to the Barnards, but perhaps you can do it when you are in the States.

Our very, very best wishes and warmest affection to you, your wife... and the boys

(signed) Dorothy

DOROTHY TAIT LETTER TO KEN COLYER 2 JUNE 1957

Dear Ken,

First, I want to say thank you so much for your letter! Then say "hello and I miss you" to yourself, Delphine, and all the boys.

Then I want to ask a question that I want you to shoot an airmail special delivery answer to immediately. How long can you stay in the States? Then, after you've sent the letter or card off, you can sit down and prepare to spend a weekend reading this lengthy epistle!

I am working like a Trojan to try and make it possible for George and the band and you to play the Newport Jazz Festival. It means an awful lot to ANY jazz musician, here or anywhere... it receives international publicity, it's the biggest event of the year, and from the standpoint of a jazz musician is of even greater— much greater—importance than the Aspen, Colorado date (which means prestige among the academic crowd and the long hairs). The Newport Jazz Festival means fame and recognition in EVERY circle. The band has been asked to play it.

I know Lyttelton and that he's coming over... but if we can make that Newport Jazz Festival on July 4 (our biggest national holiday) H.Lyttelton will be drooling all over his old Etonian tie with envy. I know no foreign musician has ever played it.

The problem, of course, is that it's on the east coast... and transport costs will run into four figures that we haven't got. Hence, I'm trying to line some things up that will at least partially take care of it. The festival is non-profit and won't pay transportation!

Let's don't get the BMU or the Federation all excited again, or say anything till the last minute. BUT if we get New port your first nite might be in Newport, Rhode Island instead of San Francisco. You'd arrive in plenty of time… and your ticket will permit a stop-over, of that I am sure. Thence maybe to the West Coast via a Chicago concert or two. THEN a good possibility of a straight week theatre engagement in L.A.

Hence the urgency to know how long you can stay.

So much for that. Now to less pleasant matters. As you can see by the above, I am proceeding on a "business as usual" basis… I wrote Paddy and told him what I'm about to tell you, asking that he keep it in strict confidence… and asking that if he told you, he ask you to keep it in just as strict confidence… even from George's boys in the band… for reasons I'm sure you can well understand. I am tired of sending frantic denials of George's demise across the water… also the publicity could be adverse as far as a band tour is concerned.

The second day after we sailed out from England George suffered a blood clot in one of the major arteries of his right leg. It was a critically dangerous thing, and the ship's doctor laid him out like cold Sunday night supper flat on his back in bed… not permitting him to walk even to his own private bathroom. The poor lamb was only above decks on the *Mauritania* for 24 hours! He was taken off in a wheel-chair… Spent two more days flat in bed in New York, then home to New Orleans. He is still forbidden to walk… except from his front door to a cab… and then with a cane. But improvement is reported.

In about a week I expect to hear from his doctor… but it is another problem on this concert business, for I MUST plan then with the minimum of strain on George… it is only by the grace of God the clot was in the artery of the leg and not a coronary artery. However, the doctor has given me a green light as far as plans are concerned with a hopeful prognosis, only instructing me that every effort must be made to see that he has the least possible strain and exertion.

He, George, doesn't want me to tell anyone. But I had to tell Paddy and you although he doesn't know that I have.

Am not going on at any greater length as I want this, if possible, to catch a late afternoon plane. Keep your fingers crossed and say a "prayer." I'm looking for what they call an "angel" over here to give us a boost on this thing financially…

My very, very best to all the boys… sure hope that if and when a band exchange works out it will be at separate times so that you won't be over here while we're over there!

And let me know pronto, toot sweet, right away and with all dispatch the date of your return deadline!

Very best regards, (signed) Dorothy

P.S. Can you tuck a pint of bitter in your back pocket?

P.S.2 Tell Bob Kelly that no one in my immediate circle of friends ever says that they're tired any more. They're all "fair wobbit."

BERTA WOOD LETTER TO KEN COLYER 17 JULY 1957

2904 ¾ Hillcrest Dr., Los Angeles 16, Calif.
Dear Ken,

I had no intention of neglecting you so long but things did pile up. All hell broke loose over the *Ebony* article here. Everybody jumped on me. *Record Changer*, *Down Beat*, *Ebony*'s readers and even people I do not know, took me to task, hauled me over the coals and what not. Of course I had GOOD answers to everybody and I answered them all. That's what I have been so busy about.

I think I summed the situation up when writing to Traill about Dr. Souchon's beef in the Sweet Letters. He's a charming old boy and I was very careful not to offend him and at the same time clear myself of his rather confused charges. I wrote to Traill, "I do not need to be so delicate with you because you are not involved in the guilty conscience of this country and have no need to circumvent the truth."

Alton Purnell was quite active in the New Orleans racial hassle. He is here now and I have letters and clippings proving that 150 clubs did not parcipitate in the Mardi Gras this year and lots of jazz musicians did not play the Mardi Gras this year in protest. The N.A.A.C.P. has been outlawed in New Orleans so the clubs brought the Rev. King in to a mass meeting. The tension is very bad there now.

I am not in direct contact with the Lewis band now. I was hoping that you might get to play the Newport Festival with the Lewis band. I would like to know how your deal with them worked out..

Panassie has printed the parts of the chapter *Ebony* did not use and I still hope it will do considerable good. Panassie said it was great, bless him. We see eye to eye on almost everything. Incidently, *Ebony*'s editor changed a few things and added a bit here and there so that a couple of the things did not ring true but I let it go. Still can't get an editor for my book of collected columns and articles. They're still touchy about racial issues here but I hope to find an editor brave enough to publish it.

Let me hear news of you and what you are doing. Traill cut the part about you out of the Lizzie Miles article. I had to ask him not to make so many changes in my stuff as he has made several mistakes that are embarrassing to me.

Alton has left the Lewis band. Joe Robichaux is playing piano now. Bob Thomas on tram; the trumpet player on the Newport and New York trip was Jack Willis. I am not sure but I think Alton

Sightseeing! Jimmy Asman and Ken show London off to Dorothy and George

said that he had played with Freddie Kohlman. Alton said he is a good trumpet player but he doesn't know the Lewis book.

Let me hear welcome news from you, and wishing you good going.

(signed) Berta

MIKE SLATTER LETTER TO KEN COLYER 19 JULY 1957

Sixty-One Broadway, New York 6, N.Y.
Dear Ken,

It was good to see you again and to hear the band. The tapes that I made have really turned out quite well and if you have time when you are in New York you might like to hear them. I must warn you to bring the hottest [coolest?—Ed] clothes you can find when you come here; for the past week the temperature has reached well into the 90's every day. Even at night it does not go below 80.

Don't forget to let me know your flight no. and expected time of arrival, also how long you expect to remain in New York.. Will

you be playing at Newport? You must also do your damn best to go down to N.O. I will do anything that I can to help. Look forward to seeing you and I can probably provide a bed if you need one, though from what you told me you will be staying over in New Jersey. Can't write any more, the heat is killing me—I'm off home to grab a beer.

All the best, (signed) Mike

DOROTHY TAIT TELEGRAM TO KEN COLYER 21 JULY 1957

BAKERSFIELD CALIF 62 20 LT =
COLYER 99 THE DRIVE ISLEWORTH-MIDDLESEX =
DISASTER DOGS US GEORGE ABSOLUTELY UNFIT FOR TWO WEEK STEADY ENGAGEMENTS DOCTORS CERTIFICATE AVAILABLE IF UNION REQUIRES MUST CANCEL COAST JAZZ CONCERT THEATRE DATES AND SET UP FOR LATER GEORGE WILL ATTEMPT NEWPORT

DATE BUT HAVE ONLY THAT USE YOUR OWN JUDGEMENT BUT SUGGEST WAIT TILL GEORGE IMPROVES AS NEWPORT DATE LOUSY DEAL FINANCIALLY BEST REGARDS = DOROTHY +

DOROTHY TAIT LETTER TO KEN COLYER 31 JULY 1957

Dear Ken,

The enclosed letter is one which I just sent to Paddy, with the medical certificate enclosed. By sending you carbons of my letters to him (I asked him to send you a carbon of the last one) everyone knows just what the situation is. And I found your new address... I had carefully written it in my address book, under "K" for Ken instead of "C" for Colyer.

Ken—the first bad thing that happened was when I learned that the Central Plaza had a new policy since the last time I was in New York. Liquor is served, and there is dancing. The Federation said "No!" That left only the Newport Jazz Festival on the East Coast—and it pays practically nothing.

As things worked out, Louis Armstrong behaved so badly and raised such a "sand" (as George would say) that all the publicity went to him (and all of it bad!) But George was pretty much overlooked on that opening day shindig BECAUSE of Louis' attitude, and actions. Will get the real dope from George one of these days. NOW—the bookings on the West Coast were in a theatre and HAD to be consecutive bookings, every night. Two shows a night. Then I learned he wasn't doing so well. It was absolutely out of the question to put him up against that, so soon after suffering an embolism in his leg. There was no assurance the clot had absorbed...

At the Central Plaza I insisted on their retaining the other band. Hence, he played half hour sets... half hour intermissions... and he only played four dates in ELEVEN days. Any playing George does between now and the time we set up some concerts will be under the same or similar circumstances... Either in conjunction with another band—or well-spaced casuals.

My letter to Paddy, when you read it, will convey the general plan for the future. The reason the carbon's so messed up is that I took it out of the typewriter, and when I put it back in I didn't line me up right. My last letter to Paddy (and ask him for the carbon if he didn't send it to you) and these, plus the medical certificate, should clarify the situation—and we can start with a clean slate to plan for the future.

As I pointed out to Paddy—Hotel reservations for you had all been made... concrete evidence of our good faith...

This MUST get off now for the early afternoon plane...

My fondest regards to your wife and every one in the band... George's too...

(Signed) Dorothy

Enclosed letter
Wednesday, July 31

Dear Paddy,

The enclosed came special delivery late last night. I've had the feeling all along that it would be the better part of discretion to let well enough alone and not press St. Martin. I think I was right—I do not like this "several months" phrase. Reading between the lines of the letter which accompanies it he would seem to be—and I think justifiably—annoyed. His attitude is that the man had a blood clot in an artery—he has a previous history of a coronary occlusion, albeit a mild one. The problem in this case was the wisdom of making bookings for consecutive concerts of three hours—one to one and a half hours playing, a brief intermission and a second spell of playing on the feet, as weighed against half an hour playing, half an hour rest, and two nearly forty-five minute intermissions—I insisted when consenting to the Central Plaza date, that he play only IF the other band was retained—thus he played only a very few half hour sets... And the Federation forbade a foreign musician.

The next move would seem to be this: ascertaining when Ken would be free... notify me... I will see what can be done for concerts during his free period... then seek, immediately, the doctor's approval.

ANY engagements that George does in the interim will be done under the same conditions as the New York... few and SHORT sets.

Here is why I MUST know Ken's free time: first, concerts are hard to come by in this country for traditional groups... if we were Brubeck or Kenton it would be a different picture. Second, when a concert is arranged the contract MUST stipulate the number of men. If we say "seven men" and then later come back to them with the word that it will only be six, they will immediately take advantage of the situation to cut the price. If we say SIX men and then come back to them and say "So sorry— it's seven men"—they usually refuse to up the price.

If we promise a British musician and then withdraw him (the next part is illegible)—but if we can arrange them in such a way that there are no one-night stands consecutively—(unless in the same city)—we can bring Ken over—But I HAVE to know when. My hope is that if we DO have concerts they will be in the east and Al Kershaw will be among those present.

Then yesterday I drove to Los Angeles and talked with Kenning, who is Petrillo's right hand man, and who saved our bacon in the previous contretemps. I told him the whole story— even brought a carbon of my letter in which I stated that possibly we could offer Ken additional concerts on the LA date—plus a letter from the hotel in Hollywood acknowledging reservations for George, Joe, Drag, and Ken Colyer... and one from the hotel in New York acknowledging reservations for the entire band AND Ken Colyer. Our good (the next part is illegible). He assured me that he would contact Petrillo—in fact put in a call to him to call back while I was there but was unable to reach him and left word for him to call back—and would place the whole story before him... as I had placed it before Harvey Ratcliff.

I was keenly disappointed that Ken would not

have the opportunity to play the Newport Festival. Believe me—Louis Armstrong behaved so wretchedly and abominably that ALL the publicity was concentrated on Louis shenanigans—and poor George (except for brief notices) was lost in the shuffle. When, as, and if I ever see George again I'll get the REAL story, for he was backstage and heard the whole thing. The like has never been heard of at ANY festival, as nearly as I can make out!

I don't want to take the time to have a photostatic copy made of this certificate—if you can show it to the authorities without relinquishing it, it would be fine. Would like to keep it on hand.

Must get this off as quickly as possible.

Get back to me with some word of Ken's schedule.

Best wishes to yourself and Ron—and the lovely little lady with the dimples—Heather! We simply do NOT grow dimples as enchanting as hers in the United States!

(signed) Dorothy

Saturday

Dear Ken,

Your letter came with uncanny speed—arriving in this morning's mail—and the first thing I want to do is shout a loud and transcontinental "Hooray!" for you and Delphine and the baby I did not know was en route! WHEN is the estimated date of arrival?????? Also Mac's???? Hooray for all of you.

This letter may seem a bit sticky and stupid—inasmuch as we are in the midst of our annual September hot spell—before the day is over it will no doubt be 105 degrees... and by the end of the summer I get very fed up with the heat and very cranky and cantankerous!

On top of which, of course, I am still desperately worried about George.

Ken—never, never believe anyone who tells you George SEEMS fine or SAYS he is fine! Forty-five minutes before he collapsed on the stand in New York with virus pneumonia he sat at the table with me and Joe Watkins and informed us that he felt "jes fine," and he'd been walking around with pneumonia for three days!—blowing every night—and his haemoglobin blood count was down to just below 60%, so low they wanted to transfuse but didn't dare. So beware of our George and his "feeling fine!"

I am still awaiting word from the doctor who cared for him in the hospital. They have another hospital there now for coloured people—it's the Flint-Goodrich. It used to be for accident (compensation insurance) cases only. Now it has been taken over by the Negro university there—Dillard—and they are trying desperately hard to make it a good hospital for colored. Certainly, George received A-1 care and treatment apparently.

I talked with him two hours after he got home—and Peter was there, and I also talked with him. Peter said George was very weak and incredibly thin. Inasmuch as he is incredibly thin in moderate good health, I shudder to think what he must look like now. George told me his blood count once again was very, very

low, when he entered the hospital, which is probably why he was so vulnerable to the virus bug.

Ken—there is no knowing just what the future holds. I dare not even predict. In New York, two and a half years ago, the doctor who cared for him told me that if he ever had another attack of pneumonia it would be curtains. Well, once again George fooled 'em and pulled thro. With that indomitable spirit of his. However, I understand that he had a heart attack while he was in the hospital. I have not yet had confirmation from his doctor about that—inasmuch as he has already had one coronary occlusion—another might really put him on the shelf. I just don't know—and I am frightfully worried.

I wrote Paddy yesterday and told him the whole story—and I also wrote to some of the British trade journals (music) so that wild rumors would not start once again. Better that they get the straight story. I did NOT mention a heart attack—sure as you're born folks would be burying poor George again if I had, as they did before—and beside, I do not have definite confirmation of [part missing—Ed] he had to be kept in an oxygen tent for five days.

Anyhow, Ken—I asked Paddy please, unless he wants me to go into whooping hysterics which would be heard clearly over here, not to press us at this point on the concerts.

The question now is not, "When will George be able to play again?" It is "Will he?"

NOW, if he DOES make a come-back from this, which will be a near-miracle, and is given permission to play again, before we can plan any concerts I MUST try, somehow, willy-nilly, to line up one or two short club dates to provide enough money to even buy the transportation for concert gigs. The few casuals George has been permitted to play have of course meant nothing financially. The past four months have been a dead loss as far as money is concerned—and this last illness has really blacked us out—and we face any engagements in the red.

He may not be permitted to play club dates. IF he is, Ken, please understand that these are essential to any plans for concert so that I can manage to scrape together enough reserve for concert engagements. I don't blame Paddy for this—but I did not know (and this was probably my own stupidity) that he was insisting on a twelve day tour to enable him to take advantage of the 14 day plane excursion rate. He knew that George could NOT ever play twelve consecutive concerts.

However—I am not worrying too much about it, for I know you and I understand each other on that score.

But I do plead for your understanding that should he be permitted to play steadily again and you hear that he is playing a club date... remember that it is ESSENTIAL that we get one or two of these under our belt so that we can embark on the concerts... even if they are only two weekend club dates. I'll write you just as soon as I hear from the doctor—I do not believe she (it was a woman doctor) will make any definite commitments until he has been out of the hospital awhile and his heart watched, and several blood counts taken... so it may take a while.

I asked Paddy if he thought he could do anything about England's winter climate! How I wish it were a mild one—I would then become a pistol-packin' mamma, rob a bank, and—with the doctor's permission—get George on a boat and have him convalesce over there! Never since I have known him has he been as happy and contented—and that means a whale of a lot in the uphill road he faces now in getting well.

Ask the boys in the band to send him a card—or a note—he'd be so happy to get them—and it would give him a tremendous lift. Can't you still hear him saying, up there on the platform... "Now me an' my boys will try to play *St. Philip Street Breakdown...*"

You will be hearing from me again soon—my love to the boys in the band—and very best to Delphine –

Cheers (even tho I do not feel exactly cheery!)

(signed) Dorothy

Thursday

Dear Ken—

Lyn is probably keeping you up to date on our correspondence re. Europe—This is to tell you that Paddy is now offering the last two weeks in January and 1st in February, 1959.

This time I'll take nothing for granted—such as Paddy notifying you regarding the tour. I sent Lyn a letter yesterday—Please pass this information on to him—He didn't mention any band.

Very hastily—and with regards to all!

(signed) Dorothy

MIKE SLATTER LETTER TO KEN COLYER 27 AUGUST 1957

1928 East 70th Street, New York

Dear Ken,

Many thanks for your letter. Unfortunately I cannot answer your questions about Newport and Armstrong, though I have up to date news from Sam Charters regarding the improved health of George Lewis. I am enclosing Sam's letter and have pencilled his address at the top—638 Royal Street. I must say that his news really makes me feel envious, but my annual pilgrimage draws nearer now that summer is over. I expect to be down there for Christmas as I was last year. In my last letter I told Sam that you would be writing to him, and I feel sure that if anyone can get a copy of the Red Book he can.

Still disappointed that your trip didn't come off. Hope it will be possible later on.

You remember the tapes I made of the band when I was in England? I would like to have someone competent, like John Reddihough, get hold of the same machine that I used and make me up some more tapes. If for any reason John could not do it, perhaps you know someone who is familiar with that type of recorder who could supervise the recording. Naturally I would cover the expense. But the tapes I made were so surprisingly good, even of the skiffle numbers, that I think that it is important that we should make some more. You can be quite certain Ken that any such tapes would never leave my possession.

The coverage that you are given by Decca is totally inadequate and I feel that if I can build up a good collection of the music you are making today, it may well be possible, say ten years from now, for you to select some of the best pieces for general release. I would never do that on my own account, but you never know, you might be glad that a more representative collection is preserved. Having listened carefully to the tapes that I have got I must say that the music is far better than any that has been specially recorded by the record companies. This is possibly because my recordings are made under less formal conditions, with a large and appreciative audience.

Ken I'd like you to give this idea considerable thought and see if you can come up with somebody to make the recordings. Done discreetly at such places as Eel Pie Island, there would be no risk of running into union difficulties, and of course I ran into no trouble at Studio 51 either. It is important that whoever does the recordings really knows what he is doing—poor results are not worth the effort. I think it is best to set out to record an entire evening that I found just about fills up two seven inch reels.

If you think the idea workable and can put me in touch with someone reliable, I will really go to work on it. I believe that the machine I used was a "Magnagraph" and I tried it at a place just off Oxford Street—Hamburg Place—it's not difficult to find anyway. What I have in mind is to record one or two complete sessions every month and so obtain a history of the band's development, repertoire, style changes etc.. The value of such a library would increase steadily and there are new techniques being developed in the States of preserving tape and prolonging its life.

Well I shall be interested to hear your ideas.

For "form" I am enclosing a couple of photos taken last Christmas Day of George Lewis' mother Mrs. Alice Zeno. Bill Russell and I visited her that morning—something I will never forget.

That's about it for now Ken. Look forward to hearing from you soon. I'm glad that things over there have picked up again. Please give my regards to Bill, Bob and all the boys. I may be sending over some drumsticks for Colin shortly and will mail them to your address.

All the best Ken, Yours, (signed) Mike

DOROTHY TAIT LETTER TO KEN COLYER 30 AUGUST 1957

Dear Ken

Am rushing this off hoping it will arrive at your place in time to catch Peter Deuchar before he leaves—and it is for you also—so you can share it if it arrives before he goes.

A matter of hours, practically, after mailing my letter to Peter in care of you I received a special delivery letter from George's daughter, Shirley, that George had been rushed to the hospital last Sunday night suffering from double pneumonia, and had been in an oxygen tent ever since. She said he would be out of the tent and home in a few days.

I don't mind telling you that I have never in my whole life been so frantic with worry. Then a letter from Joe Watkins said that it had started with an attack of the Asiatic flu, which went into pneumonia.

There is only one hospital in New Orleans that admits Negroes—and that is Charity Hospital. George has been fortunate enough thro the intercession of others there, to have the services of Dr. Maurice St. Martin, one of the best heart specialists in the country. As you know, none of the white doctors treat Negroes as a rule—and few of the Southern-trained Negro Doctors have the background—thro no fault of theirs—to be much good. However, St. Martin could not treat him after he got into the hospital—and while it is a fine Hospital (Catholic) as far as coloured is concerned it is treatment en masse with 25 to 30 in a room, and interns rather than full-blown graduate physicians. St. Martin couldn't treat him there.

Honest-to-Gawd, Ken and Peter, I swear I lost ten pounds in 24 hours! They have no business letting a man as frail as he is go home in less than nine days after double pneumonia—but they run them in and out of there like cars on an assembly line and demand for beds is so great that perhaps they have to.

But if he had ten million dollars in the bank he couldn't go anywhere else, so I can only pray—and believe me my friends, I've been doing some praying! You know the old saying—or rather the saying that originated in World War Two: "There are no atheists in a fox-hole..."

But I did want Peter to know about it before he went down. I know George, and he'll be so damned tickled and happy to hear from someone in New Orleans fresh from England—one of his friends (which to George means practically everyone on the British Isles—but some, like you and Peter, in particular) that

he's apt to leap from bed and go into town or something...

Anyhow, am going to suggest that Peter call him when he gets in and find out how to get over the river to see him, and go see him. He'd be the happiest little man in all the world. Also I'd like to have you—Peter—if you will, drop me a note and tell how he seems to be. He'll lie like a Trojan, God love him, and tell you he feels "fine," so use your intuition (am typing this on both sides of the paper to save weight.)

The last months have been for me, and for George, too, the toughest I've ever put in financially—or I would get him out here on the desert where he has three times previously been cleared of lung conditions in three days' time. **He seems to get along in New Orleans alright in the Winter time, but the doctor has warned him about being there in the hot, humid, tropical summers, in that marshy damp climate. GAWD! How I hate that place!** However, convalescing here, which might do the trick, seems out of the question at the moment—but a miracle may happen. Will shoot this off right away—and—Peter—please drop me a line from New Orleans, Air Mail.

All the best to you both, (signed) Dorothy

Thursday
Dear Ken,
No definite news as yet—should know by Tuesday, Feb 18. Will write Air Special at that time—Meanwhile, don't say anything about it till we know for sure—Will write you first of month.

Regards, Dorothy

PETE DEUCHAR LETTER TO KEN COLYER 19 SEPTEMBER 1957

St. Paul Hotel, Bourbon Street, N.O., La.
Dear Ken,
Sorry I couldn't see you the night before I left, but there was one hell of a rush to get the plane at the last moment.

Things out here are very quiet most guys just playing once per week. The only coloured band playing every night is the Bill Matthews band at the Paddock Lounge and this band is not really good listening. The "Lewis Band" plays there on Tuesdays. I put the quotation marks round the words because this is the palest of pale imitations; except for the rhythm section choruses. Robichaux surely drives and everything seems to drop when the front line comes back in. Of course, George hasn't played since he came out of hospital. The first week Joe Thomas (Brother Cornbread) sat in; and the second Andrew Morgan took his place. George is going to play next week.

Kid Sheik sent you a Christmas card, but as he only addressed it to Fulham,

London, he got it back.

Nevertheless I gave him your address and he will write again.

Everyone has been very nice and helpful and all ask after you and hope that you can get back sometime.

Evidently it is just a matter of time that Jim Robinson will rejoin George as Jim has had to scuffle for some time now.

I am managing to play every Saturday with the Kid Thomas Band out in the country on the other side of the river. Thomas has Manuel Paul on sax and Louis Nelson on trombone., and a real driving rhythm section, it's a lot of fun playing those waltzes etc.

My, being in New Orleans certainly does change your views!

I was lucky enough to meet up with Sam Charters before he left for California, and he was able to introduce me to a lot of guys which was very helpful.

Must sign off now, Yours, (signed) Peter

P.S. Try to send Bill Russell your latest LP and Brass Band recordings.

PETE DEUCHAR LETTER TO KEN COLYER UNDATED 1957

St. Paul Hotel, Bourbon Street, N.O., La.
Dear Ken,

Thanks for your letter just received. Congratulations at you becoming a Father. I will ring George in a few minutes and tell him. George hasn't played yet since I have been here, but he may play tomorrow. I have been around with Sheik a great deal and he knows everybody, which is a tremendous help. A friend, Ralph Collins from Canada, goes round to the coloured Musician's Union about 3 times a week, and most everyone comes in there.

I hope to record with Kid Thomas' band next Sunday at a party at Sammy Penn's house, he is the drummer.

Yesterday Ralph, Bill Russell and I saw two parades and a funeral, all in the one day. There was the Gibson Band, which is non-union playing a parade to the old Economy Hall, which is now a Baptist Church. Then a couple of blocks away John Casimir's Young Tuxedo struck up with Jim Crow and Albert Warner on trombones, John on clarinet (E*b*), and Kid Howard , trumpet, they went past the church which had a garden party on the lawn. During this time Picou tuned up and was raving around in the garden. The Gibson band came past the gate and stopped and blew right at the Tuxedo, that was really something. Louis Keppard, at 69, was running around taking pictures.

We then drove out to Algiers and picked up the Eureka way out on a dirt road, playing *West Lawn Dirge*. And the way Manuel Paul played the sax part was just like the record. Manuel incidentally plays with Kid Thomas, raves all the time! Eddie Pierson replaced Albert Warner on trombone, otherwise it was the same with Percy Humphrey, Willie Pajaud, & Sheik on trumpets.

Afterwards we went round to the Union and had a blow with Sheik and some fabulous guitar player. Manuel Manetta dropped in and played piano.

I did a broadcast with the Almerico band over CBS and it was a whole lot of fun. They gave me two choruses solo in *Panama*. That band really can swing; much better than Sharkey or any of those other Bourbon Street Bands.

Bill Russell's address is 600 Chartres Street. Alvin Alcorn is sitting in with the Bill Matthews Band and we shall go along there tonight, as he certainly changes that band!

The Pierson Band, which is Celestin's old group, have asked me to ride up in their bus to an Air Force Base in Alabama on Wednesday. I heard the band at the Steamer job at the Poydras Street Wharf. I think that you would remember that, and it really is excellent. As a matter in passing, New Orleans as a whole, and the Vieux Carré in particular, is the most perverted place I have ever seen. There are more homos, lesbians, cripples, beggars and other weird characters, than ordinary people. (But no old bags!!)

I am glad that you have Ray Foxley, we did a little session with him at your club last year, as I lap up the Jelly Roll style and he really can play.

All the best Ken, From Peter

P.S. I am taking lessons from George Guesnon and he really is a slave driver. His price for two lessons is a pint of whiskey!!

P.P.S. Hope you can read all this!!

MIKE SLATTER LETTER TO KEN COLYER 27 NOVEMBER 1957

158 East 70th Street, New York.
Dear Ken,

My apologies for not having written for so long, but I have been making plans to move down to New Orleans not just for a visit but permanently. As I think I told you before, I had intended to pay a visit at Christmas time. Now I have decided to quit my present job in January and without having anything definite, to arrive in New Orleans and start looking for a job there. From the enquiries that I have made, it should not be too difficult to find something suitable. My friends down there will no doubt be of considerable help. Anyway I will keep you posted and notified of any change in plans. It's a big decision and I just hope it works out. If you have the time you might drop me a line telling me what you think of the idea. I have been hoping to hear that your trip to the States is going ahead, what chance is there now of its coming off?

I would be interested to hear if you have heard from Sam Charters and whether he has sent you the Red Book. I will be writing him in a day or so to let him know I am on my way down to New Orleans.

Little of interest has happened here in the past few months, though I have heard both Turk Murphy and Wilbur De Paris, neither of whom impressed me very much I'm afraid. **Their music seems to me to be sterile and uninspired. I**

think that this can be accounted for by the poor quality of the U.S. audiences who come to hear and expect to hear a noise. The louder the noise the better. I feel the places in which the musicians play has a lot to do with it too. Mostly they play in bars, where the attention of the audience is far too easily distracted. The whole attitude of the public is too casual and they do not come to hear jazz at all. In New York at least the musicians do very well and for that reason their music suffers. They try to put on a spectacle which is what people want and therefore what they get. I find the whole thing rather discouraging I'm afraid.

Being in New Orleans I should be able to make a few tape recordings and I will certainly try. I wish you could be persuaded to get John Reddinghough to make some further recordings of the band. Decca do it an injustice by not making more records and anyway the standard of their recordings is very low in my opinion.

I hope that all goes well with you Ken and that you will find time to drop me a line or two. Remember me to all the boys and let's have some more of that wonderful music. I will be taking the recordings that I made down to New Orleans with me when I go and I will make sure that they receive a good hearing.

All the best Ken, Yours, Mike

WALTER EYSSELINCK LETTER TO KEN COLYER 1 DECEMBER 1957

My Dear Ken,

No, I can't wait any longer—damn the work, but I have to write to you first. The reason why I didn't get in touch with you earlier (besides loads of work, acting, and my new play, called *Poor Butterfly* after Bunk's moving version of it) is that I have had so much material which I hoped to turn into a few articles for your, and possibly another, jazz magazine. I intend to get this done during the Xmas when I move back to the remote quietness and the snow(?) of Vermont. While I was in New York, earlier in September I heard most of the traditional and "would-be" traditional bands that were in the city. It's amazing how few people know anything about their own music in this country, and how carelessly they listen to it. Poor musicians—I saw people like Hank Duncan and Cliff Jackson playing during intermissions, nobody listening. The audiences are so bad—aren't you lucky back in Great Newport Street. Although so many things keep me very happy I really wished I could fly over and spend Xmas with you, Delphine, the band, and our mutual jazz loving friends—just like last year.

The worst place, if we leap back to N Y for a while, is the Metropole. I don't care much for someone like Hawkins personally, yet it pains me to see a great man like him forced to play for a bunch of idiots who only drop in to drink and shout for noise, more noise, and another *When The Saints*. Buster Bailey told me that they (lined up above the bar like a preview of a circus) are forced by the management and the customers to play

so loudly that they can't even hear each other. Imagine people like that sensitive Buster Bailey, Higginbotham, Zutty, and even lesser gods like Tony Parenti, Louis Metcalf have to sell their music in a place like that. No pity for that screaming Red Allen—he seems to enjoy vulgar noise and cheap showmanship—plenty of it. And yet there are some moments of fine music, even there.

I was happily surprised when I heard Turk Murphy's band. They sound much better than on record: they—particularly Turk himself—take their music seriously and although their approach isn't ours, one must admire their stubborn idealism in a musical jungle like this one. Some of their sessions were really good and I particularly liked Turk himself and Lammi on banjo. The one exciting place, I think, is Jimmie Ryan's where the De Paris Brothers are playing, with Omer Simeon and Lee Blair—oh, isn't he great! This again isn't exactly the sound I've been longing to hear, but it's so virile, so fresh and original. Simeon, Lee, Wilbur and Sidney really are a well of information for me.

The men do hope to get a chance of playing at the Brussels World Exhibition and it would certainly be one of the most sincere and homogeneous New Orleans bands America could send us—except, of course, our Crescent City Saints we've been worshipping for such a long time.

How I long to get to New Orleans. I shall definitely spend all of next Summer there—I'll get in touch with the people you mentioned—I bought a decent tape recorder—so let's hope.

Blame your own music, the Club Session I just HAD to buy to convince some of my American friends, if this letter turns out to be too incoherent.

Yes, record hunting provides you with another example of how the American public reacts to jazz. I've been to dozens and dozens of places in New York and elsewhere. **Can you believe that in all of these shops, except for one or two (one actually had a few very interesting things) they had never heard of a label called American Music?**

Have you heard the Bill Matthews band on one of the GTJ albums recorded in New Orleans? Very much like the Celestin on Bandwagon, Excellent Burbank (I found a few 78's which have Burbank and Lee Collins, others Herb Morand)—great Matthews and astonishingly good Cagnolatti (much better than in his session with Barbarin). I've never been too fond of Barbarin but his sides in this set rank about the finest things he recorded—the rhythm doesn't sound as heavy and stilted for a change. Pleasant Sharkey—one good Johnny Wiggs side out of three—rather poor Girard—Pierson's band... well... all right; the clarinet (Humphrey) spoils a great deal—the rest insignificant. But where are people like Kid Thomas and Barnes in all this? Have you had a chance to hear the Folkways album of recent recordings of the Memphis Jug Band, their music I still find very exciting. I've met a friend who has a very large collection of early records from which I'll be taping down a lot, jug bands etc, (P.T.O. again)

Handwritten: Ken, don't treat me the way I've treated you—

please write soon. Have you recorded anything of late. Could you please send me a copy. I'll send you any A.M. record you want. Give my kindest regards to the band and everybody, particularly John and Bill. Tell him I'm writing very soon. Have a nice Xmas. By the way, you never mentioned the new Colyer's name! Bye for now—lots of love to you and Del.

(signed) Walter

RAY JACKSON LETTER TO KEN COLYER 12 DECEMBER 1957

820 North Karlow, Chicago, Ill.
Dear Ken,

At last I got around to answering your very welcome letter. Glad you found my news on the jazz situation here of interest. Of course Brunies is still playing the most wonderful trombone. Although he clowns around a lot and is almost as good a comedian as a jazz man, he can still prove he is "king of the tailgate" any time he likes. He has now left his club up on the North Side and has been playing in The Loop for the last 6 weeks or so. Unfortunately the group he has there is not so good. He leaves on tour shortly. I believe he goes first to Las Vegas.

Too bad about the tour of the USA falling through, it must have been very disappointing for you and your band. And of course it would have been great for me to meet you and the boys out here.

I must tell you of a benefit I went to out here in aid of Big Bill at the K.A.M. temple, which turned out to be a synagogue on Drexel Ave well into the South-Side. I wasn't even aware that Bill had been ill. A letter was read out at the concert, that was sent from London by Lyn Dutton, so I suppose you were all aware of his illness. He must have many friends here in Chicago as the place was packed out and people had to be turned away before the concert could get under way. It was just about the most wonderful musical experience I have ever had.

You will realize just how wonderful when I tell you that the performers included such amazing artists as Mahalia Jackson & Little Brother Montgomery—who treated us to a rolling version of *Pinetops Boogie* that had the audience spell-bound.

Also we had Sunnyland Slim who I had never heard of before but he sung and played some down to earth vocalising with piano.

A most amazing woman singer, Odetta, gave us some Leadbelly-style blues and songs. She has a most masculine and powerful voice and has been appearing here recently at the Gate of Hope. **But the singer who had everybody eating his every word was Pete Seeger. I had no idea he was such a magnetic personality.** He sung a wonderful song to the tune of *Oranges and Lemons* about the working conditions in Wales as sung by the Church Bells in most of the Cathedrals of that land. He told us that he found the poem and fit it to the tune. I am hoping to get a recording of some of these things. It is difficult for me to convey my reactions to this sort of thing in a letter, but I hope to tell you about it when I return to England in the summer.

Thanks very much for your information on New Orleans. I have decided now to work through until April and then when the weather is better I shall start travelling. Just now the climate is pretty grim here, the temperature has been down to zero the last two nights and we are to expect worse before the winter is over.

The employment situation is not as good as it might be here. There are more unemployed now in the U.S.A. than since 1949 and it said that the figure will be up to 4 million by February. If I do get fired from my job I shall be home before the summer. If there is going to be another depression I would rather have mine in England.

I don't doubt that I shall have difficulty making myself understood in New Orleans—it is bad enough here in Chicago. When one lives in London most of the time one is apt to think that Cockney is some sort of unnatural language. When I first arrived here I thought people would understand me better if I spoke with an Oxford accent so I did my best to do a George Sanders. But this was no good at all. I thought I was doing O.K. until one day I asked for a pork-chop and got a bowl of chilli! But I thought it was the limit when some old bastard who has been an elevator driver for over 50 years—where I work, told me "Why don't you speak English!!" Of course most people understand you immediately down in the Loop. And the strange thing is most coloured people understand every word you say.

But all you get from these Clerk St. bums when you ask them for something is a very curious look as if you had just come down from Mars. I had to repeat the word "knife" three times in a restaurant this evening before I got one, even then some other cook had to act as interpreter. Hope that your band is still intact and that everything is going OK for you. Looking forward to hearing that sound at the 51 on my return,

All the Best, (signed) Ray Jackson

LIZZIE MILES LETTER TO KEN COLYER 21 DECEMBER 1957

N.O. La.
Merry Christmas and Happy New Year Ken. Received your letter, always happy to hear from you. These planes are travelling so fast these days that a letter gets to Europe fast as it takes me from here to Calif. Well I have no kick cause I am not working cause when I work I get a nice salary so I can afford to work now and then. I did a TV show Sept. 29/57 called *Crescendo* paid me $1000 so I don't have to work every nite but I like to sing and then the more I sing, well the better my voice. Laying off I get rusty. Got another big TV N.B coming up in N.O. but it don't pay as much as N.O. is a very cheap place for talent. You get more money anywhere than you do in N.O. **The States is gone with the wind. Every where the same. More places closing. I am told there is more and better dixieland in Europe than over here.** Do you hear many

of my records over there? Have you come across the one I made at the Hangover Club with Joe Robichaux and George Lewis. Tell me all the records you hear of me over there, won't you please? I didn't re-sign with [the label] so I'm not making for any due. Did you like Rosetta Tharpe.

Do you think I could get placed, me and Joe, in a couple like for intermission. I need a steady job, no one nite stands. Gunter Bras used to write me all the time, he don't write any more. Did he used to run a club in Frankfurt? I hear Spencer Williams the author of *Basin St. Blues* [missing text—Ed]. Well if you don't get to the States I don't think you will be missing anything.

Got a Christmas card from Lee Collins the trumpet player who was dying with TB. He's doing alright. He's home from the hospital. Geo. is not doing anything much here. The union ought to stop these people making tapes of you while you're working then make them into records and you get nothing. Names is all they want whether they can do something or not and most of them don't do nothing. And they want you to pack and jam a place and don't give you a chance to check any publicity. Advertise some cheap way and expect you to draw.

Bourbon St. has got nothing but strippers. Sharkey is the best thing on the Street and I don't think his band is a Dixieland band like he'd like to have. Tony's band is gone with the wind. There's a little 15 year old boy from the country has 'em all beat. Plays Dixieland like Louis and George Girard. He can play, but he can't work yet in any place just as a guest. Merry Christmas to all [missing text—Ed] again some time,

(signed) Lizzie Miles

MIKE SLATTER LETTER TO KEN COLYER 27 DECEMBER 1957

New Orleans,
Dear Ken,

Thank you for your last letter that I received just before leaving New York. I was very sorry indeed that you too cannot be here in New Orleans, but perhaps it will be possible before long. Well I've lots of news and hope that I shall be able to get some more tapes of both the Eureka and Kid Thomas. Sam Charters has some more tapes available and I hope to be able to send them with the help of John Bernard. Keep your fingers crossed anyway. It certainly is wonderful to be here again, my passion for New Orleans grows more intense with every stay. It must be simply a matter of time before I get down here for good. You were quite right about George Lewis—he was here visiting his Mother for Christmas and I went over to her place on Dauphine and St. Philip with Bill Russell. George was pleased to hear of your recent concert success and I gave him your best wishes. He left yesterday for the West Coast again, but I was very happy to have finally caught up with him.

Bill Matthews and the boys are still appearing nightly at the Paddock, except on Tuesday nights when Kid Howard and his band hold a session there. Jim Robinson is still with Kid Howard.

Down the street at the Dream Room Sharkey is playing and at Pier 600 Paul Barbarin is doing a great job. Incidentaly, Paul is very interested in the possibility of a band exchange with you. I will keep in touch with him and suggest that he writes to you to see what can be done. I shall make a further effort to see Herman Deutsch to remind him of his promise to help you get back to the U.S. I talked to Percy Humphrey yesterday and am just hoping that someone will obligingly die before I go back to New York so that we shall have a funeral. There is a parade next Sunday and John Casimir and the Tuxedo Brass Band will be providing the music.

On Saturday night and possibly on New Years Eve I shall go to the Moulin Rouge to hear Kid Thomas. Mahalia Jackson has been doing some very powerful and beautiful church singing which has moistened many eyes.

I hear that Lizzie Miles is doing very well and has been offered an engagement in Alaska at $700 per week. Lawrence Marrero is still in town and I hope to hear him, possibly this evening. There is to be an informal session and Punch Miller will be on trumpet with Louis James on bass. Who the other musicians will be remains to be seen. I hope to write you a more detailed report of Christmas in New Orleans together with a few pictures so that you may be able to use some of the material for your advertising or something like that. By the way, if I do get some more tapes you must be very careful not to let them fall into the hands of anyone else. Apparently the union got wind of the last one I sent you and Percy Humphrey was afraid that there might be trouble—still all should be OK if you are discreet.

As regards the two numbers whose names you wanted to know, the dirge apparently has no name, it is simply known as *Number 51*. I believe the other one you refer to is a spiritual called *Sweet Fields* but I can't be SURE it's that one you refer in your letter. This will certainly be the most memorable Christmas that I will ever remember and one that I shall never forget. Well I've five more days and I will try and drop you another line before I leave. Best wishes and all success in 1957,

Yours (signed) Michael Slatter

MIKE SLATTER LETTER TO KEN COLYER 28 JANUARY 1958

158 East 70th Street, New York.
Dear Ken,
At last I can confirm what I told you in my last letter. I am

leaving New York on February 28th for New Orleans. I have resigned from my present job and only hope that I will be able to find something suitable when I get settled. I will write and let you know my new address.

Although I have been watching the listing of new records, I have so far seen no mention of your Omega Band record, I hope that it will be available soon as I know that many of the boys in New Orleans will be interested to hear the band.

Sam Charters has moved to California, and I am enclosing a letter that I have just received from him. His address is:

2213-11th Avenue, Sacramento 18, California.

You might let me know if you have been able to get a copy of his skiffle record, if not I will arrange for someone to bring it over to you. I am hoping that it will be possible for me to get further recordings of the Eureka Brass Band and all the others, but it may take me a little time to get the confidence of the boys, as there have been attempts to exploit them in the past. At least I can count on the help of Bill Russell, so we will see what can be done.

Do make a special effort to make same good live tapes of the band, as I hope that I will be able to get some time on one of the New Orleans Radio Stations. I would like to do a programme on "Foreign Jazz," provided I can interest someone. It may sound over ambitious, but you never know. It may be several weeks after my arrival in New Orleans that you hear from me, as I am anxious to find work as soon as possible. If I can, I will try to find somewhere in the French Quarter to live. It is pretty central and not too expensive.

Perhaps I will be able to do something to help you to make another trip to the Crescent City. We must give the idea some serious thought. I hear that Lyttelton may be coming over here, but nothing definite so far.

See what you can do about some more tapes Ken. As I suggested before, it would be easy for you to hire a good recording machine for about a pound a day. All you need then is a few reels of tape and a competent operator.

That's it for now Ken, as you can imagine, I am very much looking forward to the Holy of Holies. You can be sure that I will keep you informed of all happenings there.

Best Wishes, look forward to hearing from you,
Yours, (signed) Mike

DOROTHY TAIT LETTER TO KEN COLYER 3 FEBRUARY 1958

Dear Ken

It seems as though all I do is write apologies (when I finally do write) for not having written before! Things have been confused and upsetting as far as the band and George's health is concerned.

You've probably talked with Peter Deuchar since he returned—and know that George had another blood clot in his leg during his convalescence from pneumonia. I'm almost positive that occurred before Peter left New Orleans. After that he appeared to be getting along very well indeed. Then he caught cold, and we're on the merry-go-round again.

I had a letter from the BMU querying about the tour. I wrote them exactly what had happened. It was a very nice, understanding letter, by the way—they were quite understandably upset, but very courteous and British about it!

His first real engagement was two weeks ago—a recording date, and a five day date at a club in Chicago. The morning after they closed at the club he had a hell of an attack of emphysema— we had to rush a doctor up there to the hotel, and he had to have intravenous injections of aminophylline to get him breathing again. Yesterday I talked with him long distance—he seems to be doing well, but his doctor in N.O. to whom he reported immediately found that he was very anaemic and is going to stick needles full of liver and vitamins into his frail frame twice a week to try and build him up.

Meanwhile, the Rev. Al. Kershaw is trying to plan a series of concerts in April in Eastern Colleges. How many I do not know. George is supposed to play a date in Columbus, Ohio, the first part of March—whether he can or not I don't know.

Yet—in Chicago that horn of his sounded as full of vitality and spirit and heart as though he'd never been sick a day in his life! Quite a guy, our little George!

Ken—what are your commitments for April? The last half. I have not written Paddy and won't until I hear from you.

Now—just between you and me and for no-one else's information—I KNOW George can't play any twelve concerts on the road. Unless by some miracle half of them were within half an hour or so of each other travel-wise. This is well nigh impossible. However, we discussed this situation in England and I know you understand that we may have to be a little devious.

By the time I hear from you Al. Kershaw may have definite word on whether or not he can swing these concerts—and I may know better about George's health.

If everything is going well—Al's plan and George's health— I'll write you a formal letter, with a carbon copy to the union and one to Paddy McKiernan, offering you the concerts.

IF YOU CAN'T MAKE IT IN APRIL—then it's possible (probable) that we'll be able to work some out later on. BUT I WANT TO GO ON RECORD AS HAVING OFFERED THE CONCERTS IN APRIL, if you can't make it, then WE'LL be free to take the concerts—and set some up for you at a later date. Savvy?

I wouldn't let George do a concert tour without protecting ourselves in that way. If you can't make it, we'll try later.

Whether we do them in April or later—we've got the whole business of visa application to go through again. Does this make you shudder as it does me? I thought we could just renew it. But no—the same process has to be gone thru again. Can you send me air mail the JACKET of one of your records? I had to have one before and had to have photostatic copies of it—but Norman Pierce, who gave it to me, wanted to keep it, and I have none.

Ken—I have some tapes of a concert here in Bakersfield that George gave a few years back—and access to about four hours of taped music the band made in Oxford, Ohio—(Miami University). He's signed with Norman Granz and we shouldn't release them here. I think some British Company might jump at the chance—tho' believe me, they are not being given away. These tapes are the last recordings made with Big Jim Robinson, Lawrence Marrero, Kid Howard in the band. The last.

Some day they'll be worth a tremendous amount. But I'm not interested in making money for George Lewis' Estate—I'm interested in having George reap some of the benefits from them now, while he can enjoy them.

Do you have any suggestions? Am writing to several people over there. Someplace along the line I may get a nibble.

How is Delphine—and the future greatest British cornetist with the distinguished middle name? Congratulations to you.

My very, very best to the gentlemen of the ensemble. In Chicago, when George and I were reminiscing about England I jokingly suggested he might consider living there after his Mother is gone and Shirley perhaps married. Do ya know he took me seriously—and said "there's no place I'd rather live. Those were the happiest days of my life when I was playing over there with Ken." And he meant every word of it.

All for now. Can you get back to me fairly soon?

Very best wishes to you, Delphine, the boys in the band, and every one in the British Isles.

Sincerely, (signed) Dorothy

Write me at: Post Office Box 3042, Bakersfield, Calif.

KEN COLYER [*from the sleeve notes for KC LP1, a recording from the 1957 tour*] I have just been listening to these recordings after 30 years. I have never listened to my own records for pleasure, I am too self-critical and can only hear what is wrong, and what could be improved on, so it was a pleasant surprise to hear so many good moments captured, that were also in safe hands.

Mike Slatter was the man responsible.

He was an ardent fan and was more aware than I that as much of this music as possible must be preserved.

Tape machines weren't readily available in those days, and few people owned one in our circle. Mike would rent machines at every opportunity and record what he could, wherever we were playing. I now realise his endeavors paid huge dividends. He has captured more great moments than are on any studio session. Some of this music will come as a tremendous surprise to you, as it did to me, and fill the air with a joyous sound.

One evening as we were setting up at Eel Pie Island Hotel and all was quiet I said to the boys, "This is as close as you will get to New Orleans in England, the atmosphere and feel is here, I have never experienced it so strongly anywhere else."

The Hotel had run to seed, its heyday long gone, when it was a famous and favourite place for people to go in the summer, to relax by the Thames and enjoy themselves and partake of the Eel pies which gave the island its name.

It took on a new lease of life for a few years when a jazz club was established there, and people flocked to hear the good music. It was dark and dingy, nobody bothered much to take their glasses back to the bar, but a fellow used to go around once the crowd were in, with a large wicker basket and a torch, taking them back to the bar. This is the only place I have ever seen this happen.

I have said before that playing hot New Orleans music is like walking a tightrope, you daren't slip, but the odd slips are bound to happen. They are worth taking the risks for though, and it is far more rewarding than playing the cardboard music that passes for jazz.

Jazz is a small club music, always was and always will be. Though a band may play well in concert it will rarely build the atmosphere that it can achieve in a club that is conducive to the music. It doesn't matter with cardboard music but it is vitally important to the creation of good music.

This band is considered by many to be the best I ever had. This is possibly true but I have always striven to get the best out of the men around me and get a good unit sound. The boys I have here (two unfortunately dead now, Johnny Bastable and Mac Duncan) were together for quite a long spell.

This is important, for what sometimes seems casual is the result of working and developing together.

The short but beautiful session with George Lewis is another story.

We drove straight from the 51 Club, Great Newport Street, London, W1 after finishing the session to Manchester Airport as George was coming in on an early morning plane and we wanted to be there to greet him before commencing the now famous tour. This was his first time in England. The arrival time kept getting delayed but when the airport manager discovered what all the people were waiting for (there were also musicians and fans from Manchester and elsewhere) he was very cooperative.

When the plane's arrival was definite he allowed us to set up by a hangar.

He must have radioed the pilot as the plane stopped by the hangar, and George and his manager were allowed to disembark, the plane then taxied off to its usual stopping place.

Though it was a dismal morning, we brightened it up with a couple of rousing numbers and George was delighted.

The only opportunity for a quick rehearsal was that afternoon so we got to the hotel and grabbed a couple of hours sleep.

I found a pub that would allow us to use their small upstairs room for a couple of hours.

I can't remember who suggested that it would be a good idea to tape the rehearsal solely as a memento but I sent Ian Wheeler off to try and find somewhere where he could hire a machine for the two hours.

We started playing and it went from the word go, everybody was enjoying themselves.

After a couple of numbers George said, "We don't need no rehearsal we're musicians."

I knew that, but I also knew that that was the only chance we had of a quiet get together.

Poor Ian had had a terrible time trying to locate a machine.

He had finally succeeded but there was only a half hour left and we had to vacate the room.

As I said, I had not heard these four numbers for so long I had forgotten how good they were.

I would go so far as to say, never has the New Orleans sound and all that goes to make it, been captured so well by six white Europeans and one New Orleanian who was one of the finest clarinetists who ever lived.

There is every danger that this timeless music in a few years' time will be gone forever, except on record.

DOROTHY TAIT LETTER TO PADDY McKIERNAN 19 FEBRUARY 1958

1630 First Street, Bakersfield, California
To: Mr. Paddy McKiernan, 30 Heaton Moor Rd., Stockport, Cheshire, England
Dear Paddy,

You cannot realise how great my pleasure is in being able to offer you at this time the long-deferred concert tour for Ken Colyer.

Ken with Jim Robinson

Before I go into details, I want to express our deep gratitude and appreciation to you and the British Musicians Union for your patience and understanding during this very trying period.

While George's health is by no means robust even yet—we are planning a tour of Eastern Colleges with the Rev A.L. Kershaw, with the first concert scheduled for April 15. There is the possibility of an earlier starting date (April 8), but it would be Ken's choice as to which date he preferred to start on. At present let us leave it at April 15.

Details of venues etc. will be forthcoming a little later. The schedule is still in the process of revisions and additions.

I am assuming that it will be proper for us to stipulate that this tour is being offered under the terms and conditions of the previous agreement which we were unable to live up to at the time because of George Lewis' physical condition.

A copy of this letter will be sent to Mr. Harry Francis of the British Musician's Union, who has been most understanding and tolerant during the past months.

I will communicate with Ken Colyer immediately regarding the steps it is necessary for him to take in order to procure another visa.

Again, our thanks to you, and with kindest personal regards,
Cordially yours, (signed) Dorothy F. Tait,
Representative, THE GEORGE LEWIS JAZZ BAND
Please address reply to: P.O. Box 3042, Bakersfield, California
c.c.: James C Petrillo, Mr. Harry Francis, Ken Colyer

P.O.Box 3042, Bakersfield, California
Wednesday, February 19, 1958
Mr. Harry Francis, Musicians Union, 29 Catherine Place,
Buckingham Gate, London, S.W.1, England
Reciprocal Exchange: George Lewis-Ken Colyer
Dear Mr. Francis,

The enclosed carbon copies of letters mailed today to Mr. Paddy McKiernan and Mr. Ken Colyer are self-explanatory.

If you will recall, in my last letter I said that George Lewis was taking a five-day date in Chicago in January—his first engagement of more than one night since his return from England. I asked your further indulgence until we could see how his health stood up under the engagement.

He did not do too well and was forced to refuse an extension of the engagement because of an attack of emphysema. Since then he has been under treatment for persistent accumulation of fluid in his lungs, a result of his pneumonia last fall, and his cardiac condition.

However, his doctor has stated that in all probability the intense cold we ran into in Chicago was mainly the cause of the attack, and has given guarded approval to a concert tour in April.

Consequently, we are now in a position to offer Ken Colyer the long-deferred tour. My letter, copy of which is enclosed, to Mr. McKiernan will give you the details.

It is difficult for me to find adequate words to express our gratitude to you, and to everyone concerned, for your patience and understanding.

I have told Mr. McKiernan that I am assuming it will be proper for us to stipulate that this tour is being offered under the terms and conditions of the previous agreement.

Again-our thanks and appreciation to you.
With kindest regards,
Sincerely yours, (signed) Dorothy F. Tait,
Representative, The George Lewis Jazz Band
c.c. Mr. James Petrillo

DOROTHY TAIT LETTER TO KEN COLYER 19 FEBRUARY 1958

THE GEORGE LEWIS JAZZ BAND
1630 First Street, Bakersfield, California
To: *Mr. Ken Colyer, 99 The Drive, Hounslow, Middlesex,*
England
Dear Ken,

The two enclosed carbon copies of letters to Paddy McKiernan and Mr. Harry Francis of the British Musician's Union are self-explanatory.

You'll note that I told Paddy McKiernan that there is a possibility of some concerts preceding the New England tour—and if they come through and you prefer to come over a little earlier you could participate in them. These would be during the week of April 17.

However, for the time being we must proceed on the basis of the first concert falling on April 15, at Dartmouth College, in Hanover, New Hampshire. Details of the concerts to follow that will be forthcoming soon.

I see no reason at this time why you should not be in the clear for a May 1 engagement back in England. We are arranging the concerts in such a way that they will fall as close together as possible, geographically, so as to place the minimum of strain on George.

As you can well understand, Ken—after the series of disasters that have befallen us during the past year, I'm a little jittery. The doctor has given guarded approval of these dates for George, urging, however, that they be planned for a period of milder weather. It was the intense cold, the doctor believes, which resulted in our difficulties with George in Chicago.

If it all goes well, the tour should prove very interesting for you—it will be in a lovely part of our country, New England—and with us will be the Rev. A.L. Kershaw, our Episcopal minister who has won international fame in traditional jazz fields.

He is, incidentally, the chaplain of our band. I wonder if we're the only band in the world with a chaplain!

Will write you in more detail about applying for a new visa, et cetera. How good it will be to welcome you on this side of the Atlantic!

And—thanks, Ken, for your understanding and sympathy during these past months! With best wishes to the boys in the band, to Delphine—and to the newest Colyer! [Russell]

Sincerely (signed) Dorothy Tait
Box 3042—Bakersfield—Calif

Monday
Dear Ken

You've probably been anxiously awaiting this letter, after my last one. However, I don't mind saying that after all the tragic events of the past months I'm jittery—and I wait until I had a definite confirmation from Al Kershaw in Boston—and also dates. Altho I was confident it was OK when I wrote you and Paddy and the BMU. Still—

So, to recap:

Either the jacket of one of your records, or three photostatic copies of a jacket showing biographical notes about you. Air Mail.

Any newspaper clipping you may have about yourself—three copies of one clipping would be perfect. Air Mail. Check with American Consulate on exactly what steps to take, and ascertain if you must once again file Form Eye 2-12. And—God willing—we'll be saying, "Welcome to the USA" before too long!

Just keep your fingers crossed for George.

Very best regards and wishes to all—I wish that you, Delphine, the baby—and all those nice guys George calls "my boys" could come too!

Cordially, (signed) Dorothy

P.S. When you go to the U.S. Consulate take my previous letter with you as proof of employment.

DELPHINE COLYER It wasn't the music really. I had what they now call post-natal depression, and I just couldn't take anymore. It was a hard decision really. We were destroying each other.

We used to have long periods—like two or three days—when we didn't speak to each other. We'd still go down to the club together, and we'd still eat together... That is, provided I made steak and kidney pudding.

Dear Ken

Have been anxiously awaiting word from you—here's the dope: Tomorrow—Monday, March 10, I leave for Boston. Am stopping in Chicago briefly but will be in Boston on Wednesday.

If there is a letter from you—or the Photostats—en route to me now, they will be forwarded to me the day they arrive, and I'll get them fairly soon.

If, however, you send them after you receive this letter—here's my itinerary: From March 18 until March 29

Broad Lincoln Hotel, East Broad at Jefferson Streets, Columbus, Ohio.

One reason I am going to Boston is to take care of this visa business personally.

Have had no word from Paddy either, and will write him this same information. I suppose to satisfy the union and the labour ministry I'll have to dream up an extra concert or so! Or eight or nine! We lost out on any dates the first week in April because of Holy Week and Easter—all colleges closed . So the first one is on April 16 at Brown University, very near to Boston.

I will let you know where I will be after March 29, so you can notify me when you are coming and how, etc! This is brief, but want you to be sure and have it in ample time.

The best as always (signed) Dorothy

A cable sent to me here after I've left probably would never reach me...

MIKE SLATTER LETTER TO KEN COLYER
UNDATED

98 East 70th Street, New York
Sixty One Broadway, New York 6 N.Y.
Dear Ken,

I have heard indirectly that you run into trouble with the U.S.Embassy concerning your visa. Now I shall be going down to Washington on March 29th for the weekend and if you think that I could do anything to help please let me know right away. From my own experience I know just how difficult the immigration authorities can be and the sooner you can sort out your differences with them the better. Presumably this set back will delay your arrangements for an exchange with George Lewis which will be a big disappointment to everyone.

Ralston Crawford is leaving for England on March 20th and it is possible that he may be able to help in some way. I will discuss things fully with him before he leaves. He expects to be in London for about ten days before continuing on to the continent where he will remain until August. He intends to make his way back to the States via London and you will probably see him again in August or September. My own plans have been carried a step further, though unfortunately the New Orleans job with the Consulate is off.

I intend to come over to London in two or three months' time for about two or three weeks and hope to hear plenty of that great music.

> I have promised my friends in New Orleans to obtain some tapes of the band to bring back with me. As they have been so generous I would hate to let them down and am determined that no union or recording company will prevent me from taping one or two sessions.

My own equipment is far too heavy to bring with me and I propose to hire the best that is available in London.

I hope that I can count on your support as it means a great deal to all of us over here. **If you can see your way to turning a blind eye I'm sure we could make some very worthwhile recordings. If Studio 51 is too public a place, we could perhaps do an equally good job at one of your out of town appearances.** We must do everything possible to overcome all the difficulties. I feel that this is something very important. It is a tragedy of the first order that Decca is preserving so little of the music, almost none in fact.

I feel so strongly about it that I am prepared to deal with risk and expense and will certainly ensure that the music is kept alive for all time.

I may have mentioned in an earlier letter that I have bought a

▶ 238

A SON'S PERSPECTIVE

AN INTERVIEW WITH
RUSSELL COLYER

WHEN I WAS A VERY LITTLE BOY he would come when I went to bed. I wouldn't get a story read to me, he would play his guitar and lullaby me to sleep in my little lime-green box at The Drive. Everything at The Drive was mainly green: Even when they bought me a racing bike once for Christmas—it was hidden in the front room—it was lime green. I never lost that bike—couldn't lose it anywhere; it stuck out a bit!

On Mondays, after a weekend of gigging, I suppose, it would be up to Kew Gardens, and where the fairground used to be at Kew Bridge there was a little ferryboat across as well. And he would take me across on the ferryboat so he got his little kick going on a boat, and then I would play around on Kew Green there and he'd keep an eye out on me from the pub, and then a little walk around Kew Gardens, look at all the plants and that sort of thing. But as a little boy, you're more interested in charging around and just being a little boy, really.

But that was our once-a-week little treat—I suppose that was his wind-down as well, from being up all hours of the morning to go and have a nice walk around the park and then back on the bus.

IT WASN'T A NORMAL CHILDHOOD, GROWING UP, obviously, with Delphine going when I was very young and Vera [Ramshaw] then coming—she came as the housekeeper to begin with and then became the mother to me and she still is. I think he would have gone off the rails a lot earlier if it hadn't been for Vera, because dinner was always there even if it was three or four o'clock in the morning. His favourite was braised oxtail, 'cause it could sit for hours—the longer it sat, the better it got. So she looked after him a lot, especially when there wasn't a lot of work. She'd be working at Woolworth's, bringing her wage in—it all came into the household, really. I didn't really used to see that much of him because I was around in the daytime and he'd be working all night and he'd come down at five o'clock in the afternoon and we'd have the family dinner then he'd be off to a gig somewhere and come home at whatever hour, then I'd be up and off to school, so we didn't really spend a lot of father-and-son time together.

I first heard him play, I suppose, when he used to do the parades down Hounslow High Street. I used to sit on the floats and collect the money in the early sixties, during the CND period. The only indication I got of his stomach cancer would be when he would be moaning about the poor treatment, how they got it wrong and what had happened afterwards.

Then there would be the riverboat shuffles that used to go down to Margate. We'd all get off the boat and me and my cousin Robbie would go to a little funfair. We used to go and run around and play there. Then I remember one, when we went to Marlow from Windsor. They pulled up at Marlow, where the big green is, and they wouldn't let them tie the boat up on the side where the green was—they said "Moor it on the other side." I remember the Old Man getting a pint glass and just jumping into the river and they all jumped in and just swam across and all went into the pub. Thank you, Marlow Council! I think they manoeuvred the boat back, 'cause they'd been in the pub a couple of hours.

I used to go up the 51 Club quite a bit. Pat and Vi—one big lady and one little lady. I was a little boy looking up at everybody dancing around having a good time.

They would set up the instruments and then they always used to go over to the Porcupine opposite for a quick livener before. And I used to sit and crash around on Colin Bowden's drums. He showed me how to do the snare drum. I'd sit there bashing around, then they'd come back and it would all start, and then I used to run around and collect all the Coca-Cola bottles up and mingle around, really. I would have been up quite late for a kid. It must have been a Saturday, as it wouldn't have been a day before school. Omar would be there with his microphones, recording away...

IT WAS QUITE A SEPARATED CHILDHOOD, REALLY, because the hours of work kept you apart. When I wanted to go and do something it would be: "Well you can't because he's just got in from driving back from god-knows-where." I got my pocket money—had to clean the Volkswagen band bus. Talk about passive smoking! Roll-ups everywhere—they used to buy St. Julien best and I'd clear up the debris in the back and wash it. I'd wax it, polish it—and got a couple of shillings for my pocket money.

Dad had his highs and lows: he liked a moan, but then if you had Morecambe and Wise on the television that'd be it, he'd be laughing—and at Monty Python. The only sport he really ever liked was golf—watching it on the TV. A lot of musicians, their real life doesn't start until they actually get on the stage. When they're on there, that's their life.

Other than the garden and things like that he really didn't have a lot of other interests other than the music. I wouldn't say he'd get embarrassed easily—you can't be that shy to get up

on the stage in front of a big crowd, or a small crowd. He remained on the path he did and others wanted the glamour side of it and financial rewards, maybe—to be up there on a pedestal.

> We didn't really have father/ son conversations ever, really. There was no real time for it— just growing up and schooling. If you imagine having someone, your father, on a permanent night-shift at the factory...

My tastes in music, naturally, were more modern, the newer things. His opinion of anything electric? Well, I used to have my collection of records when I was a teenager, and I

Ken and Russell

discovered once he'd thrown them on the floor and was stamping all over them!

They were all scratched and ruined. About the only time a modern record came into the house was *American Pie*. That was the only one I can remember as a modern record at the time; just the one—not an album of it.

So our relationship wasn't, "Sit down and let me talk to you, son," about the world or this-and-that. It was quite a distant one in a way. Even when we used to have parties he wouldn't be holding court; he'd just be there, really.

I used to be football mad. Once I was playing football in the garden and he said, "I'll have a kick around with you, son." I had a big, heavy leather football so I gave it a good stomp towards the kitchen door and he put up his hand to stop it. I was not in his good books for some time after that: It sprained his thumb and he couldn't play properly, so I was cursed!

I was growing up a bit more by then and getting a bit more mischievous. I used to have a big Frankenstein poster—it was 6 feet tall. One night I got it and and stuck it at the top of the stairs. In the dark at three o' clock in the morning all you heard was "@!#$#%*!"

It didn't stay at the top of the stairs for long.

BECAUSE OF COMING FROM THE COUNTRY IN THE first place, he believed that he knew country ways and that sort of thing. I came back from my grandparents in Somerset once and they gave me two ducks. Two ducks, live, on the train, in a box! So I got home: "What's in the box?" "Two ducks!" These ducks grew and grew. They were Muskovy ducks with big red beaks. We cleared out the old coal bunker—that's where they lived. They used to go wherever they wanted. They didn't really eat stuff in our garden; they used to clear off to other people's gardens, so we used to get a few complaints.

He said one day, "I'm sorry, son, we're gonna have to get rid of the ducks. They've got to go; I'm having too much trouble. Come with me, I'll show you the old way of wringing their necks." So off we went. One of the ducks was round there. They were tame. Maybe it expected to get some corn. He was wrestling with this duck—trying to get it round the neck. The other duck came round the corner, saw what was going on and leapt on his back and started pecking at his head.

They were rolling around by the coal bunker—Dad and the two Muskovy ducks! I was just sort of standing there and said, "This is how it goes, is it? This is how you wring their necks?"

After a bit of muttering he said, "We'll do it the other way." We had a very powerful airgun so he shot them—then he ate them! If he saw a wood pigeon or something like that around he'd say, "Go and shoot 'em and put 'em in the stewing-pot."

Then we used to have the grapevine, and someone kept nicking the grapes, so what did he do? He got a little bit of laxative and mixed it up and sprayed the grapes.

One year we had some new neighbours move in. We had a bit of trouble with them. He used to have a friend with a pig farm. Then a truck arrived with a huge amount of pig manure and it was placed in a big pile in the garden and the neighbours stopped being a pain. They just said, "Can you move that pile of shit?" and he said, "Can you stop being a nuisance?"

It was then scattered around the garden to fertilise his plants for the gardening he liked to do. We used to have a couple of greenhouses. He would often go down to the greenhouse—a bottle of gin, a bottle of tonic—sit down there, do a bit of practising. I remember on one occasion obviously he'd had a little too much gin and marched back up the garden, parade-style, playing because he'd found a new song!

WE WENT ON A FAMILY HOLIDAY TO PORTUGAL, down in the Algarve. We rented a little villa out in a little fishing cove. He was practising playing in the garden and a woman put her head over the fence, with this girl: "You must come down to the bar on the harbour front and play down there!"— an MP's daughter, the Tory Reginald Maudling. Within a week he'd formed a little band! That's the last family holiday I can remember.

I think maybe he took people's word too easily. If they told him something he was a bit too trusting in some ways. He always used to buy junk out of the newspapers, the new plasticky gimmicks—they'd obviously last two minutes and then break.

You'd see: "The revolutionary new tape recorder" etc. He was there to be consumed, really. If he was in the modern era, the cutthroat industry of these days, he'd have been gobbled up. He was still trying to live the original dream.

In the seventies there was always a beer or a drink around on a shuffle or in the 100 Club days. Around 1973, the time of the power strike, he'd sneak me around to the Coach and Horses in Hounslow —"I'll introduce you to beer"—so I'd be taken round there and then they used to have pint glasses with a bit of cardboard with a string into the cooking oil for a little light! It was very dingy during the power strike. It was fine by me, I didn't mind.

Family-type events? The only one we really used to have that I can remember was the annual fireworks night round Bob and Cathy's [brother and sister-in-law]—we always used to go round there. They'd have a good bonfire and fireworks and everything like that. At Christmas Ken used to carve the meat—Vera would do all the cooking. It wasn't a close family, by no means. Vera used to go and see Cathy and Ruby quite a lot but I don't remember Ruby hardly at all.

He wasn't a strict father. I could do as I please, really. He wasn't a disciplinarian or anything like that. When I was at the junior school he'd come over to the parents' evening and those sort of things. He even came to Sports Days a couple of times. We always used to go swimming once a week down to the Hounslow baths. He always had green Speedo swimming trunks, and when I didn't go swimming he'd still go. It was about the only exercise he really got. He used to do that on a regular basis.

THEN I MOVED TO THE SENIOR SCHOOL, SUDDENLY with big, rough boys at a comprehensive. Then he wanted me to learn guitar—to be a Spanish Flamenco player; "You will learn properly." But he relied on the educational system. The music teacher's favourite thing was to give you a quick whack with the hammer from a piano. Walking through the school with a guitar you just got bullied: "Poof! Blah, blah,blah!" But I was very good at football. Didn't like this guitar business, did not like it! Then one day I came home and made the announcement: "I'm not gonna do the guitar any more, I'm gonna play football," and that was it. Because of the way things were going at school I then found out that if you were good at sport you rose up through the ranks, and the guitar was put to one side—so I ended up playing football to a semi-professional standard.

I imagine my dad would have had quite a few connections if he'd wanted me to learn guitar in the proper way. He might have got me a real guitar teacher, like going for piano lessons. He

couldn't show me himself because he was left-handed. I was trying to read but he couldn't read music, so with a song-sheet it was very difficult.

It just went downhill then. I've met people since—hurtful in a way—who'd say, "Oh, I didn't even know you exist." It was almost as if I didn't. Then that just continued. We didn't used to talk or do anything really immediate—it was like people leading two separate lives in the house at the time. It didn't really help, either, because then at that time I'd strayed into the punk era. He didn't really appreciate me sitting at the dinner table with blue hair! He didn't really like that too much. It didn't go down well.

He did actually say, "Well, I took my part in my life and I made it my way—wherever he's gonna go, he will do it." So in the more influential years, when you're becoming a teenager, I wasn't given any assistance or guidance or poked in a direction even. At fifteen I know what I was going to do at school. Gerry White said, "Pipe fitter/welder, that's a great job." So my dad said, "Oh, well, he can go and do that." He did say, "Before your football or anything like that you can go and do an apprenticeship and get that behind you first"—which I did do.

BY THEN THERE WAS VERY LITTLE CONVERSATION. In the end I left home. I got a council flat and I moved out. In that time he didn't ever visit once, but I'd come home to visit Vera. He always used to moan about how cold the house was in

Ken swims at the Beaulieu Jazz Festival

The Drive—so a pipe fitter/welder puts pipes in! So I used to do the work on the building-site in the day and then go back to The Drive in the evenings and be installing central heating. Then he used to moan because it made so much noise doing it! But I put the whole house back together and it worked fine.

I don't think he really wanted me to follow in the jazz footsteps, but as a musician he thought I might have made it but, then again, he didn't put that much input into it. "You'll go to school, you'll go to the music teacher and you'll learn Flamenco guitar." But you're not gonna learn that off some second-rate comprehensive teacher.

We actually formed our own punk band—we played at Waterloo in a proper rehearsal room, but that slowly fizzled out—everybody drifted away. I think I would have done it anyway, whether I'd been Ken Colyer's son or not. Lots of kids did it anyway. I liked all the conventional bands like the Rolling Stones and all those sort of people, Rod Stewart—I think he came to the house once, many years ago. What Vera did tell me was, when the Beatles were first coming to town they wanted a spot to play at and they offered to pay off the Old Man not to play and they would take his Sunday spot—and he wouldn't have it...

Interview by Mike Pointon, June 3, 2010

fine old silver cornet which is said to date back to the civil war. I propose to bring it to London with me when I come and let you give it a try. I am told that it is an E♭ instrument and hope that that won't throw you.

Daily now I am hoping to receive that new record of yours—I wish those damned Decca people would get in the groove. I suppose they are too busy with Elvis Presley and people like that.

Well Ken that's about it for now. Don't forget to let me know if there's anything I can do to help.

All the best, (signed) Mike

DOROTHY TAIT LETTER TO KEN COLYER UNDATED 1958

Peterborough, New Hampshire
Dear Ken

Thank God you wrote that letter! No cable has come from Paddy, and I have been chewing my fingernails clear up to the elbow! First to get your travel arrangements (then the gee-tar and clothes).

I wrote to Paddy and asked him to book you into Boston on the 15th of April. Here's the reason: On April 13 the band will be blowing their little heads off in Cincinnati, Ohio. It is terrible to have you come and no one to meet you.

I dare not leave the band when it is on the road, because of the precarious condition of George's health. Things can happen so fast with him—ALSO, I am leery of this Cincinnati date and need to be there at its conclusion in the event of what George calls a "humbug"—and he is utterly unequipped to handle that type of fuss, especially now.

Can you call the airline and see if they can get you a reservation into Boston on the 15th??? I have already made reservations for George and me, to fly from Cincinnati on Monday so as to be in Boston to meet you on Tuesday the 15th,

OR—if you want to leave things in status quo, I will make a reservation for you at the HOTEL BOSTONIAN, 1138 BOYLSTON STREET, BOSTON—to arrive on Sunday the 13th. Take bus from airport, then taxi—maybe the bus will take you to the hotel.

OR—if you want you could continue to New York and spend a day or two there, and fly to Boston on the 15th—or take the train (which is easier).

Will you do this: CABLE ME AT THE HOTEL SINTON, CINCINNATI, OHIO or have Paddy do it NOT LATER THAN FRIDAY DELIVERY.

You can say "arriving as per schedule" and I will know you're going to go to the Hotel and will wire for a reservation on the 13th. Or "Arriving Boston 15th from England" and we'll meet you at the airport—or "arriving Boston 15th from New York."

We will be at the Hotel Bostonian as of late afternoon or early evening of the 14th. If you should go to New York—wire me there when you arrive from New York.

Perhaps I'm a little at fault—I asked Paddy to have you arrive a day or so ahead of time—I guess I said "not later than the 15th." At that time I did not know about the Sunday night gig.

George will have conniption fits at the idea of your arriving with no one to meet you. I'm scared to tell him! Yes—bring dinner suit. All the concerts will be played in dinner jackets. As you know, there are only a few—but I think it will be fun, anyhow. If only the weather improves! It is horrible now. There's a saying in New Hampshire that they have eleven months of snow, and bad sledding in the twelfth.

Guitar—as you like. It would be great to have the guitar with the band—but I know you have to watch the weight of luggage carefully... and it's not necessary, and we might have to let the aesthetic considerations go!

You'll have time in Boston, if you arrive the 13th or 15th to buy the mutes. Or if you decide to go to New York and spend a day or so there you can get them there. The first concert is the 16th. As for the remainder of your clothes (a WARM coat for New Hampshire and Vermont) and just an ordinary street suit should see you through nicely.

If we have an informal session here for the Reverend—slacks and warm sweaters will be OK—it will probably be in a barn

Must rush to the Post Office with this—am leaving early in the morning—you should get this not later than Thursday—will be anxiously awaiting a cable.

Am mortified and ashamed that if you arrive on the 13th you will arrive without anyone to meet you. And I hate to think of you in Boston by yourself from the Morning of the 13th until George and I get there on the afternoon of the 14th. If that does happen, there's a nice place to eat—a small, tavern type joint—called McNiff's just down the street from the Hotel.

Will be awaiting word!

Very best wishes, (signed) Dorothy

DOROTHY TAIT LETTER TO KEN COLYER 18 MARCH 1958

Dear Ken

Colin Hogg's letter came today—so did Paddy's—and so did official approval of your Visa! Quite a day!

I am enclosing your copy of the approval—arm yourself with this and trot down to the Consulate about the end of next week (March 20-21) and see if the State Department in Washington has sent through the Visa.

I am sending Paddy today a contract—just like the previous one—and I cannot conceive how the Ministry of Labour or the union over there could require anything further.

It might be well, however, to keep a copy of the contract on your person just in case you are asked for it.

However—the American Federation of Musicians and the State Department both said they would not require a contract. But better safe than sorry—and I'm sending Paddy three copies, signed by George.

Please plan to get to Boston not later than the morning of the 15th of April—there'll have to be a little time rehearsing.

You know, of course, Ken, what the score is on the NUMBER of concerts.

George arrived in Boston last week for some visits to the five colleges involved—and 24 hours after he got there had another (his third) blood clot in his leg, and has been flat on his back ever since. The doctor gave him the green light today to get up and continue with his tour. After the tour is over he may stay in Boston and have blood vessel surgery on his legs to prevent recurrences of these potentially fatal attacks. Poor lamb!

You have my itinerary—as soon as your visa is received in London cable me—giving dates of arrival, airline, and time and place.

The contract covers all points covered in Colin's letter.
We'll be seeing you if—as George says—God spares!
Regards, Cordially,

P.S. They tell me that even tho your visa approval reads "It is unnecessary to take further steps—etc." that you had better go to the Consulate personally to check from time to time. This approval expires September 13—YOU may enter this country ANY TIME BETWEEN NOW AND SEPTEMBER 13 for a period of three months.

MIKE SLATTER LETTER TO KEN COLYER 19 MARCH 1958

721 Govenor Nicholls Street, New Orleans, La.
Dear Ken,
Greetings from New Orleans. I have been here since the first of the month. And moved into an apartment at the above address. Now I am busy trying to get a job before my resources run out. My efforts are not aided by the current business recession that we are going through. With luck I will be able to hold out until something turns up.

In one respect at least my move was well timed. It turned out that Sam Charters had come here for Mardi Gras and I was glad to find him still here when I arrived. He had stayed on to hold a recording of the Eureka to complete an L.P. of the band. **Sam, myself and another friend drove all over trying to find a hall. Finally we managed to find a small Lodge Hall which is used daily as a school room. It was only a small room and the band practically filled it.** Sam was using Doc Souchon's AMPEX, the Doc himself supervising. Although they had trouble with mix—the session finally got underway. It was magnificent, Percy was superb! One of the numbers they played was called *Trombonium*— it was the first time that I had heard it. Sam afterwards told me that he has the music and could send it to you. A couple of days later Sam took off for New York. I've no idea when he will be back. He talked of trying to come to England in the fall.

George Lewis is feeling much better and I have heard him play a couple of times. He left for the North last week, telling me he will be seeing you in Boston on April 15th. This is the first I have heard of your proposed trip. If it is possible Ken, for heaven's sake come down here while you are in the States. It may be years before you get another chance. Besides, I am sure that you can make a record or two with Bill Russell or Joe Mares. Dick Allen and I will see that you don't starve to death.

Last Thursday I talked to Sheik at a funeral and he was delighted to hear that you are coming over. I know that he hopes to see you.

Most people here have now heard the tapes that I made in England last summer. They were very impressed. We anxiously await the Omega Band record.

Well Ken keep your fingers crossed that I get fixed in a job. Hope to see you soon. Drop me a line before you leave. When things are arranged you can expect to hear from me regularly. From New Orleans there is always plenty of news.

Yours ever, (signed)Mike

DOROTHY TAIT TELEGRAM TO KEN COLYER

COLYER HOLD FOR ARRIVAL. HOTEL BOSTONIAN 1138 BOYLSTON ST BSN=
GREETINGS AND WELCOME GEORGE AND I WILL FLY TO BOSTON LATE MONDAY AFTERNOON MEET YOU AT HOTEL TERRIBLY SORRY NOT ON HAND TO GREET YOU BUT UNAVOIDABLE ENTIRE BAND SENDS GREETINGS= DOROTHY
LT COLYER THE DRIVE HOUNSLOW—MIDDLESEX 12 AP 58
DID YOU RECEIVE LETTER CABLE IMMEDIATELY CARE BARNEY RAPP SINTON HOTEL CINCINATTI OHIO DETAILS ARRIVAL IF BOSTON SUNDAY GO DIRECT TO HOTEL BOSTONIAN 1138 BOYLSTON GEORGE I ARRIVE BOSTON MONDAY AFTERNOON= DOROTHY

DOROTHY TAIT It was nearly a year after his first tour of England before George was able to fulfil his contract calling for an equal number of concerts in the United States for a British Musician. The contract had stipulated thirty days. It was three-hundred and sixty-five before Ken Colyer stepped from a BOAC plane in Boston, Massachusetts, to join the Lewis band for a three weeks tour of New England colleges with the Rev. Alvin Kershaw—the men's beloved "Rev."

Mr. Kershaw was now the rector of All Saints Parish in the lovely town of Peterborough, New Hampshire, and the tour was given under the auspices of an interdenominational Christian fellowship group, with branches in the majority of large colleges.

REV. ALVIN KERSHAW I remember clearly Ken's time with the George Lewis Band in April of 1958. We had a birthday party for Ken at my home. Joe Watkins, to commemorate the

birthday, prepared—of course—red beans and rice. We diligently went from meat market to meat market to find pigs' feet, which Joe Watkins held as essential. Regrettably, pigs' feet were not part of New England culture, so we had to settle for salt-pork. Joe explained to Ken that the secret of red beans and rice was to stir frequently "to angry-up the beans!" It was a joyous if not hilarious event.

We held concerts at a number of schools and universities under a variety of sponsors: deans of student affairs, individual contacts and several by Christian student movements—no music departments—also two independent concerts; one at the Eldreges in Peterborough, New Hampshire and one an open date at the Peterborough High School. The Principal was vigorously opposed to having the band appear; he was coming to jazz as part of the New England puritan affliction.

Finally, faculty members and community leaders and I convinced the Principal that this was a rare, unique happening. He began by telling the packed auditorium that any demonstration would end the concert. I followed him to introduce the band and told the faculty and the students that the band was saying something personally to them—and if there were no response it would be an insult to these great artists. After two numbers the place was alive and swinging. And then—oh horrors—George announced that the next numbers would be sung by Ken Colyer: *Corrinne Corrinna*, *Where did you sleep last night* and *Easy Rider*. I knew we were finished. Then a miracle happened—Ken's brogue was so thick no one could understand a word he sang. All of us—George included— gasped with relief.

The following review comes from the *New Hampshire Scene*, the house newsletter of the New Hampshire Ball Bearing Company

OLD HANDS AT JAZZ

The man shown right (Joe Robichaux) is one of six who came here from Louisiana last Wednesday to offer school children in Peterborough and surrounding towns a short course in manual training. They were able to show the youngsters that the best music is handmade.

Joe Robichaux, shown making piano music by hand, is one of the George Lewis Jazz Band now on a tour of the country, making fresh waves of appreciation for real old fashioned New Orleans folk music.

He and the other five members of the band were introduced to the children by the Rector of All Saint's Episcopal Church, the Rev. Alvin Kershaw, who seemed to be particularly pleased later with the way they manufactured *When The Saints Go Marching In*. The Reverend Kershaw is considered to be an authority on jazz. We have spoken of him here before. He was an early winner on the $64,000 TV program, and so he knows what he is talking about when it comes to jazz.

He says that the music these men made was the real thing. It ought to be, they are old hands at it and it takes old hand,

Ken tours the US in 1958 with George Lewis

naturally, to make the best jazz.

George Lewis is a particularly old hand, and Alcide Pavageau, who plays bass-fiddle, is all of seventy.

Ken Colyer is not quite so old and is disguising the fact behind a beard. He is the only man who was not from New Orleans. He comes from London, England, where jazz is going over strong right now.

The other men are Jim Robinson and Alvin Alcorn. Joe Watkins plays the drums.

George Lewis and his associates had no more than begun the first piece on their program when the youngsters started in to clap time to the rhythm.

It began quite naturally, without any prompting, and by the time they finished playing *Who's Sorry Now?* everyone in the hall was sorry because there was no more music to inspire the handiwork.

So the visitors started in to play *I scream, You Scream, We All Scream for Ice Cream*, and it was all you could do to hear the instruments.

The only time the youngsters stopped clapping all through the concert was when Joe Robichaux, the piano player, stood up and walked down the keyboard then almost sat down again about eight inches beyond the end of the piano bench.

They had to stop clapping then. They laughed so hard they had to borrow their hands long enough to keep their sides from splitting.

It was more than just the enthusiasm of youth, too that ran so like wildfire through the crowd. The Jazz Band played another concert Wednesday night at the home of Arthur Eldrege's; an informal affair, with as many as one hundred staid New Englanders for an audience.

It was a little more of a challenge to the visiting Jazz Band. The older folks were able to sit still a little bit longer. They did not lift a finger all of the way through one piece and part way through the next. But then the instinct caught hold of them and before the band were well into the third piece the elders, too, had begun to have a hand in the performance.

It created a problem, of course; when the concert was over, the audience was all clapped out, and the only way that was left to show their appreciation was to stand up and shout about it.

REVIEW OF KEN WITH GEORGE LEWIS 1958

George Lewis Concert: Bearded Ken Colyer sat in with the band for three sets and (as far as I am concerned) was the outstanding highlight of the evening. This was a far different Colyer than the one we have been accustomed to hearing by means of records. Ken played with feeling, power and technique which would have made any native New Orleans horn man a trifle jealous. His playing was so spirited that it seemed to spread to the rest of the band; with the result being some of the finest traditional music anyone has ever heard. Colyer himself sounded as though he had been playing with the group for quite a while, so well did he fit in. His enjoyment in playing with George Lewis'

group of New Orleanian's was so very evident in not only his playing but his general demeanour on the bandstand

GEORGE LEWIS/KEN COLYER IN CONCERT
by Larry Cohn

On a Sunday afternoon of March this year, Jack Crystal's Central Plaza was the scene of a bit of old New Orleans in New York. The occasion was a memorial concert dedicated to the late W.C. Handy and the George Lewis aggregation was the featured band. With George was Big Jim Robinson on trombone, Alvin Alcorn trumpet, Joe Watkins drums, Alcide "Slow Drag" Pavageau on bass and Joe Robichaux piano. This was truly a native New Orleans group—something our town has lacked for quite a while.

The concert itself was a rousing success (musically, that is, for only about 170 persons attended.) This was the finest Lewis concert that I have ever heard. Last summer, when the band gave a concert at Central Plaza (prior to its appearance at the Newport Jazz Festival) I walked out in the middle of the third set, I had never heard such poor and loud playing, with Watkins the prime offender.

But our Handy Memorial Concert was to be something else. The sound that characterized the concert was as close to the American Music records as was possible without Bunk himself being present. The band played many of the tunes that have become identified with George Lewis and Jim Robinson. *Over The Waves, Ice Cream*, and *Burgundy Street* were some of the numbers that were played. The men in the band were in great form. Lewis, with his beautiful tone, singing out over Big Jim's deep down, gutty tailgate and Alvin Alcorn's pleasantly subdued trumpet (A welcome change from Kid Howard's horn playing).

Joe Watkins was not overly loud, and this itself lent greatly to the success of the music. "Slow Drag" was as powerful as ever on his old bass fiddle—despite his years, he is still the most spirited bass player that I have ever seen. The pianist, Joe Robichaux (of the old Jones and Collin's Astoria Hot Eight sides) brought the house down with his infectious chording which the audience of traditional jazz lovers seemed to be hearing for the first time.

Not only was the audience fortunate in hearing this group in top form, but they were also in for an unexpected treat—a visitor from England.

Bearded Ken Colyer sat in with the band for three sets and (as far as I am concerned) was the outstanding highlight of the evening.

This was a far different Colyer than the one we have been accustomed to hearing by means of records.

left to right: Ken with
Joe Robichaux, George Lewis,
Slow Drag Pavageau, Alvin Alcorn,
Jim Robinson and Joe Watkins

Ken played with feeling, power and technique which would have made any native New Orleans horn man a trifle jealous. His playing was so spirited that it seemed to spread to the rest of the band; with the result being some of the finest traditional music anyone has ever heard. Colyer himself sounded as though he had been playing with the group for quite a while, so well did he fit in. His enjoyment in playing with George Lewis' group of New Orleanian's was so very evident in not only his playing but his general demeanour on the bandstand. (How about some record company recording Colyer with the Lewis Band?)

There were many other musicians present at this tribute: Wilbur De Paris, Danny Barker, Zutty Singleton etc. At one point in the Concert Tony Parenti and Lewis were on the stand together. Parenti told the audience how he and Lewis grew up together within a few blocks of each other in New Orleans. He also made mention of the fact that they were both hometown boys trying to carry on the great tradition of New Orleans music.

WALTER EYSSELINCK LETTER TO KEN COLYER
18 MAY 1958

Dear Ken,

While I am—finally—writing to you I am listening to one of the most moving, most fascinating records that has ever been made—a Folkways album of the Eureka Brass Band (FA2624). Except for *Panama*, which might well be one of the tunes you have on your tape of the band, (*Trombonium*; *Just A Little While, To Stay Here*; *Lord, Lord, Lord*; *Eternity*; *Maryland my Maryland*) were all recorded March 3, 1958, by Samuel Charters. This man has recently published a very interesting book: JAZZ; NEW ORLEANS, 1885-1957. I only glanced through it the other day as I was visiting Marshall Stearns, but it seems the precious complement to such works as JAZZMEN and SHINING TRUMPETS. I hope that you'll be able to get that record soon or that you'll be able to get hold of a copy. The Eureka has never been more brilliant and never been better recorded.

What a team Percy Humphrey (leads the marches), Willie Pajeaud (unique in the dirges) Kid Sheik, the relentless trombone duo of Sonny Henry and Albert Warner, Red Clark (sousaphone), Manuel Paul (ts,) Ruben Roddy (as), Alfred Williams (snare drum) and Robert Lewis (bass drum). This record makes up for a year that has been particularly poor in terms of new issues on the jazz market. A few months ago I met a collector who has some fascinating blues material. I copied a great many of his records on tape so that we shall all be able to listen to it once I get back.

The more I listen to people like Blind Willie Johnson, Robert Johnson, Jim Jackson, Barbecue Bob, Bo Carter, Blind Boy Fuller, Blind Gary, and the recordings made by the Library of Congress in various pens and State prison farms (John Lomax' recent release on Tradition only gives one a vague idea) the more I am moved by them. Furry Lewis is probably one of the greatest. I also came across some Bunks with Wade Whaley, some George Lewis' Gospel Five (same group that did *Far Away Blues*) and some Wooden Joe's with that amazing Kid Avery on tb. Furthermore I copied several records of jug bands (their *KC Moan* is incredible) should be re-released.

I told you earlier, I guess, how poorly people react to jazz in this country. Yesterday I went back to New York for the first time in months. I visited the usual places—Condon's, Nick's, Metropole etc. but only Jimmy Ryan's has anything that is worthy of the term New Orleans jazz. The more I listen to Lee Blair, the more I am convinced that he is the greatest banjo player (along with Marerro of course) since St. Cyr and Bud Scott. Sydney De Paris is capable of some real dirty cornet. When he waves that tin hat in front of his cornet things often start happening. He combines great power with good taste and beautiful ideas. Sydney impresses me as being very serious about his music and I like that exciting simplicity of his style.

Omer Simeon was in great form last night. He did a *Shreveport Stomp* that really reminded me of his Jelly Roll Morton days. He is fascinating to talk to and so happy when anyone starts digging into that Red Hot Peppers past. But you walk out of Jimmie Ryan's and there is nowhere, absolutely nowhere else to go.

Ken, before I go on tell me about the band, about your music, about our friends., I can't wait to hear the Omega Brass Band recording. What else is new? How's John? Tell him that I am still waiting to hear from him, but that I shall write again. The year has been frantic and successful. Most probably I'll stay at Yale for another year, while I'll have to start trying to sell some of my recent work.

In about ten days I am off to New Orleans. I won a special scholarship which will enable me to spend most of the summer(until the end of July) in the South writing. Charters' book will probably make it unnecessary to write something similar, but I am more and more fascinated by the idea of trying to write the first music drama about the origins of jazz, and about the legendary characters like Buddy Bolden. **Before I leave I'll probably meet Rudi Blesh. He is one of the only**

critics who speaks our language, and he ought to be able to give me some more information. I intend to stop at various cities and small towns en route, hoping to hear some skiffle and rural blues singing. From what various people tell me, Mississippi ought to be quite rewarding. I shall also do...

[The rest hand-written and illegible]

WALTER EYSSELINCK LETTER TO KEN COLYER JUNE, 1958

Walter Eysselinck, 931 Chartres St., New Orleans, La.
Dear Ken,

Thank you very much for your last letter; it was forwarded to me from New Haven. Yesterday I received confirmation that the School of Drama wants me back, so that I'll be here for another year.(I might end up making London my home.) My stay here has been crowned with wild excitement, and deep happiness, but also riddled with bitter disillusions. **I realise better than I ever did before that there are many musicians left, capable of playing some of the greatest music that has ever been recorded. But where do they get a chance to do so? There is no audience left for their relentless beauty;** they have to make compromises wherever they come, and low budgets tear them apart into small quartets drowned in the horror of an electric guitar.

Poor Luthjens—I just re-read your letter where you describe the joint and the music you heard there. All that is left are the streamers and the colourful week-end crowds. The trumpet player there, Walter Robertson, has a nice tone, but how can you possibly judge him if he is just wearily coasting through the long hours along with a drummer, a fair pianist and an electric guitar. ("Yeah, I can play the banjo... but that was in the old days") But when you hear Burbank, or the Eureka, you realise that the music is most reluctant to die. What we have to do is find money, lots of money, and then let groups of these great old men rehearse and then record them.

If I had been deeply moved by the Eureka the first time I heard them, I was completely overwhelmed the second time I heard them play a funeral. They had their more regular line up last Friday, and you know what four trumpets like Sheik, Kid Howard, Peter Bocage and Percy Humphrey can do. The Eureka really embodies the essence of any pure New Orleans music: collective improvisation even along the rather rigid lines of some of their orchestrations. Something must have hit Peter Bocage, because he suddenly started playing—in a tender, deeply inspired whisper—underneath the beautiful solo of Manuel Paul on *Westlawn Dirge*.

The most beautiful harmonies you can imagine. He smiled when I ran over

to him afterwards and congratulated him. "Well, you just have to prove a little musicianship once in a while. But I can also play the rougher stuff."

Now here's one example of a man who should be recorded, a man whom over forty years of playing hasn't worn out. Or take Sheik. Kid Howard was in great form, too, and there is nothing like that lead trumpet of Percy. They "play together" so well; there never seems any attempt from anybody to out blast the other. Last Friday I went with them to cemetery and back. I discovered a tune which I thought had been dead for years—*The Saints*. Last night we drove over to Westwego to hear Kid Thomas. Two or three long numbers in a couple of hours, things like *Dippermouth* or *Just A Closer Walk*, the fiery intensity of those two great horns, Kid Thomas and Louis Nelson, when they suddenly get a chance to play what they like and wave battered sauce pan or a beer-glass in front of their instrument—it makes up for every moment of sad disappointment, Joe James sang and played some great, rugged blues with delightfully naughty lyrics, and Manuel Paul convinced me that a saxophone can sound very nice in a New Orleans band. The electric guitar had one merit: it wasn't too loud. In fact when Kid Thomas and Louis Nelson really get started you don't hear it under their boundless vigor.

Do let me know if you want anything for the magazine. I've been jotting down all these chaotic impressions, and I'll type up a few things for you if you wish.

Yesterday we heard (Bill, Ralph—nice but no brains—Mike, a boy from New Orleans—had lived here all his life, but never heard a funeral; he only knows the Celestin music and clowning) a program of the N.O. jazz club on the radio. It was rather silly—dealt with different streets that were used as titles for some of the tunes. And you know what? They included your *La Harpe Street*. Mike and I started cheering like drunks (we were in the car driving to Kid Thomas; Bill had just suggested that we have some ice-cream, and we let *La Harpe Street* play as loud as we could).

[Handwritten] I've never seen any fools more fired, more unhappy than Louis Melola? But when they get a request for jazz he wakes up, his face radiates with enjoyment. What a monster! Much better than on the day.

Earlier in the afternoon Mike made me listen to some of your tapes, and I'm afraid I haven't heard much music in N.O. So far there has only been the Eureka, Burbank, Kid Thomas band that can stand comparison with those two tapes. They are much better than the trial Decca recording job. Ken, may I please copy a few of the things Mike has? You know me; I'll see to it that nobody ever gets the chance to start bootlegging or so.

It's just that the music is so beautiful (the band has improved so much since I last heard them—your music is so wonderfully alive). I'd love to be able to listen to it on my tape-recorder. Mike would definitely let me, but it stands to reason that I would ask you first. I also wonder whether you could spare a copy of that private Lewis-Colyer record, strictly for home use of course. George Lewis will be back in town tomorrow, but I know he won't play at the Paddock the way he played with you, with all the emotion of his earlier records. I can pay you with a money order or records—whatever you prefer. I trust I'll be able to get your recent Decca issues here at one of the New Haven stores. If not, I'll write to Charing Cross Rd.

In case you have a copy of that historic concert left, please send it. I'll be here until approx. July 19. Then through Sept 3 my address will be Bennington College, Bennington, Vermont, and finally from Sept 3 onwards it's 1 Hillhouse Avenue, New Haven, Conn. Again.

I do hope I shall hear from you soon, and that you will give my kindest regards, to the band and to our mutual friends.

As ever, (signed) Walter

I must run now; there's a parade with the George Williams band. (P.S. Did you ever hear Alfred Williams on snares with the Eureka? Isn't he wonderful?)

THE GEORGE LEWIS JAZZ BAND LETTER 5 JULY 1958

3327 DeArmas Street, Rt, 1, Box 10D, New Orleans, 14 Louisiana
TO WHOM IT MAY CONCERN:

My Manager, Miss Dorothy Tait, has my power of attorney to negotiate and sign any contracts, and to handle all business matters for me concerning engagements, tours, recordings or any other activity connected with my profession.

(signed) George Lewis

MIKE SLATTER LETTER TO KEN COLYER 10 JULY 1958

Dear Ken,

I had meant to write you much sooner, but things have been rather tough for the past few weeks.

Unfortunately I have become the victim of a political purge as a result of which I had to resign from my job. In consequence, I am rather anxious to get something else as quickly as possible and have not really had the time to keep up with my correspondence. I am typing this letter on Walter's typewriter and I expect that he will be adding a few lines at the end. Then we are both off to a funeral across the river which is being played by the Tuxedo Band.

The other day Bill Russell was going through some sheet music that he has and I made a note of the Rags of which he is prepared to give me copies. If you would let me know if any of them would interest you, I will obtain them from Bill and send them over to you. I can let you have the following:

By Scott Joplin *Felicity Rag*
The Easy Winners
Antoinette
The Rosebud
Elite Syncopations
Swipesy (Cakewalk)
The Favorite
March Majestic
By James Scott *Frog Legs*
Victory Rag
By Joseph Lamb *Excelsior Rag*
Bohemia Rag
Reindeer Rag
By J.Russell Robinson *Minstrel Man*
By Ed.Hudson *Nitric Acid Rag*
By Arthur Marshall *The Peach*
By Maurice Kirwin *African Pas'*

We are now eagerly awaiting your two new records, The Omega Brass Band one and *They All Played Ragtime*. I just received a long letter from your brother Bill, the first in a year. I had sent him the new Eureka record of Sam Charters asking him to get it to you in due course. I believe Walter has already told you of the program that I did for the New Orleans Jazz Club on which I played a number of your records, mostly old ones I'm afraid. Harry Souchon tells me that the response was most encouraging and that he would like me to do some more. So I hope that Dobells will send off your two latest records right away. I asked Brian Harvey to send them immediately in a letter that I sent him some weeks ago, but so far have heard nothing from him whatever. If you should happen to go to the shop, you might ask him about them will you?

Well Ken, that's all from me for the moment. I am going to turn it over to Walter to finish off. As soon as things are back to normal I will write you at greater length.

(signed) Mike

Hello Ken!

Let me first of all thank you very,very much for your kind permission to copy some of your tapes. They are wonderful, not only in my opinion, but that's the way Kid Sheik, Lawrence Marrero (he is starting a family band with Paul Barnes Eddy Marrero etc.—I admire the courage of these great old veterans so much) and George Lewis. I spent a whole afternoon at the De Armas St. the other day, and it was really one of the greatest moments in my life. George said (I'll have the complete tape of all this) that it would be hard to find a band—anywhere—as good as yours. John Reid might have shown you the copy of my letter to Brian Harvey. This is only a start because I am determined to... [illegible]

(signed) Walter

COLIN BOWDEN Ken loved Percy Humphrey. Playing in the parades, Ken's playing would soar above the band. That's where

he got that from—Percy Humphries.

MIKE SLATTER LETTER TO KEN COLYER 25 JULY 1958

530 Royal Street, New Orleans, LA.
Dear Ken,

Here are the Rags that I promised you. Professor Manuel Manetta and I picked them out yesterday afternoon. I have sent four Rags instead of three, so that you will have enough material for another 45 RPM record. I have promised to let Manetta hear them, so you had better get weaving. You may wonder why I have not included any Joplin stuff, but I felt that it was probably easier for you to get that over there, so we picked out Rags by less well-know composers:

African Pas' by Maurice Kirwin
Nitric Acid Rag by Ed. Hudson
Bohemia Rag by Joseph Lamb
Excelsior Rag by Joseph Lamb

I hope that the sheets arrive in good condition, but they are all pretty old and brittle. What I find so intriguing are the comments on the back of the sheet of *African Pas'* also the lists of Rags on two of the others. If you want any of those listed I will try my best although I am not sure that Bill will have them. He does have a great deal more material than I mentioned in my letter, but they are mostly originals or very rare ones that he will not part with. However, he has agreed to let me have Photostat copies made.

That's it for now Ken, these should keep you busy for a day or two. By the way, how is the Eb Cornet coming along?

Yours, (signed) Mike

DICK ALLEN When Ken went to Bill Russell's record shop at 600 Chartres Street in the late fifties to meet him, Bill ignored him. Looking back, Bill disliked English Jazz fans who idolized Colyer but had never heard Freddie Keppard. This certainly was not Ken's fault. He helped quite a few New Orleans musicians become well-known, but Ken added to their fame. Ken did not just create original music in the New Orleans idiom. He encouraged older musicians too. Bill Huntington showed how he helped younger ones.

MIKE SLATTER LETTER TO KEN COLYER 24 JULY 1958

530 Royal Street, New Orleans, LA
Dear Ken,

Many thanks for your letter that I received yesterday. As you can see from the above address, I have moved from Governor Nicholls Street, and am now sharing an apartment with an English friend of mine. Thanks to the promptness of your brother Bill, I have already heard both the Rag record and the one by the Omega. Last night I was over at the Bernards and played both records for them. They thought that the Rags were better than the Brass Band, though they enjoyed both very much indeed. Most of the other people that have heard them thought that the Ragtime record is the better of the two.

Charlie Love was very intrigued with the Rags and said that he had not heard music like that for years. Raymond Burke, although he never heard Bolden himself, thought that that was probably how the Bolden Band played. Sheik has heard the Omega record and liked it a lot. It so happened that when he heard it, he had his horn with him and he made me play the Dirge over again so that he could play along with it. Bill Russell put on his tape recorder and the result was most amusing. Walter took the tape with him when he left and I think that he may well be sending it to you.

The main criticism of the Brass Band was the weakness of the bass drum. When you hear the new record of the Eureka, you will see what I mean. Your drummer makes none of the double and triple beats that characterises the drumming of Bob Lewis of the Eureka, nor is it nearly as powerful. The Tuba too was rather weak, but on the whole everyone thought that you had achieved a remarkable success and we hope that it won't be too long before you make another record with the Omega.

I was delighted to hear that you made a tape at Harringay on July 23rd and can't wait to hear it. My brother, who has been away in Cyprus for the last seven months, is due back in England in August and I hope that it will be possible for him to make some tapes of the band. I think that you did meet him briefly on one or two occasions, and if you have no objection I will see if he can contact you as soon as he can get away from the army and see if it is possible to make one or two tapes as I did. Remember Ken that the tapes I made have never left my possession except with your permission when Walter dubbed them. I will always be ready to make them available to you whenever you should want them.

But as I have told you before, I do not feel prepared to wait on the generosity of Decca records, they have exhausted my patience a long time ago, as I expect they have exhausted yours. At the same time I am aware that in permitting tapes to be made you are running certain risks and if you feel that they are not worth taking, I shall well understand.

Did I tell you in my last letter that I am no longer working? I had the misfortune to become the victim of local politics and was ousted from my position with International House. All is not yet lost, as I have been able to get one or two powerful allies and there is still a faint possibility that I may be able to get back with them. Meantime, though I can ill afford it, I am going on a two-month visit to Mexico and Central America with the guy I am sharing the apartment with. For him it is a business trip and my own expenses should be pretty small.

When I get back I shall really have to tighten my belt. If the plan works out as it is supposed to, we will be leaving New Orleans next Friday. I will keep in touch with you while I am away, and before I leave, I am going to try and get three of the Rags I mentioned in my last letter from Bill Russell and mail them to you. From what you said in your letter I have understood that all of the Rags listed would be of interest to you. But after looking over the first three that I send, you will be in a better position to tell me whether it is worth sending the others. Bill Russell will be particularly pleased if you are able to make something of them and I hope that you will be able to persuade Decca to put out another Rag record, as it looks as though the first one is going to be a great success.

By the way, talking of Bill Russell he felt that the Omega would sound better if you could find the right man to play Alto and Baritone horns, it would be a real triumph if you could do it. Another thing I almost forgot. Ian must try and get himself an Eb clarinet for the Band music, he does not come through as he should on an ordinary Bb. If there is any problem of obtaining an E flat in England, I expect I could lay my hands on one here, at least I am prepared to try.

Well Ken, I hope to get the new records to Harry Souchon before I leave for Mexico, and I hope to do another program for the New Orleans Jazz Club. I will pass on to you any comments that are received. This Sunday I shall be hearing the George Williams Band for the first time, in the past I always seem to have missed them for one reason or another.

Sorry to hear that things seem to have slowed down in England, it must be something to do with the recession. George Lewis, who recently injured his finger, seems to have completely recovered and is playing as well as ever. What is the position of his coming over to England again?

All the Best to you and the boys, will write soon probably from South of the border!

(Signed) Mike

RAY JACKSON LETTER TO KEN COLYER 9 AUGUST 1958

820 North Karlow, Chicago, Ill.
Dear Ken,

Sorry I didn't see you when you were here on your tour with George Lewis. It would have been great to have seen you over on this side. I was in San Francisco myself in May and thought that I might have had some news of you there but no luck.

Mugsy and Earl Hines were there but unfortunately for me they were on vacation while I was there. I did get to hear the Bay City Jazz Band at the Sailor, but it had all the faults of the Watters band only more so. Rhythm section was as uninteresting as all the West Coast revivalists have been.

Here in Chicago it is rather more interesting. As you will see by the leaflet I have included jazz is still very much alive in this city. Although of course it would have been wonderful to have been here in the twenties.

I have been over to the Red Arrow many time to listen to this group, and I think Shoffner is a most interesting and affable person. He is playing fine lead trumpet still sounds to me much the same as those Oliver Dixie Syncopators. The group itself has something of the late Oliver sound.

Shoffner is a real gentleman, and is more than willing to talk about old times with Oliver. And at last we have it straight from the horses mouth that the choruses on the Syncopators Dippermouth are by Joe himself.

He says that Joe was a great guy and man that always put the band first and as we well know believed in collective playing. It was the agents who finally finished him as most of us are aware. What with them sucking his blood and the depression of the 30's it was too much for a sick man. Bob Shoffner himself says that he stopped playing in 1941 because he says that after paying agents fees it just wasn't worth it.

But now they have this nice set-up at the "Red Arrow" with some one-night stands or travelling of any sort and they are really packing them in out there—young people mostly—although no one is allowed in a bar in this state until they are 21. that makes it a little awkward and keeps out many people who would like to listen.

Shoffner tells me that he works as an accountant in the day time so I hope he is making plenty of it. I asked him about George Mitchell and he says that George is working here in Chicago as a manager and can't blow anymore as he has a very weak heart.

Lee Collins is in hospital here in Chicago and many old-time musicians went along to the hospital to give a benefit for him. I think he is pretty sick and they say it is unlikely that he will get much better.

Of course as you know if you have seen Reddihough's letter that Brunies is still blowing like mad at the 11,11, club. He says he has had a group in there for seven years. He has part ownership. I suppose he has been there since he left Condon's about 1950.

He is just about the most raving egomaniac that I have spoken to for sometime. Although he has not yet claimed to have invented jazz, I'm sure he would if Jelly Roll hadn't beaten him to it.

He did tell me, however, that his Brother Henry Brunies who is dead now, was just about the greatest trombone ever, but even so this is keeping it in the family.

There were some great nights at this club when "Wingston" Mannone was in town. Those two together are just about the best comedy act you could wish for. Wingy's boast is that he is just about the only man who can insult "Big Head" Brunies and get away with it. And he really does.

We have Jack Teagarden coming here to the Brass Rail and Bobby Hackett comes to the Blue Note but I am still waiting for George Lewis again and must hear his group even if it means going to N.O.

I do intend to go to New Orleans before coming home next spring. Could you give me some advice on the best time to go. Do you think that Mardi Gras in February would be a good time to hear the bands or would it be catering too much for tourists at that time.

Would be much obliged re advice on this from you.

Hope you find this all of interest and am looking forward to hearing from you,

All the very best,

(signed) Ray Jackson

WALTER EYSSELINCK LETTER TO KEN COLYER 14 AUGUST 1958 (EXTRACT)

Dear Ken,

I am back in New England now, but my mind is constantly wandering across the colored sections of the Crescent City where the summer has given me so many joys, and also so many disillusions But I've mainly been taught one thing: we have to act, and act immediately if more of this precious music is to be preserved for posterity. It seems rather doubtful if the young musicians in New Orleans will carry on the tradition and as George Lewis says in the course of a long interview which I taped down on one of the occasions when he invited me to his house (isn't his mother a grand old lady?) it's only a band like yours which will carry on the real tradition. George's interview is really interesting, and with his consent, I might publish it in one of the magazines, along with some pictures.

I also interviewed (on tape) Kid Sheik, Peter Bocage, Willie Parker (who founded the Eureka) and that wonderful Picou (I went to hear him play the last Sunday I was in New Orleans—the song of his clarinet is as lovely as ever) and the great Charlie Love. When I went to see Mr. Love he was practising, reading some delightful Rags from the famous little red book. I recorded some of this as well. The tapes of Mike you let me copy have given several musicians as much delight as myself. Marrero when he first heard some of it, thought it was the Lewis Band, Sheik imagined he heard some Bunk records, Bocage insisted I tell you how fine he thinks your music is—I could mention several others who were all greatly impressed by your music.

Even dear old Bill Russell (it's about time some legal action be taken against all these people who have stolen his music), despite his prejudice against European Jazz, had nice things to say about your music.

Sheik and I were at Bill's store when Mike brought over your last records (the Omega and *They All Played Ragtime*). I think that the rags on that EP can stand the comparison with the very best Rags ANYBODY, absolutely anybody has ever recorded. Such graceful tenderness many of the finest bands that played ragtime could well have envied you, and Charlie Love thought they were wonderful. Having the sound of the Eureka, the Young Tuxedo, the Williams in my ears, I was quite as excited by the sound of the Omega, largely because Decca had to live up to all expectations and do a horrible recording job. As a matter of fact, I think they have surpassed previous efforts to mess up a band, and you… [missing] from one mike to another. The trumpet section I liked best. Sheik and I had just come back from a project out on the colored golf course. It had really been Sheik's day, and he had played wildly, passionately and beautifully. He had been so sensational that Percy had them play THE SHEIK and let Sheik lead the band in a good many tunes. Percy himself was in great form those last few days. We had all been shouting "Sheik, Sheik" and the afternoon had really caught fire. Now at the store Sheik wanted to play some more. As he was listening to your records he grabbed his horn and played along with you people. I have the result of this on tape—*Just A Closer Walk.*

Another unforgettable evening last week was spent at Mama Lou's (Sister Washington) Sanctified Church, where Kid Howard was playing with the Handy Brothers and Alec Bigard. I've heard all kinds of gossip of Howard, I've been told he can't play any longer, but who the hell was that man in a low-ceilinged, tiny wooden hall, who played these eternal spirituals and hymns with such fervour? Who was it that had this strong, clear tone on a Saturday afternoon when I went to see him when he was just having a little fun, playing with a pianist? **Those damn critics. I'm so sick of reading all these cute, little stories, all this gossip: They merely use jazz to assert themselves, and many of them could do with a good psychiatrist.** Well, no use getting angry here. I better put in a few hours printing more of my negatives now and then get back to my writing. Let me hear from you soon, and give my kindest regards to all our friends. as ever,

Is there anything I can send you? A copy of my New Orleans Diary will be forwarded by the end of August when I finish typing up my notes.

(Illegible hand-written message)(signed) Walter

CUFF BILLETT Bill Colyer remarked (or someone that I was in conversation with) saying that after he made the two records that specifically got some exposure in New Orleans—either by Ken sending copies to old friends like Dick Allen or maybe Bill Russell, people he knew over there—that he thought that the one they would like would be the one that he made with the Omega Brass Band. That didn't create any kind of enthusiasm with the people in New Orleans at all, but the one which did was the—and I see why, because I think it has a feel no-one else had of a turn-of-the-century ragtime orchestra at the time before the New Orleans Ragtime Orchestra came on the scene—the EP *They All Played Ragtime.* Which was just four tracks.

They did rags at various times on LPs and things, but it never quite capped that. The good thing about the EP is it's the same style, but it wasn't of one band doing rags and then doing blues, and changing styles, it was four quite disciplined and lilting-sounding, tasteful rags, played musically good as well. Everything about those I can't think of anything about those four sides which you could say "Oh…" and be critical. They were all really good.

And I think they were liked in New Orleans, because there was no-one in New Orleans doing that. And people remembered when it would have been like that, and said "Listen to that. Do you remember when they played like that?" Charming band, so I think that was why—perhaps slightly unexpectedly—that went down much bigger in New Orleans than his brass band. The reason the brass band didn't I think was because the beat was wrong.

RAY FOXLEY When we made the *Ragtime* CD, he decided that he'd like to add Joplin's *Fig Leaf* to the ones we already knew well. He had only a vague idea of the number, so he said he'd come around to my house and we'd run through it together. The day before the recording we spent a long afternoon working on it—I'd play a phrase on the piano and Ken woud slowly emulate it. It was an arduous and painstaking business. *Fig Leaf* is not an easy number, having four quite complex strains. Finally we managed to struggle through the entire thing. "That'll do," Ken said. I was uneasy. How would he remember all that the next day? I needn't have worried. In the studio he sailed through it as though he'd been playing it for years and it took its place in "They All Played Ragtime," which subsequently became a collector's item.

CHRIS BARBER He had a very, very good ear, and a very good memory. I mean, I taught him several tunes in 1951; I played the cornet, and I remember I taught him *Heliotrope Bouquet* by Scott Joplin, which years and years later he played me back exactly as I'd taught it to him.

PETE DYER I thought that *that* band with Mac Duncan and Ian, some of the best things they did—particularly Mac Duncan—was on the rags. They seemed to be quite suited to that—it all gelled.

SAM CHARTERS LETTER TO KEN COLYER 12 SEPTEMBER 1958

Dear Ken,

I would have answered sooner, but a roaring Newcastle banjo player—Peter Duca (which is as close to the spelling as I can come)—has been here since last Wednesday. We've been playing a lot and seeing a lot of musicians. He's interested enough. Maybe he'll do a little research. I am leaving New Orleans in the morning and will probably not be back until Mardi Gras. **I've been waiting 3 weeks for the money to record the Eureka—Folkways is going to do it—but they** couldn't get the money together. Probably will get it done at carnival.

The "Red Back Book of Rags." I'm going to record five of the Red Back Book numbers in the last week of October. *Grace and Beauty, The Cascades, Chrysanthemum, Sun Flower Slow Drag,* and *Easy Winners.* I'm going to use a full 11 pieces. I'll play cornet. I'll send you some of the music if you think you can use it, but for your band I really think it would be more trouble than it's worth. The scoring is for 5 strings, flute, clarinet, trombone, cornet, piano, and drums. The melody is played by the flute, first violin, and piano, with the clarinet occasionally doubling the violin. They were orchestrated by different men and the style varies. Most of them are for cornet and clarinet in A. You would have to spend so much time working on them transposing, arranging, etc., that I don't know how much you'd gain. I've heard some of your recorded rags and thought they were fine. The Red Book arrangements are pretty dull. I'm recording them as part of a Ragtime Documentary for Folkways.

I don't have much Brass Band music. I got the Eureka parts for *Trombonium*—a brass band rag—the Folkways thing—and a dirge that Red Clarke particularly liked, #77. I'll record *Trombonium* at the same time I do the Red Back Book.

The scoring I've been working on for ten months is for s documentary LP of "New Orleans Musical Styles—1900." I'm doing a quadrille, some polite society piano and vocal music, the "25" trio (accordion, bowed bass and valve trombone), Rice's quartet (violin, cornet, guitar and bass—will do a rag), The Olympia Orchestra and the Bolden Band. I have the melody for only 2 of the Bolden tunes, but I've got the two complete for guitar, bowed bass, valve trombone, cornet and clarinet.

The music here is very discouraging. The union has raised scale for parades and funerals. Billie and Dee Dee are drinking so badly the music has been pitiful. Emile Barnes is no longer playing. You probably heard about Ernest Rogers' death. Vic Gaspard died three weeks ago. George Lewis just got out of the hospital here—pneumonia—and he looks terrible. He's still too weak to play. I've told everyone that you might get over here again and they're all waiting for you. You might get a little music.

If you want to write me again better write to 2213 11th Ave, Sacramento, Calif. My mother will know where to reach me.

Regards, (signed) Sam Charters

JOHN GRIFFITH Ken would always denigrate his own efforts, in reverence and respect for New Orleans jazz as he knew and loved it, and the players that he also personally knew and loved. I think, though, there were times when he *did* indicate—I mean, I remember the comment when he heard the stereo *Standards*; Paul Adams sent him that when he was down in France. And he said, "The best New Orleans band ever. Wonderful stuff."

And I think this was Ken saying "Hang on. Maybe my

life was worth something. Perhaps I really *did* achieve something remarkable here."

He knew he had to get the best out of the players that he had with him at the time. Which is absolutely professionally the right way to look at a situation. When he got to this retirement position, though still playing with pick-up bands—that end of retirement, and the actual final days down in France then I think he felt free to really evaluate what his life had been about. And that's when I think he probably opened up. And we noticed on the back of the K.C. records as well, he was talking very affectionately about Mac and Johnny and so forth. He knew damn well that that was really something quite astonishing.

TONY LEPPARD I remember when Ian and Mac left the band, we all stood in the 51 and said "It'll never be the same," and in reality, it never was the same; but it was just as good. It was just as good, because if you listen to some of those recordings that have recently come out on CD of the band with Graham Stewart and Sammy Rimington on them, and with Ray Foxley and even when Colin had left—there are some great recordings—there's some wonderful music. I was playing some the other day, and I thought "This band doesn't get the credit that it really deserved, because it's hidden behind this 'classic' jazz band."

And to be truthful, I don't agree with this 'classic' jazz band title, because if you call it the classic jazz band you've more or less said that all the rest weren't really up to it. And there were some very, very good bands who followed that band. But, they didn't sound the same, they sounded different. And I would accept that, yes, when Ian and Mac were there, there was something there, wasn't there?

The interaction between the three front-line was never to be achieved again; it was a great band. And I guess, like so many others when I go back to think "What shall I play?" then I tend to go and pick a Mac Duncan/Ian Wheeler one in preference... And of course, that was wonderful skiffle stuff as well. I mean, go and listen to that Lake skiffle CD, and go through that, and there's some wonderful, wonderful stuff on it.

And it comes to it, what was it that Ken had? Ken had that essential something that you try to put a definition on, but how can you define it? It was almost... indefinable.

Ken had something extra. He had something extra, and when he played, I could go and listen to some sessions where there was not a particularly good band surrounding Ken, but I'd be listening to Ken; I could almost block the other musicians out and just listen to Ken. And it was the way he played. I don't know—I've been asked this before, and it's....trying to put it into words. It was there—it was some gift. He was a natural. It was a gift that he'd got and... you *do* get people in all fields of music and entertainment that have a gift. The Tommy Coopers of this world. It's different—how do you define it?

I think this is probably one of the reasons why I concentrated more on Ken than the trad boom, because the trad boom just hadn't got what Ken was giving me. And it was something completely different. And the trad boom, in a way... that's not entirely true—I *was* keen on Acker's early band, very, very keen. And those early recordings of Acker's with some of those lovely tunes—*Blaze Away* and... that was a super band, and I got a lot of pleasure from Acker; I *did* enjoy that band. It was two bands—Acker and Ken. Seems a strange thing to say now looking back on it, but it's true—we DID enjoy Acker. But Ken had that wonderful something.

He was different. And the way he did it at the end, he would say things like "You've been listening to a session with the Ken Colyer Jazzmen," and it was so simple—there was no sort of showmanship about it; it was so simple "...and we hope to see you again sometime in the future." And you made jolly sure you were there, seeing them again sometime in the near future, and it was so natural, and it was so unsophisticated. But it was... wonderful times.

TONY PYKE He would come to Leicester, and Nottingham and all those places in the Midlands, and then I caught them live in Leicester. I remember it well, because it was the line-up - we like to call it the classic line-up. It *was* an exciting band, let's face it: Ian Wheeler, Mac Duncan, and funnily enough, Micky Ashman was on bass, and I've spoken to Mickey about that since, and he remembers it well. He was filling the gap between Dick Smith and Ron Ward.

He was filling the gap, because Ron Ward was very nervous about joining the band and kept putting it off, so Ken kept asking Mickey which he was glad to do.

It was a men's club, a jazz club. And of course, Colin was on drums and Johnny Bastable, and no piano in the band, but they had Bob Kelly on interval piano. And he did a bit of boogie with the band when they came back on—lovely.

And then I used to get day-return tickets on the train and travel down to go to the 51 on the Saturdays.

Mac was a lovely guy. Really, very friendly. I used to think at the time, though—because I always remembered his lovely tailgate style with the Colyer Band—but with his own band, I thought he was just getting a little bit out of his depth. Possibly. I mean, he was looking to go down another road. You know. Nothing against Eddie Condon and Dixieland, but that was more the route he wanted to take, I think; I felt that. He'd try some of these licks on trombone that he couldn't cope with. I thought; "Why not stick to your tailgate?" which he could do bloody well. Stick to that.

I remember him saying—actually referring back to his Colyer days—and he said, "Well, I'll never play another bloody spiritual as long as I live." You know, because he'd had a gut-full of it all—playing spirituals day-in and day-out, and he just said he didn't want to play another one ever.

It was later on when poor Mac took his life, and I'd played a gig with Mac—something like two or three weeks before he committed suicide—and I remember clearly. It was a pub near the airport, and we sat down together in an interval and he said—because I'd already been with Ken at that point, and he was reminiscing with me, and saying what an awkward bugger he could be, and I said yes, well we all know that. But he said "You know, I didn't really want it to be like it was. I would have gladly made up with him, but he never wanted to know."

COLIN BOWDEN The Hamburg concert. Well, we finished our concert and we had to travel all the way from Düsseldorf to Hamburg. Was it February time? And Snow—thick snow.

And we had a Ford mini-bus with a trailer with all the instruments in. We must have left about ten o'clock and we got to Hamburg about twenty minutes before the session. And we hadn't stopped to eat or anything.

It was freezing cold, and I went and set my drums up on this beautiful old wooden stage—massive stage, solid wood. And I thought, "There's gonna be a good sound in here." And then I went back to the dressing-room to change, with only about ten minutes to spare. When I get in the dressing room, they had this huge bottle of Doppelkorn. It's a sort of German whiskey—very strong.

And this bottle went round six of us twice and was gone. The next thing I can remember—half-remember—is I've got changed and I was standing in the wings, and I really didn't know where I was—Bastable's behind me. And they'd announced—it must have been Ray Foxley. And Ray had gone out and started playing.

And Ken used to announce the band, and Foxley would start a slow blues, and Ken had announced me and I hadn't heard him, and the next thing I know is Bastable's giving me a shove, and I walked out onto the stage—or staggered out, really—and they'd put foam down because they were doing a recording, and it was like walking through the Sargasso Sea. And there was a spotlight reflecting off of the rim of my tom-tom, and it was like the Star of David, and I sort of headed for this and finally got there, and a round of applause as I sat down and I don't remember anything of the session. And that was the last time I got—as far as I was concerned—too drunk to play. That was a real day and a half, that was!

IAN WHEELER Then George brought his own group over in 1959. That time we had a band to meet them at the station. Once again: finally to hear these people that we knew only from records, it was simply just great. The two I became really friendly with were Joe Watkins and Slow Drag, although Drag I could never understand! But Joe used to translate for me. Drag was the master of the Creole Patois. Good Lord... the programme from the event [handed to Ian by Mike—Ed].

They were staying in an hotel in Russell Square. Now my (then) girlfriend, Maria—who later became my wife—had a flat in Guilford Street, which is just around the corner and, after hours, they used to come back to the flat, where we'd have these long, all-night discussions—just talking and drinking with Joe and Drag.

During that time I learned that Drag played guitar, so one night I arranged for one of Johnny Bastable's guitars to be there. At that time I had a big tape recorder that Peter Goodwin had made for me, and I used to record all these sessions—just let the machine run and run and run.

So this night Drag picked up the guitar and started to play and sing *Eh la Bas*. It would not be recognised as *Eh la Bas* as we know it, but that it was! Much to my amazement, he sounded like Bill Broonzy—maybe not as practised as Broonzy but definitely there, with the bass pumping all the time. So, if ever I get to find and edit those tapes...

COLIN BOWDEN When George first came over he liked the band, there's no doubt about that.

I think I had one conversation at breakfast when there was nobody else about. Because usually there were so many mumpers about—people that always wanted to be seen with George. They never turned up at sessions when he wasn't there, and they appeared out of the woodwork on those tours, and then disappeared again.

So remember having a lovely conversation with George; he told me how to make a bass-drum pedal, which I made for Humph's Bolden programme—and it worked. George used to call me "Mr. Colins."

The whole Lewis Band came over in 1959.

DOROTHY TAIT "The greatest welcome ever extended a visiting musician," the British press said.

There had been no mix up in arrangements that made it necessary for the conductor to ask the men to remain on board for a few moments, at least not in the commonly accepted sense of that term. There had simply been too many people for an official greeting party to reach train-side, too many people to handle without sending for additional police, too exuberant a crowd to permit the band to alight from the train without guidance and help.

When they did leave their compartment, they saw ahead of them, as far as their eyes could reach, an exultant, laughing, shouting sea of people yelling welcome.

There were brass bands—how many I do not know—and among them, shouting it most gleefully, the Ken Colyer band. All of the bands played at once—each of them played something different—and the sounds of their horns and drums rose above the noise of the crowd.

Harold Pendleton, who not only arranged the tour but handled every detail of it, was trying valiantly to work out some orderly way to get the men to the cars that were waiting for them outside.

The men stood on the platform, bewildered, unable to speak. "You'll find lots of friends in England," their leader had told them, but they had never dreamed of anything like this, And one of the most amazing features of that tumultuous day was that the welcome had not been organised in any way, but had sprung from the hearts of those who took part in it: A small notice in the papers, word passed around in the jazz clubs that the band would arrive that day, and the demonstration had snowballed.

COLIN BOWDEN It was wonderful. I remember standing behind Joe Watkins and wondering, "How can he play with such drive and yet so simply?" Watkins is terribly, terribly under-rated... the last of the real driving New Orleans drummers. There are so many who to me are just Dixieland drummers—Louis Barbarin is the exception (I caught him at The 100 Club). Cie Frazier was OK but he didn't have the power. When he played with Wooden Joe he was essentially playing like Baby Dodds, because that was the fashion. But to me the last of the powerhouse, swinging New Orleans drummers was Joe Watkins.

Ken told me once to play an off-beat like Joe Watkins. It was at that dance-hall at the top of the Strand—the Lyceum, with the revolving stage. But basically I'd found a band that I could play Baby Dodds with. Basically, I wanted to play a certain way, and it was what he wanted, I'm sure.

RAY FOXLEY The concert recordings made when George Lewis toured alone with the band in Germany on that 1959 trip were fascinating to listen to after all those years. Despite the hectic touring schedule of the previous fortnight, the band and George were still going strong. The gem of the Bremen concert

Inside the newspaper: **JAZZ NEWS** — Far and Wide — PRICE SIXPENCE PUBLISHED EVERY OTHER FRIDAY JANUARY 30, 1959 — Chris Barber to play N.Y. Town Hall concert — Humph & Kenny Baker for mammoth BBC concerts — Basie - 10 London concerts — **KEN COLYER SPECIAL**

George Lewis backstage, 1959 UK tour

was surely George's clarinet feature: a medley of blues and *The Old Rugged Cross*. Starting off meditatively, he gradually becomes quieter and more introspective, as though soliloquising in an empty room. With that magnificent woody tone, it's quite magical. The audience was absolutely still and the spell is only broken when George, as though waking from a dream, suddenly blows out at full strength, bringing in the band for the finale. Even so, the music was nearly drowned out by the rapturous applause of several thousand people.

A little "Touch of Lewis in the night," and a glorious swansong. I'm glad I was there.

It has been said that this period of the 1950's was Ken's "finest hour." The New Grove Dictionary of Jazz describes this particular line-up as "The leading British Revivalist band of the decade. Widely imitated."

However, if we were riding high on that tour, jazz was as always the great leveller. Forty-eight hours later later we were home and playing our first return UK gig—at Dagenham.

GEOFF GILBERT I can remember when George Lewis and his band were on tour, and Ken's band was playing the opening set of the concert, and I can remember standing in the wings and George Lewis saying, "That man has got a beautiful tone. Listen to that tone." And I thought, "Well there's a really wonderful thing to hear." I mean, I didn't ever say it to Ken, and he didn't know that it was said, but it was something that stuck in *my* mind. And George obviously knew Ken well enough to be able to say that sort of thing to me; and I only knew him because I was driving the bus.

MIKE PETERS We were actually playing at the Colyer Club at the time, and we were rather late back. But then most of the audience were at the concert anyway. What got me at that time was what beautiful tones there were. And they didn't play loud. Because we were inclined to just, you know... volume is exciting, sort of thing.

Ken was complete— the Guv'nor, absolutely, on that. And he never played loud, he never played fast, but he could play so, so slow. I remember hearing him at the White Hart in Southall once, Bill was on washboard. And I forget the number they were playing, but they got to such a height of excitement and you'd think "He can't do it..." and he went on and on and on, chorus after chorus with waves of excitement. And beautifully controlled. It was the most wonderful thing I've ever heard, one of the most moving things ever. With Mac and Ian and John on banjo.

COLIN BOWDEN Ken was very anti-agent, I know that. Whether he handled everything himself or not, I don't know; I don't see how he could have in those days.

He wanted to do things on his own terms in his own way, there's no doubt about that. You wonder, if he'd met a sponsor he could trust, whether it would have changed him; I don't know. I don't know who did the bookings. Bill Colyer did for a time, and then they parted company, and I don't know who did it after that.

One minute Bill was there and the next minute he was gone, as far as I was concerned. Bill was the one that guided Ken. I don't know who got all the American records over here, but if it was Bill he did a very good job. Bill was on the right track as far as American jazz and blues records were concerned.

Ken wasn't God, but he had a tremendous influence. His ideas and his concepts of what he wanted to do influenced a lot of people. Whether it was his skiffle stuff or his band.

The classic band was a high-point. Ken had a unique trumpet line; it was a one-off, and consequently his band was a one-off. The band with Ian and Mac—those two were something else; they really were. It jelled. It wasn't polite music at all.

RAY FOXLEY SLEEVE NOTES 504 C.D.

1989. Listening for the first time to some of our recordings, cut thirty years ago, I felt a few powerful old reflexes stirring. Ken's music has always had that effect on people. They either love it or hate it. For his musicians, or at least those of us who understood what he was at, the relationship with the man and his music was ambivalent—frustration and euphoria went side by side. You loved it when things went well and you hated it when things went wrong FOR THE SAME REASON AS BEFORE. Repeated defects could have been eliminated with a quick rehearsal, but Ken didn't believe in rehearsal. "It'll sort itself out on the stand," he'd growl at anyone bold enough to "make a point." Sometimes it did—in many ways it never did.

> One thing you could be sure of in those days: Our performance was rarely mediocre, or "competent," or "polished." It was either very good or just terrible.

And this was a great deal more exciting than playing in a predictable band. After all, on any night serendipity could suddenly break through the anguish and make you perfectly happy. This was all part of the turbulence that was the essential Colyer make-up. The only possible comparison in the jazz canon that one can think of is Charles Mingus, with his determination to make it happen "on the spot" and let his musicians find their own salvation.

And this was something you had to do. As Ken's first and last pianist (with a considerable gap in between), I soon discovered my own unique set of perks and frustrations with varying solutions, from the outset, with no "easing-in" period. I had to learn a great deal of the repertoire "on the job." Frequently I was out of hearing range of Ken's sotto voce comments; my only signals were the inaudible mutter, the foot-stomp and we were in.

If it was something I knew, the automatic pilot would take over from bar two while I was thinking "What the hell's it called?" If it was one I hadn't heard before (Ken was good at springing surprises) I'd flounder a bit at first. But Ken's melodic sense was so strong that the shape and the essence of the tune would be carried over from the ensemble into his solo, and, by God, you'd really know that number by the end and you never forgot it either. It was a good way to learn.

Ken didn't know (or need to know) about chord changes: his concept of melody and harmony was infallible. **He could see the number as a "whole"—how to blow it, then distil it, then pick it up and shake it. Unerringly he pinpointed the heart of a melody, transforming a show tune into a folk song.** Listen to "Cheek to Cheek" on this record (That means I got the right chords going and then suggested a rough working shape). His improvisations are straight down the line New Orleans— "Always keep the melody going some kind of way." This is not theme with variations in the decorative sense: The tune stays there all the way through, but Ken pulls it about like a comfortable old sweater until it fits him perfectly.

I suppose you could liken him to a sculptor working in the public eye, and if a bit fell off occasionally nobody would notice it in the finished product. His harmonic sense was entirely instinctive and owed nothing to the rulebooks, but it was "right," so that his variations grew out of the melody, sometimes just subtely remoulding the tune and often taking off into something startling and quite individual.

KEN SIMS I played with Ken's band for a little over a week while he was in hospital. That was before I joined Acker.

And when I used to go and sit-in with them, Ken used to go across to the Porcupine for an hour or two. Nobody fought anybody, it just clicked. But I think after five-and-a-half years they wanted out. I mean, at that time I couldn't stand being with any band for much longer than two years, because by that time I knew what everyone was gonna play...

Ken was quite strict, musically, and it's what you do night after night after night, and I think they just needed a change.

The Colyer and George Lewis bands during the 1959 UK tour

Now Ian was quite happy playing the way he played, but Mac—he wanted to be something else. But that Sims/Wheeler band didn't last that long. We smashed the bandwagon up at 140 m.p.h...

IAN WHEELER Mac left the band in rather strange circumstances; Mac and I had an altercation in the band-wagon coming home from a gig—it only lasted a couple of minutes—and we always remained very good friends afterwards. And we stopped to drop Mac off at wherever it was, and as Mac got out, Ken said, "You're fired." He said, "I'll send you a cheque." Anyway, that was it. Ken fired him.

We assumed because of the little fight that we'd had, but I always thought in the back of my mind, "Did he want to get rid of Mac for some reason?" I don't know, I've never found that out. As I mentioned earlier, Mac and I had become very close, and I was personally very upset that Mac was no longer in the band. So, I said to Ken, "I'm not very happy about this. So—either one thing or the other thing has to happen".

The upshot was that I left the band. I didn't particularly want to leave Ken at that time, but there were various factors that were driving me in that direction. I decided to form a band with Mac in it, so I started looking for musicians, and suddenly discovered that someone else was looking for the same musicians, and that turned out to be Kenny Sims, who was just about to leave Acker. We were both after the same people, you see. So Kenny and I decided to amalgamate so that we could get all the people we both wanted! That's how the Sims/Wheeler Band came into being, and that was in 1960.

And then, I decided—because Ken was having problems with the booze at that time—and I thought for a while, and I said the worst thing I could possibly say to the man, **I said, "Ken, I think you should stop drinking." And he said, "Nobody tells me what to do, man." I mean, I shouldn't have said it, but I'd made up my mind I was going to leave if he didn't stop drinking. So I left. I gave in my notice.**

KEN SIMS I thought the band he formed after Ian and Mac left was at least as good, and probably better.

The 'breakdown' group:
Ken, Alexis, Lonnie, Bill and
Chris. Contrary to general
belief, the first recorded
evidence of the word skiffle
seems to be Jimmy
O'Bryant's Washboard
Band in 1925, with 'Chicago
Skiffle' for Paramount

CHAPTER TEN
SKIFFLE

JOHN BEECHAM One part of Ken Colyer's work that had huge influence was skiffle. His was the first skiffle group and, whether he would have wished it or not, his work in the field led to the popularity of bands like The Beatles and The Rolling Stones, who would very possibly not even have started to play had it not been for skiffle.

Mick Jagger, speaking of his own influences, has said, "there was traditional jazz and there was skiffle. People tend to forget how enormous that was... English rock 'n' roll really started with skiffle groups."

The Beatles were originally a skiffle group—The Quarrymen. When Ken and Lonnie Donegan played together in Ken's first skiffle group, Ken introduced Lonnie to the music of Huddie Ledbetter. Lonnie recorded Leadbelly's *Rock Island Line*. Because of the huge success of that recording, and Lonnie's subsequent stardom, a new craze for learning and playing skiffle took hold.

It was a new DIY way of learning to play an instrument: you didn't need to be super-proficient technically or to read music. The new DIY musicians who followed Lonnie—the Beatles, the Rolling Stones etc.—ad-libbed their music, and followed Lonnie's influence. Brian May of Queen said of Lonnie: "He was at the cornerstone of English Blues and Rock." But arguably none of this would have happened in anything like the way it did if it had not been for Ken, because there's a direct line from Ken (with his admiration for, among others, Leadbelly) via Lonnie to what followed.

Bill Wyman of the Rolling Stones says of Chris Barber: "By providing a base first for skiffle and then for the blues, Chris Barber was virtually a founding father of what came next—a British Rock scene." But, again, although great credit is due to Chris Barber, skiffle would probably never have played the part it did had it not been for Ken Colyer.

KEN COLYER I first heard Huddie Ledbetter on a BBC *Jazz Club* broadcast. This was about 1942, and though I was an avid jazz fan, this was a strange sound to my ears.

I bought my first guitar in Montreal about 1947, whilst serving aboard the *Port Sydney*, one of the last of the old coal-burners. The chippy [ship's carpenter] bought one at the same time. I had got him interested in jazz in the course of a couple of previous trips. His name was Ken, and like me he was left-handed.

We started together trying to learn to play right-handed but finally both had to give it up and string the guitars for left-hand playing. If the left-handed compulsion is strong enough it is almost impossible to hold the guitar properly the other way, never mind play it.

We didn't make much progress until a young Liverpool fireman named Hank Hanlin joined the ship. Hank idolised Jimmy Rogers, played Rogers' guitar style and knew most of his numbers. He taught us the basic chords and changes and we started getting somewhere.

A trip later we made a memorable visit to New York. I managed to buy the Leadbelly Asch album of 78s and started to soak them up. Leadbelly's *Good Morning Blues* had made a deep impression on me and I spent hours practising the runs and many more hours before I could sing the melody line across the boogie bass.

His impact on me was tremendous, and the crew probably thought me slightly mad as I went around constantly hollering *How*

Long and *Good Morning Blues*, trying to emulate Leadbelly.

Les Mullocks was another shipmate I introduced to jazz whilst on the *Port Sydney*. He had an accordion on which he could play a few tunes, but by the time we got to Montevideo he had decided to switch to banjo, so he sold the accordion and we had a night out on the proceeds.

When we returned to London we went to Shepherds Bush market and bought a G banjo. We used to have some uproarious sessions on the next trip, sometimes with trumpet, banjo and Bill Colyer on suitcase (played with wire brushes) and sometimes with two guitars, banjo and suitcase.

We first had a skiffle group with the Crane River Jazz Band and at party sessions would use tin-whistles, jugs and washboard besides guitar and banjo.

SONNY MORRIS Where skiffle really started in this country was in 1949 at John R.T. Davies' house. John used to play—I think— mandolin, Ben used to play banjo, Ken used to play cornet, and Bill used to play brushes on a suitcase. And that was our first skiffle, that was the beginning of that, because Ken was really into the blues, and the Big Bill Broonzy's and that sort of thing. So I would say it was probably definitely the forerunner of the skiffle time. I don't think he liked the word skiffle, but there you are; it turned into it.

DICK SMITH Skiffle developed almost straight away when we went to Germany, because in Düsseldorf we had to have other things; the band couldn't play six hours a night. But he'd already been playing skiffle with Chris, which was really good. Breakdown groups, that's what we called them then. But I'd heard him playing skiffle with Chris.

COLIN BOWDEN It was Ken playing this American blues stuff that produced the skiffle craze and the onslaught of the Beatles etc. Although he looked like the figurehead, it had nothing to do with him, because it was other people trying to play what he did. Ken wanted to emulate people like Leadbelly and Broonzy as accurately as he could.

KEN COLYER The skiffle boom, like most musical booms, limelighted the spurious more than the authentic, but the authentic always manages to survive. A music critic at the time said that our brand of skiffle sounded to him more like "Old Time Jazz" and he hit the nail on the head.

People often complain that they can't understand, or misinterpret the words. Pete Seeger tells of when Leadbelly first came North, his fellow Americans had difficulty understanding his dialect, and many a Southern blues wouldn't sound so hot if it were sung in correct English (which I don't speak very well anyway!).

PAUL ADAMS Ken would have no truck with what was popular and what was not. He simply plundered the repertoires of folk music/country blues/gospel/old timey to give him his version of skiffle. Whereas others changed it, smoothed it out, introduced vaudeville and Music Hall songs and generally commercialised it, Ken, in his own cussed way, did it the way he had always done it.

DELPHINE COLYER I suppose the first time I remember Alexis Korner was down at 14 Greek Street. They had a skiffle group, with Lonnie and Alexis and a bloke named Cyril Davies. Yes, Cyril used to come down. And then there was the Roundhouse, and a lovely Australian washboard player—Hall or something.

I remember Ewan MacColl and all that lot—an Irish Tinker lady called Margaret Barry. You'd got all these microphones all over at the Festival Hall. She had them all switched off—she didn't want any of that; and she filled the place. Skiffle music's an intimate sort of thing.

Alan Lomax turned up at the Roundhouse in Wardour Street. But the Roundhouse tended to be a sort of pick-up… people turning up. And that was on Thursdays, and that seemed to be our night off, so we'd usually go up there.

And Ken would sing and Rambling Jack Elliott and people like that would turn up there. Ken and Alex got on extremely well. And it was really Ken that encouraged Alex to sing, because he was a little bit shy about it, I think.

THE NEW SOUND
From *Jazz Journal*
The skiffle Group which takes over during the intervals at the London Jazz Club is obviously going to be the success of the year. It's getting so that more people flock into the club for the interval than for the rest of the session.

The group varies its personnel, but is always based on the guitars, banjos and vocals of Ken Colyer, Alex Korner and Lonnie Donegan. Other recent participants have been Chris Barber and Jim Bray on bass, Ron Bowden on drums, and Bill Colyer on washboard.

The idea came from Alex Korner and Ken Colyer, and was first suggested before Ken went to New Orleans, but neither of them could have guessed what a large potential audience there was. The repertoire includes such numbers as Trixie Smith's *Freight Train Blues*, *Long Gone John* and Woody Guthrie's *New York Town*. If you don't believe that this kind

Ken looks on as Alexis talks to George Lewis

of music could be a draw in London—and I don't blame you for doubting—drop in and feel the electric atmosphere that builds up during Lonnie Donegan's version of *John Henry* or Ken Colyer's *How Long*. Any time now the Library of Congress will be coming across from Grosvenor Square, to take the whole thing down on tape for Alan Lomax.

DAVE FRANKLIN So one Saturday night I caught a train from South Harrow station and headed for Bryanston Street. Outside Marble Arch station I remember asking a newspaper seller directions. "Up the Edgware Road and turn right," he said.

I found the street and walked up to the chuch and joined a queue in front of some iron railings. The people were filing down a concrete staircase and in through a pair of doors at the bottom. Looking around I thought I must be the youngest there and prayed you didn't have to be sixteen like for the cinema.

I was getting quite excited by this time and wondering what it was going to be like. Just then the band kicked into a good tempo number.

I shall never forget that moment as long as I live. The depth, power and driving force of the rhythm section seemed to lift the pavement from under my feet. Ken's trumpet was leading the way

and cutting through the front-line. This was my first experience, and I couldn't wait to get inside to see what I was hearing.

The doors at the foot of the stairs were swinging open and closed. This was muffling the sound at one moment and then letting it all out to full volume the next.

I got to the door and paid my entrance fee across a small table and asked if I could join the club. I was told to come back later when they weren't quite so busy. It was a small hall with dancing at the back, rows of chairs in the front of the stage and a gangway in the middle where people were sitting on the floor. **The music was simply stunning and seemed to get right inside me. It was so moving.**

When the band returned after the interval Ken got on the mike and said they would normally only play skiffle on Sunday nights, but this week they would be having a Saturday session. He introduced the group: Bill on washboard, Chris on bass, Tony and himself on guitars.

They started with *Alabamy Bound* and after a few more numbers finished with *Old Time Religion*. I remember singing it all the way home.

GRAHAM BOATFIELD
from Skiffle Artificial, *Jazz Journal,* **April 1956**

The fact that records by English "skiffle" groups, so-called, are popular enough to merit performance on the BBC request programmes makes it necessary for us to look more closely at this phenomenon.

For the moment, two only claim our attention, those led by Ken Colyer and by Lonnie Donegan, but their success, if such it is, will no doubt encourage others to follow in the same path. I should state first, without demur, that to me this music is painful in the extreme. It is infinitely less galling to hear a singer of the calibre of Frankie Laine, Tennessee Ernie, or Tex Ritter, mangling a folk-tinged ballad than to hear the efforts of Colyer or Donegan with the "skiffle" label attached. There is no personal animosity here; I have a liking and respect for some of these revivalist musicians, and have for some time looked on Ken Colyer as a jazzman of some consequence.

BACKROOM BOYS

The idea behind these groups is not new; over the post-war years there has been a fair sprinkling of "blues blowers," "backroom boys" and similar combinations. What is new is the mis-applied label, and the fact that some people take this stuff seriously. Colyer as a singer is nothing new; no-one could really object to the sort of ragged chant he used to lead when the Crane River Band was in full flood, and although their attempts at harmony might have caused any respectable

barbershop to put up the shutters, that remarkable Decca L.P. *Going Home* (stet) is not to be despised.

Ken's singing has grown from his jazz. Donegan, however, is a cat of another colour, and I can remember early sessions at Abbey Wood when he regaled us with Jimmie Rodgers numbers in the neighing voice of a jukebox hillbilly.

We must turn now to look more closely at these groups. In Colyer's case five men are used; apart from the leader's guitar and voice, he employs one other guitar, banjo, bass and washboard, all producing assorted vocal effects. Second guitar can double as mandolin when copying the early negro groups which used this instrument. (If Mr. Kruschev's visit to this country takes place, possibly a balalaika section could be added.) Donegan's group follows another pattern, with four men who play between them guitar, banjo, piano, and drums.

When it comes to repertoire, these two groups follow different roads: this no doubt accounts for the fact that while Colyer gives the effect of a bankrupt pier-show of black-faced minstrels, Donegan sounds like a number of intoxicated hillbillies returning from some over-lengthy orgy. Colyer copies mainly negro music, having a preference for that of a melancholy nature; Donegan alternates between the bouncier Leadbelly numbers and established white folk-song. One feels that Donegan is really on the threshold of the Big Bill Campbell territory, which artistic scruples or delusions of grandeur prevent him from entering.

Songs of a religious nature are, for some unaccountable reason, featured by both groups. It would be interesting to know if this is the outcome of religious feeling or merely a copying of earlier works of this nature. Of course, not all of those who play *When The Saints* take the words literally.

ARTIFICIAL

Both Colyer and Donegan are far from the real skiffle groups, from whom the name has been lifted; if for no other reason, their rhythmic incoherence demonstrates this point. Nor can they claim to be "jug bands" as they do not favour that notable bass instrument. Possibly "spasm band" would be a better term for what they are trying to reproduce, although paroxysm or seizure might more accurately convey the impression of what gets on to record.

Curiously, both groups sound forced, and do not appear to be enjoying themselves.

Jazz music may be universal; I know it is often claimed by those that have a liking for or an interest in European musicians that this is so. On the other hand, folk music is intensely national, even parochial. Once one has an ear for the genuine, it is impossible to stomach copied folk songs. Even to the casual listener this becomes apparent when a singer attempts to cross not only national but racial barriers.

To leave our skiffle groups for a moment and to look at singers of a vastly different standard, we can all hear the false note that is struck when Josh White sings a "white" song, or Burl Ives sings anything negroid.

Our skiffle groups, however, seem unaware that they are doing the impossible when it comes to copying music which is the very personal property of Negro convicts, Alabama sharecroppers, or even persons of Anglo-Celtic origin long gone from the British Isles. By their preoccupation with "deep" music, which IN ITS ORIGINAL FORM generated a considerable degree of emotion, they possibly imagine that they can create the same effect by a process of association.

It may be of interest to turn, for a moment, to the USA, to see if other white musicians or singers have attempted a parallel approach to this type of music. Mistily antique New Orleans street bands (never recorded), players of illegitimate instruments, such as Buglin' Sam De Kemel, the Mound City Blue Blowers and other Chicago groups featuring Red McKenzie, have all proceeded in that direction, but never to the extent of using mock-negro music and attempting to copy the work of blues and folk singers.

The nearest approach one can find is in the approach of Jimmie Rodgers, who was much given to blues performances, using tags of folk origin apparently current in the districts over which he had worked in the course of his employment on the railways. But all Rodgers' work was tinged by his singular personality, and while he paid a sort of perfunctory tribute to the blues material on which he drew so extensively, in reality he treated it lightly, merely as a frame for his yodelling and other improvisations, and never attempted to reproduce the Negro flavour of the original.

COPYISTS

Can we find any American singers or vocal groups who had so little regard for their own talents that they copied the work of other jazz performers, or even filched their songs? Possibly, but their work has most certainly not lasted. In the instrumental field, we can look at the Chicagoans who copied Negro jazz, or even in some cases copied white musicians whose style derived from a partially negroid environment.

But whatever the faults of the Chicago school, or of similar New York groups, they retained a flavour of their own; their personalities are apparent to us today. The same cannot be said of the rumpty-tumpty revival bands—either if the Lu Watters school or in Europe—for very few of their musicians have formed enough individual style to enable them to be distinguished from a number of others.

Oddly enough, it has been left to this country to produce white singers who aim to follow the great Negro singers Leadbelly and Broonzy, a form of presumption not apparently found in their own country. At this point, too, we can cast a look at the female side; something is sadly wrong when we find

Bill gives his opinion of Lonnie, Dobell's record shop, Brighton 1957

white girls trying to sing like ageing negresses, attempting the throat growls which are one feature of the Negro voice, and deliberately mangling vowel sounds into a false semblance of US Negro dialect.

An acquaintance with the work of minor figures such as Mildred Bailey or Teddy Grace may help to get the picture in perspective; at least their records show their own personalities, as do the records of scores of others, of both sexes, who have never copied great ones.

We have gone some way from the "skiffle" groups with which we are blessed at the moment. But it all boils down to one or two simple considerations. Jazz music can, apparently, be transplanted—but only if allowed to develop in its own way; if it is only a copy, either the master or the disciple packs up after a while, and someone is left high and dry.

The voice, being much more individual than any instrument, cannot really be copied, and folk song—which the skiffle groups are attempting—can under no circumstances be either transplanted or copied. London voices, probably best naturally employed in singing *Knees Up Mother Brown* are not quite happy with *Midnight Special*.

BEN HARKER [Ewan] MacColl was not only an established solo performer and the singing partner of A.L. Lloyd, but also a member of "Ballads and Blues," a loose coalition of like-minded jazz and folk musicians that emerged from the 1953 radio series. The fluid line-up variously included MacColl, Lloyd, Isla Cameron, West Indian guitarist Fitzroy Coleman, jazz clarinettist Bruce Turner, concertina player Alf Edwards, and musicians borrowed from the jazz bands of Humphrey Lyttelton and Ken Colyer. Early appearances included guest slots at Humphrey Lyttelton shows, Sunday night Theatre

Workshop benefits at Stratford East, and a financially disastrous Scottish tour in February 1954. The ensemble's finest hour came on Monday 5 July when the Ballads and Blues gave a sell-out benefit concert for *Daily Worker* at the South Bank's newly built Royal Festival Hall.

He and Bert Lloyd delivered rousing sea shanties; MacColl later joined Ken Colyer's Jazzmen to perform American convict song *Another Man Done Gone*, complete with a spiralling clarinet solo by the *Daily Worker*'s occasional jazz correspondent, Bruce Turner...

The Colyer Skiffle Group played a half a dozen songs that night. Trumpet player Ken Colyer had long admired American folk music, particularly Woody Guthrie and Leadbelly, and took to "skiffling" this material, with guitars, washboard and upright bass during interludes in his full band's performances. The formula offered by skiffle—raw, rhythmic, exuding authenticity—became a hit at Colyer's shows and beyond. Skiffle managed to combine all the exotic glamour of American culture with a visceral, DIY, anti-commercial ethos, and quickly caught on with the nascent folk scene, which had always insisted there were two Americas—one of big business, Hollywood, comic books and cultural imperialism, the other of Joe Hill, Leadbelly, Woody Guthrie, and the cultural resourcefulness of the regular working man.

By 1954 the new skiffle sound could be heard in London pubs, including the Perseverance on the Tottenham Court Road and the Princess Louise in High Holborn; within two years skiffle fans could find sessions seven nights a week at the Skiffle Cellar on Soho's Greek Street, the Gyre and Gimble behind Charing Cross Station and newer coffee shops like The Partisan on Carlisle Street and The Troubadour at Earls Court. MacColl and Bert Lloyd sometimes dropped in, and cast a curious eye over proceedings.

Before long they could listen to the new music without leaving the house: the Lonnie Donegan Skiffle Group's raucous rendition of Leadbelly's *Rock Island Line* reached number eight in the charts in January 1956. A rash of commercial releases followed, weekly radio's *Saturday Skiffle Club* drew audiences of two and a half million, and skiffle was transformed from a Soho subculture into a two-year-long national craze of music-making.

Jazz purists hooted with derision at the "neighing... jukebox hillbilly" Donegan, who was vulgarising noble music he didn't understand, but MacColl, Lomax and Lloyd were more paternal than puritanical. This wasn't exactly the revival they'd envisaged—American culture was supposed to be resisted rather than spread—but MacColl still regarded the outburst of DIY music-making as "a unique and extraordinary awakening," in which British youth was rightly rejecting crooners Tony Bennett and Dean Martin for more proletarian heroes like Guthrie and Leadbelly.

"I have the greatest confidence in the world," Alan Lomax wrote of the skifflers, "that their mastery of instruments will increase, that they will get tired after a while of their monotonous two-beat imitation of Negro rhythm and that, in looking around, they will discover the song-tradition of Great Britain."

ANDREW L KAYE AND MATTHEW BARTON Between 1949 and 1958, Alan Lomax lived in London, where he continued his multifaceted career as writer, broadcaster, performer, producer, and ethnomusicologist.

Lomax was also active as a performer while in England, giving occasional concerts and staging his ballad opera, *The Big Rock Candy Mountain*, which premiered in December 1955 at Joan Littlewood's Theatre Workshop and featured the American folksinger Ramblin' Jack Elliott. At the same time, he formed a skiffle group called Alan Lomax and the Ramblers that featured Ewan MacColl, Peggy Seeger, and Shirley Collins, among others. They recorded for English Decca and made several appearances on Granada Television.

ALAN LOMAX It was natural that the resultant Afro-British products should become popular with the youngsters of skiffle —they had already succeeded in pleasing the racially prejudiced people of British descent in the South.

They have the driving African beat that has made jazz and South American dance music internationally popular in the last twenty years.

The music of all the world is being Africanized in our century. There is nothing wrong with this, so far as I can see, since the Africans have the richest and most joy-filled folk music of any people on earth. Certainly the skifflers should not be reproached for liking to play a part in this.

This American-amalgamated, British-derived Africanized music has already filled a large vacuum in the musical life of urban Britain.

Before skiffle, even three or four years ago, relatively few people in London made their own music. Singing and playing was a thing for show-offs or professionals.

Pub singers mulled over and over the dry bones of the Cockney music-hall songs which had little meaning for the younger generation.

Nowadays the young people of this country have songs they like to sing. They have the confidence to sing them. They are not ashamed of making music, but enjoy it.

Singing appears to be on the road to becoming again the National pastime it was two or three centuries ago, before the

Ken and Lonnie

industrial revolution forcibly muzzled the naturally emotional, expansive and musical peoples of these islands.

EWAN MacCOLL The annual ceilidhs organised by Hamish Henderson for the People's Festival in Edinburgh were important, as was the plugging of the songs of Woody Guthrie and Leadbelly by the jazzman Ken Colyer... Indirectly, it was Colyer's jazz group which broke the mould of exclusiveness.

Colyer, a fanatical admirer of the folk-poet Woody Guthrie, instituted a half-hour spot in his weekly band-sessions during which the songs of Guthrie and Leadbelly were performed by a vocalist backed by guitar, bass, washboard and, occasionally, clarinet. It was this group which gave rise to the spectacular skiffle movement.

PEGGY SEEGER Ewan did know Ken Colyer and had great respect for him, but once he got involved with Ballads and Blues any connection with jazz kind of went out the window... Ewan loved the laid-back ease of the jazz clubs but didn't care for the social chaos that went with it—but neither of us were regularly in that scene.

PETE FRAME Early in 1956, when Lonnie Donegan was being fêted as a star and skiffle was beginning to take off nationally, *Melody Maker* canvassed Colyer for his comments. By then he

was already feeling somewhat prickly and embittered, like a bloke who's discovered a goldmine, only to be swindled out of the rights to it—so who couldn't forgive him for injecting a tart note into his overview? "Skiffle came about in Chicago in the rent parties of the prohibition era," he explained. "When I was with the Crane River Jazzmen [*sic*], we started the first skiffle in this country, playing it chiefly for our own amusement."

"Personally I don't give a damn if the craze for skiffle doesn't last," he concluded. "The style has not produced any worthwhile talent. There is no originality. One good thing has come out of it, however: we have built up a market which at least encourages the record companies to issue the genuine material."

SAMMY RIMINGTON We used to do the evening session, and the all-night session with another band or something, you know. Of course, it was all young people there. All kind-of beatniks... And they're all asleep on the floor. So... then we did the skiffle group—I was playing mandolin with Ken. We're wandering around amongst bodies on the floor.

So I had quite a lot of knowledge of that. You know, all the Leadbelly things and Ken did Sleepy John Estes things, and Broonzy things, and that kind of thing. And so, I *was* aware of that, yeah. I mean, I was involved with that before I heard the jazz.

Well, Alexis Korner used to do a lot of the sessions down the 51, and we played with him a lot. Ken, at one point, he brought a lot of the other guys like Memphis Slim and Speckled Red, and a great session was with Sister Rosetta Tharpe. We played with her.

So she was down the 51. And well, Champion Jack [Dupree], of course. I remember he sat in on *The World is Waiting For the Sunrise* and it was like a twelve-bar. There were no diminished chords or nothing.

BILL WYMAN On 3 March 1963 we played... an afternoon session at the Ken Colyer Club, Studio 51, in Soho. It was ironic that we were given a great welcome by the ladies, Vi and Pat, who ran this stronghold of New Orleans-style jazz, whereas the jazz snobs at the Marquee and elsewhere saw us as upstarts who should not be encouraged.

BILL COLE Yes, I used to sit in with them [The Rolling Stones] down there at the 51 Club. They were the Sunday-afternoon group. And then one day— you remember Pat and Vi who used to run the club?—Vi called me over, and she said, "What do you think of this rhythm and blues group?" And at the time they were one of the finest Chicago rhythm and blues groups I've ever heard, other than on record.

So Vi said, "Look, I'm thinking of promoting these to a Monday night, but I don't want them to fall flat on their faces, so here's half a dozen free tickets a piece. Can you give these out as complimentary tickets to make sure we've got bums on seats for their first Monday night?" Somewhere around in my scrapbook I've still got one of these tickets as well. But occasionally I'd sit-in with them, and then on the folk-and-blues all-nighters that Alexis Korner used to run.

They were at the 51. The jazz and blues sort of thing merged into one in the end. When Ken was playing there on Saturday night and the Sunday night, I used to leave my bass

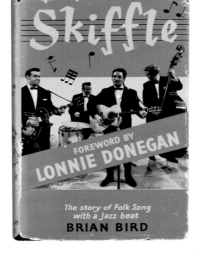

overnight, and so a lot of people used to come down—guys from the Rolling Stones, people like Jo-Anne Kelly, Long John Baldry and Rod Stewart.

Rod Stewart—one of the finest country blues guitarists; nearest thing to Big Bill Broonzy I'd heard in London at that time. And we used to sit-in and play with all of those guys. There were all sorts of people that used to turn up down there. But, that was great—mainly I used to stay there because I'd missed the last train home and things like that...

Alexis had a band down there—a sort of mainstay band— which included the late Cyril Davies on harmonica, who sadly died of leukemia very early.

But we all liked that stuff, you know—the country blues, the Delta blues, the Chicago electrified blues. We were all listening to that stuff long before the general members of the public. None of us could have foreseen that it would take off in the way that it has done today.

There was an article in one of the tabloid papers—can't remember which one it was— tracing all these sort of family trees of this. And it all went back to skiffle, and Ken Colyer introducing skiffle. Give them their due, they at least gave Ken his due for introducing skiffle, and from this Barber and Donegan and people, and so and so and so... All this down to the Beatles and that. And Colyer's only comment on this—"Oh, they blame me for everything."

DAN PAWSON
Review Of Decca Skiffle LP Sessions (Lake Records)
Skiffle was a curious hybrid embracing elements of Country blues, Urban blues, American Folk music, Jugband music, Old Timey, Bluegrass, Country, Gospel, Spirituals, Vaudeville, the social comment of the songs of Woody Guthrie, and, at its most commercial, Music Hall and specially written novelty numbers. Overall, it was a typically British concoction and one which slightly preceded the Bill Haley Rock and Roll

Ken, Bill and John Bastable

invasion. It created quite a sensation at the time and was successfully commercialised to provide people like Lonnie Donegan and Chas MacDevitt with chart hits. With this trend, however, the sincerity and principles that Ken Colyer displays on this album were often sadly missing and Ken, who originated the idiom, was denied popular recognition and shared no part in its commercial success.

Colyer sang as he spoke—with an instantly recognisable and often-imitated personal drawl. There was no deliberate or exaggerated attempt to sound American and in fact there was more than the occasional hint of his Norfolk background. Nevertheless his voice seemed to fit perfectly the idiom that he was creating and at all times sounded natural and expressive. On this album he sang and played guitar with some of the most popular traditional jazz rhythm sidemen around at the time to give him the backing he wanted. It is interesting to note, however, that the delicate mandolin strains of the earlier sessions emanate from none other than Alexis Korner, who was later to become a highly respected authority in Blues and Rhythm and Blues circles. There is a significant difference between the earlier and later sessions being enriched by the addition of Bob Kelly on piano, whose bluesy background chords helped to mellow the sometimes stringent washboard beat.

I find this record to be a welcome reminder of the scene in Great Britain during the mid-fifties. It was an era when everything seemed simpler and more straightforward. It was the era before the rise of pop culture which subsequently swamped any music that might not provide a big enough financial return for the people who were beginning to control it. It was also an era that stimulated many of the musicians

playing in Europe tody in the New Orleans style. This album is worthwhile having, not just for nostalgic reasons but also because it should serve as a reminder that in one way or another we all owe a great deal to "The Guv'nor."

TREVOR TODD I remember going on the 1964 North Sea Shuffle over to Holland. The outward trip happened to be one of the roughest crossings on record, and for a while the jazz had to stop because the drum kits were rolling all over the place and the musicians couldn't keep their balance. So many people were being seasick that an appeal went over the tannoy for helpers—many of the stewards had been taken ill as well! I happened to notice that John Bastable was in a particularly bad way, leaning precariously over the rail.

Well, of course a bit of "choppy sea" never affected an old sailor like the Guv'nor and he arranged an impromptu skiffle session in one of the bars. I've never suffered from seasickness and was fortunate enough to witness this memorable occasion. Ken gave a bit more "background information" about each number than he usually did and it began to feel like he was giving an intimate session in someone's living room rather than a massive bar.

I recall asking him to play *Midnight Special,* assuming he would give us the version off the recording. He answered with "Yuh know it's got over seventy verses, man—I don't think I've got time to sing all of 'em."

I've always remembered that from 46 years ago. It would never surprise me either, if 20 or 30 others who witnessed that beautiful session still hold fond memories of the music this tireless man gave us on that stormy afternoon.

265

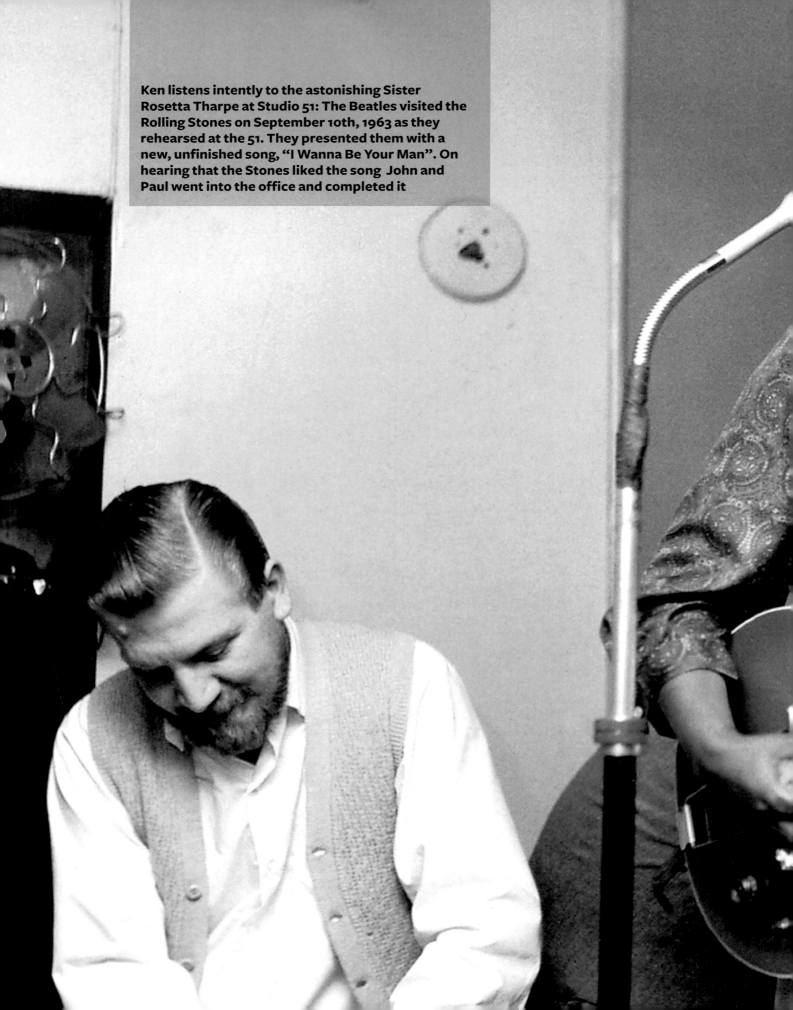

Ken listens intently to the astonishing Sister Rosetta Tharpe at Studio 51: The Beatles visited the Rolling Stones on September 10th, 1963 as they rehearsed at the 51. They presented them with a new, unfinished song, "I Wanna Be Your Man". On hearing that the Stones liked the song John and Paul went into the office and completed it

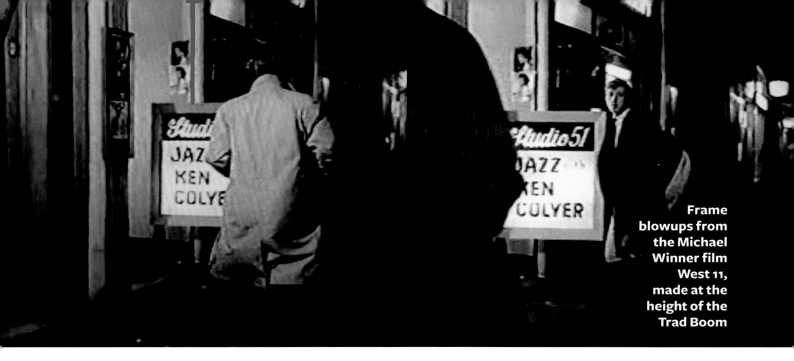

Frame blowups from the Michael Winner film *West 11*, made at the height of the Trad Boom

CHAPTER ELEVEN
THE TRAD BOOM AND BEYOND

BOB WALLIS Among the hardcore of traditionalist fans Ken Colyer was the shining light of purity throughout the muddied commercial years of the "Boom." He consistently refused to adopt "gimmicks" or a colourful uniform. He wore working men's plaid shirts which were dubbed "sincerity shirts" by the musicians in his band. He was not against uniforms; he says, "we wore derby hats and fancy waistcoats on TV before Acker Bilk took to them... What matters is the way a band sounds. Wearing glad rags is only a means to an end."

MIKE PETERS And he knew what band to put together, and he didn't go roaring around doing traddy sort of stuff. He was absolutely *amazing*; he was the most amazing player; he used to come up with the most subtle little phrases. And I think everybody got on a Ken Colyer kick—I know I did.

JOHN KEEN I should imagine around 1960, when the Trad Boom was at its height, there was an awful lot of commercial pressure on Ken to do certain kinds of records. I mean, some of

the records he made around 1961 had what appears to me to have a kind of echo on them. Over-recorded banjo—and he didn't like it. In other words, Acker had it, and it was a standard thing at the time, and I suppose he had to put up with it. He wanted to do his own stuff. He was a proper folk-artist in that sense.

But one has to admire him for it. I mean, how would *we* have coped? Those kind of show-business pressures don't exist for us now, thank goodness. We can play what we like with whom we like, what tunes we like.

KEN COLYER – BLOWING IS ALL THAT MATTERS TO ME NOW, MAN.
Owen Bryce, *Unknown magazine*, July 1960

You might be forgiven for thinking that Ken Colyer had a chip on his shoulder. Knowing the facts, you might almost forgive Ken for having one. Because here's one jazzman who's really been through hard times... who has been much misunderstood by friends, musicians and critics.
PURISM

It is true to say that the Colyer brothers, with their early band, with their writings and their publicity, started a

Gag shot of Sammy, Colin and Ron with George Lewis

movement which hundreds still believe in ardently. "Purism, that's the thing. I'm not after a trad sound."

Ken gets very cross about people who distort the sound of bands in order to make their records appeal to the trad collectors. He has always used a piano.

"To me, blowing is living. The rest of the time you just go through the motions. But man, up on the bandstand with the horn to your lips, you're living. That's it. The atmosphere. Doesn't matter whether there's one hundred or five hundred... or even fifty... or even if there's any money. Blowing is all that matters, man."

SAMMY RIMINGTON I was working as a postman with a motorcycle around London, and that's when Ken called me out. I was playin' with Barry, and he called me up and he says, "I was just wondering... you've been sitting-in with the band, and I was wondering if you'd be interested in joining the band in two weeks."

And I turned it down at first, because I said, "I'm quite happy with Barry Martyn's band," which I was, and I probably preferred to play with Barry's band than Colyer at that time, because I was more into that music. But I didn't say I didn't want to. And then he said: what changed my mind, he said "I've got to know, because we're doing a big concert tour in Switzerland with George Lewis as the guest, and I've got to get a replacement quick." And I said, "Well, I'll call you back tomorrow," or something like that. And I called him back and I said "yeah, I'll do it."

And then, I remember we flew to Switzerland—it was my eighteenth birthday, on an aeroplane—the next day. And we did a two... three-week tour. I can't remember whether it was two or three. Colin Bowden will know that. And we did a fabulous tour, and Dorothy Tait was on the tour as well, so I got to know her. It was great.

Graham Stewart *was* a bit difficult. I don't know if it was jealousy or not, but he used to knock George Lewis a bit, you know, and pick on the things—the usual things: out of tune, and all this.

He'd heard things like the Delmarks. And somehow he would pick on that because he knew that I liked it; there was a bit of friction there—it wasn't terrible. But when he heard George in Switzerland live, he changed his tune, totally. He said, "Oh yeah, he's coming out with great stuff. He's coming out with influences of Johnny Dodds, and Jimmie Noone, and..." He realised, see? And when you hear these people live, it *is* a lot different, isn't it?

COLIN BOWDEN I think "trad" evolved because people found that they could play a sound that attracted audiences, and they found if they played loud and fast they got more applause.

KEN COLYER I've said it so many times: I have no problem with having a hit record provided it's my music in undiluted form that's making the grade. But I'm not about to do a pop/trad arrangement of *The Teddy Bears' Picnic*, when that would be misrepresenting my music. Why would I make fun of what I believe in just to sell records to people who have no understanding of what I'm striving for?

Having said that, we've almost done it on occasion. *They All Played Ragtime* made the hit parade, so did *Take This Hammer*. I did *Maryland* as a single just to please that Lansdowne lot [Columbia's Lansdowne jazz series], but I'm glad that didn't make it. The music was OK but, God, what they did to the overall sound! To catch the public's ear with really good music is very, very difficult, and you need a lot of luck to make it happen. But once you start making pop records for a mass market, you're caught in a trap because then everybody thinks that's what you do, and that's all they want to hear when they catch you live.

Look at all those Kenny Ball records; jazz content nil! But I'm sure he doesn't give a damn; he's copped a lot o' loot so good luck to him. I like to make records, but only if the jazz is as good as I can make it. If it clicks with the great record-buying public, then fine, it'd be very nice, but the music's gotta be on my terms! If a record gets away, it's money for old rope, you've done the work. But with my music it's unlikely to happen. That's why my brand of skiffle didn't catch the mass ear; we couldn't make it bad enough!

Most people only want to hear bang, bang, bang—what Melly called the unrelenting chugging of trad. Your average listener or dancer simply can't appreciate counterpoint, contrapuntal harmony in the front-line or that subtle shifting of beat and dynamics, light and shade. The general public mustn't strain their ear too much, they can't take it. Look at the current pop music—beat music so-called— if you want proof of what I'm saying.

THE STRANGE CASE OF KEN COLYER
Unknown magazine, undated
"I've had brushes with producers"

The past year has seen an unprecedented demand by radio and television networks for Britain's trad bands.

The boom is reckoned to be at its peak.

Jazz clubs are packed; concerts are generally well attended; festivals are often sell-outs. And steam radio and television companies have risen to the occasion magnificently.

There is more "exposure time" for British jazz than there ever has been – and probably more than there will be again.

But are our jazz bands getting a fair crack of the whip in relation to their popularity? Broadcast and TV appearances mean a lot to a band's morale.

'GUV'NOR'

Granted the BBC and television networks can hardly consider the happiness of six musicians when they are trying to satisfy millions of listeners or viewers.

But consider the strange case of Ken Colyer—"The Guv'nor" to the sizeable purist faction among jazz fans. IN FOUR YEARS, HE SAYS HE HAS HAD ONLY TWO BROADCASTS, AND IN THE PAST YEAR TWO TV SPOTS.

Colyer's name might not mean so much to the audience of *Easy Beat* and *Saturday Club* as the Top Twenty crashers like Acker Bilk and Kenny Ball.

BUSIEST

But talk to jazz club promoters and disc chiefs, and one realises Ken's Jazzmen are a big draw.

His band is one of the busiest in the country. He has a big, loyal following. They are by now resigned to the fact that Colyer's name is not regarded by producers as a profitable advertisement.

Ken is typically philosophical about the situation.

"It has got to the point now where I have just about given up hope of getting airtime. I have one or two ideas why I have

been left out," he says.

"Once or twice I've had brushes with producers about reproduction of the band in the studio.

"Generally I have got on all right with most of the producers. And the chaps in the band know my attitude. I'm not going out to chase broadcasts.

"They wouldn't do us any harm – we'd welcome a broadcast now and then. But there seems to be some grudge or bias against the band."

MYSTERY

"The only thing is that the fans want to hear us on the air a bit. It is for them, more than for the band, that we could do with a spot."

He added "Anyway, good jazz isn't played in a TV or radio studio. You can't turn it on like a tap. Atmosphere means everything to me and the rest of the band." Ken thinks this may be the reason for the apparent boycott among radio and television men.

"Perhaps they realize that, above all, we have to be in the right environment to play. Is that why they are less favourably disposed to us?

"In a way, I hope so. It's a mystery to me. I've given up worrying."

If proof were needed that the Colyer of today is still packing in the crowds, it is supplied by Midlands promoter Bill Kinnell, who runs a network of jazz clubs.

"Ken Colyer" he affirms, "is still the biggest draw—the most reliable band—for a good crowd in a club."

PRINCIPLES

For a comment from the BBC we asked *Saturday Club* producer Jimmy Grant.

"On my programme" he said, "I have to use bands that have very wide appeal. I know that Ken Colyer is a musician with very high principles, which he sticks to. This doesn't mean that the bands I use don't have to have musical principles.

"But I see no real sign that Colyer has that wide appeal. It's nothing to do with record success either.

"We are not dictated to by discs among trad bands."

There may be other reasons for the lack of Colyer broadcasts.

But it seems that his fanatical following will have to seek out the band in person, for there are no signs of more air time for Colyer in the future.

KEN COLYER Melly saved it [*The Story of Trad* TV Show]; it would have been terrible if it hadn't been for George. Stirling Moss came out with a few good comments—he knows his music. As to my remarks, they chopped them out when the thing got a network airing, so there you go!

I'd just started speaking and they cut the sound. That's what you get for speaking your mind. That's why I don't worry about television; I've managed to get along without it. If your

After Hours

face and your attitudes don't fit, forget about it; which I was perfectly happy to do! 'Cos unless you're paying a manager to chase these phony producers, nothing's gonna happen. You don't just get picked on merit. We've survived well without the great god television.

I'm not saying I wouldn't like to do it if there were a sympathetic producer with the guts and imagination to understand and present jazz properly, and try to get something intelligent, which the music deserves. Maybe one day, there's always hope. But those producers: talk about a lot of sheep; whatever's popular at the moment. They pander to whatever is perceived public taste instead of trying to break new ground. Radio has gone the same way… makes you sick!

If the argument comes up as to why they are not using certain bands—and it's not only us, there are lots of good bands that don't get any air time—they can only talk about their high standards in the face of the lie of all the rubbish churned out day after day, week after week. It's not a black list, but there is a list circulated among all the producers, and if your name's not on it, you're not gonna be approached.

It's not strictly true that I'm unapproachable; it's true in the sense that I've often spoken my mind and I'd stick to whatever I've said—would withdraw nothing. All I'm doing is championing my music to try to make people understand what I'm for. The trouble is people tend to agree with you at the time even if they really don't, and that's unjustifiable. If you disagree with what I say, then have the guts to say so! I've never fought or argued with any producer.

Back to Ted Heath: he has really blown his top sometimes with television and radio when it doesn't go his way. I guess he figures he's big enough to get away with it.

Lyttelton has several times criticized what's happening with jazz on radio and television, and Melly does it too in his clever way; George can be so good but you have to read between the lines.

MIKE PETERS We were doing a gig—we were sharing the bill with Ken; he was on second, and we were first. And the idea was, we were playing *Over In Gloryland* and Ken would walk on and join us, and I was supposed to walk off, then the trombone player would come in and our man would walk off.

Ken was a bit pissed, surprisingly! And he walked through, straight off the edge of the stage, which was about ten foot high, and landed on this marble floor, and I thought, "We might as well play a dirge or something now. He's bound to be dead." And he got up, and came back again, and stopped before he got to the edge of the stage.

KEN COLYER Look at it this way: There were a lot of men capable of playing better stuff than they were playing at that time. It just seemed that everybody was after the one thing: hit parade status, fame—and usually at the expense of the music, which got compromised every which way.

An exception was Acker, a very good clarinet player, otherwise I would not have had him in my band. But in a sense his publicity machine ran ahead of him and he may have got cornered into playing a more commercial music than his heart told him he should have been playing.

But Acker will always come back to the truth 'cos essentially he's a very good jazzman.

His band actually never strayed that far—always played some sturdy jazz—and he's aware of that: He never slammed any doors behind him and can slip back into the music any time he chooses, provided he's in the right company. He did these other things with Leon Young but he always kept that string stuff separate from his jazz, and there was never any confusion; two separate careers essentially.

But there's another angle: "musical conscience" you might call it—and I'm probably notorious in this respect, or hopefully *famous* for it! If everybody strayed from the path, even for a short time, to cash in, where would the music be? I've tried to be true to my original ideas, to develop my talent and my band's talent to the ultimate of my ability and just play this beautiful music. Others purported to have similar ideals in the early days, but how quickly they went out of the window when there was a buck to be made by distorting the truth.

I'd like to think I've been an anchor. They use fancy phrases for me, like "The Keeper of the Flame," but I think even the modernists understand that the New Orleans style is the Root Music. I'm not saying it's the be-all and end-all of jazz and that's all that should be played, because that's just not so; there's plenty of room for all the various styles of jazz, and much wonderful music has emerged from the different periods in which specific styles evolved and stages that jazz has gone through.

But I come back to the same point: Although I like and enjoy other styles and forms of jazz, for me the essence and the root is the New Orleans style; at its best this music fulfils everything that I want from jazz and what I consider good in jazz.

I personally don't need to step beyond or outside the idiom to find total fulfilment and endless scope for self-expression; and I sense that the men who gather around me to play feel that I'm on the right tack, together with my faithful flock!!

BILL COLE I'm always very ambivalent about this. The one side of me sees him as being Mr. Grumpy with the audience—

very short-tempered with people who didn't understand what he was trying to do (not that some of us understood that either, but…). Another time, I got the impression, in a way, that there was a little bit of the quite deliberate side of that, that he was doing the anti-showmanship.

We didn't wear bowler hats and stripy waistcoats and silly uniforms like that, you know, so I sometimes felt that Ken had decided that that was the way he was going to go—the non-showmanship route.

Ken just sort of said, "Well, if that's the way they want to go, they're making money—that's fine, you know. That's their business, not mine." And he wouldn't have wanted to go that way at all.

SAMMY RIMINGTON Oh, he hated trad. He didn't like to be involved, and I didn't. I remember doing a big thing at the Albert Hall. And Colin was on that, and Johnny Bastable. I mean, thousands in there. It was an all-night concert, and that was the time when Johnny Bastable went off to sleep and Colin dug him with his drumstick before Colyer turned around. But, all them bands, one after the other, you know—there was Terry Lightfoot among others—and they're all jumping on the bandwagon, and all dressed up in their hats and etc.

We didn't get involved with it, really. We just kept out of it.

I found Ken was very philosophical, you know, about different things. And quite wise, in a way. He wouldn't say much, but when he did say it, it meant something. It was very relevant to what he was talking about. I mean, he had his strong beliefs. I respected Ken a lot. I had a lot of respect for him.

CHARLES FOX "Trad"—that bowdlerised version of New Orleans music—brought fortune as well as fame to those performers who were willing to project their music straight at the pop market. Between this Scylla and this Charybdis, unheeding the perils of of adversity and affluence alike, Ken Colyer has pursued a straight, undeviating course. The result is that he is respected by most of his fellow musicians (including, I would say, a surprising amount of modernists) and also an artist who has succeeded in communicating with audiences on his own terms.

Percy Humphrey is still one of Ken's idols, one of the handful of New Orleans trumpet players whom he singles out as his favourites (the others, incidentally, are Bunk Johnson, Papa Mutt Carey, Joe Oliver and Lee Collins). Just as the bands in New Orleans have always performed pop songs of their own day and of yesteryear as well as the accepted repertoire of jazz standards, so does Ken Colyer.

KEN COLYER Just say we're trying to capture the sound of New Orleans music. We're not setting out to reproduce classic records or anything like that. It's the functional warmth of the music we're after, what you might call the New Orleans "bounce."

Some soloists are good but most of them can't sustain, they can't keep things moving inside. And you've got to leave room for spontaneity, you've got to leave chinks. It's not exactly improvisation, it's extemporisation, a kind of embellishment. You never know what's going to happen.

Our aim with recording was to make it seem as natural as we could, to get something as close to the way the band sounds in a club. We didn't want any of those over-loaded echoes. We also wanted the music to be spontaneous, with as little arrangement as possible.

COLIN BOWDEN When I joined Alan Elsdon, it took me about three days to summon up the courage to go to Ken's house. I just turned up at the house and knocked on the door, and he said, "Oh, hello Col." And I just said, "I'm gonna leave the band in…" I can't remember how long. I don't think I worked any notice; he just decided to get Pete Ridge straight in.

The previous year Kenny Ball had asked me to join his band; I used to enjoy doing jam sessions with Kenny up in North East London. So one year I turned Kenny down, the following year Alan Elsdon phoned me, and I just said, "Yeah, I will." I remember at the time saying to a friend of mine—who knew me pretty well—"I think I've made a mistake!" He said, "No, you haven't, it was inevitable."

When you think back about it, Ken was a very intense person, and after a time you just have to get out from underneath it. There comes a time if you are also intense when you start to suffocate. It's not simply a question of whether a musical style is right or wrong for you, there comes a point when you need a change.

AFTER 13 YEARS KEN IS STILL LOYAL TO N.O.
Unknown magazine, 1960

Ken Colyer has trod a lonely path through British Jazz. But through his unswerving loyalty to New Orleans Music, he has gained a reputation as a sincere jazzman and one of the pioneers of his style.

To the massive purist following in the jazz clubs, Colyer's name is important.

His aims and his jazz are the same today as when he formed the famous Crane River Jazz Band with his washboard-playing Brother Bill in 1948.

They include "an honesty of approach to the music" and good swinging New Orleans Jazz played with some feeling.

He helped form the Christie Brothers Stompers in 1951, and a year later went to New Orleans to play alongside George Lewis and other famous jazzmen.

Returning later that year, he found that Chris Barber and Monty Sunshine had formed a band for him to join.

In 1954 the band split up and Ken has since had several personnel changes. But he still plays the same fiery jazz. Trumpeter Ken's band includes:

Graham Stewart (trombone) who led his own band until

last year. His successful "Seven" toured Germany and Scandinavia. He has also played in Moscow and Poland.

Sammy Rimington (clarinet) the most recent addition to the band—he joined it nine months ago. Aged 18, Sammy is a fervent George Lewis-Johnny Dodds admirer. He started playing clarinet three years ago, and has played with the groups of Barry Martyn, Kid Shillito and Dave Reynolds.

Johnny Bastable (banjo) has been with Colyer for five years. Formerly with the Trevor Williams Band, he is a Lawrence Marrero disciple.

Ron Ward (bass) joined the group four years ago after playing with the old Sonny Morris Band at Cranford. He was another New Orleans pioneer in Britain. Favourite bassist: Pops Foster.

Colin Bowden (drums) has been with the bands of Sonny Morris, Trevor Williams, Jeremy French and Cy Laurie. He joined Colyer five years ago and his choice of drummers includes Baby Dodds and Zoot Simms [sic].[Probably meant Zutty Singleton—Ed]

SEE THEM: Tomorrow at Worthing Town Hall, on Sunday at the Royal Forest Hotel, Chingford, and regularly at the Ken Colyer Club, Great Newport Street, London.

GEOFF COLE I was still in Exeter. I read all about it, and I heard subsequently from Johnny Bastable that Mac had been causing a lot of trouble. He was getting very obstreperous in the bandwagon, and wanting to fight people and generally being anti-social, shall we say…

I remember reading in the *Melody Maker* that Graham Stewart had joined. I was quite surprised at that, but quite pleased. OK, different approach. I knew that Graham played good classic jazz trombone in the Ory style, and I caught the band. I came up on holidays, as was my wont, and had a sit-in. Ken was always very kind and asked me to sit-in. Sammy was there by then. And he and Graham didn't get on at all. Graham called him "that little boy."

Graham had been sick, in February '61, for about ten days. And Ken asked me to do it. And I did all the deps.

So I did the jobs. I don't think I probably did all that well, but I must have done well enough. Of course, then Graham came back and I'd still sit-in, and then Graham decided to join Monty Sunshine's band.

WHAT I FEEL ABOUT JAZZ
Ken Colyer, *Jazz News,* May 31, 1961

I'm not much of a hand at this sort of thing. I'd rather play than talk or write about jazz but as I've been asked how I feel about jazz I may as well say exactly what I feel. There's been a lot of talk about technique as far as I'm concerned. There's been a lot of people said that I've no technique and that I rely on sincerity. But I've found that my technique is adequate for what I want to do; sometimes my ideas get ahead of me but usually I can say on my trumpet what I want to say.

Sincerity is something that should be taken for granted. If you don't feel it then you shouldn't be playing jazz. I'd like to say something else that I feel should be said and that is: you don't have to be noisy to be powerful. I wish more musicians would realise that. People say I sometimes play too quiet, but that's the way the old New Orleans men played. No one instrument should play more than the other. It's taken me years to find out just how I wanted to play trumpet.

When I've played I've always filled in just a little bit here and a little bit there where I feel it needed. I can play a straight lead if I want to, but this is how I feel New Orleans trumpet should be played.

The important thing is not to pattern yourself on a musician or a band. Pattern yourself on a sound. I think the George Lewis band or the Kid Ory band or the Bootblacks are the best of New Orleans jazz, but I remember Sam Morgan's band. That was a really great band—a big, warm sound and it's marvellous how they managed such a swinging front line with such an unwieldy instrumentation. They had two sopranos, two trumpets, two saxes and rhythm. When I went to New Orleans I was lucky to hear the Lewis band in its finest flower. People who had been in New Orleans for a long, long time said the band was playing greater than ever.

My visit to New Orleans strengthened my beliefs. I didn't know what to think before I went. There were so many anti-Colyer fans that I began to think that it might be me that was wrong, but I found that I was right in what I thought about jazz.

In those days I was intense about jazz. I won't say I was fanatical because fanaticism doesn't have to have any thought behind it. I was intense. I think I've been honest all along and I've never tried to kid anyone. I don't mind the way jazz is going now. If it's getting more popular—fine. There's no reason why it shouldn't be popular, so long as it doesn't get out of hand. I've played all kinds of tunes—pop tunes, folk music and all that. That's the kind of music the New Orleans musicians used to play. The trouble is when the means becomes more important than the end. There's no use chasing the Hit-Parade.

I think we play good jazz over here. All the Americans that come over have proved that. George Lewis was dumbfounded when he came over. He didn't know what to expect and he was knocked out by the reception he got.

I think if a musician has absorbed enough of the idiom he can play a pop tune and still make it jazz.

New Orleans jazz is a funny thing. I read an article that Buck Clayton said that New Orleans men were great musicians but when you put them together they couldn't stop arguing.

Personally, I don't want to argue any more about New Orleans jazz. I've got my own ideas and I want to play them. **I like to listen to other people. I think Billie Holiday is great. I could listen to her sing all night.** Some of the things I've heard come direct from New Orleans. McKinney's Cotton Pickers, the greatest big band I've heard, took a lot from New Orleans jazz, and Woody Herman took a lot from the Cotton Pickers. All that shake trumpet that the Basie band featured and all the other bands started copying came from New Orleans trumpet players like Mutt Carey. All these shakes and trills and bent notes come from New Orleans.

A lot of people have forgotten what jazz is meant to be. A journalist the other week gave the band a good write-up but he said that "an unusual feature of the band was the lack of solos." He missed the point, I think, because Buddy Bolden's band didn't feature any solos at all, only breaks... That's what went wrong with Dixieland. I like a lot of Dixieland—Bob Crosby's Bobcats playing *South Rampart Street Parade* was one of the first records I ever heard—but there were so many solos in Dixieland that the original form got lost.

KEN COLYER I've enjoyed sitting-in with Alex Welsh 'cos I do enjoy that Chicago style. But I'd never consider playing that style in my own band. For me, if I'd started dabbling or experimenting with other styles I'd have lost my way, I'd have wound up nowhere. I might have become a very proficient, very clever instrumentalist, but jazz-wise that wouldn't have meant a thing, you know?

You can't shift from one style to another just to show how bloody clever you are. My goal was and is to get as close as possible to the ultimate in New Orleans playing; there could be no deviating from that path.

At the risk of repeating myself, I can say everything I want to say within the New Orleans framework. That's not to say I'm one hundred percent there. I'm fully aware there are things to be achieved that we are not achieving right now; whether we ever will have the ability to get there one hundred percent I just don't know.

Maybe it's expecting too much to have that aspiration. What's one hundred percent? Well, you just listen to the best of the Kid Ory records and the Jelly Roll Morton stuff, to George Lewis and Bunk Johnson and right there you have my ideals defined. That rhythmical accent the original bands achieved is so important, and all too often we don't get that right in our bands—not as a unit, as a whole.

Actually, New Orleans jazz is the most difficult music there is to play at its ultimate best.

So we may never get there. But even New Orleans musicians don't always agree with me. I was expounding these

Playing in Australia at the Holywood Barbeque in Campsea

ideas to Kid Howard and he didn't seem to know what I was talking about! Kid said to me, "You've got a great band now, what're you worried about? It sounds real fine."

New Orleans music is a moving music; it doesn't stand still as long as there are creative players with the right empathy. I simply know there are aspects we are not achieving, but even if we did and I was able to say, "Right, we're playing perfect New Orleans jazz!" that wouldn't be the end of the road, because as long as you remain creative within the idiom, there's always something more to say through the music.

Some of the qualities I still strive for are intangible and very difficult to explain. And that's why it's so difficult… with musicians I've just about given up trying to articulate what extra I'm looking for and trying to achieve. If it's not in them, you're not gonna get it! If they don't get it for themselves… You can only guide a man. You can influence him to a tremendous degree by playing with him, as I've proved time and time again with the men I've had around me over the years. But in the end, if they can't find it for themselves—if they just don't have that ability in them—you're hitting your head against a brick wall.

Don't misunderstand me: We can and do play a very good brand of music—of a pretty high order—even though you may not be achieving that elusive special enhancement that could make it the ultimate.

MEET KEN COLYER

17th Australian Jazz Convention programme, 1962

Ken Colyer has established a reputation for playing only New Orleans jazz, and although he has many 'pop' numbers on his repertoire, the audience can always rely on this band to play these numbers in the New Orleans style.

KEN COLYER I went into hospital after being told I must go in as soon as possible. I explained to the Dutton agency that I would be out of action for a couple of weeks, but promoters

275

could take the band with a dep. Most declined (pleasant fellows). I kept the band on full pay and they as good as had a holiday whilst I was being operated on. Ken Sims, Nat Gonella and Keith Smith depped for me. One promoter was going to sue me for non-appearance because I had signed the contract for the job some time before.

When I came to after the op, I didn't feel too bad apart from feeling as if I had been put through a wringer. I seemed to recuperate well and was itching to get out of hospital. Then I was casually told I must immediately report to the Radiotherapy Department of the Middlesex Hospital on leaving the West Mid.

I went to the Middlesex, sections of my abdomen and my back were carefully marked with indelible pencil, and I was told not to bathe whilst I was undergoing treatment. No explanations were given. I might as well have been a piece of machinery.

I put two and two together and realised I had cancer and that it had spread. I had radiation treatment five days a week and soon began to feel steadily worse. When I told them, they gave me some seasick pills. I have never been seasick in my life. I had a weekly blood test to check my white corpuscle count.

One weekend, I flew with the band to Berlin to play the Sportspalatz. I had signed the contract months before. I felt terrible and didn't blow very well. I felt even worse on the Monday when I went for my treatment. The radiation is completely painless at the time, but the cumulative effects are disastrous. I wish doctors had to undergo the same treatment they give others. Then they might be more sympathetic.

I had my blood checked and went up to the treatment rooms, which are lead lined. They don't want any of their bloody radiation.

I gave the nurse the result slip. I never used to bother to look at it, as it meant nothing to me. Then the panic was on.

She came rushing back. "What have you been doing?"

"Nothing." I omitted to tell them I had just returned from Berlin. **My count was dangerously low. I read later that the average count should be 12,000. Mine was 2,000. They cut the treatment down and I had to have a blood check before every session.** My wound, instead of healing, became full of pus, which didn't seem to bother them, but it bothered me.

I couldn't play for more than fifteen minutes. Keith Smith came around with me and blew the bulk of the session and I did a couple of spots. I was determined that no other son of a bitch was going to threaten to sue me for non-appearance.

Ian Cuthbertson wrote me a letter in 1962 inviting me to the Jazz Convention to he held in Sydney that year. The idea, he said, was to be the guest musician, meet and play with the various bands and generally have a good time.

I had finished my radiotherapy treatment and was feeling progressively worse. I think it should be banned. They squawk when there is the slightest leak of the stuff anywhere, power stations, etc., and I read recently that the death rate was around ninety per cent through the treatment I was having. I would sooner have taken my chances.

I thought it would probably be one chance in a lifetime so agreed to go. The thirty-six-hour flight was very unpleasant and far too long. When we arrived at Sydney airport, I was shocked and a little frightened at the mass of people. I would sooner have quietly slipped in unnoticed.

The Captain of the plane hurried up to me and apologised for not knowing I was on the plane, and could he have my autograph.

Geoff Bull's brass band was there, but I couldn't play. I was too tired and too nervous. However, I revived enough by the afternoon to start sitting-in with the bands.

The Convention is a wonderful idea. They sensibly hold it at Christmas. All the boys are on holiday and of course the weather is wonderful. They came from the length and breadth of the country to play and have a good time. I wish there was something like it in England. It is practically all amateur, free and easy and relaxed.

They used a fine old wooden hall with a handy pub just across the road. Fortunately, I hadn't lost my taste for beer. I was to lose my taste for everything sometime after. I would have a few beers in the pub with anybody and everybody. Then Mel Langdon would arrange for me to do thirty-or forty-minute spots with various bands. I didn't know how many bands I played with each day, but we had a good time.

I wished I had been on better form, but didn't bother to make excuses or explain.

Some of the critics were extremely vicious, but then they seem to be with any artist from what I have read. However, one showed great sympathy and understanding. Adrian Rawlings wrote a piece that showed insight and perception, and he said, regarding the others, "What's the use?"

FRANK JOHNSON There are two types of fools in the world: those who think something old is always good, and those who think something new is better. Well, the cultists brought in the dreadful traddy-pop thing in the late 1950s. The style of band I'm thinking of is that led by the English trumpet player Ken Colyer, whom they used to call the Governor [*sic*]. Here we used to refer to it as "underwater music".

All those bands that played in that pseudo-New Orleans style were really doing nothing. You could never sit in with them: they didn't want to know, and they guarded their jazz as closely as a mongrel dog guards its burrow. There was no hope of any kind of free exchange. They didn't want anyone to play with them at all, because they believed, in their incredible egotism, that there was only one type of jazz—the sort of jazz that had been played around Burgundy Street in New Orleans. They thought they had found the Holy Grail. It was cultism carried to the nth degree.

KEN COLYER One fan observed the routine one day. I first met in the pub with whoever was there, had a chat and a few beers. Mel would arrange for me to play and tell me to be ready in half-an-hour's time. I would sort out four or five tunes, play the set and go back to the pub. I was off food and having difficulty holding anything down, except maybe a cheese sandwich. This didn't bother me too much as I have never been a big eater. I didn't find the beer particularly strong and the schooners went down easy. The day progressed. The session finished around ten in the hall. This fellow followed me over for the last session of the evening.

"I expected you to fall flat on your back; instead you blew like a lion," he said. But I don't expect there were any critics around then.

I knew Mel Langdon well from the time the Graeme Bell band were first in London. He dug the Cranes and was frequently down the 51 Club and so heard the times when the band was on top form. We often met of a lunchtime for a chat and a beer. He was fond of stories and a great raconteur. I have spent many a pleasant hour with him.

I thought the Convention went well and there were some nice moments. I have always said, "It's the moments that matter." The Yarra Yarra was the best band I played with and I thought one or two sessions were pretty good.

I took the plane home and began to feel progressively worse. The drag was on.

COLYER IS STILL FIGHTING SUCCESS
Scene No 12, November 29, 1962

Ken Colyer's name can start war among jazz fans. Worshipped—or ridiculed—he isn't, says Charles Fox, quite the purist fanatic everyone thinks.

Two huge electric fans whirred like lacquered sunflowers, one on each side of the stand. Couples pirouetted while aficionados tapped their heels to the music. The band was halfway through *The Saints*.

A "trad" band playing to a "trad" audience? Not exactly. Ken Colyer's band plays New Orleans music, not "trad." The difference is rather like the handiwork of craftsmen and a branded product. The latter may be efficient but it lacks character.

A sleeve-note writer once compared Ken Colyer to a Crusader questing for the Holy Grail. The history might be faulty but the analogy was more or less correct. With his fair hair and short Imperial, Ken even looks a bit like Richard-Coeur-de-Lion. He's also dedicated and courageous.

He has the most dedicated fans in the British Scene, although not the most.

He must, for one thing, be the only Englishman to have gone to prison for jazz. It happened after he turned seaman in 1952 especially to visit New Orleans, where he jumped ship. Not only did he blow his trumpet alongside Big Jim Robinson and Percy Humphrey in the George Lewis Band, he ended up doing thirty-eight days in the Parish gaol for over-staying his visitors permit.

Back in England, Ken formed a band that included Chris Barber on trombone, Monty Sunshine on clarinet, Lonnie Donegan as banjoist. When that group broke up he used Acker Bilk as his clarinettist. He also featured what was really the pioneer "skiffle" group, with yet another of today's bandleaders —Alexis Korner—playing mandolin.

Yet although so many of his sidemen have gone on to fame and fortune, Ken has no regrets because his band doesn't get its records into the Top Twenty. In fact, he shies away from easy success.

"People say to me, 'Why don't you aim for a pop market for just a couple of years. Then you could take it easy and play the way you want to.' They don't understand. You can't do that and keep the music intact.

"The present-day scene? Well, it's a mess, isn't it? A few years ago some of these musicians were ardent jazz players. Dedicated. Then something happened."

What British bands does he approve of?

"Mike Daniels' group," he said. "And—oh yes—Steve Lane's Southern Stompers. Both those bands are doing something with style and form."

Style and form—and dynamics. These qualities lie at the heart of Ken Colyer's jazz philosophy. He believes passionately in the subtleties of the collective sound, the ensemble pattern.

Some soloists are good, but most of them can't sustain, they can't keep things moving inside. And you've got to leave room for spontaneity, you've got to leave chinks. It's not exactly improvisation, it's extemporising, a kind of embellishment. You never know what's going to happen.

What about the slickness, the glossy surface of bands like Kenny Ball's and other "trad" groups in the Top Twenty?

Ken smiled.

"What was it Big Bill Broonzy used to say about anything he didn't like? It's all right for Opera!"

And what, I persisted, about the 'trad' practice of recording such unlikely tunes as *Happy Talk* and *Bali Hai*?

"The approach is wrong. They're doing it just to get a disc into the Hit Parade. Now, my band has a wide repertoire. We often play old pop tunes but we don't cod them. We try and make them into good jazz vehicles."

Who are his favourite trumpet players?

"They're still the same—Bunk Johnson, Papa Mutt Carey, Joe Oliver, Percy Humphrey, Lee Collins.

"The way Bunk still gets attacked is ridiculous. I read a damn fool article only the other day. What a musician he was! For one thing his memory was amazing. He remembered all the old New Orleans tunes. And how he could play rags!"

Ken Colyer himself happens to be an extremely fine player of both rags and blues. Wasn't the combination rare, I asked him—especially in Britain?

"That's because the musicians here don't bother," he said.

People like Bunk and Mutt, they took the trouble to learn. One of the good British ragtime players, though, is Chris Barber. We still play some of the arrangements he wrote when he was with the band."

KEN COLYER You have to distinguish between authentic ragtime and lots of other very good tunes that are called rags but are actually played as jazz numbers, not in ragtime at all. They're what I call pseudo-rags, written loosely in ragtime form but played as you would approach any jazz number. The authentic ragtime—based on the tunes of Joplin, Lamb and Marshall—they must be worked out and played as correctly as possible.

That's the art of the music and, again, it's a very difficult music to play well. That's probably why there's so little ragtime played; very few bands are prepared to tackle ragtime.

If you play them within a small band setting, such as mine, there is very little scope for departure from the written piece, particularly as far as the lead is concerned. The other horns can free-wheel to some extent, but not the trumpet. Just as Bunk said, "Ragtime is good as written," not to be messed about. Professor Manuel Manetta told me he had not heard ragtime played that well for 40 years. He was really impressed by how well we had played those four tunes on the Decca EP. Charlie Love is a ragtime expert, or was in his prime; he liked the record very much—thought we'd made a very good job of it. I was pleased, of course!

DAD COLYER
by Charles Fox, *Unknown Magazine,* **1962**

I was curious about the marching bands Ken played with— first the Omega Brass Band, now the New Teao Brass Band. He'd been seen marching against the Common Market as well as for Banning the Bomb. Did he parade only for causes he believed in?

"Not really," he said. "You just can't pick and choose. There's little chance normally to play marching music, for you need police permission. It just happens that most of these affairs are protests of one kind or another.

"New Orleans parade music is wonderful, unique. I don't know a musician who doesn't get a kick out of playing it. Your mind is free, you feel great. Once, that is, you've learned to march and blow at the same time. There's a knack to it."

KEN COLYER The various members of the Omega Band became spread far and wide, so that it was virtually impossible to get them all together. When I did try it, it was a real headache. But that band did produce some wonderful parade music. The more that essential line-up played together, the better it became. But parade music can fail mainly due to lack of experience on the part of men who just haven't played it enough.

Being another facet of jazz music, once again it takes an

intimate knowledge of the music if it's going to be played well. Mind, I still find it enjoyable even if it's a little bit ragged. Unless I can get a parade group together and rehearse weekly or fortnightly, it's not gonna happen. It's a shame because there's still room on the scene for a fine parade band.

DAD COLYER

by Charles Fox, *Unknown Magazine*, 1962

Men with strong opinions are usually misunderstood. Ken Colyer is no exception. He laughed when I mentioned the popular image of him as a fanatic listening to nothing but the purest New Orleans jazz.

"I'm only one-track minded about what I want to do," he said. "Actually, I enjoy hearing all sorts of jazz. The jazz bug hit me while I was at school and I absorbed a variety of things.

"The Woody Herman band, for instance. Not only that wild group which made *Apple Honey* and *Caldonia*, but the earlier band, the one with Joe Bishop in it. Now there was a musician, the *only* flugelhorn player for me!"

KEN COLYER Bruce Turner had some interesting things to say about experimental jazz; some of these modernists borrow an idea or two from the classical side and think they're being so clever or so complex. In actuality the classically trained guys could leave them standing if they chose to. Classically trained men work for years to attain a degree of ability and skill to aspire to a symphony orchestra; the abilities they acquire and expect of themselves make most of these so-called modernists look ridiculous.

What you're alluding to is a gimmicky thing—it doesn't have much to do with jazz in my book; they're just dabbling to make themselves look clever; doesn't mean a thing. Those kinds of experiments don't help to progress jazz in any way, won't lead to any kind of fruition or development of the music. I think a lot of them sense it themselves. They go out on a limb, find a dead end, then revert because they want to get swinging again. You see it all the time with some of these men.

Duke Ellington? I have heard the Ellington band in concert. I do prefer the earlier stuff, which I suppose is natural for me— I know the bands so well from that much earlier period. Unfortunately Tricky Sam's not there anymore, nor some of the others associated with the early bands. And of course Duke's writing style has changed to some extent. The sound is bound to be a bit different, but the overall Ellington sound is still there. Fortunately he's got no boppers with him—and I feel the same way about Count Basie: The presence of boppers definitely detracts and doesn't help their kind of music. It sticks out like a sore thumb if somebody starts bopping within bands of that type. But some of the early magic was there in the Croydon show; *Creole Love Call* was lovely, for example.

I do like many of the big bands but almost always it's their early work I admire most. All too often these days the band seems to be there merely to provide a backdrop for soloists. That's what's so good about the earlier material: The whole band was playing, riffing, getting that wonderful ensemble sound. But there has to be room for improvisation, for expression, even within the confines of an inevitable amount of arrangement for big bands.

You can have a skeletal arrangement—almost a head arrangement—and those guys in the Ellington band are just so good they seem to know instinctively what Duke wants and expects, almost uncanny in their ability to freewheel within the written chart and make it sound so polished... and I mean "polished" in a good sense. The Basie band comes across to me in the same way.

> It's an astounding thing— and puzzles me no-end: Men who should know better always seem to get the fame and stardom but know nothing about the music.

Ted Heath is a good example: If he's running a big band he should know more about the big bands, but he doesn't. He gives the lie.

The first time Basie came over here I was at the premier concert at The Royal Festival Hall; everybody who was anybody was there! Ted Heath was quoted there: He'd never heard Count Basie before! Now isn't that astonishing? He also said, "We can't take jazz to America—we've got to give them something else, we can't compete with this." How about that? Our top big band leader to come out with a remark like that!

Harking back again to the early players, think of Tricky Sam [Nanton] and Bubber [Miley] and Cootie [Williams] and their mute work. But it all stems from the New Orleans style; think about King Oliver's mute work. I've always used mutes of all kinds in my own bands—they're very important in helping get the light and shade, the dynamics you strive for. It's just as important as varying tempos in different tunes. In a small group especially you achieve colour variations with proper use of mutes.

You can't achieve proper shading without using mutes to get the ideal sound. I've always striven for this. So many British bands go just for one level of sound—all too often at maximum volume—and that's an emptiness, a barren sound contrasted with real playing.

Another angle on using mutes: I've always maintained that jazz is a vocal music. Just as you vary the pitch, the level, the volume, the overall sound of your voice in speech, you have to strive for similar effects when you're playing. It's like a musical conversation between the instruments in the front line.

Dippermouth Blues? It's difficult enough trying to play it like Oliver did. That is the only way to play that number, and the same goes for other classic performances of tunes that are so good you just have to play it the way it was done on the original recording. That's not copying, it's saluting.

I've never been tempted to add anything of my own to that Oliver trio of choruses, particularly the muted choruses. I find it so difficult to play them well that there's no need to add anything; they're perfect the way he did them. If I can knock that solo out really well maybe one time in six, then I'm satisfied.

Thelonious Monk? A very intriguing man! There's definitely something there—something behind his playing. He's a true individualist for sure and deserves to be studied and listened to. But to be honest I don't feel qualified to comment on a lot of the modern men. I so rarely hear them; don't buy the records; don't go out of my way to hear them. Take Mingus. I haven't listened to him but, from what I've heard and read, he's a musician deserving of respect. There was this club, apparently. During his gig he got exasperated with the audience and told them just what he thought of them—the great American public!! Apparently he got a round of applause when he'd finished.

DAD COLYER
by Charles Fox, *Unknown Magazine*, 1962

Did he pay any attention, I asked, to the school of thought which claims that Nick LaRocca and the Original Dixieland Jazz Band were playing jazz long before the Negro pioneers?

"I didn't meet LaRocca when I was in New Orleans," he said. "They told me he was crazy and living off the royalties from *Tiger Rag*. All wrong! It's a pity, for I'd like to have seen the old boy. That was a good band, even if it didn't invent jazz."

It was time for him to get back on the stand. A few couples had already started up that country-dance variation of jiving that you come across only in purist jazz clubs. Not a single twister was in sight.

"When you boil it down," Ken said, edging his way to the clear space between trombone and clarinet, "what jazz really wants is more good bands. People playing different types of music, but all of them feeling it. None of them selling out."

KEN COLYER—FORGOTTEN MAN OF TRAD JAZZ
by Ray Coleman, *Melody Maker*, Ocober 14 1961

October 14, 1961. MELODY MAKER—Page 3

✻ THE NAME THAT'S MISSING FROM THE ROYAL VARIETY SHOW

KEN COLYER
—forgotten man of trad jazz!

THERE is a trad name missing from the bands chosen to appear at the Royal Variety Show. That name is Ken Colyer. Of all the personalities who deserve some recognition for dedication to British jazz progress over the years, Colyer ranks high.

They all circles, there is a warm affection for this bandleader, who can claim a sizeable slice of British jazz pioneering. Many musicians, including Acker Bilk, Chris Barber and Monty Sunshine, have passed through the band over the years.

They all gained from Colyer's fervour and sincere beliefs about how jazz should be played.

Yet as the trad boom gathers

says .....
RAY COLEMAN

'I don't go for all that phoney publicity.'

Colyer band's 'Isle of Capri' disc. It got many broadcasts on Jack Payne's "British Band Box."

In the Crescent City, Ken sat in with dozens of jazzmen, and

crowd. They are genuine jazz fans."

Ken's club in the West End—a trad landmark—does excellent business. Colyer, affectionately referred to by his fans as "The

in all those gimmicks," says Ken. "There's a wild rat race to reach the top."

FITTING

At a time when musical integrity seems to be disappearing in favour of rabble rousing, British jazzmen and fans might take note of the Colyer dictum: no compromise, no gimmicks.

There is a trad name missing from the bands chosen to appear at the Royal Variety Show (1961). That name is Ken Colyer. Of all the personalities that deserve some recognition for dedication to British jazz progress over the years, Colyer ranks high.

In trad circles there is a warm affection for this bandleader who can claim a sizeable slice of British jazz pioneering. Many musicians, including Acker Bilk, Chris Barber and Monty Sunshine have passed through the band over the years.

They all gained from Colyer's fervour and sincere beliefs about how jazz should be played.

Yet as the trad boom gathers momentum and the tongues wag about Bilk, Ball and the Temperance Seven crashing a new barrier for trad, Ken Colyer has taken a background seat.

He has always missed the limelight.

Nobody wants to deny Bilk, Ball and the Temperance Seven the honour of Royal selection, but in these days of heavy emphasis on several so-called "top traddies," the imperturbable and often forgotten name of Ken Colyer deserves the spotlight.

He deserves a Royal Show as much as the current "ravers."

KEN COLYER
Reading Star, 7 February 1964

The few real fans of early jazz that are still around—those are the ones not driven away by the Trad Fad—probably know that Ken Colyer and his band appeared at the Olympia on Tuesday. The combo certainly swung, and though the crowd was sparse, Ken was pleased with the results.

He said "Whether there are five or five hundred, if the music's good, that's all right."

Ken has played outstanding music in the New Orleans manner for fifteen years. His has been one of the few fully professional bands that did not change its style for the sake of promoters' pockets.

"Although the so-called trad boom is over" he explained, "there is still much work for the good bands. If a lot of groups can sober up from their soak in commercialism, and we can get the small clubs going, then everything will start ticking."

To many, the name Colyer is synonymous with the Revival movement and the cult of purists—the band of critics and players who think that all jazz worthy of note was played before 1930. So I asked Ken whether he did, in fact, appreciate any of the more modern jazz.

It turned out that he is a big admirer of Duke Ellington and the Woody Herman Orchestras.

"I don't get much chance to hear other jazz, but what I do I can appreciate, although I can't say that I really 'like' a lot of it. I enjoy Charlie Parker." What does such a staunch supporter of the original jazz think of its "enfant terribles," like John Coltrane and Ornette Coleman? These men are from farther space, as far as music is concerned. To them, things like the theme and chord structure have ever diminishing importance.

His reply was, to say the least, unusual. "I must admit that Ornette Coleman reminds me of the Colyer band's earlier stuff."

GEOFF COLE The first record I ever made with Ken was the conclusion of his contract with Lansdowne, which was for an EP, which we recorded—I forget where the studios were now; somewhere in Kensington—and we did *Postman's Lament* (which became the title of the EP; they all had names in those days), *Too Busy*, *Maple Leaf Rag* and *Cielito Lindo*. We also at the time recorded *Darkness On The Delta*, but it wasn't issued. And Ken said (there was a postman strike. Remember Tom Jackson, Post Office Union leader?), "We could just cash in on this, with a bit of luck, make a bit of money too: *Postman's Lament*."

He would have loved a hit but he would insist that it was on his terms. His music—he was so sincere about the music; nobody could be in any doubt about that whatsoever. He knew the way he wanted to play. He knew the way he wanted the band to play. He didn't want to make *any* concessions whatsoever to what he deemed as outside pressure. I mean, commercialism to him—it doesn't matter what form it took, it would be an outside pressure on his music. The only thing he would go to would be to wear a uniform—evening dress. For important concerts.

ALEXIS KORNER Singing and playing, Colyer reveals his dignity, his restlessness, his authority and his sorrow. We know, from experience, that he is incapable of mechanical playing, which has enabled many British jazzmen to survive, even to flourish exceedingly.

The stubbornness of his "pure" New Orleans style is concerned not with chastity but with honesty. What you hear Ken Colyer play is, unmistakably, Ken Colyer's music.

On form, he is one of the two finest blues players in Britain (the other is Sandy Brown). He can be a most moving musician but, most of all, he is a JAZZMAN without pretentiousness, without pretence.

GEOFF COLE *West Eleven* was directed by Michael Winner. And when he asked Ken to do the film *West Eleven* it was because he'd always said "If I ever make a film and I can get a jazz club in, I want to use the Ken Colyer Club." And he came down the 51, and you weren't allowed to park with vans in the street outside the 51, so he had guys take photographs and re-built them in the studio in Boreham Wood—identical!

So he wrote some dialogue, and he gave me and Sammy and Pete Ridge lines to say. So we were filmed walking into the club saying, "Well, how can you tell? Anyway, she's five months gone." "Oh, gerraway, she's..." So Sammy had to say "Gerraway." And he couldn't. It took him about seven takes to get it right. And then Pete Ridge said something, and when they showed the bloody film, at the premiere, they'd dubbed other people's voices on. Winner was friendly with us all, he was very friendly with Ken.

KEN COLYER They didn't give us much time, but for the limited period we were on, we felt it was worthwhile. It didn't do us much good in terms of attracting an audience, but film is a tough game to get into anyway on any terms. It was pure luck that we got onto it, 'cos Michael Winner knew me from his Cambridge days, when he was a student and remembered us playing there on many occasions. He'd always been a fan, wanted a jazz band in the film in a club scene, and immediately thought of me.

It's a shame they went to all that bother, and then didn't exploit it as well as they could have done. If only there were more producers wanting to use jazz in the way that was used, incorporating jazz into real-life scenes, instead of the woeful depiction of jazz on film and television the way it is now. It seems nobody has the right idea, or any imagination of how to integrate jazz into other art forms; it runs to a bunch of blokes blowing and tapping their feet—well, really!!

SAMMY RIMINGTON *West Eleven*. Oh well, that was something. We had to be at Elstree Studios—of course—about seven o'clock in the morning or something. I think we were there for quite a few days, considering we didn't have to do

much. And we had to say a few lines. I remember my lines were "Gerraway, that's three blokes she's dating to my certain knowledge."

It was about making some woman pregnant, and we were talking—the three of us—just walking from the back of the 51 up to the stage. But they dubbed all the words—they put other voices in. We had to start there, and I'll always remember, it was a replica of the 51 Club, in the studio. We were drinking in the bar on the day, right loaded, because it's a bit boring, laying around, you know. And when you walked up the stairs—you know the 51 Club came out on Great Newport Street—so we walked up the stairs, but in the film studio it was just a drop; there was nothing there.

And I had to stop Johnny from walking off the top stairs. We were looking at the photographs—you know the photographs as you go up the stairs—and suddenly realised at the top of the stairs that there's a drop there.

MICHAEL WINNER Ken was a lovely fellow—a sweet fellow, very unassuming, very professional. The film was shot in 1963.

GEOFF COLE One day Ken and Bob and somebody else got drunk in the dressing room upstairs—we had a long time to wait around; we were just miming. We'd recorded it onto film—the soundtrack—not onto disc. And then they played it back while they did the scenes with Alfred Lynch. And one day we just started playing, you know. Ken said, "Come on, let's play something." And Michael Winner suddenly came in: "Ken, Ken... we're going through the dialogue!"

When I said to Ken, "Some of us have got some dialogue. Do we get extra money for that?" the shit hit the fan. I got severely told off for mentioning money.

KEN COLYER As I seem to be saying more and more these days, with New Orleans music—as really with any music—the importance is the moment it happens, the creative moments, the really good moments that occur when a group of men is really swinging, really driving it down. That's what's good. I can say that with every group I've had I've achieved this. I've always been able to get them to gel, to play together, admittedly under my dominance, but that's something you must have if you're to succeed. If a band doesn't have a leader with that ability to dominate and lead the whole thing musically, you just can't achieve that wonderful ensemble sound.

Although you have an idea, you can't ever really know what's going on in a musician's mind or how he's feeling while he's playing. There can also be personality conflicts affecting the music that listeners are unaware of—it's just as well that they are! Fans suddenly see a man leave the band and it's "Oh! Why would he leave?" or "Why did you fire him? Best bloke you ever had on such-and-such an instrument; it sounded marvellous!" That may seem true from the listener's perspective, but if things aren't working out internally, then changes happen.

It's true that I'm a stickler as far as the music's concerned. I can become unhappy over some fine points of a man's playing which aren't necessarily noticed by the average listener but are vitally important to me; it's not as casual as it appears, you know. Underneath there's a very strict discipline governing how the music's to be played. But the musicians have to understand that discipline and respond voluntarily to what I want.

SAMMY RIMINGTON I found Ken very, very, very fair as a leader. He was extremely fair, especially when we went through the hard times. You know, after the trad boom, it had a big dip, you know. And he was paying out of his own pocket. 'Cos he put us on a wage. I think it was every week he used to pay. I remember it was 45 pounds a week during the trad boom, which was a lot of money.

And then he dropped it a little bit, when it slumped after that, but he would still pay the musicians. He'd feel responsible, you know. Like somebody owning a big firm or something.

I think Colyer was just paying his own wage-packets, not via a big agent.

GEOFF COLE Ron Ward was the next to leave. What happened was that out at John Boddy's club at Reading, we were playing away, and at the end of the evening, I was out in the Gents, Ron came in to take a leak and said, "I've left the band." And I said, "What?" And he said, "No, Ken said the rhythm section sounded bloody awful, and I said, 'Is it me?' and Ken said, 'The rhythm section sounds wonderful when I'm drunk, but when I'm sober, it sounds awful.'"

And Ron, who suffered from a terrible lack of confidence, chucked it in very quickly, and said, "Alright, I'll hand my notice in." Just like that. And he left very, very quickly in about a week, I think. He knew he wasn't a brilliant bass player. In fact, I remember one German bloke who came once and said, "What's happened to the man who stands in the corner?" Of course, it was Ron Ward. He ignored the fact that he was playing the bass, he was standing in the corner.

BILL COLE When I joined the band the line-up was Johnny Bastable, of course, on banjo—exceptionally good banjo, and became a very firm friend of mine. The front-line was Sammy on clarinet and Geoff was on trombone. It was Pete Ridge on drums at the time.

DAVE BRENNAN On one of the Colyer band's visits to Sheffield I remember John Bastable discovered Whitbread's Barley Wine, which he obviously enjoyed very much. In the final set he kept falling asleep and Colin Bowden had to keep lashing him awake with his drumstick. Finally, when Ken was droning *Sweet Lorraine*, J.B. fell off his chair.

The following morning we called at the grandly named Empire Hotel where the band was staying. We met a dejected John Bastable. "Colyer's sacked me," he said, "the bastard's sacked me." A little while later Colyer reeled in. J.B. grovelled up to him. "Don't sack me, Ken. I'll do anything you want. I'll give up drinking." "There's no need to go fucking mad," was Ken's brief reply. And that was the end of the matter.

CATHY COLYER Bob and Ken worked together. It was me that made him stop with Ken. I'd got Robbie at school. Robert never saw his father, basically. And one night they came home from a gig at Hayes somewhere, and they'd both been knocked down the stairs because Ken wouldn't sign a contract. And Bob got a black eye, big as he was.

Bob could fight, but there was a crowd of them. And they were knocked down the stairs, and I said to him,

> "You've got to pack up this jazz and get a decent job, or you move out, because Robert doesn't see you, I don't see you.

I go out in the morning to work, you come in and go to bed, I come in and you're gone." And that was the situation.

And that was the existence for all the years he was there with Ken. It was no way to live. I mean, the drink and that went with the job, but...

Bob wasn't earning the money. It was about twelve pounds, I think.

GEOFF COLE Then Pete Ridge left the band. I think what had happened was this: He might have seen the writing on the wall. Ken kept the wages up to thirty quid until Pete left, and then they dropped after that. So, he went back—prior to becoming a professional musician he worked for a vending machine company. Ken got him because he knew he played good snare drum.

So Pete left first, and Brian Hetherington had been around the place and he suddenly came in and that was that.

BILL COLE Pete didn't stay that long after I joined. He was a gourmet chef and decided to spend more time building up his restaurant business, and so on, until eventually he sadly died.

SAMMY RIMINGTON I got Richard Simmons in on piano. I knew he was available, because we were real mates, Richard and me. First of all he didn't know what to do. And I said, "Well, come in," you know. Anyway, he didn't last so long, Richard. I can't remember what happened there.

GEOFF COLE Pat Hawes had been seriously considering joining the band. There was a stage when he would come and sit-in quite often, and I loved it. When he sat-in, playing all that Buster Wilson, I really enjoyed that. I'm not sure that Johnny Bastable liked it all that much, though. Because Pat would go on about all the passing chords and, well, you know what Pat's like… he's a lovely character.

TONY PYKE It was Bill Cole and Brian Hetherington. They pushed for me, in fact, and then Ken said, "Well, ask him to stand-by." You know, that was all I got. To stand-by for this fortnight, which is what I did, and I did the gigs. And then the same the year after—'65—again that was a fortnight. And then in November of '65, Sammy left, and Ken asked me to join.

You had Monty Sunshine with *Petite Fleur*, and Kenny Ball had *Midnight In Moscow* and whatever, and Acker had *Stranger on the Shore*. They all had their hits, in a way. And Ken said, "I'd give my right arm to have a hit—a number in the Hit-Parade. Don't think I wouldn't want that, because that would keep the band together and the wages going. But what I will not do is stoop down to a lower level. My vision is down a certain path—New Orleans-style music—and I certainly wouldn't worry one way or the other. But, if we had a hit by doing our style of music, then that's fine."

My first official gig with him was up to a club in Bedford. And I couldn't believe it: It was an awful night weather-wise; it was blowing a gale and storm, and we got there and—without a word of exaggeration—we were in a hall over a pub and playing to something like six people. And I didn't say anything about it at all. He was obviously upset about this when it happened from time to time. We'd go into these places and play to virtually no one.

Well I know we've always said things like, "Well, if it came to it, I'd play to an empty room," because we loved doing it. But this was a band—a fully professional band—that he's trying to keep going on the road, you know. But I could not believe that. But then the next night it was—I think we were down at Hayling Island—and it was completely packed out.

MIKE McCOMBE On 13 January 1967 the band was booked to appear in Brighton. It was a bitterly cold day, and by the time the gig ended ice had formed on the minor roads. On the way home we hit a patch of ice, Ken lost it and the van ran up the side of the banking on the side of the road and overturned. It spun a couple of times on its roof and then the back end slid neatly into someone's drive through the open gates. The clamshell back windows opened and my drums were ejected (I had no cases at the time) and the cymbals slowly stopped revolving noisily in the driveway.

We were all trying to sort ourselves out in the van. I think I ended up with Geoff Cole sitting on my face, and as we emerged we started to look for assistance. At this point a light came on in an upstairs window of the house whose drive we had just entered. Ah, we thought, help is on the way. The window of the upstairs room was opened and a guy stuck his head out. "Serves you right for driving so bloody fast!" he shouted, slammed the window shut and went back to bed!

A hire-car was eventually provided, the van was towed away, and we all ended up back in London a bit shaken. As a result of this, Ken had to hire a small van with which to haul the instruments, and Tony Pyke offered the use of his Mini until such time as we got the van back. As I was the junior member it was decided that I should have to ride in the van with Ken while the others went in the Mini.

This turned out to be an incredible experience, because Ken never stopped talking! On our journeys up and down the country he told me his complete life history, about growing up in Norfolk, about his parents being in service, his Dad working as a chauffeur and about the variety of cars that he drove. He told me about his seafaring days and the New Orleans experience, he just never stopped and my one regret was that handheld tape recorders hadn't been invented yet!

All this happened over 40 years ago and I can't remember half of what he told me.

COLIN BOWDEN I'll tell you a story about the hearse. Ken had bought this Rolls-Royce hearse and converted it into a bandwagon. We used to do the Bath Jazz Festival, and it was all-night. And I think we came through Maidenhead and we were all lying in the back flaked out. And there were all these people looking in. There was a traffic jam, and we were just lying there, and I remember opening my eyes seeing all these people looking at us lying there.

CATHY COLYER Well, that hearse was most strange because I had it parked outside my house. And Robert wasn't well at one time and the doctor came, and he said, "Who's is that Rolls-Royce out there? So I said to him, "Never mind about the Rolls-Royce, my son is sick!"

GEOFF COLE It was just before Christmas. We were playing at the Nottingham Dancing Slipper, Bill Kinnell's place. And Bill gave us a bottle of scotch for Christmas. He gave Ken a bottle, and he gave the rest of the band a bottle as well. And we were driving back—Bob was driving—and the bottle was going round. What happened was that we were going around the bend—we weren't all that far from Nottingham and we ran out of road, and we went round and went on the grass verge, and there were all these posts, and we went bom, bom, bom, bom like a set of dominos, and eventually we hit a wooden telegraph pole, and the van spun around and went over on its roof.

And… there was utter silence. And Pete Ridge was the first one out, and he got out of the side door, went around to the front, and he said he could see two pairs of feet sticking out from where the windscreen had been. And then he heard Ken's voice

saying, "Bob, we can't afford to do this sort of thing too often." Pete Ridge heard him, because he came back and told us.

BILL COLE Eventually Brian left, and to this day I still don't know quite what the story was behind that—whether he'd had enough or Ken had had enough, or they'd both had enough. But Brian left, and we had various people after that. At some point Mike McCombe, who you probably know from the Grand Dominion Band in Canada, held the chair down for about six months, I think. But then we suddenly found ourselves without a drummer, so Ken was using dep. drummers.

Quite a lot of them—mentioning no names, but some of them were playing what they thought that Ken wanted to hear, rather than what he did actually want to hear, and what would be the appropriate thing. You know, people riding out the last chorus on woodblocks, for instance. Totally out of order.

But then we had some very fine drummers, like Laurie Chescoe for instance. And he just turned around to Ken and said: "Ken, I cannot sound like Baby Dodds, so I'm not going to try." And Ken said, "Thank God for that. I wouldn't want you to. You just play the way you normally play, and the band will swing." And it did.

Eventually, we ran out of drummers, and we turned up one night at the 51, and Geoff said to me, "There's no drummer at the moment. Who do you think we've got on drums?" And Geoff, of course, was getting a little bit fretful about this by this time, and he said to Ken, "Who have we got on drums tonight, Ken?" "We haven't got anybody. We're not using a

drummer tonight. We're a five-piece." And so Bastable and myself were the rhythm section. We carried it through and it had a nice, light, swinging sound to it. So for about probably a week or so we didn't have drums.

MALC MURPHY I first started to sit-in with Ken's band at the Il Rondo Ballroom in Leicester. Late 1965-66. After that, Ken contacted me by letter asking if I would be interested in auditioning for the "drum chair." That was 1967. I went down to his house, then we went to the 51 Club on a Saturday night—at that time it was a regular session unless the band was on tour or had a weekend gig elsewhere. He offered me the job, which I was very pleased to accept. When Ken asked me to join the band, I knew no one in London, so Ken put me up in his front-room for about three months. That was at 99 The Drive.

While I was staying with Ken, I slept on the settee in the front room, in a sleeping bag. Anyway, one Sunday morning after coming home from the Manchester Sports' Guild the night before—we got in about 4.30, had some rabbit stew which Vera had left on a low light in the oven, and went to bed. Anyway, about 11.a.m. there's a knock on the front door, and finally I heard Ken coming down the stairs.

So I looked through the slightly opened door and saw Ken standing there in his faded red long johns, a check shirt and his hair all ravelled up as if he'd been dragged through a hedge backwards. So I heard a man's voice—there were two of them in suits and ties, and one of them was holding a black book. So he starts off by saying about the religion he represented—Jehovah's Witness—and asked Ken if he was religious. Ken waited 'til he finished speaking—about three minutes—and then said: "Do you know this is a Sunday, which according to most religions is a day of rest. Are you two people Christians?" And one replied, "Yes Sir." Then Ken said, "Well, do the Christian thing and Fuck Off," and promptly slammed the front door. I looked out of the front window and saw them hurrying away in a state of Jehovah's Shock.

TONY PYKE We were in Denmark and we went through into Sweden. We did Gothenburg—the University down at Gothenburg—and we were playing. We'd finished a set, and we'd come back into the band-room and the promoter came in and started talking to us. And Ken wasn't there. And he said, "Tell me boys, why is the band so cheap, when it's so popular? For example, for Papa Bue I have to pay x number of thousands of Kroner, and for Chris Barber x number of thousands of Kroner" (and I can't find the figures—I've forgotten) "but for you—you are just one or two thousand Kroner. And it's so much cheaper. Why is this?"

Well, somebody in the room—when Ken came back in—somebody in the room brought his attention to this, and Ken flew into a wild temper, because he was more or less saying "Keep your nose out of my business." But all that was trying to be made—the point to be made—was telling him for his own good. Because all he had to do really was to come back home, speak to Don Aldridge—talk about it—and get this business put right. But he didn't look at it that way, he thought you were having a personal go at him, in some way. And that wasn't how it was at all. We were trying to help the man, and he wouldn't be helped in that respect.

GEOFF COLE We had to leave it all to him. It was almost as if we were impugning his honesty, I suppose. Whenever anybody came into the band, at some stage in the proceedings—within the first few days—some question of money would crop up. And we always said to any newcomer, "Don't mention money to Ken whatever you do, don't say anything about money—just leave it be."

There was one occasion at the end of a tour when Ken had a big contract and he wanted to get someone to read it as he couldn't understand German hardly at all. And he got Tony Pyke to go through it, and he put a piece of paper over the fee the band were getting. But Tony said that he did actually see it before Ken put the piece of paper over it. He really didn't want anyone to be aware of the amount.

But, he used to tell us in the bandwagon: "I had to go to the bank manager again today to get an overdraft to pay the wages this week. It's not going very well." And Richard Simmons was in the band then, and he was carrying on with only half wages. He thought things can't get any worse, but they did. And in the end he had to leave.

BILL COLE Well, I used to find him great to be on the road with. A grumpy old sod at times, as you well know, but when we were on the road—particularly when we were abroad—he was a totally different person. Because I used to do a lot of the navigating. After his brother Bob left the band, we split the driving between us. I used to do all of the navigating, and calling the pick-up times and things like that.

And of course, when we went abroad, there were only two of us in the band that spoke German; that was Geoff Cole and myself. I spoke German and French and Dutch, of course, through playing in Rudy Balliu's band in the old days in Ghent. And so I used to more or less—well, between Geoff and myself

we were more or less roadies, when we were on the road there. And, somebody once said to Ken, "Oh, Mr. Colyer, how do you get on when you go abroad?"

And Ken said, "Well, it's easy for me. We get down to Dover, and we get on the boat, and when we get off, Bill knows where we're going, and when we get there he speaks the language. End of story." It was somewhat of an exaggeration, but…

TONY PYKE But Ken could be pretty nervous in the way that he could be pretty ratty with you, if you said the wrong thing. I learnt very quickly to watch what I said. I remember we were on one of the German tours, and we were at the Deutsch Museum in Munich—which is very famous, where Adolf Hitler did some of his famous speeches on the very same stage.

It was a huge place—seven or eight thousand, maybe more. And the "acowstics"—as he used to call them—were really bad, and I actually said to him up on the stage, "Cor blimey, the acoustics up here are really dreadful."

"Well, what do you expect me to do about it? Get on with it." And I thought, "Oops." You had to be very, very careful what you said to the man. He'd just explode for nothing.

KEN COLYER There are some OK bands having a go in various parts of the country, but you don't really get to hear them to make a proper assessment. There was a group we played with in Llanelli the other week; they're a Cardiff-based band and have been plodding along for years. They came up with some surprisingly good moments at that gig. They're not brilliant, only get a chance to play once a week, I think.

It's an odd thing: Wales has never been good jazz territory, I dunno why. Nothing has ever really built up in Wales, and the same goes for the West Country. Bristol was good at times, when Acker was going strong, and before he came to London; but once you go further west, it's as dead as a doornail. I feel sorry for that Cardiff band, they're cut off from everything, and they're genuine, sincere blokes, completely unconcerned with trad popularity, sticking to their guns and trying to play an authentic New Orleans style. They'll keep playing because they want to, and there are similar outfits around, more than you'd realise.

It's very important that there are these groups dotted all over the country. They're not deterred by the fact that they're operating only in a small way; there's a determination to try and play the music as best they can and keep it going. As to Keith Smith and Barry Martyn's bands, they're both good. We more or less share the same ideas, and they each put their own interpretation on the music, which is as it should be. Keith is good; he's still young, still has a lot to learn, but if he goes the right way he's got a good chance of being a fine player and leader.

Words like "improvisation" can get a little out of line. You can't expect jazz musicians to come up with something totally different, totally fresh, number after number, night after night. It just can't be done. People don't always realise that a lot of what we play now has been built up over the years; things that do happen spontaneously... if they're good and they work, you keep them in.

But it really comes down to head arrangements. You have an outline—a skeleton—keep it fairly loose and leave room, leave chinks for spontaneity. The leader has to know the melody, the others have to know the chords and work with the leader. In some choruses I'll play the melody pretty straight, in others I'll play around it.

Bunk Johnson teaches a very important lesson in this regard. It's not exactly improvisation, more extemporisation —a kind of embellishment. But having said all that, you will never, never hear my band play the same tune exactly the same way twice. But if the man behind the gun—the leader—doesn't have the imagination to go for that degree of embellishment, then he doesn't play jazz, and that's where a lot of your trad from the so-called Boom comes from. It has nothing to do with jazz—it's an effect, a pastiche.

If you've got anything in you—and if you're thinking all the time (which you have to do)—then every time you play a tune you'll find something just a little bit different to do with it, so the music never loses its interest for the real listener.

Believe only half of what you read and then disregard 95% of that. I've read everything I could possibly lay my hands on about jazz over the years. Even if the musical evidence isn't there—there simply are no early records of Negro jazz to substantiate what is generally believed to be true—men before the ODJB were obviously creating and developing this music, and it must have developed very quickly once it got away.

So it must have been Bolden, probably not in isolation. We're pretty sure there were other men contemporary with him—most unlikely the music was the brainchild of just one man. The frustration is there's so little known about Bolden, and that elusive wax cylinder has never been found!

The absolute proof is missing, sure, but it must be more than a myth. I don't know why people like Brian Wooley—and that really surprises me; he's a good cat and I've played with him many times—can't go with the broadly accepted theory. Joe Robichaux claims to have heard Bolden at Lincoln Park, but he was just a toddler at the time. He was honest about it; he said "I can't really remember... my daddy used to take me out to the Park when Bolden was playing there, but I don't remember the details or the sound except they were blowing up a storm."

Take Glenny—he was knocking on a bit, nearly 90 when he died, but he was an older man than Bolden and had worked with Bolden. He reckoned Bolden was the ultimate in power: louder than Armstrong with the microphone full on. But look, think about it from a common sense perspective—it all worked out through the basic American folk root: the blues,

the work songs, the spirituals from the plantations and churches. When instruments became available, that same folk root was converted to an instrumental form of the same music. How can people really believe that the ODJB picked up their horns and said, "Right, we're gonna play a new music never heard before" and just played it? Nonsense! Who could accept such a preposterous notion?

Jazz is the American Negro root... rock 'n' roll, R&B, beat, and whatever the current fad is—it all stemmed from jazz with consequent degradation of the music in the process. [CKC]

BILL COLE Playing with George Lewis was one of the greatest experiences, and Ken and George had a rapport—they *definitely* had a rapport. We did a recording from Manchester. In fact, we were all dying of 'flu at the time. How that recording ever got made, I'll never ever know.

But it turned out nice, and it was just as though George had been a member of Ken's band for years. That was something really strange, and I remember we were on one tour George played *Burgundy Street Blues* just with Johnny Bastable and myself—Digbeth Town Hall in Birmingham. And, well, if anybody asks me to mention a highlight in my playing career, I think I would have to say that that was it. Just an absolutely transfixed audience, and George—no drums, no piano, no horns—just Bastable, me and George. Wow!

JOHN GRIFFITH So I was backstage, and George Lewis was there, with his manager, and I just wandered up and thought, "Well, people can only tell me to go away." So I actually sort of introduced myself briefly to George, and he was all beams and smiles and very, very nice to talk to. Then after a while he turned away and just listenend to Ken. And I thought, "This is my exit; I'd better go now. I don't want to over-do it."

Then he turned back to me and sort of said, "That tone, man, that tone. Where does he get that tone from?"

And I suddenly thought, "Christ, this is the man who has heard every trumpet player of any meaning or worth anywhere at any time. And he is still fascinated, hooked on Ken's tone and his playing." I thought, "This has to mean much more than just sounds" you know. I mean, this is a terrific evaluation. It was not a performance, it was George being natural.

FREEDOM AND SELF-DISCIPLINE
SAYS KEN COLYER
Unknown writer, *Melody Maker*, undated

Jazz has several definitions but to my mind there is still no more rewarding form of it than New Orleans music—for human and emotional outlet, actual musical colour and sheer fire.

New Orleans jazz has a lot of knockers. They say that to play it you don't have to have technique and all you have to do is to listen to early records and copy. It's rubbish.

It is such a human and personal thing that to put down on paper how you set about playing is very difficult.

Perhaps the most important thing is records. Nobody has yet found a better way of getting inspiration.

From a trumpeter's viewpoint, there's a wealth of good New Orleans music on record. I'd advise any budding musician to get hold of any early ones.

Soak them up as much as possible till it's coming out of your ears; anything by Mutt Carey or Bunk Johnson.

In absorbing all the stuff on these early records one thing stands out; a trumpeter's attack is terribly important.

But you must never sacrifice a good ensemble sound.

Individuality, swing and attack; these, then, are the three big things. It's naturally important to develop swing from the start—but it's impossible to say how you do that.

About this business of copying. I guess it's the first thing any traditional jazz musician does.

But there IS such a thing as playing freely in the New Orleans style without necessarily slavishly copying every nuance of your particular favourite.

The trumpet is the logical lead instrument, but I can't stress sufficiently the need for all the musicians to play as a unit and complement each other. It's also important for each player to have terrific self-discipline and know what the other player is up to.

In N.O. jazz the actual band sound is the end product—nobody is the star.

If a band knits together well, the musicians reflect each other's statements musically.

The real beauty of N.O. music is that there is such a wealth of individuality, yet they express themselves together while retaining, in my opinion, unmistakable personal styles. Listen to any early records by any of the greats of N.O. and you'll find that controlled acceleration is often a big factor.

Controlled acceleration heightens the climax and excitement of some tunes but not all.

This is particularly evident from Kid Ory in *Get out of here and go on Home* and from the George Lewis band on several occasions.

But the word "controlled" needs emphasising. Use your own taste and judgement in this, but don't be afraid to accelerate the tempo when the excitement calls for it.

It's yet another wonderful part of New Orleans music. What form of music offers the marvellous variety of blues AND powerful build-ups?

I've noticed that there is not enough attention paid today to counterpoint—countermelodies by the front-line instruments—even by N.O. men.

This is where the clarinet comes in particularly. There's no end of scope here for the great colour of the music to blossom.

To play N.O. style jazz properly requires more skill than a lot of the knockers realise.

It's all very well sitting down and saying "I think I'll play trumpet or clarinet like that."

But when you hear a N.O. musician, there's a whole lifetime of experience, wisdom and sometimes depression, coming through that horn.

To anybody starting with a trumpet in jazz, I'd say—buy a good instrument. Spend around Seventy pounds on it.

If you take it seriously enough to want to start playing, invest in a horn that will make playing easier and the tone more pleasant. Then there's the argument of trumpet versus cornet. On this score, I agree with Louis Armstrong.

He said "There's no difference between the two—the cornet just makes you work harder."

This is entirely a matter of personal taste. The cornet needs more "lip" and wind. Many trumpets, to my mind, produce a cornet sound. Tommy Ladnier, particularly.

You can learn a tremendous amount from records, but you come to put your own interpretation of it on your music.

New Orleans jazz has more freedom of expression, rich beauty, sensitivity and depth than any music form.

I must say that if you haven't got that something inside you—that fire, spark and genuine human feeling—you will not only be unsuccessful but you will not get the right reward from playing.

Absorb the idiom and re-create it. That way, New Orleans Jazz is full of richness.

KEN COLYER I know things couldn't happen again in the way the Revival blossomed out. But the music is there and I'm sure that a future generation will go back to the base and realise how good it all is.

Things really are sadder in the States than they are over here. But there are one or two young bands—like the Hall Brothers, whom Sammy Rimington worked with while he was over there.

But New Orleans jazz is a difficult music to play properly. It's taken me more than half a lifetime to learn about the complexity of the music. I think the band I have now is pretty damned good, but it didn't just happen that way, it has evolved. We are getting towards the sound I want, but there are always problems to be solved—the old problems, rhythmically and tonally. I've always complained about these pastiche sounds, these surface sounds that many bands get when they think they are playing the music. You have to dig a lot deeper than that to understand New Orleans music.

SAMMY RIMINGTON Regarding what he learned in New Orleans, mostly he talked about ensemble playing—not so

Ken plays a club session with Mike McCombe on drums

much solos, ensemble playing together, and what an art-form it was.

And relaxation, of course.

But it's also the emotional thing, like feeling a little bit excited there, and then being relaxed there. So if you get a little bit excited it might go up a little bit. It's reflections of emotions going on. Controlled acceleration? Well, I think he made that up. But it *does* happen. If you listen to a lot of the bands, even Jelly Roll Morton, when he's doing solo things, he *does* speed up.

Because he probably listened to a lot of bands and he noticed it, you know. Like in a lot of folk musicians. He was into folk music a lot—Leadbelly—and they went up in tempo a lot, and—well, the Lewis band went up in tempo. I mean, there's a lot of bands that go up in tempo. So you can't say it's wrong, because there's some great musicians have done it, but it's not conscious. And because it's gradual, you don't notice it—it's human, and you don't notice it.

If it was pre-programmed, you'd probably notice it. Because it would be this sudden jerk—it wouldn't flow, it wouldn't have that fluidity.

It's got to be unconscious—totally unconscious. There shouldn't be any conscious thought about it at all—because it's a human thing. And if you're working with a metronome, it's not human. And if you're conscious of keeping time on its own, its gonna sound metronomic, and it's not gonna swing.

It's like a drum machine. If you play with a drum machine, it's mechanical like this, and you're tied down to this inhuman thing; there's no human element about it.

COLIN BOWDEN Controlled acceleration? Bad playing. I think it was just Ken's defence. I think it was because Johnny Bastable would always push the beat, and—if I wasn't drunk—I would hold him. But if I wasn't playing properly, I couldn't hold him. I mean, it depends to what degree bands *do* shift. You can hear the Ellington band change—move tempo. But, I think sometimes we used to speed up too much, really. And Ken called it controlled acceleration, but that was just his defensive way of talking about it.

BILL COLE We were doing one of these sort of society, university gigs up in North London— Hornsey/Haringey way, somewhere like that for the North London Police. And at the time you'd have a dance band, a beat group, a folk singer, a trad band, a raconteur and various things like this. And somewhere along the line there was an almighty cock-up. The contracts had all been sent out with an hour's different time.

So everybody turned up basically on time according to the contract, but it was an hour late. Now the silly woman that was organising this, instead of saying, "Oh, well, we'll run the whole show an hour late," got into a complete and utter tizzy and was arguing with the bands, accusing everybody for turning up late, unprofessional conduct—all this-that-and-the other. Well, we were on—we'd done a gig already somewhere else, probably down the 51. And we went on, and we were supposed to do something like one o'clock in the morning 'til two o'clock in the morning.

And then our second set was going to be four o'clock in the morning 'til five in the morning. And by this time we were a bit tired, and well away. We did our first set and it went down brilliantly. Then we asked about the refreshments and where the band-room was.

And this woman rounded on us, accusing us of being !#*@$#! musicians, freeloading, turning up late, unprofessional etc., etc.

By this time, I'd got—let's say—somewhat emotional about it, and Johnny Bastable was with me, and he was half way down a pint of Guinness and bitter. So I snatched it out of his hand, and I chucked it over her. She was wearing a lovely white ball gown at the time, as I recall. Her husband said to me, "I say, I say, you're just a musician, you can't do that to my wife!" So I hit him. And he went over a couple of tables. And I thought, "I'm sorry, but this professional life is not for me. I'm not really interested in this way of carrying on." So I walked downstairs—full evening dress—picked up my bass (I hadn't got a case for it in those days, got a carrying strap), slung it on my back, and walked out. I was in such high dudgeon that I walked from the Haringey area down to Waterloo Station. And that was on, I think, the Saturday night.

On the Monday, I'm at home, and the phone rings. "Bill, it's Ken." I said, "It's alright Ken—I resign." He said, "You can't resign. I've rung up to fire you." I said, "Ken, I've already resigned. You can't fire me, because I'm not a member of your band." "Bill, I'm firing you—you were out of order last night." I said, "Yes, Ken, I know I was out of order, that's why I've done the decent thing, and resigned."

He said, "You can't resign, because I'm firing you'. And I said, "No Ken, you can't fire me. I've resigned." Anyway, this banter went on for about five or ten minutes. So there was a slight pause in the conversation at both ends, and this hiatus was interrupted by: "Bill, who's paying for this phone-call?" I said, "You are, Ken." "In that case you're fired." Slam! Down went the phone. And that is the true story of how I was fired from the Ken Colyer band.

KEN AMES John Keen—I must thank him for that—he mentioned me to Ken, and then there was a chance to be sort of considered for the band, and I let it go by for one or two reasons, and then a bit later on Ken had Derek Jones. Eventually it was fixed up for me to go and audition at the George in Morden. So I arrived—**I had a VW Camper van, the same sort of thing as the Colyer band had, and I was having trouble, and Ken came out and had a look at it for me. And then I realised later he wasn't quite the mechanic that I hoped he might be.**

So I went and auditioned. Ray Holland was on bass—well, he was depping and filling in, but obviously Ken had booked him for sort of safety reasons. Anyway, so I turned up, and I did the second half, and then at the end of the session, Ken turned around and said, "Well, do you want to come in with us?" That was an offer to join, so I got the gig. I said, "Can I just go home and chat about this?" "Yeah, don't leave it too long."

So on Christmas morning—that was a couple of days later—I rang up Ken and said, "Hello Ken. Ken Ames here." I said, "Happy Christmas, Ken." And he said "What?" So I said, "Yeah, I'd love to join." So I joined, and immediately we sort of started recording the Joy stuff—almost immediately, in about one week. Ken was waiting to record, and he just probably didn't feel the band was ready.

So I joined, and I can remember playing at the Manchester Sports' Guild and getting back at about six in the morning, staying at Ken's—because I hadn't moved up to London at that point. And Ken knew I was a chiropodist. He said, "There's some stew in the oven—rabbit stew." Now I'm not a rabbit stew fan. Six o'clock in the morning, a bit of toast would have done me. So out comes this steaming bowl of rabbit stew. I sat there, and—I don't know how he did this—suddenly I'm sitting there, and up comes this bare foot, and he said, "What do you think of that, then?" Six a.m., barefoot, rabbit stew; what a day!

JOHN McNICHOLAS In the latter part of 1970, I was in Hamburg, Germany, with the Colyer band. Ken had asked Ray Smith to do a stint of ten concerts with the band as part of a lengthier band tour. I motored out there in a borrowed car. Each of the concerts was played in a different town.

The first night in Hamburg saw the first of the concerts. It was a disaster through Ken being much the worse through drink. He lost the beat a number of times and I remember that once, during *Riverside Blues*, he stopped playing for a few seconds before starting again. It was very embarrassing, as the rest of the band were floundering as they tried to keep together. There were some catcalls from the audience, and after the last number Ken attempted a mumbled apology to the crowd. Afterwards Bastable told me that in his 15 years with the band that was the first time that Ken had ever been given the bird.

The following evening the band played another town—I can't remember where except that they played in a school assembly hall. As if to make up for the previous evening, Ken was in top form, with *Over The Rainbow* being outstanding.

MALC MURPHY When you were a new boy in the band you shared a room with "the Guv'nor" whilst on tour, and for a couple of years that was me.

Here's an incident while on tour in Germany. I was sharing a room with Ken: two single beds, spread out. We'd been playing and were invited to a party after the concert—in evening dress, of course. Normally, Ken would be the last to leave, but this time he left an hour or so before it broke up. So I'd said to Ken, "Leave the bedroom door unlocked," as there was only one key. Anyway, I found the room, opened the door quietly so as not to wake Ken, and as I opened the door and crept in, I could hear this muffled sound—a voice mumbling something which I couldn't make out.

So I switched the bedside light on, still hearing this muffled sound. Ken's bed was empty, so I looked in the wardrobe. Nothing in the wardrobe, so I bent down and looked under Ken's bed, and saw that there was a bundle under the bed with the muffled sound coming out of it. I lay flat on the floor and with my feet I eventually rolled the bundle out from under the bed. As it unfurled, Ken rolled out, still in full evening dress with bow tie. He must have rolled himself up in the duvet and rolled off the bed, and then couldn't get out. I said, "What were you saying, Ken?" He said, "I was saying 'Help, get me out of this tangle!'"

KEN AMES I can remember at one stage, he couldn't really express what he wanted from the music side. I mean, I suppose in a way you're supposed to know, but at the same time there's that element of not being able to actually put it together and say, "If you could just do something a bit wider or..." I mean, he could say on one of these Ellington things (*Saturday Night Function*), he just wanted one note played through a whole chorus on the bass.

JOHN McNICHOLAS We were in Wuppertal, where the band had a night off. A German jazz collector had invited us to his house for a drink. It was on this occasion that I had a chance to talk to Ken for a while sitting with him for an hour or so. I remember asking him if, when he first started playing, he ever had any doubts that he would get his playing right. He nodded vigorously to this, saying that you must keep on with it until you do get it right.

He also told me an amusing story concerning his school days. "Even then, I was a bit of a weirdo," he said. Apparently Ken was more interested in American jazz heard on the radio than in attending to his studies. On one occasion, when the teacher said, "You know, Colyer, if you paid more attention to your school work instead of that American jazz music you're always on about, it would be very much to your benefit. I, for one, do not like it."

Ken replied that if the teacher cared to listen to next week's radio programme he might just change his mind about jazz.

About a week later Ken was again in trouble with the teacher. After being reprimanded for some wrongdoing, the teacher finished by saying, "Oh, and by the way, Colyer, I listened to that programme, just like you had suggested, and I still don't like American jazz music." Ken thought this highly amusing.

KEN AMES One of the first things that Ken said to me was—I don't know why he said it to me; must have thought I was some kind of intellectual—he said, "I haven't really had a great education." So I said, "Well, yeah, but here we are!" It was quite embarrassing really that he was telling me that. But Ken had that determination, and in his case—and some others—to be a maverick and an individual, ploughing your furrow, you're always going to get detractors, aren't you?

And he got through a lot of that. I mean, we know he could be a grumpy individual, but the thing is, you can't take away the fact that he had a lot more music in him than some people give him credit for. And the whole extent of his repertoire, from the rags, right through to *Ghost Soldier* and all those tunes. I mean, that repertoire—not many people can equal that.

JOHN McNICHOLAS The last day of the ten concerts was in Oldenburg, and we were to travel home the next day. A short while after the end of this concert I found Ken and Malc Murphy in a restaurant seated at a table and in a noisy argument with each other. I don't know what they were arguing about but I chose a bad moment to try and talk to Ken. I went over to thank him for an enjoyable ten days and to say that we were off home the following day.

He completely misunderstood what I was saying and replied, "If you don't like it out here you'd better not come again. All of you Irishmen are the same; everywhere you go in the world you cause trouble." At the mention of the word "Irishmen" Malc Murphy leaned forward and half shouted at Ken, "What did you say about Irishmen?" That was my cue to leave.

RAY SMITH I went out to Germany three times with the band, beginning, I believe, in 1969. Ken seemed to be drinking heavily, particularly on the last tour, sometimes with disastrous results. On one occasion we played a jazz club and the promoter had laid on a champagne party. Members of the orchestra persuaded said promoter that this was not a good idea before the session, and he gracefully postponed it until the next morning.

We had something like a six-hour drive the next day and reckoned that Ken would have time to sober up during the journey. Unfortunately, when we eventually clambered into the bandwagon, it became apparent that Ken had appropriated a couple of bottles, and I vaguely remember the sound of his voice reciting Kipling during our journey.

Came time for the concert, and we assembled onstage. Ken stomped off, and unfortunately was suffering from "champagne lip"—no sound emerged from his horn, but the drums were rolling and everyone was wondering what they were supposed to be playing. Eventually we all got together on what I thought was a slow version of *Swannee River*. I mentioned this to Geoff Cole in the interval, and he replied, "That wasn't *Swannee River*—that was *Lonesome Road*."

After the interval, a small girl was to present Ken with a large bouquet onstage. Although very young, I think she understood that he was not quite himself—there had been a bit of a shout-up during the interval—and she was visibly nervous as she approached Ken with the flowers, thrusting them into his hands and departing fairly quickly. **Ken, who of course was sitting down, stared at the flowers for what seemed like an age, eventually selected one and started eating it.** There was a stunned silence, until Johnny Bastable said, "Can I have one, Ken?" Ken duly handed them around the members of the orchestra and announced to the amazed audience that they were the best chrysanthemums he'd ever tasted.

TONY PYKE Well, in Germany, I remember a little girl bringing a bouquet of flowers up on stage to present to him. And he hardly said a word, and took them from her, and started eating them. On stage. In front of three or four thousand people—a concert stage.

It didn't seem to go down very well, and he more or less reduced the child to tears.

JOHN LONG The thing was, Ken went on alarmingly about his disappointment with Decca and Columbia, and all the big lot. Then he got onto President Records. And he got onto that because Malc's girlfriend—Carol—was a secretary there, I think. Bob Martin was a part of President Records. She introduced him to Ken, and they did this series of recordings. He wasn't totally happy about those, but the thing was that he knew he was going to disband that band.

And it was like starting with a fresh sheet, you know, he could start again. And we were talking and he said what he wanted to do. He wanted to record an LP of ragtime numbers. And he said, "It's going to be a bit arduous," and Terry, the guv'nor of the Thames Hotel, gave him use of the place. I think it was on two Tuesday evenings when there was nothing happening. So we had, shall we say, two lots of three hours to do what we will.

And my neighbour had started to be interested in coming to the jazz club with us, and he used to live literally next door to us in the maisonette over in West Ewell. I did all the talking to Ken, and Ken said what he wanted to do and this guy owned a Revox; he'd got a mixer, he'd got microphones and all the leads and the stands, and we decided to do it. So Ken booked the Thames Hotel through Terry, and we went down there on these two Tuesday nights, I think in August 1970, with just the band, and the Rosenbergs, who promised to keep quiet. And so the date was booked.

And in the intervening period leading up to it, Ken started to give it more thought. He said to me one afternoon at his place, "You know, in some ways I'm not looking forward to this, because even I get all these rags mixed up. And if I've got to concentrate, and something goes wrong and we have to keep repeating a rag, I don't know how long we can keep this going." So I thought about it, and I said, "Ken, why don't you play a couple of hymns or spirituals then a ragtime tune, then a couple more hymns and spirituals. The band will relax with the hymns and spirituals, and if we take them by surprise with a ragtime tune..." And he said, "Yeah." He said, "That sounds great."

So we spent two evenings, and in the end it worked so well, that we not only got *Ragtime Revisited* but we got a double-album of Hymns and Spirituals. Because the band were relaxed, there was no pressure; the band were relaxed, and we recorded it all.

GEOFF COLE It was Malc's turn to drive. He knew it was his turn to drive, and he came drunk. We drove to Colchester—a really hairy drive. Terrible. It was before the M25—right through the centre of town, and weaving all over the bloody road. And we got there, eventually, and Ken said, "Right. You're never driving this bandwagon again." So the other two drivers—Ken Ames and Tony—looked at each other in horror.

On one occasion we went up to Oldham Cricket Club. And this could have been a contributory factor as far as packing the band up. Tony did the first part. Ken did the second part of the drive after the stop for a cup of tea, up to Oldham. Ken drank profusely while we were playing. Good session. You know, everybody cheering and glad to buy you drinks and, you know, probably six or seven pints and a few scotches and what-have-you.

When we all got in the bandwagon, Tony and Ken Ames got in the back, and Ken came out and got in the driving seat. And he drove off down the road, and down the M6, and he was weaving all over the three lanes, going eighty miles an hour.

And we went past an accident. There were a couple of police cars and a fire engine and cars and whatnot, and we were still weaving all over the road. And it took them a while to catch up with us, but they caught up, and they breathalysed him. Again. That was the second time he was breathalysed.

So they carted him off, and we were just sitting there, you know. And eventually he came back, and the policeman said, "Well, this man's not fit to drive." And Ken Ames took over, 'cause he didn't drink much in those days. And he drove home. It wasn't very long after that that Ken packed it in. So I think Ken felt it was about the last straw for him, you know.

Also his health was obviously starting to give problems. At the time he said he was packing the band in for health reasons. Because I remember reading that Eric Silk packed in his band at that time and said for health reasons, and we thought, "Oh, he's copying Ken."

Ken kept a few gigs. He said, "I'm keeping a few gigs for myself that I've got in the book." There was the Nottingham Rhythm Club which he did with Barry Palser's band.

KEN AMES We knew Ken wasn't well, but probably because it was cancer... I mean, he certainly got through whatever it was, but he never talked about it, you see. He would not open up much.

I think it's like a lot of other things in life; they run a course. And I think one of the arts of life is actually knowing when to stop doing something. Because we do things in our lives because we're habitual, and really we need to review where we're at. And I think Ken, probably, with his reflective personality, reached a point where he thought, "I've been doing this for a long time, I'm not very well, I could probably enjoy myself more being free from the responsibilities of being a bandleader." Which I think was probably his key.

He'd done it for a long time, and he was ticking over, and I think with the house, and running a band, and the cost of everything and all that, I would say that those factors are probably the key thing. I don't think personalities were entirely to do with it.

TONY PYKE He usually paid us out on a Wednesday—in pay-packets. Twenty-five quid in a pay-packet. I remember it well. We were at Amersham—The Crown at Amersham. And he paid us out the money as we were getting the instruments out. And he just said, "Oh, and by the way—I'm folding the band." There was a deathly hush as we were standing there, and it was sinking in. And somebody—I don't know who—not me, said "Well, why? What's prompted this?" And he said, "Well, I've been told to take it easy—the doctor's told me I can't do this any more. On the road."

KEN AMES It was a bit of a surprise. It was Amersham, and as it happened, I went to the toilet, and by the time I came back, Ken had announced to the assemblage that he was folding the band. I can remember Geoff Cole sighing very deeply as I went up. And I thought, "What's happening?" And that was it—suddenly everybody's drinking halves. But then of course we continued under Bastable's name and kept it going with John Shillito.

RAY SMITH I was playing the interval piano spot at Amersham that night, and heard all about what was happening. At the end of the evening Ken asked me if I could write music down on paper, as he was involved with someone who was intending to write a show using New Orleans music. It was a bit vague and nothing ever came of it, but I remember him saying at the end of our brief conversation, "One door closes and another one opens... sometimes."

THE END OF AN ERA
by Max Jones, *Melody Maker,* May 15, 1971.
KEN COLYER, the guv'nor of Britain's trad jazz scene, is quitting at the end of the month after 20 years as a bandleader. He talks to MAX JONES about his decision...

The news reported in last week's *MM* that Ken Colyer is to pack up band leading is a shock to the nervous system of the family of New Orleans jazz followers. It signifies the end of an era.

Ken is known as the Guv'nor, not only for his conception of New Orleans trumpet but also for his dedication to an ideal and his strict observance of what he sees as the vital New Orleans traditions. **He is more than a musician; he is a point of view.**

And now we hear he is to play his farewell date with Colyer's Jazzmen, formed in 1952, at the end of this month—probably at the Cambridge Festival on May 30.

Not that he is giving up playing altogether, of course; just the worries of band leading. And that is only because it is absolutely necessary.

"If over the next couple of months I can take things easy, fix up two jobs a week or something like that, I should feel all right. As long as I can stay at home and just pootle along."

Colyer was talking at his home in Hounslow. He handed me a note from his doctors saying he was suffering from a chronic illness and needed complete rest.

"I'm looking for guest spots with any bands. It wouldn't be practical for me to continue with my old band. That's just what I want to shed, that responsibility.

"The trouble is, the situation gets progressively worse. As things have got tighter workwise and financially, we've had to do more work. Today it is almost impossible to run a full-time jazz band and pay the musicians any sort of money. It's one long headache. I've seen this surgeon and he says I've got some damage, you know, from the heavy dose of radiation I had and must take a rest.

"So that's it. I'm just running out of gas. The state I get into now, it takes me 12 or 14 hours to get eight hours of proper rest. Sometimes, on tour, I've laid in that bloody motor all day, I've felt so shattered.

"If I relax now, apart from having the odd tootle, I'll probably feel tons better soon. If I don't, I get the feeling I'll be in dead trouble."

As for the future of the Colyer Jazzmen, Ken says the obvious thing is for them to carry on. Banjoist Johnny Bastable will take over leadership and, in Colyer's words, it will probably be "a bit difficult all round for a period."

What about the past? What thoughts sprang to mind as he looked back over a couple of decades? Ken smiled a bit wryly and reflected that nobody, all those years ago, could possibly have predicted the way the whole music business was going to go.

"So many ideas got shattered before they even got started; maybe it has to be that way."

Has the upsurge of modern pop had a decisive effect on the popularity of jazz?

"It must have, because one thing hinges on another. The kids are still like sheep, a bit, you know. They do follow the "in" thing. We get quite a few youngsters hearing the band, and they seem to like it—once they get a chance to listen.

"And there's the point. They don't often get the chance because with their crowd, today, it isn't the "in" thing to listen to New Orleans jazz. This obviously must affect business.

"I'd say that if anything the audience is worse, but in all probability the figures have remained static—which makes it seem worse. I mean, look at it from our point of view: everything goes up except our income.

"The cost of everything skyrockets, but they still expect their jazz on the cheap. Promoters want to pay us the same money they paid years ago."

Some bands have modified or completely altered their musical policies because of shifts in public taste, but Colyer has never been a big modifier or compromiser.

"Our band sound was bound to change slightly," he explained. "You have that freedom within the idiom, the freedom of individuality within the confines of the New Orleans style. There's no end of variety possible, and make no mistake... nobody outside New Orleans has mastered the idiom yet, not by what we know of the best examples of New Orleans music."

And how has the Colyer band rated? "A very good attempt," was Ken's summing up. "We've genuinely attempted to emulate the music. That's all I've tried to do and there are not many doing that, here or over there."

He is not giving up because he feels disillusioned.

"I'm not bellyaching at all. Looking back, I'd do it again. There's no other life I prefer. The music has been a way of life to me, and playing full-time you learn to take the bad times with the good."

CHAPTER TWELVE
FREELANCE DAYS/FINAL BANDS

BILL WILKINSON The kindest thing he ever said to me—we had finished a gig at London Zoo with Sammy Rimington and others. It was one of those nights when it was really cooking. We had a beer afterwards. He had just packed up being a bandleader, and said that if I had ever joined his band he would never have packed it in, which was a generous thing to say. He'd asked me several times to join but I always felt it would be too constricting.

RAY HOLLAND During the early seventies jazz clubs in London were encountering many problems, due mainly to an upsurge of free pub jazz. One such club to suffer a decline in attendance was the Morden Jazz Club, run for many years by Steve Duman at The George. Ken Colyer's Jazzmen had played this venue on numerous occasions and had always been exceptionally well received, so it was no surprise when Steve approached Ken about taking up a residency every Tuesday, instead of the usual format of a different name band each week, in an attempt to prolong the existence of the club.

Ken had disbanded his professional band by this time due to ill health, but by popular demand was guesting with many bands and was also forming bands himself for various sessions. The band formed to play at The George, which Ken decided to call his Handpicked Jazzmen, was one such band. Sadly, it was this band's task to play the last session ever at the famous 51 Club in Great Newport Street, the club that Ken had made his own.

The musicians he picked were Dave Bailey (clarinet), Tony Scriven (drums), Ray Holland (bass)—all of whom were playing together with the Mac Duncan Jazz Band—Mike Sherbourne (trombone), who was with the Bill Brunskill Jazzmen, and Stu Morrison (banjo), who had recently left Chris Barber's band.

To play with Ken on these Tuesday night sessions brought great pleasure to us all and taught us a lot.

ROGER HORTON Ken Colyer worked for me for donkey's years. He wasn't always a 100 Club band—he worked at Studio 51, his own club in Great Newport Street, and in fact he never played the 100 until the 51 shut down in 1972. When it did, I approached him and said, "Ken, you will need a West End base, come over to the 100 Club." That would have been in the early seventies, and he ended up playing about 250 gigs for us over the years.

STU MORRISON I'm surprised how unerringly Ken tapped the majority of the numbers in exactly the right speed. When he was wrong (which wasn't often) we in the back line were treated to a shake of the head and a dogged carrying-on to the end of the number. Speeding up was not allowed and was never to be confused with "intrinsic acceleration," which was left to the discretion of the rhythm section. But you had to do it right.

I don't think that there was any doubt in anyone's mind that that particular back-line gave it a pretty heavy 4/4 but although none of us (Colin Bowden, Ray Holland, Pat Hawes and myself) could hardly be described as delicate, Ken as a rule seemed pleased and we were left pretty much to our own devices, and the whole thing swung along pretty well.

The nearest Ken came to criticism was one night when we were fired up on enthusiasm and Gold Labels [Barley Wine— Ed] and the fireworks were going off all over the place in, I think, *That's A Plenty*. Ken beckoned me in mid-number and whispered, not too quietly, "It's... busy on Tyneside tonight!" Now tell me who didn't have a sense of humour!

LEN BALDWIN Roger Horton phoned me and said, "We've got this band on a Wednesday night at the 100 Club, could you come down and have a blow?" So I went down and it was Ken: my hero. At last, playing with him! The first band I played with was myself, Ken (obviously), Sammy Rimington on clarinet,

Stu Morrison on banjo, Annie Hawkins and Colin Bowden. As you know, Ken didn't talk a lot really.

I remember about three or four tunes in, he called *Careless Love Blues*, he kicked it in and said, "George Lewis version," which is, of course, a twelve-bar blues for the first few choruses—and I didn't realise it. So I went in and started playing *Careless Love* and suddenly realised that it was twelve-bar and so that was fine.

We finished that, went into the main tune—and he pointed to me to take a solo and I just played the melody. I finished the solo and we finished the tune and he turned to me and said, "Don't ever do that again. I (a strong emphasis on the word 'I') play the melody!"

Anyway, we played the rest of the evening and when we finished he said, "See you next week." That was it really, and then I was there all the time for the next eight years. There was no contract, there was nothing. But gradually, from this Wednesday job, things developed. Suddenly, Ken came down one evening and said, "By the way, I've got a gig coming up, are you free?" "Oh, yes. Where is it?" "Leicester." This was on a Tuesday night. Don't forget that we were working during the day, but I didn't want to miss it.

ROGER HORTON A guy came up to Ken at the Club bar in the interval one night and said, "Ken, I just want to say how much I enjoyed that first set—absolutely marvellous. I haven't listened to the band for ten years, but I thoroughly enjoyed that," and Ken said to him, "With fans like you it's not surprising I'm living in the gutter!" He could be like that— and other times he could be as nice as pie.

STU MORRISON Throughout Ken's life and more so after his death, a great many people have come forward with what must be one of the most unfair labels that can be applied to anyone, and that is that he was unapproachable.

This just wasn't so, and anyone who says it was is way off target and had never taken the time to do anything except bash Ken's ear about their opinions on all things jazz orientated. Just like all of us, Ken liked a break now and then and off stage during these breaks could and would converse about all manner of subjects with all manner of people.

I first talked to Ken at Shoreham Jazz Club in Sussex. I was a fat schoolboy and, not surprisingly, we talked about the local shipping, the harbour, etc. He was interested and interesting. The years rolled on and we "yarned" on all sorts of subjects from the French Colonial penal colony to the short stories of Joseph Mitchell, especially *McSorley's Wonderful Saloon*, which was read by Eli Wallach on Radio 4's *Book At Bedtime*. We talked about beer, cooking and, very memorably, gardening.

It was during a break at the 100 Club and Ken was cursing the plague of greenfly that were attacking his dahlias. I was working during the day on the gardening staff at London Zoo and was suggesting what Ken might try to kill them off. It was at this point that a "fan" intruded into the conversation with the usual drill about micro-tonal flattening of the fifth and seventh notes, the Spanish Tinge, etc.

If he had been a little more sensitive he would have been conscious of what I christenend Ken's "Basilisk gaze" being turned upon him and the dark flush spreading up from Ken's collar. The blistering tongue lashing that the poor guy endured can be imagined, delivered, as it was, in Ken's "straight-forward" manner. The upshot was: "Would you please not interupt me when me and my side-man are discussing gardening during our break!"

Don't forget that anyone deserves a few minutes off during the working day (or night) and it's only fair for an audience to respect this and to allow the professionals who they are employing for that evening to relax between sets. That's not to say that they must not be approached or talked to; that's all part of being a pro. The actual wording might not be exactly right but Ken once said to me, "I'll talk to anyone about anything, but I won't be talked *at*!"

I'm sure that anyone with any sensitivity can see what the difference is.

BARRY MARTYN I think he [Ken] believed his own publicity. I've been living in New Orleans since the seventies. Went back there, so I came and went, and I learned a lot. I think Ken Colyer wanted to be the English Messiah, in that given field, but I never paid much attention to his band or him. It didn't come in to me very much.

BILL STOTESBURY The only real time I remember talking to him was when he actually came and played with Chris Watford's band. He had a little band that played at the Rose and Crown. I think that was the first time that I had any real conversation with him.

I was very grateful, because I was struggling like buggery

for the first set, because it was pretty dreadful—Chris Watford's wife on the piano doing this chord stuff, and it was not very good at all.

I was terribly embarrassed, because he was my hero, actually sitting-in with us and we didn't know what we were doing. But he was wonderful. He actually said to me, "I like what you're doing, man," you know. And I was pretty heartened by that. At least he was listening to what I was doing. And of course, you learn that you listen... he never missed a trick, did he?

I think he played again at some time. I know he'd got Maeve and Les [Rosenberg—long-time loyal fans] to get my address. And it was pretty soon after that, actually, that he rung me up and said, "I want you to do a job for me." So... that was interesting, really.

CHRIS WATFORD Having booked Ken to come down as a guest artist to play with my Elite Syncopators earlier in the year at Wrotham Heath, Kent, I decided to book him again, but to also book Ron Weatherburn on piano and Trevor Richards on drums, to keep Ken amongst friends he knew.

The room was packed, and John Long had set up his recording gear in the central corridor midway down the hall. We played two or three numbers to get the crowd warmed up. I then introduced Ron to the crowd, and then Ken Colyer, who ambled up to the band amid tumultuous applause. Before we could do anything, Ken put his mouthpiece in, and stomped off into a mournfully slow number without telling anyone what tune it was or what key we were in!

It sounded dreadful, and after going on for what seemed like ages (probably on a 32-bar sequence), Ken pointed at the local trombonist to take a solo. He didn't know what tune we were playing, so busked away as if he were at his own funeral, trying to follow the chords that my local banjoist Bill Stotesbury was playing. Unfortunately, Bill didn't know what tune we were playing either, and was trying to follow the trombonist! Ron tugged at my sleeve and shouted at me, "What are we playing?"

I said "I don't know," to which Ron shouted "Well ask him!" With great presence of mind I turned to Ken, who was busy fiddling with his mutes and said, "Ron wants to know what we are playing"— duly landing Ron in the proverbial!

"*What Am I Living For,*" came the reply. Thinking it was a question I replied, "I don't know, Ken," to which he growled, "That's the name of the tune!"

When the dirge-like number finally finished, it was greeted with absolute silence—the audience clearly were completely baffled. Needless to say, the rest of the session rapidly improved, and the music got better and better, so a good time was had by all.

Ironically, the next day Bill Stotesbury phoned me to say he wouldn't be playing with me again, because Ken had just rung him to invite him to join his band full-time!

BILL STOTESBURY The first gig—it was quite an experience—was at Nottingham. The Dancing Slipper. I had to go to Ken's house in Hounslow. Hardly ever seen him, really, by then. I went into the house, and we chatted, I think. And then the Clappers, Les and Maeve, arrived outside and hooted, and out we went in silence. And I sat in the front—Ken sat in the back with Maeve. I started talking—a bit of talk, but nobody seemed to want to talk, so I shut up. Stopped after that for Maeve to go to the loo, and then went up to Nottingham. First number was *Somewhere over the Rainbow*.

The band was Annie, Colin and me—no piano—and the front line was Len; I can't remember who the clarinet player was.

> I mean, it was so thrilling to play with him. I mean, he always took you, I suppose, two choruses beyond where you'd think you could possibly get to.

I mean you'd think, "Oh God, it's coming out, and the whole thing's riding out," and then he'd ride across that middle tune to the next chorus, and drive you up and up, and I've never experienced anything like that even with Tony or Cuff.

JOHN GUY When Ken ceased leading a full-time band in the early seventies he made several appearances with local bands in the Cambridge area. We had become friends when I wrote the sleeve notes for his *Ragtime Revisited* album. Some late-finishing gigs meant that he was occasionally grateful for a pallet on the floor. Chatting at family meal times he revealed a wide range of interests, and a dry sense of humour. **We were shown his new vehicle, standing parked outside my house. "I'll be a poor man for five years while I pay for that."**

The Clappers (Les and Maeve Rosenberg)

Louise, aged five, took his remarks to heart. She designed some publicity posters for him, and with the aid of a kind person who worked at BUPA, had them photocopied. Sales to jazzers raised five shillings and fourpence farthing, the money duly sent to Ken.

"How old is this child?" he asked and responded with avuncular warmth. "I wrote her a letter in my best round schoolboy hand, and sent her a record."

The album *Out of Nowhere* has some lovely moments. It still stands up today.

PETER MORCOM After Ken gave up leading his band I played with him on several gigs in East Anglia. Some of these were with the Savoy Band (with Colin Bowden) and others were ones that I had arranged, at the Quay Theatre, Sudbury and the Electric Palace, Harwich, to quote two examples.

On one such occasion I picked Ken up in my car on a bright and sunny afternoon in June. We had been travelling for some ten minutes when Ken broke the silence with: "Ain't ya got a heater in this car?" That was the only time I was on the receiving end of one of his put-downs. The first time we played at the Quay I had to explain to Ken that we had no PA. Ken was worried about the vocals, but when he experienced the "acowsticks" he was thrilled to be able to sing without a mike with the band playing so quietly behind him.

JOHN WURR And then there was a bizarre gig we did for John Boddy. Woolworths were re-launching their image, with a big TV campaign (remember the *Wonder of Woolworths*?) to show off their new range of stuff, including women's clothing.

They held a fashion parade at the Savoy, and we were the music. We had to wear waistcoats and bootlace ties (a bad idea), had to share cramped changing accommodation with the models (a very good idea) and were supposed to match the music to the colour of the clothes being displayed (a terrible idea, as it meant we had to change tunes as

soon as a new item appeared on the catwalk).

Ken completely lost the plot. We ended up playing *Red Sails in the Sunset* to a blue swimsuit, and *Blue Skies* to a green sequined dinner gown. In addition, we had to play the *Wonder of Woolworths* jingle, which at that time we had never heard.

As the only reader in the band, I was handed a piano score, from which I had to extract melody and chords, and teach it to the band in about 30 minutes. Ken was less than co-operative, and I later pondered on the complexity of a character which often led him to resent those who were in a position to help him the most. I certainly earned my money, and an earful of abuse, that day.

LEN BALDWIN John Boddy had by this time linked up with Ken and was acting as his agent and was getting him the jobs.

JOHN BODDY When I first started booking Ken, I'd do all the European stuff for him. But I didn't do all the English stuff. I used to work with Karl Heinz Lehmann, and also Dieter Nentwig, who I encouraged to become an agent.

LEN BALDWIN The thing with Ken, as I said, was that there was never a contract. You were in the band **but you never knew whether you were in the band because he never said anything. It was just the same guys that he would ask to do the gigs.**

PETE LAY Barry Weston put a note in to the 100 Club—you know, addressed it to Ken Colyer via the 100 Club, and said, "Would you be interested in doing a guest spot with the band?" Just to basically get the club off the ground, you know. And he responded and said yeah and said how much he wanted, which, in this day and age, was a pittance for a guest fee: fifteen pounds or something. You know, ridiculous.

And he came down to the British Legion Club, Chatham in August '72. And that was the first time I played with Ken, and it was a six-piece band with piano and no banjo. Derek Cook was on bass, Colin Martin was the piano player, and Norman Halliday on clarinet, Barry and Ken.

He just said hello, and we chatted at the bar, and... the usual platitudes and all that before the session, and: straight in. *I Can't Escape From You.* He called the tunes and that was it. *I Can't Escape From You* was the first number.

I dunno... ever since, of all the sessions I've ever played with Ken, it was one of those things. You just felt at home, and knew exactly what was going to happen. There was never any uncertainty about his lead—the way he led a band. You never failed to see the signals in his playing. There was none of this showmanship about him—the signals were in the playing.

The way he used to lead-in some choruses, you know.

Time as well. The tunes he picked. I found sometimes he played four or five tunes—the same sort of tempo, same sort of thing; same... pop-standard-type things. And he'd be working on that audience, and then all of a sudden he'd drop a bombshell in it, and it would be like a ten-minute blues. And all of a sudden, you'd find the audience would be with him. And from then on, he used to get them eating out of his hand, somehow.

It was a good session....considering. You know, as a mere starter-out. Obviously indoctrinated by the Colyer music, I knew what had to happen, but would it happen? It was just like putting on old slippers.

I get shivers now thinking about it, because it was that... It felt at home straight away.

COR FABRIE The Storyville Jazzband started to tour with Ken in Holland in 1972. The music was broadcast on the radio each month for two years. **It was always wonderful to play with Ken. His beautiful singing tone, his (always) fantastic timing, his high standard of taste, his wonderful vocals and enthusiasm for the music.**

Ken said about the band: "The Storyville Jazzband is one of the few good New Orleans bands in Europe." I miss Ken. There is nobody with his quality. Butch Thompson played the tour with Ken in 1976 and we recorded together in November of that year.

RAY SMITH He put a band together to go to Zurich for a month to play at a well-known club called the Casa Bar in 1976. It was a small, narrow, dimly lit clip-joint, with a bandstand that could best be described as intimately diminutive. Mike Sherbourne on trombone, clarinettist Brian White, Paul Rosenberg at the drums, bass player Lindsay Cooper and myself on piano completed the line-up.

We played every night, eight until twelve o'clock, and the atmosphere was relaxed. We relaxed so much after the gig every night, I unfortunately have very little recollection of what we talked about. There were bits of the Colyer humour that surfaced during the month.

On one session he had a request to play "The Louis Armstrong version of *St Louis Blues*." His reply —delivered whilst rolling a cigarette— was: "Well actually... we play the Peruvian version."

Bassist Lindsay Cooper used to take the occasional solo-chorus, which he did humming his improvisation whilst playing, à la Slam Stewart. Ken's verbal encouragement came out as "Play it again, Slam."

Unfortunately, Ken was given a cheque for the month's work on the penultimate evening of our gig, and on presenting it to the bank the next day, the cheque bounced. When the owner of the club appeared that evening, Ken made a beeline for him and the resulting shout-up rather spoiled the atmosphere. The matter was finally settled satisfactorily, but the damage had been done: He had been made to feel like a criminal in a foreign country—once again.

LEN BALDWIN We did some German tours, three I think. When he was there he was a bit stressed and strained. I didn't realise it at the time, but don't forget that on and off at times Ken had internal complaints.

JOHN BODDY I was with him in Hamburg and he was probably a bit apprehensive because he was going to be on with the Barber band, and Papa Bue and Monty Sunshine's band. So I thought, "I've got to keep sharp for this." I heard the door open shortly, and he said "I'm going to get my head down," and I said "So am I."

There was a card in the room where you got a free cocktail, so I knew what was going to happen. So I thought, "I won't have a shower, I'll sit here." Three or four minutes later I heard the door go. So down I go and he's in the cocktail bar, and we had the cocktail, and I said, "Come on Ken, get your head down now, you've got a concert tonight."

And we go upstairs, and we do the same thing again, and I heard the door go again, and he'd gone off like a bullet. And anyway, I got down off the lift, and I saw him disappear round the corner, so I caught up with him and I said, "Where are you going? You don't want to start—it's only two o'clock. We can give it one after the gig."

Anyway, I talked him into going into one of these places where they do all the chicken, and he had a good meal and he went back, and on the gig I said, "I'll tell you what I'll do, Ken. I'll get some bottles of champagne." So anyway, I got these bottles, and he said, "Ah, we can put them in the dressing room."

And I said, "No, no... I put it in the fridge, Ken." "What did you do that for?" "It's got to be cold." So he kept saying, "Is that champagne ready yet," and I'd say, "No, no... It's not cold enough yet." And we get about twenty minutes before he's due to go on, and I said, "Now I'll go and get that champagne." And he said, "Oh, good idea, man." So I got the champagne, and we had about two glasses before he was going on, and it went an absolute storm.

RAY SMITH One night in the mid-seventies the band played at a pub in Harlesden. Gerry Turnham came round to pick me up, and we were the first to arrive. The piano was a half-tone flat and impossible to get in tune with. Gerry had a tuning fork in his clarinet case and tuned to that, whilst I—foolishly—elected to play everything in a different key to everyone else. This was not the wisest decision of my life, but the alternative was not to use a piano. So Len Baldwin arrived and tuned up to Gerry and so on until Ken arrived.

"Piano's flat Ken—you'll have to tune up to Gerry," which he duly did without question or comment. We started, I remember, with *Painting the Clouds with Sunshine*. The piano playing was pretty awful, and I was glad when the session ended—I sounded like Eugene Quills underwater.

Whilst we were packing up Gerry said to Ken, "I think Ray did very well tonight, don't you, Ken?" Ken's quizzical expression indicated that perhaps he thought Gerry Turnham had lost his mind. "What d'ya' mean, man?" asked Ken. "Well, he was playing in different keys to us... because the piano was a half-tone flat." Gerry had to repeat this, and suddenly Ken understood—came over to where I was and uttered the classic line: "I'm sorry man, I thought you were pissed."

JOHN BODDY And another time in, I think it was Hanover. We had to go the next day to East Berlin. And Ken had a bloody good jazz club session, and then Ken and I had gone off. Anyway, we went to this place, and again he found a band playing, and again he got up on the guitar, and he was well pissed—so was I—but he's doing all the Woody Guthrie numbers and Jimmie Rodgers things and we're having a ball and they're clapping, and we came out and Ken said, "Great evening, John," and it's about 4.30 a.m., and I said, "We've got to be out of the Hotel at six, we'll have to get back," and he said "Well, get a cab...."

RAY SMITH On the next German tour, by which time Tony Pyke had rejoined the band, Ken decided he wanted to start the skiffle group up again. I wasn't terribly enthusiastic, as it would mean playing tunes in unfamiliar keys such as D, E, and A. However, Ken arranged to come around to the flat one day to rehearse with just guitar and piano.

It just happened that I was feeling rather fragile on that particular day, and certainly couldn't manage anything stronger than a twelve-bar in B♭, so when Ken asked for an A to tune his guitar, I played a B♭, which device meant that instead of those dreadful keys, I could play safely in familiar keys, albeit a half-tone higher than Ken would be used to.

Once I'd committed myself to that deception there was no turning back. After sailing through *Go Down Old Hannah*, *Streamline Train*, and *Midnight Special*, Ken said, "You've got them natural keys down good man, but I don't know what's the matter with my voice." I never owned up to that, I'm afraid, but have now.

KEN SCAMMELL I had different bands on at the club at Brentford—all sorts of bands. And we never got anybody down there. And I think it was Bill Wilkinson used to play, and Bob Ward. And I think it was Wilkie said, "If we got Colyer down here, we might get somebody." And he was playing over at Thornton Heath with him, I think.

And he got in contact with Ken, and Ken came down. And I was paying the band fifty pounds—all of 'em.

I hadn't met him until then, no. And, although he lived in Hounslow, I knew a lot about him. Later on, when I got to know him, he told me that he used to go out during the night cycling, because he couldn't sleep—because he was a very edgy person.

I was really amazed when he accepted the gig—I couldn't believe it, you know, and I said, "Well, I can't pay any more." And then after that he loved playing there, and every time if there was a change of date, he never missed one of them. He was always there, you know. I mean—I thought it was amazing. And he *did* like playing there, and of course, he used to get lifts, because he was off the road for part of the time there... in fact, most of it I think. Until the gig moved up the road with Tony Morgan, then it went to the Rugby Club.

I thought he was a very shy and introverted person— doing an extrovert job.

But he *was* an introverted type. I think that when he sacked people, he didn't know how to do it, so he used to do it in an odd sort of way. But I mean, underneath it all, he was just an ordinary guy, and—well, I thought he was a nice guy. The way I look at it is he was always great with me. And the way he played, so I've got no qualms about him. **He'd front the band, and as soon as he fronted the band, the band played with style. I still don't know how.**

How did he get that? I don't know how you get that. But he had this knack of making them all play his way. But then, even some musicians who weren't really in his class, he'd still get them to play that way.

Then the band revolved a bit. First of all it was Bill Wilkinson with Bob Ward, Graham Paterson and Alan Ritchie.

Tony Pyke was in the band. The drummer changed from Bill to Paul Rosenberg then Brian Chadwick; Ray Smith was on piano, sometimes Pete Dyer on trombone, Bill Stotesbury playing banjo.

Ken had a newsletter he put around, but I don't know... I never ever saw one, but that's what I was told—that he would get people down through his newsletter.

JOHN LONG Fred Shaw—we used to groan whenever Ken said he was handing over to Fred Shaw. And then one night Fred Shaw sat down and played an incredible *Canal Street*. And I said to him afterwards, "Fred, where did you learn to play *Canal Street* like that?" and he said, "Ah, that was the Guv'nor." And I said, "What do you mean, that was the Guv'nor?" And he said, "Well you know the last time we were here, he had car trouble, and I took him home, and he invites me in for a drink. And he sits me down with a whisky, and he says, "Fred, when you come in, bring your horn in. We've got work to do. Fred, I'm going to have you playing one tune properly if it's the last thing I do. And so we were an hour playing *Canal Street*."

KEN COLYER George Chambers has run his own band for many years in Belfast and has done much to keep the scene alive through the years. I have had some good times with him.

He had been phoned once from a place called Cushendall, regarding his band. He explained that it was a New Orleans Band.

"We know."
"What time do we start?"
"Any time you like."
"Intervals?"
"Any time you like."
"What time do we finish?"
"Any time you like."

I did the job with him. We drove through the beautiful Glens of Antrim on the way. It must be some of the most wonderful country in Ireland.

JOHN LONG Ken was off to play with the Climax Band, first

in Toronto and then New Orleans. I took him to Gatwick Airport, couple of days before we were going. We went to New York, hired a car, and drove down the East Coast, taking about four days. Arrived in New Orleans, knew where he was going to be, walked around to the hotel, and it had these swing-doors. And as we swung into them, you could hear Ken's voice in the bowels of the hotel, in the bar. And we went in there, and he was with the Climax Band from Toronto. And they were all sitting around enthralled, listening to the great man talking.

And as we came around the corner, he stopped and he said "This is John and Renee. These are the guys I told you about," and he went on with his story.

RENEE LONG When we left the hotel, he would walk with his eyes on the ground.

JOHN LONG I'd hired a car, thinking that he would want to go to places, and show us around, but no. Stayed in the hotel. Walked to the gig.

I got on the phone to Dick Allen, who didn't know Ken was back in town. And the look on Ken's face when, at the Esplanade Cafe, Dick Allen walked in—I knew he was coming, but didn't say a word—and Kid Sheik, Kid Simmons, Preston Jackson, Cornbread Thomas—they all came in to see him.

KEN COLYER [With] Louis Nelson in Basle, Switzerland, **I was explaining how the ghosts of the past had haunted me on my last visit to New Orleans. "I believe I know what you mean, Ken."**

MIKE CASIMIR Many New Orleans celebrities had considerable respect for Kent, as they called him, although at times he appeared to fail in offering them a greeting or an acknowledgement. The fact that he admired and adored the New Orleans musicians and their music made his behaviour even more incomprehensible.

BUNK-UM

Tom Bethell, *Jazz Journal*, March 1976

Colyer was scheduled to play for three nights at Cafe Esplanade on Bourbon Street with a jazz band from Toronto, and the first thing that struck me when I walked into the place was that the band sounded exactly like Ken Colyer's Jazzmen back in 1957, which was when I first heard him play. JUST the same, which was odd considering he was touring only briefly with this Canadian group. Colyer's influence USED to be enormous in England. And with these Canadians, obviously it still was. Ken looked thinner, rather shrunken, and a touch scholarly in wire-rimmed glasses. The orange T-shirt did not seem quite right, though.

I told him I wanted to write something about his return to New Orleans. He just took out a tobacco pouch and rolled himself a cigarette, just as I had always remembered him doing, and then poured himself some beer from a pitcher into a plastic cup.

"Are you going to see the sights while you're here?" I asked. He gave me a sidelong look which said, in effect, that he had suspected this was going to be a waste of time and now he knew it. "I've seen all the sights," he said, sighing. (*Will they never learn?*) "I've seen things you'll never see... Been all around the world..." He paused, puffed and considered. "I AM one of the sights," he said finally.

Dutifully, I asked Ken to tell me what he thought was the most important thing about New Orleans music, expecting, perhaps, a homily on the virtues of playing together as a team.

He thought for a bit, took a drink and said, "I'd 'ave to say the Bunk Johnson American Musics." He was referring to the recordings made in the 1940s of the trumpeter Bunk Johnson and issued (by local jazz connoisseur William Russell) on the American Music record label. Bunk Johnson, it should be explained, is to the visiting foreign jazzmen as the trunk of a tree is to its outermost branches. The clarinettist in Bunk's band was George Lewis, and after Bunk's death in 1949, Lewis carried on with the rest of Bunk's band.

"That's the best music there ever was," Colyer explained. "They talk about contemporary New Orleans jazz, but there's no such thing." He refilled his cup with beer and asked me, "There's no contemporary Michelangelo, is there?"

..."It's nice to come back, of course it is," Colyer said, "but I carry a bit of New Orleans wherever I go. It's not a passing fancy with me.

New Orleans jazz is here to stay. You can play within the idiom, within the style, and if you've got anything in you, it'll come out. Doesn't have to be CONTEMPORARY..."

RAY SMITH We went out to play in East Germany in 1978—the Dresden Jazz Festival. The concert on the Saturday night was televised and recorded. Paul Rosenberg was the drummer on the trip, but unfortunately he wasn't around when we were due to go on. Ken was nervous, and after much agitation, Ken was lucky to secure the services of a German drummer from one of the other bands, but he was still not a happy man. As I remember events, the stage was set in the style of a Mississippi Riverboat. When the time came for our entrance—probably because of the general chaos—we clambered over the sides of the boat, not realising there was a door centre-stage.

Having settled in our seats, Ken suddenly announced to Len Baldwin that he'd forgotten his tin-mug, which he used as

a mute. He left his seat, returning a couple of minutes later, and we played our forty-minute set. It must have been fun to watch on television. After the session was over, Paul Rosenberg turned up full of apologies—he had fallen asleep on a seat in front of a church.

DAVE BRENNAN Near the end of the tour, the whole band had to appear on television for an interview. However, they only spoke to Ken. Under the blaze of lights, I'd no idea of knowing whether it was live or not, but the high degree of tension being shown amongst the TV crew led me to believe that it was live. We were sitting casually in a row, Colyer was at one end and I was at the other.

Ken was asked to introduce the members of the band, and say what their jobs were. The interview immediately became farcical, as Ken gave us all spurious professions, including brain surgeon, astronaut and so on.

He was asked by the lady presenter what it was he liked about Dixieland jazz. "I hate Dixieland jazz, I can't stand it," Colyer said.

"It's just a racket," he replied to a bemused young lady presenter. It should have been obvious to Ken that she was using the term "Dixieland" in the American sense to include New Orleans-style jazz.

The embarrassing interview continued to follow these lines, until the presenter tried another tack, asking Ken why he played it. Eventually Ken explained that he played New Orleans jazz, which was "beautiful music" and then for about the fifth time he said that Dixieland was "just a racket!" She obviously took all this as direct criticism of the Dresden Dixieland Festival, and finally in desperation she asked, "Would you come back to Dresden, Mr. Colyer?"

Ken muttered something in a low voice, and the band doubled up in embarrassment, covering their faces and looking at the floor. I leaned over and whispered to Ray Smith "Did he say what I thought he said?" Ray whispered back to me "He said, 'Yeah, in a fucking Lancaster!'"

Afterwards the lady interviewer, who was a lovely friendly person, said that she'd get the sack for that. There was Colyer, he had adoring fans and an uncritical media, and he threw it all back in their faces.

RAY SMITH So we filed into the TV studio. The band were seated whilst Ken was standing in the front with the East German interviewer and an interpreter. Questions were asked, interpreted, answered by Ken, and then his answers interpreted yet again. It was a long process, and after the first question—"What do you think of our Dixieland Festival, Mr. Colyer?"—Ken assumed his W.C. Fields aspect.

"We don't play Dixieland, we play New Orleans jazz," came the reply. Sensing that it wasn't going to be an easy interview, the next question was, "What do the members of your band do for a living, Mr. Colyer?" This was an unwise question, and

Ken's reply was surprisingly good humoured:

> "Well, our trombone player, Len Baldwin, is a dustbin collector, and Gerry Toinham here is a brain surgeon. Ray Smith, our piano player, is a wall-of-death driver in the circus."

The interviewer realised that she was being put-on, and—before Ken had time to complete his survey of suitable means of employment for the chaps—asked the even more absurd "And what do *you* do during the day, Mr. Colyer?" Ken hesitated, and then said, "Not very much... I sit at home with the blinds drawn, drinking gin and tonic." "And why is this, Mr. Colyer?" "Because I don't feel very well."

We were ushered out of the studio pretty quickly, and later—at the open-air jam session at which we were required to play—the East German interviewer was tearfully telling John Boddy that it was the worst interview that there had ever been on East German televison. I thought it was pretty good, but Ken was being duly reprimanded and, feigning anger, walked away from the shout-up, and whilst walking away started singing—to a well-known melody— "...*Falling Down Drunk Again, What Am I To Do*..." He looked over in my direction, with a slightly satisfied gleam in his eye. He often *did* put people on, in a Colyer-ish sort of way.

JOHN LONG So... we're on our way to see John Vianicci, who ran a New Orleans-style jazzband in the South of France in a place called Toulon. Ken had always been on about his fear of being poisoned by garlic, and we stopped half-way at a lovely little seaside resort called Le Lavandou, and we found a restaurant with seats overlooking the sea, and Ken said to me, "Go in and look and see what you can find."

And, I got a copy of the menu and found that there was the famous Salade Niçoise, which never had garlic in it. It looked like a meal in itself. So I was able to assure him that Salade Niçoise was the thing—dish of the day, and it wouldn't have garlic in it. So we all ate it. But, having found that out, he wouldn't go in a restaurant after that unless it had Salade Niçoise.

Ken was lucky in that our friend Louis, who did jazz programmes on Radio Malta, knew anybody in Malta who was likely to be able to play jazz. And we got some gigs for Ken where he could sit-in with resident bands. We found a little quartet that played at a restaurant in a hotel, and they played every night, and they invited Ken to join them whenever he

wanted to. This was going extremely well. About half way through the holiday, Louis decided to throw a party for our party and his own family...

And so Ken went over there, and we're all sitting around in this large room enjoying ourselves, when Louis goes to his office and comes back with a book, a book called *Teach Yourself Jazz*. And he plonked it down in front of Ken, and Ken gave it a quick glance and shut it at once.

And Louis wasn't very happy about this, so he picked it up and said, "Mr Colyer... this book... Are you aware of it?" And Ken said, "Never a day goes by that I have to refer to it." People in the room weren't sure whether to laugh or not, because they knew that Louis didn't understand that it was a joke.

JOHN BODDY We did the Middle East tour, 1981. Someone got on from the British Council and asked me for some ideas, because they'd had Stan Tracey over to do some things. So I went and saw them, had a chat and told them a bit about Ken and what he'd done for music in Britain, and represented—obviously—something that was unique; it was American music like Stan was playing, but it was unique: Ken was still expressing British culture. And we got the gig. And it was terrific, actually.

Well, the audiences were very good, but I mean... everywhere was packed out. We started in Beirut and then on to Kuwait, which was absolutely wonderful. We stayed on a ship, and it was cemented-in—an American ship; they'd cemented it in to the side, and just when you came off, across the road was a sports place with a swimming pool which Ken liked, and we'd have saunas and all that, and the food there was absolutely fantastic.

And of course, the British Council kept us supplied with booze—the guys turned up every day with a box with some bottles of gin in it. When Ken and the band played in the restaurant there, it was packed—every night. But all the people that worked there—in Kuwait—they'd make this booze from typewriter cleaning fluid. And they'd got chemists there who would come along and distill it all. And they'd come along with their bottles and I drank some of it, and it would take your head off.

So they'd put those bottles under your chairs, and the waiters bring around the Coke and everything. But, it was the first band to be on Sudanese TV. They brought cameras into the grounds of what used to be the British Library, and they filmed the band playing there. It went out on Sudanese TV.

TONY PYKE A three-and-a-half-week tour to the Middle East. Lebanon—Beirut; then up to Kuwait; Syria, for a few days; Jordan, then down to Sudan.

Mainly expatriates, but a lot of Arabs, especially in Khartoum.

You know, it was a pleasure to be sharing a stage with him

again as far as I was concerned. I enjoyed it. Had a great time.

BILL STOTESBURY And first stop was Beirut, and we couldn't believe it because the airport had been bombed and there was all these ruins. And we were whisked off, and we went through the customs and Ken had a bottle of gin, I think. And it was OK.

We had a Cultural Attaché bloke with us and I think we would have got through because of that. And anyway, we got there and we had all these bus-type things to travel in and we snuck into Beirut with roadblocks and everything else. I didn't realise what we were coming into. And then of course, British Council tours are well organised, because you're treated as if you're royalty. And when you arrive in a country, you're met by the Cultural Attaché. You do your concerts, and the day you fly out you have a completely free day again, where you get a Cultural Attaché. So I mean, you're really well looked after.

The whole idea of the British Council is to spread the gospel according to England. And I mean, that was quite incredible. And the audiences loved it. Drove across the desert to Petra. Ken didn't do that. That was a shame, because he was an intelligent bloke, you'd think he'd want to see these places.

RAY SMITH When I asked Ken why he wasn't coming to Petra with us, his reply was simply, "I've seen it." "Oh, when was that Ken?" "1949. National Geographic Magazine."

BILL STOTESBURY We all looked like terrorists, with beards: Paul Rosenberg, Arthur Bird, Tony Pyke, Johnny Beecham. After Jordan, we went to Syria, and they took us up into the mountains and went down to the temples, took our shoes off. And we walked up and down the Souk in Damascus. We had to change hotels—the first hotel was the one that Lawrence had stayed at, where he had those big conferences. And it was absolutely alive with bed-bugs or something. And so we moved to a new hotel. **And at the end the guide said how anxious he had been because we all had beards and the only people that wear beards in Syria are the Bedouins.**

RAY SMITH On the last night, after the concert, we were all having dinner in the hotel as guests of the British Council official, one John Semple. John Semple was quiet and unassuming, and a bit afraid of Ken for some reason; he'd led a sheltered life. Anyway, a local string group were playing with guitars and things, and during dinner Ken was trying to listen and becoming rather agitated having to answer questions every so often.

It just happened that he had brought his guitar out to the Middle East, but so far no one had asked him to play, and I could tell he was contemplating sitting-in with the local group that were playing.

> Suddenly, Ken finally had enough of whoever was asking him a question, swore, stood up and announced: "I'm going to get my axe!" John Semple turned a peculiar colour, being convinced that our leader had finally snapped. Ken, of course, returned some minutes later with his guitar.

JOHN BEECHAM Some of the people who have been in Ken's band were so deeply respectful of Ken, and so cautious of his bad temper, that—frankly—they were scared of him. When I was in the band the guy that got on best with him was the pianist, Ray Smith, and this was because Ray was more natural around Ken—more able than the other guys to share a joke with Ken.

For my part I respected Ken tremendously, and I was thrilled to be in his band, but I don't feel that I was so much in awe of him that I didn't enjoy his company; and when we stayed in hotels on tour, it was usually Ken, Ray and myself who would sit up drinking and yarning, as Ken called it, and Ray would wind Ken up in a way that would be far too familiar, too disrespectful, for some musicians to contemplate, and of course, Ken *knew* that he was being wound up.

Ray would say, "The trouble with you, Colyer, is you pander to the audience. You're too commercial." And of course nothing could be further from the truth, and Ken would laugh at this—heh, heh, heh—and Ray would say, "Who do you think you are, Colyer? Chris Barber?" And Ken would love it.

BARRY PALSER Amersham Jazz Club, mid-seventies. The place was packed. There were very few chairs so lots of the punters were standing; the band were sitting down and there was no stage. Therefore the horns were playing straight into the bodies of the people in the front (any trombone player will tell you what a pain in the proverbial that is!).

Half way through the session and halfway through a typical twelve minute "Colyer Blues" (can't remember which one though I can remember the old sod made me play Ory's *Creole Trombone!*) Ken was in a trance delivering his heartfelt vocal when there was a disturbance at the far end of the room. A rattling noise—quite loud, bit like an old wooden tambourine. I couldn't see what it was because of all the bodies, but I could

Ken with, left to right, Tony Pyke, John Beecham, Paul Rosenberg, Arthur Bird, Bill Stotesbury and Ray Smith

see a deep frown appear on Ken's face!

The rattling got louder and suddenly three Salvation Army Ladies burst through shaking their collection boxes. The furrows of the frown got deeper and *"if looks could have killed..."* The ladies finished up right in front of the band, shaking the boxes and not prepared to move until they got some money.

Ken, not to be sidetracked, continued with the usual full Colyer Blues format whilst the ladies continued to rattle (Out of tempo I might add)! Finally we stopped playing; Ken put one hand on his knee and leaned forward eyeball to eyeball with one of the rather diminutive ladies. A strange silence filled the room as everyone knows what the Guv'nor can be like!

There was a stern look on his face and he said: "What are three nice ladies like you doing in a Den of Iniquity like this?"

There was a collective sigh of relief!

KEN SCAMMELL I was quite amazed that he was coming out with all this other stuff. And, of course, his guitar playing and that, which I didn't know anything about.

I went round to his house a couple of times, and he had all these bottles—he was making sloe-gin.

Well, I mean... I took a bottle of gin around there, because that was my tipple at the time. So we just knocked that out and had quite a nice time round there.

TONY LEPPARD Ken was asked to go and play at Lonnie Donegan's Anniversary down at the Fairfield Halls. Oh, it was a great evening. They all seemed quite matey together. And Bill was there of course, and played on the washboard. To me, in many ways, Ken was an enigma.

JIM BRAY Oh, it was very pleasant. I think the first reunion was a concert at the Fairfield Halls in Croydon with Ken and the original band. I think that was it... can't remember what anniversary it was.

RAY SMITH We were playing a gig in the Cambridge area a couple of days after that Fairfield Halls Reunion Concert, and Jim Bray was on bass that night. I'd travelled with Ken to the gig, and he and I were sitting at the bar before the session started. Jim arrived and walked over to where we were sitting. "Evening Ken, evening Smudger. Good concert on Friday, I thought, Ken." "Yeah, Barber doesn't change much," to which Jim replied: "Neither do you Ken, neither do you."

MONTY SUNSHINE We called it "Ken Colyer's Band." And it was called that because we were playing all sorts of places.

We played one place where there was Ella Fitzgerald, and all sorts. But Ken would be fronting the band. Then Ken'd ring me up and say, "Chris wants us to play with his band. Can we go along there?" So I'd say, "Fine." I said, "I'll come along and I'll pick you up." And I used to go and pick Ken up, and go along and play with Ken's band. They had Lonnie there as well. And Jim, and Ron. It was quite good.

Except towards the end. Chris had said something over the radio or television and Ken took it wrongly. And he picked the phone up—we played at Southend, and he said, "I'm not going to do it." And Chris said, "But I've announced it!" And Ken said "Don't talk to me." Anyway, I said, "Leave it to me," and I got round at Ken's place, and eventually I said, "Oh, for Christ's sake, how old... we're all grown up." He didn't mean what he'd said—they'd got it all wrong. "You're causing friction; don't be like that."

"OK." It was just as simple as that. Yeah—he didn't understand him. You know, he was more like a child—he wasn't the same as that, but he had that sort of attitude.

He was a very sensitive guy. But he was seeming to be a tough guy, and so on; but he wasn't, really. Not to me... not to a lot of people.

TIM PHILLIPS I said, "Ken. You know, obviously, you have this great love of music and the philosophy behind it. How close do you think you've ever got to what you are trying to achieve with these bands?" And of course we talked about the different line-ups and all that kind of thing. "Well, I think one of the best bands I ever had I may have got to forty percent."

Now I thought that that was a really brave, if possibly drunk, thing to say. And he said part of it was to do with the fact that he was surrounded by people who wanted to be in the Ken Colyer band and not necessarily trying to recreate what *he* was trying to recreate. And I'll never forget that moment because I just thought it was really quite humble.

LEN BALDWIN Just before 1979 I had to leave the band because I was going through a messy divorce and I didn't play for a year or so, and Johnny Beecham joined until I came back for a very short period of time. By that time the thing that eventually killed Ken was beginning to hurt, because he was very awkward about a number of things. He sacked me at the 100 Club on a Wednesday night. "Sorry, man. I don't think you can do this now and I want to do something else," he said. And within a short period of time Arthur Bird, the bass player, went. Then somebody else went and the band just changed and Ken was just doing odd things.

I certainly noticed a difference in him over the period of time that I was with the band. During the period when I first joined in and into the mid 70s, at times Ken played as well as he ever played. After that, although he was still playing well, it was in bursts rather; he had deteriorated slightly.

He had also got into the habit by then of the band always playing the same way. It would be two choruses to start and then two choruses of clarinet, two choruses of trumpet, two choruses of trombone, two choruses of piano, whereas prior to that he would vary things a bit. He got into a bit of a routine.

> But every so often he would come out with this stuff that nobody else could do really. That was the beauty of playing with him.

JOHN LONG On one of our holidays in Malta, Ken asked one day if I could find somewhere in Malta that specialises in fish. So I looked up the handbook and found that there was a hotel on one of the seafronts that specialised in seafood, and we went off down there, and went in and spoke to the restaurant manager, and he said, "The people staying at the hotel are eating at the moment, but when they finish perhaps we can look after you then. Would you like to come in the lounge?" He arranged some seats around a table, and he laid a tablecloth on this table, and a waiter came in with a vase full of carnations, and said, "Would you like to be our guests and have a drink?"

So we order and the waiter goes off, and Ken leans forward and takes a carnation, bites the head off, and puts the stalk back in. And by the time the waiter comes back, there are only stalks in this pot. And he's sitting there in khaki shorts, grey socks and sandals, a string vest and a green eyeshade. And I said to him before we left the flat, "You can't go to a hotel for dinner dressed like this." "I can," he said. "Tell them I'm an eccentric millionaire."

PETE LAY By the time mid-August had come, Mac Mackay had gone off and drunk himself stupid and died, Keith Box had left, and Len Baldwin had sort of come in to cover those gigs.

And then Keith Box didn't want to travel all the way up from Bristol, and he used André Beeson. And he played brilliantly. He said, "This isn't my music." But Ken was happy as Larry with him, because he just played good clarinet. So for about two or three months, André Beeson was doing the 100 Club sessions. Actually, at that time, Ken was only doing the odd gig out at jazz clubs and basically the 100 Club. Because he'd just started up that thing with Max Collie—the Mardi Gras—at about that time.

So he had a lot of commitments with Max. But by the end of August, Bill Stotesbury had been given the sack. Brian Mitchell came in on banjo. All over silly things, when you look back in retrospect. It was all over silly little things. I think at that time Ken was writing the book, he didn't need anybody letting him down at that time. He needed guys then around him that would say: "Well, Ken, we'll be here. We'll play with ya." And he didn't need people messing him about saying, "I can do that one, I can't do this."

And I think it was the loyalty thing that came into play. You know: "These guys will turn up and play with me on every session."

JOHN LONG Well, the worst period that I knew Ken was in the three or four months when he was writing that book [*When Dreams Are in the Dust*], because he wouldn't speak to anybody. He turned his back on everybody—just turned up at gigs and played and didn't say a word, and it was very, very difficult.

KEN COLYER LETTERS TO MIKE POINTON UNDATED

Mr. K. Colyer, 99 The Drive, Hounslow TW3 IPW Middx
Dear Mike.

Many thanks for the publishing info: It looks interesting and I will make enquiries.

I am blowing a little better but things still aren't right. My osteopath says its like having a load of sand in the gear box, but he's working on it.

Edward Black is trying to get Pete Windows of the BBC to do some programs of my narrating excerpts from the book but he says there is no news yet. Do you know either people?

Thanks again, Ken

Dear Mike,

Thanks for your letter and advice. I haven't heard from Brian yet but might try Quartet books if his deal doesn't come to fruition.

I think the book is going to be longer than I thought, but I won't have it chopped about. I've seen one job of butchery done. The book should have general appeal, but not to morons. As you say they must be the ones who buy these best selling books that are unreadable to an intelligent person.

RENEE LONG He said—afterwards—all the demons came out. He lived on sherry, coffee and fruit, and he hardly slept. And then one night at the Centaurs, he had finished the book, and he came in and saw us, and came over and said, "Would you like a drink?" and chatted as though nothing had ever happened.

TREFOR WILLIAMS Max Collie asked Ken to do the [Mardi Gras] show. I thought it would be daunting, but there were no problems at all—he was lovely, he really was. We were doing all these concerts and Max arranged for him to have his own dressing room backstage, but he didn't want that; he wanted to come in with the boys.

And he came in with us, and he was full of jokes and stories—great fun. He used to bring garden clippings in, and plants and things like that for us, and he was always great fun

to be with. And afterwards, I mean, he'd be on his little tipple of gin and tonic, going back after a gig, and sometimes you'd be in the bandwagon, and he'd start singing to us.

And Max would turn around and say, "That sounds a bit like Bob Dylan," and Ken would say, "Bob Dylan? I taught Bob Dylan everything he knows."

Yeah, he brought his guitar along, and did a little spot on the shows. He did it solo. He played cornet with us—with the band.

He had an amazing thing: Whoever he played with—no matter who they were—he had a strong influence over them, and it turned out the Ken Colyer Sound. Whenever, whatever line-up it was.

JOHNNY PARKER What had happened, we had a whole week with Graham Stewart, and he asked me to fix some jobs. I managed to fix a whole week, and Alan Elsdon was on horn right up 'til the Sunday. Well, we did the Portman Hotel on the lunchtime—brunch, as they called it—and the 100 Club at night. And Ken was on those. So they were the only ones that Ken was on. And unfortunately, well, the lunchtime session, he said he'd pick up Dave Evans. When we got there there, was no sign of Dave Evans; we were waiting, and after about half an hour, Ken said, "Oh, I think I said I'd give him a lift."

So I rang through, and sure enough, Dave's still waiting to be picked up, because he doesn't drive. So I said, "Well get a taxi, get here as soon as you can, and whatnot, and I'll go and see the management and explain." So I went to see the management and explained there had been a misunderstanding. And they said that's fine. So we went across to the bar, and when Dave turned up, he was in a panic. So I said, "Don't panic. Sit down and have a beer." I said, "It wasn't your fault, so just relax." And so that was all a bit dodgy to start with. So we finished there, and then we went down the 100 Club in the evening—some of us came back here and some went back with Alan Cooper. And Alan Cooper had decided to carry on drinking during the afternoon.

I couldn't hear what was going on on the other side of the stage, because I had Graham next to me and then Ken and then Alan Cooper over on the other side. And, well, if you hear the record, you'll hear. And Ken, unfortunately, was a bit under-recorded—I mean, the balance isn't particularly kind to him—and Alan Cooper's over-recorded, and... it's a pity.

ALAN COOPER He rang me up the next morning, and I said,

"Christ, Ken, before you say anything, I just want to tell you that last night's session was recorded." And he said, "That's

Ken seen here in the fifties, enjoying an informal session with Alan Cooper

why I'm ringin'. You loused it up. I want you to join my band." And so I thought that was a tremendous honour, and it would have been wonderful.

JOHNNY PARKER And when I told this to Wally Fawkes he said, "Oh what, as punishment?"

KEN COLYER Parker is one of the best pianists I know, and I really enjoy working with him. A perfect band would be a delight beyond dreams and it has always eluded me.

KEN AMES The quartets with Paul Sealey. I enjoyed those—they were nice. In fact, I think *How Long Blues* is one of my favourites of that. You know, if you're going to say, "What did you like of your recordings?" That was an unrehearsed thing—we just turned up and played.

PAUL SEALEY We did the recordings for Steve Lane with Jean-François Bonnel with the Quartet down at the Pizza [Express] in '85. Very nice. And all those nice tunes like *Cheek to Cheek* and *You Took Advantage of Me*. I always felt he wanted to play those tunes. *He* was the one who wanted to do those, and he played them very well. His style was unique.

I wouldn't go so far as to say that I'd buy into some of the mystical stuff about knowing things unknown to man—the kind of stuff that people like to make out about these people, but he had an approach—a style—to my ears that was different

from others. We know he liked Percy Humphrey and Mutt Carey, but he always sounded—to me—as if he was going towards some of the small-band players of later years, like the young Buck Clayton and Taft Jordan and Joe Newman.

He didn't have the same harmonic insight as maybe they had, but there was something about his playing—the way he played across the bars and his phrasing—that wasn't as obvious as a lot of the other people I have played with. There's nothing wrong with being an obvious player like Max Kaminsky or Muggsy Spanier; it's just straight down the line. But there was more than that. I have worked with people—like Ken—who *were* untutored and they hear someone's playing that they like and they get the spirit of it—or some of the spirit of it—without going all the way, and you feel like that's the direction, they're going but they seem to stop.

But there were New Orleans players like that: Red Allen, Kid Shots, Herb Morand, Lee Collins, Kid Howard. It's a little bit away from Louis, but I've always felt there was a line—and certainly a line to people like Joe Newman. When I hear him in the Basie band with the mute, playing some of those controlled solos with not too many notes, it reminds me enormously of those muted King Oliver things with Clarence Williams. So there's a line. There's an intensity in that simple playing, and there's an element of that in Ken's playing that I heard, but I wouldn't suggest that it was anywhere near as advanced as that. But those recordings we did with the quartet were unique, I would say.

The only anecdote I can think of was... he sent me a letter with the tape of his guitar/vocal things, asking for my opinion. The letter says, "When you receive it and play it let me know what you think, as soon as possible." Well I *had* played it once and I was intending to play it again and a few days had gone by and I hadn't contacted him, and he phoned me up, and the only time he was ever so slightly annoyed, to say, "You haven't phoned me back to say what you think." And I felt that this was very, very important to him, and what he did was very important to him.

I mean, the fact that anybody that played in that style, the sort of blues guitar—he was a big fan of Leadbelly's, and I was—we were both enormous fans; and people like Big Bill, Blind Blake—and was interested in all this poetry, it was quite a wide range for someone who some people thought of as some old New Orleans trumpet player. I certainly think he was very serious about all these things—he really was into this on a serious basis.

KEN COLYER LETTER TO PAUL SEALEY

99 The Drive, Hounslow, TW 3 1 PW, Middx.
Dear Paul,
Please find enclosed a cassette with a run-down of what I want to do on the recording.

Sweet Mabel is about the right length but could be extended. I have put two renditions down of *Weeping Willow* because I can't get the darned thing absolutely right and have kept trying to get it down clean. This is the complete version as I want it (apart from mistakes). *Sentimental Journey* is about right but could be adjusted. *Going Down Easy* could take another chorus with the vocal comeback on the middle eight. *Dark is the Night* could be extended. *The Long Trail* is a Kipling poem I've loved from my Merchant Navy days and I've wanted to record for a long time. I have put a melody theme at the end (should have done it first) that I would like to run through the backing. *Dusty Rag* could be extended. There is another theme; Ray Smith plays it with the band, but I don't know it. *G and B Blues* would have to be extended. Like I said, I have never been able to think of any more verses to it but it could add a touch of humour. *Feeling Low* could run to according how we hit it. Forgive the whistling on *Early One Morning*, I was just adding the melody line. We don't have to do it but I think it could work out quite nice. Also, *John Henry*. Please let me know what you think of the material and any suggestions you might have.

There is no recording date set but we would need one or two rehearsals to get the numbers whipped down. I haven't made my mind up about the bass, piano and washboard yet but I think some of the tunes would go well with just two guitars, though I must bow to the German market and put a bit of the old skiffle sound in. I am sending it recorded delivery as I have had a lot of stuff go astray in the post this last year. Would you let me know when you get it? And what you think when you have run it over.

Best Wishes, Ken

Running Order
Side 1

	Tape course	Time (Min/Sec.)
SWEET MABEL	99	4.16
WEEPING WILLOW	198	5.7
SENTIMENTAL JOURNEY	268	4.9
GOING DOWN EASY	323	3.38
DARK IS THE NIGHT	375	3.47
THE LONG TRAIL	465	7.5
LONG TRAIL THEME	471	
Side 2		
DUSTY RAG	85	3.24
G & B BLUES	120	1.36
FEELING LOW	165	2.14
EARLY ONE MORNING	191	1.17
JOHN HENRY	247	3.16
WEEPING WILLOW	322	

PETE LAY We did a session at the Pizza Express with Acker—great admiration between the two of 'em.

They were like two old buddies, chatting away in the corner before the recording session started up. It took some

Ken's suggested repertoire for a Paul Sealey recording session

INTERLUDE VOL. 1.
THERE'LL COME ANOTHER DAY
WRAP YOUR TROUBLES IN DREAMS
I'M IN A DANCING MOOD
MOOD INDIGO
SWEET MABEL
DARK IS THE NIGHT
GO TELL IT ON THE MOUNTAIN
ONE FOR MY BABY
GOING DOWN EASY   GOING DOWN SLOW
WEEPING WILLOW   RAG
THE LONG TRAIN

persuading to get the two buggers up on the stand to do the recording session.

Considering it was only about eighteen months from his last session, as such, he wasn't in bad form really. And I think, again, Acker stirred him up. And similarly, the way Acker played—he responded to what Ken wanted. And Acker was saying, "Well, you know, I haven't played these tunes since I was with you, Ken." Didn't show—he just created his own things out of it. I think Acker's a very underrated jazz musician.

TONY LEPPARD Brecon is a small Welsh town nestling in rolling countryside on the edge of the Brecon Beacons, which each year since 1984 has been the venue for the Brecon Jazz Festival. Ken had been booked to play as a solo artist with four different bands.

On the Friday evening Ken's first engagement was at an out-of-town location, the Mountains Motel, with the

European Classic Jazzband. The Classic was an International band. The Swedish leader, Tomas Ornberg, on clarinet was living in Holland, Bent Persson from Sweden was on trumpet, Mike Pointon, from London, was on trombone, Ray Smith, living in Holland, was the pianist, Paul Sealey played banjo and guitar, the bass player, Goran Lind, came from Sweden and the drummer, Kabe Rau, was from West Germany. In addition, Belgian Fapy Lafertin was a guitar guest. My recollection is of a most satisfying session which left Ken, the other musicians and the audience very happy.

It was, therefore, a happy, relaxed Guv'nor who joined us in the evening for dinner at the Wellington Hotel and agreed to come with us to hear the European Classic Jazzband play the late session at the Castle Hotel. During the interval, Tomas invited Ken to play a few numbers with the band, but Ken told him that he had not, unfortunately, brought his horn with him. I could see that Ken was keen to play, and I suggested that I drive him to his hotel to get his cornet. Ken jumped at the offer and we set off in great haste. I don't think I ever saw Ken more excited at the prospect of playing, and certainly for me what followed was something to live in the memory.

Ken played only three numbers with the Classic before he had to stand down to accommodate other guests. But those numbers were something very special.

PETE LAY Ian Turner came in on clarinet and Pat Hawes was still there. Of course, Julian Davies was the regular bass player, and Brian Mitchell. So we had the foundations of the rhythm section working together for a while, and once Les Handscombe and Ian—well Ian was another person who had been brought up on Ken Colyer, so there was no problem there. Les Handscombe always liked playing with Ken.

MIKE BROWN It is very well known that Ken was enthusiastic about the New Orleans brass band. If a trumpet player unknown to him was mentioned to Ken, his stock response was: "Yeah, but what would he sound like on the street?" Ken was a great admirer of Percy Humphrey, the leader of the Eureka Brass Band. And also Willie Pajeaud, second trumpet with that band. He had seen the Eureka on his famous New Orleans adventures in the fifties and it made a lasting impression on him. He would probably mention Willie Pajeaud and the Eureka playing *Our Director* more than anything else when we were talking about brass band stuff. Other regular topics were his love of 6/8s and his ambition to play the full version of *If I Ever Cease To Love* with a really big brass band. I think this goes back to the original trip to New Orleans. It is after all the Mardi Gras anthem and was often played by massed bands.

I always thought Ken sounded more like Peter Bocage than anyone else in his later years. I told him this once and got a big smile in response (unusually).

Ken came in and happily played second or third trumpet on a number of brass band gigs over several years, whenever we were stuck due to unavailability of one or more regulars. He played all types of event with us, and the full repertoire including concert dirges (something he never expected to do, he said). On some concerts a jazz band was required in addition to the full brass band. Ken very happily led the short band, including four-piece front-line with the late John Lewis on tenor sax. Predictably, it sounded like a Ken Colyer band.

Which brings me to a unique story. In July 1981 the Excelsior Brass Band was booked to play the Bracknell Jazz Festival; a midweek evening, early start and crises in the trumpet section. The only regular available was Sonny Morris, who had not led the trumpets before, augmented by Ken and Bill Brunskill (who surprisingly had no brass band experience). The opening parade was played and needless to say Sonny, Ken and Bill played great. Our second set was due mid-evening. During the break Ken produced a tenor sax and said he would like to join the reeds for the second set. We knew he had acquired the instrument a while back and had been practising with some help from Tony Pyke. We did not know he was planning to make his inaugural appearance with us at this event.

Fortunately Rod Ellis had arrived and took on Ken's trumpet spot. I mentioned Ken's pending debut in the green room to Sammy Rimington. Sam's reaction was, "I can't be left out of this; OK if I join you on alto?" So a three-man reed section became five men: two tenors, two altos and an Eb clarinet. The only communication from Ken was: "I suppose you'll do the usual stuff?" I nodded and that was that.

It is believed that this was the only public outing he ever made on tenor. I know he was aware of his anti-sax reputation and think he chose this opportunity to repudiate it publicly.

He certainly got a reaction. Beryl Bryden, in her usual overbearing manner, collared me afterwards, demanding full details of what was going on, and I was summoned to do a one-hour live interview on the Radio 210 Jazz Show on the following night. The presenter seemed to assume that Ken had disappeared after the break-up of the co-op band with Chris Barber!

It took the full hour to convince him that Ken had an internationally successful band, recordings, etc. post-Barber. So much for the media jazz-experts. Ken had a good laugh

Acker and Ken at the Pizza Express

when he heard the above. So that is my memory of Ken: not easy, never boring, very fixed in his view of New Orleans music, from which he never deviated. His music provided me with a great deal of pleasure over the years, and he did it his way.

LES HANDSCOMBE I got on great with Ken and we had an instant empathy from the first time we played together; we wanted the same things in life—to have fun playing the music we loved. Forget the money and the long distances we travelled, it was always worth it for me to see Ken having a good time and a quiet joke. Yes! He had a very keen sense of humour which belied the reputation he seemed to have acquired. Ken liked sincere people and suffered fools not at all. On one occasion he announced the band would play *Chloe*. I said, for a laugh, "The Spike Jones version?." He said out of the corner of his mouth, "The Colyer version, man."

BERNIE THIELE The concert of the Crane River Jazzband with Ken Colyer, Sonny Morris, Monty Sunshine, John R.T. Davies, Pat Hawes, Ben Marshall, Julian Davies and Colin Bowden at the Bakehouse in Gifhorn, Germany, on 9 May, 1986 was completely sold out, and the Bakehouse was bursting at the seams with over 250 guests. Even jazz fans from Berlin, Hamburg and Hannover had come. It was amazing with how much commitment and physical effort the Cranes played and how much fun they had themselves.

The band were taken back to Hannover without loss of time on Saturday morning and flew back to London without Ken. He later flew to Sweden, where he had a commitment at a jazz festival as special guest. So he and I went to Hannover airport alone at lunchtime in my car.

My impression from the beginning was that Ken was in low spirits. He did not participate in conversation, answered my questions reluctantly, looked unwell and seemed apathetic and sick, not only to me. He had even fallen asleep during dinner at the restaurant the previous evening. But he had turned into a different person during the gig on Friday night. Jazzing made him come alive and blossom.

I therefore told Ken when saying goodbye that he had a friend in Gifhorn who would help him whenever he might be in serious trouble with his health. I then wrote my name, address and telephone number on the paper napkin which lay in front of us on the table and said, rather boastfully, that although not a physician myself, I employed seventy of them at my hospital in Gifhorn.

Two months later, I received the first letter from England from Ken, who told me how grateful he was for my offer of medical help should he ever need it. He had only just had a medical checkup and the results had given him no reason for concern.

PETE LAY November '86 we got that German T.V. thing. We got to the 100 Club and he said, "Oh, we've got this guy from Germany. We went down to the Pizza Express last night, and I did a thing with Wally Fawkes and Ian Christie and Brian Brocklehurst, I think—Johnny Parker." And he said, "We recorded at the Pizza. The guy wants to record the thing at the 100 Club tonight. Are you up for it?" So we said, "Yeah." So the guys came down and recorded it.

And that session we had Jim Searson on clarinet, because Ian couldn't do it, which—in some ways—the film was fine, but what happened was, he tried to get the balance of the music through the camera mike, and it didn't work. So he had to come back—I think it was February in '87—and redo it, by putting a recording system in, and re-filming it, but re-film it taking it out of the van out at the back, and recording it as a live transmission. So, we had a proper miked-up recording session, so it was basically a proper recording session, but done live at the 100 Club. But that was with Ian on clarinet, so it *was* the last band.

I think it would have been late '86—when he was having problems with his embouchure, and he was finding it a little bit difficult, and he was changing keys on certain tunes to accommodate the embouchure problem. He was playing *Thriller Rag* in E♭, and things like that, slightly changing things to accomodate. And he deliberated about going into the Alexander technique. He said he went and had a couple of meetings with these people but didn't find that was beneficial to him. He spoke with Phil Parker [Jr]. He spoke with them and they put him onto Tommy McQuater.

He went to see Tommy to get some lessons about how to sort of build another embouchure, in effect. To overcome the problem, by creating another embouchure. There were times when you could hear he was regaining the power again in his lip. It did certainly put him at ease for his playing, because he was getting these pains here as well—in his jaw—and things

like that. Probably all to do with the cancer.

He was losing weight then, too. He was starting to... he *did* maintain a *certain* amount of body weight up to a certain time, but he was, at that time, starting to lose weight.

And then, really, things were going very well. We had quite a lot of work in the book, and things were picking up. Ken's Mardi Gras thing was coming to a close.

He used to thoroughly enjoy working with Max. He got on very well—he got on well with Denny Ilett, who had joined the band in place of Phil. He enjoyed working with Jim McIntosh, Trefor... Pete Cotterill had joined on drums then. He enjoyed working with the band. I know he only got to play three or four numbers and the skiffle.

MAX COLLIE Ken was a lovely bloke to work for. They always thought that when we got the Mardi Gras show together he would only last for about five seconds. Instead of which, he was fine; he was great. And he said to me... "I'd do anything for you guys," and he was perfect. And he was never pissed. Until on the very last show when he was dying on his feet, over in Hannover. Of course, in *Mardi Gras* he did about three hundred shows.

TREFOR WILLIAMS He wasn't a forceful guy, to say "You've got to do it this way!" and ram it down your throat. He was very quiet, and just sat there and played. And I think everyone had so much respect for him that they listened to what he was doing...and caught on to what he was doing. And it came out the Ken Colyer Sound... every time. I think our trumpet player at the time was Denny Ilett, and Denny sat out, and Ken came on... and the whole band sounded like the Ken Colyer band for those numbers, and then Denny would come back, and it would be the Max Collie Band again. It was funny like that.

Ken and Cy Laurie never got on very well. I think it went back a long way, before my time. Certain things he'd say... One thing he *did* say to Cy, he said, "You went off to Tibet to stand on your head and left me holding the fort." I didn't know quite what he meant by that, but I know that Cy went off for a few years, didn't he?

Well, yes, I suppose just looking at him, he was losing weight and he was losing power in playing. And yes, he *was* going down hill; we could tell, although he wouldn't talk about it. But we knew that he wasn't too well. I was actually on the last session that he ever played with a band, and that was in Germany. He was living in France then, and he came from France into Germany to do this one festival, and he looked dreadful—he really looked dreadful.

And he'd cut his own hair, and it was all tufts here, there and everywhere, and he looked dreadful, and he generally... he looked awful, and he couldn't really put much together then.

He wasn't happy, he wasn't happy at all. I don't think... I think he knew that he was on the way out, and he knew that he

Ken with German TV director Fritz Peters during filming at the 100 Club

couldn't play like he could—he was frustrated about that, but... It was very sad to see.

MAX COLLIE Well, it was a no-brainer really. I thought "I'll get Ken in and Cy Laurie." I'd already spent about three thousand pounds, and that—in 1984—was a lot of money. Posters and designs, and I was still spending money even before we got to doing a show. And we went to the first rehearsal. That was down at not a very nice area, near the Elephant and Castle. In a rehearsal room there. And Ken came along and I thought it might be a bit strange with Ken and Cy.

And Cy comes in and says, "How's my old mate Ken?" And Ken says, "You ain't no old mate of mine. Going off to India to stand on your head and leaving me to hold the fort." And I thought *Oh shit—all my money's gonna go down* and I said, "Oh... that's enough of that. And now let's get on with what we're gonna do." And I just overrode it all.

Ken didn't trust Cy, I found out later. I wondered why Ken was so against Cy, but Cy could be a very annoying character. Very bigheaded, you know. Terribly bigheaded—I fired him three times, over the years. Didn't seem to make any difference. To him.

When Ken saw him, you know, all this bile came out. But I found out later that one of the real reasons there is he knocked back Ken when Ken wanted him to join his band. And Ken never forgot that. He asked him to join his band.

After we changed from the marching band, Ken would do a bit of skiffle. Yeah, he had different things. He'd come on and he'd do it with the band, and then he'd go off, and in the parade band we had Denny and Ken. Cy wouldn't listen, you know. But Ken was fine. He was wonderful.

He was dedicated to his jazz, and he couldn't abide anyone who was just full of chat, you know. That was of no interest to him whatsoever. He'd go out to the cemetery and sit amongst the graves. To get away from it all. Because it was so quiet there. His local cemetery. And he liked gardening too.

JIM McINTOSH A funny thing happened that Ken said to me when he called a tune, *Winter Wonderland*. And I actually tapped Ken on the shoulder and said, "Ken, I don't know it," and he said, "Now's your chance to learn it." Luckily, somebody—it might have been Mike Sherbourne or Len Baldwin or someone—they were mouthing the chords to me.

Ken joined forces with Max eventually in this New Orleans Mardi Gras show. And he used to have to do a spot in it. He did a tune on his guitar, singing, and he did two numbers with the band; one was *Curse Of An Aching Heart*, and I can't remember what the other one was. And Ken said, "You're getting a few power strokes in, I'm pleased to see." And he quite liked me. He really took to me once when I came into the changing room. And I was putting my uniform on, or taking it off—I can't remember—and I was stripped to the waist, and I was

Ken with Ian Turner and Jim McIntosh

preening in the mirror, seeing how slim I was, and his voice came from the back of the changing room: "McIntosh—you're a fat cunt and you always will be; come and have a gin and tonic." And that's when we actually, I would say—if you could be friendly with Ken—became friends.

So Max was going on about, "Yeah, well we'll do this and we'll do that, then we'll have the parade." And just out of the courtesy of being slightly inquisitive I said to Ken, "What should I be doing on banjo in a parade, Ken?" And he said, "Banjo? How many more misconceptions must you labour under? There's no banjo in a marching band."

DELPHINE COLYER But the last time I saw him—talked to him—was down at the Brew House down here [Taunton]. And we had a very nice conversation. Yeah, I always went to see him when he was down here. He was with Max Collie and Cy. But I had seen him on other occasions. There was a place called The Camelot at one time. **I turned up—it was quite a lot of years ago—and all of the rest of the band saw me and thought, "Oh my God—not another fight!" And Ken came over just as if he'd seen me the day before: "Do you want a drink?"**

STEVE LANE Well, he came over to see me on a number of occasions. You see, he had this recording that this bloke did up in Nottingham. I don't quite know how he did it, but he had the original tape. I've forgotten the name of the bloke that did the recordings at The Dancing Slipper. I don't think it was Kinnell who did the actual recordings. But I think he was difficult to get the tapes from. But anyway, Colyer got hold of the tapes

for this session, and cleared it with the bloke. And Ken came to V.J.M. and said, "Will you put it out?" Well, of course, I recommended that we put it out. And that's what happened, but in the course of it I passed the tape over to Johnny Wadley, and he made a test-pressing, and so Ken had to come over and check it out—listen to it several times.

And while he was here, Mum would make him a cup of tea or something, and he would start talking to her—and they would disappear into the front room here, and I didn't see them for the rest of the afternoon; and my mum confided in me a lot of things, later, when she was bed-ridden.

She used to tell me about these things. It was amazing, really. You can't imagine two people being less compatible. My mum was a person who could chat to anybody, and it just worked out. And as I say, he came over on the day before he went to France. Well, I think he may have come over to see her. I don't think there was any excuse, you know—he was very unhappy and in a bit of a state himself.

I think he'd come over to say goodbye. But there was a much better connection between him and my mother than between him and me. I mean, I respected him, but I wouldn't say that... we got on alright, but it wasn't the same sort of attraction.

JOHN GRIFFITH My last sighting of Ken was one of the last gigs he played in this country, and it would have been at a little pub in Hampton, although I can't remember the name of the pub. And he was playing with—don't think it was a full line-up, I think it was a sort of quartet or quintet. And it was a very strange situation, and Ken was... I don't think there was any money in it for him, and there was no bandstand or anything, and I think he was actually playing sitting halfway up some carpeted stairs in the pub, and they'd turned that into a bandstand. I wasn't playing, I just knew he was there, and just turned up, because I knew that Ken was planning to go to France by then.

TREFOR WILLIAMS A lot of things he said you could take offence to, but I think he had a lot of tongue-in-cheek with some of the things he said. But he was a wonderful man, he really was. He was a great player, and I count myself lucky that I *did* spend some time with him.

PETE LAY The very last session at the 100 Club—June '87. I think it was the 21st of June. The last session, we turned up and he said, "Oh, Ray Foxley can't play piano tonight. He's gone up to Birmingham."

Ray Foxley had taken over from Pat Hawes. And Ray was doing this little show—a ragtime show. And he said, "Oh, I've booked T.J.—this young guy from Max's band—to come and play piano." Obviously, there was this young kid down from up North. We'd never met him before. But he made a big impression on me, because he was such a good sort of blues-type piano player. The first thing we said was, "Will he be alright with the tunes?" and he said, "Oh, he said he can read chords. It's not a problem—as long as I bring the chord-book."

But the session, I thought, was fine. And Ken let him sing some blues from the piano, featured T.J. within the band, not as a soloist, and that was T.J.'s first and last gig with the Ken Colyer band.

I thought we'd built up quite a good relationship with him. Like all things—I think with all of his bands, you didn't sort of all get round him. We all did our own thing in the intervals, and things like—it was always passing conversations, you know. You probably had more conversation at the beginning of the evening, 'cause Ken always arrived early—hat, trumpet, on the stand, go to the bar. So, it was those times, I think... early evening was the time you actually got to speak, but never during the session, because you were talking to other people, and Ken would be talking to other people too. Roger would be, you know, "banjos ringing, tills singing..."

In May, we'd done a benefit for Bill Colyer at the 100 Club. Bill was a bit down on his uppers at the time. Ken was not particularly enamoured with the idea of doing a benefit for Bill. Roger had suggested it at the previous 100 Club session. He said, "We're thinking of doing a benefit," you know. Ken intimated that Bill had bled off him—"All my life!" you know. So there was a little bit of animosity going on... typical brothers, really.

But then when it came to the Benefit night, everything was hunky-dory, and it was one of those occasions where a lot of musos turned up. We ended up with the Colyer band, and then there were enough guys to do a set in the middle, and then we had Sonny and Ken up doing two trumpet things with the band, so it was a good evening. But then that moved on, and the Longs took Ken away—they used to take him to Malta, didn't they, on holiday?

He came back and did the 100 Club, and he'd had a good trip, and he seemed to be on fine form; we were looking forward to the gigs we had in the book—we had quite a few in for the summer.

So we did the 100 Club; we did another gig with him at the weekend; then he was going up to do Louth, in Lincolnshire—I can't think of the guys in the band; I know Tony Peatman was in the band. But it's the Lincolnshire musicians that—Louth Jazz Club—they did release a tape; they called it the Last Ever Recordings of Ken Colyer. And he came back, and Ken was at the 100 Club with T.J., and I said, "How did the weekend go?" and he said, "Oh, it wasn't too good. Didn't enjoy myself—wasn't a particularly good session." Not explaining why.

I know, later, he wasn't particularly well, and he didn't play half the gig, but on that session, it wasn't noticeable that he was feeling ill at all. His playing was as—of that time—as good as you could expect from him.

JOHN LONG It would have been mid-'87...

RENEE LONG Well, the last time we were at the 100 Club, they actually ignored each other. It was Ken's last appearance at the 100 Club, and...

JOHN LONG Bill was still very upset about it, because he came over here, and stayed with us for two or three days after Ken died.

RENEE LONG I never thought I'd see this—it was dreadful. Everyone had left the club at the end of the session, and Bill was still there. And he called out to Ken, "You're a sad sack," and Ken turned and he started to follow Ken, and it got worse and worse, and Bill wouldn't let him go. And Bill went on and on, and Ken was about to pack his horn away, and Ken picked up his horn and threw it to the back of the stage, and shouted at Bill, "Go away. Don't you ever, ever speak to me again." And his most treasured possession—his trumpet!

KEN COLYER Bill Colyer (no relation); I was saying why Collier is a twit (Louis Armstrong biographer James Lincoln Collier). Bill said, "You're a sad sack." I had a nervous and physical breakdown the following Saturday. Twenty-one years and my elastic band had finally broke.

2. KEN COLYER

CHAPTER THIRTEEN
THE CRANES FLY AGAIN

SONNY MORRIS I was running a band at the Grey Horse in Kingston and, round about our 25th anniversary of the Cranes, Ben Marshall decided it would be a good idea if we had a reunion. He phoned everybody and all were quite happy to do it. Without any real publicity, the turnout was amazing. They were queuing-up right down the street to get into this pub with the whole of the Original Crane River Jazzband (except for Ron Bowden; unfortunately Ron didn't make it—he was otherwise engaged in those days).

We had a wonderful night with the reunion. Then Monty—

ever the entrepreneur—decided we could do well with this, so he started arranging gigs for us around the country.

BEN MARSHALL Sonny was playing regularly at the Grey Horse in Kingston. Had a band there, and we were having a nag during the interval. And I said, "What's Ken doing?" and he said, "Oh, I dunno. Not much," 'cause he'd not long before had the illness.

I said, "Has he not got his regular band?" "No, no, he hasn't." So I said, "I wonder if we could arrange a get-together." (Just a sort of throwaway.) And he said it would be nice if we could, and then I think I wrote to everybody else, but I rang them and said,

Colin, Monty, Pat, Ken, John R.T., Ben, Sonny and Julian

"Would you be interested, if we could set it up? Be a nice idea for old times' sake if we could all get together, just for a knock."

Everybody was all for it, so I said "Right. I'll set the date and a place and be in touch." And so I did that and we fixed the Grey Horse, 'cause Sonny was already there and the guv'nor was all for it. And I sent out to all of them a photograph—written on the back was the place and date. And everybody turned up. That was a fantastic evening; I think it was better than the Festival Hall, really.

We'd asked Colin Bowden because I'd spoken to Ken about what we were going to do about drums, and he said, "Well, how about Colin?" So we asked Colin, and he said yes. And I went over to Ken's a couple of times. I borrowed this banjo; I hadn't played for twenty years. And we did some run-throughs on things, you know, to remind me of what it was all about—just he and I. And then we had this night, and turned up there, and bloody hell! *Well* before time, it was jammed. They were all queuing out the front of the pub, because the word had got around and you just couldn't get in the door. It was jam packed.

COLIN BOWDEN I'd started doing sessions with Ken again somewhere around 1972. John Long had got us together again. I started doing quite a few sessions with a band built around Ken. And it was the 25th anniversary of the Cranes. The Grey Horse in Kingston—we went there and just played an ad-lib session, and obviously people thought, "That's a good idea." And the first job I think we did was Nottingham, where Ken announced to the audience that I should have been around when the Cranes first started, which was very nice of him.

JULIAN DAVIES Colin had been playing with Ken for a long time, I mean that's why he was such a bloody good drummer. Pat and him would play *Tea For Two*, and then after two choruses Pat would get off the stand, and Colin would do twenty-five choruses of *Tea For Two* and was absolutely brilliant, and he was never at a loss. I remember when he lost a stick, and he got a solo for a one-armed drummer—brilliant!

JOHN GRIFFITH History! It was like it was all happening all over again. We asked Ben what was the difference between the revival sound and the early sound? And Ben said it was mind-blowing. Just as if it was happening the other day—a week ago.

I remember this famous quote of Ken saying to Colin: "Where were you first time when we needed you?"

BEN MARSHALL I was interviewed by Max Jones, I think, from the *Melody Maker*. And I said, "Just like that, it felt just like we'd played last week, at Cranford." Exactly like that. And there was Julian walking across the pub. I'd not seen Julian for almost twenty years, and my wife Dot was with me, and he says, "Hello, how are you?"

He gave us the big hello, and, carrying his bass up on the stand, he said "You still with Dot?" and I said yeah and he said, "I'm on my third." I'll never forget that. And that was a night! Fantastic!

317

Just took off. And we all said after, "We've gotta do this again. Can't forget it now."

JOHN GRIFFITH I wasn't there on that first gig, I was certainly there on the next one—because I'd heard about it. But I missed that first one.

I think that Ken was far more relaxed with the Cranes' band. He wasn't leading as a bandleader. He was obviously leading musically. Another trumpeter, so he could relax more, and I felt he seemed a lot happier than, I'm told, he had been for years.

MONTY SUNSHINE Oh, that was terrific. They started playing I tell you, it was good. It was better musicianship—it was tremendous. **I enjoyed the Crane River reunions. The records probably prove it.**

BEN MARSHALL We were only doing things now and again because it was very awkward to do it. There was—what—four bandleaders in that band, and to get them all free on the same time... I was the sort of link-man, so someone would write to me and say "We'd like the band."

"When? What date? Have you got an alternative, in case?" Then you'd ring one, and you'd get through six of them, then the next one would say "Oh Christ, no—I'm in Germany."

Oh God, here we go again—another date, and go all the way around until you'd got all seven of them.

LEN BALDWIN The first reunion I was not involved with, because they were trying to get all of the original people back, which they succeeded in doing. Most of them were there, I think. Ray Orpwood was the original trombone after John R.T., but he was dead by then.

John R.T. had been doing some of the trombone work, but they then did two or three big gigs—two in Germany, I think—and then what happened was that John R.T. started having—it wasn't depression but he reckoned he couldn't breathe properly. Therefore, he couldn't play the trombone, but he could still play the alto saxophone (I'm not quite sure how that works). He obviously didn't want to play the trombone, that's what it was all about.

So they had some gigs lined up and Ken asked me—I was playing with him at the time—to do the gigs. Which I did, two or three of those in Frankfurt, and I enjoyed it. Ken obviously enjoyed it as well; he got on very well with Sonny Morris.

Monty was always slightly aloof, as Monty always is. Because by that time he had been a bandleader in his own right for many years. So, of course, along the front-line there was a little bit of a clash of egos, because there was Ken, Sonny—who had his own band—and Monty. I'd notice on one or two tunes that there was vying for who was going to do what, when and why. However, the overall sound was very good.

I think it was probably the fact that they were two very contrasting styles of playing. Ken was very content to interweave and play that style while Sonny was very direct, wasn't he? So it just gelled. Obviously they had played together quite a bit with the original Crane River before they had gone their separate ways, so I think they had got used to doing it. The tunes I played with them were all the original Cranes' tunes: *Sad Night In Harlem, Miner's Dream Of Home* and those sort of tunes.

BEN MARSHALL The reason for Len Baldwin joining was... John had these dreadful headaches. I don't know what it is—they call it suicide-headaches or something, the pain's so awful. And I've seen him nearly go potty on stage.

Round at Colchester once, he got off the stand, and ran across, hunched... killing him. And he used to suffer, and apparently he was talking to this specialist about it, and telling him what went on, and the specialist said, "Well, probably all that back-pressure you're getting from blowing on that trombone isn't doing you any good. I suggest you pack that up for a while."

So John told us this, and we said, "Well, what can we do? Let's get another trombone in, and John go on saxophones." It had been going on for some time. So that's what we did, and Len joined us. We had some nice publicity pictures done of that band which included Ray Smith at the piano—because, at that point, Pat didn't want to know.

But happily, Pat came back in not too long after that. I think Ray only did a couple of jobs with us, but one of them was a trip to Germany, I think. And Pat returned, which was fine, but unfortunately, when we did the next German trip with him, all the publicity pictures were with Ray Smith!

RAY SMITH Ken asked me to join the band some time in 1976 after Pat Hawes had left suddenly after a session, I believe, at Hatfield jazz club. I didn't last long, and suddenly Pat was back. I realised afterward that Ken didn't actually have the right to ask me to become a permanent member and he was quite embarrassed at having to tell me not to turn up any more. But it *was* exciting, and I enjoyed playing with the band.

COLIN BOWDEN Ken and Sonny—it was amazing. They used to pick up on phrases. First Sonny would lead and then Ken lead, and then one of them would play an improvisation and take over the lead. But it wasn't a

worked-out thing; it was something that they just did. It was as if they had their own blueprint.

I think it evolved because they were both learning to play, and neither of them were tutored—both self-taught. I think it was a case of it evolved naturally—they didn't have to work at it.

John R.T. knew where the boundaries were, if you like. They'd played together as learning players. It was a very natural band to play with.

SONNY MORRIS With Monty's contacts in Germany, he arranged for us to go to Germany at a big concert in Hamburg, with a promoter called Karsten Jahnke. We played in this massive, massive hall—I think there were 3,000 people in there. It was a programme of mainly British bands: Humphrey Lyttelton, Chris Barber, Dutch Swing College. We went on, and you cannot believe the reception we got.

BEN MARSHALL Now that was the thing that was the highlight above the Festival Hall—way above the Festival Hall. Ken just started announcing the band: "You've just been introduced in garbled German." And he realised what he'd said, and then he said, "And I'd like to introduce the band in garbled English."

It was tremendous, it really was. We were introduced singly, and just walked on stage, you know. The Congress Centrum—it was just very similar to the Festival Hall, where you got about three or four yards before the first row of seats.

And this space was just jammed solid with photographers. Never experienced anything like it. And we kicked off, and we did—I'm sure we did *Maggie* for the first number.

There were four other English bands. All of them were in the wings. Because—you know—the Cranes had re-formed, and probably most of them hadn't heard us anyway, and were probably thinking, "Well, what was all the fuss about? Let's have a listen."

And then, you know, Ken did the spiel and Pat started to come in, and that was all impromptu—as he was introducing each member, they would join in, right through the band, until he finished up.

COLIN BOWDEN This is the programme: Rod Mason/Ian Wheeler band, Max Collie's Rhythm Aces, then Humph's band

with Kathy Stobart and Bruce Turner, and the Barber Blues Band with Pat and Chris and John Crocker and Graham Burbidge, bless his heart.

And then the Cranes go on and that was Sonny and Ken, John R.T., Mont, Pat Hawes, Ben Marshall, Julian Davies and yours truly. And I'll never forget it because it was "Hot Jazz in Britain Today," the whole concert. And all those bands were in the wings looking, to see what the Cranes sounded like.

And we sort of played the first tune, and there was a stunned silence for a fraction of a second, and then the biggest roar I've ever experienced in my life, louder even than the George Lewis concert in Manchester—it was that type of sound. A wall of sound hit us and we knew we'd cracked it. And we just sat back—wonderful.

JULIAN DAVIES During that weekend, we made a broadcast which was the one that came out on the CD *Storming Session*, and a straight recording session. And then the concert. So we played quite a bit, and also Karsten—who ran a brewery—provided all the beer. So when we came to do it in the evening, we played so well because we'd played so often, and it just went a bomb.

We went on the stand and we did those—I thought we did more than three numbers, but we started off with that *Snag It*, and it got it off. Ken introduced the band as we came on and it went like that—no arrangement—and we just go on and do our bit and so on and it built up and built up and built up, until you get the trumpet breaks and it really... blossomed.

And when we came off, all the other musicians—we had an absolutely standing ovation—and all the other musicians were standing in the wings, and Humph grabbed my hand and Chris Barber said, "How the hell am I gonna follow that?" It was absolutely brilliant, and it was just one of those things.

PAT HAWES When the original Cranes disbanded, we still kept in touch, but I was still surprised when a letter arrived from Ben Marshall in 1972 suggesting a get-together for old-times' sake. Realising that we needed a drummer, Colin Bowden (no relation to Ron Bowden) was invited to come along. We had all worked with Colin in various situations and had the highest regard for his powerful New Orleans-style drumming.

We had hoped to have this reunion at the White Hart, Cranford where the Cranes had run their own club (1949-1951)

in a hall at the rear of the pub. Sadly the building was unsafe structurally and an alternative venue was arranged—the Grey Horse, Kingston, which regularly put on traditional jazz—Sonny Morris played there frequently. There was a less than sensational piano, a large stage and plenty of room for an audience.

Frankly, I had my doubts as to who would bother to turn up. I arrived an hour early to put down a pint or two and meet some friends who had promised to come. To my astonishment, the place was packed, with a long queue outside trying to get in!

Gigs began to come in. We had a rehearsal or two and the enthusiasm of audiences for the band, so apparent at the Grey Horse reunion, was apparent wherever we played. Obviously gigs with the Cranes had to be fitted around other commitments—Monty, with plenty of contacts, looked out for work and Ben Marshall acted as our contact man.

Word of the band's renaissance reached promoter Karsten Jahnke in Germany. Karsten was planning a big concert in Hamburg and the Cranes were invited to be on the bill, joining the bands of Humphrey Lyttelton, Chris Barber, Max Collie, etc. The concert, "Hot Jazz Meeting," was held at the Congress Centrum, Hamburg, on the night of May 15th 1973.

We flew out from Heathrow on Friday May 14th, returning to London on Sunday May 16th. A busy schedule was arranged which included not only the concert appearance, but also a studio recording for Happy Bird Records, plus a broadcast for Nordwestdeutscher Rundfunk (German Radio RDF, today NDR).

In a perfect world, someone would have kept an accurate diary of the events that were crowded into that busy weekend. Unfortunately jazz musicians are not noted for attention to apparently unnecessary detail and the exact sequence of events can't be established for certain.

It's surprising, however, how certain things stick in the memory. A short while before this trip there had been an air crash involving a British Airways Trident jet, with heavy loss of life. Sonny was apprehensive about flying anyway, saying "I bet it's a Trident." Sure enough, when we disembarked from the airport bus, there was a Trident sitting on the runway. Sonny's face was a picture! On take-off, a German priest sitting opposite crossed himself repeatedly—just about the last straw for Sonny! In the event, nothing untoward happened on the way to Hamburg—it seems very funny now, much less so at the time.

The Davies Brothers are fairly certain that we were met at the airport and were whisked off to tape the broadcast before going to our hotel. The Happy Bird recording session was probably the morning of the 15th May, the same day as the concert. One thing that is certain was that the hospitality was overwhelming, much of it of the liquid variety—German beer, topped up with frequent glasses of schnapps, a potent memory eraser!

Ken and Monty were no strangers to the German scene—they were *big* there, with a large following of traditional jazz fans. Colin Bowden too, knew from experience the kind of reception we were likely to get. To the rest of us it came as a complete surprise—the Hot Jazz Meeting was a sell-out.

Happy Bird recorded the parts of the concert by bands who were not under contract to other companies. Happy Bird LP 5003 coupled three titles recorded live at the concert—*Snag It, I Can't Escape From You, Panama*—with *Moose March, Sometimes My Burden Is So Hard To Bear, When You and I Were Young, Maggie*, which were studio-recorded that same weekend. I have the remaining titles from the concert on tape, unfortunately in poor sound quality and at low volume, recorded by someone in the audience, not suitable for issue.

Snag It was the Cranes' first number. Starting with just piano and Ken introducing each member of the band, who then joined in (an idea inspired by Orson Welles' introduction of the Kid Ory band on the 1944 Standard Oil Broadcast).

The Cranes were certainly the hit of the evening. It was good to see the Humphrey Lyttelton and Chris Barber bands standing in the wings watching the proceedings. It was at this concert that I experienced for the first time a truly unique German audience phenomenon. In Britain, the slow handclap has always been reserved for an unsatisfactory performance—different countries, different customs! At the end of each number, the audience began slow handclapping, gradually accelerating, reaching a thunderous climax, an accolade only given for an outstanding performance.

John R.T. and I once discussed this strange manifestation and John remembered a similarly unnerving experience when the Temperance Seven, playing Londonderry, Northern Ireland, for the first time, had money thrown at them, a gesture of real approval, but certainly in the East End of London a mark of disapproval and frequently a precursor of violence.

COLIN BOWDEN There were rehearsals at John R.T.'s, because he recorded the rehearsals, being John R.T. There was Mont, doing the impresario bit, Ken doing the prima donna bit, Sonny laughing his head off. It was good—a good atmosphere. I did my usual thing; I would just disappear if there was any problem. I thought the music was wonderful.

JOHN LONG I was delighted that it was going to happen, and I was able to record the full band down at the 100 Club but, within a few months, Ken was disillusioned by it, because he said "It won't work for much longer, because they've all become prima donnas."

JULIAN DAVIES I think Ken felt like he'd come home. Yes, I think he loved it—nobody had to prove anything, and Ken was at ease.

BEN MARSHALL Some of the happiest times I remember

were in the early days, and also one of our trips to Germany, when we'd done the job, and it had gone quite well, and we were sitting around having a few jugs, and everybody'd get talking. Then Ken would start talking—getting involved in the conversation and, relaxed as hell, telling stories—some a little bit over the top; one in particular.

Well, it was just—it shocked me a bit at the time, and thinking afterwards, I thought, "Oh, it was probably the drink," 'cause he'd had a few. He was drinking; he had a bottle of Irish Mist there—I can see it clear as day—and he was offering it around and he offered me one, and I said, "No, I don't drink spirits, Ken."

"'Come on, come on—you've got to have some of this, man." I said "I don't drink spirits."

"Tiny drop, tiny drop. Come on, come on." And he tipped a bit of it. And I had a little sip, and it *was* rather nice and I said "Yeah, that's lovely, Ken." "I told you, man, I told you. You listen to me, man." And then he's telling us about when he was in New Orleans. And things that went on and "I was playing here, and I was going in there" and he said, "I bet those guys were really wondering what's going on with this blonde Messiah that's come among us."

BEN MARSHALL I think they called it the Manor House, but it was the Nottingham Rhythm Club. Quite a nice club, and Ken had been on holiday in France, and I think this was his first job when he came back. And he came into the dressing-room and he changed his shirt, and he was tanned, and I said to him, "I've never seen you looking so good. Do you feel good?" So he said, "Yeah, I don't feel bad, man."

So I said, "Great, you look well. Take care of yourself," because he'd let himself go a bit.

That was the last time I saw him, although I did talk to him on the phone before he returned to France. He sounded pretty bad.

CHAPTER FOURTEEN
THAT LONESOME ROAD

PETE LAY It came as a shock when we went to the next 100 Club gig for Roger to announce that "I've got some bad news for you. This morning, Sonny took Ken to the airport." The sequence of events had happened that particular weekend. And there was this talk to Roger, "Can you do this for me? Can you sort these sort of things out." And Roger said, "Why are you asking me? Because it's not really my affair" you know. "Maybe you should talk to Sonny." So there was a triangle of conversations going on about sorting out affairs. He wanted the house sold, there and then, as you know. And all sorts of things. He said, "I've got to go— gotta leave."

> I think in the circumstances Ken had felt he couldn't perform anymore. The one thing he could do, he couldn't do anymore, so he had to get away, go to somewhere where he couldn't be contacted.

But then, obviously, after a few months, people did make contact with him. Which was fortunate, because it then gave the impetus for a benefit night at the 100 Club for him and the start of getting some of those recordings that are done with the band with George Lewis to be released officially. He said, "There's some good stuff on reel-to-reel," you know. But he wasn't happy with that LP that came out with George Lewis with his band— there were five or six tracks from the concert and on the other side was the tracks with Marrero and Jack Delaney.

I don't know who put it out, but it was things that Mike Dine had done and he wasn't happy about that. Because they weren't supposed to have been put out. Whether Bill had something to do with that or not, I don't know. Because who would have got hold of the tapes? And that was another thing that Ken told me; the session at the 100 Club that was released by George Buck, with Johnny Parker. Now Ken was not happy with that being released, and I understand it was Bill sold the tape to George

Buck. And I think that was one of the issues that he'd taken with Bill, why he wasn't happy about a benefit for him.

So Ken wasn't at that final gig. Sonny was there. Roger told us, and Sonny played. And Sonny led the band during the summer, until, basically, those who had wanted to play with Colyer, didn't want to do the gig anymore. And so they said no. Basically out of that Sonny teamed up with Bob Ward and formed the Delta Jazz Band.

PETER MORCOM My last contact with Ken was just before he left for France in 1987. He phoned me three times in the ten days before the Sunday gig at the 100 Club. This was not the Ken I had known. It was only when I turned up for the gig that I learned that Sonny had taken him to Heathrow that afternoon. Hindsight explains a great deal.

KEN COLYER LETTER TO TIM NEWMAN 17 JUNE 1987

99 The Drive, Hounslow, Middx TW3 1 PN
Dear Tim,
Just a line to let you know that I won't be able to play the club next year as I am going into dry dock for a while to try and mend my health up.
Best Wishes, (signed) Ken Colyer

PAUL ADAMS We did have quite a big bust-up, actually, which was a bit spectacular. He wasn't well, which was one thing, and he said something about me and Decca lining my pockets, which sort of came out of the blue because he'd been so cooperative up until that time, and I had met up with him when he was doing the Max Collie thing and sort of doing a little bit.

And so it was all very strange. I got very miserable about it, for about twenty-four hours, and then I just went "Right, I'm coming out with both barrels blazing."

So I pointed out to him that if anybody was lining their pockets, it might be Decca. Because Decca were charging me two thousand pounds advance royalties, and we never sold enough copies for me to start paying them, so we never recouped the advance royalties, so, you know, I thought I was hardly lining my pockets.

And I was angry, having got very miserable about it. I was really angry, and I suppose I didn't really know Ken so I didn't know the sort of ins and outs of his character very much. So, you know, I wasn't prepared for this.

And what happened was I got a letter by return of post apologising. And Jimmy Asman said to me, "Ken never apologises to anybody—where has that come from?"

And then he was ill and he went to France, and I'd got a reasonable collection of country blues recordings. So I used to dub them off onto cassette and send them to him. And I got these little notes back saying "I really like getting stuff from you, because you're one of the few people who aren't after something." And again, I don't know what that meant. You know, it was Ken being Ken. You know, you just got "Yeah… whatever," you know.

KEN COLYER LETTER TO DAVE SMITH 6 JULY 1987

Dear Dave,

I hope this reaches you alright. Left in hurry— so sick couldn't think of everything. Thought I had your address in my pocket. Well I have had a pretty disastrous time since I have been here, but some people have been very kind. Eventually ended up in hospital for three days. Don't recommend French Hospitals. They thought I had bone disease or virus infection. Both proved negative. I remember Mike Read saying he had to pack up thro' overwork. Went on luxury holiday and everything went wrong with him. If I could have stayed here in May I think I would have been alright. But returned home and felt sick within days.

Damnable weather. I really like it here and hope I am on the mend after a week of hell. I am very weak, can hardly walk, but will take it easy. My son Russell is coming tomorrow, has been very worried about me. Good kid, didn't think he cared too much. Maybe like me, doesn't always show true emotions. But I don't want to see anybody else until I am better. Despite all, have written what I think is a good book. Partly to take my mind off the pain and partly driving urge. Mind crystal clear apart from slight hallucinations probably through lack of sleep, but am not worried about it. Noise is the thing that drives me up the wall. My nerves have been on razor's edge. Did snap (elastic band broke) but have managed to put a knot in it. Am moving to quieter place as soon as I can— really nice— address will be:

LE DATTIER E9, Route-De-Bagnols-En-Foret, 83600 FRÉJUS, FRANCE. Keep it to yourself, tell no one.

I know why so many great painters liked it here. Getting exploited but where I am going is more exclusive. Worth the extra money. Have some great records coming out— date sheet will tell you.

Didn't realize how good we were thirty years ago. Musician heard I was here sick. Told fellow he would walk here (60 miles) just to shake my hand (nice). OTHERS HAVE TREATED ME LIKE DIRT AND IT HURTS. But I feel in better frame of mind and hope things work out. Otherwise it is the finish.

Am selling my house. Pity you couldn't transfer the garden to your place, but mustn't look back.

Best Wishes to your wife and children

Sincerely, Ken

KEN COLYER LETTER TO DAVE SMITH 9 JULY 1987

La Dattier E9, Route-De-Bagnols-En-Foret, Fréjus, France
Dear Dave,

I wrote to you but guessed the address. I did not realise I had your card. I have had a pretty bad time but am feeling better now. I love it here (more than the natives). Am going home tomorrow to wind my affairs up. No good leaving it to others (useless). Then I will be here permanently.

GIVE NO ONE MY ADDRESS.

Post very bad here. Always used AIRMAIL

Might have some joy on book in Germany. HAVE WRITTEN ANOTHER, BLOWING THE WORKS,

Best Wishes, (signed) Ken.

KEN COLYER LETTER TO DAVE SMITH AUGUST 14, 1987

Holiday Green, Fréjus, France
Dear Dave,

Thanks for your letter. I have been very ill, but am mending up now. The weather's fine and doing me the world of good. Have still got financial problems, but mostly it's a case of getting money transferred here from England. Modern business and banking is run on ineptitude, as you probably know.

I am hoping to move once I have got the finance, just down the road. I will never live in England again, the climate would eventually kill me. So I would sooner die here.

But I might need to come over some time later, to earn a little money. Some darned German keeps talking about God's Gifts, but God didn't ever give me any money, I have told him, it's not hogwash I need at the moment but finance.

I might start looking around here for some work, but it is the old story, what passes for music, darn near drives me mad.

I am getting a little boat, so that I can really get away from Bedlam for awhile, each day. I haven't seen your friend, but it has been the height of the holiday season, and the roads have been choc-a-block. I will start easing off now.

The first record should be out (of 30 years ago, terrific stuff, nobody playing like it today) by the time you get this. My books

(2 now) I am still having trouble with. It's a printer I want, not a publisher, to hell with them. I will finance it myself. The damn fools think that I am completely unknown. Whereas there is a market been waiting for years.

Will let you know, if, and when I decide to return for a short period,

Best Wishes, (signed) Ken

KEN COLYER LETTER TO TREFOR WILLIAMS 15 AUGUST 1987

Holiday Green, Fréjus, France
Dear Trefor,

Was nice to hear from you. I am glad to say that I am mending up, though these lesions are still plaguing me, but with painful manipulations, I think I am dispersing them. Legs are weak, could hardly walk a while back, but again they are slowly strengthening up. I am as brown as a berry. Tell Pete I am blond again, but I have chopped most of my hair off, just a nuisance. My main problem at the moment is untying my finance. I need the money here, it's unbelievable how these banks and people can fuck you about.

They take it easy enough, but create all sorts of problems when it comes to giving it back.

I want to settle here and just maybe come back for short trips to make a little money. Tell Max I should be alright for Australia, if it is still on. I didn't think I would be fit for anything ever again awhile back, but I knew a year here would work wonders. And it is working in a couple of months. But I will never get on the treadmill again. It would be fatal.

I now have two books to get published. Being fucked about as usual, though I want to finance them myself, as I am sure they will sell well enough. If they don't, too bad. The L.P. is just appearing of glorious music of 30 years ago. Again, I know it is going to sell, and want to put maybe two more out. At least Tony Leppard is being very helpful. Most of the 'others' it's, "A handful of Gimme, mouth full of much obliged." (Estes) You say they are on my side. Horseshit. They are a bunch of mealy mouthed fucking bums. The type that would kick a dying dog.. I won't go into what has gone on, but you get the picture.

Did you get Pete to see to that drum head? The drum is worth looking after, and you play it good. Better than the supposed New Orleans thickheads.

I have explained more fully what constitutes good New Orleans music, how to listen, learn and maybe play it, in my second book. I call it 'Master Class'. But feel it is too late, unless a miracle happens, but you never know. There is the 'Long Hope.'

Guess that's all for now.

TONY LEPPARD Sunday 13th September 1987— a day I shall never forget. I'd been out to a bottle fair at Dorking in the morning and decided that I would relax in front of the television in the afternoon.

I had just sat down with a cup of tea when the telephone rang. When I picked up the receiver, the voice from the other end simply said "Hello Tone, it's Ken." This in itself was no surprise; the Guv'nor had been constantly in touch with me since his departure from England to his new home in France, and telephone calls at any time of the day and night had become routine. However, what followed was anything but normal.

"Can I see you?" said Ken. This took me aback as I knew that Ken was soaking up the sun in the South of France. How wrong I was. "Certainly Ken, where are you?"

"Victoria Station. I can be at Hounslow East in about 45 minutes." "OK Ken, I'll be there to meet you."

The station at Hounslow East is an elevated affair, and from the barrier I had a good view of the whole platform. When Ken's train arrived, therefore, I immediately spotted him as he alighted from the rear carriage.

Many things were to happen during the next few hours that I shall remember for the rest of my life, and the sight of Ken limping along the platform (he had twisted and sprained his ankle) was one of them. He had a nice, suntanned colour; I could not remember when I had seen him looking in such good health. A roughly trimmed beard and a wide-brimmed, straw panama hat reminded me of Hemingway.

The only possessions he had with him were the clothes he stood in and the contents of a tote bag, which hung from his shoulder on a dog's lead he had found during his travels in France and contained a few essentials including duty-free cigars and a bottle of gin.

Another surprise awaited me when we got into the car and Ken removed his hat. His appearance had undergone a remarkable change. Gone was the well-groomed hair. No longer creamed and bleached by the sun, his hair had returned to its natural fair colour and, as he had trimmed it himself, it was spiky and, by past standards, rather on the untidy side. It was quite obvious why he had been called 'Blondy' during his Merchant Navy days.

When he left England in July 1987, Ken went to live in a mobile home he had purchased on a camp-site near Fréjus. This turned out to be too noisy and not at all to his liking, so he soon moved out and took up residence in a small boat he was negotiating to buy, moored in the harbour of a small fishing village called Les Isambres. It was here that he had met a French couple (a pair of the Good Samaritans that Ken often talked about). They realised that Ken had serious financial problems and had loaned him sufficient money to get him back to Hounslow to arrange a bridging loan until his house was sold.

We spent the rest of the day at our ease, mainly listening to Ken's tales of some of his outrageous adventures in France. He had a pretty jaundiced view of French hospitals, in one of which he had spent a few days after he collapsed in the street immediately upon his arrival in France. Later on it was discovered that Ken had an enlarged heart and, looking back, I feel sure that on that occasion he suffered a heart attack.

Ken outlined his plans for the future. His immediate concerns were to get himself fit to be able to undertake a concert with Max Collie in Hannover in December and a trip to Australia in 1988, also with Max, and to sort out his finances. He needed a loan of six thousand pounds to see him through until the sale of his house was completed. If this could be arranged, he could finalise the purchase of his boat and settle some debts he had incurred. One of these was for ten Francs, about one pound, that he owed to a lady who worked in a petrol station. This had arisen when the lady in question had not understood Ken's own form of Esperanto and had put more petrol in to his car than he had money to pay for. Typical of the man, this small debt concerned him as much as any other.

I had been in contact with Ken's bank, Barclays in Hounslow High Street, on a number of occasions, and had built up a good relationship with some of the people there. I agreed, therefore, that I would go to the bank with Ken the next day to help with the negotiations.

As soon as Barclays opened at 9.30 I phoned for an appointment and explained what it was that Ken needed. We had to be at the bank at 11.00 a.m. With time to kill, Ken and I discussed the future K.C. Record releases, and this led me to play to Ken a recording of the Jazzmen made by the late Peter Godwin at Studio 51. It opens with a fine rendering of *Muskrat Ramble* and progresses with *Riverside Blues* and other superb tracks until *Wolverine Blues*. Ken listened intently and pointed out to me aspects of the music that were to him both good and bad.

At the end of *Wolverine Blues* I made the comment that it was a pity that the usual coda ending had been omitted. "That doesn't matter," Ken replied, "Jelly would have been pleased with that." **I noticed that Ken had moist eyes and I realised then that what we had been listening to had gone forever and that Ken knew it.** Sadly to say, that was exactly the way things turned out.

The time came for us to keep our appointment with Barclays. As we walked in we must have looked a bit comic: me in a suit trying to look smart and businesslike; Ken straight from a beachcombing foray in his 'Hemingway' outfit.

Now, it is probably an understatement to say that Ken did not like, or cope well with, officialdom. He immediately showed signs of anxiety, and I thought he might become aggressive.

I told him not to worry and to leave the talking to me, which he seemed quite happy to do. To my enormous relief, as soon as we were ushered into an interview room, the very young bank official announced that, subject to Ken signing the necessary documents, the requested loan was in order.

Ken quickly signed as requested. "I'll get you a banker's draft," said the young man. "No," replied Ken, "I want it all in cash; French Francs." "Oh, I don't think we have that much." "Then I'll take it in Dollars or Deutschmarks." Maybe Ken had a certain reputation at the bank, I don't know, but after a number of telephone calls to other banks in the area, the Francs appeared.

A large pile of banknotes sat before us: 60,000 French Francs. Ken suddenly seemed to lose interest in the proceedings, leaving me to take care of the money. So I stood up, and started stuffing bundles of money into my pockets. Ludicrous really. The bank man leaned over and asked "Would you like a bag, sir?" and immediately produced a large manila envelope. Bless him, I think I would have ended up with most of the money inside my shirt. With that trauma behind us, we strode forth into Hounslow High Street. Well, I did. Ken still limped along in his sandals.

"Let's have a cup of tea." Into the first restaurant we came to. Tables set for the lunchtime rush and this odd couple bowl in and order "Two cups of tea, one strong." To his credit, the waiter took it all in his stride, and quickly served our tea. Then, still clutching the bag of money, I followed Ken out of the restaurant and into Marks and Spencers to get him a box of extra-strong teabags. Into a nearby baker's for a couple of sandwiches for lunch and then to a travel agent for a one-way ticket on the next flight from Heathrow to Nice.

By the time we got back to Rydal Gardens, Kay was home from work. A quick lunch and it was time to leave for the airport where, after booking-in, we said our farewells.

I shook hands with the Guv'nor and it's strange to look back on that, because it was the only time I can remember so doing. Off he went, into the departure lounge, without a backwards glance, still limping, his tote bag—now containing 60,000 Francs beneath a box of cigars and a bottle of gin—hanging from his shoulder. Kay and I were convinced that he would be mugged before he got home. Our fears were unfounded. He telephoned a couple of evenings later to say that all was right in the world.

Although we remained in contact by telephone and letter, that was to be the last time we saw Ken, and the last time he came to England.

KEN COLYER LETTER TO JULIAN DAVIES 24 SEPTEMBER 1987

Villa Maica, 198 De Ronde, Parc du Corsaire,
83360 Les Issambres, France
Dear Julian,
Thanks for your letter and cheque.

When you are suffering the 'Agonies of the Damned', you don't feel too kindly towards anything or anybody. I must go into hospital soon but can't even do that without finance.

I have met some 'good Samaritans' here who are helping me.

I am trying to sell everything in England, but thanks [part missing] the ineptitude of the bank, have been left in a mess. Slowly getting it sorted out.

I have my guitar with me, and a cornet, so thanks for the offer but should be O.K. for instruments.

Will let you know how I get on.

Best Wishes, Ken

KEN COLYER LETTER TO JULIAN DAVIES 5 OCTOBER 1987

Kreiskrankenhausen, 3170 Gifhorn, Germany
Dear Julian,

I said I would keep you posted. Am being thoroughly examined here. Have had polyps removed from lower colon, but there may be more on further exam.

It's a beautiful hospital in lovely woodlands and I am receiving first class treatment, thanks to Bernd Theile (Bernie Teeler).

I long to get back to Les Issambres, but must be patient and see it through. Nerves are still on a razor's edge, but it is peaceful and quiet here so they will probably improve.

Weather has been good for the time of the year, though they forecast rain for tomorrow.

Have been playing guitar to much appreciation (good practice too). Had a little try on cornet yesterday, didn't feel too bad.

Am rooming with a wonderful man (76 years of age), went to his house. He has incredible talent; painter, sculptor, lovely work in ceramics etc: He has been three years writing his autobiography. I would like to read it. He went all through the last war, is covered in scars, blown up by hand-grenade and goodness knows what else, was on the Russian Front and many other places and campaigns.

We have very interesting conversations and have mutual admiration and camaraderie.

Hope this finds you and Joyce well, and the weather clement,

Best Wishes, Ken

KEN COLYER LETTER TO DAVE SMITH 11 OCTOBER 1987

Kreiskrankenhausen, 3170 Gifhorn, Germany
Dear Dave,

In dock once again, had a polyp removed from my colon. They found my heart is enlarged (I wonder why?) but I don't think it is a problem. They can't find out what my muscular trouble is but are giving me excellent treatment here and I hope to be in better shape when I leave, but I don't know when that will be. I started this letter before I received yours from Holiday Green. The best address to write to when I leave is

PORT FERREOL 83386, LES ISSAMBRES, FRANCE.

But they will forward mail from here.

I got the cheque from Lance, which was very welcome, and have written to him.

A few weeks ago I had lost faith in all humanity, but glad to say, I *am* more compus mentis now and this naturally will help my physical problems.

Also, a Frenchwoman fell in love with me, from a distance, at Port Ferreol (a beautiful little place). We have got it together, and after many years, the love life is good. It's not a casual affair, and I'm very happy about it. She is about 50 and absolutely delightful. Very intelligent, very passionate (It's true what they say about the French). She is with me at the moment, and has helped me a lot through my tribulations.

I laughed at some of your letter, but know how the infection must have been as I have had so much damned pain myself.

Cy is a 100% shit so I need say no more about him.

I hope you have success with your business contract, but know all about bureaucracy gone mad, it has damned near driven me mad, trying to get MY money transferred from Barclays Bank in Hounslow. It is stupefying that they are so inept. I desperately need certain funds and just cannot get them, yet they won't give me a short-term loan (been banking with them for 35 years, treated like a bloody con man)

Still let's hope everything will work out in the end, but life certainly is a 'two edged sword.'

Keep in touch,

Best Wishes, (signed) Ken

KEN COLYER LETTER TO JULIAN DAVIES 18 OCTOBER 1987

Altea Hotel, Port Ferreol, 83380, Les Issambres, France.
Dear Julian,

Have just returned from Hospital in Germany. Malignancies removed from colonic area successfully. Drove there (Gifhorn 900 miles approx.) in 20 hours. Terrible weather returning as you probably know. Took 3 days coming back, impossible to carry on. But had a beautiful French woman with me, so despite jet lag, had some pretty good moments. She fell in love with me here when I was in deep trouble and I didn't know!

She is a 100% and I am now in love with her. She is the most delightful woman I have ever met. Even likes and knows (reads) Steinbeck, Hemingway, etc... Loves the music and has uncanny intuition. I am 59 and not just infatuated (she [Nicole] is about 50) Who cares!

I am still having attacks of terrible pain, I wouldn't wish it on my worst enemy, but it's due to severe disability and nervous breakdown. Doctor recommended anabolic steroids. I will try and get some tomorrow. I am about 20 lbs. under weight, and weak as a kitten. I just hope (and I think it will) that this part of the country and the new love in my life will fix things up. It will take time, but I have got plenty of that ("If We Survive," as Fields used to say.)

I have switched to cigars (Wild Havana, La Paz favourite brand). Have told her, beautiful woman, good cigar, good gin and tonic (also good wine), what more do you want in life? Like I said (more or less) to hell with the rest, they can have it. If these pains would only leave me alone, life would be perfect. Still swimming here in the sea, good exercise and the air has ambience. Obviously, can't make any jobs in England for some time. Keeping in on guitar but not cornet. I might be able to fix up a band job here next summer. Got friendly with a favourite 'drinking hole' which would be a nice spot, but didn't talk finance; might know more, May or April next year.

All the best, Ken

P.S. Finances still in a mess, but hope to get them sorted out next week.

KEN COLYER LETTER TO DAVE SMITH 19 OCTOBER 1987

Mon 6 a.m. Altea Hotel [headed notepaper],
Port Ferreol, 83380, Les Issambres, France.
Dear Dave,

Just a line to let you know that I am back at the above, after two hazardous days of driving. You probably saw reports of storms in Germany, worst driving conditions I've ever

Nicole cutting Ken's hair

experienced, not good for a sick man and feel pretty beat up, though Milady is wonderful and we laugh a lot. She is so understanding, it is fantastic.

Weather is good here and we are swimming again, which is good exercise. I am sure I will recover, but will try and see her doctor today. I must get something for these terrible muscular attacks. Feeling much better mentally but I am worn out and can't stand the pain anymore.

I hope Derek can do something positive about printers. I must get my books printed. Tony Leppard (63 Rydal Gdns. Hounslow, Middx. Tel: 01 894 4218) will be back from holiday about 24th Oct. He is a very good friend. Will you keep in touch with him? I hope I can get some capital today, them useless gits have messed me about long enough. I can get a 20,000 pound mortgage on my apartment once I get my capital. This money I can use for books etc. I am not worried about the future. It will look after itself. I hope things are going along all right with you, and your project.

Say hello to your children and good wife for me.
(signed) Ken

MAX COLLIE I got Roger [Horton] to put on a benefit night for him. I made sure that I got hold of the money and nobody else did, because they have a bad habit of losing some of the money at some of these benefits. And I sent the money down to Ken. We raised three thousand quid. And he'd say "Oh... Nobody likes me..." type of thing, you know. But, I've heard all this before.

And I said "Now look here. There's lots of people come up and give me money and things for you. And they were all there, and they all turned up for you, so don't say that. They all love you." And then he went all quiet then... "Oh yeah... alright."

I knew he was on his last legs. Because I'd already told him we'll cover him, and he really tried, you know. He really did try—he was that sort of bloke and it wasn't too bad at all. He really tried hard, and he lost the trumpet, and I had to chase round to the hotel where we were staying, which was next door and they couldn't find it.

I found the trumpet in the hotel. It's the only time he got pissed on any of the shows—all those hundreds of shows. They had to take him off the stage.

After the gig I put him in the car with Bernie, and they took him to hospital.

BERNIE THIELE I received two letters from Ken at the end of August 1987 from the South of France. He told me about his physical complaints, his destitution and despair, and that he needed money and my help. One of these letters seemed a little confused to me and I suspected that he might not only have physical but mental problems.

Tuesday, 29th September, was a chilly autumn day with the mucky weather typical of Northern Germany when Ken arrived in Gifhorn in his car from the South of France. He was overtired, and I took him directly to the ward and to bed so that he could get enough sleep and had some nurses to look after him.

Ken's liver was 'clean' but there were polyps in the intestinal tract that had caused some haemorrhaging. Professor Gillich—Ken's surgeon—was able to remove these endoscopically up to the small intestines. The doctor's orders were: control checkup in two months' time, latest. After one week, Nicole Demay came from Paris to Gifhorn for a visit. Ken seemed like a different person, and no trace was left of his depressive mood. I heard him laugh for the first time! **Nicole stayed at an apartment at the nurses' home. It was touching how she looked after him, and I could get some decent sleep. Anyone could see that the two were head over heels in love.**

Nicole and I conversed in English, which she spoke better than I. She told me how she had met Ken. He had had a heart attack on the market place in Fréjus. She found him—literally—in the gutter and saw that he got emergency care. When Ken had been defibrillated and discharged a few days later, she invited him to her beautifully located holiday home in Les Issambres.

I saw Nicole as a charming Parisienne, warm-hearted, compassionate, generous, and of a slightly depressive nature.

Ken was discharged from the hospital on 14 October. He had said neither goodbye to his attending physician, Professor Gillich, nor to the nurses on his ward or thanked them for their generous support. I was thoroughly disappointed and angry — I told him so in no uncertain terms when I sent his medical report to Les Issambres on 22 October, 1987.

In view of his merits for New Orleans jazz, my love for his music and my reverence of his brilliant talents as a musician and bandleader, I forgave him his tactless behaviour. However, I doubted that Professor Gillich and Ward nurse Regine would be so understanding. I was wrong again, and underestimated the generosity of both of them.

Ken had had a commitment with Max Collie since the beginning of the year as 'special guest' at a jazz concert on 11 December at Hannover Town Hall. He was planning to come by plane. Professor Gillich generously offered to perform Ken's due control endoscopy in Gifhorn at that time. And so I went to Hannover by car on 11 December accompanied by our club friend Renate Eggeling, and we enjoyed the jazz concert by Max Collie and his Rhythm Aces with Ken Colyer as guest star. Ken played the trumpet. But what impressed me more was his solo performance with the left-hand Ovation guitar.

He sang and played the blues *Go Down Sunshine* alone in the spotlight on the stage— little did I know then that this was to be his last public performance.

Ken with Bernie Thiele

MAX COLLIE When we did the gig in Hannover—the last Mardi Gras with Ken—when he said "That's the last time you'll hear me," all the women in the audience started to cry.

High drama, I'll tell you. "This is the last time you'll hear me play." It was a big crowd too—two or three thousand. It was the Jazz Tag in December. I think it shocked everyone. I think it was '87, just before he died, because I brought him up from down on the French coast, down South.

He'd more or less packed in playing and he was coming up to go to this hospital—the Community Hospital in Gifhorn—and I said "Do the gig'" and he said, "I don't know if I can play properly." And I said, "Don't worry about it, Denny'll cover you." And he'd actually stopped before that. But he was playing guitar down there, trying to get a bit of money out in the restaurants. Because he was completely broke. We had the fun-raiser for him at the 100 Club.

BERNIE THIELE Ken was Professor Gillich's patient at Gifhorn Hospital for the second and last time from 12 to 20 December, 1987. The control endoscopy did not yield any conspicuous findings. The neurological examination by Dr Straub because of his muscular aching was also without pathological results. I received my last letter from Ken on 22 February, 1988. It was the first time he wrote me something positive, that he was much better than recently.

KEN COLYER LETTER TO TIM NEWMAN 26 DECEMBER 1987

198 Chemin De Ronde, Parc Du Corsaire,
83380 Les Issambres, France
Dear Tim,
Have been seriously ill and near death once or twice since

coming here, hoping to recuperate.

Have had cancer of the colon operations, and lesions on the brain, which they are still trying to sort out. It gave me muscular paralysis and terrible pain. Anabolic steroids injections have helped. I am 20lbs underweight and living on hospitality at the moment. I have never had to beg in my life before, but if you could raise a few bucks, it would be appreciated as I am in dire financial straights.

I have had one or two very helpful friends, but many have let a sick man down.

Best Wishes, (signed) Ken Colyer

Best wishes to the boys. (signed) Ken

KEN COLYER LETTER TO JOHNNY PARKER 29 DECEMBER 1987

198 Chemin De Ronde, Parc Du Corsaire,
83380 Les Issambres, France
Dear Johnny,

Just received your letter. I wondered why you hadn't replied. Looks like we've both been in a fix. I have had cancer operations on the colon, which is clear at the moment but must have further control in 3 months time. I also have some sort of lesion on the brain, which has given me terrible muscular pains. I am still waiting for a neurologist's report on this.

I am very weak and debilitated; 20lbs underweight and can't eat very much. I am on my own at the moment. Nichole is in Meudon, Paris. I miss her very much, but she has problems too. If life wasn't always a two-edged sword.

The sale of my house has been messed up, but I am hoping to get my share in January. I have to give Vera 50%, which cuts my reserves drastically. I am managing on what Nicole has borrowed for me. **Never had to beg in my life, now I am tired and ill, I have to. French language is a damned problem here, but I have been on the point of suicide and death three times and feel I will die if I return to England.**

I have a good man working on my book, but I need money to launch this. I think it will sell, but it will be some time before I see any profit.

Tony Leppard put the money up for the first issue of wonderful 1957 tapes, but it is not showing a profit yet.

There is great skiffle material on second, which John R.T. Davies is working on, but where are all the JAZZ LOVERS, to buy the stuff?

If it weren't for Nicole I would be dead now, and wouldn't have to worry, she saved me when I had made a final decision to finish with it all. You get plenty of 'well-wishers' but what bloody use are they? That's the trouble of leading a life making music, and not money.

I hope this finds you in better shape than I am in at the moment.

Cheers (signed) Ken

KEN COLYER LETTER TO TIM NEWMAN 9 JANUARY 1988

198 Chemin De Ronde, Parc Du Corsaire,
83380 Les Issambres, France
Dear Tim,

Many thanks for your cheque. My health is very poor at the moment, same as finances. I think it will take a long time to recover both.

Max Collie said he would talk to Roger Horton about a benefit at the 100 Club. I think I have done my share of benefits for others in the past, so it would be very welcome.

Have you heard the 1957 record? With George Lewis; wonderful memories of the past. There is more on tape that could be issued. Hearing it after 30 years I realise how good we were. There is no band playing like that now.

Hope things are better, next time I write.

Thanks again, (signed) Ken

KEN COLYER LETTER TO DAVE SMITH 10 FEBRUARY 1988

198 Chemin De Ronde, Parc Du Corsaire,
83380 Les Issambres, France
Dear Dave,

Thanks for your letter, cheque, (sterling would have been O.K.) and dressing down, I will try and take heed, and eat a little more.

I am feeling better than I did some weeks ago.

I have been in touch with Derek, and sent him the photographs.

I have tried practicing on cornet, but jaw muscles still feel clapped out.

Best wishes for now, and thanks again,

(signed) Ken

JULIAN DAVIES Ken was to write to me. And to telephone. Not straight away. Initially I wrote to him and he was in a bad mood and he just wrote 'Bollocks' all over the letter and sent it back.

GEORGE CHAMBERS In the March issue of *Jazz News* I reported the illness of Ken Colyer and wished him a speedy recovery. Well, shortly after going to press, the worst happened when, on 11 March 1988, the Guv'nor passed away just a few weeks before his 60th Birthday.

JULIAN DAVIES So Russell, Ken's son, asked me to go to the funeral. And we all met on Waterloo Station, or wherever it was, and travelled all the way down to Nice, and Nicole met us.

It was distressing for all of us. And Nicole—when we got to the hospital to pick up Ken, she said, "Do you want to see him?" He was lying on his back in the bed. He was fully dressed and the doctor who examined him said he just died of natural causes, and he would have just gone to sleep. If you'd have been in the room you'd have never known...

BERNIE THIELE The Crematorium, which had just been built, was situated to the north-west of Nizza in a picturesquely located little valley in the mountains. The five of us—Ken's son Russell, his brother Bill, his best friend Julian Davies, Nicole and myself—stood silently around Ken's coffin in the oratory, while soft music was playing. Only Nicole cried and said from time to time "Poor Ken..."

Nicole Demay took her own life in 1992. She had not been able to get over Ken's death.

CATHY COLYER It was so strange at the memorial service [at St Paul's]. The three women there. Vera was there, Delphine was there, and the French lady was there—Nicole. And I thought to myself "There's this one quiet man and you've got these three women all madly in love with him." It was a strange situation.

CHRIS AND BILL STOTESBURY After Ken's funeral in France, a few of us felt there should be some sort of 'memorial' in England so that friends, colleagues and fans could 'show their respects'. Many ex-sidemen were approached and asked to write a few word about Ken. This was difficult for them as many of them were still shocked by his passing, but from the replies it was possible to put together a eulogy of sorts.

The Very Rev David Elliott, rector of St Paul's Covent Garden (the 'Actors' Church) agreed to hold a service for us and it took place on Saturday 8th October on a chilly but dry day. The assembled congregation was made up of family, musicians and fans and I believe there was standing room only.

Ray Smith played the piano as we all arrived and then Ken's family had chosen the hymn *Lead Us Heavenly Father Lead Us* to open the service, followed by the Crane River band recording of *I'm Travelling*.

Kevin Sheldon read the tribute very movingly and then a recording of *Lord, Lord, Lord* was played. It was strange to hear Ken's distinctive voice telling us, "you've sure been good to me." Many people knew that Ken's favourite poem was by Rudyard Kipling and it was thought fitting to ask Robin Hunter to do a reading of it. Unfortunately there are two poems with similar titles and I chose the wrong one... I think Ken would have been amused by my discomfort when I was told this after the service.

Leaving the church we were all pleased to see and hear Sonny Morris leading a Parade Band including many of Ken's sidemen. Fond stories were told and good times remembered.

It seemed fitting later, to watch the jugglers and other entertainers on the square outside the church and remember happy sunny days with the Jazzmen playing on that same square.

HOUSE OF COMMONS: NOTICE OF MOTIONS 21 APRIL 1988

Ken Colyer, Jazzman

Mr. Pat Wall	*Mr. Barry Jones*
Mr. Frank Cook	*Mr. John Fraser*
Mr. John Cummings	*Mr. Ronnie Campbell*
Mr. Bob Cryer	*Mr. Dave Nellist*
Dawn Primarolo	

That this House deeply regrets the reported death in France of Ken Colyer, an inspiring contributor to the post-war jazz revival, who did so much to improve the standards of British traditional jazz and above all for the links he established with the then much neglected surviving New Orleans jazz musicians; and as a tribute to his life hopes that at long last the Arts and Entertainment establishments will fully recognise the enormous contribution jazz music and jazz musicians have made and are making to humanity's cultural heritage.

RUSSELL COLYER I was away from The Drive from about the age of twenty. I had very little contact after that. I remember I had a girlfriend and Dad used to play in a rugby club at Isleworth and I lived in Brentford. I said, "We're doing nothing tonight. Dad's playing down there" and he saw me in the audience. He was a little embarrassed.

I remember going up to him at the bar and he had his back to me. I said, "Would you like a drink?" "I'll have a gin and tonic," and that was it. No "Hello son, what are you doing here?" or "Boy, what are you after, you got a problem?" or anything like that. If I'd had problems I would have gone to Vera rather than Dad. I wouldn't say he was that approachable on sensitive things, father-to-son matters. The thing I resent more was the lack of support as a teenager—it did upset me quite a lot.

So I hadn't had any major contact for nine to ten years—and then suddenly the start of the exodus to France and the mobile home. It wasn't the coming together of a father and son. It was more "Sort it out and help me!" He was in Nottingham, he played a gig there. Vera might have rung me and said "That's it—he's gone mad."

He broke down in Nottingham. She said he was rolling around on the floor, crying like a baby. Then he jumped in the car and drove home. It was "fuck the lot of you!" Vera stayed in Nottingham with Gerry [White] and Mavis.

The first mobile home that he then went and lived in was in Fréjus. Then he'd gone down to get away from it all. He'd got no work: "Sell the house—sell my house!"

So I'd now gotta come in and start picking all the pieces up—but it was nothing to do with me in the first place! So he was down there. He went into hospital there a couple of times. I went to visit him in there. On one of my visits he was in the first mobile home and he collapsed on me. We were alright one minute, we were just sitting down having a chit-chat about everything—not about the past, never went back into the past—and he went down in front of me and then I had to get the medics.

I went up to reception and then we got him up to the gate at Holiday Green. Then he went down again in the car park so they got the medics and the ambulance and all that and he then came out. It must have been a physical thing rather than a mental thing as he was still aware of what was going on because the medic was bending over him and said "Are you alright, sir?" and he looked up and said "If I was fuckin' alright I wouldn't be laying here!" It was pitch black in the dark and they took him away.

The guys in Holiday Green, on the reception, I got to know them quite well. I used to ring them up regularly: "What's he up to now? Is he alright?" "Yeah, he's alright, he's pottering around doing this and that…"

All this is happening and we're still trying to get the money to him as he had no money. **I think that's really when he turned quite bitter. He wasn't getting any financial help by the jazz world, family—nobody.** I'd just got a job on the council and if I had a tenner or something on a Wednesday that would get sent. But it was a very limited amount of people who helped. I think he was very, very angry by then and frustrated. I mean he was never the happiest of souls—he was a bit on the grumpy side.

I used to sneak off on a Friday morning, get on the night train, get off at Fréjus in the morning—get on the bus, be at Holiday Green half eleven the next day. Bunking off a brand-new job, sneaking off—doing that!

I wasn't involved in any of his health side of it, the organising of that at all. Bernie was more involved… At the hospital, he got out of bed; it was a lovely sunny day.

> ## "Your father, he's been in the hospital shop, he's now sitting outside, gone into the shop with no money, picked up a load of groceries and sat outside having a picnic!"

I did visit him in the hospital. There was an old chap in there and he used to share the last bits of baccy he had with dad. It was sort of up-and-down but I was more trying to sort out the practical side. The problem with Holiday Green—Vera had bought this mobile home, meant to be ideal. I think the reason for it was to get away from the English weather.

He'd moved on to a holiday camp—it wasn't a residential site—and, of course, there were screaming kids and shouting; the last thing he wanted. And that's when the boat idea started coming in. He would get the boat so he could get down there and get some peace and quiet.

He got a little sailing boat. He didn't sail it anywhere he just went and sat on it. But it was very, very, small inside.

So from the age of 20 to 29 I had not really had much contact with him at all and suddenly… but it wasn't a "please" or a "thank you," it was more of a—"get it sorted!"

As his health got worse I spoke to our family doctor, Dr Cusack, and he said, "We're going to have to section him. He is a danger—dangerous." (Just before, Dad'd said, *I've got a gun*, etc.) I'd spoken to the doctor and he'd said "Well, he's got mental problems and we'll have to get him into a hospital and do something."

So then I had to go and meet our family doctor in a little layby. I was hiding with the doctor in his car at 8 o'clock in the morning and we were gonna wait for him to come out 'cause he was gonna drive back to France but he couldn't drive like that. We had to wait and we'd have to pounce on him, jump on him… but he didn't show! Where is he gone? Has he committed suicide?

I said "Well, the only place he could ever do it round there would be the London Apprentice, Isleworth. He loved that pub, and the river there was very dangerous. So we sped down there but couldn't find him. So I got back into the house and he was there. Because we hadn't sold the house quick enough I was then the evil one, trying to stitch him up. It was nothing to do with me, really. All the people that had been reasonably close to him were then the enemy! So I went through it, with not really understanding it—just functioning to just try and do what he was asking. He was trying to drive back to France.

I said, "You can't drive." We had a screaming row. I said "You're barking. You've lost the plot; we've got to get you in hospital!" Then he jumped in the car in the garage, the little Nissan Cherry. "I'm off!" It wouldn't move!

He said, "You bastard, you've sabotaged the car!" ('cause I used to build little motorbikes, things like that.) And then he produced a load of flowerpots and proceeded to bombard me with them. He was gonna get the police. Then I think he got maybe the RAC round to unsabotage the car. The bloke got in and said "Sir, your handbrake is on." He was in such a frenzy: "I've gotta go!" "Sir, the handbrake's on!"

The first mobile home had become too noisy then I heard he was gonna buy another another one. I'd been up and down a few times by then to sort things out and keep it all under control as best I could. I got to know the blokes who sold the mobile homes 'cause they had a little football team which then I started to play for.

I spoke to the Old Man. I said "Why don't we take this mobile home you've got. I'll go and see the boys. We'll put it on a lorry and we'll move it to a quiet site. Why spend thirty thousand pounds when you can spend a grand?" That second mobile home never materialised, so the deposit was wiped out.

[signature]

Russell and Bill at the crematorium

Then we moved the mobile home and that's when I think Nicole became involved. I had to site the new one. I had to re-plumb it in, and do everything. Because he'd been wandering around Les Isambres he found Nicole who was staying in her villa nearby. Later on, after he died, I had to go back down with Nicole and we met her at her and her husband's apartment in Paris.

I got a phone call from him. I must have known about the loan, or money from the house and I think he was in Marseilles. I said "Is that right you've got a bag of cash with you? Do you think you could go and put it in the bank or somewhere?"

"Oh, that's alright!" I was trying to sort all the practical problems out and Bernie was looking at more the health solutions and then one morning I heard the news.

Nicole did all the legal side of it: arranged for the cremation paperwork, everything.

So all we had to do was go down there for the cremation. I already knew Julian would come down there and it was "And your Uncle Bill's gonna go."

"Uncle who?'"

"Uncle Bill."

"I know he's got a brother Bob."

"And Uncle Bill."

I'd never met Uncle Bill. Maybe once. Now I'm thirty years old, suddenly I've gotta meet Uncle Bill.

So we all got on the train, all went down to Fréjus with Nicole who arranged to put us up. I was driving the old Nissan Cherry around. It was an overcast day and we did what you do there—me, Bill, Julian and Nicole. And that was it.

So then I started to clear all the stuff out of the mobile home and I went back down to sort the boat out. The harbourmaster said, "You've got to move it." I loaded up the Nissan and I got the box with the ashes in. He'd always told me that in the event of his death he would like to be scattered at sea.

I was quite obviously naïve to all this sort of thing on how, legally, it has to be sorted out. So Nicole said "We'll go down to the Mediterranean and we'll scatter it together," because of her love of Ken.

> I said, "I don't really want to do it into the Mediterranean, to be honest with you. It's a sea that doesn't really go anywhere. I'd like to put it into some sea that can go anywhere in the world— he's a free spirit and can go wherever he wants."

So after some negotiating—because she's now crying, and it's a very emotional time—I negotiated with her that I would take the brass plaque off the top. I said, "I'll give you this—you can have the plaque as a memory. I can't thank you enough. But if I give you that you can keep it, OK? Thank you very much." And that was accepted.

So now I've got the casket. What am I gonna do? I've loaded the car up and everything. It was only afterwards, driving back, I found out what I did was quite illegal—moving a body from one country without licence is illegal, and disposing of a body is also illegal. So I didn't know what to do.

I was on the ferry going across from France. Perfect. I'm in the Channel— the Channel goes everywhere. I got out the Swiss Army knife, took the screws off. On my own. Stood on the back of the boat, looked at it, took the top off. Said the Lord's Prayer, "Off you go!" Tipped the lot into the Channel.

Then when I got into the Customs, they ripped the car to pieces! Just a random search. But I'd already done the deed! I thought I'd come through in the end for him...

CHAPTER FIFTEEN
LEGACY

KEN COLYER Jimmy Rushing said, "You know how to play the blues. I interrupted my conversation to listen to you." (I was playing the slow version of *Canal St. Blues.*) Roosevelt Sykes said, "It's the real McCoy," Albert Nicholas said, "You're playing the truth." One of the Harlem band in Toronto stopped and said, "That's the truth." And this is the truth.

Some people seem to go through life continually searching for something for nothing. I have had to pay heavily for being "The keeper of the flame. For the Gods they are jealous Gods." I don't see any light at the end of the tunnel at the moment but "Fear the worst and hope for the best." And so be it

JOHN BEECHAM With regard to the mythical figure Ken Colyer has become, there may be some weight in the concept that lots of people have a need for heroic figures who they can put on a pedestal, and that in K.C.'s life there were certain ingredients that have turned him, in people's imagination, into a quasi-religious figure. These ingredients might be said to include: a pilgrimage to a holy city; epistles; disciples; miracles; a holy book; a holy relic; rights and ceremonials; testifying and icons.

PILGRIMAGE TO THE HOLY CITY: NEW ORLEANS. Especially significant because of the adversity and hardships endured—as outlined in the Holy Book When Dreams Are in the Dust—which involved the pilgrim going almost round the world in the wrong direction and the glamour of jumping ship before the arrival at the Holy City.

THE EPISTLES. Ken's letters to "Brother Bill," which were published in the *Melody Maker*—creating the first renown of the Pilgrim and highlighting the expectancy of his return (George Melly wrote: "Ken Colyer returned to England an heroic figure.")

THE DISCIPLES. Although Chris, Monty and Lonnie would not have seen themselves as disciples, Ken claimed to have "taught" the band that was formed for him to lead on his return. Certainly Ken turned Chris Barber on to the music of Bunk Johnson and George Lewis, and it was Ken who introduced Lonnie to the music of Huddie Ledbetter. Ken wrote of the members of this band: "All they wanted from me was a little reflected *glory*"(my italics).

THE MIRACLE. That absolutely any bunch of musicians who happened to sit down with Ken to play would wondrously sound like "The Ken Colyer Band." (We, the musicians, know it didn't work quite like that, but that is the impression some fans have.)

THE HOLY BOOK. The main reason for the creation of the Ken Colyer Trust was to get *When Dreams Are in the Dust* published and, significantly, it was stated several times in Trust newsletters that this book was totally Ken's own work, and that not one word of it could be changed, as if any editing would have been thought of as compromising its authenticity.

HOLY RELIC: THE HOLY BOOK#2. Ray Smith told me of an encounter he had in Holland shortly after Ken's death. A Dutch musician unveiled a bound photocopy of the chord book that Ray had made up many years previously for Ken's use when he [Ken] was guesting with bands all over the place.

"Look at this, Ray," the bloke said with great reverence. "This is Ken's chord book, written by Ken himself."

And Ray said, "Afraid not; I wrote all those chords out—and some of them may be wrong." And the bloke said, "But bands all over Europe are using this book because it's in Ken's own writing." Then Ray told him that actually Ken didn't really know about chord sequences, and that the book had definitely been compiled by himself, and the bloke was all crestfallen and said, "Oh no, say it isn't so."

There's an obvious danger here of the chord book becoming a sort of gospel according to one of Ken's disciples.

RITES AND CEREMONIALS, INCLUDING THE RITUAL OF THE G & T. On informal gigs, like the 100 Club, there would be a sort of mini-interval every three numbers or so, when Ken would roll a fag. (I sometimes half expected some of the more timid members of the band to roll fags too, out of reverence for Ken, even if they didn't smoke.)

When I first started playing in Ken's band I thought that these breaks interfered with the flow of the music, but then I realised that they were all part of the occasion, and perfectly acceptable to Ken's audience, who would mostly sit quietly while Ken smoked, and an air of expectation would hang over the 100 Club.

It was at these times that one member or another would approach the stage and lay the offering of a gin and tonic at Ken's feet, murmering at the same time a request for their favourite number, and then backing respectfully away. (Ken's response was often "I can't stand fucking lemon slices in my gin.") ICONS. With the commendable object of financing projects such as the posthumous publishing of Ken's book, the Trust began marketing sweatshirts and such, bearing Ken's image. I think that in their heart-of-hearts everybody concerned would have had a pretty good idea of what Ken's reaction would have been to the marketing of tea towels and coffee mugs with his face on them—had he been alive.

But of course he was dead by then, which is always an advantage in mythical or religious matters, because the figurehead can grow in majesty in the collective imagination without the inconvenient presence of the living, fallible human being.

PAUL SEALEY A bit like Bunk, really, you have to look at what he did in the context of the time—it was in England, not in New Orleans; it was years later; he was the only one, as far as I'm aware, that was trying to play that revival New Orleans as opposed to what I would think of as classic jazz.

And I would think from that point of view he was certainly the first and I don't think anybody has done it any better. There are others who have done it *as well*, like Cuff [Billett] for example, and there are other players who've gone further in some ways with that particular style, but the tragedy was that we're all striving to do something that's not natural to us, so I always say how could a white boy from Watford be expected to play like a black man who couldn't go into a hotel or get a drink of water a hundred years before? It's very difficult to put yourself socially in their minds, that's the main problem.

But Ken had this approach, and speaking to my old bandleader Chris Barber—we spoke a lot about this—and

although they had the break-up, Chris never blamed Ken, oddly enough, about it. He said the rhythm section stirred it up a bit and it was a case of him or me, sort of thing. And Ken, in retrospect, and I think quite rightly, said that they weren't playing the New Orleans music the way he wanted, but of course, they couldn't.

And Chris said that Ken wasn't always able to express exactly what the problem was. But I thought afterwards, "How can you?" When it's a feeling thing it's very difficult to put it into words. And Chris went on to that urgent traddy thing and Ken spent the rest of his life trying to reproduce it.

He got close at times with this band with Ian and Mac, and without being disrespectful to the later bands, he got further and further away from it in many ways, and never got back to it again to the same degree.

There were moments, but I think it was a struggle. We never really discussed about whether he was frustrated about that, but I got the feeling that he was from his attempts to sort of re-invent the band.

The last time I played with him would have been in Brecon in 1985; Jean-François sat-in with us, I remember. Ken seemed to enjoy it. He was thinner than I remember, but he didn't seem to have any problems—he seemed to be OK.

EDWARD BLACK Ken, like Dylan Thomas, put all that was good in his life into his art and tended to foul up his personal relationships; the quality of Colyer's art was more consistent and less derivative than DT's.

On the debit side, Ken had a severe personality disorder. When in his final tormenting illness he aimed to offend friends and colleagues, I told him they were saddened by the self-destructive side to his nature; he controlled the anger of his response.

He remained bitter at Decca and other recording companies, and for those who profited from or pirated his work, while allowing him a pittance... and for those insensitive recording engineers who messed up the finely balanced and changing tonal qualities, such as the unreal clarinet in the superb *Club Session*. Bill told me (I was a schoolboy at the time) they could either get the clarinet right or the trumpet!

He was hurt by the BBC choosing Humph to recreate Buddy Bolden. He lived a hard life and received many blows which marked him and would have crippled a lesser man. He had problems with musicians he felt were unappreciative of his nurture and making them names—and their later hostility.

Racked by illness and pain at the end, he felt his friends had turned away.

MAC ROBINSON In thinking about Ken Colyer, it is important to keep in mind two things: Firstly, Ken should be remembered not as a man who, many years ago, merely made a contribution to European jazz;, but rather as a man who

DIED 1988

Christina Onassis, 37, unhappy million-heiress

Divine, 42, gross actor with Female Trouble

Robert Mead, 48, master dancer and teacher

Percy Thrower, 75, the popular gardener

Felix Wankel, 86, the alternative engineer

President Zia Ul-Haq, 64, for 11 years the hard man of Pakistan, in an air crash with five generals

Gil Evans, 75, great jazz composer and arranger

Ken Colyer, 59, brought New Orleans to Britain

Lord Ramsey, 83, former Archbishop of Canterbury

Ann Ford, early 70s, seamless stocking tycoon

Lord Peart, 74, Labour minister of Ag and Fish

Baroness Wootton, 91, a passion for social equality

Geoffrey Household, 87, Rogue Male and more

Dr Arnulfo Arias, 86, much ousted president of Panama

Sir Denis Hamilton, 69, Sunday Times's mastermind

Henryk Szeryng, 69, Polish born violinist from Mexico

Hamish Hamilton, 87, publishing house founder

Errol John, 64, West Indian playwright and actor

---

continued throughout his lifetime to keep alive an ideal; always playing, always travelling, continuously influencing young musicians and inspiring them to want to play the music.

Secondly, Ken was never a re-creationalist in a scholarly, pallid sense of reproducing classic records note-for-note. He took delight always in taking pop tunes (usually tunes from the classic 1930's "standards" era that lent themselves well to the New Orleans treatment) not normally associated with a traditional jazz treatment and giving them the Colyer sound.

KEITH SMITH Thinking of Ken shortly after he died, one thought continually came to mind and rang increasingly true the more I reflected upon his life. Long ago, during an interview, I heard the actor Michael Caine confess, "I invented myself. I didn't have a personality until after I was twenty, and then I became what I am now and I can't go back."

He was a law unto himself, but the price was high and his life a lonely one. And, apart from brief spells, his bands were never the success that this perfectionist had originally craved and striven for, although many fine sidemen emerged along the way.

PETER HUNTER I don't know whether I should say, but hell, he would find it amusing, as he did at the time. He was playing down at the 51 Club, and any of you who have ever been down there would know that they had the most dreadful 40-amp speakers stuck up on the wall, and the microphone—God, it

was a dreadful thing!

Ken was playing *Snag It* and, as was his wont, he had been in the Porcupine previously and perhaps had imbibed slightly more vodka and tonics, or gin and tonics, or pints or whatever, and he came to do his break in *Snag It* and stepped forward to the microphone and got it stuck up the end of the trumpet and nothing whatsoever came out.

We got to the end of the number and Ken, with his mouth how it used to twist up at one side, leaned forward and said "Well, sometimes you make it and sometimes you don't—that's jazz!"

MONTY SUNSHINE He wasn't frustrated—he was sensitive. And anyone else tells me that he was not, well...

TREFOR WILLIAMS He was... a joyful guy when you got to know him. But a lot of people found that there wasn't a lot of joy in him. I don't know what it is, but he wouldn't suffer fools. He knew exactly what he wanted to do, and if people weren't in tune with what he wanted to do, he got frustrated with them.

PAT HALCOX But he had a showmanship of his own, didn't he? A bit like Miles Davis, really. Not quite back to the audience, more like back to the wall. I feel that Miles was a bit like that too—frustrated.

RAY SMITH I think that Ken was happy with his own playing and his concept of the music. What frustrated him was other people's playing and lack of concept, and what he perceived as lack of taste. He prided himself on his good taste, you know.

SAMMY RIMINGTON He didn't say a lot—he didn't speak a lot, so it was very hard to get to know him, really.

He was always very kind to me. And even when I went to New Orleans the first time, during the band holidays in '62, he said, "Well, soak up as much as you can, have a great time."

BILL COLE Oh, he was an absolute romantic. Oh, definitely. He could wax lyrical about all sorts of subjects... things you probably wouldn't even imagine. He'd look at a flower or something—he was quite keen on gardening, you know. And I think there was a romantic streak. Talking in those terms, I tell you what he reminded me of: some of the French romantic poets and some of the romantic painters and that sort of thing.

He wasn't a Philistine.

GERARD BIELDERMAN Ken's time at sea left him with the outlook of a sailor. At times he was rude, taciturn and inaccessible. These features, however, hid the real Ken Colyer, a friendly enough person. And so he stayed during his lifetime: one time disagreeable and impudent, the other time mostly friendly, helpful and talkative.

IAN WHEELER The session came to an end, and I went up to Ken to say tarra, and all that, and I put my hand out, and he said, "Don't want any words, man; don't want any words." That was the last thing he said. And that was it. I was out, I was gone. Later on we got quite friendly again to the extent where we discussed possibly forming a band to do a few concerts.

I believe it was in Mac's lifetime, but it may have been after. But there were still some of us around, and... I drove him home a couple of times from gigs, you know, and we talked. It was quite friendly again. He'd forgiven me, obviously.

BEN MARSHALL He seemed reluctant to allow anyone to get too close, even people who only had his welfare at heart. Maybe he had tried it and been hurt too often.

As a well-known clarinet player once put it: "Ken was a disciple, just like the rest of us." True I think, but he has left a far bigger shadow on jazz history than the rest of us will.

RAY FOXLEY In the old days we never really knew much about Ken at all. Small talk was out. Conversation was limited to question-and-answer unless, late at night, Ken in his cups would decide to expound on his beloved New Orleans music and then you listened but never argued. So naturally we assumed that this was his one and only passion.

It was only in his last years (and I renewed acquaintance less than two years before his death) that he became more outgoing and revealed a rare intelligence and a wide range of interests.

BILL COLE To be honest, we used to argue a lot, and fall out, but we always got on. I keep coming back to this word "ambivalent," which I'd never really thought of until now. I think he was a major figure, an influence—well, you've only got to look round and see the things that the Ken Colyer Trust puts on to see how *much* a major figure he was. Whether he was appreciated for what he *did*, or what he represented, I don't know. It's one of those things I'm never too sure of.

I don't regret the time that I spent with Ken. A lot of it was hard going—particularly on the road. It was hard work, but at the same time, I suppose I made my name out of it. And in a way, his words keep coming back to me: "I'll be famous after I'm dead."

I almost feel guilty—sometimes—about things that I'm doing now. I'm one of these that's living off his back. I mean, after all I've been left—I was with his band for five-and-a-half, six years—and I've now been left thirty-eight years. And I'm still being advertised as "ex-Ken Colyer".

MALC MURPHY Ken was, as a musician and a man, hard to get close to, but I don't regret in any way joining him. I learnt so much about the approach he had towards the music, but I also had my own deep feelings for the New Orleans jazz music. We recorded around ten LPs while I was with the band, broadcast regularly both in England and in Europe. We usually played six nights a week on average in the UK, and tours: Belgium, Holland, Germany, Sweden, Denmark, Norway etc.

Ken was a good and fair bandleader and as long as the band played well and up to the standard he set, he was content.

Ken, in my opinion, did so much to bring the way he thought New Orleans jazz music should be played to this country and his legacy will carry on.

TONY PYKE There were occasions like when we did Hampton Court—The Thames Hotel—and I was driving him; just he and I. And I'd say to him, "There's an episode of *Sergeant Bilko* on television, starting in ten minutes. Do you fancy seeing it round at my place?" And he'd say, "Oh, yeah!" He loved Bilko, and so did I.

So we'd come in, and I used to brew my own beer in those days, and he'd say, "Have you got one of your home-brewed beers?" I said, "Of course I have." So I poured out a home-brewed beer for him... he loved all that. So we'd sit and watch

Ken Colyer

KEN COLYER, the most unwavering and dedicated of British jazz traditionalists would have been 60 next month. His place on the jazz circuit seemed unshiftable by fashions, economics or mortality. From the early Fifties, when the civil war between the factions of modernists and traditionalists was gathering steam, Colyer led bands that behaved as if Louis Armstrong, let alone Charlie Parker, had never existed. It was a form of musical fundamentalism that was never so assiduously observed by any other British bandleader, and few anywhere in the world.

Colyer's preoccupation was the sound of Bunk Johnson, a trumpeter from the pre-recording period of jazz whose music enjoyed a resurgence in the Thirties as part of the backlash against Bebop. Louis Armstrong had liberated the role of the soloist in jazz with an abundance of spontaneous melodic ideas that inevitably led to the creation of star improvisers fronting rhythm sections. Colyer was devoted to the New Orleans music that preceded Armstrong, a collectively improvised contrapuntal music in which no one stood in the spotlight. It was also rhythmically far closer to the marching bands and funeral bands of turn-of-the-century New Orleans. George Melly wrote (in Owning Up) that Colyer "intended to sound like an old man who had never left New Orleans when they closed Storyville". He began performing like this at a time when even the addition of a saxophone to a New Orleans revivalist ensemble could occasion heated abuse from purists. But to less obsessive fans a more modernised remake was attractive. Colyer hated such mutations. He formed the Crane River jazz band in the early Fities, which he named after a stream running near his home in Hounslow. He was nicknamed "the Guvnor" by all the serious adherents of the idiom, and rejoined his old service, the Merchant Navy, in order to wangle a trip to New Orleans.

He deserted once he got there, played with many of the surviving veterans of the music, was gaoled and deported back to England — to a hero's welcome from the cognoscenti. Chris Barber and Monty Sunshine formed a band in readiness for his return but, characteristically, Colyer rejected it complaining that it was too commercial.

Colyer acted as a curator of a style now recognised as a cornerstone of jazz. Because of the lack of recording facilities at the time, few people had the chance to hear it. Even veteran Americans recognised his dedication as an invaluable living history lesson for younger jazz fans, and more open-minded British musicians, like Humphrey Lyttelton, listened with a kind of reluctant admiration to Colyer in the Fifties. His devotion to purely musical values and his indifference to compromise were an example even to players light years away from his style.

John Fordham

Ken Colyer, born Great Yarmouth, April 1928; died March 10 in the South of France.

Bilko together, supping my home-made beer.

Yeah... He loved W.C. Fields, Bilko, Groucho, and Mr. Magoo. He loved them.

JOHN GUY The last time I saw The Guv'nor was at Max Collie's Mardi Gras gig at the Cambridge Arts. He was backstage, wielding "a good broom to sweep with. I like to leave the place as we found it."

We chatted over old days, old friends. "My advice to you, is write. Write about music, write about me, write about anything you like —but write!" I have gained much from this advice.

Thanks, Ken.

PAUL ADAMS Well Ken's heroes—it's quite interesting actually, because... I did have a lad working for me in the old days when we did LPs, and the LPs used to come, and the sleeves used to come, and somebody had to put the two together. And I used to pay somebody to come and do that, and I had this lad who lived locally who was doing this for me.

And while we were doing it I used to play sample copies to make sure they were alright, and it was the skiffle one. And this lad said to me—I'd gone into the other room—and he said "Frank's finished." And I said, "What do you mean 'Frank's finished'? It's Ken Colyer."

And he said "Naaaa... sounds like Frank Sinatra to me." And I said, "Right... well, OK then." And I mentioned this to Ken, and he said that Frank Sinatra was one of his heroes. And when you get that piece of information, lots of things click into place. You listen to his phrasing when he sings, and he phrases when he sings exactly the same as when he plays the trumpet. And you can hear the Sinatra phrasing.

You get people who are singers who've not got particularly good voices, but it's what they *do* with that voice that's important, and Ken wasn't a technically accomplished trumpet player. What *did* drive Ken on was this still striving for something. What that was, in a sense, I suppose—his problem was his difficulty in surrounding himself with people that he felt were of a like mind, and he appeared to have mixed views about that, you know. It was a very strange thing.

From my point of view, I think he *did* achieve what he wanted to achieve. Whether *he* felt that is a totally different thing. Because it is a bit sort of intangible, isn't it? You could find any number of better trumpet players, but it's what he did within his limitations that was a significant thing. And I think that's what's important.

ALAN COOPER He felt that he had been maligned or defamed or whatever it was. Not that he would have anything to worry about, because his name will be remembered with affection and respect where other names will have just gone down the plug. That was the man that had been doing things to the end... as is of course Ed O'Donnell.

BEN MARSHALL Sonny and I talked about getting a band together to play in the manner we talked of with Ken and the others back in the early days, about the whole band acting like a rhythm section, concentration on ensemble work, seeking the inner rhythms, dynamics, swing, lift, energy, passion—all the things we talked of for hours on end. Sonny, Terry Giles, Bob Ward, John Sirett, Colin Bowden and me—"Sonny Morris and the Delta Jazz Band."

KEN COLYER I said to a fellow musician once: "You might as well play to the desert air." After a pause he said, "Let me know Ken, when you're going. I'll come along and listen." I like that.

Contemporary music came along with disastrous effects

upon any development of the true sounds. Much of it is so lacking of the true contents. True New Orleans music is highly complex although it sounds simple.

I have proved that people listen to it and can't hear it. One said to me once, "I have more New Orleans records than you." Of course he had, and he couldn't understand a note of it. I pointed out George Lewis's marvellous blue note which magically changes the whole tune. He had listened to the record many times and never noticed it. This makes bunkum (which Sinclair Traill said I talked) of the "I know what I like" people.

You don't know what you like until you take the trouble to learn to appreciate what you like. The more you know about art the more you appreciate great paintings. Some have an instant impact, like Toulouse Lautrec, but this is intentional. You can't appreciate Van Gogh until you know about the man and a little more about perspective, and so it goes.

You have to learn to appreciate a good thing. Very few people have a natural perception for immediate appreciation. I didn't like jazz when I first heard it. I had some ear for melody, but it was only after constant listening and learning to play *Riverside Blues* on a chromatic harmonica that the liking for jazz grew on me. It was no instantaneous thing.

I have often thought it's not the music that lets you down, it's the people. Somebody asked, "Don't you get tired of playing?" I get tired physically and mentally and I get tired of people, but I never get tired of the music.

DIZ DISLEY Well, he achieved a lot. He achieved skiffle. But he had a great influence, I think, apart from anything else. We had a mutual respect.

RON BOWDEN We all admired Ken, you know. And what he'd done and sort-of envied him that he'd been to New Orleans and played with those guys. And he mentioned guys' names that we'd never heard of, who he met out there, and played with out there.

JOHN BEECHAM Ken wrote in his book that on his return from New Orleans, "my sole intention was to carry on playing somehow or other." I think that he continued to succeed in this aim for the rest of his life. When Ken first took up the cornet there really wasn't much music, if any, in Britain that he could use as a reference: it was mostly all dance bands and light popular music. All he had to go on were records and the wonderful live music he'd heard in New Orleans, and that was probably enough to show him where he wanted to go.

He never really changed: The Ken Colyer heard on the earliest Crane River and Christie Brothers records is

the same player to be heard at the end of his playing life. It seems that Ken Colyer, the cornet player, emerged from nowhere in the 1940s and stayed the same.

He certainly seems never to have *tried* to change his playing, and so I think he achieved his ambition to "carry on playing." This, of course, meant carry on playing professionally, and to do so was no small feat, considering that he was a shy, taciturn individual with no aptitude for self-promotion and no show-business savvy. He stuck to his guns and made a living without compromising his music in any way—quite an achievement given his circumstances.

TONY O'SULLIVAN I don't think I was ever a Colyer copyist—any more than I have copied the many other trumpet players who have influenced me over the years—**but I will always remember and pay tribute to Ken for channelling my youthful enthusiasm and idealism into a creative activity** which has enriched my life enormously and hopefully brought a bit of enjoyment to that of others.

GED HONE He was always calm and self-composed, with complete intense concentration, whilst communicating his musical thoughts and feelings to the band in a telepathic way. Everyone who played with him seemed to be under a magical jazz spell

COLIN BOWDEN I talk about Ken being a grumpy old sod, but… listen to his music. He used to say, "We don't want any prima donnas in this band" but of course, he was a prima donna himself, absolutely. And that's just the way he was. It's like his trumpet playing: It's just wonderful, end of story. I mean everybody's got chinks in their armour, and which bits do you look at?

CHRIS BARBER I liked Ken's playing. In fact, I liked his attitude to the music—he liked the same things as I did, actually, in music. Very much the same things. I think he was a very genuine person playing the music which he loved, and he played it very well. But it didn't work out between us. It's a shame.

JOHN BODDY Ken had that aura. He was a little bit different. He didn't say a lot, but I mean he had that sort of magic quality and he had it in his playing, and what more could you ask? You can't always expect someone to create magic moments. If you got it once a week when you were on tour with him, it was worth it. It was... a knockout, you know.

KEITH INGHAM He had a much wider knowledge of jazz than most people think. We played some gigs together at the Rose and Crown in Limehouse in the late sixties, and I was surprised at the tunes he knew: *This Year's Kisses* and a lot of those old Billie Holiday numbers.

I was Red Allen's pianist when he was over in England in 1967. Red went down to hear Ken several times. He said it reminded him of the old days in New Orleans—he heard something in Ken's music that took him back to his young days listening to the bands there.

> Ken had that working-class attitude to the music—like an artisan. I liked Ken as a person and I had a great deal of respect for his integrity as a musician.

RON BOWDEN I loved to play with the band. And I loved playing... Alright, some nights you didn't want to—everybody gets those nights, don't they? But it was great, because we were touring and working nearly every other night. And playing the music I loved.

STU MORRISON "So it could be said, Ken," said the interviewer, walking towards the steel jaws of the gin-trap, "that you are the Father of British Rock and Roll and British Pop Music." To which Ken said, "Christ, if I thought I was the father of a bastard like that, I'd go someplace quiet and shoot myself!"

LEN BALDWIN I don't think Ken ever really achieved what deep down he wanted from this particular sound. Also, perhaps, he was on an impossible mission anyway, because he was playing with us people who were all British and hadn't come from the sort of background that could produce the music he wanted.

JOHN BEECHAM A significant achievement of Ken's is that he was the titular leader of a band that made a new sound in jazz, a sound which had a huge influence on the way bands have played ever since. Arguably this wasn't the sound Ken wanted and I think there are two main factors that made the band sound the way it did.

Firstly, it seems that when musicians play in a way that is

Bill with the plaque made for the 100 Club

heavily influenced by their idols, they end up sounding like themselves anyway. The Rolling Stones were blues fans, especially their original leader Brian Jones, and they imitated Jimmy Reed, Howlin' Wolf and Robert Johnson, but very soon they sounded unmistakably like The Rolling Stones.

Maurice Ravel said, "When I copy, I innovate." Although the first Colyer band didn't *copy* Ken's New Orleans idols, they were heavily influenced by them. One important influence was the instrumentation of the first K.C. band: They were the first band in Britain—I think—to feature on record a pianoless rhythm section including banjo à la the line-up on George Lewis's Climax Session, and the spare, straightforward sound made by this rhythm section impacted on the sounds of traditional jazz all over Europe.

> But the outcome of the influence Ken and the others in his band felt from the New Orleans musicians was a new sound rather than a likeness or replica.

Secondly, it was the difference between Ken and Chris. When brought together—combined in one band—that made this new sound come about. Ian Wheeler, interviewed by Mike Pointon, identifies very succinctly the differences in musical approach of the two men. Ken says in his book "I tried to meet Barber halfway…" and this is pretty much what he did. And this *halfway* point is where the music found its unique identity. It wasn't entirely the way Ken wanted it, it wasn't *precisely* the way Chris wanted it.

It wasn't New Orleans jazz—although it was greatly influenced by the New Orleans musicians. But what resulted was—in my opinion, and based on listening to the album *New Orleans to London* and other recordings they made, because I never heard the band live—grand. And what began with this band was British Traditional Jazz as a new style.

And I don't think that Ken hated the sound of this band. I know—because he told me—that he was proud that they had a hit record with *Isle Of Capri*, and later in his career he was prepared to participate in reunions of the band's original lineup. If it were anyone else but Ken Colyer it could be argued that he did this for the money, but that would be completely out of character in a man who was always so little swayed by commercial considerations.

GEOFF COLE Ken once said, "I'm like Duke Ellington. Music is my religion."

DEREK WINTERS If you listen to Ken's music it is like a textbook of how to try and approach playing the music we love, New Orleans jazz.

PAT HALCOX Ken had his own ideas of what to do and he went and did it. You've got to admire people like that.

KEN AMES I'm sitting around the meal table, and everybody's knocking Ken, and the final things this particular guy said (he doesn't know anything—he plays in a jazzband, but he doesn't know anything about New Orleans). And he says "Oh, isn't Ken Colyer the trumpet player who played badly deliberately?"

And I thought, well if Ken had been there he wouldn't have been sitting in that chair for a lot longer. So I thought, "Well, I'm outnumbered here." And anyway, a bit later on I did a tape up for this guy—complete mixture, everything from Artie Shaw to Colyer. The one Colyer track on there was *Sweet Lorraine* from the quartet. I just slung it in. And when I saw him he said, "Oh yeah, I enjoyed that tape. And it was nice to hear that Tommy Ladnier/Sidney Bechet version of *Sweet Lorraine*. So I said, "It was Ken Colyer."

LONNIE DONEGAN As the band went round the clubs the reception was exciting. You could never ask for the same sort of self-satisfaction again in life—once is enough; it was marvellous.

MONTY SUNSHINE In the long term, in fact, every known jazz band owes something to him. In Europe. You see… when Ken—in the early days—brought the music to some form of acceptance, there was this lovely pilgrimage he made—on his own—to New Orleans. And of course, he came back with this charisma of having been to Mecca, as it were.

But this changed a hell of a lot of people's views, because in those days, with all due respect to your Sid Phillipses and Harry Golds and Roy Fox and so forth, they hadn't quite attained this gruffness… this gruffness, and this melodic and rhythmic approach of the New Orleans musicians. **And Ken brought a lot of understanding back in an aural sense and in a musical sense.**

And I think a lot of people picked these things up. Everybody really. I mean he was… he was playing tunes that really you and I wouldn't have thought of.

His technique *was* this forthright approach. You couldn't but realise that what he… the moment he played two notes that there was a contribution to jazz, whereas a lot of guys play hundreds of notes and it means nothing. That's the difference.

PAT HALCOX He played music—you've got people that impart a feeling, an emotion, and he could do that. He wasn't what I would call a classic New Orleans trumpet player, because he sounded better when he had good musicians around him—people that knew the part they had to play. Because he played his part very well. If you hear the part, you can complement it, and the band sounds great.

But sometimes, you know, he did not have such good musicians, and he couldn't really lift them, because he didn't really play that sort of straight-ahead, authoritative style. But he had a beautiful tone and would have played great on any instrument, I think.

Timing was splendid, absolutely splendid, that was his great strength: timing and melody.

JULIAN DAVIES **Mind you, I always loved the guy, but he communicated basically through the music, you know.** We didn't spend much time talking. I never went round to his place, and he never to mine. Well, I did when I'd pick him up for a gig or something like that. But that's… it was never to go round there to a party or anything.

I don't think he was interested in achieving more than being able to play the music. He was really only interested in his own ability to play. I don't think he… he wasn't the least bit impressed by the adulation. He, at the end of every gig, would get up, turn his back on the audience, and put his cornet away in the box—not because he didn't respect the audience, but because he wanted them to applaud the music and not him.

SAM CHARTERS So I meet Ken in London. We go out to the pub, we talk... endlessly talk about New Orleans. Wonderful moustache. He was dead serious, and yet I was aware that there were undercurrents. I mean... the very qualities that made Ken so important, were the qualities that made him difficult.

You know, the essence of popular music is compromise, exploitation, adaptation. In my long career I've seen it with New Orleans jazz, folk music, blues, rock and roll—you name it: Whatever it was that we managed to put together and get people to notice, instantly came thundering in the people who simply wanted to make a lot of money.

And so we seemed to be beside the point, but then they always put us in the shadow, so it made it difficult for us to make even a living, when they were turning it into a show. The incredible show-business side of trad jazz, which still goes on to an extent, made Ken angry.

I think that Ken was very important, of course, for everything that he did for New Orleans afterwards, but all this was important for Ken as a musician.

It wasn't just a moment that he'd been there. I think it left deep roots in Ken himself. He had heard the music *as a living music*, not as a show.

He'd heard it as... neighbourhood bars, he'd heard it as sounds people sang, he'd heard it as music that people who weren't necessarily professionals or developed skills played because other people wanted to hear it. It was as simple as that, and he never lost that. For me, he never lost what he'd learned in New Orleans.

CHRIS BARBER Ken was very, very sincere about the music— he certainly had a name for his sincerity. What he was proposing was a certain branch of the revived archaic New Orleans jazz syndrome at a time when nobody much else was talking about it. He was very charismatic about the music— in fact his whole idea was very charismatic.

I suppose he was a prophet of the thing which became important at the right moment. So he became the person who was held to be responsible for it. He loved that music but he liked loads of other things too.

JOHN PETTERS I think, from what I observed, he believed passionately in what he was doing—so there was that to it. But he actually delivered. He did what he wanted to do and that was that. For me, Colyer and Acker got the closest to generating the heat of American Jazz.

JOHN WURR Given all the hype and idolatry it's tempting to overestimate Ken's legacy. We have to remember that we Europeans were only borrowing a music which had already nearly fully run its course. Yes, I do think that the best non-American musicians breathed some new life into it, and I would place Ken among those. His legacy is mainly, I feel, as an inspirer of people like myself and countless others of my generation. Unlike so many of his contemporaries, Ken was perceptive enough to identify the essence of jazz music, and we were fortunate enough to recognise it.

MAX COLLIE He was doing his book *When Dreams are in The Dust* with us. And from the beginning he'd get very shitty about people. And he said "Oh, don't worry about me... I'm just reliving all those things."

He was like a folk-hero, really. I'd have to say that. Yeah... no doubt about it.

JULIAN DAVIES He changed my life. Absolutely. I probably would never ever have had the chance—the chance he gave me all those years ago—and I don't know how I would have got into playing jazz if I hadn't had that chance. Because he taught me to play bass, you know. From nothing. I can't imagine how else I would have... and it made such a difference to my life.

KEN COLYER The story is done. I've got to go now to begin a journey in my head—"There's a whisper down the field."

THE LONG TRAIL (L'ENVOI) *by Rudyard Kipling*

There's a whisper down the field where the year has shot her yield,
And the ricks stand gray to the sun,
Singing: "Over then, come over, for the bee has quit the clover,
And your English summer's done."
    You have heard the beat of the off-shore wind,
    And the thresh of the deep-sea rain;
    You have heard the song—how long! how long?
    Pull out on the trail again!

Ha' done with the Tents of Shem, dear lass,
We've seen the seasons through,
And it's time to turn on the old trail, our own trail, the out trail,
Pull out, pull out, on the Long Trail—the trail that is always new.

It's North you may run to the rime-ringed sun,
Or South to the blind Horn's hate;
Or East all the way into Mississippi Bay,
Or West to the Golden Gate;
    Where the blindest bluffs hold good, dear lass,
    And the wildest tales are true,
    And the men bulk big on the old trail, our own trail,
        the out trail,
    And life runs large on the Long Trail—the trail that is
        always new.

The days are sick and cold, and the skies are gray and old,
And the twice-breathed airs blow damp;
And I'd sell my tired soul for the bucking beam-sea roll
Of a black Bilbao tramp;
    With her load-line over her hatch, dear lass,
    And a drunken Dago crew,
    And her nose held down on the old trail, our own trail,
        the out trail
    From Cadiz Bar on the Long Trail—the trail that is always new.

There be triple ways to take, of the eagle or the snake,
Or the way of a man with a maid;
But the fairest way to me is a ship's upon the sea
In the heel of the North-East Trade.
    Can you hear the crash on her bows, dear lass,
    And the drum of the racing screw,
    As she ships it green on the old trail, our own trail, the out trail,
    As she lifts and 'scends on the Long Trail—the trail that is
        always new?

See the shaking funnels roar, with the Peter at the fore,
And the fenders grind and heave,
And the derricks clack and grate, as the tackle hooks the crate,
And the fall-rope whines through the sheave;

> As mentioned in *When Dreams Are In The Dust,* Ken had discovered a "yellow, musty copy of Kipling's *Barrack Room Ballads,*" and, aboard ship, had tried to learn a verse each night of The Long Trail, as he felt that he and his shipmates were "living what it was all about." His own version can be heard as the last track on the CD included with this book

It's "Gang-plank up and in," dear lass,
It's "Hawsers warp her through!"
And it's "All clear aft" on the old trail, our own trail,
    the out trail,
We're backing down on the Long Trail—the trail that is
    always new.

O the mutter overside, when the port-fog holds us tied,
And the sirens hoot their dread!
When foot by foot we creep o'er the hueless viewless deep
To the sob of the questing lead!
    It's down by the Lower Hope, dear lass,
    With the Gunfleet Sands in view,
    Till the Mouse swings green on the old trail, our own trail,
        the out trail,
    And the Gull Light lifts on the Long Trail—the trail that is
        always new.

O the blazing tropic night, when the wake's a welt of light
That holds the hot sky tame,
And the steady fore-foot snores through the
    planet-powdered floors
Where the scared whale flukes in flame!
    Her plates are scarred by the sun, dear lass,
    And her ropes are taut with the dew,
    For we're booming down on the old trail, our own trail,
        the out trail,
    We're sagging south on the Long Trail—the trail that is
        always new.

Then home, get her home, where the drunken rollers comb,
And the shouting seas drive by,
And the engines stamp and ring, and the wet bows reel and swing,
And the Southern Cross rides high!
    Yes, the old lost stars wheel back, dear lass,
    That blaze in the velvet blue.
    They're all old friends on the old trail, our own trail,
        the out trail,
    They're God's own guides on the Long Trail—the trail that is
        always new.

Fly forward, O my heart, from the Foreland to the Start—
We're steaming all-too slow,
And it's twenty thousand mile to our little lazy isle
Where the trumpet-orchids blow!
    You have heard the call of the off-shore wind,
    And the voice of the deep-sea rain;
    You have heard the song—how long! how long?
    Pull out on the trail again!

The Lord knows what we may find, dear lass,
And The Deuce knows what we may do—
But we're back once more on the old trail, our own trail,
the out trail,
We're down, hull down on the Long Trail—the trail that is
always new.

APPENDIX ONE
KEY RECORDINGS

REVIEWED AND DISCUSSED BY BILL COLYER, KEN COLYER, PAUL ADAMS, JOHN GRIFFITH, RAY SMITH AND MIKE POINTON

THE CRANE RIVER JAZZBAND

(Cadillac SGC/MEL CD 20/2)

Bill Colyer I think that of all the groups on the scene in the very early fities the Crane River was the most outstanding. As these recordings show, they had quality, maturity and a certain conviction which transcended all their technical shortcomings. It is not difficult to establish a reason for this. Ken Colyer was the reason—and I know that all the musicians involved would agree on that. All the truly exciting and pacemaking groups in this wonderful music called jazz, function in the same way.

A burning conviction in the rightness of their music and a tremendous group spirit and a faith in the nominal leader of the group. While this lasts the group is unbeatable whatever the style in which it chooses to play.

When the Cranes were not rehearsing in the fields of Cranford, where London Airport now sprawls, they were invariably listening to my record collection (or sinking large quantities of the brewers' output).

As my collecting had started In 1935 or thereabouts, and jazz was known as "hot" and hadn't yet been compartmentalised, what more natural to start a record session with say a Lionel Hampton favourite, follow with a Duke, then maybe Leadbelly, Wild Bill, Morton, Artie Shaw, Goodman, Joe Turner, Basie. From this wide and rewarding background came feeling for tone, timbre, vibrato, swing and all the good ingredients that go into the melting pot to make jazz music. What Ken brought to the Cranes was the belief , the conviction that the New Orleans framework of group playing was the most rewarding and the most logical way of making jazz music.

It had nothing whatsoever to do with recreating an old style, or imitating musicians of a past era and different environment. Ken and the Cranes believed that the music they loved came from people—working, living everyday people, and since they were that themselves, what more natural than to play music that way.

The session that produced *Miner's Dream, Do What Ory Say,* and *Uptown Bumps* took place at the famous hut which housed the Cranes' own Cranford Jazz Club next to the Bath Road hostelry The White Hart. It was recorded on several GPO telephone microphone inserts and I remember having to hold the vocal one in my fingertips a few inches from Ken's lips for the vocals. *After Dark* and *Just A Little While* deserve their own accounts, but I cannot easily summarise the rather involved stories! Suffice to say that I still get a kick from Ken's solo on *After Dark.* John R.T. shines on this one to, and it is, incidentally, his own composition.

Shortly after the Pete Payne Delta Sessions, which gave us *Moose March,*

Kentucky Home, and *Gypsy* came a highlight for the Cranes when, on a live session, Pat Hawes pulled off a wonderful treble— superb piano and a great vocal on *Winin' Boy* capped with a storming washboard on *Maryland.*

The final track, *Creole Song* was made some considerable time after the rest of the numbers and shows admirably how, at virtually the end of the road for the Cranes, their purely instrumental technique had improved without losing one iota of their wonderful spirit and feel for New Orleans music.

Here then is a collection of recordings covering a period in my life which will never be forgotten... I am proud to have been a part of the original Crane River Jazz Band.

CHRISTIE BROTHERS' STOMPERS (Cadillac SGC/ MEL CD 20-1)

Ray Smith The background to both the formation of the band and the recordings has already been covered in Chapter 5. These recordings were a vital part of the development of Ken's ideals, and it's interesting to note that his playing on these tracks is almost totally Mutt Carey-inspired, an influence that he subtly assimilated into his playing in later years. Comparing these tracks with those made ten years later with the Graham Stewart/Sammy Rimington version of the Jazzmen reveals probably why Ken wasn't content to remain within the straight-ahead approach offered by the Christies, good though it is. Both Keith and Ian Christie were searching for (and found) their own musical identities which differed from Ken's. Much the same situation was to present itself three years later.

KEN COLYER IN NEW ORLEANS
(504 CD 53)

Mike Pointon Despite the undeniable quality of many of his later recordings with his own bands over the years, perhaps the most enduring part of Ken Colyer's prolific recorded legacy will be the sessions he made in New Orleans after his incarceration in the Parish Prison before he was deported back to England.

The best-known is the series of sides from February 23/4 1953 originally released by Vogue (now reissued as *Ken Colyer in New Orleans: The Complete 1953 Recordings* on 504 CD 53) which, despite technical shortcomings, have a relaxed ambience demonstrating how well the young Englishman integrated with the New Orleanians. Emile Barnes' quicksilver, edgy clarinet and Harrison Brazlee's ruggedly driving trombone complement Ken's inspired lead perfectly.

The youthful Billy Huntington capably reflects his tuition by Lawrence Marrero and the presence of Albert Glenny, who had played with Buddy Bolden, gives a living link to the early days of the music. Albert Jiles lays down just the kind of down-home beat that Ken always strived for in later years. A palpably joyous spirit prevails throughout.

Paul Adams I think the Vogue transfer—the original transfer—of the first-generation chosen takes of Ken in New Orleans are absolutely mind-blowing. Yeah, they're wonderful. Billy Huntington, of course, learnt the stuff so well. They're magical and very important. And anyone

NEW ORLEANS TO LONDON
(Lake LACD 209)

Ray Smith This recording session marked a turning point for British traditional jazz, and the impact these recordings made at the time had repercussions that perhaps are still with us today; it was a new sort of music, really, fusing elements of the "classic jazz" style with the looser approach Ken must have witnessed in New Orleans. The band was co-operative musically as well financially and it's success was surely a group effort; Ken's band was still playing this version of *Cataract Rag* in the late seventies, which I know was Chris Barber's very fine arrangement, as was *Harlem Rag*.

The sound of the band was more recognisably British than later Colyer units, but this shouldn't detract from an appreciation of how good the music was—they were all British after all—and every track is a classic in its way. Polite and tidy rather than wildly inspired, we are fortunate indeed to be able to listen to history in the making.

Sinclair Traill Review from *Jazz Journal*, March 1954. The notes on this LP sleeve say that Ken Colyer must feel very gratified to have achieved this wonderful result, and well he

that has those Vogue LPs should hang on to them, because the sound of those was so good. The Decca engineers at the time did absolute wonders, and lo-fi though they are, it doesn't matter.

Mike Pointon A further selection of recordings, generally of a better standard

may, for this is an excellent record by any standard. The material is well chosen, the front line finely integrated and, wonder of wonders, the rhythm section (sans piano) play with a delightfully relaxed beat.

The front line of Colyer, Chris Barber (trombone), and Monty Sunshine (clarinet) have an excellent rapport and a very obvious real feeling for New Orleans jazz. I shall not single out anyone for special mention as the playing of all three is worthy of the highest praise.

Neither shall I pick out any special tune, as every track has something of interest to offer. Tunes are: *Goin' Home, Isle of Capri, Harlem Rag, La Harpe Street Blues, Stockyard Strut, Cataract Rag, Early Hours, Too Busy*.

Well done, Ken well done everybody—and that remark includes an unknown but obviously sympathetic Decca recording engineer.

Berta Wood American Jazz Scene from *Jazz Journal*, August 1954

I carried my copy of *From New Orleans To London* to San Francisco and told the story of Ken's journey to New Orleans in order to listen to classic jazz. Alvin Alcorn recently from New Orleans and playing with the Ory band, remembered Ken and knew the story.

Turk Murphy played both side of the LP between sets at the Italian Village and was so impressed by it that he said Ken could have a job playing with the Murphy crew anytime he wanted. I looked at Bob Short to see how he was taking it and he jumped up saying that it was okay because he preferred staying with the tuba and not doubling on cornet. I asked Turk a second time to be certain and said that he had better be careful because this Colyer cat might might jump on a merchant ship and

technically, were made and released on 504 CD 23 as *Ken Colyer—the Unknown New Orleans Sessions* with Raymond Burke 1952-1953. Several tracks feature his mentors Edmond Souchon and Dick Allen as well as trumpeter Albert Artigues. Fine trombonist Jack Delaney, pianist Stanley Mendelson and drummer Abbie Brunies play on several this time he might not have to go around the world to get here—San Francisco being a sort of crossroads of the world and wide open to the sea.

PLAYS LIKE SO-AND-SO

Some jazz fans came to our table and asked, Who is it? And we were happy to tell them. Turk wanted a copy of the record and Bob Short wanted one and a certain Barney Crosby who deals in foreign records has possibly ordered them by this time. I don't know why this should happen but it does. People who have heard a playing feel strongly called upon to say He plays like so-and-so. Or, he reminds me of such and such. Everybody did it. But always with the implication that Colyer is far more than a copyist and always with only the greatest musicians in mind.

Of the more-or less sharpies and hipsters, two were reminded of Papa Mutt and his deep Blues for Jimmy style. He reminded Turk of George Mitchell. Alvin Alcorn and Albert Burbank agreed that they heard the Kid Howard horn and George Lewis tempos and a style close to that of the George Lewis band. While listening they smiled their agreement. Everybody thought the Colyer music remarkable. The most popular tune was *Goin' Home* and it got to me too.

LEWIS' BAND LISTEN

On *Isle Of Capri,* George Lewis remarked, with his wonderful, soft spoken authority that the Colyer solo was played remarkably like Elmer Talbert played it and he was smiling and nodding his head in time as he listened. "Yes, it is very good," he said. Slow Drag was patting his foot in time and nodding too, and he was smiling with that abundant, Frenchy, Creole, New Orleans sweetness. And oh, what I would have given for a camera to have caught Lawrence Marrero as he listened! He was standing deeply absorbed and motionless in the middle of the floor. The all-out smile on his

face was so deep, so wide, so strong and there was so much of it that it was like a definition of Jazz itself. Because Colyer knows Lawrence personally he will know what I mean. Alton Purnell was quietly listening and deep in thought and I would have liked knowing something of what was on his mind.

A COMPOSITE?

There were half-a-dozen jazz wigs present at this playing and most of them were moving in one way or another with the beat and one of them heard some Wooden Joe Nicholas in the Colyer trumpet. Now if Ken is a kind of composite production of Elmer Talbert, George Mitchell, Papa Mutt, Wooden Joe and Kid Howard plus himself and his own style, you had better treat him nice and treat him kind—give him everything he wants—because you have hit the jackpot in New Orleans trumpets.

It was interesting to watch the interest in the playing subside and drift while the rags were on, (*Harlem Rag* and *Cataract Rag*) and then come back again for more careful listening to the Blues. Nobody plans it that way. It just happens. If the more overbearing of the intellectuals ever tend to get out of hand, it will most certainly be while the rags are playing. (Time out for chuckling).

Goin' Home has all I ask of good jazz. Aside from the profound and beautiful lyrics which, alone, would have made this tune stand out, it has a tempo de (sic) lowdown. Kate could have shimmied to this one. It is a happy thing!

It can be said that the music is as sensitive as New Orleans Jazz although not as strong as native New Orleans Jazz which is not a criticism. New Orleans Jazz itself is not as strong as it once was. Again I am reminded of George Lewis saying, "We only try to play like the fellows used to play." And it looks like a sure bet that musicians like Ken will, in the future, be playing the very best New Orleans Jazz to be heard...

BACK TO THE DELTA

(Lake LACD 209)

Paul Adams Well, it was a weird thing, you see. Originally, when I got the matrix sheets from Decca, all these tunes—apart from the skiffle ones—were listed twice. I thought, "That's very odd." So I got in touch with them and said, "Why are these tunes listed twice. Are they different takes?"

They didn't really know, but what they did say to me—because they hadn't got them in their library—was, "Oh well, no; they're just the same takes that have been listed twice."

And then it came to light, actually, that the American version of that ten-inch was different. It had different banjo on it, and

different drums on it, and different bass. Then it emerged that they'd had this recording session which, according to folklore, Ken wasn't happy with and sent everybody home. The sides were rejected apart from the skiffle ones, because it was the skiffle ones that were issued; the band tracks were rejected.

They went back sometime later and re-recorded the same tracks, with Stan Greig on drums this time and Disley on banjo. And that was the session that was issued. But the American branch of Decca—London—they wanted to issue it over there.

And again, as far as folklore is concerned —as far as I understand—the wrong set of master tapes were sent out; the first set were sent out, not the second set. And that's how that happened. So I mean, it was just an interesting thing. But the master tapes certainly don't exist in London anymore, and where they are overseas I don't know, so it was a question of getting hold of a decent copy and cleaning it up.

---

tracks and two members of George Lewis's classic rhythm section are also included—Lawrence Marrero and Slow Drag Pavageau—although, due to union restrictions, Ken was unable at that time to record with George. But clarinetist Raymond Burke, a truly creative and original musician Ken admired, is on top form

throughout. When Lewis visited Britain, touring as a guest with the Colyer Jazzmen in 1957, several informal recordings were made which can be heard on 504 CDs 50 and 51. In 1959 when the Lewis band toured Europe, George also recorded with Colyer's Jazzmen in Germany and tracks were released on 504 CD52.

KEN COLYER'S JAZZMEN AND SKIFFLE GROUP 1956
(Lake CD LACD 241)

Ray Smith Of all the many recordings Ken's band made, perhaps the singular most important track early on, as far as I'm concerned, was the stunning version of *Dippermouth Blues* recorded for Decca in March 1956. The intensity, drive and sheer joy engendered by this version makes it one of the high points in Ken's recorded output, and fully captures the ensemble style and spirit of New Orleans as never before heard from a British band on record. The other three numbers from this session are wonderful, of course, as were the tracks recorded the previous year which were issued on two E.P.s (*And Back To New Orleans* Vols 1 & 2, LAKE LACD 236) but it's as if he realised that this was at last the band of his dreams.

CLUB SESSION WITH COLYER
(Lake LACD 241)

John Griffith The *Club Session* record, for example. It's marvellous. It is—I can understand why it's the highest-selling Colyer record of all time, which Decca claimed that it was. It is quite marvellous. I know that Ian was asked once about it, and he sort of said, "Well, it must be the tunes."

You know, everyone knew that it was an interesting and bloody good band but—it must be the tunes. It is partly because of the tunes. I mean, when it comes to making records, it is that selection of tunes that sort of becomes familiar in a collector's mind, and they do refer back to it because they know if they put this disc on, they're going to get a certain run of tunes, you know. And that makes a record very popular. Not the individual tunes, but the run of tunes.

Paul Adams But, you see, it was really funny—three times this has happened in Colyer history; not that the wrong thing has

been issued, but something has happened with the master tapes. *Club Session With Colyer*— everybody goes

"What a wonderful session it was." It wasn't a session, it was two sessions. One session was recorded live, they had problems; there's this bit of myth about—again, I don't know how true it is—about a thunderstorm outside affecting the recordings.

So they went back into the studio, and—sometime later—and re-recorded it. So, you have two distinct sounds on that album. You know, if you understand audio or you've been listening, you get two distinct sounds. One is a studio set—with some applause added—and the other is the actual live one.

COLYER PLAYS STANDARDS
(Lake LACD 144/267)

Paul Adams So that happened, then you get to the Colyer Plays Standards session, which was a beautifully recorded—beautiful in stereo—recording of the Colyer band in a club session, I think—whether it was recorded in the pub round the corner or actually just live in the studio—and those sides were rejected.

Interestingly, I ran them by Ken, because he was still alive when we found... these were found accidentally; it was John Griffith who alerted me to it. There was a compilation album put out of trad things, and it had one track on it, and it was from the *Colyer Plays Standards*, but it was in real stereo, not fake stereo—they did a lot of electronic re-processing in real stereo.

So what John had said to me, try to find if they've got the actual stereo masters. And I thought "Well, yeah, that would be really good." But there's no stereo masters listed. And then when we compared it with the actual version that was on the LP, it was obviously a different recording. So not only was it in stereo, it was a different recording. So, we kept plugging away and plugging away, and finally got a rather excited sort of telephone call from Decca saying they found this tape—box of tape—that just says "Ken Colyer." Nothing else, it just said Ken Colyer—what is it, you know?

So they dubbed it off and sent it to me, and it was the *Colyer Plays Standards* but recorded live with one tune that wasn't on the actual issued version, and the actual issued version had an extra tune that wasn't on this live session. And that was in beautiful

stereo. And I said "Well, that's never been issued; let's do that." So that's what we did first of all. So that's another session where what had happened, where Ken had rejected these stereo's, and he said—with hindsight—he can't understand why they were rejected. Ray Foxley said exactly the same thing. But they went back into the studio, and they recorded the whole thing again. So in fact, that was three times Colyer had done that. It's very strange.

And it appears that he had some thing about Decca—he wasn't happy with Decca. I don't think he was ever happy with any record company, to be honest. And I don't suspect that Decca had actually really done anything wrong. I think that what had happened essentially was that—it's a big business and Ken wasn't big business, you know. Although, again, I'm not sure whether that was part of the myth, and part of the myth that he liked to put about, because we can't escape from the fact that he did sign with Denis Preston, and he did make singles, you know. So, at the end of the day, you wonder sometimes how non-commercial he really was.

I'll probably never know the answer to that. So he wasn't terribly happy with Decca, which actually in a sense I thought was a bit sad, because the sound that Decca got towards the end of Ken's time with them—I always thought that *Club Session* was a bit of a mess in terms of that; it was a bit all over the place, but the studio and quasi-studio sessions were actually better than the early stuff that he did for Preston (I mean the actual genuine live version of *Standards*). Because the issued one—despite the fact that it's got applause on—was actually recorded in a studio, and the applause is just dubbed on. But, that was a really, really good sound, and the ragtime session, and the little EP of the street things was a good sound—the street titles.

It was a shame in some ways, but in many ways Decca was ahead of the field at the time, in terms of their sound recording. And he stayed there because, I gather—I was reading a book, and I did talk to Chris Barber about this—that people were seriously taken to task for letting Chris Barber move on, and of course, they kept Ken.

Ken obviously played quite a programme. There's another one of these myths—I still have people on recording sessions who say to me, "Ken Colyer always said if it doesn't work out the first time move on to the next tune." I have the master tapes of his recording of *Melancholy Blues* in which he had six goes at it. So again, that's

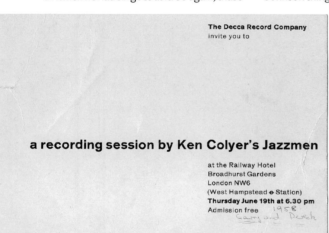

another myth that's grown up around him.

That was in '65. It's on the *Out of Nowhere* album (Lake LACD101).

John Griffith Ken would always denigrate his own efforts, in reverence and respect for New Orleans jazz as he knew and loved it, and the players that he also personally knew and loved. I think, though, there were times when he did indicate—I remember the comment when he heard the stereo Standards; Paul Adams sent him that when he was down in France and he said, "The best New Orleans band ever. Wonderful stuff." And I think this was Ken saying "Hang on. Maybe my life was worth something. Perhaps I really did achieve something remarkable here."

THEY ALL PLAYED RAGTIME
(Lake LACD 267)

Paul Adams Ken was interesting, because he was building, in a sense, on the Bunk Johnson thing. Because that way of playing ragtime, in many ways, was not part of what traditional jazz bands really did. Neither did the New Orleans bands. They might have done in the early part of the century, but they weren't really doing ragtime pieces in terms of the revival. But Bunk Johnson did—I suppose possibly the Lu Watters band did a little bit.

Of course, that opens up another avenue. Because it took a long time—it seems so obvious to me, but it seemed quite a long time before the Colyer pundits realised how much Ken was influenced by Mutt Carey. You know, they all did the Bunk Johnson thing, and yet there's miles of Mutt Carey in Ken's playing. I don't know how hard Ken had to work when he did the ragtime things because obviously he was not a reader and you've got to completely learn it.

Ray Smith Ken understood the nature of the music and had the ability to capture the flavour and charm of the rags without necessarily playing the notes as written; almost a sort of minimalist approach, but each note was placed exactly in the right place at exactly the right time, almost forcing the other players do what they did. And the result was the lovely lilting sound that the band achieved here. This involved a lot of work from all concerned, not least of all from Ken himself, but the understanding of the idiom from the band as a whole marks this as a milestone in their recorded output.

THIS IS THE BLUES
(Lake LACD 188)

Ken Colyer I was talking to Dougie Richford the other day; he's a musician who knows. He'd happened to have heard This Is The Blues, and said it was one of the best

British jazz recordings he'd ever heard; he loved the music. I was so pleased to hear him say that, and maybe the recording quality was better than on the two previous albums—still not what I'd wanted, but Dougie's remarks pleased me a great deal.

So, going back to the current recording we were discussing, my disappointment with the Columbia sessions made me insist that the final product would have "The Band Sound," the way we sounded live! Not some bad studio distortion that messed my music about. Charlie Fox summed it up on the liner note when he said we'd captured "The New Orleans Bounce... the functional warmth of the music."

We did do a test, a sort of experimental recording session at the 51 for Columbia, and some of the stuff wasn't bad—Pat Hawes was on that—and I did try to get the Columbia people back down there for an actual recording session.

THIS IS JAZZ VOLUMES 1 AND 2
(LACD 201D)

Ray Smith This Is Jazz Volume 1 was one of the first Colyer LP's I bought in the fifties, and it's difficult not to choose it in this section. Re-listening after all these years made me realise just how good this band really was: I love a piano (good title for a song) and Ray Foxley added another dimension to the band, smoothing the path between rhythm section and front-line. Listen to the wonderful interplay between Mac and Ian, the infectious playing of Colin Bowden throughout, and Ken's inspired preaching creating that marvellous ensemble sound that was the Colyer hallmark.

By the time Volume 2 was recorded, Sammy Rimington had replaced Ian Wheeler and Graham Stewart was on trombone in place of Mac Duncan. Ken decided, wisely, to try for a more Kid Ory-inspired approach. The difference is subtle but telling, and took the band on to new heights. Comparisons are unwise as musically this band was every bit as good as the previous one, and unfortunately didn't last as long, but I would say that this was one of the most satisfyingly successful of all the K.C. sessions still available.

COLYER'S PLEASURE

(Lake LACD 34)

Ken Colyer This group has been together long enough now that I can say it's as good as any of the bands I've led, definitely.

The problem with Columbia, you'd record the stuff at Lansdowne and it sounds OK or as good as you can get it. But when the master tape gets into Columbia's hands, they muck it about before they master it

onto record.

They had absolutely no idea at Columbia of how a jazz band is supposed to sound. To them it's

just all one noise—just a trad noise that they've got to try and level out so that our music sounds just the same as all the other bands... a very annoying thing! They spoiled some good music on those sessions.

ORY'S CREOLE TROMBONE

(Pastels CD 20.1651) Previously released as "*Ken Colyer Concert ...and let the music roll along*" (WAM LP 1)

Ray Smith The inclusion of this recording gives me the opportunity to talk about this band's particular qualities. This was Ken's longest serving, and arguably most consistent, unit. The addition of the piano-player probably changed the routine a bit, but the band as a whole achieved its usual cohesive sound. The dependable team of Geoff Cole's trombone and Tony Pyke's clarinet playing provided a comfortable platform for Ken's inspired lead, and the rhythm section rolls along in the best Colyer vein. The repertoire of the band at this time had grown considerably since the fifties, and Ken's intensity is well captured in the final choruses of the band numbers.

The Skiffle group is also impressive, and being a live recording, the atmosphere engendered an authenticity often missing from studio recordings.

KEN COLYER'S JAZZMEN : LIVE AT THE DANCING SLIPPER 1969

(Azure AZ CD 25)

Mike Pointon This is a fine representative session by what was effectively the longest-

lasting Colyer line-up. It includes a typical cross-section of the band's repertoire, reflecting the imaginatively eclectic choice of numbers Ken would feature .

The front line features him on top relaxed form, interweaving with the ever-reliable, fluent Tony Pyke and Geoff Cole's mellow trombone. They are underpinned sympathetically by John Bastable's rock-steady banjo, Bill Cole's sonorous bass and unobtrusive drums from Malc Murphy. *Barefoot Boy*, originally recorded by Herb Morand, one of Ken's favourite horn men, with the Harlem Hamfats, is a highlight of the album, together with Ellington's *Drop Me Off In Harlem*. *Peanut Vendor* demonstrates how such a Latin-tinged piece could ring the changes and reflects Colyer's wide-ranging tastes in music.

As Ken stated in his liner notes: "Many musicians have joined me, for many reasons, other than the essential ones. I have never made any secret of my musical intentions throughout my life and have always accepted that they were common knowledge. This should have attracted the right men, but not always so... This band was together for quite a long period and was a well-drilled professional group, with some degree of what I want in musicians.

"I consider my own playing satisfactory, in spite of the fact that my health was bad at the time and I was receiving intensive radiotherapy after a malignancy." He also reflected: "We really should have had a New Orleans school. I once said that was our great disadvantage. When we started out we had to learn by trial and error. It is all there on the records but it is not always so easily grasped... but with talent and intense concentration one can learn. Some people seem to think I went to New Orleans in 1952 and by some magical process learnt the music in a couple of months. I did learn and my playing and contribution to the music has been compared by Emile Barnes, Willie Humphrey and George Lewis to that of the legendary Chris Kelly and Buddy Petit."

THE LEGENDARY CRANE RIVER JAZZBAND (Lake LACD 57)

Paul Adams Sonny was a much more rough and ready player but, again, was very

exciting, you know. I've seen nights with Sonny, and I've played with Sonny and really been concerned that maybe he wasn't playing very well, but the audience was really loving it. He could be a bit erratic, but on form he was superb. And we did have some conversations about it, and he said, you know, everybody always links me with Ken because of the Crane River thing and everything else and I think he did, not exactly hero-worship Ken, but I think Ken was a big influence on him in lots of ways. But Sonny said, "When you actually analyse it, the amount of time I actually spent playing with Ken was very small. There wasn't actually that much we did together in the great scheme of things."

I wish I'd seen them live—I never did see them live. I think a lot of reunions don't work, but that one did. It certainly did work very well. I was pleased that somebody recorded it well, and so we had some idea of the interplay with the two trumpets, you know, which they'd really got worked out well together. How much working out went on and how much was intuitive we'll never know—because neither of them were skilled musicians in that sense.

THE CRANE RIVER JAZZBAND: "STORMING SESSION"

(Upbeat URCD 159)

Ray Smith Pat Hawes' sleeve notes to this CD—reproduced in part in chapter 4—covered the events surrounding the live concert in Hamburg, and the impact the music had on the audience and musicians alike. This was undoubtedly the highpoint of the band's career, and it is rare indeed to have such an event captured on disc; unfortunately only three numbers from the concert are included here, plus some fine studio recordings from the next day. Everyone involved is on top form throughout, driven on by Colin Bowden's sympathetically colourful drumming.

The importance of this band in the history of British Jazz—and in the journey of Ken Colyer—cannot be underestimated; this recording is part of the story.

LIVE AT PIZZA EXPRESS— KEN COLYER JAZZ QUARTET

1985 (Azure AZ-CD 33/34)

Mike Pointon This delightful session presents Colyer's relaxed, introspective cornet in a different setting from the usual New Orleans line-up he generally fronted.

Ken's mid-register playing blends well with young Jean-Francois Bonnel's fluent Creole-tinged clarinet and Paul Sealey's accomplished guitar and banjo, underpinned by Ken Ames' bass, provide ideal support. Steve Lane's notes rightly compare the session's intimate ambience and teamwork to the Bechet/Spanier Big Four.

As Steve wrote: "He may have spent time in New Orleans, absorbing the musical atmosphere, but his playing style was quite original—he was far removed from the army of trad copyists by whom he was surrounded, and his sensitivity and creativity imparted validity to the British jazz revival. It is Ken who imparts emotional power to the proceedings. He demonstrates that he has the skill and vision to make fine music in an unusual setting."

I DID IT FOR THE MUSIC- KEN COLYER AND HIS DREAM OF NEW ORLEANS

Membran Music DVD 231874

Mike Pointon This nicely -packaged DVD, produced by longtime Colyer fan Fritz Peters, is a well-compiled documentary filmed in 1987 giving a good overview of Colyer's musical philosophy with interviews with Ken himself and such associates as Chris Barber, Monty Sunshine, Acker Bilk, Lonnie Donegan, Humphrey Lyttelton, Ian Christie and Ian Wheeler. We also see Ken in action at the 100 Club in London with his final regular band and with a skiffle group including his brother Bill and Johnny Parker. Peters explains how he persuaded Ken to participate in the project and bandleader/trumpeter Abbi Hubner tells us of Ken's immense influence over the years in Germany. We get many revealing insights into how Ken was a driving force in stimulating interest in New Orleans music in Europe. There is also a bonus CD of music.

BONUS CD DETAILS

1 **Goin' Home**
Ken Colyer (guitar/vocal). Recorded at John Bernard's home in New Orleans 2 February 1953 (previously unreleased)

2 **I'm Travelling**
Crane River Jazz Band
Ken Colyer (tpt), Sonny Morris (co), Ray Orpwood (tmb), Monty Sunshine (clt), Ben Marshall (bjo), Pat Hawes (pno), Denny Coffey (bs), Bill Colyer (w/bd). Recorded live at the Royal Festival Hall in London 14 July 1951

3 **Heebie Jeebies**
Christie Brothers Stompers
Ken Colyer (co), Keith Christie (tmb), Ian Christie (clt), Pat Hawes(pno), Ben Marshall (bjo), Denny Coffey (bs), Bill Colyer(w/bd).
Recorded in London 14 August 1951

4 **Milé's Blues**
Ken Colyer and his New Orleans Band
Ken Colyer(co), Harrison Brazlee (tmb), Emile Barnes (clt), Billy Huntington (bjo), George Fortier (bs), Albert Jiles (dms). Recorded in New Orleans 24 February 1953

5 **Winter Wonderland**
Ken Colyer and his New Orleans Band
As track 4

6 **Breeze**
Ken Colyer's Jazzmen
Ken Colyer (tpt/vcl), Lonnie Donegan (bjo), Chris Barber (bs), Ron Bowden (dms). Recorded at Skovshoved, nr Copenhagen, Denmark 12 April 1953

7 **Isle of Capri**
Ken Colyer's Jazzmen
Ken Colyer (tpt), Chris Barber (tmb), Monty Sunshine (clt), Lonnie Donegan (bjo), Jim Bray (bs), Ron Bowden (dms). Recorded in London 2 September 1953

8 **Far Away Blues**
Ken Colyer's Jazzmen
Ken Colyer(tpt), Ed O'Donnell (tmb), Bernard 'Acker' Bilk (clt), William 'Diz' Disley (bjo), Dick Smith (bs), Stan Greig (dms).
Recorded in London 10 September 1954

9 **Shim-Me-Sha-Wabble**
Ken Colyer's Jazzmen
As track 8 except John Bastable (bjo), Micky Ashman (bs), Eric Skinner (dms). Recorded in London 25 June 1954

10 **Dippermouth Blues**
Ken Colyer's Jazzmen
Ken Colyer (tpt), Mac Duncan (tmb), Ian Wheeler clt), John Bastable (bjo),

Dick Smith (bs), Colin Bowden (dms). Recorded in London 8 March 1956

11 **Down Bound Train**
Ken Colyer's Skiffle Group
Ken Colyer (guitar/vcl), John Bastable (bjo), Micky Ashman (bs), Colin Bowden (dms).
Recorded in London 25 May 1956

12 **Blame It On The Blues**
As track 10 except Ron Ward (bs). Recorded live at the Railway Hotel in London 4 October & 16 November 1956

13 **Basin Street Blues**
George Lewis with Ken Colyer's Jazzmen
As track 12 plus George Lewis (clt). Recorded live at the Free Trade Hall in Manchester 27 April 1957

14 **Weary Blues**
As track 13. George Lewis (clt) replaces Ian Wheeler.

15 **Jambalaya**
Ken Colyer's Omega Brass Band
Ken Colyer (tpt), Bob Wallis (tpt), Sonny Morris (co), Mac Duncan (tmb), Mick Clift (tmb), Ian Wheeler (clt), Dave Keir (as), Derek Easton (ten), Mole Benn (tu), Colin Bowden (sn/dm), Neil Millett (bs dm).
Recorded in London 8 September 1957

16 **Kinklets**
Ken Colyer's Jazzmen
As track 12 except add Ray Foxley (pno). Recorded in London 16 January 1958

17 **Get Out Of Here And Go On Home**
Ken Colyer's Jazzmen
As track 16 except Graham Stewart (tmb), Sammy Rimington (clt). Recorded in London 23 August 1960

18 **Goin' Home**
Ken Colyer's Jazzmen
Ken Colyer (tpt), Geoff Cole (tmb), Jack Gilbert (clt), John Bastable (bjo), Ken Ames (bs), Malc Murphy (dms). Recorded in London 18 May 1971 (previously unreleased)

19 **The Long Trail**
Ken Colyer (guitar/vocal). Recorded at his home in Hounslow October 1982 (previously unreleased)

Our gratitude goes to Paul Adams of Lake Records, Mike Dine of 504 Records John Jack of Cadillac Records, Udo Schneider and Russell Colyer. The most comprehensive Colyer discography is No. 3 in Gerard Bielderman's Eurojazz Discos series.

APPENDIX TWO
COLYER: THE MAN

BY JOHN KEEN

KEN COLYER'S INTENSE EXPERIENCES of jazz music in New Orleans and of life and human nature in prison in late 1952 and early 1953 when he was only 24 years old were very significant in his understanding and playing of New Orleans jazz. He went there at a time when the musicians, George Lewis et al, were at a peak of their creativity. For one thing (or rather three) they all had marvellous tones and feeling, and incredible rhythm, and had been playing their kind of music for decades.

Ken had seen and heard them play. He had gained a greater understanding of the way the music was played. His experiences in New Orleans gave him the ability to lead, and inform and guide, and interact with others back in England. His visit gave him first-hand knowledge and contacts. It established his status as a significant player, a leader in the field.

Other New Orleans-style players had learned the music from records. He had seen how it was done to a greater extent than others and had returned with the confidence and ability to lead a band. No wonder it was difficult for him back in England to tolerate lack of commitment and of taste, poor musicianship and enthusiasm, and ignorance of the music he loved.

He wanted to play what he saw and hoped was as close as possible to the real thing, the New Orleans sound. And what he did and played on his return was hugely significant in the development of British jazz and pop music. Namely, the style of ensemble playing, the formation of six-piece bands with pianoless rhythm; his dedication to the New Orleans sound and tunes associated with the Lewis repertoire. And skiffle. All came about because of KC and his stay in New Orleans.

IN HIS AUTOBIOGRAPHY HE IS POSITIVE ABOUT THE music and musicians and the many people and situations that he meets in New Orleans, including in prison. In his young days he seemed friendly and cheerful and outgoing. Later in life he became wary, pessimistic, inward looking, defensive and superstitious.

His apparent negativity, paranoia and cynicism develop as he comes into contact with attitudes that are hostile or indifferent to his music and recordings, and as he needs to face the problems of organising and finance. It's possible he had few communication skills of the kind needed to negotiate, persuade and explain. In my view he would have benefited from a manager like Louis Armstrong had, Joe Glaser, to deal with the anxieties and diversions that develop in the jazz musician's life, allowing him to concentrate on his music.

Throughout his life Ken seemed to be conscious of, and affected by, his working-class background. In his book there is, as in Louis Armstrong's life, an underlying theme of struggle and survival. It's possible that Colyer lacked the social skills that would have enabled him to communicate confidently with middle-class, more educated colleagues, and the people that were concerned with finance, recording and promotion.

In his book he talks about drink a lot, also smoking, and there are suggestions that later in life he had little interest in food or any form of exercise. No idea or indication that he might be damaging his health. Yet his health was damaged.

Ken Colyer had great skill in ensemble playing and had a formidable technique in the sense that he could express and convey great feeling. His tone was dark, and different from trumpets with a brassy sound. It was soft and mellow yet he was still able to project through an ensemble.

He played strong lead trumpet; it was sparse, terse, yet melodic and direct, and hugely tasteful. His sense of rhythm was confident and surefooted and swinging. He played notes in front and after the beat. His tone and phrasing engages the listener. His great strength was simplicity. His music had soul and spirit. If the Chris Barber band was bright, Ken's music was dark.

His playing was inspirational. A lot of trumpet players wanted and tried to play like him and some still do.

IT IS INTERESTING TO MATCH WHAT WE KNOW OF the KC character and his achievements with current thinking and research in psychology that describe personality across five broad dimensions: extraversion, agreeableness, conscientiousness, emotional stability and openness.

CONSCIENTIOUSNESS
Individuals are reliable, hard-working, self-disciplined, strong work ethic, effective in pursuing goals. Certainly Ken was conscientious—he had the qualities outlined above.

Portrait of Ken
by Diz Disley:
"I always liked it
'cause he got
Ken's eyes perfectly;
the expression,
the humour."
—Bill Colyer

divergent thinking and cognitive flexibility.

In my view Ken was certainly open-minded and flexible in his creative life; for example, he listened to a wide range of music and though he favoured the trumpet styles of Kid Howard, Mutt Carey and Elmer Talbert, he also liked Bobby Hackett and Wild Bill. And he was innovative in his wide repertoire of tunes.

EXTRAVERSION AND AGREEABLENESS

EMOTIONAL STABILITY

Stable individuals experience fewer negative emotions and handle stress better. Less emotionally stable will have high levels of chronic stress and anxiety. Lack of emotional stability is also associated with poor health, less job satisfaction and early burnout.

It would seem that KC lacked emotional stability. He had high levels of stress associated with the band business; and there are hints that he was chronically dissatisfied with his bands and colleagues.

OPENNESS IN AREAS REQUIRING INNOVATION AND CREATIVITY

This trait is associated with individuals who have an open-minded, reflective and exploratory mindset. It allows

Ken was at a disadvantage in situations requiring extensive social interaction, had no interest in selling himself and was not good at it. However, his playing and experience and status were inspirational to other musicians, and in this his leadership was very strong; but he also lacked some of the skills needed for effective leadership e.g. communication and an outgoing personality. His single-mindedness might have made him intolerant and difficult to deal with.

Was Ken happy or content? It seems not. He should have been very satisfied with his achievements, yet somehow one knows he was not. The title of his book—*When Dreams Are in the Dust* tells us that he was not. In it he expresses feelings of disappointment, disillusionment and pessimism, of hopes unfulfilled. Yet if there was ever in the jazz world a life of creativity to be valued, it was his, and he did not recognise it.

353

APPENDIX THREE
MASTER CLASS

KEN'S NOTES FOR A SECOND BOOK

Sometime after Ken moved to France he started making notes for a second book to be called *A Masterclass of New Orleans Jazz*. Some of these notes were written on scraps of paper, bus tickets etc., and as such weren't arranged in any specific order. However, this stream of consciousness allows a rare glimpse into his methods; the important recordings—both of New Orleans musicians and others—and the musical principles that were uppermost in his mind at all times. The writing was at times difficult to decipher, but Colyerisms have been left intact: Ken uses the word 'hisself' for 'himself,' and in describing Herb Morand's playing uses the phrase 'a certain dinge' meaning , presumably, darkness of tone. As an added bonus, Ken's true thoughts about Louis Armstrong's importance are contained within these pages.

CAME FROM THE OTHER SIDE OF THE TRACKS, as did most of the great creators of the music. Have led a life that is completely foreign to them. Without my efforts, the course of the music would have taken a different course; a few realise this, but pitifully few. Where do we go from here? On a downward course to Nothingsville? I tried to build something within my ability, to have a path for others to follow, with maybe more talent than I.

I have truly seen my dreams turn to dust and despair. **The music is still there to be played and created upon. The only confines are in the imagination.**

There are no barriers. The negroes in New Orleans welcomed me, after hearing a few notes. Because they knew that I had taken the trouble to try and learn.

At certain times I am a man of few words, as they are; the communication is in the music.

MUSIC TO LISTEN TO: Blind Mamie Forehand: "Wouldn't mind dying, but I've got to go by myself." This record has a strange beauty. The slide guitar is expertly played (unknown guitar). It has a brooding quality that Monty Sunshine found disturbing. Called it voodoo music, but it is secular.

At the turn of the century you would probably hear this sort of music in small churches in the backwaters of the Missisippi Delta.

All of this type of music should be listened to by potential musicians. Let it sink into the subconscious and it will eventually come out in your playing.

TRY AND SEE TORTELIER MASTER CLASSES, probably available on video cassette. Teaches how to phrase with grace and beauty. Same rules apply to all music.

It is essential to absorb knowledge of three-part counterpoint harmony. Contrapuntal harmony. Dissonance should come naturally. The only way is to have it in your head, play, woodshed, concentrate on absorbing the right sounds. Classic examples of counter harmony that readily spring to mind are the American Music LP of Louis Nelson DeLisle. He was highly respected in New Orleans and rightly so. Many learnt from him, though individual interpretation is the freedom you have within the idiom. His counter-harmony playing is superb and produces the sound that made the music unique.

Louis Nelson (no relation) is not so effective. He DOES NOT play a tailgate counter to the lead. Peter Bocage, though pleasant enough, is no Bunk or Mutt Carey. NEVERTHELESS, the recording is very important.

THE FOUR BUNK BRUNSWICKS ARE GEMS. Well recorded, perfect tonally, and the band sound relaxed and in good form. I rate these as all-time classics.

These prove Bunk's mastery. He has to work to the 78 time-limit. (I have never timed them—could be interesting.) So like Ellington, he cleverly engineers the numbers until they become symphonies in miniature. *ALEXANDER'S RAGTIME BAND* is important, for Jim Robinson's playing is the perfect foil. Get a good brass team working and you really have something.

Add a clarinet like George and you have the ensemble sound that made the music revolutionary; naturally I include the rhythm section, for truly there must be no weak links. Every man must hold his end up. Many times I have had to work twice as hard, and feel as if I have an anchor chain around my neck. It shouldn't be. For when everything is right, there is no strain, the time flies, and though there might be tiredness, there is a nice feeling of exhilarating relaxation. This must be why the N.O.s men could work such long hours and no coasting. *TISHOMINGO* is pure essence.

It is very difficult to describe sounds. It can't really be done,

DON'T ever listen to trad. You are an idiot if you cannot tell the difference.

Traditional was the word coined by somebody or other, certainly not me. I have always thought that jazz is jazz and should need no categories.

It is always better, the closer it is to the true form. Here you must develop your ear and your own good sense to guide you. Ballet dancers sweat and grind, and torture themselves. Classical musicians practice for hours. My Uncle William Ehrhardt was a classical clarinettist of some esteem.

He could listen to jazz with an unprejudiced classical ear. You couldn't fool him, for he knew with an expert's knowledge. He really liked George Lewis. More sophisticated and technically better men didn't always impress him. I wish I had kept notes but was very young and just interested in what he had to say. He never tried to shoot the music down, and this was my main pleasure.

He would listen and give constructive criticism.

One thing I do remember. He noted that the blues were usually played in the flat keys, because you can produce more blue notes.

This may be true, but look at the New Orleans way of playing the blues in C and G. They still produce the correct blue sound, and still bend the pitch and flatten to get the correct sound.

Don't take everything as gospel.

that's why we must refer to other things to give you some idea. Beautiful music is pure poetry. A distillation of all that is good.

No adultery. It is therapeutic, it makes people feel good, not just momentarily, but helps them through life. I have saved suicidal people. One example: a successful author was on his way to throw hisself in the Elbe. He passed the club on the way to the river. Heard the music, and came in. Within a week he was a happy man, with a renewed faith in life.

Maybe it is a religion. I am not ashamed of approaching the music with a religious fervour. The very reverse.

If only people would look and see the damage done, almost from the beginning, by so-called religions. They are all fake, hypocritical, crazy, murderous. Only the Aztecs had the right idea. They prayed to the sun. 'Barbaric'? Maybe a few sacrifices were better than killing millions.

HOWEVER, BACK TO THE MUSIC. That is the only thing in life that will not play you false. It is people that let you down. You can't blame the music for that.

I DISLIKE MANY RECORDS I HAVE MADE BECAUSE THEY ARE NOT GOOD ENOUGH. Unfortunately, I have never had a band that will listen to their records, clinically analyse the faults, then play and woodshed like hell. You can be woodshedding all the time if part of your mind is always critical of what you are doing. It is the only way to improve.

Humph gave 'New Orleans to London' a very well thought-out constructive criticism. Now I thought we would digest what Humph said, iron the faults out and improve. I was wrong. They were so deluded, they resented the article.

The break-up of a potentially good band was inevitable.

If you are young and read this, and don't quite understand,

give it a chance, then one day maybe you will.

Remember Garrick (he was a famous actor): "Let's steal with honesty from one another." Then maybe there is a chance for the music and "There will come another Day."

I WISH THE WORD 'WHY' HAD NEVER BEEN PUT INTO THE LANGUAGE. Remember, it may take you minutes to read what it has taken me hours to write. So it is with the music. It may take years of hard work to produce three or four minutes of lasting beauty that will be there forever. I don't need a record collection anymore. I have it all in my head and I haven't got a computer for a brain.

Another important record is JAZZ AT VESPERS by the George Lewis Band.

I was lucky enough to be in The Rev. ALVIN KERSHAW'S town with George and the boys. To play for his, and all the town's, children. A memorable concert. They were three wonderful days I will never forget. I have written about them elsewhere.

Al is a wonderful man. George called him a 'living saint'.

And the most un-reverent Reverend I have ever met.

A true christian, and that is more important.

The record highlights many of the aspects of the music.

Jim Robinson is at his finest. I have played with him when he is playing like this, and it is truly wonderful.

There is always a danger when the leader of the band is somebody other than the trumpeter.

The trumpet must state the lead and LEAD, otherwise the music will lose its form.

I know there are exceptions. There are always exceptions to the rule, but don't be thrown by them. "Life is full of paradoxes."

And you must learn. It has purposely been made difficult, like an examination for a very high degree.

It is no good explaining everything in detail. You must learn to think for yourself. The freedom of expression the music gives you is the most wonderful thing about it.

But you must obey the rules and stay within the idiom.

But you will find there is plenty of room. The only restrictions are in the imagination.

Like a prisoner can think and transport himself far away, I sat the other night just staring at the beauty of the sunset and seeing why painters loved this part of the world. And the opening line to a song came into my head. I shall leave it there until it is ready to formulate, in its own good time.

Great men have always overcome the obstacles purposely strewn in their path.

It gives us lesser mortals encouragement.

READ MEZZROW'S *REALLY THE BLUES*. It is not only a good story, he teaches about true humility, without which you are lost before you start.

Don't worry about the snide and supercilious. They tried to pull me down all through my career. But they failed miserably. Among the many, Kid Ory's band and George Lewis's are the most important.

With Kid Ory the time the Crescent records were made is vital. Paragons. As the essential members died or departed, they could not be replaced, except with happy exceptions, like Omer Simeon when Jimmy Noone died.

Listen to *Blues for Jimmy* with Omer Simeon on clarinet. "A distillation like a rare liquid." Few musicians seem to realise that there are several blues styles. *Blues for Jimmy* was his favourite "shouting blues". A lot of thought should be put into the way a certain blues should be played BY ALL MEMBERS OF THE BAND.

Listen to Johnny Dodds' *Gravier Street Blues* and *Red Onion Blues*. Masterpieces. The clarinet is the dominant voice, but with Dodds this is acceptable. Because Natty Dominique and Preston Jackson KNOW HOW to subordinate themselves to the clarinet lead and produce some of the most fantastic polyphonic sounds on the simple three-part harmony. IT becomes another world. It still sends shivers "through my belly and breast" (Walt Whitman).

Listen to Preston Jackson on *New Orleans Hop Scop Blues*. The most remarkable shouting trombone ever recorded. No man alive could emulate it today.

THE LEWIS CLIMAX SESSION MUST BE MENTIONED. William Russell and John Hammond did more for the true interests of the music than any other men I can think of. They captured moments that are now the hard core of our knowledge.

The story goes that Bunk, "the wayward genius", had gone off on a toot on the day of the session and at the last moment Kid Howard was found. What a marvellous city. Instead of detracting from the session, it produced moments of pure magic.

Howard is a mixture of influences. Some we will never know, but Emile Barnes told me (and Dick Allen—Dick was interviewing him) that he is playing Chris Kelly ideas. Emile had worked with Kelly and considered him the best. I made him think of Chris Kelly when I played with him. Also Louis Nelson.

I think that the Ernestine Washington records with Bunk are the most important they recorded, to explain the perfect cohesion of a band playing as one. George told me Ernestine was a tyrant and wouldn't let up until she got the tempos right, but Bunk subordinated and accepted her instructions.

I have seen George telling his band off, when everything seemed alright to me. But they accepted it with an "OK George." Also saw Kid Ory constantly directing the band with a lift of a hand and a downward flourish. The band immediately responded. I have often thought that British bands *do* need a conductor. One who can listen observantly and put things right.

When I have been able to sit out for a couple of nunbers with another trumpet sitting in, I have immediately been able to see faults that could be corrected with very little trouble. But my bands have been noted for having a good internal balance, which is essential, usually alright until somebody mucks it up.

SESSION TO BE THANKFUL FOR: SAM MORGAN BAND. Morgan's was a large musical family as were several others in those days, which produced first-class musicians. The line-up is so unwieldy here, that if it wasn't for the New Orleans discipline all would be chaos. Instead, with a steady rhythm and fine-toned bass from Big Jim Little (MUST NOT BE ALTERED—STYLE OF WRITING IS INTENTIONAL—KC) acting as the underpin, we have memorable music.

People have asked, "I wonder how good Bunk was in his prime?" Let these people play *Thriller Rag, Snag It* etc. when their chops are getting beat after a hard session.

However, Lee Collins on the Collins, Jones Astoria Hot Eight must give us a good idea as to how he was playing. Bunk was renowned and very popular.

Emile Barnes, Joe Robichaux and Louis Armstrong among others back this up.

He was also a good teacher, teaching Tommy Ladnier, Louis (try and find the Louis Armstrong Anniversary Record Changer for much more honest information on Bunk) and Lee Collins, who made no pretence otherwise. His beautiful tone, phrasing, and mastery of the diminished chords cleverly interweaving them across the dominant chord structure personifies Bunk at his best.

I WOULD LIKE TO SAY A FEW WORDS ON SIDNEY ARODIN, a unique yet relatively unknown clarinetist.

I know nothing about him save his beautiful work on the Jones-Collins Astoria Hot 8's. He is on other records but I am not familiar with them.

He's been likened to Pee Wee Russell for originality, but he is much more satisfying in his will'o-the-wisp quality which I have never heard in any other clarinet.

Here, truly, is Peter Clayton's "Sense of space and wayward poetry." Though the numbers are broken up with tricky breaks and lead-ins.

They are not like most of the white bands of the time.

Joe Robichaux may have heard Earl Hines, but I don't think

so. His playing is complex rhythmically and the equal of later Hines in complexity.

Joe told me that when they recorded the tunes, the producer asked for titles. They didn't have any. Hence *Damp Weather,* which it was on the day or evening of the recording. *Tip Easy Blues* because they had to be very careful not to jog the mikes as they stepped forward to solo. *Duet Stomp* is self explanatory and *Astoria Strut.* This is where the paradox comes in. The line-up is not the usual trombone, trumpet, clarinet, but tenor and alto sax, clarinet and trumpet. Yet the sound is steeped in all that is good in New Orleans music. Backed by superb rhythm. My senses have been so sharpened by listening to these four sides that I have actually smelled the warm atmosphere of New Orleans and been transported to the city.

Herb Morand *Barefoot Boy.* Tune said to go back to Bolden. Words a bit nonsensical, but it doesn't matter. Words far more stupid in most modern songs. Morand has that unique New Orleans tone that is very difficult to emulate, wide with a certain dinge. As has Ladnier. Defies description. Construction of finale. Superb.

There is very little pure improvisation, but one lives with an ever-open ear, catching snatches of phrases from every source and storing them in the subconscious.

Then when the right moment arrives, they come together and make something original. The moments are rare, but one must leave an ever-open door for them. Hence the term "A musician's musician."

They don't have to be musical influences. There is "The blazing tropic night."

Hemingway's *The Old Man And the Sea* Laurie Lee's *Cider With Rosie.* Are sheer poetry and inspiring.

Bird song "You never can recapture." But some stays like flecks of gold in a sluice pan.

*B*runswick Series.
Coal Cart
2.19
N.O. *Hop Scop Blues*
Keystone
Gravier Street
Etc.

Some of most important ever recorded. Men on terrific form. Unfortunately Red Allen (whom I love) sides least successful. Red's style did not suit N.O. lead. At his best with Luis Russell, then excellent.

Records contain all important aspects. Terrific intense swing (mainly Zutty Singleton), beautiful solo work *and* teamwork, interplay, correct use of "three-part harmony." "Then you has jazz."

RED NICHOLLS *WAIL OF THE WINDS*. First record. HMV. Second poor. Red not on record. Beautiful moving record. I could NEVER get a band to play it. Could be transposed to three front-line format. Swingle Singers could do it.

Important to read books that are HELPFUL. Especially Biography (and Auto-) People like Hodier useless. Very little fiction any good.

Dorothy Baker *Young Man with a Horn*. Good despite slamming from various sources. Garson Kanin *Blow Up a Storm* very readable. Good insight.

Dreary technical details of no use. Rudi Blesh *Shining Trumpets*. Important. Again, technical detail not. But description of George Lewis *If I ever Cease To Love*: "Plays breaks Like Chain-Lightning." Very good articles on Bunk Band Stuyvesant Casino. Should be re-published. Most important articles and interviews.

MOST FRENCHMEN NEVER TOOK ADVANTAGE OF FIRST VISITS OF GREAT JAZZMEN. England was DENIED this chance. Musicians Union—Damned FOREVER. Would have changed attitudes and scene dramatically.

Much important learning lost forever. If Condon band I heard in Greenwich Village could have come over (1947) G.Brunis, E.Hall, S.Weis, E.Condon, P.W.Russell, W.Davison, J.Blowers. George Lewis Band (prior 1952) and many others. WHOLE concept and scene would have changed FOR BETTER.

All this written with no references. My mind teems with knowledge.

TO MUSICIANS LEARNING: Don't stuff your head with chords. Some knowledge helpful. But more important to develop your ear as much as possible. Some have better sense of sounds than others.

I developed mine as much as possible, and always wished it was better.

One MUST BE one's own critic. Part of your mind must always be your watchdog. ("The little man on the shoulder"— Sam Price), knowing when you are off-form or not progressing.

Don't get to a stage and think that is good enough. You are not playing at playing jazz. Learn how to PLAY IT. Sense of timing, beat, swing, phrasing. VITAL. ESSENTIAL.

LOUIS STRESSED THIS AND SAID KING OLIVER TAUGHT HIM SO MUCH.

Don't read or listen to nitwits like COLLIER, HODIER etc. They will teach you nothing.

You must have latent, natural talent, but hard, intense woodshedding is the thing. THERE ARE NO SHORTCUTS TO EXPERIENCE.

MEZZ MEZZROW: "Go with your cap in your hand to the music, must be humble. The music is the master. Everything else is SUBSERVIENT."

THE IDEAL BAND WOULD HAVE A THOROUGH KNOWLEDGE and ability to play in the New Orleans idiom.

But also be able to adapt and be able to play the beautiful ballads and pop tunes.

Much the same as one has to be able to adapt to play ragtime correctly and respect the form.

Think of the music, not just as notes and chords.

Duke Ellington used to paint word pictures to the band, at rehearsals, in order to get the feel of the thing, and the right mood for the tune.

NEW ORLEANS MUSIC.
It should be the TRUTH.
STRAIGHT FROM THE HEART.
Cross the bar line.
Bend the note.
Play on the beat (With swing).
Delay the phrase.
Punch the hell.
To make the sons of bitches "Wake Up."
"GET RID OF THE ANCHOR CHAIN."

There must be men to do this, otherwise the heart, the kernel of the music will be lost FOREVER. And only the crass, the mediocre will survive.

JOHN LEWIS. MODERN JAZZ QUARTET: "Every now and again we have to go back to the Goldmine." No matter how many times you go to New Orleans you will learn nothing if your heart and mind are not in the right place. You must carry it with you wherever you go. As the New Orleans men did. If I treat it as a religion, it is a far better one than Christianity.

THEY JEER AT LEGEND OF BUDDY BOLDEN being heard so far away across Lake Pontchartrain.

Sound travels long distances on a still summer's night, and especially across water, with a following breeze and no obstruction. Dick Allen and I thought of trying it one night. Pity we didn't.

Freddie Keppard and King Oliver were tremendously powerful in their prime. As was Wild Bill Davison when I heard him in 1947. People never heard Wild Bill like this by the time he came to England. But the important thing is, they had wide tones. It is not just the noise. Some trumpeters screech their heads off and it is hard on the ears. Them men played with beautiful broad tones that would shake you if you heard them today.

They played on deep cup mouthpieces that give you that broad tone, but are very hard on the chops. But look at the build of Louis and Bill. It is not just lip that you have got to

have. To Wooden Joe Nicholas playing on a very deep cup with NO PRESSURE SYSTEM (Dick Allen confirmed this.)

Bunk Johnson was bemused by the shallow cups present-day men used. Listen to his LOW register on *Franklin Street Blues*. Very difficult to play. Harry James had a fine tone all through the register. William Russell said Wooden Joe (probably why so named) was "the most powerful man he had heard in New Orleans." King Oliver blew a cornet out of tune in a month. Seems incredible. But George Wettling said the Oliver band was the "greatest ever." "Could improvise on High Society for twenty minutes!" Why the disbelief?

The Crane River Jazzband were heard in Feltham. A good three miles away. When we played down by the Crane River at Cranford.

When we finally started sessions in the White Hart Annexe on the Bath Road, people complained nearly a mile away. No amplification. So take no notice of the fools and scoffers.

Power does not mean noise. Whistling Rufus said we were too loud, then we would drop down to a whisper and really jump, before roaring into the climax.

People did not know what they were listening to. Except for one or two like Ernest Borneman and Jimmy Asman.

WILLIAM RUSSELL COMPLAINED of only being able to get poor equipment, yet worked wonders.

Kid Rena session. Rhythm section poorly recorded. Gives no indication of Albert Glenny's fine playing. But two clarinets recorded beautifully. LOUIS NELSON DELISLE and ALPHONSE PICOU. Two of the masters. Climax Session may be due to balance. Marrero's magnificent playing dominates. Yet overall music stupendous. Somebody thought Lawrence was only playing on one chord. My God! Cloth Ears!

Nick Boston session. Rest of record not impressive, but plays uncannily like Bunk on *King Porter Stomp*.

Old-time men were jealous of their music (Keppard). And rightly so. Some good men have gone astray and not been able to get back. They think they can. But usually it shows. If you develop you must guard that development very closely. It is easily lost. It is not a case of what is good for someone else is good enough for you. Arrant nonsense.

BUBBER MILEY: Played with such 'wisdom' for one so young. I feel that men like him just had to learn a Bb scale.

And they knew what it was at.

Then they die.

Self destruct.

Wally Fawkes (clarinet) said that I "knew all about that."

Once called me "monster" but with a smile on his face.

Maynard Ferguson and other big bands too repetitious. Show no imagination. Not enough variety in material. Jack Parnell on T.V. Programme. Very Good.

BIG BAND HAD ENORMOUS SCOPE.

Early Ellington and many others.

Rhythm sections now very poor.

Listen to early airshot, publicity broadcast of Chick Webb, Fletcher Henderson, Count Basie.

NOT ENOUGH SUPERLATIVES TO DESCRIBE.

I can hear where Harry James got his style from. TAFT JORDAN (Chick Webb Orchestra) Glorious stuff.

Blowing like 'there's no tomorrow'.

Cab Calloway had very good band.

Band behind Phil Harris a real swinger.

Swing has been lost. It is still there. For God's sake revive it. And let's have REAL MUSIC again.

It's hard work but worth it

For the wonderful feeling it gives.

Many musicians will testify to this.

"That's the truth, old man."

I still cannot rest for thoughts "Of Beautiful Music."

The same rules will ALWAYS apply.

LIONEL HAMPTON, SMALL BAND. *Pigfoot Sonata*. Marlowe Morris on piano.

Floats along on a semi-boogie bass pattern.

Ziggy Elman plays lovely toned horn. Very relaxed.

Records with Django and Rex Stewart, made in Paris

They take a tune like *Lady Be Good*, and completely convert it, with amazing variations. After-hours music.

Not like the boppers, who rarely contribute anything.

Musician: "I was a member of The McKinney's Cotton Pickers. The bestest damn band there ever was."

Manitas de Plata. Has only one theme, he calls *La Rumba*. Yet plays amazing, brilliant variations on it endlessly.

Fellow said we were 50%.

Colin Bowden higher % than most.

Maybe I am exceptional and have an extra bit of talent, but it proves what can be done.

George Berry the best. Flashing brilliance like George.

Palser unwittingly right Correct foil. Drummers erratic.

Sleepy John Estes, Speckled Red.

½ pint gin. Not secret drinkers.

Don't recommend trying it.

LET US SAVE THE MUSIC BEFORE IT IS TOO LATE. Best? When I listen to Red's *Feeling Drowsy* he's the best. When I listen to Louis' *Jeepers Creepers* he's the best.

Almost anything of Bunk, Mutt and so on.

Jens Lindgren: "Maybe you get something from up there?" All I have ever received from up there is barbaric cruelty.

Let's sail away and never return, with Bunk Johnson's clarion horn "Leading the way, right down the middle of the road." (Squire Gersh.)

Ghostly haunting sounds from the not-too-distant past.

I was 3 years old when BUDDY BOLDEN DIED.

Public-school boys, trying to play jazz.

The music of the common man with a little talent.

Oliver was a butler.

Bechet Shined shoes.

Bunk was a labourer in the rice fields.

I saw Glenny plastering a door-step.

Louis Nelson driving a post-office truck.

MASTER MUSICIANS.

"We are the kings" (Ludwig van Beethoven)

"Bunk drank that port-wine, and that's what came out of that horn."(Louis Armstrong)

But Louis meant "That dark, mellow, rich beauty with a golden glow."

That haunts forever.

RANDOM THOUGHTS: CRIPPLE CLARENCE LOFTON, SPECKLED RED: Are two of the most unique of pianists. No technique in the academic sense but having abilities that are above the orthodox senses. Creating harmonies and cross-rhythms that have never been written.

TRUE PRIMITIVE ARTISTS.

JESS STACY

My all-time greatest pianist. Can convert any tune into barrelhouse. Beautiful sense of true natural swing. And most important, can PRODUCE HIS OWN TONE on any given piano.

He is the only man I can immediately identify.

At one time, he pleasantky haunted me, through the day and night.

Saw the cover on a record rack. Familiar King Oliver photo, with other figures superimposed. The SWINGLE SINGERS. RAGTIME AND ALL THAT JAZZ.

Played it and was knocked out. Best breath of fresh air I had heard for a long time. Numbers beautifully and lovingly performed, of Joplin and Morton. Just could have done with a deeper bass, but minor criticism. *Weeping Willow Rag* favourite.

TO GO ON ANOTHER TACK. I have been listening to a short tape (about 17 minutes) of my skiffle group made at Eel Pie Island, Twickenham, in 1957.

It is remarkable. I can now listen to it observantly. When you are in an intense state of creation, you cannot do this.

I remember hearing it at the time and commenting that it had a good barrelhouse sound. But I was busy making the music and absorbing from the source.

I did not pay too much attention to, and did not like listening to, my own recordings. I was too unhappy with some of the results.

But now I realise that at that time we were among the greatest exponents IN THE WORLD of the music I am talking about.

Play it to one who has never heard or known of it before and I defy him to know without pre-knowledge that there is only guitar, banjo, washboard and bass in the line-up. The full sound is unbelievable. No wonder a bemused onlooker said "It is old-time jazz, not skiffle." He had only heard the weak, stupid pastiche sounds of the TRAD WORLD. My singing is the best I have ever heard and I am ON THE RIGHT TRACK.

> I have said in later years that I need all the help I can get, and have delegated authority. Always with detrimental results. Here I need no help, but am an iron man standing on his own two feet.

LOT OF THOUGHT'S GONE INTO THE WORDS. Interpretation's far better than any other records by supposed experts. There are so many facets to jazz without going outside the confines of the idiom. The early men were very aware of their music. Freddie Keppard is the classic example. He refused to record because he knew what would happen. The Original Dixieland Band did. And it did happen.

Yet at some time a Northern Company sent a fieldman to New Orleans to see what was worthwhile recording.

He wired back "No jazz in New Orleans." Thank goodness William Russell wasn't a field-man.

Henry Allen's Brass Band was still parading in the 40s. Ralston Crawford had fine photos of them.

Nobody recorded them.

We must be thankful for what was recorded, but, alas, much was missed. All New Orleans musicians weren't good. Naturally, there were the competent, the good, the very good and the elite. The elite were dangerous in a certain respect; they were exceptionally talented and the student should beware of imitating them. A good example is Baby Dodds. Gene Krupa idolised Dodds: "I was weaned on Baby Dodds' snare roll." Ray Bauduc, Davy Tough, amongst others listened and learned. Tough could swing like the wind. But they all had an identity of their own.

Sidney Bechet emulators were, and are, mostly disastrous. Although Bechet played superb clarinet, and always said master the clarinet first.

He led a wealth of musicians astray. (Bruce Bakewell is one exception I can think of) and George Berry is one of the few approaching Lewis.

The bass, unfortunately, is far too easy an instrument to fake on.

One good teacher could put them all right. (Need for a school again).

Many of the old-timers took secrets to the grave. Some passed a little on.

Lawrence Marrero told me things that helped many banjoists. But not being a banjoist myself I could not exploit them. "The power stroke" he mentioned as being very important.

I have often been likened to men other than those I am thinking of. Natty Dominique, Tommy Ladnier. The common denominator is there, and that's the important thing. As for Chris Kelly and Buddy Petit, neither recorded but I have got deep enough into the music to play "as to the manor born." (Humphrey Lyttelton). Kid Howard: "Man, you got educated fingers." "It's been a pleasure playing with you, Mr. Colyer."(Louis Nelson)

Unknown fan: "I heard the band playing as I walked in. Didn't sound much good, but boy, that horn player knew what he was doing."

I WAS SO DISAPPOINTED WHEN I BOUGHT Ellington's record *Sunday Morning Blues*, Billy Eckstein vocal. Billy seems to be the forerunner of the non-blue blues singers. The band lacks the old rich sound. The Duke knew that he was losing irreplaceable men and just had to make do with what he had got. The glories must have lasted into the late thirties, then the edge was gone.

Harry James made a lusty fight with his first band and made some fine records. Jack Gardner on piano is second to Jess Stacy and rocks the band, coming out with fine barrelhouse solos as did Bob Zurke with the Bob Cats.

Art Hodes is worthy of special mention. Art developed his piano playing the hard way

I think he was influenced by James P. Johnson at an important stage. And produced a tone of his own. It seems impossible that the inanimate instrument like the piano can produce an individual tone, but it can be done by exceptional men.

Somebody pressed on me a classic record of Rubinstein.

I patiently played it through. He hasn't got a clue, and to quote Eddie Condon, the piano is saying "Please take your clumsy hands off of me."

I wish he had gone to hear Stacy before he touched a piano.

As far as emulation goes, the nearest I have ever heard to Bunk is a record of Nick Boston, with pianist, playing *King Porter Stomp*. Now this may not be intentional, so much the better.

The original record is by King Oliver and Jelly Roll Morton, both giants, and contemporaries of Bunk.

A good New Orleans lead can pull a mediocre band together. But, if the anchor chain is too heavy—can't be done.

Bill Wilkinson: 'When it's really going, it's like trying to control a team of thoroughbred horses.'

Until more musicians have the guts to ignore fads or fashions, things will change only for the worse.

Artie Shaw got into trouble for calling Bobby-soxers morons when they started knocking the musicians' instruments out of their hands and taking over the stage.

I got into trouble for the same reason when Lyn Dutton ran the 100 Club, or whatever it was called then.

LOVELY MOMENT WHEN WE STOPPED THE COACH WAY UP IN THE YORKSHIRE MOORS. Got instruments out and played down into the valley.

Sheep turning their heads, miles away.

Wrote from Montreal 1947 extolling the virtues of Oscar Peterson when he was unknown in Europe. Played much better then, Barrelhouse, boogie-woogie

GEORGE LEWIS CAME TO ENGLAND AND THE WHOLE BALL GOT ROLLING.

Went to New Orleans Bier Bar, Dusseldorf, and Hamburg. Got the whole ball rolling. Everybody else cashed in. Decca ignored my pleas to record in Germany. Was under contract, they refused permission. Didn't know what was going on. Dumbkopfs.

The Graeme Bell band who played an insipid form of jazz, but were very popular.

Couldn't be bothered to come to the 51 Club, until Mel Langdon, their manager, forced them. By having taxis standing by in the interval. They came, were very condescending. I couldn't believe that a trumpet could be played so weakly as Roger Bell played.

WOODY GUTHRIE *NEW YORK TOWN BLUES* has taken the tune of Gus Cannon's *K. C. Moan* and made yet another lovely song, like both equally. Story line is contained in whole of song. Pure poetry.

A writer once said the music was created because the Southern Negro needed it and it should be left that way. But it has such a universal appeal that it has become an international language. But much of importance got lost on the way.

The pastiche is easy to play and means nothing.

Like Benny Goodman imitators. I always say "It's Benny Goodman," it doesn't matter who it is.

Same with Armstrong imitators. It's Louis, they are adding nothing, and cannot produce his majesty and mastery. Just pale copies.

They might sound like George until you listened to George.

Then they were nowhere. One has to copy and emulate.

But mix enough influence and a little of yourself and the results can be interesting.

To hear supposed jazz musicians joking about their cliches because they have nothing to say is pitiful. If they wracked their brains a little instead of becoming automatons they would find the music more stimulating and interesting. A few mistakes are inevitable but acceptable if a man is working like

"The sweating , coatless trumpet player,
Riding out of this world for nobody's sake,
But his own."

History cannot repeat itself. There can never (be) eras like we have had in the past.

That is the way of things, but I still maintain there is no such thing as contemporary jazz. The form was created.

The closer you stick to it, the better it will sound. There is plenty of freedom WITHIN the idiom. That is the beauty of the music.

There is a wealth of variety. The limitations are in the individual.

Talking to Buck Clayton: "Mutt Carey taught us. He was like a Father to us youngsters."

RE-PHOTO ON WALL: "Move your hand a bit this way.
Poor bugger, he's had it."
Recording techniques were better in the early days.
Engineers in America know the music and did their best to transfer it to wax.
Always problems in England.
Low Fidelity is adequate for capturing music—-listen to early records.
Faithfully reproduced.
Equipment supposedly improves.
Engineers clueless.
Situation hopeless.

FEMALE SINGERS: Alas, a breed to be feared. Almost none have the quality of voice desired, cannot sing in band keys, have no sense of syncopation, rhtyhm or anything else.

We just can't produce them. Exceptions that spring to mind: Judith Durham when she used to sit-in with me at the 51 Club (Chris Barber had nothing to do with the place while I was in charge of musical activities. The man who wrote Michael Camus' story seemed to think so. He had a research team to help him, and they got all their facts wrong. I wrote to him complaining of this. Wrote a nice reply completely ignoring my complaint. Probably knows I can't sue for plagiarism. Barber probably shitting and smirking.

Then I'm told I have no right to reply and have got to watch

what I SAY. To hell with them. Scum. Let them take ME to court if I am wrong. I am sick and tired of it. Judith had great success with the Seekers. Very good 12 string guitar player. Difficult instrument to play, but tho' musically perfect, far too smooth and sophisticated. For my taste. She later formed her own band, "The Hottest Band in Town." It was far from that. In fact, hopeless from a jazz point of view.

I hate these stupid bragging band names. The numbers they played, supposedly original, were completely uninteresting. Rimington joined, then complained. "Well leave them," I said. "The money's good" was the reply. Calls himself a jazz musician. Waste of ONE VERY WORTHWHILE SINGER. Jan Sutherland, I only met once. Molson Festival, Toronto. Was impressed. Got all the right things going. Sang a terrific *Delta Bound* with Johnny Parker on piano. Queenie Watts was a good, belting pub singer. There were probably more like her in the old days. Good gutsy singers more like blues shouters than these no-hopers.

SAM PRICE was guest one night at the 100 Club. Sat listening to the first set chuckling to himself. Sam knew the men that had "The little man on their shoulder." Played his first set. I foolishly forgot and left my horn on the chair. Vibration jarred it off chair, bent it. Nobody bothered. It cost me a few quid to have it straightened out. Put it in case after 2nd set. Sam said "You're coming back, aren't you?"

Swung into last set, and Sam was in on piano, having a ball.

Sam Price behind Rosetta Tharpe *Up Above My Head*. SUPERB SWINGING NUMBER. Cy Laurie with Max Collie's rhythm section. Bloody Travesty. Should not be inflicted on your worst enemy.

Louis Armstrong's answer to all French and Italian speakers was "Sea Food, Sea Food, Sea Food." GOOD IDEA. If an artist makes one outstanding record, it is enough to prove his quality. Red Allen's *Feeling Drowsy*. He doesn't quite get it on the other takes and I argue that they should not be issued, if they detract. Of course, the parasite record producers do not care.

Bix Beiderbecke's *Singin' the Blues* is a gem, and I need nothing else to prove to me that he could play some 'magic horn'.

Nevertheless, there is some truth in Benny Green's book "The Reluctant Art". One of the most important books in the jazz library.

Little Brother Montgomery's *Vicksburg Blues* ranks among the finest blues tunes ever written. He admitted to me that it was difficult to play. And no wonder. The cross-rhythms are complex to the extreme, and the tune is entirely unique.

I am sure Little Brother knew nothing about madrigals and such, yet the influences go far beyond the basic blues theme.

It makes you wonder about reincarnation. Was he a musician in some other age? In an entirely different setting?

Some blues men have only one tune and there is nothing wrong with that, but others show amazing diversity. As I have

said before, there are no limitations within the idiom.

Billie Holiday's *Ghost of Yesterday* is one of the most poignant, aching themes I have ever heard. The backing is kept to the minimum, and her voice is allowed to carry the tune. The musicians show her great respect.

I WISH I COULD GO TO THE CANYON SOMEWHERE IN CALIFORNIA, where musicians used to go to practice at dead of night because the accoustics are perfect.

Talking to Robin Tankard (bass) at Bowness. "I like to be able to sit down for at least half an hour before a session to compose my thoughts." Robin: "Ooh, must do that." Fine bassist.

Some people brag about how many times they have been to New Orleans. Some live there. They might just as well go and stay in Brighton. Recharge their batteries! Phooey.

You have to carry it around with you, wherever you go. "The heavy burden, the soul of an artist."(Dorothy Baker) "That's the Blues, old man"(Johnny Hodges)

Max Jones: "I think you have done your share of benefits, Ken."

Denny Ilett, discussing a certain musician: "He's a poseur."

"Comes the dawn, comes the day.
I've been a million miles trying
to drive my blues away."
—Ken Colyer.

INDEX

ACKNOWLEDGEMENTS

The Ken Colyer Trust's gratitude goes to the late Peter Wilcocks, a member whose generous donation helped make the financing of this book possible.

The authors are grateful for the encouragement shown by Julian Davies, Barry Price, Renee Long and Kay and Tony Leppard of the Trust who have often acted well beyond the call of duty. Chris Stotesbury's assistance has also been invaluable.

Delphine and Russell Colyer have been of special help in perhaps more ways than they realize. John Griffith has also been a continual source of information and assistance for us.

Others who have aided our project include, in no special order: the late Richard Baker, the late George Melly, Mike Stanley, Barry Palser, Udo Schneider, Geoff Gilbert, Diana Clark, Tony Morgan, Jim Godbolt, Bernd Thiele, Claes Ringqvist, Richard Rothwell, Joanne Penn of Norfolk Family Search, Andy Simons of the British Library and David Nathan and his colleagues at the National Jazz Archive.

Above all, we wish to thank all those contributors who kindly agreed to being interviewed or wrote their impressions of Ken for us.

MIKE POINTON AND RAY SMITH, London & Holland, August 2010

SOURCES

MAGAZINE AND NEWSPAPER ARTICLES

Ken Colyer Trust Newsletter Issues of December 1992, March 1993, September 1993, March 1994, September, 1994, June 1997, September 1997, June 1998, Autumn 2002 and Winter 2002. The Rev. Kershaw article "Old Hands" is from the Ken Colyer Trust Newsletter of March 1996, and was originally printed in The New Hampshire Scene.

Melody Maker, issues of March 21, May 2, April 4, May 1, May 2, August 1, September 5, September 12, all 1953; May 23 and June 5, 1954; January 8, 1955; July, 1960; March 4, 196; March 3 and October 14, 1962; March 30, 1963; December 20, 1968; May 15, 1971

Jazz Journal issues of June 1953, July 1956, March 1976

Coda, issue of June 1995

The Gramophone, issue of January 25, 1954

Jazz News, issue of May 31, 1961

Ken Colyer Club Magazine, 1955 issue

New Orleans Item, February 15, 1953

Scene, issue No 12, November 29, 1962

Reading Star, February 7 issue 1964

Ken Colyer Scrapbook, courtesy Julian Davies

A Ken Colyer Miscellany (Chiltern Pub., March 1998)

BOOKS AND MANUSCRIPTS

Ken Colyer, When Dreams Are in the Dust (Ken Colyer Trust, 1989)

Ann Fairbairn [aka Dorothy Tait], Call Him George (Bantam Books, 1971)

Pete Frame, The Restless Generation (Rogan House, 2007)

Ben Harker, Class Act: The Cultural and Political Life of Ewan MacColl (Pluto Press, 2007)

Ken Harrison, Internet ms

Alan Lomax, Selected Writings 1934-1997 (Routledge, 2003)

Ewan MacColl, Journeyman (Sidgwick & Jackson, 1990)

George Melly, Owning Up (Weidenfeld & Nicholson, 1965)

Keith Smith, The Albino Kid (unpublished ms)

Bruce Turner, Hot Air, Cool Music (Quartet Books, 1984)

Mike Williams, The Australian Jazz Explosion (Angus and Robertson, 1981)

Bill Wyman with Ray Coleman, Stone Alone (Penguin Books, 1991)

ARCHIVAL TAPED INTERVIEWS

Ken Colyer recorded at 99, The Drive in 1964. Interviewer unknown. Transcribed by Mac Robinson

Ken Colyer interviewed by Barry Palser, 1970s

Ray Foxley interviewed by John Keen, 1990

Sonny Morris interviewed by John Keen, 1992

Whatever Happened to Bill Brunskill (Thames TV documentary 1984)

SLEEVE NOTES

Columbia SEG 8180 E.P.
Vogue EPV 1102
Decca L.P. LF 1196
504 CD 52
K.C. Records KCT 2R
Upbeat C.D. URCD 159
Membran Music DVD 231874 I Did It For The Music
Cadillac CD SGC/MELCD 20/2
Cadillac CD SGC/MEL 20-1

LETTERS

Donated by Bill Colyer, Delphine Colyer, Julian Davies, Tim Newman, Johnny Parker, Mike Pointon, Paul Sealey, Dave Smith, Trefor Williams

MISCELLANEOUS

Bob Wallis dissertation, Revivalism to Commercialism: A Study. Courtesy of National Jazz Archive/Mrs Joyce Wallis

Brian Harvey An Electric Night. HJC's Sunday Supplement

Ken Colyer: He Knew. BBC Radio 2, broadcast March 2008

PHOTOGRAPHS

We would like to thank Terry Cryer for the use of his great photographs, especially the front cover portrait.

We would like to thank all of the photographers and magazines whose work is printed here: the Bill Colyer Collection, Russell Colyer, Delphine Colyer, Martin Colyer, John and Renee Long, Tony Leppard, The Ken Colyer Trust Archive, Pete Dyer, Ian Christie, Mike McCombe, Roger Horton, Bernie Thiele, Dick Smith, Tom Parks, The late Reverend Alvin Kershaw, Jimmy Hankinson, Hans Harzheim, Diz Disley, Pete Vince, Sonny Morris, Trevor Glenroy, Geoffrey Paddon, John Brock, Ronald Howe, John Bernard, Bill Smith/Coda Magazine, Geoff Bull, Susanna Schapawalow, The Daily Express, Southern Photographic Service, Tunbridge Wells Advertiser, General News Features, New Musical Express, Jazz Journal, Melody Maker, Steve Turner.

It is very difficult to track down the original photographers, especially those who worked for now-defunct press agencies and newspapers. Many fan photographs have been donated to The Ken Colyer Trust, often not attributed. We feel that their use in this book is in the spirit in which they were donated: to keep alive the memory and influence of Ken Colyer. Apologies for not crediting these donations individually; it would have been too daunting a task. Any mistakes will happily be corrected in future editions.

Thanks to Toby Buchan for his advice.

The painting by Diz Disley on page 353 is courtesy of Roger Horton.

The painting by George Melly on pages 76-77 is courtesy of Michael Woods and Diana Melly.

Cartoon by 'Trog' courtesy of Wally Fawkes and Dave Bennett

Martin Colyer would like to thank Michèle Colyer, Gabriel Colyer, Steve Caplin and Hugh Kyle.